Lecture Notes in Computer Science 14056

The series Lecture Notes in Computer Science (LNCS), including its subseries Lecture Notes in Artificial Intelligence (LNAI) and Lecture Notes in Bioinformatics (LNBI), has established itself as a medium for the publication of new developments in computer science and information technology research, teaching, and education.

LNCS enjoys close cooperation with the computer science R & D community, the series counts many renowned academics among its volume editors and paper authors, and collaborates with prestigious societies. Its mission is to serve this international community by providing an invaluable service, mainly focused on the publication of conference and workshop proceedings and postproceedings. LNCS commenced publication in 1973.

Hirohiko Mori · Yumi Asahi · Adela Coman ·
Simona Vasilache · Matthias Rauterberg
Editors

HCI International 2023 – Late Breaking Papers

25th International Conference on Human-Computer Interaction
HCII 2023, Copenhagen, Denmark, July 23–28, 2023
Proceedings, Part III

Editors
Hirohiko Mori
Tokyo City University
Tokyo, Japan

Yumi Asahi
Tokyo University of Science
Tokyo, Japan

Adela Coman
University of Bucharest
Bucharest, Romania

Simona Vasilache
University of Tsukuba
Tsukuba, Japan

Matthias Rauterberg
Eindhoven University of Technology
Eindhoven, The Netherlands

ISSN 0302-9743 ISSN 1611-3349 (electronic)
Lecture Notes in Computer Science
ISBN 978-3-031-48043-0 ISBN 978-3-031-48044-7 (eBook)
https://doi.org/10.1007/978-3-031-48044-7

This Springer imprint is published by the registered company Springer Nature Switzerland AG
The registered company address is: Gewerbestrasse 11, 6330 Cham, Switzerland

Paper in this product is recyclable.

Foreword

Human-computer interaction (HCI) is acquiring an ever-increasing scientific and industrial importance, as well as having more impact on people's everyday lives, as an ever-growing number of human activities are progressively moving from the physical to the digital world. This process, which has been ongoing for some time now, was further accelerated during the acute period of the COVID-19 pandemic. The HCI International (HCII) conference series, held annually, aims to respond to the compelling need to advance the exchange of knowledge and research and development efforts on the human aspects of design and use of computing systems.

The 25th International Conference on Human-Computer Interaction, HCI International 2023 (HCII 2023), was held in the emerging post-pandemic era as a 'hybrid' event at the AC Bella Sky Hotel and Bella Center, Copenhagen, Denmark, during July 23–28, 2023. It incorporated the 21 thematic areas and affiliated conferences listed below.

A total of 7472 individuals from academia, research institutes, industry, and government agencies from 85 countries submitted contributions, and 1578 papers and 396 posters were included in the volumes of the proceedings that were published just before the start of the conference. Additionally, 267 papers and 133 posters were included in the volumes of the proceedings published after the conference, as "Late Breaking Work". The contributions thoroughly cover the entire field of human-computer interaction, addressing major advances in knowledge and effective use of computers in a variety of application areas. These papers provide academics, researchers, engineers, scientists, practitioners and students with state-of-the-art information on the most recent advances in HCI. The volumes constituting the full set of the HCII 2023 conference proceedings are listed on the following pages.

I would like to thank the Program Board Chairs and the members of the Program Boards of all thematic areas and affiliated conferences for their contribution towards the high scientific quality and overall success of the HCI International 2023 conference. Their manifold support in terms of paper reviewing (single-blind review process, with a minimum of two reviews per submission), session organization and their willingness to act as goodwill ambassadors for the conference is most highly appreciated.

This conference would not have been possible without the continuous and unwavering support and advice of Gavriel Salvendy, founder, General Chair Emeritus, and Scientific Advisor. For his outstanding efforts, I would like to express my sincere appreciation to Abbas Moallem, Communications Chair and Editor of HCI International News.

July 2023 Constantine Stephanidis

HCI International 2023 Thematic Areas and Affiliated Conferences

Thematic Areas

- HCI: Human-Computer Interaction
- HIMI: Human Interface and the Management of Information

Affiliated Conferences

- EPCE: 20th International Conference on Engineering Psychology and Cognitive Ergonomics
- AC: 17th International Conference on Augmented Cognition
- UAHCI: 17th International Conference on Universal Access in Human-Computer Interaction
- CCD: 15th International Conference on Cross-Cultural Design
- SCSM: 15th International Conference on Social Computing and Social Media
- VAMR: 15th International Conference on Virtual, Augmented and Mixed Reality
- DHM: 14th International Conference on Digital Human Modeling and Applications in Health, Safety, Ergonomics and Risk Management
- DUXU: 12th International Conference on Design, User Experience and Usability
- C&C: 11th International Conference on Culture and Computing
- DAPI: 11th International Conference on Distributed, Ambient and Pervasive Interactions
- HCIBGO: 10th International Conference on HCI in Business, Government and Organizations
- LCT: 10th International Conference on Learning and Collaboration Technologies
- ITAP: 9th International Conference on Human Aspects of IT for the Aged Population
- AIS: 5th International Conference on Adaptive Instructional Systems
- HCI-CPT: 5th International Conference on HCI for Cybersecurity, Privacy and Trust
- HCI-Games: 5th International Conference on HCI in Games
- MobiTAS: 5th International Conference on HCI in Mobility, Transport and Automotive Systems
- AI-HCI: 4th International Conference on Artificial Intelligence in HCI
- MOBILE: 4th International Conference on Design, Operation and Evaluation of Mobile Communications

Conference Proceedings – Full List of Volumes

1. LNCS 14011, Human-Computer Interaction: Part I, edited by Masaaki Kurosu and Ayako Hashizume
2. LNCS 14012, Human-Computer Interaction: Part II, edited by Masaaki Kurosu and Ayako Hashizume
3. LNCS 14013, Human-Computer Interaction: Part III, edited by Masaaki Kurosu and Ayako Hashizume
4. LNCS 14014, Human-Computer Interaction: Part IV, edited by Masaaki Kurosu and Ayako Hashizume
5. LNCS 14015, Human Interface and the Management of Information: Part I, edited by Hirohiko Mori and Yumi Asahi
6. LNCS 14016, Human Interface and the Management of Information: Part II, edited by Hirohiko Mori and Yumi Asahi
7. LNAI 14017, Engineering Psychology and Cognitive Ergonomics: Part I, edited by Don Harris and Wen-Chin Li
8. LNAI 14018, Engineering Psychology and Cognitive Ergonomics: Part II, edited by Don Harris and Wen-Chin Li
9. LNAI 14019, Augmented Cognition, edited by Dylan D. Schmorrow and Cali M. Fidopiastis
10. LNCS 14020, Universal Access in Human-Computer Interaction: Part I, edited by Margherita Antona and Constantine Stephanidis
11. LNCS 14021, Universal Access in Human-Computer Interaction: Part II, edited by Margherita Antona and Constantine Stephanidis
12. LNCS 14022, Cross-Cultural Design: Part I, edited by Pei-Luen Patrick Rau
13. LNCS 14023, Cross-Cultural Design: Part II, edited by Pei-Luen Patrick Rau
14. LNCS 14024, Cross-Cultural Design: Part III, edited by Pei-Luen Patrick Rau
15. LNCS 14025, Social Computing and Social Media: Part I, edited by Adela Coman and Simona Vasilache
16. LNCS 14026, Social Computing and Social Media: Part II, edited by Adela Coman and Simona Vasilache
17. LNCS 14027, Virtual, Augmented and Mixed Reality, edited by Jessie Y.C. Chen and Gino Fragomeni
18. LNCS 14028, Digital Human Modeling and Applications in Health, Safety, Ergonomics and Risk Management: Part I, edited by Vincent G. Duffy
19. LNCS 14029, Digital Human Modeling and Applications in Health, Safety, Ergonomics and Risk Management: Part II, edited by Vincent G. Duffy
20. LNCS 14030, Design, User Experience, and Usability: Part I, edited by Aaron Marcus, Elizabeth Rosenzweig and Marcelo Soares
21. LNCS 14031, Design, User Experience, and Usability: Part II, edited by Aaron Marcus, Elizabeth Rosenzweig and Marcelo Soares
22. LNCS 14032, Design, User Experience, and Usability: Part III, edited by Aaron Marcus, Elizabeth Rosenzweig and Marcelo Soares

23. LNCS 14033, Design, User Experience, and Usability: Part IV, edited by Aaron Marcus, Elizabeth Rosenzweig and Marcelo Soares
24. LNCS 14034, Design, User Experience, and Usability: Part V, edited by Aaron Marcus, Elizabeth Rosenzweig and Marcelo Soares
25. LNCS 14035, Culture and Computing, edited by Matthias Rauterberg
26. LNCS 14036, Distributed, Ambient and Pervasive Interactions: Part I, edited by Norbert Streitz and Shin'ichi Konomi
27. LNCS 14037, Distributed, Ambient and Pervasive Interactions: Part II, edited by Norbert Streitz and Shin'ichi Konomi
28. LNCS 14038, HCI in Business, Government and Organizations: Part I, edited by Fiona Fui-Hoon Nah and Keng Siau
29. LNCS 14039, HCI in Business, Government and Organizations: Part II, edited by Fiona Fui-Hoon Nah and Keng Siau
30. LNCS 14040, Learning and Collaboration Technologies: Part I, edited by Panayiotis Zaphiris and Andri Ioannou
31. LNCS 14041, Learning and Collaboration Technologies: Part II, edited by Panayiotis Zaphiris and Andri Ioannou
32. LNCS 14042, Human Aspects of IT for the Aged Population: Part I, edited by Qin Gao and Jia Zhou
33. LNCS 14043, Human Aspects of IT for the Aged Population: Part II, edited by Qin Gao and Jia Zhou
34. LNCS 14044, Adaptive Instructional Systems, edited by Robert A. Sottilare and Jessica Schwarz
35. LNCS 14045, HCI for Cybersecurity, Privacy and Trust, edited by Abbas Moallem
36. LNCS 14046, HCI in Games: Part I, edited by Xiaowen Fang
37. LNCS 14047, HCI in Games: Part II, edited by Xiaowen Fang
38. LNCS 14048, HCI in Mobility, Transport and Automotive Systems: Part I, edited by Heidi Krömker
39. LNCS 14049, HCI in Mobility, Transport and Automotive Systems: Part II, edited by Heidi Krömker
40. LNAI 14050, Artificial Intelligence in HCI: Part I, edited by Helmut Degen and Stavroula Ntoa
41. LNAI 14051, Artificial Intelligence in HCI: Part II, edited by Helmut Degen and Stavroula Ntoa
42. LNCS 14052, Design, Operation and Evaluation of Mobile Communications, edited by Gavriel Salvendy and June Wei
43. CCIS 1832, HCI International 2023 Posters: Part I, edited by Constantine Stephanidis, Margherita Antona, Stavroula Ntoa and Gavriel Salvendy
44. CCIS 1833, HCI International 2023 Posters: Part II, edited by Constantine Stephanidis, Margherita Antona, Stavroula Ntoa and Gavriel Salvendy
45. CCIS 1834, HCI International 2023 Posters: Part III, edited by Constantine Stephanidis, Margherita Antona, Stavroula Ntoa and Gavriel Salvendy
46. CCIS 1835, HCI International 2023 Posters: Part IV, edited by Constantine Stephanidis, Margherita Antona, Stavroula Ntoa and Gavriel Salvendy
47. CCIS 1836, HCI International 2023 Posters: Part V, edited by Constantine Stephanidis, Margherita Antona, Stavroula Ntoa and Gavriel Salvendy

48. LNCS 14054, HCI International 2023 - Late Breaking Papers: Part I, edited by Masaaki Kurosu, Ayako Hashizume, Aaron Marcus, Elizabeth Rosenzweig, Marcelo Soares, Don Harris, Wen-Chin Li, Dylan D. Schmorrow, Cali M. Fidopiastis, and Pei-Luen Patrick Rau
49. LNCS 14055, HCI International 2023 - Late Breaking Papers: Part II, edited by Qin Gao, Jia Zhou, Vincent G. Duffy, Margherita Antona, and Constantine Stephanidis
50. LNCS 14056, HCI International 2023 - Late Breaking Papers: Part III, edited by Hirohiko Mori, Yumi Asahi, Adela Coman, Simona Vasilache, and Matthias Rauterberg
51. LNCS 14057, HCI International 2023 - Late Breaking Papers: Part IV, edited by Vincent G. Duffy, Heidi Krömker, Norbert A. Streitz, and Shin'ichi Konomi
52. LNCS 14058, HCI International 2023 - Late Breaking Papers: Part V, edited by Jessie Y. C. Chen, Gino Fragomeni, and Xiaowen Fang
53. LNCS 14059, HCI International 2023 - Late Breaking Papers: Part VI, edited by Helmut Degen, Stavroula Ntoa, and Abbas Moallem
54. LNCS 14060, HCI International 2023 - Late Breaking Papers: Part VII, edited by Panayiotis Zaphiris, Andri Ioannou, Robert A. Sottilare, Jessica Schwarz, Fiona Fui-Hoon Nah, Keng Siau, June Wei, and Gavriel Salvendy
55. CCIS 1957, HCI International 2023 - Late Breaking Posters: Part I, edited by Constantine Stephanidis, Margherita Antona, Stavroula Ntoa, and Gavriel Salvendy
56. CCIS 1958, HCI International 2023 - Late Breaking Posters: Part II, edited by Constantine Stephanidis, Margherita Antona, Stavroula Ntoa, and Gavriel Salvendy

https://2023.hci.international/proceedings

25th International Conference on Human-Computer Interaction (HCII 2023)

The full list with the Program Board Chairs and the members of the Program Boards of all thematic areas and affiliated conferences of HCII2023 is available online at:

http://www.hci.international/board-members-2023.php

HCI International 2024 Conference

The 26th International Conference on Human-Computer Interaction, HCI International 2024, will be held jointly with the affiliated conferences at the Washington Hilton Hotel, Washington, DC, USA, June 29 – July 4, 2024. It will cover a broad spectrum of themes related to Human-Computer Interaction, including theoretical issues, methods, tools, processes, and case studies in HCI design, as well as novel interaction techniques, interfaces, and applications. The proceedings will be published by Springer. More information will be made available on the conference website: http://2024.hci.international/.

General Chair
Prof. Constantine Stephanidis
University of Crete and ICS-FORTH
Heraklion, Crete, Greece
Email: general_chair@2024.hci.international

https://2024.hci.international/

Contents – Part III

Information Design, Visualization, Decision-Making and Collaboration

The Pendular Graph: Visualising Hierarchical Repetitive Structure in Point-Set Representations of the POP909 Music Dataset

Chenyu Gao[1(✉)] and Tom Collins[2,3]

[1] University of York, York, UK
chenyugao.cs@gmail.com
[2] University of Miami, Coral Gables, USA
[3] MAIA, Inc., Davis, USA

Abstract. Structure in music can mean many things: repetition, tonality, the existence of and focus on different "musical dimensions", such as rhythm, timbre, etc. Here, we are concerned with repetitive structures in music, such as sections that repeat within a song (verses, choruses, etc.). We are also concerned mainly with hierarchical repetition (e.g., within a verse, there may be a phrase or riff that recurs multiple times). Existing annotated music datasets tend to be either small in terms of items in the corpus, but with detailed annotatations, or larger as a corpus, but with linear annotations only. In this paper, we 1) develop a method for taking a linear annotation as input, and converting it to a hierarchical annotation as output, where such hierarchies exist in the input, and 2) introduce a web-based interface (https://pendular-graph.glitch.me/) where hierarchical annotations of 909 songs can be explored and played back, in synchrony with a visual representation of note content.

Keywords: Visualisation · Structure · Music · Graph

1 Introduction

The word "structure" has multiple meanings in music theory, from repetition to the existence of and focus on different "musical dimensions" (e.g., pitch or rhythm). In this paper, we are mainly focusing on hierarchical repetitive structures in music. For example, there are sections (verses, choruses, etc.) that repeat within a song, in which there may be a phrase or riff that recurs multiple times within a verse. If a piece of music is annotated as "intro, verse, verse, chorus, verse, chorus, chorus" (or, more succinctly, "ABBCBCC"), this is a *linear* annotation (not hierarchical), because it contains no indication of smaller-scale repetition of phrases within a verse, and the existence of a larger section is only implicit (e.g., the substring "BC" occurs twice).

Comprehending musical structure has been shown to help people remember or understand music better [14], and could be especially useful for people

H. Mori et al. (Eds.): HCII 2023, LNCS 14056, pp. 3–16, 2023.
https://doi.org/10.1007/978-3-031-48044-7_1

listening to a piece for the first time. Visualised structure also provides a way to communicate intepretations of music, as different people may annotate the same song with different structural labels [3]. A lot of music structure visualisation tools have been developed [5,16,17,19,20,24,31], but many of these tools suffer either from a lack of interactivity, or are now unusable due to software dependency or maintenance issues. In this paper, we develop a Web-based hierarchical repetitive pattern visualisation tool based on the PatternViewer [24]. In our interface, the hierarchical structure of each song is visualised as a pendular graph, and repetitive phrases can be played by clicking nodes on the graph. Figure 1 shows an outline of our interface.

Existing music structure visualisation tools are highly relied on annotated data, while existing music datasets with structural annotations tend to be either a) small in terms of items in the corpus, but with detailed annotatations [6,27], or b) larger as a corpus, but with linear annotations only [12]. So, we define hierarchical structural annotations from an existing set of 909 linear-annotated popular Chinese songs.

The contributions of this paper are to 1) develop a method for taking a linear annotation as input, and hierarchicalise it to provide a hierarchical annotation as output (where such hierarchies exist in the input, such as with "BC" in the example above), and 2) introduce a web-based interface where hierarchical annotations of 909 songs can be explored and played back, in sync with the note-level content.

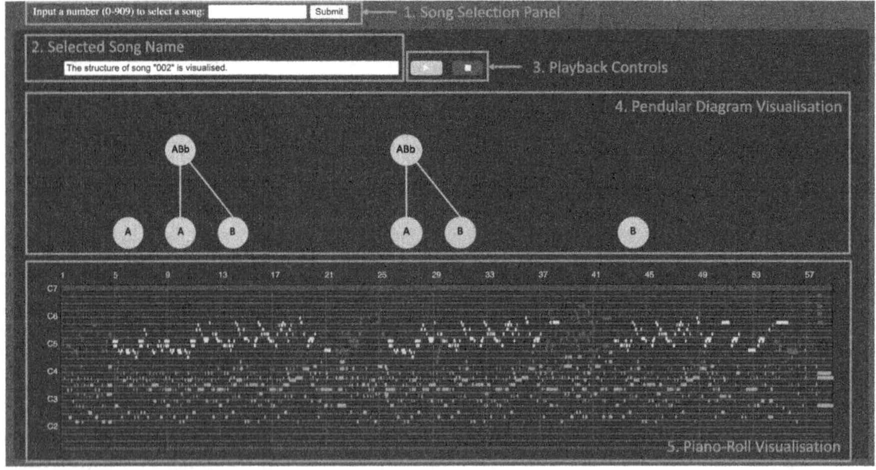

Fig. 1: A screenshot of our interface.

2 Literature Review

This review is split into three parts: first, we provide a brief survey of relevant music representations and file formats; second, we consider previous work on preparing and publishing music datasets with structural annotations; third, we look to methods and tools developed for the visualisation of music-repetitive structure.

2.1 Relevant Music Representations and File Formats

Mainly, this paper will overlook **audio** representations of music. Automatic transcription methods are improving [2, 18] and offer the prospect of deriving note-level details from arbitrary audio inputs, but in this paper we are concerned with a dataset whose representation is symbolic (at the note level). Much work on symbolic music processing in the music information retrieval literature begins with melodic – or at least sequential – representations, such as ABC [28], viewpoints [9], or pitch/interval strings [10]. While some of the examples we include below from other researchers' work constitutes melodic or monophonic (meaning one note at a time) representations, generally, we are concerned with music where multiple notes can begin/end at the same time (polyphonic).

Musical Instrument Digital Interface (MIDI) is means via which certain electronic instruments or devices can communicate musical information. MIDI files contain the trace or record of people playing on such instruments, but they can also be created by someone inputting notes with a mouse or keyboard, using software such as a digital audio workstation. Note events belong to tracks that are associated with certain instruments, with the MIDI note number describing the pitch of a note, and "Note_on" and "Note_off" pairs indicating the start times and durations of notes. As such, MIDI does support polyphonic representation of music. Although other information, such as tempo and velocity (loudness), are also contained in MIDI, MIDI provides slightly different information to that contained in staff notation or sheet music (e.g., direction of note stems, voicing, pitch spelling, etc., are absent from MIDI files but present in staff notation).

MusicXML and MEI are hierarchical markup languages for representing staff notation, in much the same way that HTML represents text documents. They can also represent polyphonic music. Another difference between MusicXML and MIDI is that MusicXML describes musical events relative to one another whereas MIDI events are encoded in absolute terms. E.g., to calculate the start time of a note in a MusicXML file, it is necessary to know or calculate the start and end times of all preceding notes, whereas in a MIDI file it is not.

Composition, Instrument, and Production objects are three JSON-based file formats used to bridge audio and symbolic representations of music.[1] As implied by their names: a Composition object contains similar information to a digital score encoding or MIDI file; an Instrument object contains information about

[1] https://musicintelligence.co/api/maia-spec/.

sample-based or synthesis-based sound generators; and a Production object contains information about audio effects that might be applied to instruments over the time course of a piece. For the purposes of this paper, we can focus on an example Composition object, given in Listing 1.

We will not go through the example in Listing 1 in full detail, but only mention the most relevant components. Lines 2–8 can be considered metadata, while lines 9–31 are the main musical data of the Composition object. The `layer` property straddles the categories of metadata and data, containing staff information as well as annotations of the piece of music. For instance, the `hierGt` property is an abbreviation of "hierarchical ground truth", and will be explained further in Sect. 3, since it is a new contribution of this paper. Each note in the piece is specified by an element of the `notes` array (lines 11–24), with properties that encompass both MIDI and MusicXML formats, depending on the source from which the Composition object is created. For example, if a Composition object is created via MusicXML import, a property such as `pitch` will be defined unambiguously; but if it is created via MIDI import, then `pitch` would have to be estimated from the context. On the other hand, if a Composition object is created via MIDI import, then there may be many tempo and/or control changes (such as sustain pedal), which can be stored in `tempi` and `controlChange` properties, respectively; but if it is created via MusicXML import, then the `controlChange` property is not likely to be populated.

2.2 Music Datasets with Structural Annotations

A classical music dataset named JKU-PDD [6] has repetitive theme and section (generally, "pattern") annotations. Ground-truth patterns in the JKU-PDD dataset are based on sectional repetitions marked in the score, as well as and music analysts' annotations [1,4,25]. A strength of the JKU-PDD is that it contains **hierarchical** patterns (e.g., an annotated theme may occur within an annotated section); a weakness is that only five pieces of music are labelled. Repetitive pattern annotations of another six pieces of classical music are provided by Tomašević et al. [27]. These six pieces are labelled by multiple annotators when studying to what extent different annotation tools and the background of annotators influence the annotation process. Similarly, the weakness of this dataset is that it only contains a handful of pieces.

The POP909 dataset [29] contains piano arrangements of 909 popular Chinese songs in MIDI format, with phrase-level repetitive structure labels [12]. So, in contrast to the JKU-PDD and Tomašević et al.'s annotations, a strength of POP909 is its size; but a weakness is that the annotations are not hierarchical – the labels are attributed at the phrase level only.

In the repetitive phrase labels, melodic phrases are labelled with capital letters, while non-melodic phrases are labelled with lower-case letters. A non-melodic introduction phrase is labelled with "i", a non-melodic ending phrase is labelled with "o", and other non-repetitive phrases are labelled with "X" and "x". The phrase length (the number of bars) is indicated by the number following each phrase label. For example, the song "123 Pinocchio" by Hey Girl in the

Listing 1 Simplified example of a Composition object for "123 Pinocchio".

```
{
  "id": "002",
  "name": "123 Pinocchio",
  "composers": [...],
  "layer": [
    ...,
    "hierGt": {...}
  ],
  "keySignatures": [...],
  "timeSignatures": [...],
  "notes": [
    {
      "barOn": 1,
      "beatOn": 1.5,
      "ontime": 0.5,
      "duration": 0.33333,
      "mnn": 75,
      "mpn": 68,
      "pitch": "D#5",
      "staffNo": 1,
      ...
    },
    ...
  ],
  "tempi": [...],
  "miscImport": {
    "midi": {
      "controlChange": [...]
    },
    ...
  }
}
```

POP909 dataset is labelled "i4A4A4B9b4A4B9b4B9X5o2", where "A4" means phrase "A" consists of 4 bars. Each time "A4" appears in the sequence, there is an exact or inexact repetition of the phrase "A" in the song.

In contrast to the JKU-PDD, with POP909, we do not know whether all or just some of the notes occurring in the four bars labelled "A4" belong to (are a repetition of) "A". But the size of POP909 and the potential for turning the annotations into a hierarchical repetitive structure (see Sect. 3) make it an interesting dataset.

2.3 Music Structure Visualisation Methods

The Shape of Song [30] is an application of arc diagrams [31], in which the repetition of a contiguous pitch sequence is connected to the previous occurrence with an arc. Figure 2 shows an example of the arc diagram, where the largest arc connects bars 1–2 with bars 5 and the first three pitches of bar 6. Two more D's in bars 3 and 7 could be considered included in the largest repetition, since the patterns are still perceptually similar after adding these two notes. However, the arc diagram limits repetitive patterns to be consecutive. If applied to polyphonic data, it would be necessary to define a sequential ordering of notes before the arc diagram could be calculated and constructed – and again, there could be issues with perceptually similar material not being annotated because of slight differences between occurrences of patterns. Similarly, the Infinite Jukebox [20] also connects repetitive patterns with arcs, but a song is visualised as a circle. The interactivity of the Shape of Song and the Infinite Jukebox is limited, and the arc diagrams become dense and difficult to interpret when the length and complexity of the music grows.

Fig. 2: "Mary Had a Little Lamb" visualised by using the Arc Diagrams [31].

Endrjukaite and Kosugi [16] visualises both repetitive patterns and changes in volume by using coloured cylindrical diagrams. Each song is represented by such a diagram, where repetitive patterns are drawn in the same colour, and the diameter reflects the volume. Similar to [16], Chen and Su [5] and Hayashi et al.

[19] also represent repetitive patterns in the same colours. Further, [5] introduces a clustering method to visualise the role of these repetitive patterns in the context of the whole piece of music, while [19] focuses on repetitions between different MIDI tracks. These visualisations suffer from limited interactivity.

By contrast, Songle [17] is more interactive, visualising both the repetitive structure of note and chord content of songs. Songle uses horizontal panels to represent structure and content. For example, one panel contains an automatic transcription of the note content, another an automatic transcription of the chords, while a third panel uses differently coloured oblongs to indicate repeated segments, with oblongs at the same vertical position and of the same colour being perceptually similar. But repetitive patterns are not organised by hierarchical structure, which makes it difficult for users to comprehend the overall structure of songs. Furthermore, mistakes in the automatic transcription can obscure relationships between song segments (e.g., a repeat chord sequence Em, G/D, C, B, D mistranscribed on occasion as Em, C7, Cdim7, G/D will not be identified as sufficiently similar to be highlighted visually).

PatternViewer [24] visualises the repetitive music structure in a pendular graph, and notes currently playing are coloured according to the estimated key. In a pendular graph, G, each vertex (or node) v in the set of vertices V represents a pattern occurrence $P_{i,j}$, where $P_{i,j}$ is a set of points belonging to a point-set representation of the entire piece. An occurrence set is denoted $\mathcal{P}_i = \{P_{i,j} \mid j = 1, 2, \ldots, m\}$, and in a visualisation of G, members of the same occurrence set $\mathcal{P}_i$ are shown as nodes with the same vertical location, with horizontal location determined by their order of appearance in the piece. Members of the same occurrence set are perceptually similar to one another – sometimes (but not necessarily) transnationally equivalent. Patterns containing more points are visualised vertically higher up, while patterns containing fewer points are lower down. An edge e connects two vertices u, v if the pattern occurrence $P_{i,j}$ associated with v is a subset of the pattern occurrence $P_{k,l}$ associated with u.

In PatternViewer, users can click nodes in the pendular graph to listen to a corresponding part of music. Unfortunately, only a handful of pieces were prepared to be visualised (due to the time-intensive nature of defining precisely which notes in a time window do/not belong to a pattern occurrence), and the current version of macOS does not support the installation of PatternViewer, since the software is no longer maintained.

3 Hierarchicalisation of the POP909 Annotations

Repetitive phrase labels for the POP909 dataset are proposed by Dai et al. [12]. The labels are only linear, however, while (in)exact repetition in music tends to be full of hierarchy. For instance, Fig. 3 summaries the repetitive patterns of "123 Pinocchio". The largest repetitive pattern 'A4B9b4' appears twice, highlighted by the red bounding boxes. The labelling along the bottom part of Fig. 3 is the same as that discussed in Sect. 2.2. The nodes and edges above this constitute an example of a pendular graph (see description of the PatternViewer at the end of

Sect. 2.3). For the sake of clarity, when displaying the graphs, we dispense with the bar numbering aspect (i.e., "A4" becomes "A").

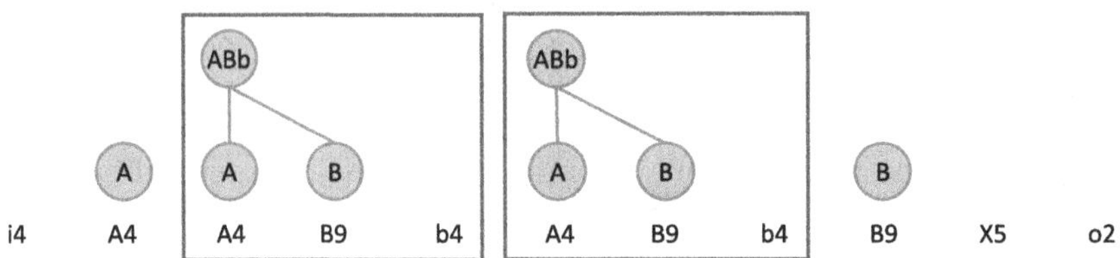

Fig. 3: Hierarchical structure analysis of "123 Pinocchio", Hey Girl. The smallest repetitive phrase is labelled by a letter followed by the number of bars. Phrases labelled with the same letter are (in)exact repetitive, and larger repetitive patterns are highlighted by bounding boxes. The nodes and edges constitue a pendular graph.

Algorithm 1. Hierarchicalises linear repetitive pattern labels.

Input: Linear, phrase-level repetitive pattern labels ($\mathbf{P}$) of the POP909 dataset
Output: Hierarchical repetitive pattern labels

```
for p ∈ P do
    Separate phrase labels and bar counts into two arrays as V_Phr and V_Bar.
    V_Rep ← get_repeat_subsequences(p)
    for v ∈ V_Rep do
        if Non-repetitive patterns (e.g., "X", "x", "i", and "o") involved in v then
            Filter out v
        else if v only appears in larger patterns then
            Filter out v
        else
            if An occurrence of v overlaps the previous occurrence then
                Filter out the current occurrence of v
            end if
            if The occurrence count of v > 1 then
                Push v into V_Out
            end if
        end if
    end for
    return V_Out
end for
```

In this paper, inspired by Deutsch and Feroe [15], we propose an algorithm to convert linear, phrase-level repetitive pattern labels into a hierarchical labelling. Repetitive substrings with the longest length will be labelled as a new pattern. E.g., phrases "ABb" in "123 Pinocchio" will be gathered as a group. On the other hand, substrings that never repeat (such as "i", "X" and "o") or substrings that appear only in a larger pattern will not be labelled. For example, "b" in "123 Pinocchio" will not be labelled since "b" never occurrs independently of "ABb". The outline of our algorithm is given in Algorithm 1. This algorithm takes linear pattern labels ($\mathbf{P}$) of songs as an input, and outputs hierarchical repetitive pattern labels.

When processing a sequence of letters and numbers p from $\mathbf{P}$, our algorithm begins by separating phrase labels (letters) and bar counts (numbers) into two arrays $\mathbf{V}_{\mathrm{Phr}}$ and $\mathbf{V}_{\mathrm{Bar}}$. The function `get_repeat_subsequences()` will return substrings of $\mathbf{V}_{\mathrm{Phr}}$ that repeat at least once, in descending order of length, as well as the index arrays where the first letter of these substrings occur in the entire string as $\mathbf{V}_{\mathrm{Rep}}$. For example, when inputting "abcabda", the function `get_repeat_subsequences()` outputs repetitive substrings "ab", and "a", and "b" and the index arrays of occurrences $[0, 3]$, $[0, 3, 6]$, and $[1, 4]$.

The following steps filter out repetitive patterns $v \in \mathbf{V}_{\mathrm{Rep}}$ that involve non-repetitive phrases (lines 5 and 6 of Algorithm 1), or appear only in larger patterns (lines 7 and 8). For example, "b" in the input "abcabda" will be filtered out, as "b" appears only in a larger pattern "ab". Occurrences of v will be filtered out if they overlap previous occurrences. Then, the number of occurrences of a repetitive pattern will be checked again after the filtering is complete, and only patterns whose occurrence count is larger than one will be pushed into the array $\mathbf{V}_{\mathrm{Out}}$. Finally, $\mathbf{V}_{\mathrm{Out}}$ will be returned for the piece of music. An example hierarchical structure annotation processed by our algorithm is shown in Listing 2, which is stored in the `layer` property of a Composition object (see end of Sect. 2.1).

The contents of lines 2 and 3 of Listing 2 should be compared with the bottom part of Fig. 3: it is the linear annotation; meanwhile, the contents of lines 4–23 contain the pendular graph rendered in the top part of Fig. 3.

4 Interface

Our interactive interface visualises the repetitive patterns of songs hierarchically, as a graph consisting of vertices and edges. The web interface is developed by using JavaScript packages: the client side is built mainly using p5.js; the server side is developed with Fastify and the Node Fetch APIs. The MAIA Util package [8] is used when processing music data, and Tone.js [22] enables the songs to be played back dynamically in the browser.

Figure 4 shows an architecture diagram for our interface. The process starts with a user inputting a number into the Song Selection Panel. The user's input will be sent to the server, and the Change Piece block will check if the input is an integer between 1–909. If the user's input is a sensible number, then a corresponding Composition object will be requested from the Database, and the Composition object as well as a message indicating the song is selected successfully will be sent back to the Song Selection Panel on the client side. Otherwise, a message with the reason for the failure selection will be sent. After getting the message back from the server side, the Song Selection Panel will parse the message, and decide whether to update the Pendular Graph visualisation.

Listing 2 A hierarchical structure annotation example of "123 Pinocchio".

```
"hierGt": {
  "pLabel": "iAABbABbBXo",
  "bars": [4, 4, 4, 9, 4, 4, 9, 4, 9, 5, 2],
  "pendularGraph": {
    "ABb": {
      "edges": [
        "A",
        "B"
      ],
      "subsetScore": 0,
      "occ": [2, 5]
    },
    "A": {
      "edges": [],
      "subsetScore": 1,
      "occ": [1, 2, 5]
    },
    "B": {
      "edges": [],
      "subsetScore": 1,
      "occ": [3, 6, 8]
    }
  }
}
```

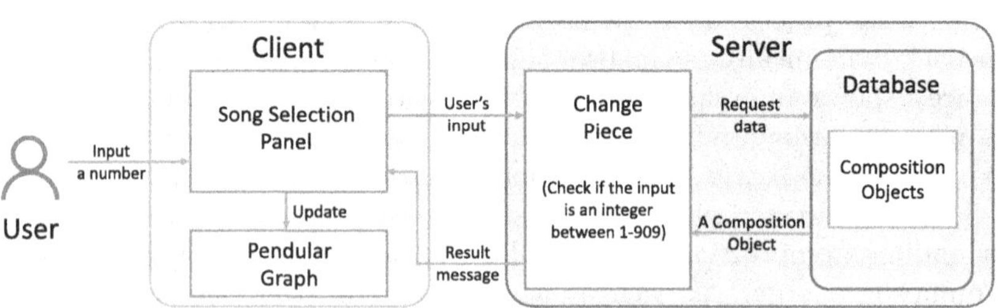

Fig. 4: An architecture diagram for our pendular graph system.

A screenshot of our interface is shown in Fig. 1, which includes 5 elements:

1. **Song selection panel** at the top of the page. A user can enter a number between 1 and 909 in the text input box to select a song to visualise. Once the user clicks "Submit", the server side will read and process data of the selected song, and send it to the client side. Then, content related to the song structure visualisation will be updated.
2. **Selected song name** panel below the song selection panel, which tells the user which song is selected and visualised.
3. **Playback controls** can be clicked to start/pause and stop a song.
4. **Pendular graph visualisation** is the main component of our interface, so-called because the vertices/nodes resemble pendulums. The code behind this component parses the hierarchical structure labels annotated by our algorithm (Sect. 3), and draws them as a pendular graph, where each vertex represents a repetitive pattern. Horizontal location is determined by appearance in the piece; patterns containing more points are visualised vertically higher up, while patterns containing fewer points are lower down. An edge will connect two vertices if one pattern's point-set representation is a subset of that of another. Users can click nodes in the graph to listen to the corresponding part of the music.
5. **Piano-roll visualisation** at the bottom of this page, in which the melody is coloured in yellow, the secondary melody/lead instruments is coloured in purple, and the accompaniment is coloured in orange.

5 Discussion

It has long been suggested that composers introduce repetitions carefully to emphasise music ideas [26]. Recognising repetitive patterns is also an important step for understanding music [21,23]. Visualising the structure of music can enhance audiences' understanding of music, especially when they are listening to a piece of music for the first time [13].

In this paper, we describe the development of a web-based interactive interface, via which hierarchical, repetitive structures of 909 pop songs can be visualised, and repetitive patterns can be played back by clicking nodes of the constituent pendular graph. Compared with some existing music structure visualisation tools, our interface has better interactivity, and it can also visualise more music than many other existing music structure visualisation tools.

During data processing, we noticed that the input MIDI files need to be quantised before use. For example, the downbeats of MIDIs in the POP909 dataset are not aligned to barlines correctly, and time signatures are missing. So, we first align the downbeats according to Dai's annotations [12]. To calculate the time signature of each song in the POP909 dataset, we assume it is in either $\frac{3}{4}$ or $\frac{4}{4}$. We obtain the number of bars for a song by using the phrase-level annotations as a reference, and the total count of crotchet beats can be calculated from the corresponding MIDI file. Our program estimates the time signature of each song by determining if the count of crotchet beats calculated by "bars × beats per bar" matches that in the MIDI file. We find that the time signature of over 95% of songs in the POP909 dataset is $\frac{4}{4}$, while only 28 songs are in $\frac{3}{4}$ time. Quantisation for some symbolic data could be more complicated still when MIDIs are recorded by using a MIDI keyboard for playing input. Thus, a general quantisation method for symbolic data needs to be developed.

A lack of structure is a common problem in music generated by deep learning-based models [11]. In this paper, we developed an interactive interface for visualising the hierarchical structure of the POP909 dataset, which is a quite popular dataset for music generation model training. We hope our interface could inspire researchers in music generation model design to enhance the structure of generated music.

5.1 Limitations and Future Work

While deriving and sharing hierarchical annotations for 909 songs represents an order-of-magnitude increase in the availability of such annotations, it is at the expense of relatively coarse levels of definition – i.e., pattern occurrences begin/end at bar beginnings/endings, and they are defined temporally, meaning all notes existing between two time points are assumed members of a pattern occurrence. This is less precise than with the PatternViewer visualisations [24].

Another limitation of our work is that visualisation is restricted to the labelled POP909 dataset. The current version of the interface does not allow users to upload an arbitrary song to visualise its structure. Future work to incorporate pattern discovery algorithms (e.g., [7]) into this system will enable users to visualise the structure of uploaded songs. Also, the incorporation of pattern discovery algorithms will also address the problem of pattern occurrences beginning/ending at bar beginnings/endings.

As mentioned in previous sections, existing datasets with structural annotations are either small in number of pieces but with detailed annotations, or large in number of pieces but with linear labels only. This lack of data for evaluation restricts the development of pattern discovery algorithms. In future, the hierarchical version of POP909 annotations introduced in this paper can act as a ground truth to evaluate pattern discovery algorithms.

References

1. Barlow, H., Morgenstern, S.: A Dictionary of Musical Themes. Crown Publishers (1948)
2. Benetos, E., Dixon, S., Duan, Z., Ewert, S.: Automatic music transcription: an overview. IEEE Signal Process. Mag. **36**(1), 20–30 (2018)
3. Bent, I.D., Pople, A.: Analysis. In: Sadie, S., Tyrrell, J. (eds.) The New Grove Dictionary of Music and Musicians, 2nd edn, vol. 1, pp. 526–589. Macmillan, London (2001)
4. Bruhn, S.: J.S. Bach's Well-Tempered Clavier: In-depth Analysis and Interpretation, vol. 4. Siglind Bruhn (1993)

5. Chen, T.P., Su, L.: The musical schemagram: time-scale visualization of repeated patterns in music. In: 2018 Asia-Pacific Signal and Information Processing Association Annual Summit and Conference (APSIPA ASC), pp. 1642–1648. IEEE (2018)
6. Collins, T.: Discovery of repeated themes and sections (2013). https://www.music-ir.org/mirex/wiki/2013:Discovery_of_Repeated_Themes_%26_Sections
7. Collins, T., Arzt, A., Flossmann, S., Widmer, G.: SIARCT-CFP: improving precision and the discovery of inexact musical patterns in point-set representations. In: Proceedings of the International Society for Music Information Retrieval Conference, Curitiba, pp. 549–554 (2013)
8. Collins, T., Coulon, C.: MAIA Util: an NPM package for bridging web audio with music-theoretic concepts. In: Proceedings of the Web Audio Conference, pp. 47–52 (2019)
9. Conklin, D., Witten, I.H.: Multiple viewpoint systems for music prediction. J. New Music Res. **24**(1), 51–73 (1995)
10. Crawford, T., Badkobeh, G., Lewis, D.: Searching page-images of early music scanned with OMR: a scalable solution using minimal absent words. In: Proceedings of the International Society for Music Information Retrieval Conference, Paris, pp. 233–239 (2018)
11. Dai, S., Yu, H., Dannenberg, R.B.: What is missing in deep music generation? a study of repetition and structure in popular music. In: Proceedings of the International Society for Music Information Retrieval Conference, Bengaluru, pp. 659–666 (2022)
12. Dai, S., Zhang, H., Dannenberg, R.B.: Automatic analysis and influence of hierarchical structure on melody, rhythm and harmony in popular music. In: Proceedings of the Joint Conference on AI Music Creativity (2020)
13. De Prisco, R., Malandrino, D., Pirozzi, D., Zaccagnino, G., Zaccagnino, R.: Understanding the structure of musical compositions: is visualization an effective approach? Inf. Vis. **16**(2), 139–152 (2017)
14. Deutsch, D.: The processing of structured and unstructured tonal sequences. Percept. Psychophys. **28**(5), 381–389 (1980)
15. Deutsch, D., Feroe, J.: The internal representation of pitch sequences in tonal music. Psychol. Rev. **88**(6), 503 (1981)
16. Endrjukaite, T., Kosugi, N.: Music visualization technique of repetitive structure representation to support intuitive estimation of music affinity and lightness. J. Mob. Multim. **8**(1), 49–71 (2012)
17. Goto, M., Ogata, J., Yoshii, K., Fujihara, H., Mauch, M., Nakano, T.: PodCastle and Songle: crowdsourcing-based web services for spoken document retrieval and active music listening. In: Information Theory and Applications Workshop, pp. 298–299 (2012)
18. Hawthorne, C., Simon, I., Swavely, R., Manilow, E., Engel, J.: Sequence-to-sequence piano transcription with transformers. In: Proceedings of the International Society for Music Information Retrieval Conference, pp. 246–253 (2021)
19. Hayashi, A., Itoh, T., Matsubara, M.: Colorscore: visualization and condensation of structure of classical music. In: Knowledge Visualization Currents: From Text to Art to Culture, pp. 113–128 (2013)
20. Lamere, P.: The Infinite Jukebox (2012). https://eternalbox.dev/jukebox_index.html
21. Lerdahl, F., Jackendoff, R.: A Generative Theory of Tonal Music. MIT Press, Cambridge (1983)
22. Mann, Y.: Interactive music with Tone.js. In: Proceedings of the International Web Audio Conference (2015)

23. Meyer, L.B.: Emotion and Meaning in Music. University of Chicago Press (2008)
24. Nikrang, A., Collins, T., Widmer, G.: PatternViewer: an application for exploring repetitive and tonal structure. In: Late-Breaking News and Demos of the International Society for Music Information Retrieval Conference, Taipei (2014)
25. Schoenberg, A.: Fundamentals of Musical Composition. Faber and Faber (1967)
26. Schoenberg, A.: Style and Idea: Selected Writings. University of California Press (2010)
27. Tomašević, D., Wells, S., Ren, I.Y., Volk, A., Pesek, M.: Exploring annotations for musical pattern discovery gathered with digital annotation tools. J. Math. Music **15**(2), 194–207 (2021)
28. Walshaw, C.: The ABC music standard 2.1 technical report (2011). https://abcnotation.com
29. Wang, Z., et al.: POP909: a pop-song dataset for music arrangement generation. In: Proceedings of the International Society for Music Information Retrieval Conference, Montreal, pp. 38–45 (2020)
30. Wattenberg, M.: Shape of song (2002). http://www.turbulence.org/Works/song/
31. Wattenberg, M.: Arc diagrams: visualizing structure in strings. In: IEEE Symposium on Information Visualization, pp. 110–116 (2002)

Using Perspective Taking and Information Paucity to Explore Alternative Realities

David A. Illingworth[1(✉)], Ashley Lawrence[2], Michael R. Dougherty[3], and Rick P. Thomas[2]

[1] California State University, Long Beach, Long Beach, CA 90840, USA
david.illingworth@csulb.edu
[2] Georgia Institute of Technology, Atlanta, GA 30332, USA
[3] University of Maryland, College Park, MD 20742, USA

Abstract. The reported experiment examined perspective taking and information paucity as candidate interventions to enhance performance in a counterfactual forecasting task. We hypothesized that these interventions would increase the number and diversity of hypotheses generated in support of counterfactual reasoning and, in turn, improve accuracy in forecasting. We also examined whether the manipulations influenced the retrospective estimates of criteria relevant to a historical event and the accuracy of future forecasts. Participants were tasked with completing two historical counterfactual exercises-the first involved the West African Ebola outbreak, while the second was related to the Financial Crisis of 2007-2008. Participants in an information paucity group did not receive the full description of the historical event at once. Instead, they received a summary of the historical event followed by four troves of information, organized by topic, sequentially in random order. Participants in an immersive perspective-taking group were asked to take on three perspectives: 1) healthcare professional, 2) economist, and 3) legislator. There was also a third experimental group that received both interventions and a control group that did not receive any of the interventions. We found that sequential presentation and perspective-taking increased the number of counterfactual Hypotheses and the diversity of the generated counterfactual Hypotheses across both scenarios. Unfortunately, the differences in counterfactual reasoning did not translate to differences in the forecasting accuracy of the participants.

Keywords: Counterfactual Reasoning · Forecasting · Hypothesis Generation

1 Introduction

Counterfactual reasoning is an ubiquitous process that involves imagining alternative scenarios to a realized sequence of events [1–4]. Counterfactual forecasting (CF) assesses the probability of a counterfactual outcome via its plausibility within the constructed alternative scenario. Developing conceptual models

Supported by The Intelligence Advanced Research Projects Activity.

H. Mori et al. (Eds.): HCII 2023, LNCS 14056, pp. 17–31, 2023.
https://doi.org/10.1007/978-3-031-48044-7_2

of counterfactual worlds involves "mentally undoing" the past-changing critical variables in the realized causal scenarios and recalculating their impacts on both intermediate events and final outcomes to understand what might have happened when changing the states for those critical variables.

Although people naturally engage in CF, they are often narrow in their considerations [1]. Human cognitive limitations cause people to be unsuccessful when performing counterfactual reasoning and incorporating their reasoning into their beliefs. For example, due to the hindsight bias phenomenon, people consistently ascribe a higher probability to an event after it has occurred than they would have estimated before the event [5,6]. People have difficulty generating counterfactual hypotheses (i.e., alternative causal scenarios) about the world and understanding how those hypotheses can lead to different outcomes. They instead focus on a minimal set of hypotheses or causal scenarios—often on a single hypothesis or explanation, to the exclusion of other non-zero utility alternatives [7]. Thus, there is a need to develop methods to support multi-path reasoning—the generation of more than a single hypothesis [8–11].

The goal of our experiment was to investigate the degree to which the number and breadth of counterfactual hypotheses increase with manipulations of perspective-taking and information paucity. Also, the experiment examined whether the manipulations influenced the retrospective estimates of criteria relevant to a historical event (counterfactual forecasts) and the accuracy of future forecasts.

Information Paucity, as operationalized in this experiment, involved the presentation of independent subsets of information for a realized event. Participants were only provided a new subset of information after attempting to generate hypotheses for previous subsets. The conceptual basis of the information paucity manipulation is that starting with independent subsets of information can seed different semantic defaults, which has been shown to improve hypothesis generation and counterfactual generation and reduce hindsight bias [7,9]. Stated more simply, information paucity prompts decision-makers to consider different aspects of a counterfactual scenario by controlling (or restricting) access to the information available in the complete counterfactual Scenario.

Immersive perspective-taking was operationalized as prompting participants to take on a different role or persona (in terms of thoughts, values, and feelings) from the current perspective [12]. The conceptual logic of immersive perspective-taking is that it can facilitate multi-path reasoning because the perspective switch may provide a new way of framing a problem, thus, augmenting the knowledge and inference processes brought to bear to facilitate new outlooks on a scenario [7].

2 Method

There were 560 participants recruited via Qualtrics, but 134 failed to finish the experiment, leaving a sample size of 426. We will address the attrition for this experiment in the discussion section. All participants were required to have a college degree and a background (via education or professional domain) in finance or public health. The participants were randomly assigned to one of eight independent groups defined by crossing Scenario (2014-2016 West Africa Ebola Outbreak vs. the 2007-2008 financial crisis), Information Paucity (all information vs. sequential presentation), and Perspective Taking (no perspective vs. sequential assignment of immersive roles). After the presentation of all materials and the opportunity to generate as many different potential consequences resulting from the counterfactual, the participants provided three counterfactual forecasts and one predictive forecast relevant to the domain of the historical event they received. At the end of the experiment, the participants were administered the Cognitive Reflections Test [13] and the Berlin Numeracy Scale [14]. An illustration of the experimental design and flow of the experimental protocol is provided in Fig. 1.

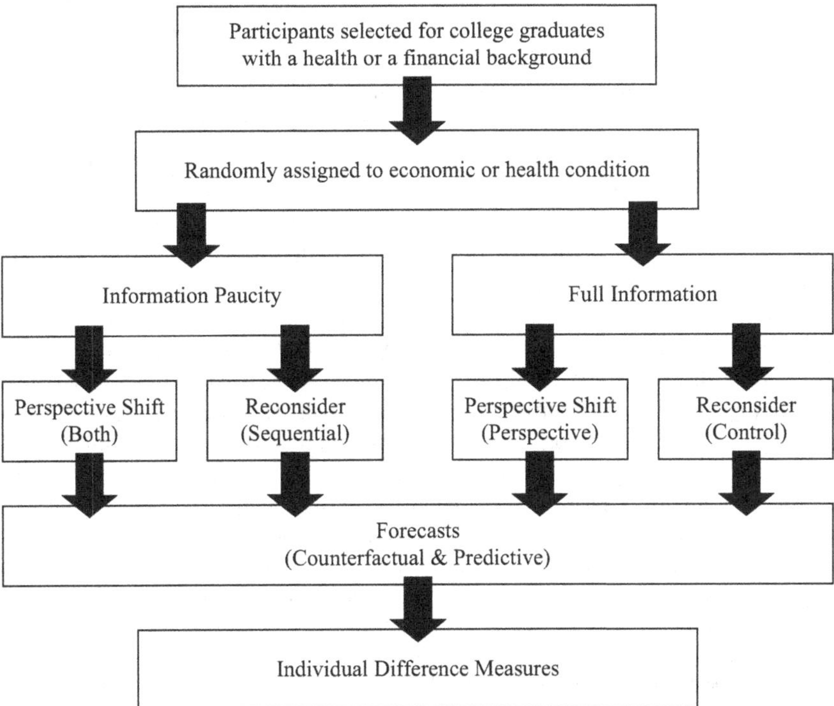

Fig. 1. Experimental design and flow.

2.1 Paucity Manipulation

Participants in an information paucity group did not receive the full description of the historical event at once. Instead, they received a summary of the historical event followed by four troves of information, organized by topic, sequentially in random order. For the West African Ebola Scenario, the four troves were transmission, healthcare infrastructure, public health practices, and the effects on healthcare workers. For the Financial Crisis of 2007-2008 scenario, the four troves were lending, financial institutions, government policies, and consumer factors. The participants received a prompt to generate counterfactual hypotheses after being presented with each trove of information describing an aspect of the historical event. After receiving the summary and all four troves of information, the participants were prompted to reflect on the complete description of the historical event and to generate new counterfactual hypotheses.

2.2 Immersive Perspective-Taking Manipulation

Participants in an immersive perspective-taking group were asked to take on three different perspectives: 1) healthcare professional, 2) economist, and 3) legislator. The perspectives were assigned in a random order, and immersion in the perspective followed a series of steps. First, to measure the participant's knowledge relevant to a specific perspective, the participant rated their self-knowledge on seven dimensions relevant to the domain of the perspective. For instance, items from the healthcare perspective included questions about health program policy, disease transmission principles, etc. Similar self-rating items were given to measure knowledge for the economist's perspective (e.g., "How knowledgeable are you about the principles of supply and demand?"). The second step, the perspective-taking immersion, was to prompt the participants to generate two recent events relevant to the perspective. For instance, from the economic perspective, the participants were asked to generate two recent economic events and how they affected individual people, communities, government institutions, and national or global economics. The third step in the immersive perspective-taking required the participants to rate the fluency of their memory for the events generated in step 2 and the ease of generating the consequences. Fluency was measured on an 8-point Likert scale, ranging from 1 ("Not at all") to 8 ("Extremely"). The final step of the immersive perspective-taking manipulation provided the participants explicit instructions to use the perspective to generate new counterfactual hypotheses. These steps were repeated for each perspective.

2.3 Individual Difference Measures

At the end of the experiment, the participants were administered the Cognitive Reflection Test (CRT, a measure of people's willingness or ability to engage in deliberative thought; [13]), and the Berlin Numeracy Test (BNT, a measure of people's ability to reason about simple numerical concepts; [14]). Overall, the distribution of scores on both measures appeared consistent with the literature (see Fig. 2).

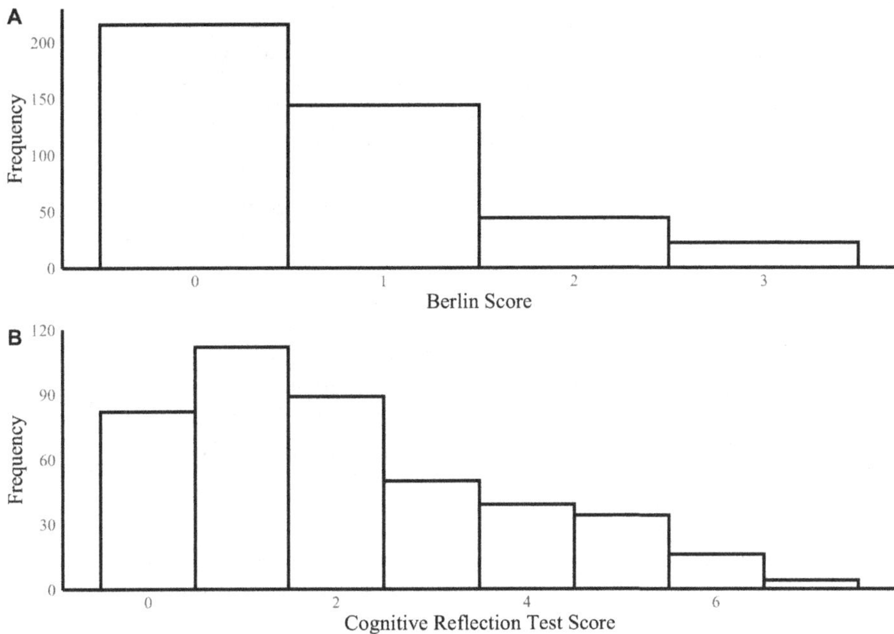

Fig. 2. Distributions of scores on the Berlin Numeracy Task and the Cognitive Reflection Test for the entire sample.

3 Results

3.1 Demographics

The participants in the experiment tended to be older (Fig. 3, Panel B), Caucasian (Fig. 3, Panel D) and educated (Fig. 3, Panel C). Although approximately equal proportions of women and men were in the study, more women had a health background (Fig. 3, Panel A). In contrast, more men had an economics/financial background. The sex distribution is consistent with the population demographics in these professions.

3.2 Hypothesis Generation

We tested if immersive perspective-taking and information paucity increased the number of hypotheses generated by the participants using Poison Regression. We also evaluated whether the background knowledge of the participant (financial versus health) influenced the number of hypotheses generated or interacted with the effects of the perspective-taking and information paucity manipulations on the number of hypotheses generated. For the health scenario, there were statistically significant main effects of both perspective-taking, $\chi^2(1, 212) = 40.96, p < .05$, and information paucity, $\chi^2(1, 212) = 69.17, p < .05$, as well as a significant

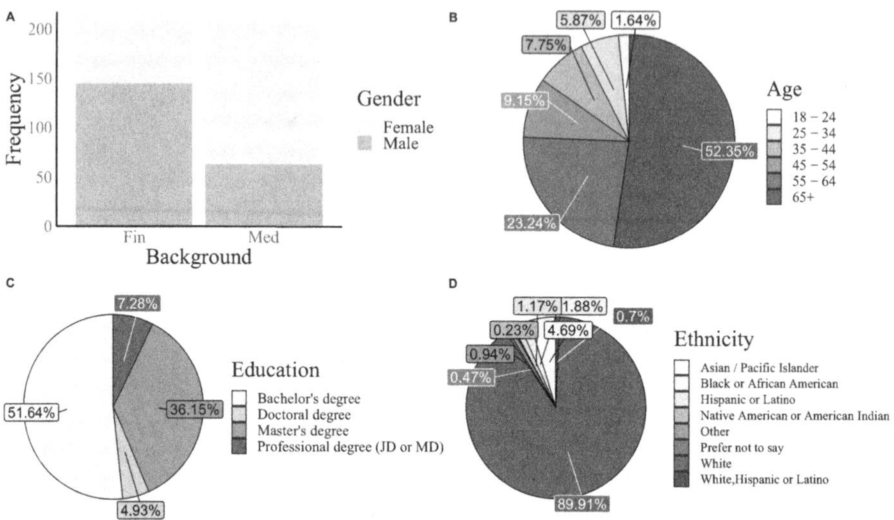

Fig. 3. Sample demographic data, including the gender distribution across background (Panel A), age distribution (Panel B), level of education (Panel C), and ethnicity (Panel D).

perspective-taking by paucity interaction, $\chi^2(1, 212) = 4.26, p < .05$. The pattern of findings was identical for the economic scenario; there were statistically significant main effects of both perspective-taking, $\chi^2(1, 212) = 23.29, p < .05$, and information paucity, $\chi^2(1, 212) = 103.15, p < .05$, as well as a significant perspective-taking by paucity interaction, $\chi^2(1, 212) = 6.18, p < .05$. As illustrated in Fig. 4, Panel A, both information paucity (sequential) and perspective-taking led to the generation of more hypotheses relative to the control condition. The significant interaction implies that the combined effect of information paucity and perspective-taking was less than additive. There were no statistically significant effects of background knowledge on the number of hypotheses generated, and background knowledge did not interact with the manipulations, $ps > 0.05$. As clearly illustrated in Fig. 4, Panel A, the both group's mean number of CF-hypotheses generated was substantially higher than the control group.

We applied Latent Semantic Analysis (LSA) to extract the semantic content from the counterfactual hypotheses generated by the participants. The analysis aims to assess the degree to which the participants explored similar versus different parts of the hypothesis space, thus, enabling us to evaluate the effectiveness of our manipulations at nudging participants to consider different factors of the hypothesis space or to increase their diversity of thought.

We derived a diversity of thought metric for each participant by using LSA to generate similarity estimates of the counterfactuals generated by each participant. Similarity scores reflect the mean of the similarities across all pairwise combinations of the counterfactual hypotheses generated by the participant.

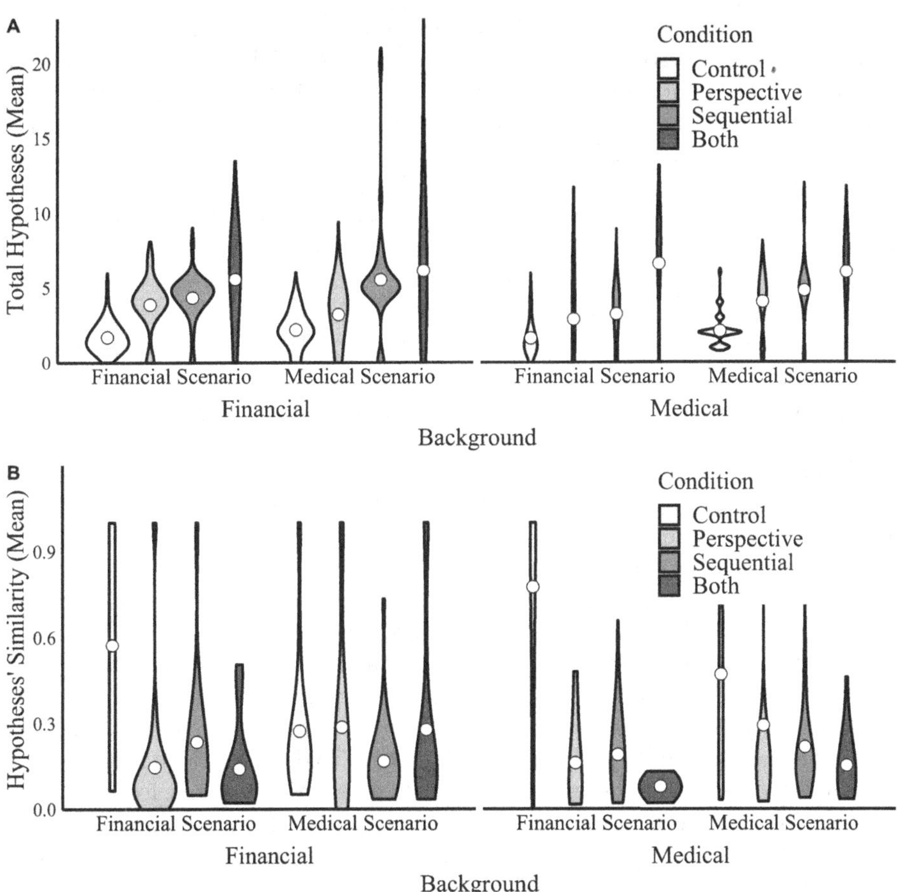

Fig. 4. Hypothesis generation behavior. Number of counterfactual hypotheses generated as a function of background knowledge, scenario, and the experimental manipulations are presented in Panel A. The similarity of generated hypotheses are presented in Panel B.

Figure 4, Panel B plots the mean similarity (diversity-of-thought- metric) across the conditions.

We tested if immersive perspective-taking and information paucity increased diversity of thought by analyzing the mean similarities using the General Linear Model (GLM). We also evaluated whether the background knowledge of the participant (financial versus health) influenced the mean similarities or interacted with the effects of the perspective-taking and information paucity manipulations on mean similarity. For the health scenario, there was a statistically significant main effect of information paucity, $\chi^2(1, 196) = 9.37, p < .05$, indicating that participants receiving the perspective-taking manipulation had lower mean similarities between their generated hypotheses, indicative of more diversity of thought than participants that did not receive the information paucity manipulation. There was also a statistically significant two-way interaction between perspective-taking and background knowledge, $\chi^2(1, 196) = 4.91, p < .05$, indicating that perspective-taking led to less diversity of thought when the participants' background was in public health than when their background was financial in the health scenario. There were no other statistically significant main effects or interactions in the health scenario. Regarding post-hoc analyses, all groups' mean similarity scores were significantly lower than the control group. The pattern of findings for the economic scenario for mean similarity was more in line with the number of hypotheses generated analyses; there were statistically significant main effects of both perspective-taking, $\chi^2(1, 174) = 38.45, p < .05$, and information paucity, $\chi^2(1, 174) = 25.43, p < .05$, as well as a significant perspective-taking by paucity interaction, $\chi^2(1, 174) = 17.24, p < .05$. As illustrated in Fig. 4, Panel B, both information paucity (sequential) and perspective-taking generally led to relatively low mean similarities compared to the control condition. The significant interaction implies that the combined effect of information paucity and perspective-taking was, once again, less than additive. There were no statistically significant effects of background knowledge on the number of hypotheses generated, and background knowledge did not interact with the experimental manipulations, *ps* > 0.05. Regarding post-hoc analyses, all groups' mean similarity scores were significantly lower than the control group, *ps* < 0.05.

We tested if immersive perspective-taking, information paucity, or background knowledge influenced the content of the counterfactual hypotheses generated by the participants. Specifically, we used LSA to derive vectors representing the semantic content of the counterfactual hypotheses generated for each participant. The LSA vectors were used to derive a distance (dissimilarity) matrix for submission to K-means clustering. We used the fit metric of inertia and the elbow method to choose the number of eigen decompositions of the dissimilarity matrix to submit to the K-means clustering algorithm and the most appropriate number of clusters to fit the data. A six-cluster solution was most justified for the Health scenario, while a 3 cluster solution was the most justified for the financial scenario.

We used log-linear regression to analyze whether the likelihood of cluster assignment differed as a function of the experimental manipulations or background knowledge. There was a statically significant interaction, $\chi^2 = 6.92$, $p < .05$, between background knowledge and perspective-taking on semantic cluster assignment in the financial scenario (see Fig. 5). No other effects were statistically reliable, *ps* > 0.05. There were no statistically significant effects for the Health Scenario, *ps* > 0.05.

3.3 Counterfactual Forecasts

We evaluated whether the experimental manipulations and background knowledge affected the participant's CF. We calculated the Rank Probability Scores (RPS) for the three counterfactual forecasts for each historical event (See Table 1). Because CF involves predicting the outcome for scenarios that have

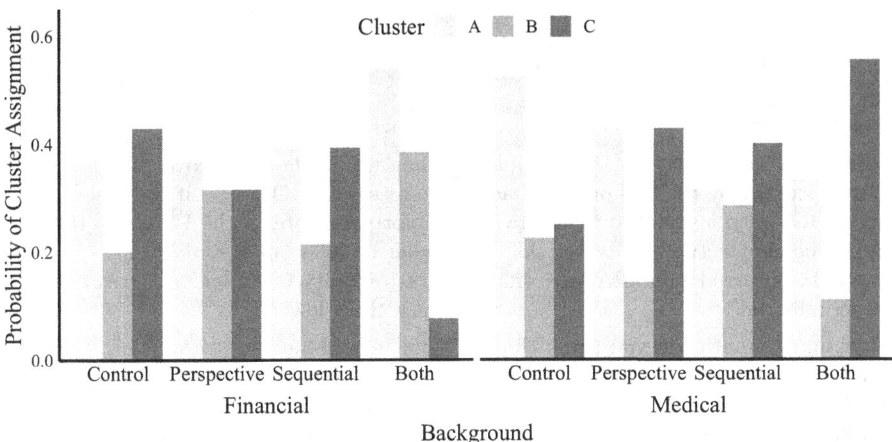

Fig. 5. Probability of semantic cluster assignment as a function of background knowledge and the experimental manipulations in the financial scenario.

not and will not be resolved, there was no objective truth to which participants' forecasts could be compared. Thus, the RPS in the context of CF can be interpreted as a deviation from the hindsight score, where higher values indicate a greater degree of disparity between the CF and the historical event's outcome. Thus, in the hindsight context, higher RPS scores might be interpreted as better. As can be seen from Fig. 6, there is no consistent pattern of deviation from hindsight with respect to the scenario, background knowledge, or the experimental manipulations, $ps > 0.05$.

3.4 Prospective Forecasts

We also asked each participant to make a single prospective forecast in each scenario (Table 2). Of course, for the prospective forecast, higher RPS values should be interpreted as usual—that the forecasted probability distribution was more deviate concerning the outcome index. Thus, higher RPS values reflect more errorful forecasts.

We evaluated whether the experimental manipulations and background knowledge affected the participant's prospective forecasting performance (RPS scores) using the General Linear Model. There was a statically significant three-way interaction between Background Knowledge, Paucity, and Perspective-taking, $F(1, 178) = 5.29$, in the Financial Scenario (Fig. 7). There were no other statistically signification effects of the experimental manipulations or background knowledge on prospective forecast accuracy for either scenario, $ps > 0.05$.

The prospective forecast regarding the Ebola outbreak in the Democratic Republic of the Congo (DRC) was not analyzed. In addition to the near record number of deaths related to Ebola, numerous additional crises arose in the DRC while we were conducting this study, including a rise in militant violence, a

Table 1. Counterfactual forecasting questions by scenario.

Health Scenario	Financial Scenario
How many deaths do you think would have occurred by the end of 2016 had the CDC's response in 2014 been twice as strong as it actually was but the response occurred 3 months later than it actually did?	When would the US recover its pre-recession GDP level if the amount of mortgage debt in the US was a third higher in 2006 but the ratio of debt-to-equity for financial institutions was a third lower?
How many months do you think the outbreak would have lasted had the CDC's response in 2014 been twice as strong as it actually was but the response occurred 3 months later than it actually did?	What would have been the peak unemployment rate that resulted from the financial crisis had the amount of mortgage debt in the US been a third higher in 2006 but the ratio of debt-to-equity for financial institutions was a third lower?
How many healthcare workers would have died during the outbreak had the CDC's response in 2014 been twice as strong as it actually was but the response occurred 3 months later than it actually did?	By what percent would net worth have decreased had the amount of mortgage debt in the US been a third higher in 2006 but the ratio of debt-to-equity for financial institutions was a third lower?

Table 2. Prospective forecasting questions by scenario.

Health Scenario	Financial Scenario
There is currently an outbreak of Ebola in the Democratic Republic of the Congo. How many deaths from Ebola do you predict by December 31, 2019? Please assign a probability to each of the categories below indicating the chance that the number of deaths would fall into each category	As of the last quarter in 2018, home mortgage debt outstanding in the U.S. was $10.88 trillion. What do you predict the amount of home mortgage debt outstanding will be at the end of the last quarter in 2019? Please assign a probability to each of the categories below indicating the chance that the outstanding home mortgage debt would fall into each category

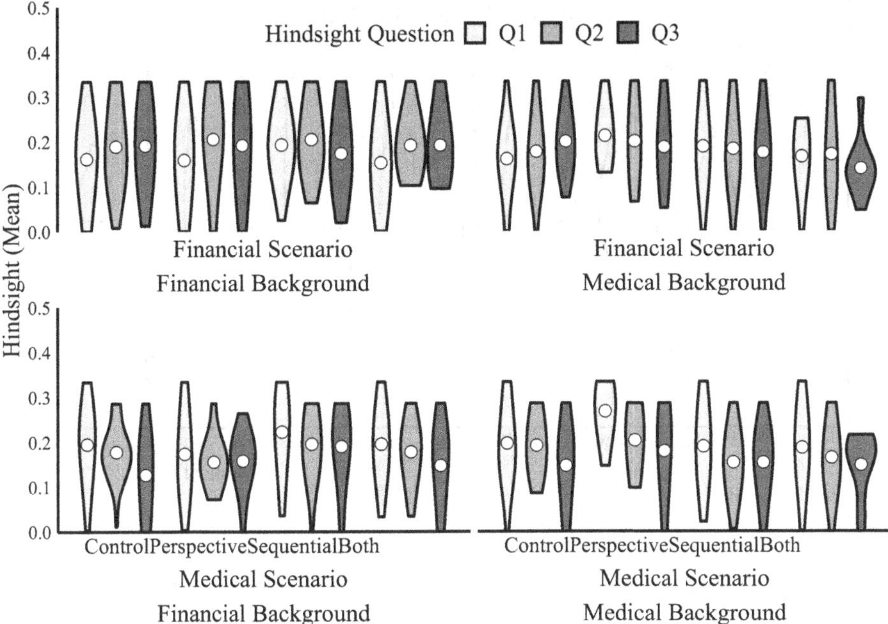

Fig. 6. Mean RPS (Deviation from Hindsight) of the counterfactual forecasts plotted as a function of background knowledge and the experimental manipulations for the financial (top row) and health scenarios (bottom row)

measles outbreak, and the seasonal malaria peak [15]. We determined that there could have been confusion regarding the outbreak in question and the final death count would be confounded by the multiple crises in the country, presenting a challenge to validating ground truth.

Semantic Differences in CF-Hypotheses: Number of CF-Hypotheses Generated and Diversity of Thought. We used both a General Linear Model and logistic regression to explore whether cluster assignment predicted the mean similarity between the CF hypotheses generated by the participants. There were no statistically significant effects of semantic cluster assignment on the number of hypotheses generated or the similarity of the generated hypotheses (diversity of thought, $ps > 0.05$). Thus, there is no evidence that the number or the diversity of the hypotheses generated by the participants affected the underlying semantics of the generated CF hypotheses relative to other participants receiving the same scenario.

Semantic Differences in CF-Hypotheses: Deviation from Hindsight and Prospective Forecast Accuracy. We used the General Linear Model and logistic regression to explore whether cluster assignment predicted the mean RPS

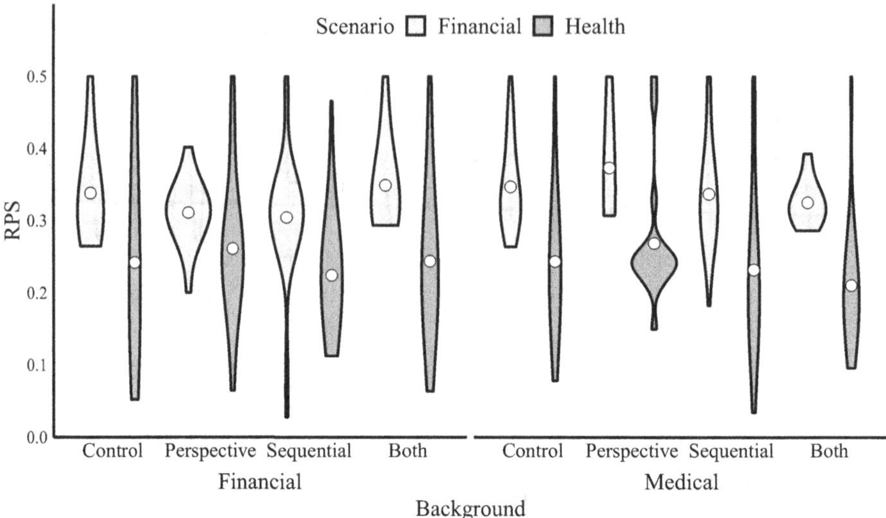

Fig. 7. Mean RPS scores for the financial predictive forecast plotted as a function of scenario, background knowledge, and the experimental manipulations.

scores for CF forecasts (deviation from hindsight) or the prospective forecasts. There were no statistically significant effects of semantic cluster assignment on the RPS scores for the CF forecasts or the prospective forecasts, $ps > 0.05$. Thus, there is no evidence that the content of the generated CF hypotheses impacted the forecast behavior of the participants in the experiment.

Individual Differences and Exploratory Analyses. Using Pearson correlation, we evaluated the association between six variables: 1) the total number of hypotheses, 2) the BNS, 3) the accuracy score on the CRT, 4) a composite measure of deviation from hindsight, 5) a composite measure of prospective forecast accuracy, and 6) the mean similarly of the CF-hypotheses generated by the participants. Table 3 lists the Pearson correlations for the two scenarios (correlations for the financial scenario are reported above the diagonal, and the correlations for the health scenario are reported below the diagonal) for the six variables. Pearson correlations that are statically significant at the $p < .05$ level are indicated with an asterisk. Consistent with previous research, there was a significant correlation between the CRT and BNS. Prospective forecast accuracy had a small but statistically significant correlation with the total number of hypotheses generated in the financial scenario, indicating that as the total number of hypotheses generated increased, the participants' predictive accuracy increased. There was also a significant negative correlation between the number of hypotheses generated and the semantic similarity of the generated hypotheses for both scenarios. Prospective forecast accuracy was also significantly correlated with the composite deviation from hindsight in both scenarios. This suggests prospective forecast accuracy improved as participants' CF forecasts deviated more from the historical event.

Table 3. Pearson correlations.

	1	2	3	4	5	6
1) Total number of hypotheses	1	−0.10	−0.03	−0.00	0.18*	−0.49*
2) Berlin Numeracy	−0.02	1	0.38*	−0.11	−0.04	−0.03
3) Cognitive Reflection Test	−0.11	0.52*	1	−0.08	−0.11	0.02
4) Comp. hindsight	0.07	−0.11	−0.15*	1	0.23*	0.04
5) Predictive forecast accuracy	−0.05	0.07	0.05	0.27*	1	−0.04
6) Hypothesis similarity	−0.47*	0.05	0.01	0.01	0.05	1

4 Discussion

Our experiment provides definitive evidence that our manipulations affected counterfactual hypothesis generation. Specifically, sequential presentation (information paucity) and perspective-taking increased the number of CF hypotheses and the breadth of the generated counterfactual hypotheses across both scenarios. That information paucity increases hypothesis generation has been reported previously [7,9], but it was important that we replicate the phenomenon in a CF context. We built on this result by analyzing the semantic content of the generated counterfactual hypotheses. Using a similarity metric, we show that generated counterfactual hypotheses are more dissimilar when our interventions are present. This result indicates that generating more hypotheses is not accounted for by rephrasing the same idea repeatedly.

Unfortunately, we have very little evidence that these differences in counterfactual hypothesis generation influenced CF or prospective forecasting in any reliable or systematic way. Moreover, the semantic content, diversity, and the number of CF hypotheses generated also did not influence the CF or prospective forecasting in any reliable or systematic way. Broadly speaking, our study was motivated by the idea that considering more causal counterfactual hypotheses would result in better calibration of the probability of likely outcomes. That increased number and the breadth of generated hypotheses did not translate into better predictive accuracy, providing evidence against our hypothesis.

As far as our more exploratory analyses were concerned, we found very little evidence that differences in domain knowledge led to differences in counterfactual hypothesis generation, CF, or prospective forecasting. There also appear to be no large or systematic effects of individual difference measures on counterfactual hypothesis generation, CF, or prospective forecasting. Additional research will be necessary to explore other manipulations that enhance CF accuracy.

This work was part of a project funded by The Intelligence Advanced Research Projects Activity, which focuses on externally valid methods. Our goal in this experiment was to isolate the unique contributions to performance from each of our interventions. Consequently, we have created a task in which time on task is confounded with our experimental manipulations. For instance, participants in the control condition had fewer steps to complete the task than those in the sequential or perspective conditions. Participants in the both condition had far more steps to complete than any other group.

Moreover, as we stated in the Methods section, 134 participants failed to finish the experiment leaving open the possibility of differential attrition across the experimental conditions: 14 self-terminated before group assignment, 37 self-terminated in the Control condition, 7 self-terminated in the Perspective group, 51 self-terminated in the Sequential condition, and 6 self-terminated in both. Because participants were less likely to self-terminate in the perspective-taking and both conditions, the perspective-taking manipulation may have motivated the participants to expend effort and maintain task participation, which is potentially important in application.

Our sample was also predominantly white, over the age of 65, and in possession of advanced degrees. Additionally, we observed that gender was not independent from academic or professional background. While these gender differences reflect the distributions present in these professional domains, some may interpret the disparity as a limitation of the study. It is worth pointing out that we do not report significant differences between the financial and medical backgrounds for any of our planned or exploratory analyses. Ultimately, our results must be interpreted in the context of the limitations listed above.

While we successfully affected counterfactual hypothesis generation in a manner consistent with our predictions, we were unsuccessful in demonstrating a mechanism by which performance on CF tasks could be enhanced. The general summary is that the experimental manipulations had their predicted influence on CF reasoning but that the differences in CF reasoning did not translate to differences in the forecasting behavior of the participants.

References

1. Byrne, R.M.J.: Counterfactual thought. Annu. Rev. Psychol. **67**, 135–157 (2016)
2. Kahneman, D., Miller, D.T.: Norm theory: comparing reality to its alternatives. Psychol. Rev. **93**(2), 136–153 (1986)
3. Kahneman, D., Tversky, A.: The simulation heuristic. In: Kahneman, D., Slovic, P., Tversky, A. (eds.) Judgment Under Uncertainty: Heuristics and Biases, pp. 201–208. Cambridge University Press, New York (1986)
4. Roese, N.J.: Counterfactual thinking. Psychol. Bull. **121**(1), 133–148 (1997)
5. Fischhoff, B.: Perceived informativeness of facts. J. Exp. Psychol. Hum. Percept. Perform. **3**(2), 349–358 (1977)
6. Lichtenstein, S., Slovic, P., Fischhoff, B., Layman, M., Combs, B.: Judged frequency of lethal events. J. Exp. Psychol. Hum. Learn. Mem. **4**(6), 551–578 (1978)

7. Dougherty, M.R.P., Gettys, C.F., Thomas, R.P.: The role of mental simulation in judgments of likelihood. Organ. Behav. Hum. Decis. Process. **70**(2), 135–148 (1997)
8. Dougherty, M.R.P., Hunter, J.E.: Hypothesis generation, probability judgment, and individual differences in working memory capacity. Acta Physiol. (Oxf) **113**(3), 263–282 (2003)
9. Sprenger, A., Dougherty, M.R.: Generating and evaluating options for decision making: the impact of sequentially presented evidence. J. Exp. Psychol. Learn. Mem. Cogn. **38**(3), 550–575 (2012)
10. Weber, M., Borcherding, K.: Behavioral influences on weight judgments in multiatribute decision making. Eur. J. Oper. Res. **67**(1), 1–12 (1993)
11. Thomas, R.P., Dougherty, M.R., Sprenger, A.M., Harbison, J.: Diagnostic hypothesis generation and human judgment. Psychol. Rev. **115**(1), 155–185 (2008)
12. Galinky, A.D., Maddux, W.W., Gilin, D., White, J.B.: Why it pays to get inside the head of your opponent: the differential effects of perspective taking and empathy in negotiations. Psychol. Sci. **19**(4), 378–384 (2008)
13. Frederick, S.: Cognitive reflection and decision making. J. Econ. Perspect. **19**(4), 25–42 (2005)
14. Cokely, E.T., Galesic, M., Schulz, E., Ghazai, S., Garcia-Retamero, R.: Measuring risk literacy: the berlin numeracy test. Judgm. Decis. Mak. **7**(1), 25–47 (2012)
15. Doctors Without Borders: Urgent humanitarian response needed as multiple crises hit Ituri, DRC (2019). https://www.doctorswithoutborders.org/latest/urgent-humanitarian-response-needed-multiple-crises-hit-ituri-drc

A Fuzzy Multicriteria Decision-Making Approach for Assessing the Preparedness Level for the Implementation of Logistics 4.0: A Case Study in the Food Industry

Genett Jimenez-Delgado[1(✉)], Monica Ardila-Parra[2], Gilberto Santos[3], José Carlos Sá[4], Vanda Lima[5], Leonardo Campis-Freyle[6], Lesvia Valero[7], Hugo Hernandez[8], Dionicio Neira-Rodado[9], and Jannys Hernández-Ureche[10]

[1] Department of Industrial Engineering, Institución Universitaria de Barranquilla IUB, Barranquilla, Colombia
gjimenez@unibarranquilla.edu.co

[2] Department of Industrial Engineering, Universidad Autonoma del Caribe, Barranquilla, Colombia

[3] Research Institute for Design, Media and Culture, School of Design, Polytechnic Institute Cavado Ave, Campus Do IPCA, Vila Frescaínha S. Martinho, 4750-810 Barcelos, Portugal
gsantos@ipca.pt

[4] Engineering School, Polytechnic of Porto, Porto, Portugal
cvs@isep.ipp.pt

[5] Escola Superior de Tecnologia E Gestão, Polytechnic of Porto, Felgueiras, Portugal
vlima@estg.ipp.pt

[6] SOLTRAF SAS, Barranquilla, Colombia

[7] Economic Science Faculty, Department of Financial Administration, Corporación Universitaria Latinoamericana CUL, Barranquilla, Colombia
lvalero@ul.edu.co

[8] Department of Industrial Engineering, Corporación Universitaria Latinoamericana CUL, Barranquilla, Colombia
hhernandez@ul.edu.co

[9] Department of Productivity and Innovation, Universidad de La Costa CUC, Barranquilla, Colombia
dneira1@cuc.edu.co

[10] Department of Humanities, Universidad de La Costa CUC, Barranquilla, Colombia
jhernand4@cuc.edu.co

Abstract. Industries must prepare diagnoses that indicate their actual state in using Industry 4.0 technologies, especially in Logistics 4.0. So then, focused on the food sector industries, designing and testing a model to carry out this diagnosis is necessary. This project aims to present a Diagnostic and Characterization Model for the Food Sector Industries of the city of Barranquilla based on multifactorial strategies that help them evaluate and make decisions to increase the possibilities of implementing and adopting technologies established under the Logistics 4.0 in your supply chain. In this context, designing and testing a Diagnostic and Characterization Model for the Food Sector Industries will be carried out, applying

H. Mori et al. (Eds.): HCII 2023, LNCS 14056, pp. 32–46, 2023.
https://doi.org/10.1007/978-3-031-48044-7_3

a multicriteria methodology as AHP-TOPSIS and thus generating a tool that allows its applicability in the medium and long term.

Keywords: Logistic 4.0 · AHP · TOPSIS · Food Industry

1 Introduction

Past industrial revolutions have widely impacted the industry. This fast-paced environment challenges companies to adapt to new concepts such as the industrial Internet, cyber-physical systems, adaptive robotics, cybersecurity, data analytics, and artificial intelligence. These emerging technologies facilitated and accelerated the birth of Industry 4.0, like the last industrial revolution.

Industry 4.0 is an emerging research topic at the forefront of new social and industrial changes and directly influences the management of human talent. It is essential that the strategies proposed to mitigate the gaps be determined with a clearer vision with the sole objective of analyzing the situation of Industry 4.0 in companies.

The current trend in companies identifies the need to apply global adaptation scenarios to consolidate value generation in operational, planning, and execution processes to offer quality products and services. This scenario has been linked to the fourth industrial revolution, focused on the use of technologies for the development of internal activities oriented to the use of components such as artificial intelligence, robotics, and IoT, among others. This scenario, risky for some in terms of employability, requires training processes that qualify the company's techniques and procedures, using digital tools that guarantee optimal management of corporate information in real-time against the work scenarios' risks, benefits, and operability.

Logistics, in a general sense, is considered one of the strategic areas that can benefit the most from each of the aspects offered by industry 4.0, fueled by the processes of shipping, monitoring, tracking, and storage of products that intensify the need for its use [1]. Today, companies and industries in the food sector must develop diagnoses that indicate their natural state in the appropriate use of Industry 4.0 technologies, especially in Logistics 4.0. Thus, designing and testing a model to carry out this diagnosis focused on this industry sector is necessary. This model will be the result of this work.

2 Materials and Methods

The economic sectors have initiated diagnostic, characterization, and execution processes that allow for establishing the requirements and scenarios in which the approach to using tools for the needs of organizations can be generated. Derived from digital maturity, degrees of investment, data analysis, and adaptation of tools, situations are defined that help provides degrees of competitiveness, developing a technological paradigm that needs to be applied gradually so as not to generate lagging scenarios compared to other companies.

Production, traditional work methods, and logistics management are, without a doubt, the fundamental pillar for creating business models that provide value to customers, product customization, and dynamic consumption. Logistics performance in the food industry sector is becoming more critical every day, facing the challenges that the market and competition have become a challenge for them, the increase in logistics costs, and the current scenario of uncertainty Marked by post-pandemic effects, the maritime transport crisis, the economic recession, and the Russian-Ukrainian war, it has led supply chain leaders to develop strategies to operate while maintaining costs without affecting the final costs of the product. The food industry deserves all the attention and technological, financial, and competent human capital updates to face these challenges.

2.1 Cause-Effect Analysis

The works carried out by Atlas Tecnológico [2] show that, concerning Industry 4.0, the main reasons industries in the food sector have not been able to count on optimal performance are difficulties in accessing technological tools and financing processes. Among the most relevant aspects obtained in the study, it is observed that many organizations do not know the available technologies and, worse, do not have the experience to integrate, develop or use each of these instruments. Faced with aspects such as automation, the sector depends a lot on the type of organization since, in some cases, manual classification determines quality. At the same time, those that have transformation mechanisms consider it a critical success factor. The study states that "53% of companies think automation is one of the five priority challenges facing the agri-food sector, the order of priority being widely distributed among the top 5 positions" [2]. The component related to the interconnection of systems is also a pillar recognized by these organizations. There is a considerable gap between large and small companies in the sector, where data is obtained manually and not systematized. Finally, this study reveals that the main barriers to Digitization and technological adaptation arise from technical problems that cannot be resolved immediately due to the shortage of suppliers and the high costs these organizations must incur [2].

2.2 Justification

According to the review of the documentation carried out previously, it was found that the food sector industries have not been able to count on optimal performance due to difficulties in accessing technological tools and financing processes. Additionally, it was observed how many organizations do not know the available technologies and, worse, do not have the experience to integrate, develop or use each of these instruments. According to Logistec [3] states that given the above, new supply chain planning and execution models will be necessary, which should consider, for example: increasing the regionalization of the inventory, bringing it closer to customers; develop faster sales and operations planning cycles; implement S&OP to support strategic planning through long-term and analysis of various scenarios to review supply chain strategies, among others continually. Today the competitive environment makes the leaders of the supply chains adopt new techniques in their processes. The advances of these techniques are appreciated with a growing interest in the themes of industry 4.0, especially in terms of the supply chain, which can be defined as a "series of related activities that involve the coordination, planning, and control of products and services, between distributors and customers [4].

One of the paths towards transformation can be through standardized processes, measurement of operational risks, or seeking outsourcing of services. In this context, the valuation of logistics outsourcing with companies that handle data analytics has become a crucial aspect in the food industry since logistics service is prioritized at a high level, as well as cost optimization; parts that require a large volume of information, because all the variables of the wholesale, retail, and large-scale retail trade for order analysis, storage, and transportation are analyzed, using data analysis in an easy and accessible way [5]. Regarding the supply chain, a vital process for logistics development, it was found that Industry 4.0, for this context called Logistics 4.0, can monitor and evaluate the risks related to quality, inventory, economy, natural disasters, losses in transit, delays in new products, cybersecurity, intellectual property, political instability or customs, using tools such as diagnostic models for the industries in the sector in question.

2.3 Literature Review

The search for knowledge related to the theme "logistics 4.0" and its implementation in organizations determines scenarios that build the base structure of this work for the definition of variables and methodologies consistent with the interpretation of results. The use of information technologies and immediate access means for analysis and follow-up with differential value are some of the logistical challenges that force us to propose quick adaptation strategies.

Currently, the work centers of industrialized countries establish guidelines and efforts to address the fourth industrial revolution aimed at adopting and implementing new technologies that guarantee greater fluidity, immediacy, and comprehensive solutions with permanent monitoring. Each of these disruptive changes is not unrelated to logistics, where an interconnected system must be guaranteed that optimizes time and resources, accompanied by a strengthening of R&D processes with a high degree of investment [6].

One of the primary efforts in terms of documentary understanding of the challenges that countries must gradually adopt from conventional to intelligent systems from logistics processes. The construction and application of technologies in industry 4.0 applied to logistics processes today mark some trends such as RFID, wearable IoT, AR, Blockchain, and drones. What each of these technological tools allows is to provide information on the technological paradigms of what has been implemented today by some sectors worldwide. These technologies represent a challenge for organizations as pillars that promote and strengthen aspects essential for enhancing competitiveness and efficiency [7]. In this same sense, and already as a practical case in the Spanish environment, an analysis of the subject was generated to venture into processes of characterization, diagnosis, and implementation of logistics 4.0 strategies in sectors such as habitat, made up of the construction area and furniture manufacturing [8].

From Latin America, knowledge in the field of industry 4.0 has been strengthened, carrying out characterization processes to determine the benefits, advantages, and weaknesses that the region's countries have to obtain a framework from this perspective—case studies such as those carried out by [9] in Mexico, Brazil, and Chile. The studies presented in Latin America also address the construction of knowledge to understand how the adaptation of strategies oriented to logistics 4.0 in the development of regular activities [10].

One of the most used technologies in the logistics context has been the implementation of the Blockchain for the application of monitoring processes and logistics operations. [11] presents a case from the agricultural sector, and [12] shows cases successfully applied in the port sector.

Understanding the context in which the theme of logistics 4.0 is handled, in Colombia, approaches have been presented on the challenges the sectors must adopt to stay in this line. Some works have given a documentary review oriented to the knowledge of the subject, such as the one presented by [13]. From this previous study, some lines of action classified in the strategic and operational reorganization of companies were proposed through diagnoses for the use of emerging technologies, as well as the development of intelligent R+D+I processes and two-way internal communication that strengthen corporate information among all participants that generate a culture and sense of belonging [14]. Likewise, Jimenez et al. [15] carried out a study on good practices and trends in the application of reverse logistics in the manufacturing industry.

The AHP, TOPSIS, and MCA strategies have been used in different contexts to facilitate decision-making, such as Research carried out by [16] in the transport sector. [17] and [18] conducted a similar study for the feasibility analysis of green data centers at higher education institutions. [19] exposes these methods for quality improvement and applying the ISO 9001 standard to the advisory process of the Research and business center in a higher education institution.

3 Methodology

This research proposal initially seeks to identify the criteria and subcriteria that affect the preparation and implementation of logistics 4.0 in companies in the food sector, as well as the strategies and benefits of logistics 4.0 in the industry, through documentary Research, the trial of experts and semi-structured interviews applied to those responsible for logistics processes in food companies. For the information gathering technique, a methodology has been proposed that combines two crucial multicriteria tools widely used in supplier selection problems, such as the Fuzzy Hierarchical Analysis technique (F-AHP) and the Order Technique. of Preference for Similarity to Ideal Solution TOPSIS.

Figure 1 shows the proposed methodological scheme, which is divided into three phases: the application of the diffuse AHP, the application of TOPSIS, and the final selection of providers: the FAHP technique has been chosen because, according to the review, it is one of the most used decision-making techniques. The TOPSIS technique is used to order the alternatives and select the best one, in this case, the best provider for the organization. This selection is made by determining the positive and negative distances of the alternatives, compared to an ideal solution, and selecting the provider that has the best indicator, that is, the one that is as close as possible to the positive answer and furthest from it—the negative solution [20–22].

The stages of the proposed methodology for the development of this project and the development of the proposed objectives are presented below in Fig. 2.

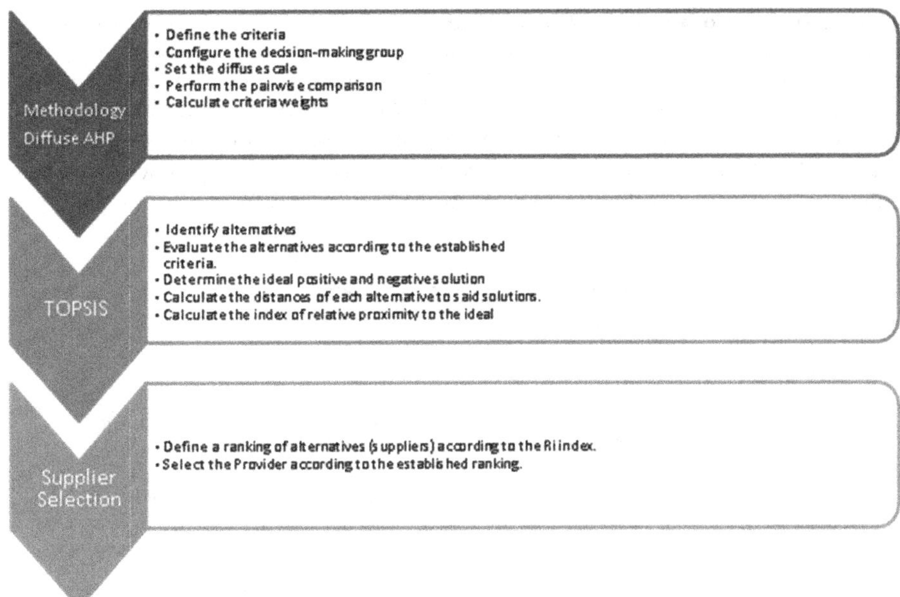

Fig. 1. Proposed methodological scheme

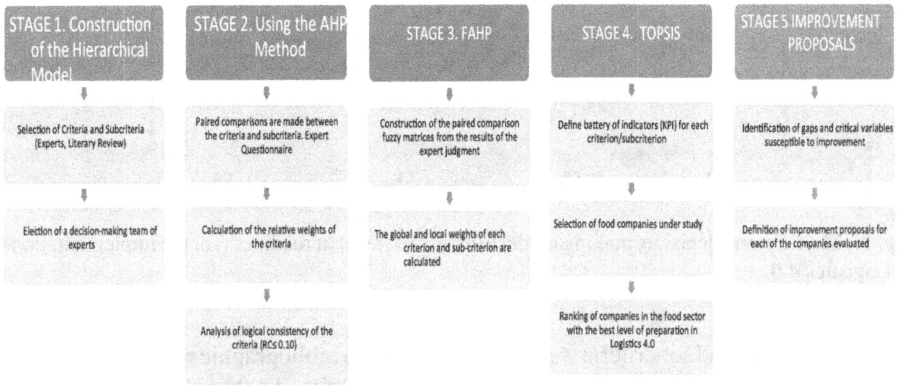

Fig. 2. Methodological approach to assess the level of preparation for the implementation of logistics 4.0 in food companies

4 Results and Discussion

The proposed Research aims to evaluate the level of preparation for implementing Logistics 4.0 in Food Companies through the combined method that uses F-AHP and TOPSIS.

4.1 Construction of the Hierarchical Model

The construction of this model is based on the choice of a set of criteria and subcriteria that allow us to assess the level of preparation for the implementation of logistics 4.0 in food companies. In this sense, the evaluation model consists of four (4) criteria and fourteen (14) sub-criteria. The final decision model is presented in Fig. 3, where we can see the requirements and subcriteria chosen as the basis of this Research.

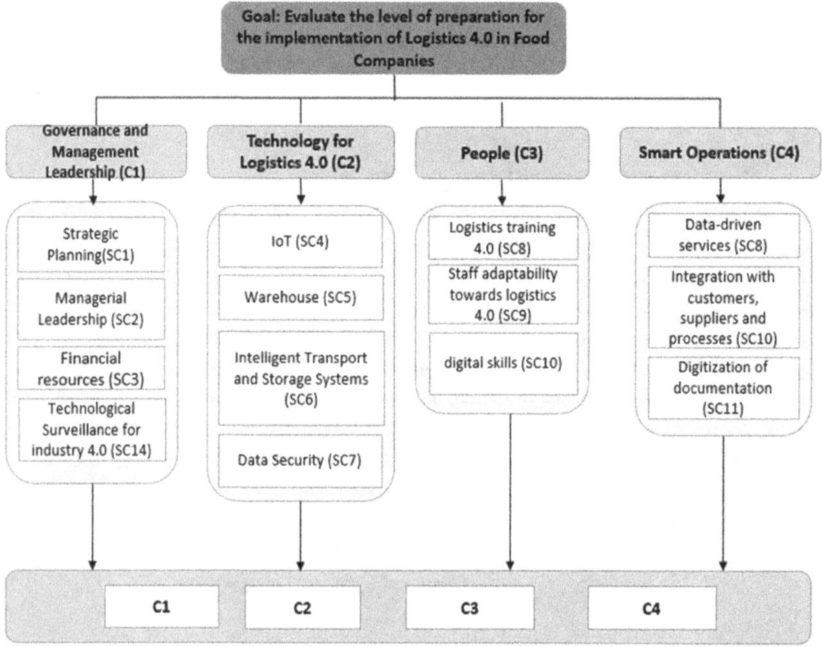

Fig. 3. Multicriteria decision-making model to assess the level of readiness for the implementation of Logistics 4.0.

These criteria and subcriteria were chosen based on a bibliographic review of the most relevant variables at the time of the implementation of logistics 4.0, with the contribution of experts and national economic reports on logistics.

4.2 Structuring of the Multicriteria Model

This Research is based on the Analytic Hierarchy Process (after this AHP-Analytic Hierarchy Process), which is one of the most widely used multicriteria techniques to determine the weightings of criteria and subcriteria. This technique was proposed and developed by [23]. The fuzzy AHP methodology helps to establish the level of importance between the criteria and subcriteria defined for selection based on a qualitative comparison between them, which is later transferred to a numerical scale that allows mathematical calculations to be carried out in the AHP method, pairwise comparisons are made using a scale to assess the importance of criteria and subcriteria. This pairwise comparison procedure starts from a square matrix in which the number of aspects defines the number of rows and columns to be weighted in this study; a five-point scale was used to facilitate the understanding of experts and reduce inconsistencies in the paired comparison process, [24] as described in Table 1.

Table 1. Linguistic correspondence and reduced AHP scale

Reduced AHP Scale	Importance	Definition
0.2	1	A lot less
0.3	2	Less
1	3	Likewise
3	4	More
5	5	Much More

The following steps were performed to develop this study while applying this methodology: Pairwise comparisons were made between the criteria/sub-criteria using the correspondence and the corresponding reduced scale of the AHP. A survey was designed and applied to facilitate the collection of the comparisons by the experts, as shown in Fig. 4.

Survey to determine the level of importance between factors and sub-factors in the decision-making model for the Evaluate the level of preparation for the implementation of Logistics 4.0 in Food CompaniesSurvey to determine the level of importance between factors and sub-factors in the decision-making model for the Evaluate the level of preparation for the implementation of Logistics 4.0 in Food Companies

Name:______________________ **Date:**______________________

Position:______________________ **Dependence:**______________________

In the following tool you will find a table for each factor of the decision-making model, in which you as a respondent, according to your experience, must select the importance of the factor or sub-factor that is on the left as regards the factor or sub-factor located to the right

Importance Level

1	A lot less	0,2
2	less	0,3
3	likewise	1
4	more	3
5	much more	5

CRITERIO		IMPORTANCE 1	2	3	4	5		CRITERIO
Governance and Management Leadership								Technology for Logistics 4.0
Governance and Management Leadership								People
Governance and Management Leadership	*Es*						*Importante que*	Smart Operations
Technology for Logistics 4.0								People
Technology for Logistics 4.0								Smart Operations
People								Smart Operations

Fig. 4. Data collection instrument applied to AHP trials

Next, the geometric means of the expert judgments were calculated and incorporated into the criteria and subcriteria comparison matrix, taking into account their linguistic correspondence, as shown in Fig. 5. The geometric means were then calculated.

The experts' judgments were incorporated into the criteria and sub-criteria comparison matrix. Subsequently, we calculate the priority vectors for each criterion, and a priority matrix is formed, multiplied by the priority vector obtained.

			E1	E2	E3	E4	E5	E6	E7	GM
Criterion	Governance and Management Leadership	Technology for Logistics 4.0	1	3	1	5	3	3	3	**2,36**
	Governance and Management Leadership	People	0,3	0,3	3	3	5	1	1	**1,22**
	Governance and Management Leadership	smart operations	0,3	0,3	1	3	3	3	0,3	**0,96**
	Technology for Logistics 4.0	People	1	1	1	3	3	1	0,3	**1,15**
	Technology for Logistics 4.0	smart operations	0,3	1	1	3	5	1	3	**1,45**
	People	smart operations	5	1	0,3	3	3	3	5	**2,14**
Governance and Management Leadership	Strategic Planning	Managerial Leadership	3	1	3	1	5	1	5	**2,17**
	Strategic Planning	Financial resources	1	3	1	1	3	3	3	**1,87**
	Strategic Planning	Technological Surveillance for logistics 4.0	3	1	3	3	1	3	3	**2,19**
	Managerial Leadership	Financial resources	5	3	1	3	3	3	3	**2,76**
	Managerial Leadership	Technological Surveillance for logistics 4.0	1	1	3	3	1	1	1	**1,37**
	Financial resources	Technological Surveillance for logistics 4.0	0,3	0,3	3	3	1	1	3	**1,14**

Fig. 5. Matrix of Criteria and Subcriteria with their numerical correspondence

Calculation of the relative weights of the criteria and subcriteria using FAHP. By applying the FAHP technique, the local and global weightings of the criteria and sub-criteria were determined to consider the importance and uncertainty of environments. The results of these calculations can be seen in Table 2:

In Fig. 6, it can be seen the classification of the criteria is based on their importance obtained from the application of the FAHP method. Taking these results into account, we can conclude that Criterion 1, Governance and Leadership, which got a global weight (GW = 34.9%), is the most relevant criterion when evaluating the level of preparation of logistics processes in food companies towards the industry 4.0:

In this sense, we can declare that organizational factors have a substantial impact on the innovative capacity of the company and its direct effect on business growth strategies, essential aspects when starting the implementation of Logistics 4.0. Within this criterion, the sub-criterion SC1 Strategic Planning stands out, which obtained an (LW = 42.03%), which allows us to consolidate the premise that the planning of processes and the evaluation of their economic, financial, and operational impact will enable us to define strategies and tactics that allow the company to draw a roadmap to achieve its objectives.

The second criterion in order of importance is criterion C3 People, with a (GW = 29.3%). People are the central axis of any implementation process. The company's ability to raise awareness, train, train and generate a favorable environment for the adaptation of personnel towards logistics 4.0 is the basis for the success of the implementation of this process.

Table 2. Local and global weights of the criteria and subcriteria

CRITERION	GW	LW
C1. Governance and Management Leadership	34.9%	
SC1. Strategic Planning	14.68%	42.03%
SC2 Managerial Leadership	9.55%	27.34%
SC3 Financial resources	5.48%	15.70%
SC4 Technological Surveillance for logistics 4.0	5.21%	14.93%
C2 Technology for Logistics 4.0	19.0%	
SC5 IoT	6.32%	33.19%
SC6 Warehouse	5.43%	28.51%
SC7 Intelligent Transport and Storage Systems	4.55%	23.89%
SC8 Data Security	2.74%	14.41%
C3 People	29.3%	
SC9 Logistics training 4.0	12.76%	43.61%
SC10 Staff adaptability towards logistics 4.0	11.36%	38.84%
SC11 Digital skills	5.14%	17.55%
C4 Smart operations	16.8%	
SC12 Data-driven services	5.58%	33.28%
SC13 Integration with customers, suppliers, and processes	8.15%	48.59%
SC14 Digitization of documentation	3.04%	18.13%

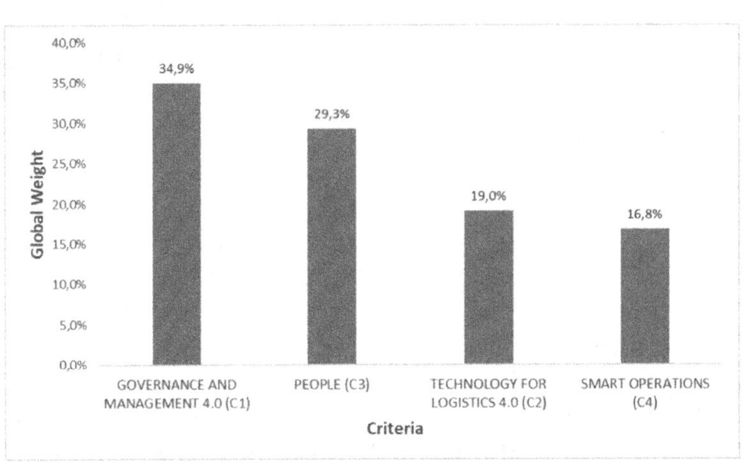

Fig. 6. Global weights of the criteria in the evaluation of the level of preparation of the logistics processes in food companies towards industry 4.0

4.3 Ranking of Food Companies Using the TOPSIS Method and Identification of Opportunities for Improvement

In this final phase of the development of this Research, the TOPSIS technique was used to classify food companies according to their level of preparation towards the implementation of Logistics 4.0. Taking into account the results of applying this technique, the critical aspects that influence the performance of each company proceeded, and, later, the intervention strategies approach to improving the preparation levels in logistics 4.0.

Authors are considering the companies' responses obtained by applying the instrument designed for collecting information. The normalized matrix R, the weighted normalized decision matrix, the separations of the positive and negative solutions, and the calculation of the preparation coefficients for each food company were obtained. Table 3 shows the data of the normalized matrix and, in the same way, the negative ideal solution (NIS) and the positive ideal solution (PIS):

Table 3. TOPSIS Decision Matrix for Logistics Readiness Level 4.0

	E1	E2	E3	E4	E5	PIS (A+)	NIS (A−)	W	Norm
PE	2	1	2	1	1	2	1	0.148	3.32
LG	2	2	2	1	1	2	1	0.101	3.74
RF1	2	1	2	2	1	2	1	0.023	3.74
RF2	2	1	2	1	1	2	1	0.023	3.32
VT	2	1	2	1	2	2	1	0.049	3.74
IT1	2	1	3	1	2	3	1	0.041	4.36
IT2	2	1	3	2	1	3	2	0.041	4.36
WH1	2	1	2	2	2	2	1	0.032	4.12
WH2	2	1	1	1	1	2	1	0.032	2.83
ST1	2	1	1	1	1	2	1	0.024	2.83
ST2	2	1	2	1	1	2	1	0.024	3.32
SD	2	1	1	2	1	2	1	0.026	3.32

Table 4 shows the classification of the evaluated food companies, considering their proximity and separation from the positive ideal solution, called for the study "coefficient of preparation." The preceding shows that the companies that obtain the lowest value in di+ when evaluating the level of preparation in the implementation of Logistics 4.0 with the TOPSIS technique are the ones that are best prepared to assume the challenge of this implementation, that is, are closer to the ideal preparation values:

Table 4. Ranking of Food Companies

Companies	CCi	di +	di-	Ranking
E1	0.75	0.026	0.078	2
E2	0.30	0.086	0.036	4
E3	0.83	0.017	0.083	1
E4	0.23	0.079	0.023	5
E5	0.33	0.081	0.039	3

Figure 7 shows these results:

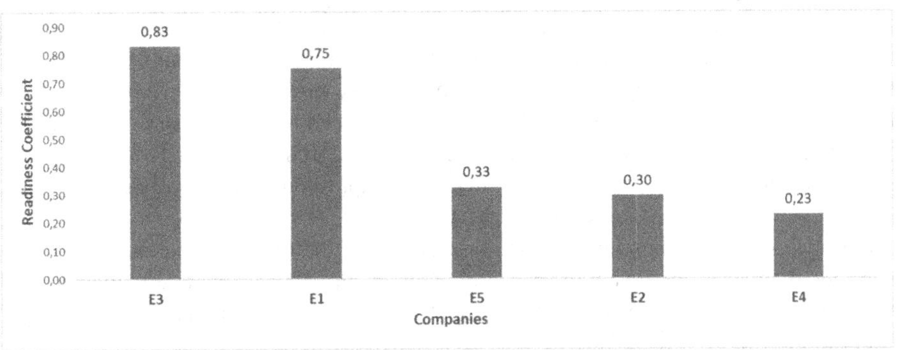

Fig. 7. Logistics Preparation Coefficients 4.0 in Food Companies

This technique showed that Company 3 obtained a higher preparation coefficient than the others, with a percentage of 83%. This result reflects that this company has more excellent preparation towards Logistics 4.0. Its processes are oriented toward implementing technology solutions based on developing a competitive advantage for the organization in logistics and supply chain operations. Compared with Company 4, which obtained a low level of preparation with a coefficient of 23%. Company 1 is in second place in the classification ranking with 75%, making it a benchmark for best practices in logistics 4.0. Companies 5 and 2 are located at a medium level with a preparation coefficient very close between them, with 33% and 30%, respectively. Taking into account the results of the application of this methodology, we observe that most of the companies evaluated have deficiencies in the indicators of the level of connectivity and use of mobile devices in the company; Systematized management of the Warehouse Management System for the management of its warehouses and inventories and digital tools for the location and traceability of the products in the warehouse and Digital skills in employees.

5 Conclusions and Future Works

This Research was carried out with the AHP-FHP-TOPSIS combined approach methodology to evaluate the level of preparation of food companies towards the implementation of Logistics.4.0. This proposed methodology includes five phases: Construction of the hierarchical model, use of the AHP methodology for the analysis of logical consistency of the criteria, use of FAHP to calculate the relevance of the criteria and subcriteria, use of the TOPSIS method to classify the companies of food and proposal of improvement opportunities.

Considering the results of this Research, we can conclude that within the study carried out, the Governance, Leadership, and People criteria are the most relevant when implementing Logistics 4.0 considering the subcriteria of Strategic Planning and Training in Logistics 4.0, respectively. These criteria obtained the highest global weights within this analysis, with 34.9% and 29.3%, respectively. Another of the most relevant results was the classification of Company 3 as the one with the highest preparation coefficient for implementing Logistics 4.0, with a proximity coefficient of 83%. As the final objective of this study, for all the companies, the critical points were identified, and improvements were proposed that can be implemented to obtain better results in the preparation towards Logistics 4.0, to improve their standards in their logistics processes and get a technological maturity that allows it to adapt to current market demands and the effective fulfillment of its service promise.

Finally, as a recommendation for future Research, the proposed methodology can be applied to other industries in the productive sector. In addition, we intend to continue developing different methods to establish and implement action plans to fill the gaps found in this study.

Acknowledgement. Gilberto Santos acknowledge Fundação para a Ciência e a Tecnologia (FCT) I.P., under the project UIDB/04057/2020.

References

1. Universidad de la Rioja, "El impacto de la Industria 4.0 en la Logística: 6 avances que yarevolucionan el sector | UNIR," (2019). https://www.unir.net/ingenieria/revista/el-impacto-de-la-industria-4-0-en-la-logistica-6-avances-que-ya-revolucionan-el-sector/. Accessed 23 Feb 2023
2. Interempresa, "La industria 4.0 alimentaria no despega por la dificultad de acceso a las tecnologías y a la financiación - Alimentación," (2021). https://www.interempresas.net/Alimentaria/Articulos/369826-industria-40-alimentaria-no-despega-dificultad-acceso-tecnologias-financiacion.html. Accessed 23 Feb 2023
3. Logistec, "8 TENDENCIAS TECNOLÓGICAS DE LA CADENA DE SUMINISTRO PARA 2022 Y MÁS ALLÁ | LinkedIn," Revista Logistec (2022). https://www.linkedin.com/pulse/8-tendencias-tecnológicas-de-la-cadena-suministro-para-revista/?originalSubdomain=es. Accessed 23 Feb 2023
4. Büyüközkan, G., Göçer, F.: Digital supply chain: literature review and a proposed framework for future research. Comput. Ind.. Ind. **97**, 157–177 (2018). https://doi.org/10.1016/J.COMPIND.2018.02.010

5. Paciarotti, C., Bevilacqua, M., Ciarapica, F.E., Mazzuto, G., Postacchini, L.: An efficiency analysis of food distribution system through data envelopment analysis. Int. J. Oper. Res. **36**(4), 538–554 (2019). https://doi.org/10.1504/IJOR.2019.104056
6. "La revolución industrial 4.0 y eladvenimiento de una logística 4.0 | Publicación | Comisión Económica para América Latina y el Caribe." https://www.cepal.org/es/publicaciones/45454-la-revolucion-industrial-40-advenimiento-logistica-40. Accessed 23 Feb 2023
7. Martínez, T.R.: Estudio De La Aplicación De La Industria 4.0 En El Ámbito De La Logística. Universidad de Valladolid (2019). https://uvadoc.uva.es/bitstream/handle/10324/36767/TFM-I-1140.pdf?sequence=1&isAllowed=y
8. Aidimme, Amuebla, Cenfim, and Cetem, "Análisis de viabilidad para la Implantación de la Industria 4. 0 en el sector hábitat," Madrid (2017)
9. Fernandes, A.G.: Diagnóstico general: nivel de desarrollo de la Industria 4. 0 enel desarrollo de una Hoja de Ruta (2020)
10. Díaz, N., Cruz, A.L., Ruiz, H.S.: Instrumento de diagnóstico y autoevaluación para medir las condicionesorganizacionales hacia la nueva revolución industrial 4.0. Revista Internacional de Investigación e Innovación Tecnológica **6**(35), 1–14 (2018). http://www.scielo.org.mx/scielo.php?script=sci_arttext&pid=S2007-97532018000500002&lang=es%0Ahttp://www.scielo.org.mx/scielo.php?script=sci_arttext&pid=S2007-97532018000500002&lng=es&nrm=iso&tlng=es
11. Caballero, R., Rivera, B.: Blockchain: una alternativa para permitir la trazabilidaden la cadena de suministro agrícola en Panamá. In: 2019 7th International Engineering, Sciences and Technology Conference (IESTEC), pp. 46–51 (2019)
12. Duran, C.A., Fernandez-Campusano, C., Carrasco, R., Vargas, M., Navarrete, A.: Boosting the decision-making in smart ports by using blockchain. IEEE Access **9**, 128055–128068 (2021). https://doi.org/10.1109/ACCESS.2021.3112899
13. Guevara, A.: Análisis De Los Retos De Logística 4.0 En Colombia Durante Los Próximos 5 Años, pp. 1–18 (2020). https://repository.unimilitar.edu.co/bitstream/handle/10654/37134/GuevaraLadinoAndersonCamilo2020.pdf?sequence=1&isAllowed=y
14. Susana, P.C.A.: Propuesta de implementación de la industria 4.0 enel sector manufacturero de bogotá. Universidad Católica de Colombia (2020). https://repository.ucatolica.edu.co/bitstream/10983/25322/1/PROPUESTADEIMPLEMENTACIÓNDELAINDUSTRIAL4.0ENELSECTORMANUFACTURERODEBOGOTÁ.pdf
15. Jimenez, G., Santos, G., Félix, M., Hernández, H., Rondón, C.: Good practices and trends in reverse logistics in the plastic products manufacturing industry. Proc. Manuf. **41**, 367–374 (2019). https://doi.org/10.1016/j.promfg.2019.09.021
16. Jimenez-Delgado, G., Balmaceda-Castro, N., Hernández-Palma, H., de la Hoz-Franco, E., García-Guiliany, J., Martinez-Ventura, J.: An integrated approach of multiple correspondences analysis (MCA) and fuzzy AHP method for occupational health and safety performance evaluation in the land cargo transportation. In: Duffy, V.G. (ed.) HCII 2019. LNCS, vol. 11581, pp. 433–457. Springer, Cham (2019). https://doi.org/10.1007/978-3-030-22216-1_32
17. Hernandez, L., Jimenez, G.: Characterization of the current conditions of the its a data centers according to standards of the green data centers friendly to the environment. Adv. Intell. Syst. Comput. **574** (2017). https://doi.org/10.1007/978-3-319-57264-2_34
18. Hernández, L., Rios, C.E.U., Pranolo, A.: Design a model-based on nonlinear multiple regression to predict the level of user satisfaction when optimizing a traditional WLAN using SDWN. Int. J. Adv. Sci. Eng. Inf. Technol. **11**(4), 1487–1493 (2021). https://doi.org/10.18517/ijaseit.11.4.14463
19. Jimenez, G.: Procedimientos para elmejoramiento de la calidad y la implantación de la Norma ISO 9001 aplicado al proceso de Asesoramiento, no. November, p. 22 (2016)

20. Shemshadi, A., Shirazi, H., Toreihi, M., Tarokh, M.J.: A fuzzy VIKOR method for supplier selection based on entropy measure for objective weighting. Expert Syst. Appl. **38**(10), 12160–12167 (2011). https://doi.org/10.1016/J.ESWA.2011.03.027
21. Hernandez-Collantes, L., et al.: An Integrated framework based on fuzzy AHP-TOPSIS and multiple correspondences analysis (MCA) for evaluate the technological conditions of the teleworker in times of pandemic: a case study. In: Stephanidis, C., et al. (eds.) HCII 2021. LNCS, vol. 13097, pp. 459–475. Springer, Cham (2021). https://doi.org/10.1007/978-3-030-90966-6_32
22. Wibawa, A.P., Fauzi, J.A., Isbiyantoro, S., Irsyada, R., Dhaniyar, D., Hernández, L.: VIKOR multicriteria decision making with AHP reliable weighting for article acceptance recommendation. Int. J. Adv. Intell. Inform. **5**(2) (2019). https://doi.org/10.26555/ijain.v5i2.172
23. Saaty, T.L.: Multicriteria Decision Making, vol. 1. The Analytic Hierarchy Process: Planning, Priority Setting, Resource Allocation, vol. 36, no. 3. McGraw-Hill (1990). http://mansci.journal.informs.org/cgi/doi/10.1287/mnsc.36.3.259%5Cn, http://www.jstor.org/stable/2631947%5Cn, http://www.amazon.com/Multicriteria-Decision-Analytic-Hierarchy-Process/dp/0962031720
24. Jiménez-Delgado, G., Santos, G., Félix, M.J., Teixeira, P., Sá, J.C.: A combined AHP-TOPSIS approach for evaluating the process of innovation and integration of management systems in the logistic sector. In: Stephanidis, C., et al. (eds.) HCII 2020. LNCS, vol. 12427, pp. 535–559. Springer, Cham (2020). https://doi.org/10.1007/978-3-030-60152-2_40

Study on the Optimization of Digital Content Reading Experience Based on Scene Theory

Xueyan Jin and Rongrong Fu(✉)

College of Art Design and Media, East China University of Science and Technology, Shanghai, China
493544402@qq.com

Abstract. In the Web 3.0 era, digital reading has become the main way to obtain information and information, and the scenario-based communication method has put forward higher requirements for product services. However, it is found that current digital reading applications still have problems such as information overload, inconvenient interaction, and easy to cause user reading fatigue. Therefore, in order to optimize users' digital reading experience, this paper proposes a method to construct target scenes and design adaptive interfaces based on scene theory, taking existing digital reading applications as an example. Firstly, based on scene theory, we initially divide the scene, and then use EEG and focus groups to extract users' visual, auditory and interactive action preferences for digital reading and build the target scene; secondly, based on emotional design, we refine the design strategy to better meet users' reading needs for existing problems; finally, we design the scene mode according to the needs of the scene, and prove through questionnaire evaluation that this design strategy can reduce users' cognitive.Finally, we design the scenario model according to the needs of the scenario, and prove through questionnaire evaluation that this design strategy can reduce users' cognitive burden, relieve reading fatigue, and realize the unification of reading scenario and users' perception. In order to test the scientificity and effectiveness of the design method, WeRead is chosen as a typical case study.

Keywords: Digital Reading · Scene Theory · User Experience · Emotional Design

1 Introduction

Digital reading, the digitization of reading, refers to the activity of using digital devices to read digital texts such as text, pictures, audio, and video [1]. The results of the 20th National Reading Survey report show that the exposure rate of digital reading methods among Chinese adult nationals is 80.1%. The 2022 Annual China Digital Reading Report shows that the scale of Chinese digital reading users has reached 530 million, of which the main user group is 19–45 years old, accounting for 67.15%. In the era of mobile Internet, digital reading has become the main way for people to obtain information. In this context, the significance of scenes has been greatly strengthened, and the essence of

H. Mori et al. (Eds.): HCII 2023, LNCS 14056, pp. 47–62, 2023.
https://doi.org/10.1007/978-3-031-48044-7_4

mobile communication is scenario-based services, providing scenario-specific adapted information or services is the core goal of mobile media services [2], and scenario-based design thinking emphasizes attention to user scenario needs and experiences. However, the study found that the current digital reading platform still suffers from information overload, inconvenience of interaction, easy to cause user reading fatigue and other problems, and the lack of scenario-based reading humanized and personalized design synoptic considerations.

In order to optimize users' digital reading experience, this paper takes WeRead (an existing digital reading application) as an example, combines users' digital reading preferences of sight, sound and action, and investigates design strategies that better meet users' reading needs. Therefore, this paper proposes a digital reading interface optimization model based on scene theory and emotional design and uses EEG experiments, focus groups and questionnaire research to assist in the optimization design of WeRead, which helps users reduce cognitive burden, alleviate reading fatigue, realize the unification of reading scene and user perception, and arouse people's interest in reading.

2 Related Work

2.1 Scene Theory Study

"Scenarios", originally applied in the field of drama, refer to certain task actions or life images that take place in a specific time and space. From Erving Goffman's "Mimetic Drama Theory" [3] to Joshua Meyrowitz's "Media Context Theory" [4], to Robert Scoble's "five forces of scenario" [5], the connotation of scenario theory keeps changing with the development of technology. Currently, there are more studies on scene theory in the fields of regional space [6], social culture [7], communication [8], and design [9]. In design, scene theory was first applied to the interaction design process.

Research on the Use in Interaction Design. John M. Carroll first proposed scenario-based design (SBD) [10]. On this basis, many researchers have continuously improved the framework of scenario-based methods in interaction design. For example, Wang Yumei clarified the concept of interaction design based on scene theory [11], that is, the use of scene description methods to describe the user's use of the product in the whole interaction design process. With the depth of theoretical research, the practical research combining scene theory gradually increases. Li Mengke explored the design of mobile reading products using scene hierarchy analysis [12]. Ocean Jiang proposed the theory of scenario-based interaction design and used it to design a small program for booking laboratory instruments [13].

2.2 User Interface Study

The interface is a level between human-computer interaction, which can be divided into two levels from a psychological perspective: sensory (visual, tactile, auditory, etc.) and emotional. Based on the principle of user-centered design, interface design should consider the user's thought process, emotion and behavior, with user experience as the main goal.

Study of Interface Design Elements. Interface design includes the overall design of human-computer interaction, operation logic and interface visualization, among which interface visualization is the part of the app that directly connects with users. In the user experience, color has a great influence on the visual effect of the interface and has an impact on the user's psychology and behavior. The more irrational the color coding design is, the more likely it is to lead to user visual cognitive errors [14]. Dianne Cyr found that website color is an important determinant of user trust and satisfaction with different cultural differences [15]. Zeming Hu studied the effect of color matching on user perceptions in terms of hue, saturation, and brightness of music playback interfaces [16]. Xu Boqin focused on middle-aged and elderly users' preferences for color elements in shopping mobile and proposed corresponding color design strategies for shopping interfaces [17]. The purpose of color use is highly related to the usage environment [18]. Therefore, optimizing the color of the interface from the scene perspective can provide users with a better visual experience.

Digital Reading Interface Research. Scholars have mostly studied digital reading interfaces from the perspectives of user groups, media, senses, and reading influences. Lu Yongsheng et al. studied the minimum legible font size for digital reading for middle-aged and elderly users [19]. Gu Xin explored the changes that occur in the visual design of screen reading from three perspectives: text, images, and layout [20]. Xue Feng proposed a digital reading interface design method based on the reorganization of multiple sensory experiences [21]. Lili Duan investigates the differences in the impact of interface layout on reading depth and experience in digital reading [22]. The design for digital reading interface usually involves text, color, layout, interaction and other factors, so it is necessary to consider the target user groups and conduct design optimization research for their preferred needs.

Digital Reading Application and WeRead User Portrait Research. Through the survey of digital reading apps in the mobile mall, according to the product positioning and digital content can be mainly divided into information category, book category, and knowledge sharing category. The information category provides users with real-time news information with concise text, mainly pictures and videos, which is easy for users to browse quickly. The book category accounts for a larger share, with the main purpose of improving users' knowledge and culture and cultivating reading habits, providing users with long-text books and magazines for reading, mostly including book list recommendations, book tables, book listening, ranking, comment sharing and other functions. The knowledge-sharing category is characterized by users producing their content, with a variety of graphic forms and obvious socialization. At present, the digital reading applications of the book category still suffer from information overload, inconvenience of interaction, easy to cause user reading fatigue and other problems, and lack of humanized and personalized design synoptic considerations for scenario-based reading.

WeRead is an official reading platform based on the WeChat relationship chain. Overall, 20–30 years old is the main user group of WeRead. As of December 2019, the average reading time of WeRead is about 86 min, with peak reading hours distributed at 12:00 noon and 22:00 Bedtime, lunch break and commuting scenes are the most common reading scenes, with book lovers in first-tier cities being the most active. Therefore, it can be found that the core users of WeRead are young and highly educated groups, who live in cities with developed economies and transportation, may be college students or newcomers in the workplace, and have a strong demand for self-growth and self-awareness improvement, so they are more inclined to read serious books, which is in line with the positioning of WeRead.

2.3 Summary

Through literature research, it was found that the digital reading interface affects users' attention, reading interest and physiological health, etc. Therefore, targeting the reading psychology and needs of young user groups in specific scenarios, the interface is optimized at the sensory and emotional levels through scenario-based interaction design methods, so that users can enjoy and feel the product service experience wholeheartedly. The subsequent research found that there is room for improvement in the existing digital reading applications in terms of information, interaction, visual design and humanized and immersive services.

3 Constructing the Research Framework

Donald Norman explained three levels of affective design from the perspective of perceptual psychology, i.e., instinctive, behavioral, and reflective levels [23]. To refine a design strategy that better meets users' scenario reading needs, this paper proposes a digital reading interface optimization model based on scenario theory and affective design, as shown in Fig. 1, using EEG experiments, focus groups to identify key design elements, and eye-movement experiments and questionnaire research to assist in completing the design practice.

The steps of the study are as follows:

(1) Construct scenarios. Based on the scenario theory, we initially divide the user scenarios, and further refine the elements of user concerns in the scenarios with high frequency of use through interviews.
(2) Determine the key design elements. Combined with the keywords extracted from the interviews, rational data analysis was conducted through EEG experiments.
(3) Design practice and evaluation. Take WeRead as an example to optimize the interface design, and finally let users experience the interface before/after optimization, eye movement experiment and questionnaire research to verify the effectiveness of this design scheme.

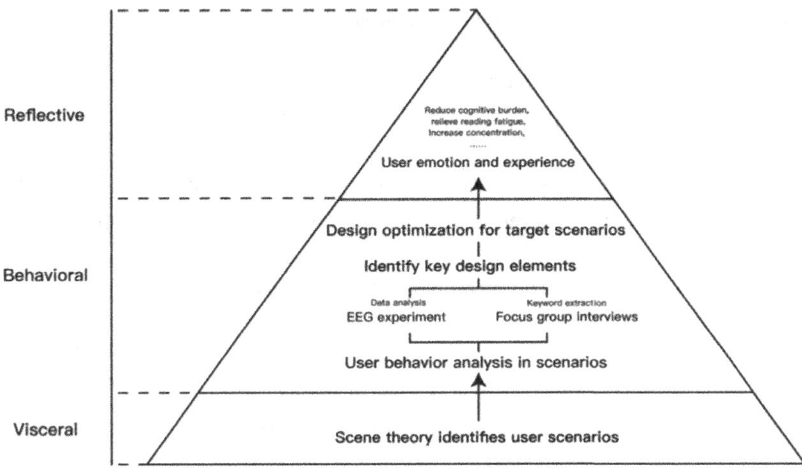

Fig. 1. Interface optimization model

4 The User Reading Habits Research

4.1 Focus Groups

Based on scene theory, the reading scenarios of Weread users are divided into home scenario, work study scenario and mobile transportation scenario based on scene attributes (public or private) and device status (fixed or mobile). The purpose of the focus group is to extract the digital reading interface elements and existing problems that users are concerned about, combine them with their behavioral habits, and provide directions for subsequent optimization. Six Weread users aged 20–30 were invited to conduct interviews. The specific interview outline is shown in Table 1.

Table 1. Interview content

Interview dimensions	Interview Questions
Reading Scenarios	In what scenario (time and place) do you usually do digital reading? What is the reason?
	What is your physical state, movement, and reading interface setting in that scene?
Visual Design	Do you think the information hierarchy and guidance of WeRead are clear? Is there a lot of content?
	Which visual elements such as layout, color, font and icon are you more concerned about when reading? Why?
	What background color do you choose when reading? Do you choose green eye protection mode? Why?

(continued)

Table 1. (*continued*)

Interview dimensions	Interview Questions
	Do you like to read other people's comments? Do you think the current commenting interface can be improved? Is it easy to use the function bar at the bottom to make adjustments?
Auditory design	Have you ever used the listening function? Under what circumstances do you usually use it? What are the reasons?
	What are the requirements for voice type, volume, and speed of speech?
Interaction Design	How is the experience of interaction process when using it? Which part is good or bad?
	One-handed and two-handed operation habits? Is the hand comfortable when reading?

Analysis of Interview Results. After the interviews, the results were summarized and summarized, and the user behavior habits and existing interface problems were derived, as shown in Table 2 and Fig. 2. The reading scenario is similar to the results of the previous study; the visual affects the users' digital reading experience more than the auditory and the action, among which color is the main influencing factor agreed by the users. Therefore, to further clarify the influence of color factors on user usage, EEG experiments were conducted to understand the user's preferred colors in different scenarios.

Table 2. Results of the interviews

Dimension	Problems	Keywords
Visual	Background green is too bright, will feel uncomfortable	Color
	Background color can only adjust the brightness, not convenient	
	The function bar at the bottom is not clear, not clear what the icons mean	Icons
	The form and content of notes are mixed and cannot be classified	Information
Auditory	In noisy environments, such as the subway, the volume will be uneven	Volume
Interaction	The comment function is easy to touch by mistake when turning the page and exiting	Gestures
	The comment page occupies the whole page, which is not convenient for one-hand operation	

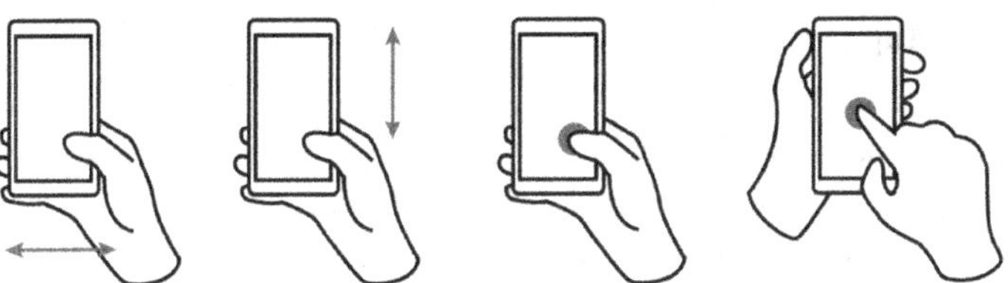

Fig. 2. User digital reading common gestures

4.2 EEG experiments

Purpose of the Experiment. Color as a perceptual stimulus, the color design of the interface directly affects the optimization of user experience. Illumination in different scenes affects hue, color intensity, saturation and the complementary relationship between colors, which in turn affects the user's visual comfort and information recognition efficiency. In order to obtain the color preference of users' digital reading in home and mobile traffic environments, this experiment is based on the principle of EEG technology, by controlling the lighting environment to simulate home and mobile traffic scenarios, and using the Muse2 EEG device to measure the user's concentration on color samples under the same experimental conditions, respectively.

Experimental Subjects. Ten digital reading users aged 20–30 were invited as subjects for the experiment. Three of them were mature users who maintained high-frequency use of WeRead, three were moderate users who were regular users, and four users who used other digital reading applications. The subjects all participated in the experiment independently, were in good health before the experiment, and did not have priori knowledge of the experimental material.

Experimental Equipment. The EEG device used in the experiment is Muse2, which uses several dry electrodes to collect EEG data, and then outputs real-time EEG information after filtering and related algorithm processing, Neutral and Calm are used as indicators of frontal area activity of the subject (Fig. 3).

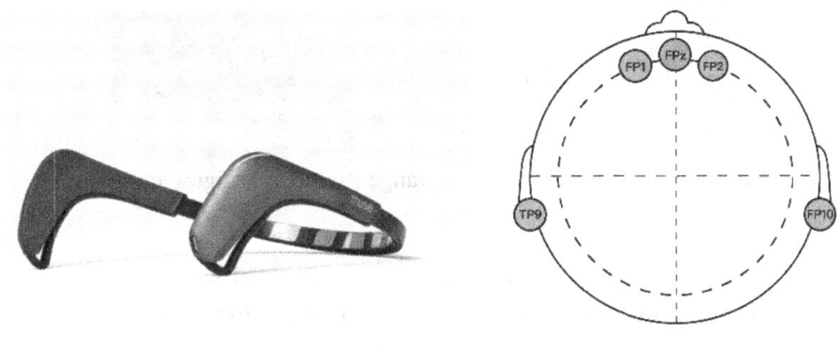

(a) Muse device (b) Device sensor electrode position

Fig. 3. Muse device

Experimental Setup

(1) **Experimental environment**

Based on the results of the previous study, home and mobile transportation are commonly read scenes, so the home scene and the subway and airplane scenes were selected for the experiment, and the scenes were simulated by artificially compensating for the light environment conditions.

Home scene: According to "Architectural Lighting Design Standard" GB50034-2013, the illuminance for general activities indoors is 100 lx. The lighting of home scene is set to 150 lx.

Subway scene: According to "General technical specification for metro vehicles" GB/T 7928-2003, the average illuminance of the subway carriage at 800 mm from the floor should not be less than 200 lx, and the minimum value should not be less than 150 lx when there is no light outside the car. The lighting is set to 400 lx.

Aircraft scene: According to the related research [24], the illuminance of the reading light in the cabin is set to 80lx under the condition of using electronic screen, which is in line with the theoretical value of the best comfort. The illumination of the aircraft scene was set to 80lx under dark conditions.

(2) **Experimental samples**

Myopia problem makes people pay more and more attention to eye protection, the most commonly used "eye protection mode" in digital reading applications, the color is generally green and yellow. According to relevant research and studies, the shorter the wavelength of light, the higher the energy, the greater the damage to the eyes. And the cell phone screen emits a lot of blue light can be increased by increasing the yellow tone to slow down the damage to the eyes. Green is in the center of the visible spectrum, so the human nervous system, cerebral cortex and retinal tissues in the eyes are more easily adapted to the relatively moderate green color, as shown in Fig. 4. Therefore, in order to study the comfortable reading color for users, yellow and green backgrounds were selected as experimental samples for use.

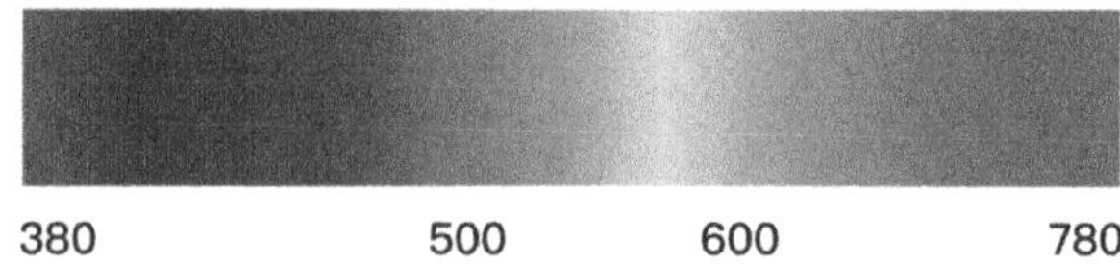

Fig. 4. Visible light wavelength range (nm) (Color figure online)

Six groups of colors were prepared as experimental samples according to the difference of hue, saturation, and brightness (HSB), with the specific values shown in Table 3, three groups for green and three groups for yellow. In addition to the background color, the content, screen brightness, text and paragraph settings remain unchanged, and Fig. 5 shows the six groups of color samples.

(3) **Experimental procedure**

Table 3. Sample HSB values

	Hue	Saturation	Brightness
Sample 1	70	27	94
Sample 2	42	45	95
Sample 3	100	38	60
Sample 4	40	13	100
Sample 5	148	40	87
Sample 6	36	42	73

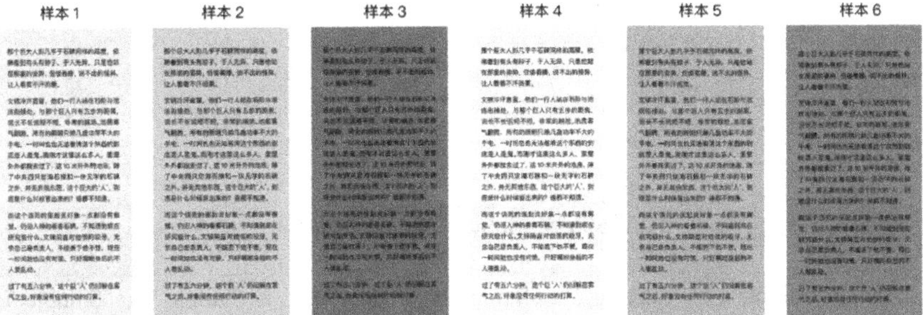

Fig. 5. Experimental samples (Color figure online)

In the preparation phase, subjects entered the prepared experimental conditions and adapted to the laboratory environment, wearing the EEG device and adjusting to their comfortable posture under the guidance of the researcher.

During the experimental phase, the subject was informed of the material to be presented for overall perception, rested for 10 s with eyes closed, then watched sample 1 for 1 min, and was presented with a gray screen for 1 min at the end of the experience, and then repeatedly presented samples 2–6. EEG data were collected continuously during the process. At the end of the experiment, the researcher removed the test equipment and the subjects left the experimental environment to wait for the next scene of the experiment.

At the end of the experimental phase, three sets of scenes were experimented, data recording was completed and data graphs were drawn.

Experimental Data Analysis. The six sample calm values for different scenarios are shown in Tables 4, 5 and 6, respectively. The higher ones in the home scenario are sample 2 and sample 4; the higher ones in the subway scenario are sample 6 and sample 4; the higher ones in the airplane scenario are sample 4 and sample 3.

Table 4. Home scenario data

	Sample 1	Sample 2	Sample 3	Sample 4	Sample 5	Sample 6
Subject 1	0	41	0	0	0	0
Subject 2	0	0	0	0	0	0
Subject 3	0	0	0	40	4	24
Subject 4	40	42	43	54	47	46
Subject 5	3	54	5	50	8	54
Subject 6	3	2	12	55	44	9
Subject 7	47	50	48	0	6	8
Subject 8	50	56	22	44	1	46
Subject 9	2	13	0	6	0	0
Subject 10	7	58	44	55	0	55
Total	152	316	174	304	110	242

Table 5. Subway scene data

	Sample 1	Sample 2	Sample 3	Sample 4	Sample 5	Sample 6
Subject 1	0	0	0	0	0	3
Subject 2	10	0	0	3	0	9
Subject 3	44	58	42	41	6	42
Subject 4	45	9	2	9	5	51
Subject 5	0	60	0	0	20	60
Subject 6	0	0	44	7	43	12
Subject 7	16	14	58	0	3	3
Subject 8	0	7	13	46	10	38
Subject 9	5	8	5	57	11	49
Subject 10	50	7	5	48	7	57
Total	170	163	169	211	105	324

Table 6. Aircraft scenario data

	Sample 1	Sample 2	Sample 3	Sample 4	Sample 5	Sample 6
Subject 1	47	4	15	9	4	48
Subject 2	9	15	14	52	48	14

(continued)

Table 6. (*continued*)

	Sample 1	Sample 2	Sample 3	Sample 4	Sample 5	Sample 6
Subject 3	32	0	0	0	0	0
Subject 4	30	30	9	43	10	12
Subject 5	0	0	0	0	0	0
Subject 6	52	58	14	41	17	7
Subject 7	41	0	11	0	0	3
Subject 8	0	18	58	0	0	0
Subject 9	6	50	54	51	4	0
Subject 10	0	6	59	50	8	48
Total	217	181	234	246	91	132

Experimental Interviews. After the above experiments were completed, the subjects were interviewed as shown in Table 7. The purpose of the interview was to do a perceptual analysis of the above experiments and record the subjective feelings of the subjects. The results show that the adjusted background color can make the subjects feel comfortable, while the subjects hope that the digital reading application can provide different scenes of mode design.

Table 7. Experimental interviews

Interview Content	Interview Results
What kind of light environment do you like when you do digital reading?	Natural light, dark environment
Which color do you like best in the above scenes?	Home, Airplane: Sample 4 Subway: Sample 6
Can these colors make the eyes feel comfortable when you read the scene?	Yes
Do these colors allow you to immerse yourself in reading?	Yes
Do you want a scene model design that gives you the appropriate context for reading the scene?	Yes

Conclusion. Through the color preference analysis of the above experiment, it was found that subjects in the home scene preferred beige with a saturation of less than 50% and luminance around 70–90%; subjects in the subway scene preferred dark yellow and green with saturation 30–40% and luminance around 50–70%; subjects in the airplane scene preferred beige or dark green with saturation less than 50% and luminance around 60%-90. In summary, subjects in all three scenes had a clear preference for yellow with low saturation. Therefore, this study takes the visual color element as the key design element of the scene mode and adjusts the background color by hue, brightness and saturation to create a comfortable and eye-friendly atmosphere for users to read in different scenes.

5 Design Practice

5.1 Design Strategy

Based on the above research and experimental data analysis, users in different scenes have different interface preference settings when reading digitally. Users usually adjust the background color and brightness according to the light of the scene to facilitate more comfortable eyes when reading for a long time. At the same time, scene attributes (public or private) and device status (fixed or mobile) influence user interaction and preference for features. Users in mobile traffic scenes are influenced by space and sound, and are prone to accept faster and more intuitive information presentation, while users in home scenes can read in a more relaxed and free state, and interact with the text in the form of taking notes to deepen their understanding of reading. In the home scene, users can read in a more relaxed and free state, and interact with the text in the form of taking notes to deepen their understanding of reading.

The scenario-based user experience optimization not only requires the functional operation to conform to the usage scenario, but also takes into account the user's psychological state of use. Therefore, this study formulates the following visual design strategies for WeRead: the optimization of the reading interface is based on user visual psychology, providing users with corresponding scene mode designs according to different scenes, and different modes recommend comfortable background colors for users in terms of hue, brightness and saturation to relieve users' eye fatigue from reading; considering the degree of information reception and operation of users in different scenes, the function bar adds text descriptions; different The notes in different forms are classified to make it easy to find.

5.2 Design Options

Scene Model Design. Combining people's digital reading habits in different scenes, especially the impact of light on the visual settings of the user interface, two modes of background settings are provided: standard mode and scene mode. The standard mode optimizes the existing standard background color of WeRead to meet the basic interface setting needs of users; the scene mode provides adapted scene backgrounds to relieve users' reading fatigue with appropriate background colors (Figs. 6 and 7).

Function Optimization. To improve the efficiency of users in understanding information in different scenarios, auxiliary explanatory text is added to the bottom function bar to help users understand the role of icons and guide them to perform the corresponding operations where needed. The text size added ensures readability and is consistent with the global content text style.

Fig. 6. Standard mode

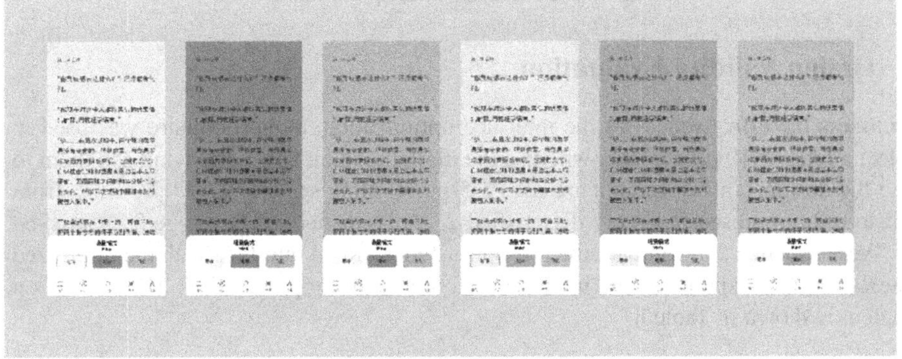

Fig. 7. Scene mode

Combining the visual characteristics of color matching in different scenes, matching the corresponding form of note delineation to achieve the unity of reading scenes and user perception. The color separation notes method divides text into various levels, and color as an index of information facilitates users to clarify their thoughts. Therefore, the classification function of notes is added to integrate the scattered notes according to color and form to quickly filter out the content users need and reduce their cognitive burden (Fig. 8).

Fig. 8. Function bar, notes optimization

6 Design Validity Evaluation

To assess the effectiveness of the interface optimization, a questionnaire was used to select a total of 10 participants who use the digital reading application and ask them to rate the design. This questionnaire uses a 5-point rating scale (−2, −1, 0, 1, 2), from left to right, representing "very dissatisfied-2", "dissatisfied-1", "average 0" "Satisfied 1" "Very satisfied 2". Compare the pre-optimized WeRead interface with the optimized interface, users experience the interface before and after optimization. The evaluation content is shown in Table 8.

Table 8. Evaluation content

	Easy-to-read reading interface	Background color comfort	Function bar optimization	Notes Classification
Average	1.64	1.79	1.81	1.69

By rating the optimized interface, the results of each evaluation ranged from 1.5 to 2 points. Based on the average values, participants rated the optimized digital reading interface more positively.

7 Summary

This study proposes a method to construct a target scene and design an adapted interface based on scene theory. Firstly, the research on the application of scene theory and the current situation of digital reading is conducted to analyze user behavior habits and construct target scenes; subsequently, scene theory is combined with emotional design to propose an interface optimization model for digital reading; secondly, EEG experiments and focus groups are used to dig out problems and needs, extract key design factors, and refine design strategies with interface color as the main focus; Finally, taking WeRead as an example, we design a scene model with different background colors to match the scene to relieve users' reading fatigue.

References

1. Song, H., Jia, X.: Progress: themes and characteristics of digital reading research in China. J. China Editorial **01**, 78–84 (2022)
2. Peng, L.: Scene: the new element of media in the mobile era. J. Journalist **03**, 20–27 (2015). https://doi.org/10.16057/j.cnki.31-1171/g2.2015.03.003
3. Erving, G.: Self-presentation in Everyday Life. Beijing University Press, Beijing (2008)
4. Joshua, M.: The Disappearing Territory. Tsinghua University Press, Beijing (2002)
5. Robert, S.: The Coming Age of Scenarios. Beijing Union Publishing Company, Beijing (2014)
6. Li, H., Jin, H., Terry, N.C., Jiang, W.: Scenario theory and its application to the conservation and renewal of historic towns in China. J. Urban Plan. **03**, 102–110 (2022). https://doi.org/10.16361/j.upf.202203014
7. Xu, X., Zhao, T., Terry, C.: Scene theory: exploration and insights into the cultural dynamics of regional development. J. Foreign Soc. Sci. **291**(03), 101–106 (2012)
8. Gao, S.: Scene theory: opening a new thinking of mobile communication. J. Journalism **17**, 44–48+58 (2015). https://doi.org/10.15897/j.cnki.cn51-1046/g2.2015.17.008
9. Bi, Q., Zhao, F., Chen, J.L.: Research on interaction design based on emotion regulation and scene theory. J. Packag. Eng. **39**(08), 80–83 (2018). https://doi.org/10.19554/j.cnki.1001-3563.2018.08.017
10. Carroll, J.M.: Five reasons for scenario based design. J. Interact. Comput. **13**, 43–60 (2000). https://doi.org/10.1016/S0953-5438(00)00023-0
11. Wang, Y., Hu, W., Tang, J., Li, S.: Research on scene theory in product interaction design. J. Packag. Eng. **38**(06), 76–80 (2017). https://doi.org/10.19554/j.cnki.1001-3563.2017.06.019
12. Li, M.: Research on mobile reading product design based on scene theory. East China University of Science and Technology (2021)
13. Jiang, H., Mei, Y., Gu, X.: Analysis and research of scenario-based interaction design theory. J. Packag. Eng. **40**(18), 269–275 (2019). https://doi.org/10.19554/j.cnki.1001-3563.2019.18.045
14. Li, J., Xue, C.: Research on color coding of digital interface based on visual perception hierarchy. J. Mech. Eng. **52**(24), 201–208 (2016)
15. Cyr, D., Head, M., Larios, H.: Colour appeal in website design within and across cultures: a multi-method evaluation. Int. J. Hum.-Comput. Stud. **68**(1–2), 1–21 (2009). https://doi.org/10.1016/j.ijhcs.2009.08.005
16. Hu, Z.: An experimental study on ERP for visual information perception in digital interfaces. Southeast University, Nanjing (2015)
17. Xu, B., Lu, Z., Li, M.: Research on color design elements of online shopping APP home page for middle-aged and elderly users. J. Packag. Eng. **42**(02), 210–216 (2021). https://doi.org/10.19554/j.cnki.1001-3563.2021.02.033
18. Xu, F.: Analysis of the dominant role of visual information in interface design. J. Packag. Eng. **36**(02), 102–106 (2015). https://doi.org/10.19554/j.cnki.1001-3563.2015.02.027
19. Lu, Y.S., Li, F., Chen, N., Shi, Y.J.: A study on the minimum recognizable font size of digital reading for middle-aged and elderly people on mobile. J. Packag. Eng. **43**(16), 243–247 (2022). https://doi.org/10.19554/j.cnki.1001-3563.2022.16.027

20. Xin, G., Jian, Z.: The visual design transmutation of screen reading. J. Decorat. **02**, 20–23 (2017). https://doi.org/10.16272/j.cnki.cn11-1392/j.2017.02.006
21. Xue, F.: The design of digital reading interface under the threshold of synaesthetic experience. J. Publish. Distrib. Res. **09**, 83–86 (2019). https://doi.org/10.19393/j.cnki.cn11-1537/g2.2019.09.030
22. Duan, L., Shi, X., Jan, D.: Research on the influence of interface layout on reading effect in digital reading. J. Libr. Theory Pract. **05**, 105–109 (2020). https://doi.org/10.14064/j.cnki.issn1005-8214.2020.05.020
23. Norman, D.A.: Design Psychology 3 Emotional Design (Trans. by, He, X., Ou, Q.). CITIC Press, Bejing (2015)
24. Lu, X., Yu, S., Pei, H.: Study on the comfort design scheme of reading light environment in the cabin of civil aircraft. J. Equip. Manuf. Technol. **03**, 19–22 (2018). https://doi.org/10.19554/j.cnki.1001-3563.2022.16.027

Decision-Making Framework to Support the End-of-Life Management of High-Activity Radioactive Sources

Rajiv Khadka[1,2(✉)], Xingyue Yang[1,2], John Koudelka[1,2], Victor Walker[1], and Kevin Kenney[1]

[1] Idaho National Laboratory, Idaho Falls, ID, USA
[2] Center for Advanced Energy Studies, Idaho Falls, ID, USA
rajiv.khadka@inl.gov

Abstract. Sealed radioactive sources are used for an extremely wide range of applications, including at various nuclear facilities, universities, hospitals, and biomedical and industrial organizations, as well as for geological prospecting and exploration. However, proper management of these sealed radioactive sources after they have reached their end-of-life (EOL) remains a global challenge. Very few field-tested mobile hot cells (MHCs) exist to support the EOL management of disused high-activity radioactive sources. One critical challenge encountered by source recovery teams at each site is that of finding adequate space–as well as access to that space—to complete the staging and recapture process by using a MHC. This process is tedious, uncertain, and time-consuming, thus making it essential to properly understand how to plan and manage the setting up and taking down of the MHC. However, no tool currently exists that can serve as an effective medium for making such plans, or for informing, educating, and communicating to source recovery teams important knowledge about the environment in which the MHC will be deployed. In this report, we present a novel approach to planning and managing the deployment of MHCs, and apply it to several different sites that rely on such technology. Furthermore, this planning tool will support collaboration, promote information sharing, and foster better decision-making processes, enabling MHCs to be more efficiently and reliably set up and used for source recovery purposes.

Keywords: Radioactive · Decision Making · LIDAR · Visualization · Mobile Hot Cell

1 Introduction

Sealed radioactive sources are used in a diverse range of applications—from nuclear medicine to metallurgy to electronics to biomedicine [15]—and the types and activities of these sources vary widely. However, proper management of sealed radioactive sources after they have reached the end of their useful life remains a challenge [17]. As demand for nuclear energy continues to grow throughout the world, so does the need to store and manage radioactive materials. Safe and secure handling of these materials is critical for their future use,

H. Mori et al. (Eds.): HCII 2023, LNCS 14056, pp. 63–74, 2023.
https://doi.org/10.1007/978-3-031-48044-7_5

as well as for the health and safety of people potentially exposed to them [13]. The current methods used by other countries do not achieve the desired levels of safety and reliability in the handling of radioactive materials [6]. Furthermore, some countries' systems and procedures for managing radioactive materials are even less safe and secure [6]. Mobile hot cells (MHCs) are designed to handle and manage sealed spent high-activity radioactive sources (SHARS) [3], and to allow for their storage, transportation, and disposal. MHCs can be used for high-level radioactive sources that are no longer required for use or are considered a safety hazard.

The stationing of MHCs at physical sites so that they can be used for storing and transporting sealed radioactive sources must be planned and coordinated in a safe, reliable manner. Transportation of the sealed sources (via MHCs) from their original locations to where they will be loaded into a transportable trailer must be pre-planned and well communicated among the various operators and stakeholders. In using MHCs to safely store and manage the sealed radioactive sources, it is critical that the location of the sealed sources, MHC assembly, trailers, and additional mechanical equipment be well understood. However, no pre-planning tools or framework exist to support operators in conducting a preliminary assessment of the physical site in order to better understand and communicate the work scope and process, the risks involved, the schedule, and the procurement and approval processes. Currently, Google Earth [7] and other similar tools are used in conducting preliminary assessments of the sites of MHC assemblies. However, Google Earth was never designed nor developed to support this type of task. This makes it unreliable for such work, nor does it provide all the necessary assistance for conducting the pre-planning tasks. In the present work, we propose and present a novel framework for providing a decision-making tool that can be used in conducting preliminary assessments of the environments in which MHCs will be assembled in order to manage, store, and transport sealed sources across diverse locations.

During a preliminary assessment, the technical team must investigate the physical site so as to decide how to move the sealed radioactive sources from their current location to the MHC and then to the transportable trailer for end-of-life (EOL) management. To reach their decision, the team must analyze the risks involved, procure the appropriate equipment, and determine the work scope and process, the time required, and the needed additional resources. It may not be feasible for each team member to travel to the physical site in order to conduct a preliminary assessment of the EOL management of radioactive sources; however, each team member must be well informed and knowledgeable about every step, process, and decision that enabled successful EOL management of the given radioactive sources. We propose employing WebGL technology so that a light detection and ranging (LIDAR) [16] device can be used to scan and visualize the physical environment [12]. This framework is discussed in detail in Sect. 3.

The novel contributions of this paper can be summarized as follows:

- We propose a novel decision-making framework for conducting preliminary assessments of the EOL management of high-activity radioactive sources.
- We demonstrate the feasibility of the proposed framework by demonstrating a prototypical implementation, supporting pre-planning tasks, and sharing knowledge among a diverse array of collaborators.

2 Background

An active radioactive source is defined as an item containing a quantity of radiation [10]. This includes sources that release highly radioactive substances such as natural radon and polonium, and also artificially generated sources such as x-rays and gamma rays, radioactive isotopes, and radionuclides for therapeutic or diagnostic purposes. Radioactive waste can be generated from various applications such as hospital, academic, and commercial testing; industrial use of radioisotopes; and the processing of spent nuclear fuels [11]. Such radioactive waste can take different forms (i.e., solid, liquid, gas, or sealed). In sealed sources, the radioactive waste is enclosed in a small metallic vessel and can "remain radioactive for several years even after just one use. Use of sealed radioactive sources is standard, with certain types (e.g., long half-life sources) being employed across a range of very low-activity to high-activity applications (e.g., SHARS). Such sealed radioactive sources still pose health hazards, even though the devices containing these sources are non-functioning. The International Atomic Energy Association has grouped these sealed sources into four categories [4]. The first category (i.e., low-hazard radioactive materials) pertains to sources that pose no health risk to humans, animals, or the environment. The second category (i.e., intermediate- or high-hazard radioactive materials) pertains to sources that can cause injury or death as a result of direct exposure. However, they pose less risk than Category 2 sources because of their low radioactivity levels. The third category (i.e., high-hazard radioactive materials) reflects the radioactive materials' ability to penetrate skin or organs (i.e., the higher the mass fraction of an element emanating from a Category 3 source, the more likely it will reach the skin or organs before being destroyed). Therefore, these sources pose a major health concern, and development of technology and infrastructure to package radioactive waste for safe disposal is critical for both human and environmental safety.

The International Atomic Energy Association has proposed using a mobile system for the conditioning and proper management of highly radioactive sources. The mobile device concept consists of a MHC (see Fig. 1 & 2) to handle sealed types of SHARS (e.g., irradiators and teletherapy heads). In turn, this MHC consists of a mobile high-containment container designed to safely maintain spent sources at low radiation levels. It employs various manipulation capabilities (e.g., robotic arms, mills, and welders) to isolate the sealed SHARS, thus protecting the operator from radiation exposure. A shielded enclosure protects operators from excessive doses of radiation from the radioactive materials. Therefore, assembly and disassembly of the MHC for storing and transporting the sealed sources must be conducted in a manner that is both safe and reliable, making the preliminary assessment a critical step in the decision-making process.

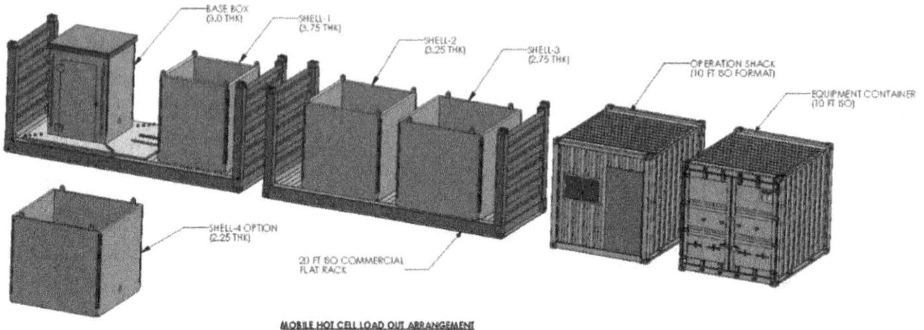

Fig. 1. Mobile hot cell load-out arrangement

This novel framework provides operators the unique opportunity to visualize, monitor, pre-plan, and make decisions regarding the use of MHCs to store and transport sealed SHARS. It enables preliminary assessments to be conducted while collaborating with team members to design the work process for the EOL management of the sealed sources including transporting them from one location to another. It provides a user interface (UI) that enables operators/researchers to virtually navigate their way around the physical site, measure the site's various dimensions, and introduce virtual objects (e.g., trailers, tables, forklifts, and cranes) into the environment.

3 Decision-Making Framework

This decision-making framework incorporates the standard process described by Lunenburg [8], but modifies it to meet our requirements and align with the nature of our work.

3.1 Process

Site Identification and Requirement Analysis. The first step in the decision-making process is for the technical personnel to identify, based on consideration of critical and/or strategic factors, where the sealed radioactive sources are to be physically located for EOL management. In reality, however, these factors serve as obstacles to finding the proper solution for managing the

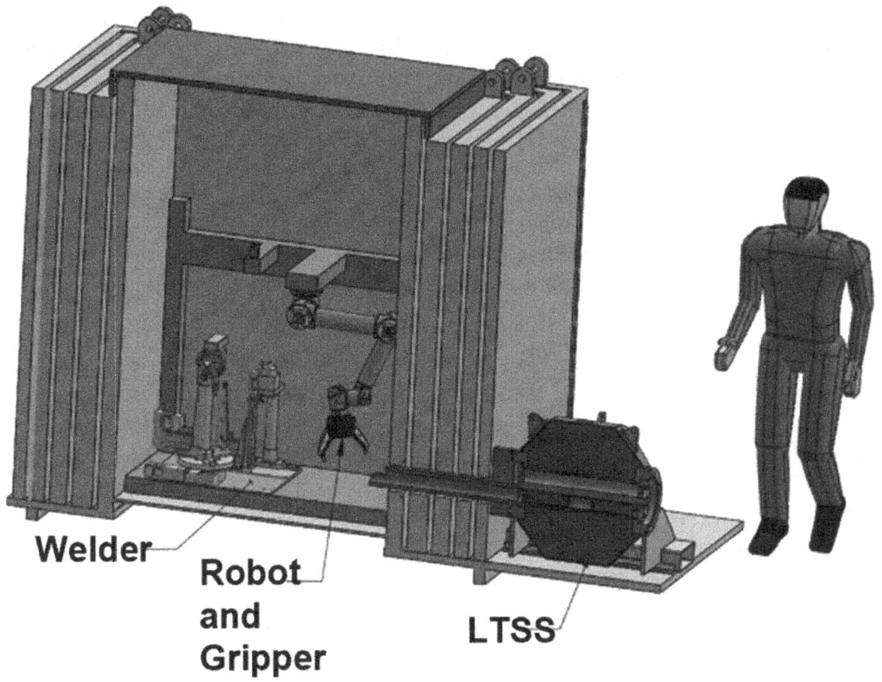

Fig. 2. Mobile hot cell prototype

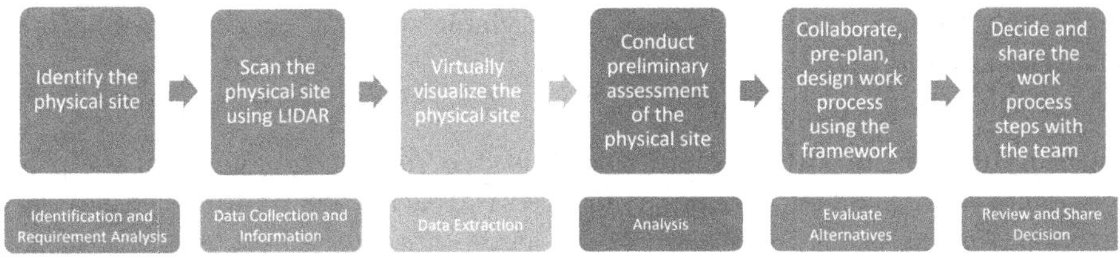

Fig. 3. Decision-making process for preliminary assessments of the EOL management of radioactive sources

entire storage and transportation process for radioactive sources—a process that entails identifying the physical site, limiting assumptions, risks involved, physical/mechanical challenges, local policies, deadlines, resources, and budgets.

Collect Relevant Information. Once the team has identified the physical location and determined the requirements, this step entails collecting any additional information relevant to the physical site. After defining and analyzing the physical site, the next step is to scan it using LIDAR. Each LIDAR scan of the site will be integrated with the UI in order to enable visualization of the site.

Data Extraction. The raw data from the LIDAR scan of the physical site are pre-processed so as to be converted into a visualizable format. It is in this step that any errors, inconsistencies, and noise in the data are removed.

Identify the Alternatives. This step entails determining and analyzing the work process plan for the EOL management of radioactive sources. The team collaborates to visualize the environment, using the novel framework to plan and conduct a preliminary assessment of the possible solutions/routes for reaching the end goal. This step helps the team determine and plan paths for transporting the sealed sources, gathering resources, procuring equipment, and recruiting additional manpower.

Evaluate the Alternatives. After analyzing the physical site by using the framework, it is important to determine which alternatives offer the best support, entail the least amount of risk, and foster maximum utilization of time and resources. This step entails identifying multiple alternatives and then weighing their potential risks and pitfalls against their possible rewards. Ultimately, those alternatives that seemingly represent good, viable strategic choices are selected for discussion and review.

Implementation of the Decision. In this step, knowledge gained in the previous steps or through experience is utilized to reach a decision, which is then carried out by someone physically present at the site selected for the EOL management of the radioactive sources. This step of the decision-making process is comprised of four sub-steps: using the framework to gather relevant information collected in the previous main steps, examining the potential alternatives, ranking the various options, and taking action. These substeps typically occur in logical sequence as more information is gathered on the possible options. When a decision is made, all user-framework interactions while visualizing, monitoring, and interacting are taken into account to determine the work process that works best for managing the sealed sources.

3.2 Framework and User Interface

Figure 4 shows the software architecture of the framework for conducting preliminary assessments of the physical sites. Cyclone 360 [1], a proprietary software, imports the site scans from the Leica BLK2GO [2] hardware. Meshlab [9] preprocess the scans, which are then fed into the Unity3D game engine software

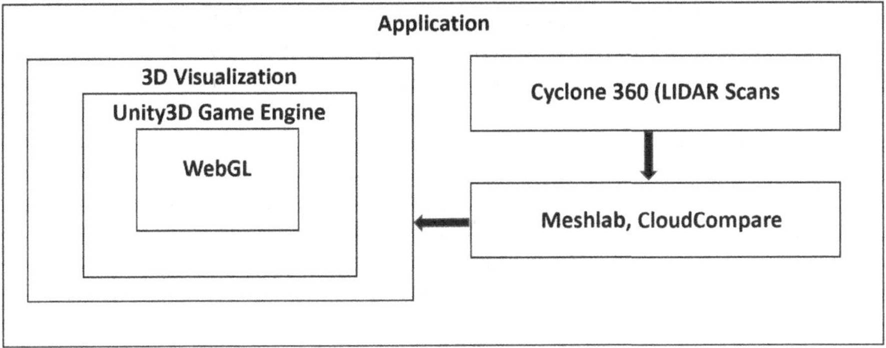

Fig. 4. Overview of software architecture

[14] and visualized using standard web browsers. We will discuss the details of the process and the technical features of the framework and UI in this section. Figure 5 shows the UI of the framework for conducting the preliminary assessment of the site. This UI shows the LIDAR site scan and the necessary buttons for conducting the assessment to support effective decision making.

Fig. 5. Decision-making process for preliminary assessments of the end-of-life management of radioactive sources

LIDAR Scan. We used the Leica BLK2Go to enable fast, easy, one-button mobile scanning of the physical site for the EOL management of radioactive sources. Minimum training is required for an individual to scan the environment and share the resulting data. Though we chose the Leica BLK2Go, our framework can incorporate scans from any standard LIDAR scanning device. The captured scans are then preprocessed in the manner discussed in the following section.

Fig. 6. The Leica BLK2Go

Data Preprocessing. We used a point cloud renderer to display scanned environments in Unity. The renderer was developed based on Potree [5], which can load and display large point clouds more efficiently. The scanned data were downloaded from the Leica BLK2Go to a computer via a thumb drive. We used the Cyclone Register 360 and MeshLab software to convert the raw data from the B2G format into the PLY format, which Potree is able to accept. As LIDAR-scanned environments may contain noise, errors, and inconsistencies, the "select outliers" tool was employed in MeshLab to reduce the noise and discrepancies contained in the scans. We also performed a manual check to clean up the scan and to visualize the scanned environment such that it is similar to the real world. MeshLab also aids in converting the scanned data into the necessary format for visualization on a diverse range of platforms.

User Interactions. User interactions play an important role in increasing the effectiveness and usability of the interfaces. The UI for this framework was designed based on feedback from technical operators who perform physical activities for the EOL management of radioactive sources. Users can interact via such things as tools, controls, and notes. Users can measure the site and place virtual objects in it by via the application-provided tools. The controls afford user navigating functions. Additional details are given below.

Measurements and Dimensions

One essential task that technical operators conduct for preliminary assessments is to measure the environment and the transportation areas. They wish

Fig. 7. Using MeshLab to remove discrepancies and noise from the raw scanned data

Fig. 8. Measuring distance using the UI tools

to be able to measure the pathways and the height/width/depth of the transportation areas in order to ensure safe and reliable transport of the radioactive sources. In our framework, Raycast is used to detect mouse clicks in the 3-D environment. The framework then calculates the distance between the two points selected within the environment (see Fig. 8). The framework also has the flexibility to increase the dimensional changes (i.e., width, height, and depth) of the virtual objects that can be added to the environment. This enables the operators conducting the preliminary assessment to gauge the sizes of the mechanical equipment that may be employed for managing the sealed sources.

Virtual Objects

Pre-planning and preliminary assessments involve discussing diverse alternatives and solutions in order to successfully reach the end goal. Users can utilize this framework to add multiple different virtual objects (e.g., semi-trucks, tables, cranes, and forklifts) into the environment, then discuss the most effective way of using them at the physical site. That this framework allows for the addition of virtual tools will aid in procuring the mechanical equipment necessary to safely transport radioactive sources via the MHC and then load them into the trailer for transportation.

Navigation

Users can employ the framework to navigate around the environment by using the keyboard and mouse, and they will have the flexibility to transport to a specific location, rotate around, and zoom in/out for a better view of the environment.

Collision Detection

A challenge faced by the technical team at physical sites is to avoid mechanical equipment collisions, which present a risk to radioactive sources during transportation. Technical operators will wish to gauge the risk of such collisions. Our framework affords the capability to automatically detect collisions—as illustrated graphically in Fig. 9—and show where exactly in the environment they occurred. This visualization of collision contact presented in Fig. 9 was rendered via particle systems in Unity.

Fig. 9. Graphical representation of a virtual lift table colliding with the surrounding area

Notes

During preliminary assessments, operators may want to take notes pertaining to discussions on specific sites and then use them to plan for the future. Our framework provides the capability to take notes on each physical site and then store them for future reference.

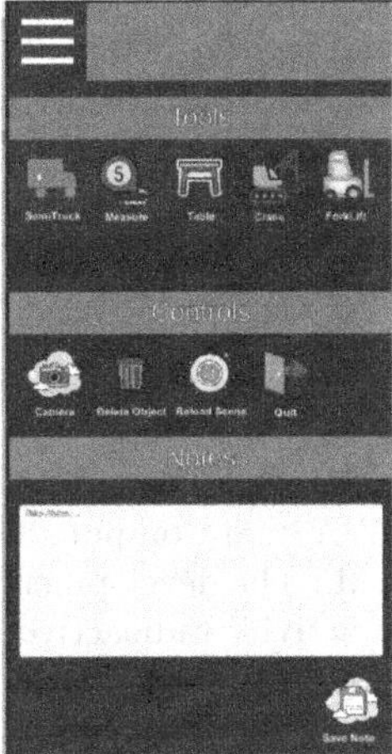

Fig. 10. Note-taking feature

Platforms

The framework was designed using the Unity 2020.3.11f1 game engine, and built using the C# programming language. It was based on WebGL, and its visualization capabilities can be accessed on modern web browsers.

4 Discussion and Conclusion

Sealed radioactive sources entail a unique set of diverse challenges, risks, and uncertainties. Furthermore, storing and transporting sealed sources from one location to another adds even more risk. Thus, it is essential to evaluate and assess each step of the EOL management of radioactive sources. Herein, we presented our novel framework for virtually conducting preliminary assessments of physical sites in order to evaluate a given area and decide what actions are necessary to store and transport sealed sources safely and reliably. This novel framework bridges the technological gap and meets the challenges that currently exist in conducting preliminary assessments and making EOL-management-related decisions in a trustworthy, reliable, and risk-reduced fashion. We believe this framework will support informed decision making, speed up pre-planning activities, maximize the utilization of resources, reduce human errors, and foster increased reliability. We plan for this framework to be open source so that it can be shared with operators needing assistance in conducting preliminary assessments for making EOL-management-related decisions.

Funding Information. This research work was supported by the Department of Energy (DOE).

References

1. AG, L.G.: Leica cyclone register 360–3D laser scanning point cloud registration software (2022). https://leica-geosystems.com/en-us/products/laser-scanners/software/leica-cyclone/leica-cyclone-register-360
2. AG, L.G.: Mobile mapping. simplified (2022). https://shop.leica-geosystems.com/leica-blk/blk2go
3. Bahrin, M.H., Rahman, A.A., Hamzah, M.A., Mamat, M.R., Azman, A., Hasan, H.: Stress analysis for wall structure in mobile hot cell design. In: AIP Conference Proceedings, vol. 1704, p. 050017. AIP Publishing LLC (2016)
4. El-Adham, K., Geleel, M., Mahmoud, N., Cochran, J.: Classification of the inventory of spent sealed sources at INSHAS storage facility. In: Waste Management Symposium, Tueson, USA (2006)
5. Fraiss, S.M., Wimmer, M.: Rendering large point clouds in unity. Tech. Univ. Wien, Bachelor Sci. Medieninformatik Visual Comput. **54** (2017)
6. Liebenberg, G., Al-Mughrabi, M.: The development of a mobile hot cell facility for the conditioning of spent high activity radioactive sources (SHARS) (2008)
7. Lisle, R.J.: Google earth: a new geological resource. Geol. Today **22**(1), 29–32 (2006)
8. Lunenburg, F.C.: The decision making process. In: National Forum of Educational Administration & Supervision Journal, vol. 27 (2010)
9. MeshLab: Meshlab (2022). https://www.meshlab.net/
10. Millar, R., Klaassen, K., Eijkelhof, H.: Teaching about radioactivity and ionising radiation: an alternative approach. Phys. Educ. **25**(6), 338 (1990)
11. Oh, C.H.: Hazardous and Radioactive Waste Treatment Technologies Handbook. CRC Press (2001)
12. Parisi, T.: WebGL: Up and Running. O'Reilly Media, Inc. (2012)
13. Rechard, R.P.: Historical relationship between performance assessment for radioactive waste disposal and other types of risk assessment. Risk Anal. **19**(5), 763–807 (1999)
14. Technologies, U.: Unity for all industries (2022). https://unity.com/
15. Vicente, R., Sordi, G.M., Hiromoto, G.: Management of spent sealed radiation sources. Health Phys. **86**(5), 497–504 (2004)
16. Wandinger, U.: Introduction to lidar. In: Weitkamp, C. (eds.) Lidar. Springer Series in Optical Sciences, vol. 102, pp. 1–18. Springer, New York, NY (2005). https://doi.org/10.1007/0-387-25101-4_1
17. Won, K., Han, J., Bonne, A.: Radioactive waste disposal: global experience and challenges. IAEA Bull. **39**(1), 33–41 (1997)

Supporting Sequential Memory to Facilitate Reading Comprehension on a Tablet

Rino Kimura and Makoto Nakashima(✉)

Computer Science and Intelligent Systems Course, Graduate School of Engineering, Oita University, Oita, Japan
nakasima@oita-u.ac.jp

Abstract. In recent years, reading through electronic books (e-books) has been increasing, but it is said that the comprehension of the contents is inferior to that of paper books. We propose two visualising bookmark methods to support the retention of sequential memory, one of the causes of poor comprehension, by focusing on the difficulty of "looking back" at e-books. To verify the effectiveness of the proposed methods, a comparative experiment was conducted to measure the degree of sequential memory retention and the ease of looking back on different reading styles. The results showed no significant differences in post-reading test scores for sequential memory retention. Still, the correlation between subjects' reading comprehension and the test scores measuring ease of looking back at pages of an e-book was closer to that for paper books than the correlation for conventional e-book readers. The post-experiment questionnaire also showed that many subjects felt that the proposed methods were comfortable to look back at, indicating that the methods were highly effective in easing looking back.

Keywords: Supporting sequential memory · reading comprehension · bookmark visualisation · partial bookmark · dual time series bookmark listing

1 Introduction

As the reading of electronic books (e-books) becomes more widespread, various studies have shown problems compared to the traditional reading of paper books. Some experiments have shown that memory retention of the order of story episodes is not as good when reading e-books as when reading paper books [5]. One of the primary causes for them is the difficulty of looking back at previous pages. In the electronic form, the "look back" operation to recheck the already-read part requires the user to turn the pages individually. To reduce this load, many existing e-book readers have a bookmark function. However, searching for a specific bookmark from the list becomes more difficult as the number of bookmarks increases. Furthermore, paper books have much information, such as the weight of the book and the sensation of turning the pages, which assist a "sense of the pathway" necessary for remembering and spatially reconstructing a series of events [7]. Such information is unique to paper books and is a sensation that e-books do not have.

H. Mori et al. (Eds.): HCII 2023, LNCS 14056, pp. 75–86, 2023.
https://doi.org/10.1007/978-3-031-48044-7_6

In this study, we propose two visualisation methods for bookmarks: "*partial bookmarking*" and "*dual time-series bookmark listing*" for a simple e-book reader available on a table to facilitate looking back and support sequential memory when reading an e-book. The partial bookmarking mechanism [6] developed for web browsers records the information, i.e., a partial bookmark, required to identify any piece of an e-book page which the user is interested in and wants to access again later. It overlays the piece content on the page the user is viewing. The user can look back without going back and forth between pages by selecting the partial bookmark icons. Utilising dual chronological bookmark listing, these partial bookmarks are displayed as clickable icons on the e-book reader with two additional pieces of easy-to-understand visual time information, i.e., which page and when it was bookmarked, that help to provide a cue for recall memory.

The experiment was conducted to examine the effects of the proposed methods on the ease of looking back and sequential memory retention. For this purpose, three groups of subjects were prepared, each of which to read with a paper book, an e-book, and the proposed system, respectively. To avoid differences in reading comprehension among the groups, a questionnaire was administered to measure reading comprehension, and the subjects were divided according to the results. In the experiment, each group was asked to read the same short story, and a test to measure the retention of sequential memory and a test to measure the ease of looking back was conducted. The post-experiment evaluation questionnaires indicated that the proposed system improved the comfort of looking back on the user's experience and was superior in usability.

The rest of this paper is organised as follows: The problems of e-book reading in comprehension are discussed in Sect. 2. The proposed methods for visualising bookmarks on the e-book reader are described in Sect. 3. In Sect. 4, we clarified the effectiveness and usability of the methods in reading e-books using a simple web e-book reader incorporating the proposed methods.

2 Issues on E-Book Reading

Now that e-books have become widespread, there are a variety of e-book readers. Many of them have features to make reading e-books more comfortable. However, from the viewpoint of this study, e-books have the following two problems:

(1) Difficulty in looking back
(2) Few clues to reconstructing sequential memory

These issues are discussed below, using the functions of existing e-book readers as examples, based on the fact that good comprehenders were significantly better than poor comprehenders at remembering and relocating the order of information in a text [3]. As for existing e-book readers, we use Amazon's Kindle, regarded as one of the most used readers in the world, as an example.

2.1 Difficulty of Looking Back

In addition to turning the pages one by one to find the page you are looking for, you can also mark the pages you are interested in and look back at them later. The following is a description of well-known marking functions.

Bookmark. This function bookmarks the entire page. Figure 1 shows an example of using bookmarks on Kindle. As shown in the left-hand part of the figure, the page can be bookmarked by clicking the bookmark button in the upper right corner of the screen. In the bookmarks area, which appears by clicking the My Note button, the bookmarks, consisting of the page number and the snippet, are listed in page order, as shown in the right-hand part of the figure. By tapping a bookmark, you can go to that page. The following is an example of using bookmarks on Kindle.

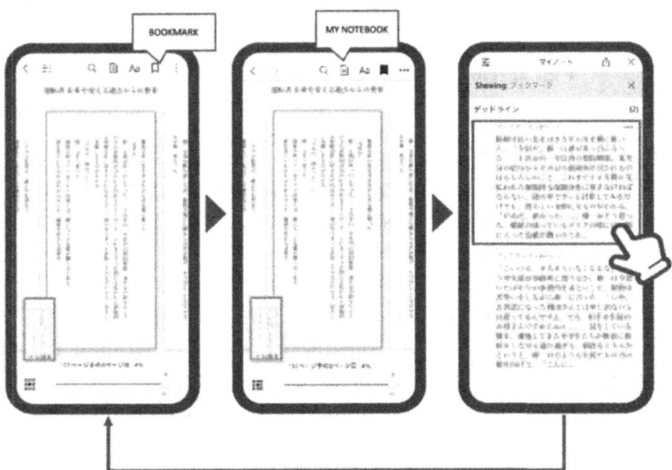

Fig. 1. Bookmarks on Kindle.

Highlights. This function saves a portion of the text. The selected sentences can be coloured with a long press and choosing the range and colour. To find the highlighted section, click the My Notebook button in the same way as the bookmark function. The display order is page order, and the entire selected text is displayed as a highlight. By tapping the highlighted page, you can go to the highlighted page. Figure 2 shows an example of highlighting on Kindle.

To look back using the above two functions, it is necessary to display the reading toolbar, open My Notebook, and search for essential information. This function is challenging to perform continuously because of the cognitive load before looking back, which makes spatial reconstruction of memory difficult.

2.2 Few Clues to Reconstructing Sequential Memory

Paper books have much information to grasp the position in the book, such as the sensation of turning the pages and the difference in the weight of the book on the left

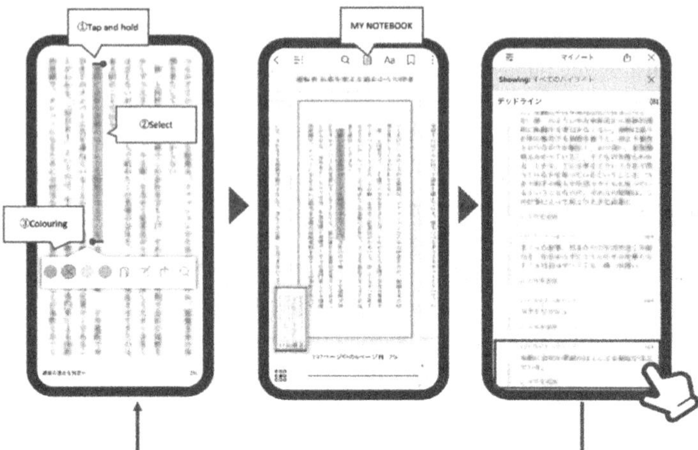

Fig. 2. How to highlight and browse on Kindle

and right hand. On the other hand, e-books have only page information, such as page numbers that indicate pages and percentages that denote the reading progress. Therefore, it is difficult to grasp the position in a book and to reconstruct the memory spatially in the e-book.

In order to solve the above problems, it is necessary to have a function that allows easy access to the looking back pages and increases the information about the sensation of the pathway to facilitate spatially reconstructing memory without interruption. To this end, this study proposes a function for e-books that reduces the cognitive load of looking back and has new visual information that can replace the tactile information in paper books.

3 Supporting Sequential Memory

This section describes the methods of visualising bookmarks on e-book readers. The point of sequential memory support is to make it easy for the user to grasp and quickly see the parts of the text that they want to return to again and again when necessary.

3.1 Partial Bookmarking

Users who bookmark a page do not necessarily need the entire page. In addition, moving to the bookmarked page when necessary is not only time-consuming but also takes the user away from the page they are currently reading. As a bookmarking method that can deal with these problems, we introduce the technique of partial bookmarking [6], which was developed for bookmarking only the necessary parts of a web page. A partial bookmark in this proposal consists of information that identifies a partial area on a page of an e-book that the user wants to bookmark and makes it available for later reference, i.e., a page number and the coordinates of the partial area. The information is used to redisplay the bookmarked information later.

Figure 3 shows examples of partial bookmarking on our prototype implementation for a simple web e-book reader. Let us assume that the area surrounded by the dotted line on the right-hand part of the figure is the area of interest the user has bookmarked on the e-book page (according to the user's choice in CLIP mode). When the bookmarked area is called up later when the user is reading a different page, it is overlapped on the page the reader is reading, as shown in the left-hand part of the figure. The display location should be freely movable so as not to interfere with reading in MOVE mode.

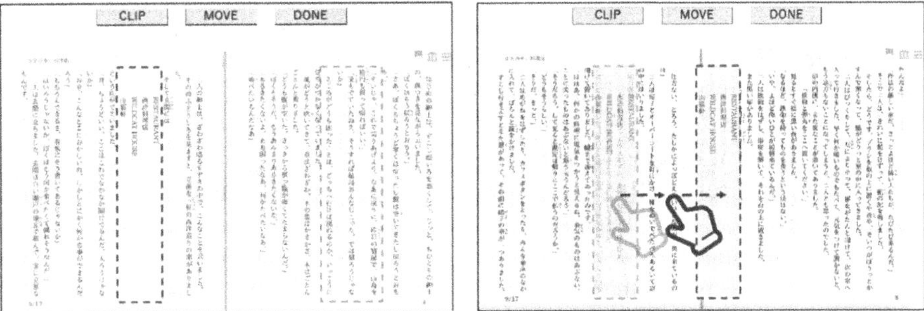

Fig. 3. Partial bookmarking

3.2 Dual Time-Series Bookmark Listing

When the user cropping of the bookmark area is DONE, these are displayed on the e-book reader screen as corresponding icons to allow easy recall of partial bookmarks. In Fig. 4, each of the coloured rectangles at the top of the screen is a bookmark icon. To provide a "sense of pathway" to the user, two types of time-series information are added to the display design of the icons to remind the user of where the bookmark was located and when it was created. As shown in the left-hand part of the figure, the former indicates the bookmarked page's position by the bookmark icon's displayed position. As depicted in the right-hand part of the figure, a colour change represents the latter information according to the order in which the bookmarks were created.

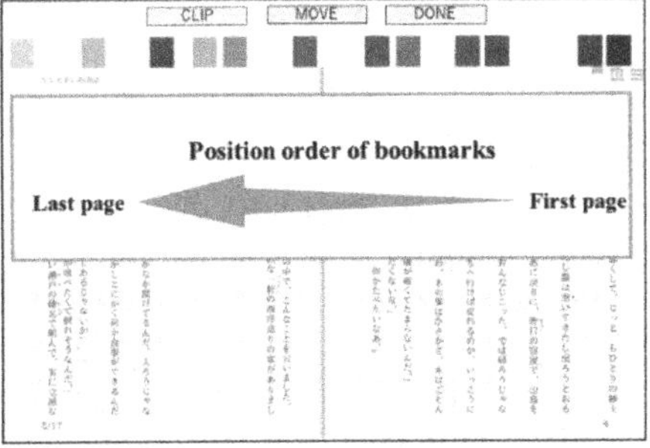

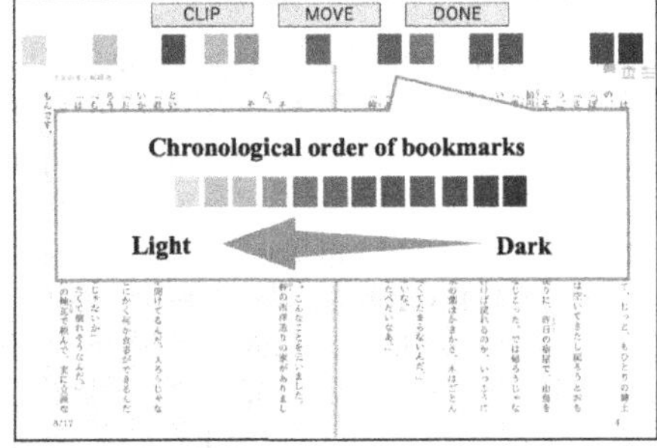

Fig. 4. Dual time-series bookmark listing

4 Experiment

A preliminary comparative experiment was conducted to clarify the effectiveness of the proposed methods in supporting sequential memory retention and improving the ease of looking back.

4.1 Settings

Three subject groups were prepared for the comparison: one group (denoted as G_u) read the specified novel on printed paper, and the other two groups read the e-book on an e-book reader (G_w) or an e-book reader incorporating the proposed methods (G_p). A total of 24 subjects were recruited from Oita University students (ages 18 through 24, 19 male, five female) to take part, and each one was gotten a prepaid card worth 1,000 Japanese yen for their time. First, they were asked to complete a pre-survey to measure their reading performance [8]. Next, the subjects were divided into three groups of eight each so that there was no difference in reading performance, i.e., the mean pre-survey scores and the homogeneity of variance of the scores of the members of each group. Each group of subjects was then asked to read one copyright-free translated novel [2] in Japanese (a 23-page short story) in different ways for each group. After reading the novel, subjects were asked to answer two tests, T1 and T2. T1 is about the sequence of events in the novel to measure the degree of sequential memory retention, which was responded to without looking at the novel. T2 assesses the ease of looking back; subjects were allowed to look at the novel to find the answers.

Grouping by Pre-survey. To avoid differences in reading comprehension in each group, a questionnaire was administered to measure reading comprehension [8]. Table 1 shows the questionnaire items. The first half of the questionnaire was divided into two parts, with the first part asking about reading habits up to the present and the second part asking about reading comprehension. All the subjects were asked to answer on a 7-point Likert scale for each item. Based on the total score of this questionnaire, each group is divided into groups so that there is no difference in the average score of each group. The average scores of the pre-survey are 38.2, 39.0, and 38.2 for G_u, G_w, and G_p, respectively.

To verify the validity of this grouping, the equality of variances was examined using Levene's test, and the equality of means was analysed using one-way ANOVA. As a result, there is no significant difference in variances ($p = 0.76$) and no difference in the means ($p = 0.98$). These results indicate the validity of the grouping.

Ways of Reading. Subjects were asked to read the assigned novel in a manner determined by each group, as mentioned in Sect. 4.1. Each of these reading scenes is shown in Fig. 5. The novel specified was the Japanese translation of O. Henry's "The Church with an Overshot Wheel" (translated by Ikuzaburo Miyake), using text data (12,331 characters) available in Aozora Bunko [2], a Japanese digital library including many out-of-copyright books. The subjects in G_u read the novel (23 pages) printed on paper. For G_w and G_p, the Web-based e-book reader [1] prepared for Aozora Bunko was used. Note that the subjects in G_w were asked to perform reading without using any of the functions provided by the reader. The subjects in G_p used the reader incorporating our proposed methods. Before the experiment, they had a 5-minute operation practice using

Table 1. Pre-survey items

Q1	Do you like to read books written in Japanese?
Q2	How often do you read paper books?
Q3	How often do you read electronic books?
Q4	How much did you read in high school?
Q5	How much did you read in junior high school?
Q6	How much did you read in elementary school?
Q7	How long does it take to finish a 200-page paperback book (if you continue reading)?
Q8	Do you consider yourself to have good comprehension skills when reading a book?
Q9	What is the percentage of students scoring in modern Japanese on the National Center Test for University Entrance Examinations?
Q10	What is the average score for contemporary writing on national practice exams?

a novel other than the one used in the experiment. For G_w and G_p, Lenovo YT-K606F with a 13-in. display resolution of 2160 × 1350.

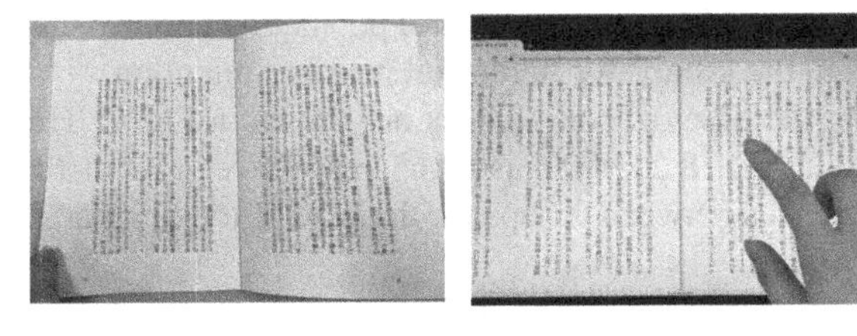

G_u (printed paper) G_w (e-book reader) G_p (e-book reader with proposed methods)

Fig. 5. Reading scenes

Post-reading Tests. To measure the effectiveness of our methods on the retention of sequential memory and the ease of looking back, two similar tests were conducted in three groups: In the first test (T1), to measure sequential memory retention, the subjects were asked to answer seven questions about the order of events in the book under the condition that they did not see the book to find the answers (the total mark is 25). In the second test (T2), to verify the ease of looking back operations by the proposed methods, the subjects were asked to describe the five events under the condition that they could see the book to find the answers (the total mark is 10). The time limits for T1 and T2 were 3 and 8 min, respectively, depending on the amount of work involved.

Post-experiment Questionnaire. All subjects were given a questionnaire about looking back during the experiment. Table 2 shows the questionnaire items. Here Q4 through Q6 were items only for the subjects in G_p. All the items were yes/no questions. The subjects in G_p were additionally given the SUS (System Usability Scale) [4] questionnaire, which evaluates usability on a 10-item Likert scale.

Table 2. Post-experiment questionnaire about looking back.

Q1	Did you look back when reading?
Q2	Did you look back when solving the second half of the question?
Q3	Did you find it difficult to look back during the reading?
Q4	Did you use the bookmark function when reading?
Q5	Did you look back at your bookmarks when reading?
Q6	Did you look back at your bookmarks when solving the problem?

4.2 Results

Figure 6 shows the score distribution for T1 for each group of subjects. The mean score for each of G_u, G_w, and G_p was 14.25, 11.25, and 11.50, respectively. The figure suggests, and further applications of Dunnett's test with G_p as the control population confirm that there are no significant differences in the groups for sequential memory retention.

The results of T2 for measuring the ease of looking back are shown in Fig. 7. The mean score for each of G_u, G_w, and G_p was 8.25, 8.00, and 7.63, respectively. As in T1, there were also no significant differences between groups for the ease of looking back.

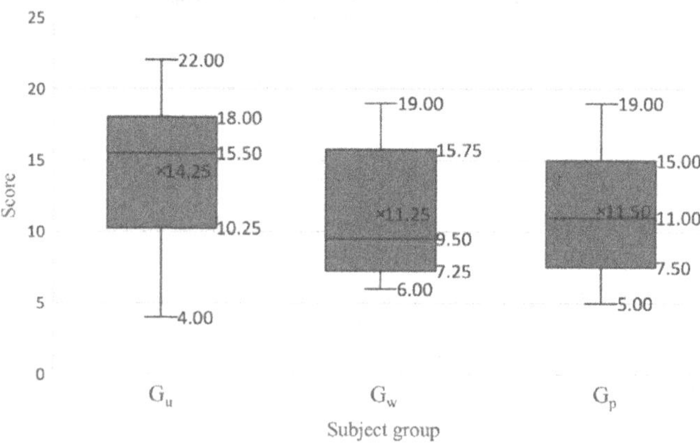

Fig. 6. Box-and-whisker plots of score distribution for T1.

Table 3 shows the results of the post-experiment questionnaire. From the results of Q1 and Q2, we can see that the ratio of subjects who looked back at the pages remained the same among the groups. From the results of Q3, the ratio of subjects who found

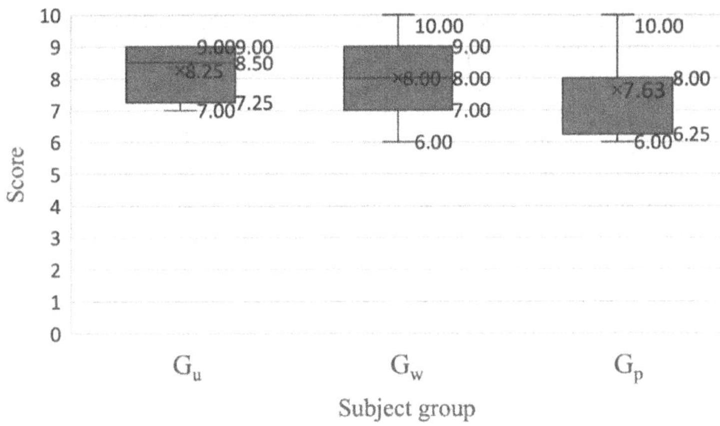

Fig. 7. Box-and-whisker plots of score distribution for T2.

it difficult to look back at the book was lowest for G_p, indicating the effectiveness of the proposed method. From the results of Q4 and Q6, we can see that our proposed methods were used without problems for creating and visualising bookmarks. Note that the average number of partial bookmarks taken by the subjects in G_p was 12.25. This means that each subject created one partial bookmark for every two pages.

Table 3. Post-experiment questionnaire statistics

Group	Answer	Q1	Q2	Q3	Q4	Q5	Q6
G_u	Yes	0.75	0.87	0.66	–	–	–
	No	0.25	0.12	0.33	–	–	–
G_w	Yes	0.75	0.87	0.62	–	–	–
	No	0.25	0.12	0.37	–	–	–
G_p	Yes	0.75	0.75	**0.50**	1.00	0.50	0.75
	No	0.25	0.25	**0.50**	0.00	0.50	0.25

The average SUS score was 80.63, with a standard deviation of 1.25. The SUS evaluation method is based on the following criteria: a score higher than 68 would be considered above average, and a score higher than 80.3 indicates good usability. It can be said that the proposed methods have excellent usability.

5 Discussion

As mentioned in the previous section, there were no significant differences in the post-reading test scores for measuring sequential memory retention (T1) and the ease of looking back (T2) among the three groups. However, there were differences in the correlation between the pre-survey scores and these test scores among the groups. Table 4 shows the correlation between the pre-survey scores and the scores for T1 and T2.

For G_u, a fairly positive correlation was found for T1 scores, whereas almost no correlation was found for G_w and G_p. This means that the better a person's reading comprehension, the higher the rate of sequential memory retention in reading on printed paper. On the other hand, the subjects with high reading comprehension on paper did not demonstrate this ability with the e-book reader.

Table 4. Correlation coefficients for pre-survey and post-reading test scores (T1 and T2).

Pre-survey scores vs	G_u	G_w	G_p
T1 scores for measuring sequential memory retention	0.49	0.01	−0.01
T2 scores for measuring the ease of looking back	−0.08	0.72	0.38

Figure 8 shows the scatter plots for the T2 and pre-survey scores for G_w and G_p. A strong positive correlation for G_w and a slightly positive correlation for G_p were found, whereas there was almost no correlation for G_u. The more negligible correlation of G_p compared to G_w, and the fact that there is no significant difference between the post-reading test scores of G_w and G_p measuring the ease of looking back, indicate that the proposed methods improve the ease of looking back to some extent and are closer to the comfort level of looking back in a paper book.

From the result of Q5 of the post-experiment questionnaire, it can also be seen that it is not easy to look back page by page in e-books. Although there is no problem with the system's usability from the SUS evaluation result, the proposed methods do not have enough functions that everyone would find easy to look back at, like a paper book. When subjects who answered that it was difficult to look back in Q3 were interviewed about the reasons for this, the following comments were made: "*Because the information in the bookmark was only text, and I could not see the original page*," "Because I could not turn the pages at once." This indicates that the visualising bookmark methods require not only a bookmark that allows easy access to a portion of the necessary information to be viewed but also other features that make looking back more flexible.

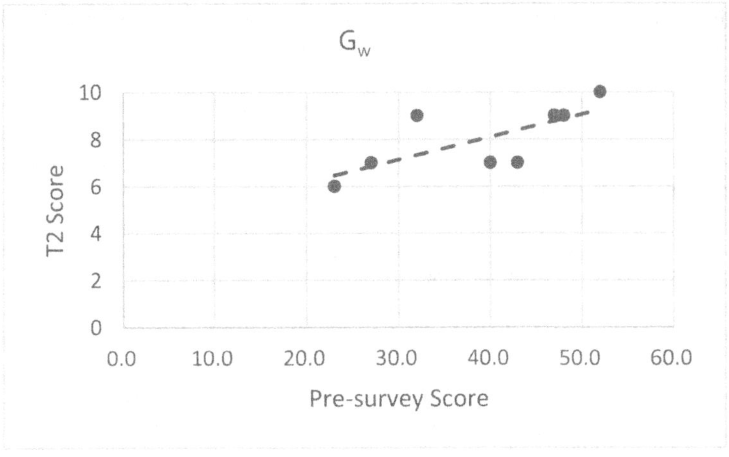

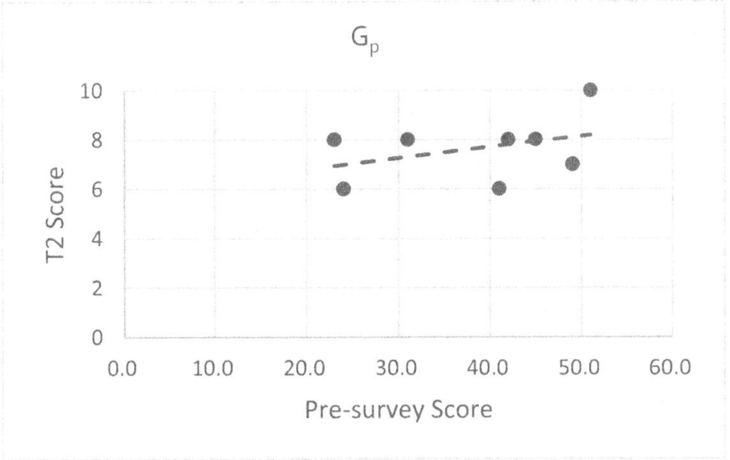

Fig. 8. Scatter plots for the pre-survey and T2 scores distribution.

6 Conclusion

While some subjects found it easier to look back on the proposed method, others did not change. Although the proposed methods received a good evaluation in terms of usability, the results of the questionnaire indicated that other functions were needed. There is room for investigation. As for functional improvements, a function that allows users to refer to the original page from a bookmark and a design that enables more accurate correspondence between the bookmark icon and the bookmark content in their minds are required. In addition, a more in-depth study of bookmarking and looking back at paper books is needed. For example, since the bookmark icon is modelled after a sticky note in a paper book, investigating how users use sticky notes may provide an opportunity to create a new design.

Acknowledgements. This study was supported by JSPS KAKENHI Grant Number JP22K12704.

References

1. Airzoshi. https://www.satokazzz.com/books/
2. Aozora Bunko. https://www.aozora.gr.jp
3. Cataldo, M.G., Oakhill, J.: Why are poor comprehenders inefficient searchers? An investigation into the effects of text representation and spatial memory on the ability to locate information in text. J. Educ. Psychol. **92**(4), 791–799 (2000). https://doi.org/10.1037/0022-0663.92.4.791
4. Lewis, J.R., Sauro, J.: Item benchmarks for the system usability scale. J. Usabil. Stud. **13**(3), 158–167 (2018)
5. Mangen, A., Walgermo, B.R., Brønnick, K.: Reading linear texts on paper versus computer screen: effects on reading comprehension. Int. J. Educ. Res. **58**, 61–68 (2013). https://doi.org/10.1016/j.ijer.2012.12.002
6. Nagatomo, T., Tachibana, T., Sato, K., Nakashima, M.: Partial bookmarking: a structure-independent mechanism of transclusion for a portion of any web page, adjunct. In: Proceedings of ACM UIST'16, Tokyo, Japan, pp. 185–186 (2016). https://doi.org/10.1145/2984751.2984761
7. Piper, A.: Book Was There: Reading in Electronic Times. The University of Chicago Press, Chicago (2012)
8. Sawasaki, K.: The relationship between university students' reading experiences and reading comprehension. J. Int. Relat. Comp. Culture **10**(2), 213–231 (2012). (Japanese)

Understanding the Design Rhythm of Vortex via Visualization

Runqing Lin[1], Aijia Zhang[1], Caihong He[2], Guanghui Huang[1,3(✉)], and Jiayuan Zhou[4]

[1] Faculty of Humanities and Arts, Macau University of Science and Technology, Avenida Wai Long, Taipa, Macau 999078, China
ghhuang1@must.edu.mo

[2] Guangzhou Wanqu Cooperative Institute of Design, Guangzhou, Guangdong, China

[3] Zhuhai M.U.S.T. Science and Technology Research Institute, Zhuhai, Guangdong, China

[4] The Chinese University of Hong Kong (Shenzhen), Shenzhen, Guangdong, China

Abstract. Vortex is a natural phenomenon with the beauty of rhythm and it is also a valuable inspiration for designers. With the continuous development of computer technology, the use of generation technology to simulate the visual effect of vortex has become a commonly used means of artistic expression. At present, though generation technology is mostly used to explore the visual effects of fluids, its design rhythm is rarely summarized. This paper starts with analyzing the motion trajectory of vortex animation. First, the dynamic effect of vortex is simulated by generating algorithm to form visual animation. Secondly, the visual characteristics and causes of vortex momentum are analyzed by using the nine-square grid. Finally, the subjective and objective double analysis system of rational collocation and sensibility is constructed, the design rhythm expression language of vortex is combed and summarized, and its metrics and application performance in visual art and design are summarized. it also provides a set of practical tools and quality evaluation reference standards for designers to cross-study the dynamic law of fluid in design.

Keywords: liquid visualization · generation design · vortex pattern · design rhythm

1 Introduction

The pattern of vortex is a typical source of design, widely used and seen in graphic design, animation and architecture. Kohei Sugiura, the world-known Japanese graphic designer, has summarized the origin, aesthetic connotation, and symbolic meaning of vortex pattern [1]. He highly recommended and referred to the vortex pattern as the most symbolic Asian icon. He put forward that the Tomoe pattern on Japanese family crest (Kamon), the swirling pattern on Chinese bronze ware, tendril pattern on Indian dress, etc. are all derived from vortex. Due to its unique charm, the vortex pattern has attracted great attention from designers and the composition rules of the vortex have been summarized by many. The specific process is as follows: sketching imitation, modeling simplification, typical extraction, induction and deformation. This mode mainly requires

H. Mori et al. (Eds.): HCII 2023, LNCS 14056, pp. 87–99, 2023.
https://doi.org/10.1007/978-3-031-48044-7_7

designers to have keen insight, observation and modeling ability as they have to extract elements from the form of nature itself, summarize the design rhythm of the pattern, and apply it to daily design practice.

However, this process has certain limitations in the digital environment. First, it requires designers to collect and sort out the material for a long time, which is a low-efficient way. Secondly, it itself relies more on the designer's own modeling skills and perceptual talent. It is not a universal mode that can enable designers to do more complex work.

With the continuous development of computer graphics, the above problems can be effectively solved by generative design. Software such as Procesing, Touchdesign, Grasshopper, etc. can simulate various fluid phenomena to varying degrees. This type of software is known for its fast creation efficiency, multiple types of generation, and strong analysis ability, which provides designers with new design thinking and design methods.

Therefore, this paper hopes to simulate the shape of the vortex through the method of fluid visualization, and combined with the auxiliary observation method of the vertical and horizontal analysis of the nine grid, to construct a rational and perceptual subjective and objective analysis system to better help designers to observe the dominant and recessive phenomena of the vortex. Through the design of a set of vortex scale tools that follow the golden proportion rule, it helps designers to understand and use the design rhythm of vortex pattern more intuitively.

2 Literature Review

In this part, the paper will review the previous literature. More specifically, it includes research on analysis of design rhythm, generative methodology of fluid animation and visualization of computational fluid dynamics.

2.1 The Analysis and Research of the Design Rhythm

Albrecht Darer proposed that an artist should learn the design rhythm of geometry and should not become a pure artist [2]. He emphasized the importance of geometric design rhythm to artistic creation.Le Corbusiery pointed out that the design rhythm in geometry are obvious to the human eye, and these rhythm are the basis of various human activities and should be used by people [3]. He strengthened the function of the design rhythm of geometry and applied the idea to the design practice.Josef Miiller-Brockmann pointed out that the proportion of various forms of elements and the distance between them are almost always logically related to the Fibonacci series that leads to the golden section ratio [4]. He emphasized that there is a design rhythm of combining mathematics with beauty in layout design.Chen Nan put forward the design philosophy of rhythm [5]. He referred to the rhythm as the basic unit to determine position, size, amount, and orientation. Starting from traditional Chinese culture, including poetry rhythm system, nine-square grid, graphic deduction system of I Ching, he figured out the framework, logic, continuity, and series of design system and concluded that designers shall pay attention to the innovation of the rules of rhythm, in addition to the innovation of form.

Zeng Rong and Anna analyzed the rhythmatized characteristics of digital interface design layout principles, and discussed the innovative ways and development path of rhythm in digital interface layout design [6]. Chen Wei explored and summarized the rhythm in agricultural products by careful observation [7].

From the above mentioned, the paper defines the meaning of rhythm as follows. Rhythm is related to a certain structure and pattern, which can be decomposed. It is also a pattern or movement that is regular and repeated. The paper also found out that the previous researchers paid more attention to the induction of history theory, evidenced by the methodology they adopted, for example, historical research, case study and direct observation.

2.2 The Analysis and Research of the Design Rhythm

The research method of fluid animation generation are mainly summarized into three categories: empirical, physical, and data-driven method [8].The early wave modelling method is based on experience. In this method, water surface is often simplified into a height field. The shape of the water surface is directly constructed after observation. From the perspective of image processing, Mastin et al. [9] used wind-driven empirical sea spectrum model and Fourier transform to filter and synthesize white noise images to obtain sea surface scenes with waves. Later a physics-based fluid simulation method is introduced. Kass M. Rapid [10] used a simplified two-dimensional shallow water equation to obtain the height field to approximate the surface effect.Monaghan [11] proposed a particle-based Lagrangian method. This method discretizes the fluid into a series of particles with physical properties such as velocity and density. It studies the changes of the physical properties of a single particle over time, and obtains the overall fluid effect by tracking the motion of the particles.Third, the data-driven method is put forward by Shang Liu et al. [12]. They proposed a structure-driven near-shore swell animation synthesis method. Taking the near-shore swell as the object, the representation and extraction method of wave morphological characteristics was studied, and controllable wave animation was quickly generated. Guijuan Zhang [13] proposes a method that users can use the key frames of structure to control the animation fluid.

This type of research mainly explores how to use Computer Graphics to truly transform the motion state of fluids in nature. It is an algorithm-based design pattern, often using quantitative experiments.

2.3 Research on Visualization of Computational Fluid Dynamics

Computational fluid dynamics (CFD) visualization involves many fields such as Computer Graphics, computer vision, and human-machine interaction. It is widely used in medicine, weather forecasting, molecular biology, nuclear science, etc.. With the aid of Computer Graphics and image processing technology, CFD converts the phenomena and calculation results generated in fluid mechanics into visual images, which are displayed on the screen and processed interactively [14].

Among them, vector field visualization technology is common in fluid visualization research. Various existing representation methods for vector field visualization can be roughly divided into points, lines, surfaces, particles and particle animation, vector field topology, vector volume rendering and texture-based methods and other categories [14]. Kenwright [15] adopted the streamline construction method. He used the numerical integration method and the dual stream function method, and found out that, though to a certain extent, the clutter of the point icon mapping vector is solved, sometimes it may lead to the disordered and discontinuous displayed image, which cannot represent the continuous distribution between point data in the vector field. Van Wijk j j [16] proposed that the particles in this method can be selected as point particles or surface particles, and the appropriate particle release time and life cycle can be selected to construct a continuous animation display. The animation display of surface particles can provide a stronger sense of three-dimensional space. The internal structure of the flow field is shown, and in addition, particles of different shapes can be used to represent different structures in the same flow field.

Due to the huge amount of data generated by CFD calculation, it is difficult to find a appropriate visualization method to display all the data on a two-dimensional screen. Post, FH visualized the characteristics of fluid mechanics, which displays high degree abstraction and less redundant information, and helps to reduce complexity so as to easily obtain high interactivity [17]. Helman j, Hesselink l [18] provided a new technology to understand the vector field structure from the global perspective. The vector field topology displays the topology of the entire flow field with less redundant information, and can be extended from the flow field to other vector fields, such as Eddy current field, pressure layer field, etc. Such a method can effectively separate the user's area of interest from the data field.

Therefore, the visualization studied in this paper is an interpretation method, which uses the computational generative design to visually organize and display the relevant information of the fluid, and help us interpret and deduce the design rhythm of the vortex. Next, the paper will describe research questions and design explorations.

3 Research Questions

Based on the above work, in addition to the general golden section ratio, there are few more intuitive and easy-to-use design rhythm and tools for the vortex shape pattern design. How to help designers have a deeper understanding of the design rhythm of the vortex form, so we try to answer the following questions in this study.

(1) Is there an implicit design rhythm for the vortex shape?
(2) Can visualization based on fluid mechanics effectively help designers understand the design rhythm of vortex morphology?
(3) Whether the nine-square grid can assist designers to observe the eigenvalues of fluid visualization, and better summarize the design rhythm of vortex morphology?
(4) Is there a quantifiable quality evaluation standard for design metrics?
(5) how to evaluate the design quality of vortex pattern in design practice?

4 Experiment Design

The paper is driven by the experiment. First, the paper adopts vortex as the research subject. Among various fluid dynamics phenomena, vortex is the most often seen element in design work.

Graphic designers usually abstract vortex wave and produce swirls, round swirls, water swirls, etc. Brand designers often choose the dynamic pattern of vortex as the base logo and extend it into other graphics. Animators also create works based on vortex stimulation. Therefore, the conclusion of design rhythm of vortex is of overarching importance for designers both theoretically and practically.

The visualized vortex is stimulated by generative design software processing and analyzed from a perspective of rationality and sensibility. In the meanwhile, nine-square grid is used to facilitate conclusion.

4.1 Generative Design Based on Fluid Mechanics

First, the paper simulates the fluid visualization of the vortex to generate animation, and simulate the velocity formula of the two-dimensional vortex and the spiral formula of Archimedes in the algorithm design. In order to try more on the vortex effect, we set three parameters, one is the module, which mainly controls the number of spirals, that is, how many lines converge towards the center at the same time.

The second is the velocity coefficient. The convergence velocity mainly affects the curvature of the spiral. The third is the modulus, which refers to the ratio of stress to strain of the material under stress. The modulus affects the curvature of the fluid. The larger the value, the stronger the stiffness and the smaller the curvature. However, affected by other parameters, there may not be obvious changes. The paper sets the parameters for generating the animation to the following three values: module: 218, speed: 0.15, modulus: 8, because this value can best restore the motion law of the vortex in the current algorithm.

4.2 Layout Based on Nine-square Grid

The paper adopts nine-square grid as the assistance tool to analyze generative animation. Nine-square grid is a kind of structural master map, which consists of both nodes and lines. It is a scientific network layout, and designers often subconsciously observe and design according to this established rhythm.

The establishment of the nine-square grid can help us observe the location, size, quantity, direction and other factors of the generated fluid phenomenon. The paper marks each square of the grid into with different letters, and each letter represents a region. On the one hand, the formation of the nine-square grid analyzes the overall characteristics of the fluid from a macro perspective. On the other hand, the nine small partitions help to observe the changes of microscopic eigenvalues.

5 Observation

Observation helps us better find a way to the design rhythm of vortex via visualization. Since the visual animation is infinitely generated, the time needs to be limited. We set the observation time to 10 s, observe and summarize the law of vortex generation animation within a limited time range.

Spatially, we put the nine-square grid into the background of the animation as an implicit network to aid in the analysis. In addition, we also set the trajectory formed by the vortex as a structure, and summarize the design rhythm of the vortex by observing the formation, development and change of the structure. This experiment mainly analyzes the spatial density of structure, the structural relationship, and the structural orientation, so as to summarize three aspects of the design rhythm of the vortex: overall layout, rhythm relationship, and momentum trajectory.

First, we use the nine-square grid as the space limit to observe the overall spatial density of the structure (see Fig. 1), and set three hierarchical units of high, medium and low for further illustration. When the animation is set below 3 s, the structure increase progressively with time, and the overall coverage region e of the nine-square grid is composed of a small number of loose structure. At this time, the structure spatial density of the vortex is low. When the animation is set between 3 s and 5 s, the overall number of structure formed by the vortex gradually increases, and the structure spatial density of the vortex changes from low to moderate. When the animation is longer than 5 s, with the increase of time, the number of structure formed by the vortex becomes denser, and the structure spatial density of the vortex changes from moderate to high.

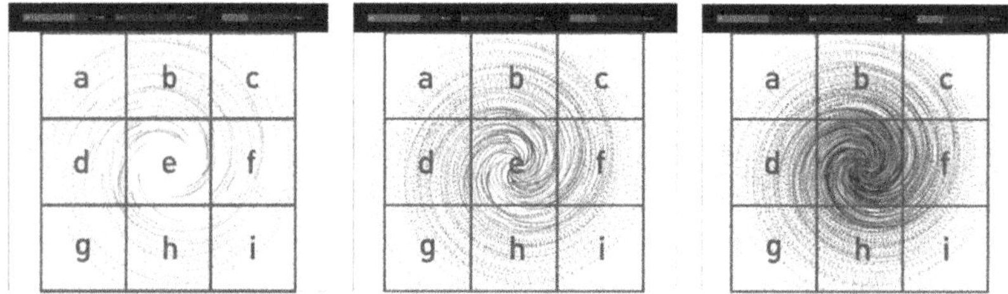

Fig. 1. The overall spatial density of the bone of 3 s, 3–5 s, and 5–10 s (Color figure online)

The second is the modular relationship of the structure. We use the change of the brightness and depth of blue to indicate the density of the structure, and finally reflect all the obtained data in a table.

When the animation is shorter than 3 s, we observe the local relationship of each area in the nine-square grid, and find that the region e in the center presents a lower blue lightness, while the other 8 letter regions are brighter than the region e, indicating that the structural density in the peripheral area is higher than that in the central area at this time, which further confirms that the current structure forms a structural relationship of loose inside and dense outside.

When the animation proceeds between 3 s and 5 s, the overall spatial density of the structure changes from low to medium at this time. In terms of local changes in each area, the blue lightness of the region e begins to become darker, gradually changing from light blue to dark blue, and deeper than the lightness of the other 8 letter regions, which means that compared with 3 s or below, the structural density of the vortex has gradually gathered from the four sides to the middle at this time, and the structural relationship formed is dense inside and loose outside.

When the animation proceeds to 5 s later, the blue lightness of the region e becomes darker and darker, and the blue range forms a clockwise divergent diffusion from the region e to the other 8 regions. We can observe that the blue at this time gradually forms a progressive gradual change in depth. The longer the time, the larger and deeper the blue coverage, which further confirms the current structural relationship of inner density and outer looseness. (see Fig. 2).

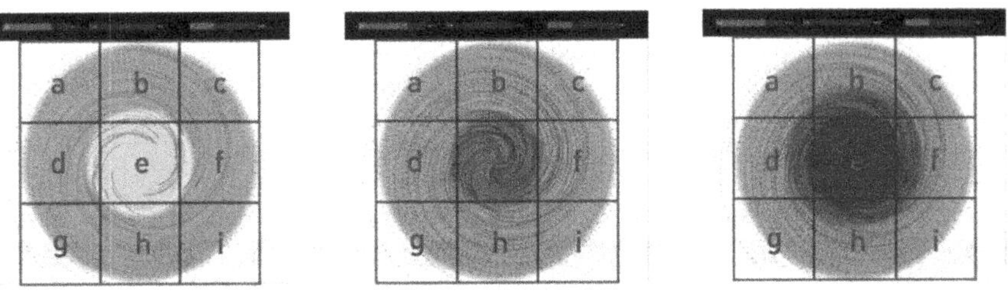

Fig. 2. The degree of bone density of 3 s, 3–5 s, and 5–10 s (Color figure online)

In the meanwhile, we further analyze the region e as a local close-up (see Fig. 3) (see Fig. 4), and draw the following results: when the animation is shorter than 3 s, the structure in the region e continue to increase to form a progressive composition. When the animation is set between 3 s to 5 s, the structure in the region e alternate regularly while maintaining the progressive increasing state, forming an undulating composition. When the animation is longer than 5 s, the whole structure continues to maintain a progressive and undulating dynamic force, so that the structure in the region e is highly intersected. A state of repetition and superposition occurs, forming a repetitive composition with the rhythm change spreading around with time.

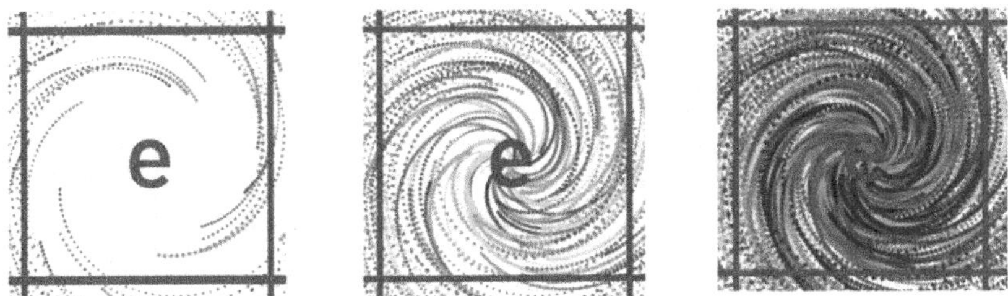

Fig. 3. E regional analysis of local features of 3 s, 3–5 s, and 5–10 s

Finally, the orientation of the structure. We use arrows to indicate the direction of the fluid. Since we set it to move at a uniform speed, the momentum of the vortex converges from the four sides to the middle from beginning to end, forming an outward-inward momentum. (see Fig. 5).

The experimental phenomena illustrate the following three aspects. First, the density relationship of structures in space continues to increase with the time, which further explains the overall layout of vortex structures change from simple to complex and from

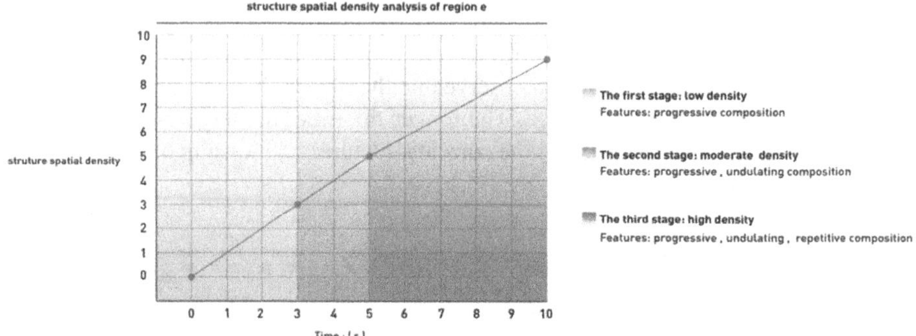

Fig. 4. Structure spatial density analysis of region e

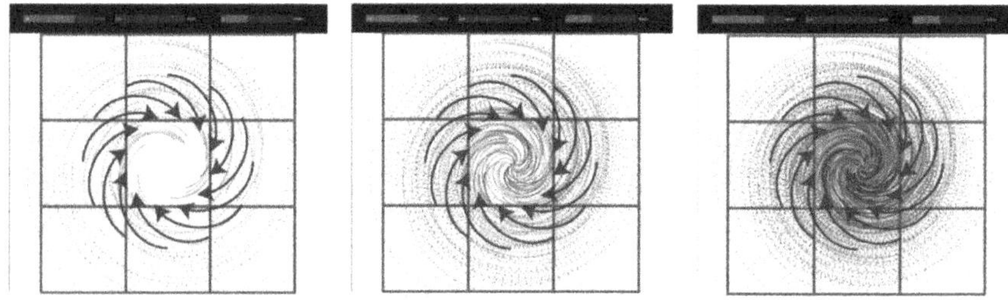

Fig. 5. The bone orientations of local features of 3 s, 3–5 s, and 5–10 s

less to more. The second is the structural relationship of the structure, which changes from loose inside and dense outside to the opposite, indicating that the structural rhythm relationship is changing alternately. The third is the movement trajectory of the structure, which is a clockwise progressive effect from outside to inside (Table 1).

Table 1. Structural analysis chart of vortex.

Time (t)	Spatial density of the bone	Structural relationship	Orientations
$0 < t < 3$	low	loose inside and Dense outside	Outward to inward
$3 < t < 5$	middle	dense inside and loose outside	Outward to inward
$t < 5$	high	dense inside and loose outside	Outward to inward

6 Application Practice Verification

How to apply the design rhythm of the vortex pattern summarized by observation to guide the design practice? Is this set of design metrics description system effective? In order to answer this kind of question, it is necessary to instrumentalize the design rhythm description system of vortex pattern. For this reason, we combine the golden section proportion rule to design a vortex pattern design meter quality measurement tool: "meter ruler". The basic idea is: take the bone sparse density of the vortex as the measurement parameter, take the sparse density reaching saturation as the full grid state in the process of vortex generation, and take the golden section proportion of the full lattice as the "best grid" standard. Skillfully convert the golden section proportion of the geometric scale into the density saturation ratio of the design grid, and establish a quantitative measurement method of the vortex design grid (see Fig. 6). Taking the bone sparse density pattern of the pattern generated by the vortex generation tool as the standard reference pattern, the corresponding density saturation ratio is marked on a straight line segment, and the bone density relationship actually reflects the white space ratio of the vortex design pattern. Therefore, the application value of the golden section principle in the vortex grid can be expected.

In the example, we design the vortex grid scale as 10 scales, and the value of each scale represents the saturation ratio of the density of the vortex bone. When the vortex line is denser, the vortex grid measurement value is larger, on the contrary, when the vortex line is more sparse, the vortex grid measurement value is smaller. Only when the vortex metric value is near the golden section ratio value, the bone sparse density of the vortex pattern reaches the best position of visual comfort. The two golden section points respectively contain the stage characteristics of the relative rapid growth of natural development and the maturity and stability of both vitality and stability.

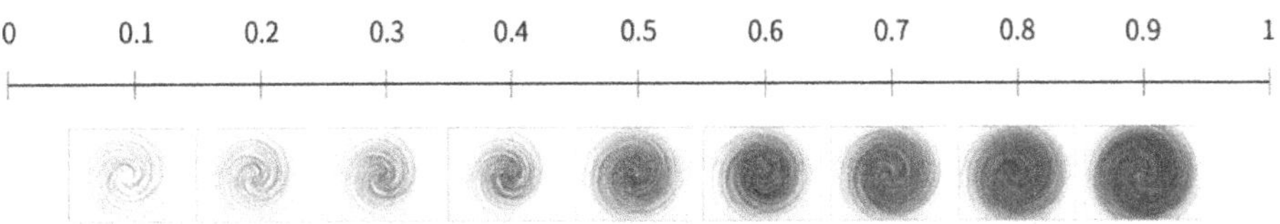

Fig. 6. Vortex design rhythm ruler

In order to verify the effectiveness of this metrical ruler, we selected the representative Japanese family crest in the graphic world for observation and study, and delineated the Tomoe pattern as the final measurement object in 217 family lineage classifications. The reasons are as follows: first, from the appearance, the shape of Tomoe pattern is very similar to the vortex. Second, from the perspective of conceptual interpretation, Tomoe pattern is interpreted as the appearance of a vortex of water, and many of the design inspiration of Tomoe pattern also comes from the vortex. We removed 52 irregular Tomoe pattern out of 94 Tomoe pattern, and finally selected 42 patterns for observation. We found that one of these Tomoe pattern conformed to the density relationship of 0.1, and two of them were in the density relationship of 0.2. There are 2 in the density of 0.3, 4 in the density of 0.4, 2 in the density of 0.5 and 14 in the density of 0.6. There are 8 in

0.7 density relationships, 6 in 0.8 density relationships, and 3 in 0.9 density relationships (see Fig. 7). Through the scale measurement, we can see that the vast majority of the design of Ba pattern is in line with the density relationship above and below 0.618, which precisely reflects the proportional relationship of the golden section (see Fig. 8). At the same time, in order to make the experiment more rational, we match the previous generated animation one by one to visually reflect the dense proportion of the vortex.

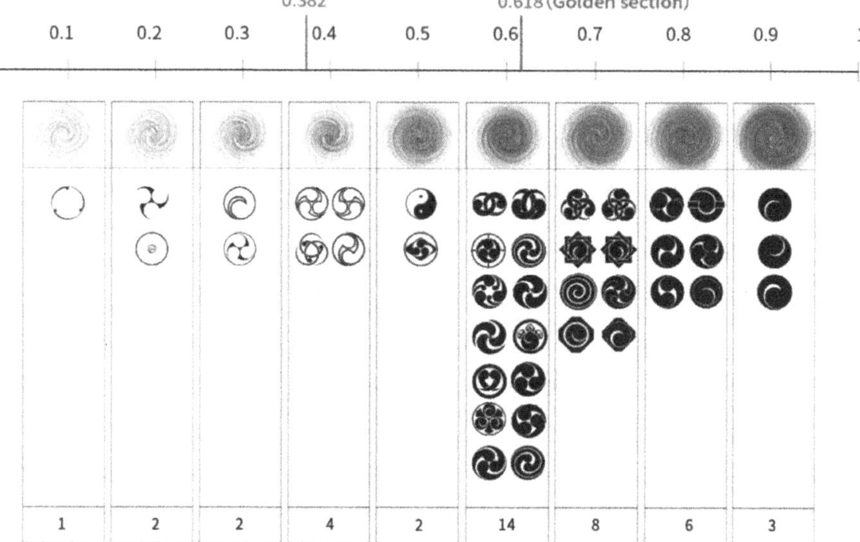

Fig. 7. Vortex design rhythm ruler corresponding to Tomoe pattern statistical table

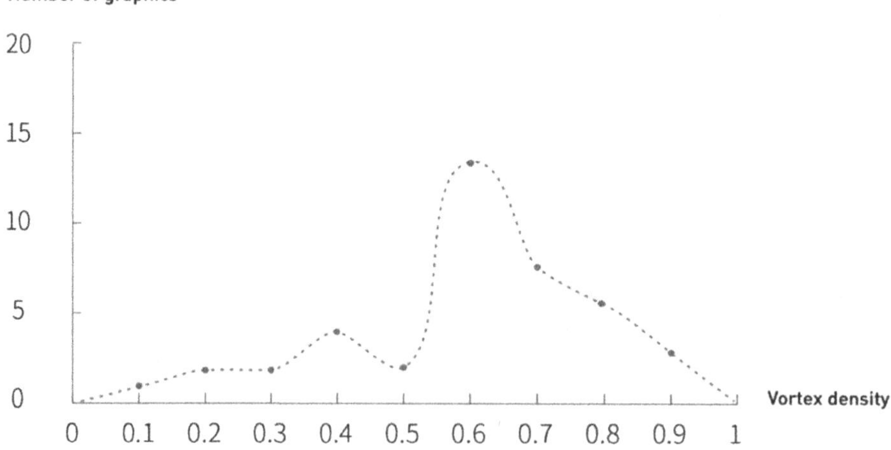

Fig. 8. Vortex design rhythm ruler corresponding to Tomoe pattern Trend

7 Research Results

To sum up, we can summarize the vortex into three pattern compositions and three rhythms, which together form its design rhythm. At the same time, through the test of the design practice with the grid scale, the proportion of the density saturation of the vortex satisfies the proportion of the golden section, that is, when the saturation ratio of the density is 0.382 and 1: 0.618 respectively, the vortex design rhythm is in the best state.

Three patterns:

(1) Repeated structure with gradual change of emission. The basic shape of the vortex gathers from the outward center, the emission point is around the screen, and it is arranged in a certain order through multiple vortex lines, and the trend of inward movement over time constitutes the structural composition with gradual change of emission.
(2) It is composed of an outward-inward spiral structure. The flow trajectory of the overall shape of the vortex can be seen as a structure composed of an outward-inward spiral.
(3) Concentric structure composition with tight inside and loose outside. Putting the structure into the nine-square grid, we can find that the lines of e are dense, and at the same time, the surrounding plates a, b, c, d, e, f, g, h, and i are looser than the lines of e. The whole structure is composed of concentric repeating form with the center of gravity and dense inside and loose outside.

Three rhythms:

(1) Repeated rhythm, also known as continuous rhythm, is recorded as: AAA. It is characterized by the repeated appearance of swirling structures and the sense of rhythm is produced by organized arrangement. It can be either a single structural repetition or a group of compound repetitions.
(2) Progressive rhythm, also known as gradual change rhyme, is recorded as: ABC. It is characterized by the rhythm, which is produced by the continuous increase of the vortex.
(3) The undulating rhythm, also known as the cross rhyme, is recorded as: ABA. It is characterized by the rhythm, which is increased or decreased by the regular alternation of the swirling structure.

8 Discussion and Conclusion

Our aim is to summarize design rhythm from a broader perspective, and to prove that visualization knowledge in hierarchical data representation can more effectively strengthen the research on design metrics.

We provide a clear way to visualize the fluid, telling designers a hidden design paradigm.

(1) This paper presents a tool to quantify the quality of design metrics: Vortex rhythm ruler. TheVortex rhythm ruler can be used as a reference for analyzing and testing the design quality of all kinds of vortex forms. This quantitative tool can be used

not only to measure the design rhythm of the vortex, but also to transfer to other categories of art.

(2) Form a rational and perceptual dual analysis system to meet the needs of subjective and objective interactive experience design and evaluation. Through the visual generation of fluid involved in the generation of design, combined with the observation method of designer thinking, we not only give better play to the sensitivity of designers to observe objects, but also increase the rational elements of the method of analyzing design rhythm.

(3) Simultaneously, we try to construct a design thinking mode, that is, rhythm is a basic underlying structure for design and creation. Further creation based on such an underlying foundation is stimulated. Experiments show that we can not only effectively understand the laws of vortex, but also control their variable values to design and generate according to the laws, and carry out higher-level creations under the basic rhythm. With objects generated, the rhythm can also help us better carry out higher-level aesthetic iteration research. (see Fig. 9)

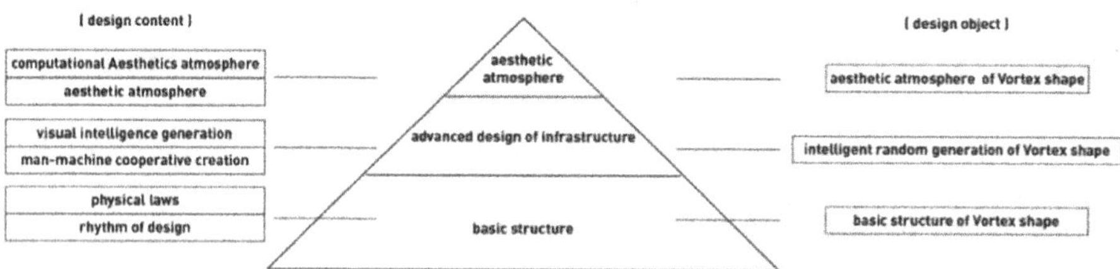

Fig. 9. Design rhythm Architecture Diagram

9 Limitations and Future Work

We find that there are still the following areas for improvement in the current research work: first, the type of fluid studied is single, and at present we only analyze one form of the vortex. Such as other hydrodynamic phenomena: ripples, ripples and other irregular fluid effects have different design rhythms, and more work needs to be done to analyze and sort out. In the future work, we will summarize more rules and related fluid animation generation according to this model. Second, for the vortex design rhythm carding, the selected Ba pattern graphic case can not fully represent all the vortex graphics, and more vortex design works can be analyzed in the future. Third, in the use of tools, we can use machine vision and deep learning methods to further interpret more vortex works in the future.

Acknowledgments. This research was funded by the "Research on Digital Art and Cultural Industry Development" project of Guangzhou Wanqu Cooperative Institute of Design (9028). We would like to thank Associate Professor Huang Guanghui of Macau University of Science and Technology for her guidance on this paper. We would like to thank Guangzhou Wanqu Design Institute for their support. We would also like to thank all the families who participated in the research.

References

1. Sugiura, K., et al.: The Birth of Modeling: Image Cosmology = Life and Modeling/Yasuhira Sugiura; Li Jianhua, translated by Yang Jing. Chinese University Press, Beijing (2013)
2. Dürer, A.: Of the Just Shaping of Letters, Project Gutenberg. Print (1535)
3. Le, C.: Towards A New Architecture. Dover Publications (1986)
4. Müller-Brockmann, J.: The Graphic Artist and His Design Problems. Niedermann Verlag (1961)
5. Chen, N.: Rhythm of design—pre-designed methodology for format system laws. ZHUANG-SHI (09), 66–71 (2012)
6. Zeng, R., An, N.: Lattice design of layout methods in digital interfaces. Art Work **2021**(02), 91–94 (2021)
7. Chen, W.: Research and application of 'rhythm and rhyme' in the modelling design on agricultural machinery product. J. Phys. **1626** (2020)
8. Zhang, J., Wang, Y., Shang, L., Zhu, D.: A review of fluid animation generation methods. Integr. Technol. **6**(01), 69–81 (2017)
9. Mastin, G.A., Watterberg, P.A., Mareda, J.F.: Fourier synthesis of ocean scenes. Comput. Graph. Appl. **7**(3), 16–23 (1987)
10. Kass, M.: Rapid stable fluid dynamics for computer graphics. In: ACM SIGGRAPH Computer Graphics **24**(4), 49–57 (1990)
11. Gingold, R.A., Monaghan, J.J.: Smooth particle hydrodynamics, theory and application to non-spherical stars. Mon. Not. Roy. Astron. Soc. **181**(3), 375–389 (1977)
12. Shang, L., Feng, X., Zhu, D., Wang, Z., Wang, Y.: A skeleton-driven animation synthesis method of nearshore surge. J. Softw. **27**(10), 2600–2611 (2016)
13. Zhang, G.: Skeleton-based control of fluid animation. Vis. Comput. **27**(3), 199–210 (2011)
14. Xiaobo, L., Zulin, H., Guojian, H.: Advances in the visualization of scientific calculations in computational fluid dynamics. Hydrodyn. Res. Progr. (Ser. A) **19**(01), 120–125 (2004)
15. Kenwright: A 3-D streamline tracking algorithm using dual stream functions. In: Proceedings Visualization '92, pp. 62–68 (1992)
16. Van Wijk, J.J.: Rendering surface particles. In: Proceedings of Visualization '92, pp.54–61. IEEE Computer Society Press (1992)
17. Post, F.H.: Global, geometric, and feature-based techniques for vector field visualization. Future Gener. Comput. Syst. **15**(1), 87–98 (1999)
18. Helman, J., Hesselink, L.: Representation and display of vector field topology in fluid flow data sets. IEEE Comput. **22**, 27–36 (1989)
19. Vanwalsum, T.: Selective visualization of vector-fields. Comput. Graph. Forum **13**(3), 339–347 (1994)
20. Jian, W.: Study of the vortex structure of the graph. Nanjing University of the Arts(2010)
21. Tian, R.: Study on the morphology of mathematical rationality. Xi'an Academy of Fine Arts (2020)
22. Muchuan, X.: Modularization and generative design. ZHUANGSHI (10), 89–91 (2012)
23. Schachter, B.: Long crested wave models. Graph. Models Image Process. **12**(2), 187–201 (1980)
24. Chen, N.: The Influence of "parametric design" on the development trend of visual communication design from the perspective of "rhythm of design. Creat. Des. **01**, 61–72 (2013)
25. Xiaoling, D.: Application of vortex modeling in graphic design. ZHUANGSHI (01), 121–122 (2007)

A Hybrid MOO/MCDM Optimization Approach to Improve Decision-Making in Multiobjective Optimization

Dionicio Neira-Rodado[1,2(✉)], Genett Jimenez-Delgado[3], Fernando Crespo[4], Roberto Antonio Morales Espinosa[5], Jonny Rafael Plazas Alvarez[6], and Hugo Hernandez[6]

[1] Universidad de la Costa CUC, Calle 58 No 55-66, Barranquilla, Colombia
dneira1@cuc.edu.co

[2] Universidad del Valle, Calle 13 No 100-00, Santiago de Cali, Colombia

[3] Institución Universitaria de Barranquilla IUB, Carrera 45 No 48-31, Barranquilla, Colombia
gjimenez@unibarranquilla.edu.co

[4] Universidad Alberto Hurtado, Santiago, Chile

[5] CEIPA, Escuela de Negocios, Carrera 57 No 72-143, Barranquilla, Colombia
roberto_moraleses@virtual.ceipa.edu.co

[6] Corporación Universitaria Iberoamericana, Calle 67 #5 - 27, Santafé de Bogotá, Colombia
{jonny.plazas,hugo.hernandez}@ibero.edu.co

Abstract. Multiobjective optimization (MOO) and multicriteria decision-making (MCDM) are critical disciplines in operations research, aiming to assist decision-makers in making the best decisions in complex problems. Nevertheless, the hybridization of the process has yet to be explored. In this case, the hybridization of the decision process is analyzed to evaluate the solution set obtained with this approach and compare it against the solutions obtained with Pareto Set. This novel approach shows that according to the decision-maker preferences, solutions could be in this solution set despite not being included in the Pareto Set. This approach gives alternatives to decision-makers without moving apart much from the best solution. A flow shop is used as a numerical example to compare the Pareto Set and hybrid approach outcomes.

Keywords: Multiobjective Optimization · Pareto set · TOPSIS · MCDM

1 Introduction

Multi-criteria decision-making (MCDM) methods provide different tools for decision-makers to assist them in selecting the most appropriate alternative in the case of multiple conflicting criteria. The main property of MCDM methods is that they manage to reflect human thinking in the decision process. This property yields more stable and satisfying solutions and alternatives to decision-makers when tackling problems with conflicting criteria [1, 2]. In this sense, it is important to highlight that MCDM methods aim to reflect the decision maker's preferences rather than determining an optimal solution [3–5], and they can handle both numerical and categorical criteria in the process.

H. Mori et al. (Eds.): HCII 2023, LNCS 14056, pp. 100–111, 2023.
https://doi.org/10.1007/978-3-031-48044-7_8

MCDM methods are easy to implement because they do not require high computing times. Additionally, they have become a popular way to address to tackle decision processes which is necessary select the best alternative considering conflicting dimensions or criteria of the problem. Nevertheless, these methods are used when the number of alternatives to be considered is relatively small.

On the other hand, there have also been efforts to represent in a better way human thinking process in the field of optimization, to get more robust and integral solutions. The field of multi-objective optimization (MOO) and goal programming aim to achieve these goals using different approaches. Nevertheless, the most common method when considering different objectives/criteria in the process, is the determination of a Pareto set containing the non-dominated solutions and determine the most suitable solution within this set. The importance of determining this Pareto set lies on the fact that on many occasions the best solution is not viable due to economic, organizational, or environmental issues. Therefore, it is necessary to give different alternatives to the decision maker so he can select the most suitable one.

Considering that MOO has been integrated with MCDM in the selection of the more suitable solution, once the Pareto set is obtained, this process may have the flaw of considering dominant solution as always be better than dominated solutions. In this sense, considering that the decision-making process require the determination of a set of alternatives to the owner of the process, it would be preferable to have the solutions that deviate less from the optimal solution. Nevertheless, the determination of a Pareto set could be challenging specially when dealing with non-convex objective function spaces. The determination of Pareto Set can be achieved with methods such as ϵ-constraint programming or variating the weights in a weighted sum method.

On the other hand, another way to deal with MOO problems is to determine the weights of each objective from the beginning of the process and obtaining the best solution (A priori approach). If the problem is solved with metaheuristics a rank of the best solutions can be made. Nevertheless, both a priori and Pareto front approaches have their drawbacks, and face some challenges in giving a solution set that are satisfying for the decision maker. In the case of a priori approaches it is important they are usually used to find a unique solution. If a rank of the solutions is obtained, this rank will be only built considering the best solutions according to the given weights but will not consider regret measures or penalize solutions when they deviate from the ideal solution. Additionally, when the objective function space is not convex they will fail in obtaining a trustable rank, or even a representative Pareto set, when used to find the Pareto front. When an uniformly distributed Pareto set is obtained, using for example ϵ-constraint programming, the decision maker in many occasions ask for other options to make his final decision. Therefore, further optimization must be made looking for diversification and intensification to improve the alternatives given to the decision maker. These problems can be improved if from the beginning MCDM approaches are involved in the process, in order to obtain a more stable solution set that better represent decision maker's wills. In order to achieve this goal, a hybrid MOO/MCDM optimization approach to improve decision-making in multiobjective optimization is proposed, in which TOPSIS proximity ratio is used as the optimization objective of the problem. The weights of the criteria (individual objectives) are set with AHP, and a rank with the best solutions is obtained so the decision maker can choose the one that better fits his requirements.

To explore this situation, a numerical example considering a flow shop is used to simulate the impact of the proposed approach in the decision-making process. The main contribution of this paper is to propose a hybrid MCDM/MOO approach that involves the human thinking process in all the optimization process, and not only at the final stage when the Pareto set has been built. The proposed method will then be applied to a 6-machine 8-job flow shop. Section 2 of this paper reviews the integration of MOO and MCDM, in particular TOPSIS and AHP. Section 3 describes the proposed methodology. Section 4 shows the numerical example and analysis of results, and finally Sect. 5 shows the conclusions of the study.

2 Literature Review

Multi-objective optimization (MOO) is defined as the process of systematically and simultaneously optimizing a collection of objective functions [7]. In this regard, Aranda and Orjuela [8] mentioned that in a multi-objective problem, there is not a single function to optimize but a set of *n* functions where there is no single global solution. Still, it is necessary to determine a location of points that fit a predetermined definition of an optimum. The MOO is a topic that has been extensively addressed and studied in the literature with applications in areas such as mathematics, engineering, social studies, economics, agriculture, aviation, and automotive, among others [9]. There are two approaches to generating multi-objective programming solution sets: the "scalarization" methods and the "non-scalarization" methods [10], among which are the Pareto method and scalarization. According to Gunantara & Hendrantoro [11], the Pareto method is applied when the desired solutions and the performance indicators are separated and produce a compromise solution (compensation) which can be shown in the form of a Pareto optimal front (POF). On the other hand, the scaling method is a performance indicator component that forms a scalar function that is incorporated into the fitness function.

On the other hand, multi-criteria decision methods (MCDM) are a set of techniques that support the decision-making process to select the best alternative or solution to a problem based on a set of criteria and sub-criteria. For the manufacturing sector, the object of this study, one of the most used multi-criteria methods is the Technique for Order Preference by Similarity to Ideal Solution (TOPSIS), successfully used in manufacturing processes such as milling, drilling, turning, electric discharge machining, abrasive jet machining, micromachining, among others [12]. According to Atul Shukla et al. [12], the TOPSIS method has been used in combination with other techniques such as AHP, Taguchi, Genetic Algorithms, or ANOVA in the optimization of the machine, input, and process parameters.

There have been some previous works, which explore the hybridization of MCDM and MOO methodologies as support for decision-making. For example, Reich et al. [13], found that a combination of AHP and MILP can help solve management environment problems such as global supply chain network design. Other works have addressed the integration of MCDM tools such as TOPSIS with multi-objective optimization techniques, which have shown greater flexibility compared to other existing models, such as the research by S. Hamdan and A. Cheaitou [14], which used the combination of AHP, Fuzzy TOPSIS and optimization techniques for supplier selection, considering Two bi-objective and one multi-objective optimization models. A recent study by H. Kilic and A. Yalcin [15] proposes an integrated methodology that includes the intuitionistic fuzzy TOPSIS (IF-TOPSIS) technique and a modified two-stage fuzzy goal programming model to address the problem of selection of sustainable suppliers in multi-element/multi-supplier/multi-period environment. From the above, it is concluded that although there is literature on the use of combined MDCM and MILP models to improve decision-making, it still requires further development and validation in realistic environments, as well as its application to problems of the manufacture. To contribute to closing the existing gap, we propose an innovative integrated framework that combines the TOPSIS multi-criteria decision method with the Mixed-Integer Linear Programming multi-objective optimization algorithm applied in a practical manufacturing environment that allows a more robust solution to the multi-objective problem—proposed, incorporating decision criteria and selection through an index of proximity to the ideal solution, with possibilities of application in other multi-objective problems in manufacturing environments.

3 Proposed Approach

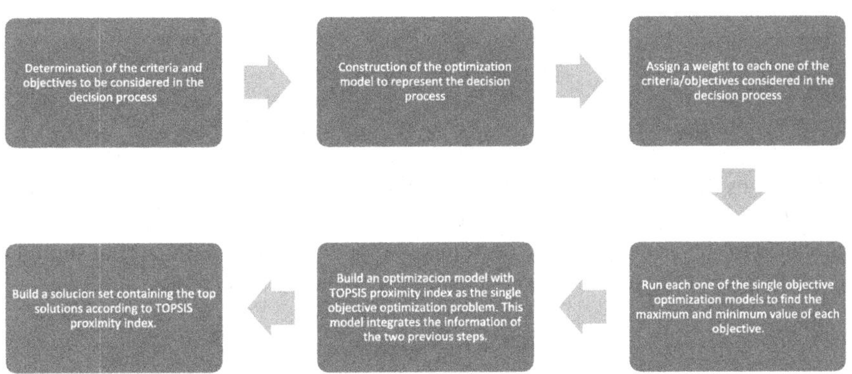

Fig. 1. Graphical representation of the decision-making process.

The proposed approach is represented on Fig. 1 and is based on the theory of MCDM as a general framework, incorporating MOO to tackle problems in which we can represent the criteria/objectives involved in the decision-making process, with mathematical models. In this case the alternatives would be all the solution space (feasible region).

The first stage of the process covers the definition of the problem and the criteria and objectives involved in the decision process. For example, in a model to schedule airplane operations a criterion could be fulfilment of the schedule. Nevertheless, this criterion can be measure with indicators such as number of delayed flights or mean delayed time. This stage includes all these decisions by the decision maker team.

Let us suppose that decision makers decide to consider n criteria represented as $C_1, C_2, \ldots C_n$, each one can be measure with different indicator so I_{ij} represents the j-th possible indicator to measure the criterion i. Decision team analyze the problem and depending on their experience, judgement and data availability select the most appropriate indicator for each criterion. Then $I_1, I_2, \ldots I_n$ represent the selected indicator for each criterion.

Once the criteria, indicators/objectives are defined, and data is available, a mathematical model to represent each one of the indicators must be constructed. In this stage is important to bear in mind, that the model will be integrated with TOPSIS, and TOPSIS require to obtain the maximum and minimum value in each one of the objectives. This situation may drive to two scenarios:

- The decision makers want to work with absolute maximum and minimum values. In this case the decision makers will explicitly set these two values for each objective.
- Decisions makers choose to work with relative maximum and minimum values for each objective. If so, then if would be necessary to adjust each model to be able to maximize and minimize each objective. This will require that decision makers have two models for each objective, one able to maximize and one able to minimize.

According to what is stated in this stage the mathematical model for the indicator associated to the first criterion is:

$$\text{minimize}\, I_1 : \text{minimize} f_1(\vec{x})$$

$$s.t.\ \boldsymbol{A}\vec{x} \geq \vec{b}$$

$$\vec{x} \geq 0$$

This means that the decision team will end up having n objective functions $f_1(\vec{x}), f_2(\vec{x}) \ldots f_n(\vec{x})$. In case they decide to work with relative maximum and minimum values in the TOPSIS stage the adjusted model for the maximization should be obtained. In case of the first criterion this model can be represented as:

$$\text{maximize}\, I_1 : \text{maximize} f_1'(\vec{x})$$

$$s.t.\ \boldsymbol{C}\vec{x} \leq \vec{d}$$

$$\vec{x} \geq 0$$

Obtaining the relative importance of each criterion (objective) with the implementation of AHP covers the third stage. Then n weights will be obtained $w_1, w_2, \ldots, w_n$. The fourth stage requires to run all the optimization problems built in stage two in the case that the decision makers have chosen to work with relative maximum and minimum values. In the case of criterion 1 these maximum and minimum values are I_1^{max}, for the maximum value obtained for $f_1'(\vec{x})$, I_1^{min} representing the minimum value obtained for $f_1(\vec{x})$. This will be the case when the criterion is of the type the higher the better. If the criterion is of the type the lower,the better, then the interpretation will be the opposite and the best value will be the one obtained with the minimization (I_i^{max}) and the worst value will be obtained with the maximization (I_i^{min}). In both cases the fulfilment of the corresponding constraints is mandatory. In case the decision team chooses to work with absolute maximum and minimum values I_1^{min} and I_1^{max}, these values will be set directly by the team. Similar logic applies for the rest of the criteria.

The fifth stage requires the construction of a new optimization problem in which it is sought the maximization of TOPSIS' proximity ratio. To achieve this, the following steps must be fulfilled:

- Normalization of each objective according to these formulations:

  If the objective/criterion is of the type the higher the better normalization should be made as follows:

$$\tilde{f_i}\left(\vec{x}\right) = \frac{\left(f_i\left(\vec{x}\right) - I_i^{min}\right)}{\left(I_i^{max} - I_i^{min}\right)}$$

  If the objective/criterion is of the type the lower the better normalization should be made as follows:

$$\tilde{f_i}\left(\vec{x}\right) = \frac{\left(I_i^{min} - f_i\left(\vec{x}\right)\right)}{\left(I_i^{min} - I_i^{max}\right)}$$

  It is important to point out, that after normalization, the values of I_i^{max} and I_i^{min} will be:

$$\tilde{I}_i^{min} = 0; \forall (i \in criteria)$$

$$\tilde{I}_i^{max} = 1; \forall (i \in criteria)$$

- Weighing each objective and their extreme values by multiplying the maximum ($\tilde{I}_i^{max}$), minimum ($\tilde{I}_i^{min}$), and the corresponding objective function ($\tilde{f_i}\left(\vec{x}\right)$) of each criterion by its weight (w_i).
- Determination of the positive and negative ideal solutions, represented as $\overline{S^+}$ and $\overline{S^-}$, respectively.

$$\overline{S^+} = \left\{w_1\, \tilde{I}_1^{max}, w_2\, \tilde{I}_2^{max}, \ldots, w_n\, \tilde{I}_n^{max}\right\}$$

$$\overline{S^-} = \left\{w_1\, \tilde{I}_1^{min}, w_2 \tilde{I}_2^{min}, \ldots, w_n\, \tilde{I}_n^{min}\right\}$$

  Considering the previously explained behavior of $\tilde{I}_i^{min}$ and $\tilde{I}_2^{max}$, $\overline{S^+}$ and $\overline{S^-}$ can be simplified as follows:

$$\overline{S^+} = \{w_1, w_2, \ldots, w_n\}$$

$$\overline{S^-} = \{0, 0, \ldots, 0\}$$

- Determine the distance to the positive and negative ideal solution of each point of the feasible region.

$$\overline{d_i^+} = \sqrt[2]{\sum \left(\overrightarrow{I_i} - \overline{S^+} \right)^2}$$

$$\overline{d_i^-} = \sqrt[2]{\sum \left(\overrightarrow{I_i} - \overline{S^-} \right)^2}$$

where $\overline{d_i^+}$ represent the distance to the positive ideal solution of objective vector $\overrightarrow{I_i}$ obtained from variable vector $\overrightarrow{x_i}$, and $\overline{d_i^-}$ represent the distance to the negative ideal solution of objective vector $\overrightarrow{I_i}$ obtained from variable vector $\overrightarrow{x_i}$. This calculation will be made for the evaluated points during optimization until the algorithm converges.
- Calculation of $\overline{RS_i}$ or proximity ratio to positive ideal solution for each evaluated point.

$$\overline{RS_i} = \frac{\overline{d_i^-}}{\overline{d_i^-} + \overline{d_i^+}}$$

This calculation will not be done for each point in the solution space. The problem will be formulated as a maximization problem as shown below:

$$\text{maximize } \overline{RS} = \text{maximize } f_{\overline{RS}}\left(\overrightarrow{x}\right)$$

where max $f_{\overline{RS}}\left(\overrightarrow{x}\right)$ is defined as:

$$f_{\overline{RS}}\left(\overrightarrow{x}\right) = \frac{\sqrt[2]{\Sigma\left(\left(w_1 \tilde{f_1}\left(\overrightarrow{x}\right), w_2 \tilde{f_2}\left(\overrightarrow{x}\right), \ldots, w_n \tilde{f_n}\left(\overrightarrow{x}\right)\right) - \overline{S^-}\right)^2}}{\left(\sqrt[2]{\Sigma\left(\left(w_1 \tilde{f_1}\left(\overrightarrow{x}\right), w_2 \tilde{f_2}\left(\overrightarrow{x}\right), \ldots, w_n \tilde{f_n}\left(\overrightarrow{x}\right)\right) - \overline{S^-}\right)^2} + \sqrt[2]{\Sigma\left(\left(w_1 \tilde{f_1}\left(\overrightarrow{x}\right), w_2 \tilde{f_2}\left(\overrightarrow{x}\right), \ldots, w_n \tilde{f_n}\left(\overrightarrow{x}\right)\right) - \overline{S^+}\right)^2}\right)}$$

This is a more general model than the one shown for $\overline{RS_i}$. As it can be seen the model is nonlinear, and its solution cannot be obtained with linear programming. Metaheuristics approach could be desirable.

In the last stage the decision team, will have available the solution of the problem. Solving it with metaheuristic approaches will imply that a rank of the solutions obtained could be constructed during each iteration until the algorithm converges. This rank can contain a desired number of solutions. This solution set will be analyzed by the decision team to pick one of these solutions, considering organizational constraints.

4 Numerical Example

The flow shop scheduling problem is one of the most addressed topics in literature [6], because of its many economic and industrial applications. In its simplest form, the flow shop problem consists of two main elements: (1) a group of M machines and (2) a set of N jobs to be processed on this group of machines. Each job can be processed on one and only one machine at a time (which means no job splitting), and each machine can process only one job at a time. Each job is processed only once on each machine. Operations are not preemptable, and set-up times of operations are independent of the sequences and therefore can be included in the processing time. The scheduling problem specifies the order and timing of the processing of the jobs on machines, with an objective or objectives respecting the above-mentioned assumptions [6] (Fig. 2).

Fig. 2. General Flow Shop Scheme

As it was mentioned above, the flow shop that is going to be analyzed is made of 6 machines and has 8 jobs that required to be scheduled. The performance of flow shops can be measure with different metrics. In this case makespan C_{max}, mean lateness $\overline{L}$, maximum tardiness T_{max}, and number of tardy jobs nt are the metrics (Criteria/objectives) to be used in order to measure the performance of sequences and make the decision of which sequence is the best. The processing times and due date of each job can be observed on Table 1. Processing times were randomly generated with $U(5;30)$.

Table 1. Processing times and due dates for flow shop

	Machine 1	Machine 2	Machine 3	Machine 4	Machine 5	Machine 6	Due date
Job 1	27	29	12	28	12	20	189
Job 2	21	9	8	16	19	26	142
Job 3	5	12	15	8	9	26	182
Job 4	27	18	5	16	29	27	136
Job 5	10	25	7	16	29	18	196
Job 6	6	20	24	22	14	17	163
Job 7	6	7	14	17	7	24	203
Job 8	11	29	6	9	9	25	168

In order to make a better analysis of the implications associated with tackling the decision making process with this approach compared with selecting the best decision among the non-dominated solution from the Pareto Set, all the possible sequences were calculated. The total possible sequences for an 8-job flow shop problem are 40320. These sequences and the values of C_{max}, $\overline{L}$, T_{max}, and nt, were obtained using RStudio. The first tests were performed using just two objectives in the process to be able to plot the solution space and understand in a better the difference between the two approaches.

The two objectives to be considered in the first scenario are C_{max}, and T_{max}. A representation of the solution space can be found on Fig. 3.

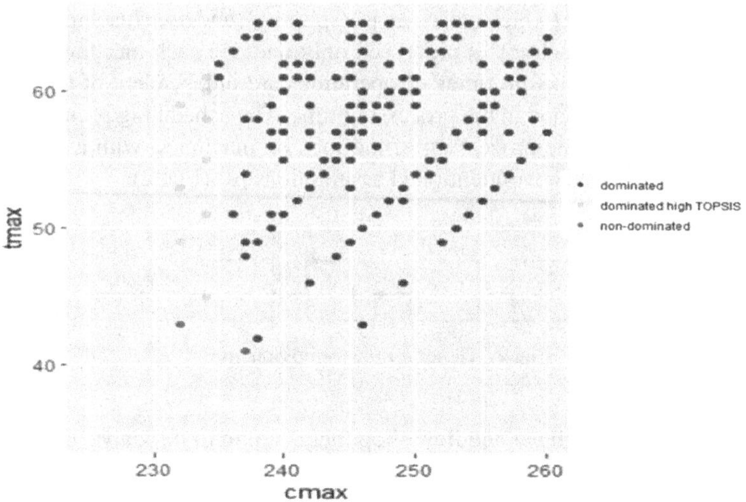

Fig. 3. Two-objective solution space characterization

Figure 3 shows solution space when addressing the problem considering two objectives (C_{max}, and T_{max}). Points were colored depending on the type of solution. As it can be observed there are two non-dominated solutions. The green points represent dominated solutions with high TOPSIS proximity ratio. TOPSIS was calculated assigning a weight of 0.8 to C_{max}, and 0.2 to T_{max}. Table 2 shows the top solutions ranked by TOPSIS proximity ratio (RS). This table also shows a comparison with Pareto solutions and a priori solutions. As it can be observed the problem has two non-dominated solutions which correspond to the Pareto set. These solutions are ranked 1 in the case of sequence V14340 and 19 in the case of solution V14339. This evidences that TOPSIS includes non-dominated solutions in the best ranked solutions. Compared with a priori method the rank differs starting from position 6 with a Hamming distance of 15 between the a priori and TOPSIS top 25 rank.

On the other hand, when the experiment is conducted considering the four objectives, the difference between Pareto Set, a priori approach and TOPSIS approach, becomes more evident. The results of this experiment are summarized in Table 3. Additionally, Table 4 shows that there are 12 non-dominated solution in this four-objective problem. Nevertheless, according to Table 3, only 2 of these nondominated solutions rank in the top 25 solutions. Finally, when ranking the top 25 solutions according to TOPSIS, there is a significant difference with the rank obtained with the a priori approach. In this sense, it is important to point out that the hamming distance between the TOP25 rank in TOPSIS and a priori approach is 23. TOPSIS ranks high solution that with the a priori approach would have been ranked 40 or worse. Similarly, Table 3 does not include solutions that are well ranked according to a priori method and as it was mentioned before, it does not include 10 of the 12 non dominated solutions in this four-objective problem.

Table 2. Top solutions according to TOPSIS (two objectives)

Sequence	S1	S2	S3	S4	S5	S6	S7	S8	Cmax	Tmax	RS	TOPSIS Rank	Apriori	Apriori Rank	Type
V14340	T3	T7	T8	T4	T2	T6	T5	T1	232	43	0.996663	1	0.9972414	1	non-dominated
V14338	T3	T7	T8	T4	T2	T5	T6	T1	232	49	0.986754	2	0.9889655	2	dominated high TOPSIS
V14344	T3	T7	T8	T4	T5	T2	T6	T1	232	53	0.980232	3	0.9834483	3	dominated high TOPSIS
V32340	T7	T3	T8	T4	T2	T6	T5	T1	234	45	0.978711	4	0.9778161	4	dominated high TOPSIS
V34860	T7	T8	T3	T4	T2	T6	T5	T1	234	45	0.978711	5	0.9778161	5	dominated high TOPSIS
V32338	T7	T3	T8	T4	T2	T5	T6	T1	234	51	0.973834	6	0.9695402	7	dominated high TOPSIS
V14320	T3	T7	T8	T2	T5	T4	T6	T1	232	59	0.970576	7	0.9751724	6	dominated high TOPSIS
V32344	T7	T3	T8	T4	T5	T2	T6	T1	234	55	0.969245	8	0.964023	8	dominated high TOPSIS
V13894	T3	T7	T2	T6	T8	T4	T5	T1	234	58	0.965413	9	0.9598851	9	dominated high TOPSIS
V31894	T7	T3	T2	T6	T8	T4	T5	T1	234	60	0.962735	10	0.9571264	12	dominated high TOPSIS
V14632	T3	T8	T2	T7	T5	T4	T6	T1	234	61	0.961369	11	0.9557471	13	dominated
V32320	T7	T3	T8	T2	T5	T4	T6	T1	234	61	0.961369	12	0.9557471	14	dominated high TOPSIS
V34858	T7	T8	T3	T4	T2	T5	T6	T1	236	51	0.956275	13	0.9528736	15	dominated
V11374	T3	T2	T7	T6	T8	T4	T5	T1	235	61	0.955209	14	0.9474138	27	dominated
V32146	T7	T3	T5	T8	T2	T4	T6	T1	235	62	0.954007	15	0.9460345	29	dominated
V14319	T3	T7	T8	T2	T5	T4	T1	T6	233	70	0.951848	16	0.9516667	16	dominated
V14337	T3	T7	T8	T4	T2	T5	T1	T6	233	70	0.951848	17	0.9516667	17	dominated
V14343	T3	T7	T8	T4	T5	T2	T1	T6	233	70	0.951848	18	0.9516667	18	dominated
V14339	T3	T7	T8	T4	T2	T6	T1	T5	237	41	0.949552	19	0.9583333	10	non-dominated
V15059	T3	T8	T7	T4	T2	T6	T1	T5	237	41	0.949552	20	0.9583333	11	dominated
V14316	T3	T7	T8	T2	T4	T6	T5	T1	237	48	0.948133	21	0.9486782	19	dominated
V14628	T3	T8	T2	T7	T4	T6	T5	T1	237	48	0.948133	22	0.9486782	20	dominated
V15036	T3	T8	T7	T2	T4	T6	T5	T1	237	48	0.948133	23	0.9486782	21	dominated
V15060	T3	T8	T7	T4	T2	T6	T5	T1	237	48	0.948133	24	0.9486782	22	dominated
V32316	T7	T3	T8	T2	T4	T6	T5	T1	237	48	0.948133	25	0.9486782	23	dominated

Table 3. Top solutions according to TOPSIS (four objectives)

Sequence	S1	S2	S3	S4	S5	S6	S7	S8	Cmax	Lateness	Tmax	Tardy Jobs	RS	TOPSIS Rank	Apriori	Apriori Rank	Type
V13894	T3	T7	T2	T6	T8	T4	T5	T1	234	-107	58	3	0.890415	1	0.893935	1	non-dominated
V14626	T3	T8	T2	T7	T4	T5	T6	T1	239	-107	50	3	0.886364	2	0.886895	4	dominated high TOPSIS
V14632	T3	T8	T2	T7	T5	T4	T6	T1	234	-107	61	3	0.885792	3	0.888763	3	dominated high TOPSIS
V34720	T7	T8	T2	T3	T5	T4	T6	T1	237	-128	64	3	0.879043	4	0.889511	2	non-dominated
V13906	T3	T7	T2	T8	T4	T5	T6	T1	241	-107	52	3	0.876377	5	0.875113	5	dominated high TOPSIS
V14556	T3	T8	T2	T4	T5	T7	T6	T1	240	-107	57	3	0.87493	6	0.870659	9	dominated high TOPSIS
V13893	T3	T7	T2	T6	T8	T4	T1	T5	240	-107	58	3	0.873615	7	0.868935	10	dominated high TOPSIS
V14590	T3	T8	T2	T5	T7	T4	T6	T1	238	-107	65	3	0.869745	8	0.8652	15	dominated high TOPSIS
V14631	T3	T8	T2	T7	T5	T4	T1	T6	234	-107	71	3	0.867501	9	0.871521	8	dominated high TOPSIS
V34762	T7	T8	T2	T5	T3	T4	T6	T1	240	-128	67	3	0.86392	10	0.871839	7	dominated high TOPSIS
V34719	T7	T8	T2	T3	T5	T4	T1	T6	237	-128	74	3	0.859529	11	0.87227	6	dominated
V31912	T7	T3	T2	T8	T5	T4	T6	T1	242	-128	69	3	0.852425	12	0.860057	17	dominated
V14589	T3	T8	T2	T5	T7	T4	T1	T6	238	-107	75	3	0.850662	13	0.847958	34	dominated
V11392	T3	T2	T7	T8	T5	T4	T6	T1	242	-107	69	3	0.84824	14	0.841636	42	dominated
V13912	T3	T7	T2	T8	T5	T4	T6	T1	242	-107	69	3	0.84824	15	0.841636	43	dominated
V34785	T7	T8	T2	T6	T3	T4	T1	T5	243	-128	69	3	0.848117	16	0.855891	22	dominated
V34786	T7	T8	T2	T6	T3	T4	T5	T1	243	-128	69	3	0.848117	17	0.855891	23	dominated
V32274	T7	T3	T6	T8	T4	T5	T2	T1	239	-128	77	3	0.847607	18	0.858764	19	dominated
V14625	T3	T8	T2	T7	T4	T5	T1	T6	239	-107	76	3	0.845671	19	0.842067	41	dominated
V32032	T7	T3	T4	T8	T5	T2	T6	T1	245	-128	65	3	0.845226	20	0.854454	26	dominated
V34761	T7	T8	T2	T5	T3	T4	T1	T6	240	-128	77	3	0.844389	21	0.854598	25	dominated
V11512	T3	T2	T8	T7	T5	T4	T6	T1	243	-107	70	3	0.84225	22	0.835746	57	dominated
V14032	T3	T7	T4	T8	T5	T2	T6	T1	245	-107	65	3	0.841113	23	0.836033	54	dominated
V14555	T3	T8	T2	T4	T5	T7	T1	T6	240	-107	77	3	0.840419	24	0.836177	53	dominated
V14274	T3	T7	T6	T8	T4	T5	T2	T1	240	-107	78	3	0.838369	25	0.834453	64	dominated

Table 4. Non-dominated solutions (Pareto Set) in the four-objective problem

	V13894	V13896	V14338	V14339	V14340	V14626	V32339	V32340	V32344	V34716	V34720	V34788
Cmax	234	243	232	237	232	239	238	234	234	237	237	250
Lateness	-107	-107	-107	-107	-107	-107	-128	-128	-128	-128	-128	-128
Tmax	58	87	49	41	43	50	42	45	55	48	64	94
Tardy jobs	3	2	4	5	5	3	5	5	4	4	3	2

5 Conclusions

The example and experimentation show that decision making techniques may give a distinct perspective to optimization problems. MOO problems are often addressed with metaheuristics, determining in first place a Pareto Set, and focusing the decision process only on the alternatives included in this set. This approach is not the best considering that many good solutions might get excluded from the Pareto Set. On the other hand, when addressing the problem with a priori approach, the best solutions do not rank well considering that the normalization approach used in a priori approaches does not properly capture the nature of human thinking. In this sense, TOPSIS works better because it considers the best and the worst possible solution in the decision criterion (proximity ratio, RS), which can sense better the feeling of regret of the decision maker. All this process is very important, considering that tackling MOO problems is a difficult task, and user are not able to include all possible constraints in the problems, such as organizational culture or preferences. Therefore, supplying a solution set with different alternatives that do not move away much from the best solution is better for decision makers because this will assure the satisfaction and success when implementing the selected solution. Finally, it is important to point out that the inclusion of MCDM from the first stages of MOO would help to make better decisions, because human thinking would be involved in all the process, obtaining a better and more stable solution set. This is relevant, especially in cases when the best solution cannot be implemented, due to the preferences of decision-makers or some organizational policies. The problem is that if the decision maker does not use the best solution, the following solution in the set is not necessarily the second-best solution to the complete problem. The numerical example showed that many non-dominated solutions can rank better considering the decision-maker preferences, generating more satisfaction with the final decision. This rank differs from the rank obtained with a simple scalarization (A priori), because TOPSIS considers each objective best and worst solutions in the process.

References

1. Drumond, P., de Araújo Costa, I.P., Moreira, M.Â.L., dos Santos, M., Gomes, C.F.S., do Nascimento Maêda, S.M.: Strategy study to prioritize marketing criteria: an approach in the light of the DEMATEL method. Procedia Comput. Sci. **199**, 448–455 (2022). https://doi.org/10.1016/J.PROCS.2022.01.054
2. Quezada, L.E., López-Ospina, H.A., Ortiz, C., Oddershede, A.M., Palominos, P.I., Jofré, P.A.: A DEMATEL-based method for prioritizing strategic projects using the perspectives of the Balanced Scorecard. Int. J. Prod. Econ. **249**, 108518 (2022). https://doi.org/10.1016/J.IJPE.2022.108518

3. Wang, P., Zhu, Z., Huang, S.: The use of improved TOPSIS method based on experimental design and Chebyshev regression in solving MCDM problems. J. Intell. Manuf. **28**(1), 229–243 (2017). https://doi.org/10.1007/s10845-014-0973-9
4. Çelikbilek, Y., Tüysüz, F.: An in-depth review of theory of the TOPSIS method: an experimental analysis. J. Manag. Anal. **7**(2), 281–300 (2020). https://doi.org/10.1080/23270012.2020.1748528
5. Ortiz-Barrios, M.A., De Felice, F., Parra Negrete, K., Aleman Romero, B., Yaruro Arenas, A., Petrillo, A.: An AHP-topsis integrated model for selecting the most appropriate tomography equipment. Int. J. Inf. Technol. Decis. Mak. **15**(04), 861–885 (2016). https://doi.org/10.1142/S021962201640006X
6. Rodriguez, J.V., Rodado, D.N., Parody, A., Crespo, F., Brugés-Ballesteros, L.: Addressing the Permutational Flow Shop Scheduling Problem Through Constructive Heuristics: A Statistical Comparison, pp. 169–181 (2021)
7. Marler, R., Arora, J.: Survey of multi-objective optimization methods for engineering. Struct. Multidisc. Optim. **26**, 369–395 (2004)
8. Aranda, J.A., Orjuela, J.A.: Optimización multiobjetivo en la gestión de cadenas de suministro de biocombustibles. Una revisión de la literature. Ingenierıa **20**(1), 37–63
9. Gunantara, N.: A review of multi-objective optimization: methods and its applications. Cogent Eng. **5**(1), 1502242. https://doi.org/10.1080/23311916.2018.1502242
10. Ehrgott, M., Wiecek, M.M.: Multiobjective programming. In: Multiple Criteria Decision Analysis: State of the Art Surveys, pp. 667–722. Springer, Cham (2005). https://doi.org/10.1007/0-387-23081-5_17
11. Gunantara, N., Hendrantoro, G.: Multi-objective cross-layer optimization with Pareto method for relay selection in multihop wireless adhoc networks. WSEAS Trans. Commun. **12**(3), 85–95 (2013)
12. Shiklaa, A., Agarwalb, P., Rana, R.S., Purohit, R.: Applications of TOPSIS Algorithm on various manufacturing process: a review. Mat. Today Proc. **4**, 5320–5329 (2017)
13. Reich, J., Kinra, A., Kotzab, H., Brusset, X.: Stategic global supply chain network design - how decisions analysis combining MILP and AHP on al Pareto front can improve decision-making. Int. J. Prod. Res. **59**(5), 1557–1572 (2021). https://doi.org/10.1080/00207543.2020.1847341
14. Hamdan, S., Cheaitou, A.: Supplier selection and order allocation with green criteria: an MCDM and multi-objective optimization approach. Comput. Oper. Res. **81**, 282–304 (2017). https://doi.org/10.1016/j.cor.2016.11.005
15. Kilic, H.S., Yalcin, A.S.: Modified two-phase fuzzy goal programming integrated with IF-TOPSIS for green supplier selection. Appl. Soft Comput. **93** (2020). https://doi.org/10.1016/j.asoc.2020.106371

Music Visualisation and Its Short-Term Effect on Appraisal Skills

Ali Nikrang[1,2], Maarten Grachten[3], Martin Gasser[4], Harald Frostel[5], Gerhard Widmer[6], and Tom Collins[7,8](✉)

[1] Ars Electronica Futurelab, Linz, Austria
ali.nikrang@ars.electronica.art
[2] University of Music and Theatre, Munich, Germany
[3] Independent Machine Learning Consultant, Cologne, Germany
[4] Muse Group, Limassol, Cyprus
[5] Independent Machine Learning Consultant, Linz, Austria
[6] Institute of Computational Perception, JKU, Linz, Austria
[7] University of Miami, Coral Gables, USA
[8] MAIA, Inc., Davis, USA
tomthecollins@gmail.com

Abstract. Music psychologists have long been concerned with phenomena such as repetition and tonality – both the internal representations formed by exposure to these phenomena, and how these representations vary with expertise. A question arises of whether less expert listeners can gain proficiency in perceiving a particular phenomenon by being exposed to representations that are known to be employed by more expert listeners. The current paper addresses this question within the domain of music appraisal. Participants with varying levels of musical expertise interacted with visualizations of two excerpts from Beethoven's symphonies. One visualization (ScoreViewer) showed the staff notation of the music, synchronized to an orchestral recording. The other (PatternViewer) also depicted the notes synchronized to the recording, as well as representations of the music's repetitive and tonal structure. Participants' appraisal skills were assessed via multiple-choice questions on instrumentation, dynamics, repetition, and tonality. Results indicated that interacting with the PatternViewer visualization led to a significant improvement in listeners' appraisal of repetitive and tonal structure, compared to interacting with the ScoreViewer. The size of this effect was well predicted by amount of formal musical training, such that less expert listeners exhibited larger improvements than more expert listeners. While further work is required to determine whether the observed effects transfer beyond the pieces studied or into long-term learning, these findings for appraisal skills indicate that carefully chosen representations from models of expert behavior can, in turn, help less expert individuals to improve their understanding of musical phenomena.

Keywords: Music · Visualisation · Appraisal · Cognition · Learning

M. Grachten and H. Frostel—Independent Machine Learning Consultant.

H. Mori et al. (Eds.): HCII 2023, LNCS 14056, pp. 112–130, 2023.
https://doi.org/10.1007/978-3-031-48044-7_9

1 Introduction

Whether at the concert hall, in front of a computer, or holding a phone, we may question: what does one look at when listening to music, and does it make any difference to our perception of the music?

Some listen to music with their eyes shut. In a live setting or music video, some people study the performers' movements, others the setting itself, and some even study fellow audience members. When listening to recorded music, computer/phone applications also offer a choice of visualisation modes. An uncompressed sound (or audio) file typically consists of 44,100 samples (values between -1 and 1) per second, which displace the membrane of the speaker(s) and give the listener the impression of hearing the music as it was originally recorded. Some visualisations operate on this data too to provide animations that appear to be synchronised with the music as heard. A screenshot of such a visualisation is given in Fig. 1A.

The demand for and popularity of looking whilst listening to music is difficult to overestimate: a visualisation application by [19] called the *Music Animation Machine*, which plays an audio file synchronised to a symbolic representation of the music (i.e., the note information present in staff notation), has over 30,000,000 views on YouTube.[1] Notes appear as horizontal oblongs in the Music Animation Machine, as shown in Fig. 1B. Time runs along the x-axis such that the starting and stopping time of each note corresponds to an oblong's left- and right-most extremities, respectively. Thus a note's duration corresponds to the oblong's horizontal extent. The pitch height of each note is represented by the oblong's height on the y-axis, with lower-sounding notes appearing lower down on this axis. The representation is known as *piano roll*, because holes punched in paper rolls according to the same (x, y)-axes were used to drive an autonomous musical instrument called the *player piano*, which reached peak popularity in the early twentieth century (see Fig. 1C).

Other visualisation apps offer a higher level of interactivity and have a stronger didactic emphasis. For instance, the *Orchestra App* offers multi-perspective video recordings of orchestral concerts, interviews with the conductor and performers, information about orchestral instruments, audio-synchronised staff notation and piano roll, and more (see Fig. 1D). The user is able to switch between these display modes whilst the piece is playing. Despite the above-mentioned visualisations, for many, the cultural facade of Western classical music remains imposing and impenetrable. Some listeners do not derive pleasure from listening to the music and/or they are unable to *appraise* it, by which we mean *to gain an explicit understanding of the inner workings of a piece*. Examples of music appraisal include identification of: orchestral instruments and their interplay; changes in dynamics and tempo, such as *crescendo* and *accelerando*; short repeated musical ideas called *motives*, which build to make *themes* and in turn larger *sections*; tonal structure such as changes in key (the note collections used by the composer over the course of a piece).

[1] https://www.youtube.com/user/smalin/.

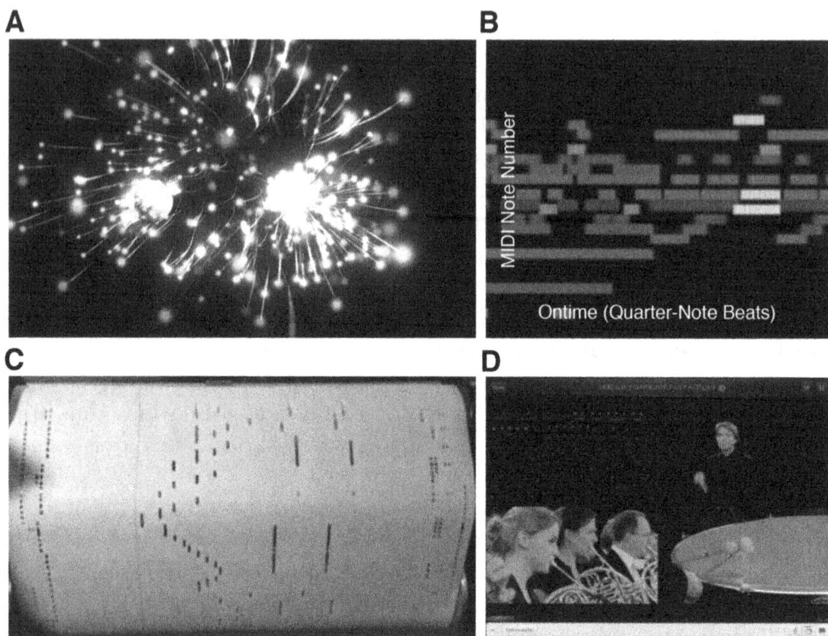

Fig. 1. A) Screen capture of a visualisation mode available with Apple's iTunes software; (B) Piano-roll representation of the Music Animation Machine [19], with axes added to indicate note on and offtimes (x-axis) and MIDI note number (y-axis); (C) An actual piano roll, where for mechanical reasons the x- and y-axes are usually flipped compared with Fig. 1B; (D) Screen capture of The Orchestra app, showing multi-perspective videos sychronised to the music audio.

As relatively little is known about the effect of attending to visualisations while listening to music, the purpose of this paper is to investigate whether an interactive visualisation application, based on 40 years' worth of psychological research into listeners' cognition of repetitive and tonal structure, is capable of enhancing music appraisal skills. We report an experiment where listeners interacted with two visualisation applications in order to answer questions that were adapted from music-appraisal examinations. The music excerpts come from the symphonies of Ludwig van Beethoven (1770-1827). One visualisation application, called the *ScoreViewer*, presents the staff notation of the music synchronised to audio; the other, called the *PatternViewer*, is also synchronised to audio and presents a piano-roll representation such as in Fig. 1B, as well as representations of repetitive and tonal structure.

The remainder of the paper is organised as follows. The ScoreViewer and PatternViewer are introduced, the next sections describe the setup and results of an experiment investigating the effect of visualisation applications on music appraisal skills, and a final discussion section sets our findings in the wider context of interacting with and understanding intellectual artifacts, and the catalytic role that experimental-psychological research can play in this process.

2 ScoreViewer and PatternViewer

2.1 ScoreViewer

ScoreViewer is a web-based application that shows the staff notation (score) of the music, synchronised automatically to an orchestral recording [13]. At the top of the ScoreViewer, there is a media control bar for play/pause and skipping to different parts of the score/audio file (see Fig. 2). The current bar is always indicated by a semi-transparent gray box. ScoreViewer is a system for listening to orchestral music accompanied by the score. In the current paper it acts as a kind of control condition for normal music listening with score, while the second visualisation presents listeners with extra information that might help them to appraise the inner workings of a piece.

2.2 PatternViewer

The second visualisation is called PatternViewer.[2] Like ScoreViewer, it also depicts the notes (in piano-roll notation) synchronised to the recording. Additionally, it contains representations of the music's repetitive and tonal structure. These representations are based on [11]'s model of cognition of repetitive structure and [17]'s model of tonal cognition.

There are five elements to the PatternViewer's display, as shown in Fig. 3:

1. As with the ScoreViewer, the PatternViewer contains a media control bar for play/pause and skipping to different parts of the piece. The control bar appears in the top-right corner, and can be clicked or dragged to navigate to different time points;
2. In the top panel is a global-scale, piano-roll representation of the piece, which is synchronised to the audio. Notes light up in the piano-roll as they are heard in the audio. Different colours indicate changing key estimates (see point 4 for further explanation). There are two reasons for the choice of piano-roll representation as opposed to ordinary staff notation. First, it is simpler in piano-roll for listeners to follow the notes currently playing in a piece [19]. Second, it is easier to render piano-roll events in different colours, which is useful for conveying key estimates;
3. In the bottom-right corner is a local-scale, piano-roll representation of active (currently playing) pattern occurrences (see point 5 for further explanation).
4. In the bottom-left corner is a coloured circle of fifths, which provides a reference for the key estimates shown in the global-scale piano-roll representation. For instance, the notes currently playing in Fig. 3 are coloured red, which represents the key of C major (red segment labeled C in the coloured circle of fifths). A modern version of Newton's colourwheel [20], as used in experiments on visual cognition [28,29], was a natural choice for the reference. The circle of fifths, in itself, is not a music-psychological representation but a music-theoretic diagram. [18] showed that the important hierarchical relations

[2] https://tomcollinsresearch.net/research/PatternViewer/.

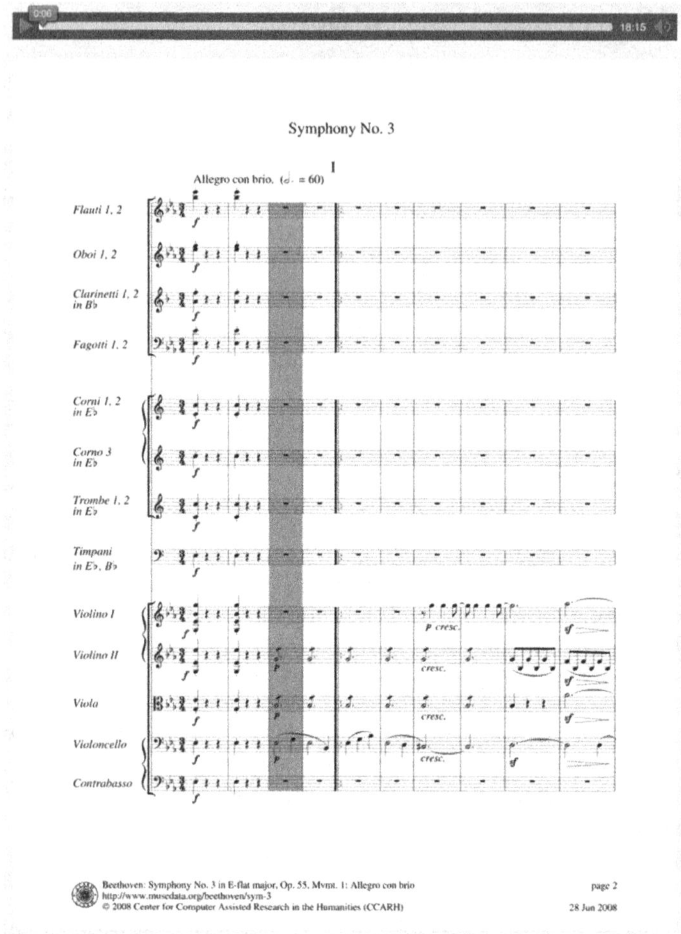

Fig. 2. The Scoreviewer visualisation. An audio file is embedded towards the top of the browser page. Below this is the staff notation corresponding to the point in the audio file, with the current bar indicated by a gray box. In this example the beginning of the main theme from Beethoven's Symphony no.1 first movement is highlighted. (Color figure online)

between pitch classes and keys enshrined in the circle of fifths are a psychological reality, however, and later [17] specified a method for estimating key based on empirical key profiles. Therefore, as it appears in the PatterViewer, the circle of fifths and perceived key estimates represent a model of tonal cognition.

5. In the top-left corner is a pendular graph, where each node represents a note collection that repeats (called pattern occurrence). As the piece plays, nodes in this graph will appear red when a pattern occurrence is active. The user has the option to hear/see the pattern occurrence that a node represents—by

clicking on the nodes in the graph, the audio and piano-roll representations will skip to and play the pattern occurrence automatically. The pendular graph in Fig. 3 is inspired by [11], and therefore the pendular graph models the cognition of repetitive structure.

In a pendular graph, a node's horizontal (x-axis) position corresponds to the time in the piece at which the pattern occurrence begins [7]. (If there are a lot of occurrences in a short period of time, nodes may be shifted slightly to the right.) All members of a specific pattern occupy the same vertical (y-axis) position. Vertically, different pattern occurrences are arranged in ascending order of duration. Therefore, large repeated sections tend to appear higher up and have labels nearer the start of the alphabet, whereas motives and themes tend to appear lower down in these graphs and have later alphabetic labels. If an edge (line) joins the pattern occurrence X_i to the higher pattern occurrence Y_j, this means that all the notes belonging to X_i belong also to Y_j. In Fig. 3, the nodes A_1 and C_1 are active (red). Node C_1 represents the first theme in the symphony movement, and its note content is displayed in the local-scale piano-roll representation in the bottom-right corner. In total, there are six occurrences of the

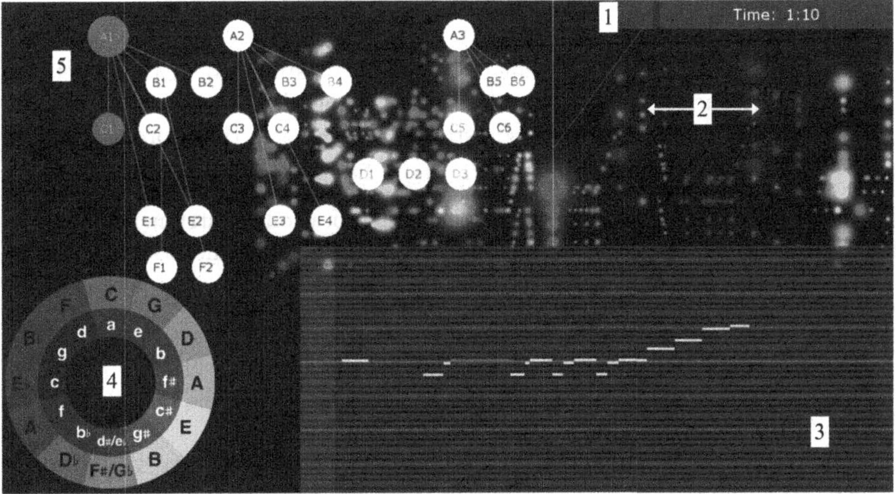

Fig. 3. The PatternViewer visualisation. Top left: a pendular graph representing the hierarchical, repetitive structure of the current piece. For instance, C_1 is the first occurrence of the main theme, whose notes are a subset of the large repeated section A_1 known as the exposition. Top right: a global-scale point-set representation, coloured by the current key of the music. A white vertical bar indicates the position within the audio, which can be moved back or forward by clicking to the left or right. Bottom left: a coloured circle of fifths, which can be used to identify the key colour shown in the top right (currently C major). Bottom right: a local-scale piano-roll representation, showing the contents of a pattern occurrence from the top-left graph (currently the main theme C_1).

theme in this movement, labeled $C_1, C_2, \ldots, C_6$ in the pendular graph. Node A_1 represents a large repeated section. The first movement of this symphony follows the conventional *sonata form*, in which A_1 is the *exposition* section. The edge (line) connecting C_1 to A_1 indicates that this first theme occurrence is part of the exposition section (as is the second theme occurrence C_2). When the exposition repeats (A_2), there are subsequent occurrences of the theme (C_3 and C_4).

In summary, the ScoreViewer and PatternViewer provide interactive , audio-synchronised visualisations of a piece of music. Additionally, the PatternViewer contains representations of the piece's repetitive and tonal structure, which are based on prominent models of music cognition [11,18].

3 Experimental Hypotheses

The main hypothesis that we investigate concerns how appraisal of the repetitive and tonal structure of a piece of music varies with use of the ScoreViewer and PatternViewer visualisations:

- **Null hypothesis.** There is no significant difference in terms of listeners' appraisal of repetitive and tonal structure, when using the ScoreViewer or PatternViewer visualisation.
- **Alternative hypothesis.** Interacting with the PatternViewer visualisation leads to a significant improvement in listeners' appraisal of the repetitive and tonal structure of a piece of music, compared to interacting with the corresponding, audio-synchronised staff notation (as in the ScoreViewer).

A secondary hypothesis centers on two aspects of music that might still be appraised effectively by studying the staff notation—instrumentation and dynamics. The following hypothesis is intended to balance the first hypothesis, allowing for the possibility that the PatternViewer is not always preferable to staff notation for appraising music:

- **Null hypothesis.** There is no significant difference in terms of listeners' appraisal of instrumentation and dynamics, when using the ScoreViewer or PatternViewer visualisation.
- **Alternative hypothesis.** Interacting with the ScoreViewer visualisation leads to a significant improvement in listeners' appraisal of the instrumentation and dynamics of a piece of music, compared to interacting with the PatternViewer.

4 Method

4.1 Participants

We recruited eighteen students from Johannes Kepler University Linz (mean age = 26.3 years, SD = 3.8, see also Fig. 4A), via the general student email list, offering €20 compensation, and mentioning that an interest (but not proficiency) in classical music was desirable. Thus our participants had varying levels of musical expertise, as shown in Fig. 4B-D. Mean years of formal musical training (instrumental or vocal) was 6.0 (SD = 4.7, see Fig. 4B). We also collected data on participants' musical activities, such as regularity of playing an instrument or singing (Fig. 4C) and concert attendance (Fig. 4D).

4.2 Stimuli

During the experiment, participants heard two excerpts from Beethoven's symphonies. The first excerpt was from Symphony no.1 in C major op.21, the opening 6:40 of the first movement (bars 1–225). The second excerpt was from Symphony

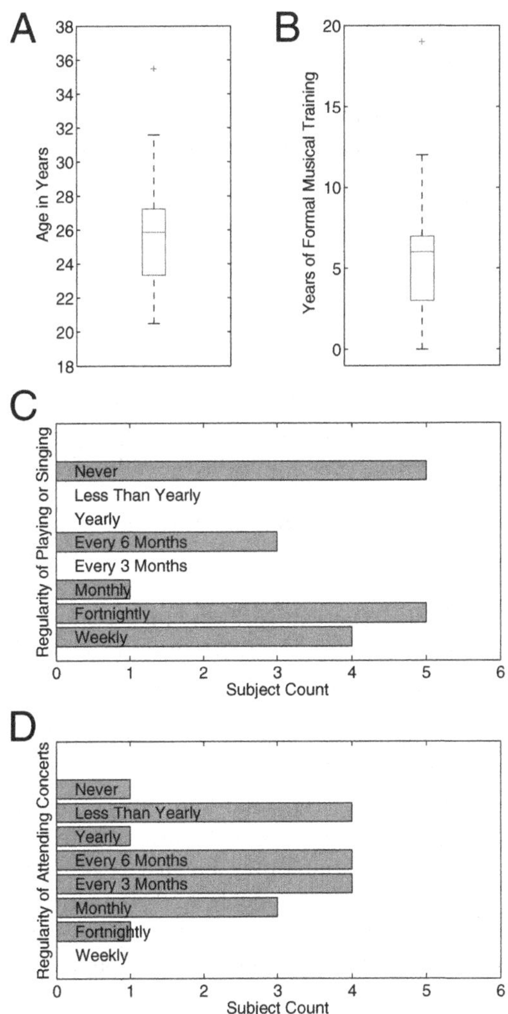

Fig. 4. Age, formal music training, and musical activities of the listeners in the study. One mature student is the cause of the outliers in Figs. 4A and B.

no.3 in E♭ major op.55, the opening 6:40 of the first movement (bars 1–158).[3] The excerpts will be referred to hereafter as Excerpt A and Excerpt B respectively. They were chosen to be matched in terms of tempo (Allegro con brio for both, following a short Adagio molto introduction in Excerpt A), overall key (major), and familiarity level amongst the listening public. The excerpts were the same length to avoid the possibility of participants listening to one excerpt more times than the other. In both cases the opening 6:40 encapsulated the statement and repetition of the large repeated section known as the exposition. Excerpt A included some of the next sections as well (development and partial recapitulation), but most questions focused on the exposition. Thus the overall form of the music heard by participants was similar also.

4.3 Procedure

In order to test our hypotheses, we need to operationally define *music appraisal skills*. Two sets of twenty questions were devised (one set for Excerpt A, the other for Excerpt B). The questions were based on past examination papers on appraising music from the UK GCSE Music qualification [1,12,21,27]. Each of the four main exam boards offer a Music qualification, which is taken as an elective course by students aged 15-16 years. Among other areas, the syllabi for these courses identify (1) instrumentation, (2) dynamics (including tempo), (3) repetitive structure, and (4) tonal structure as being relevant to the appraisal of music, and so our twenty questions were constructed by devising five questions from each of these four categories. Each question was multiple-choice, with three possible answers. An example question for each category is given below:

1. **Instrumentation.** Which of the following instruments is playing in the time window 1:46-1:49?
2. **Dynamics.** Which time window contains the most powerful (loudest) occurrence of the main theme?
3. **Repetitive structure.** Typically the first movement of a symphony begins with a large section called the exposition, which is repeated. In the current piece, at what time does the repeat of the exposition begin?
4. **Tonal structure.** To which key is there a brief modulation at 2:58?

For the purposes of analysis, the four question categories exemplified above are grouped into two topics: (A) instrumentation and dynamics (hereafter, Instr.Dynam or Topic A); (B) tonal and repetitive structure (hereafter, Reptn.Tonal or Topic B). These question categories and topics were selected on the basis that Instr.Dynam questions may be easier to answer with the ScoreViewer, where the names of the instruments and dynamic markings are stated (see Fig. 2), whereas Reptn.Tonal questions may be easier to answer with the PatternViewer, where representations of repetitive and tonal structure are provided

[3] Both were from recordings of the Royal Concertgebouw Orchestra. The first was conducted by David Zinman and the second by Iván Fischer.

(see Fig. 3). The topics, showing equal favor to the two visualisation applications, enable our experimental hypotheses to be investigated in a balanced manner.

After giving informed consent, receiving task instructions, and undertaking some training to gain familiarity with the layouts of the ScoreViewer and PatternViewer, a participant was presented with Excerpt A and the corresponding question set. To prevent ordering effects, the twenty questions appeared in a random order. After answering these questions, the participant was presented with Excerpt B and its corresponding question set (also in a randomised order). Thirty minutes were allocated for listening to and answering questions on each excerpt.

We used a within-subjects design that was counterbalanced across visualisation condition. That is, all participants heard Excerpt A first, followed by Excerpt B. One of two visualisation conditions (ScoreViewer or PatternViewer) was assigned to Excerpt A, and the other to Excerpt B, such that half of participants interacted with Excerpt A via the ScoreViewer, and half interacted with Excerpt A via the PatternViewer (and similarly for Excerpt B). Therefore, conditions were counterbalanced across pieces, and any learning effect that caused participants to perform better on Excerpt B than A would not bias our comparison of the ScoreViewer and PatternViewer.

At any stage, participants were able to ask questions of clarification, they were able to revise answers, and they were encouraged not to worry if they were unsure of the answer to a question. Instructions and questions were presented in English via a web interface, which contained links to Wikipedia and Youtube when helpful (e.g., definition of a tonal sequence or example of a clarinet sound). There was also an experimenter on hand to provide German translations of terms when necessary.

4.4 Apparatus

Participants sat at a laptop in an $12\,\text{m}^2$ room, and read and answered the question sets on this machine. The laptop was connected to a projector, which showed the visualisations on a 2×3 m wall section. The audio was presented by stereo speakers at a level of -20 dB.

5 Results

All participants had above-chance performance on the task, so no data were excluded from the following analyses. A two-way within-subject ANOVA on accuracy, with factors for Topic and Visualization type, revealed a significant main effect of Topic ($F_{1,17} = 22.64$, $p < .001$, see also Fig. 5), and a significant interaction effect of Topic and Visualization ($F_{1,17} = 6.84$, $p < .05$, indicated by the lines having different gradients in Fig. 5). The significant interaction suggests that the effect of Topic on accuracy varies as a function of Visualisation, with Reptn.Tonal questions being answered more accurately in the PatternViewer and Instr.Dynam questions being answered more accurately in the ScoreViewer.

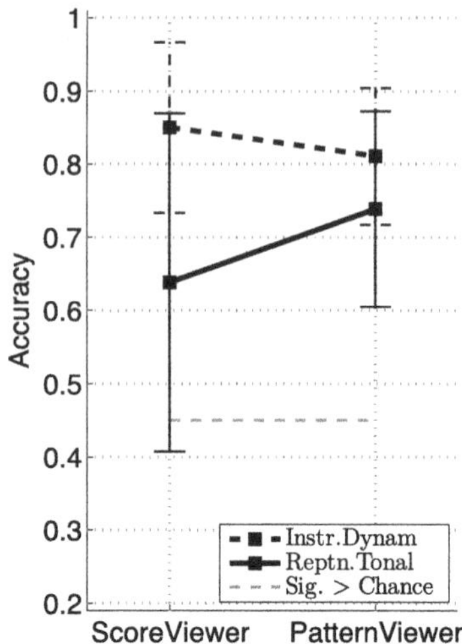

Fig. 5. Plot of accuracy varying with Topic (Instr.Dynam or Reptn.Tonal) and Visualization type (ScoreViewer or PatternViewer). Chance performance is indicated at $18/40 = .45$ by the dashed gray line. Under a binomial distribution with parameters $n = 40$ trials (questions) and $p = 1/3$ chance of success (multiple-choice question with three options), the probability of scoring more than 18 correctly is less than .05. (Color figure online)

To investigate the interaction effect more thoroughly, a planned comparison was performed on the accuracy of Reptn.Tonal answers in the PatternViewer versus Reptn.Tonal answers in the ScoreViewer. The result of a one-sided, paired t-test was significant at the .05 level ($t(17) = 1.77$, $p < .05$). Thus there is evidence for rejecting our main, null hypothesis (that there is no significant difference in terms of listeners' appraisal of repetitive and tonal structure, when using the ScoreViewer or PatternViewer visualisation), in favor of the alternative hypothesis—using the PatternViewer visualisation leads to a significant improvement in listeners' appraisal of the repetitive and tonal structure of a piece of music, compared to interacting with the corresponding, audio-synchronised staff notation (as in the ScoreViewer).

Further analysis reveals that the size of this effect is not uniform across participants, but varies as a function of musical training. Figure 6A shows Reptn.Tonal accuracy in the PatternViewer minus Reptn.Tonal accuracy in the ScoreViewer for each participant, plotted against years of formal musical training. The plot suggests that the effect size is a function of musical training, with participants' accuracy on Reptn.Tonal questions being higher in the PatternViewer than in the ScoreViewer (positive difference) if they have received approximately five years or less of formal musical training. If they received more than five years of musical training, the effect is either small or small in the opposite direction (negative difference).[4] Restricting the comparison of accuracy on Reptn.Tonal answers to those participants having five years or less of formal musical training, a one-sided, paired t-test is more significant still ($t(7) = -3.12,\ p < .01$).

Switching focus to the secondary hypothesis, concerning how participants' appraisal of instrumentation and dynamics varies with visualisation, a planned comparison was performed on accuracy of Instr.Dynam answers in the PatternViewer versus Instr.Dynam answers in the ScoreViewer. The result of a one-sided, paired t-test was not significant at the .05 level ($t(17) = -1.51$, ns), suggesting we cannot reject the null hypothesis of no significant difference in terms of listeners' appraisal of instrumentation and dynamics, when using the ScoreViewer or PatternViewer visualisation.

Again, we performed a subsequent analysis to investigate whether the size of this effect is uniform across participants or varies as a function of musical training. Figure 6B shows Instr.Dynam accuracy in the PatternViewer minus Instr.Dynam accuracy in the ScoreViewer for each participant, plotted against years of formal musical training. The distribution appears to be more even about zero than in Fig. 6A. For the Reptn.Tonal differences in Fig. 6A, it was possible to identify an exponential decay curve, $y = \alpha + \beta \exp \gamma x$, which provided a significant fit to the observations, where x is years of formal musical training, y is the Reptn.Tonal accuracy difference between PatternViewer and ScoreViewer, and α, β, γ are parameters estimated from the data. A corresponding analysis for the Instr.Dynam differences in Fig. 6B did not lead to identification of any significant linear or exponential trends. Thus the intuitive inspection that the size of the visualisation effect for Instr.Dynam does not vary as a function of musical training is supported by the regression analysis results.

6 Discussion

Of long-standing interest in psychology and neuroscience is how structured information in our environment passes through low-level and high-level representations, being transformed by as well as transforming the mind and brain. Two eminent examples of this type of information are repetitive and tonal structures in music, with listeners being exposed to music over many years, and behavioural experiments revealing that implicit sensitivities develop to these aspects of music's structure, even in the absence of formal training [24,26]. While pieces of music, like other cultural artifacts, will always be open to different interpretations by different individuals, the models of repetitive and tonal structure proposed by [11,18] respectively are particularly parsimonious. Therefore, we investigated whether presenting these parsimonious representations to listeners can help them to appreciate the inner workings of a piece, more readily than this appreciation might emerge simply by continued music listening. Our contribution was to determine how appreciation or appraisal of a piece of music varied

[4] Only one participant was at ceiling for repetitive/tonal questions in the ScoreViewer, and two other participants were at ceiling for repetitive/tonal questions in the PatternViewer, so these comparisons are not being confounded by ceiling effects.

with question topic (instrumentation, dynamics, repetition, tonality) and visualisation: we used the ScoreViewer, which automatically aligns a playing audio file to the relevant position in the staff notation; and the PatternViewer, which is automatically aligned to the audio as well, but includes representations of

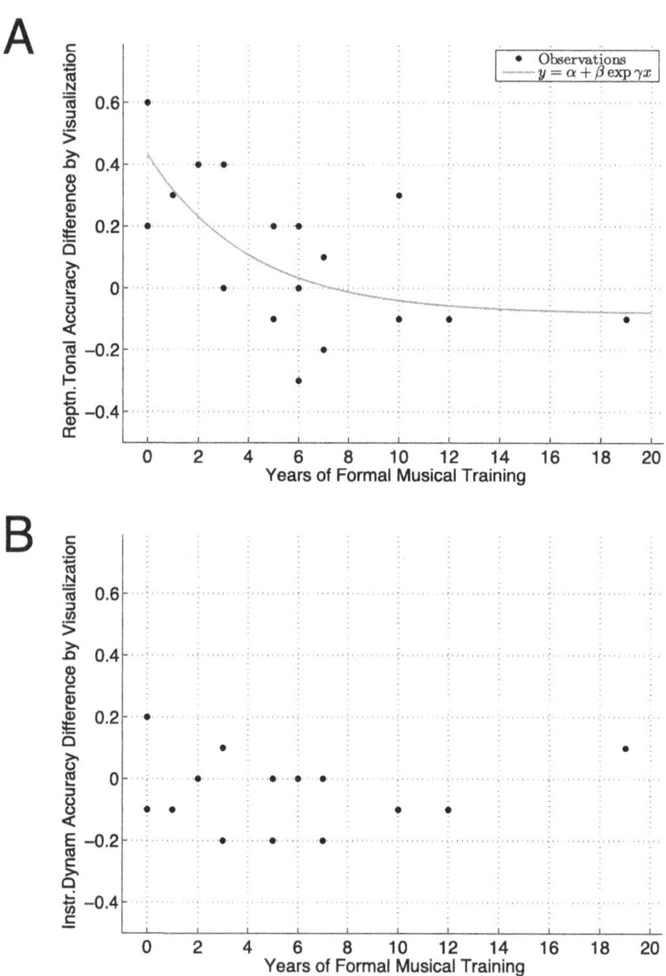

Fig. 6. (A) Plot of Reptn.Tonal accuracy in the PatternViewer minus Reptn.Tonal accuracy in the ScoreViewer against years of formal musical training. Parameters for the curve $y = \alpha + \beta \exp \gamma x$ were identified by iterating over choices for γ and performing linear regression to select optimal values of α and β. The regression of accuracy difference on years of training was significant, $F(1, 16) = 12.31, p < .01, s = .19, R^2 = .43$, and gave parameter values $\alpha = -0.08$, $\beta = 0.51$, $\gamma = -0.25$; (B) Plot of Instr.Dynam accuracy in the PatternViewer minus Instr.Dynam accuracy in the ScoreViewer against years of formal musical training. A corresponding regression analysis did not identify any significant linear or exponential trends.

repetitive and tonal structure also. As such, the first visualisation (ScoreViewer) acted as a kind of control condition for normal music listening with score, while the second (PatternViewer) presents listeners with parsimonious representations that might help them to appraise the inner workings of a piece.

6.1 Outcome of the Experiment

The results of our experiment demonstrated that listeners' appraisal of repetitive and tonal structure was improved when using the PatternViewer, compared to using the ScoreViewer. While this overall observation holds, it was nuanced by a further analysis, which suggested participants with five years or less of formal musical training showed the greatest appraisal improvements for repetitive and tonal structure questions, when using the PatternViewer compared to ScoreViewer. On the other hand, more musically-expert users showed moderate or no improvement. When modeling this accuracy-difference-by-visualisation for repetition and tonal questions (Fig. 6A), we found a proportion of variance $R^2 = .43$ was explained by just one variable: years of musical training. Our main finding invites the conclusion that exposure to carefully chosen representations derived from behavioural experiments and accompanying models can help listeners to gain an appreciation of the inner workings of pieces of music, over a relatively short period of time.

That more expert listeners displayed moderate or no improvement on repetition/tonality questions when using the PatternViewer versus ScoreViewer suggests that their habitual methods for answering such questions may have been disrupted in the PatternViewer. Most music students are taught to estimate the key of an excerpt of staff notation by reading the pitch classes of notes and determining to which key they fit best. The temporal order and rhythmic structure of the notes plays a role as well. While it is possible for trained musicians to read the pitch classes of notes in the PatternViewer, it is not as straightforward a task as in the ScoreViewer—the latter using the five staves to which musicians are highly accustomed. Being forced to put their habitual technique for key estimation to one side and to adopt the method provided by PatternViewer instead could have resulted in a processing cost, leading to the moderate or no improvements observed. A similar explanation might be offered for repetitive structure. Processing costs of this kind, where participants have to unlearn a previously successful strategy, have been proposed as an explanation for similar patterns of results in other task domains [2].

Questions from two further categories were presented (instrumentation and dynamics), which were intended to complement repetitive and tonal structure questions. That is, instrumentation and dynamics questions might well have been easier to answer in the ScoreViewer than in the PatternViewer, and so the question categories were balanced with respect to visualisation mode, allowing for the possibility that the PatternViewer is not unilaterally preferable to staff notation for appraising music. Results indicated that there was no significant difference in terms of listeners' appraisal of instrumentation and dynamics, when using the

ScoreViewer or PatternViewer visualisation. Subtracting a participant's accuracy for instrumentation and dynamics questions in the ScoreViewer from their accuracy in the PatternViewer, this difference did not appear to be a function of years of formal musical training. Based on this finding, we conclude that in terms of improving music appraisal, the PatternViewer's benefit is limited to matters of repetition and tonality. Staff notation is just as effective for conveying matters of instrumentation and dynamics.

The results regarding instrumentation and dynamics should be set in the context of (1) staff notation's longevity, and (2) its explicit specification of instrumental and dynamic information. (1) With some of the earliest surviving polyphonic music dating from 1150-1250, and maintaining broadly the same format in today's notation, it would be unlikely for a new representation of music to be unilaterally preferable to staff notation for conveying musical information. (2) Instrument names are written on the score, and so if noteheads appear in the flute part, then it is clear that a flute plays during a certain time window. Similarly, opening "<" and closing ">" hairpins that signify crescendos and diminuendos respectively are written into the score at appropriate points. It might be suggested that instrumentation and dynamics questions are straightforward to answer in the ScoreViewer, because the relevant information is made explicit. It should be said, however, that these questions can be made more complex (and sometimes were in our experiment), by asking about combinations or families of instruments, or subtler changes in loudness or tempo.

Unlike instrumentation and dynamics, only rarely are aspects of repetition and tonality marked explicitly in the score (and by extension, ScoreViewer): a key signature is given at the beginning of a piece, but still it may be in a major key or the relative minor, and usually the key signature is not modified to reflect local key changes; since the Classical period, repeated sections have been marked in the score rather than all the notes being written out a second time, but still, motives, themes, and other local repeated figures are not annotated. The PatternViewer, then, makes aspects of repetitive and tonal structure more explicit, providing the cognitive representations via which it is possible for a less expert listener to relate technical terms such as *motif* or *key change* to observable and interactive elements/events on the screen, such as nodes in a pendular graph or distinct colour changes in piano roll respectively.

Guiding the listener in this way could invite the criticism that any improvement in appraisal (such as that observed in our experiment) may be transient rather than permanent. For instance, does reading off estimates of local keys from a lookup index or diagram (such as the circle of fifths in the PatternViewer) help a less expert user to *understand* tonality any more than using a calculator to work out 6×7 fosters an understanding of multiplication? Our answer is that it depends on the topography of the index and the recurrence of its use. After interacting with the PatternViewer for a longer period of time (though substantially less time than would be required in the absence of its repetitive and tonal structure representations), a user may notice that pieces tend to begin and end in the same key, that tonicsisations and modulations tend to occur between proximal keys on the circle of fifths, that the second theme in the recapitulation of a sonata movement switches key compared to the exposition, from the dominant (or relative major) to the tonic, etc. The more parsimonious the topography of the index or diagram, the more readily these tendencies are likely to become apparent. Even for the more expert listener, it can be helpful to highlight such tendencies, since [9] demonstrated that music students are surprisingly insensitive to global key relations when listening with the score.

6.2 Experimental Psychology as a Catalyst for Understanding Intellectual Phenomena

Recent years have seen a huge increase in educational games/apps. Some of the names and claims attributed to these applications (e.g., “brain fitness workouts that can help your mind process information more quickly” [3]) imply that proficiency gains will go hand in hand with use. These claims, largely untested, have been called into question by the scientific community [22]. At a more moderate pace than the rapid growth of the applications market, educational psychologists and technologists are developing and testing electronic games that appear to enhance learning in domains such as mathematics, the natural and social sciences, and engineering [5]. The domain of music appraisal is ripe for investigation, therefore. It has been shown that meaningful interactions with structured information such as music can have a positive impact on intellectual ability [16]. In this paper, we have incorporated two parsimonious models of music cognition [11,18] into a visualisation application and tested its ability to increase proficiency for certain aspects of music listening and appraisal. The models-come-visualisations, based on behavioural data from previous repetition and tonality experiments with more expert listeners, appear to help less expert listeners, inviting the interpretation that these models act as a catalyst or go-between: a less expert listener’s intuitions about musical structure are promoted to the level/clarity of understanding required to link musical events to the correct technical terms synonymous with proficient appraisal. According to this interpretation, the role of cognitive psychology is to act as a catalyst, as a less expert individual gains deeper understanding and appreciation of intellectual phenomena [14].

6.3 Limitations and Future Work

We have been careful to set out the limitations and scope of the PatternViewer’s ability to enhance music appraisal skills. In part, this is to avoid the kind of controversy that was caused by non-replicability and partial reporting of the so-called *Mozart effect* [4], where incomplete information was provided on what questions appeared to be answered more accurately after ten minutes of listening to Mozart [23]. Here we are not claiming an increased intellectual ability beyond music—only increased appraisal abilities for *certain aspects* of musical structure. Rather than showing a general proficiency effect after mere exposure to music, of more immediate relevance to the present work would be to devise and test analogous visualisation applications within alternative task domains.

With regards the PatternViewer, future work will consist of (1) investigating whether there are other aspects of musical structure (e.g., [15,25]) for which beneficial representations can be developed, and (2) expanding the number of pieces for which we have the necessary data encodings. With regards (1), other aspects of musical structure could include harmonic progressions, textures, musical tension, etc. This work in turn may motivate new psychological experiments of the type that [10,18] performed in the 1980s, because, for instance, models of sensitivity to different chord functions in a progression, and sensitivity to different textural categories, are still to be fully developed [8].

We are cautious about including too many representations in the visualisation, however. First, the visualisation contains five sources of information already (media control bar, global and local piano roll, coloured circle of fifths, and pendular graph). Introducing more representations could lead to information overload. Second, there is a balance to be struck between the number of pieces for which the PatternViewer can be used and the depth/variety of representations on offer for any one piece. We continue to advance methods for automating aspects of the PatternViewer display, such as alignment of the audio and piano roll [13], or specification of the pendular graph [6], but there is still a bottleneck in terms of the relatively small number of pieces for which we have high-quality symbolic encodings. The developers of the Orchestra App face an even bigger challenge in this respect, since in the Orchestra App there are even more display modes for any given piece.

In future, we envisage this work could have a wider impact on people's listening experiences. New immersive user experiences in which the user can interact with music structures in a visualisation space could further promote the understanding of the inner workings of a piece. At the more compact end of the scale, another possibility could be the development of mobile apps for use in school music lessons, or for use by music enthusiasts in preparing to attend the concert hall.

Acknowledgments. Gerhard Widmer's work is supported by the European Research Council (ERC) under the EU's Horizon 2020 research and innovation programme, grant agreement No. 101019375 ("Whither Music?").

References

1. AQA: listening to and appraising music: past paper for GCSE music unit 1. AQA, Manchester, UK (2012). Accessed 13 Jan 2014. www.aqa.org.uk/
2. Brady, T.F., Konkle, T., Alzarez, G.A.: Compression in visual working memory: using statistical regularities to form more efficient memory representations. J. Exp. Psychol. Gen. **138**(4), 487–502 (2009)
3. Brainmetrix: brain training, brain exercises, brain fitness games, brain metrix (2014). Accessed 1 Aug 2014. www.brainmetrix.com/
4. Chabris, C.F.: Prelude or requiem for the Mozart effect? Nature **400**, 826–827 (1999)

5. Chen, N.S., Hwang, G.J.: Transforming the classrooms: innovative digital game-based learning designs and applications. Education Tech. Research Dev. **62**, 125–128 (2014)
6. Collins, T., Arzt, A., Flossmann, S., Widmer, G.: SIARCT-CFP: improving precision and the discovery of inexact musical patterns in point-set representations. In: Proceedings of the International Society for Music Information Retrieval Conference, pp. 549–554. Curitiba, Brazil (2013)
7. Collins, T., Meredith, D.: Maximal translational equivalence classes of musical patterns in point-set representations. In: Proceedings of Mathematics and Computation in Music, pp. 88–99. Montreal, Canada (2013)
8. Collins, T., Tillmann, B., Barrett, F.S., Delbé, C.: A combined model of sensory and cognitive representations underlying tonal expectation: from audio signals to behavior. Psychol. Rev. **121**(1), 33–65 (2014)
9. Cook, N.: The perception of large-scale tonal closure. Music. Percept. **5**(2), 197–205 (1987)
10. Deutsch, D.: The processing of structured and unstructured tonal sequences. Percept. Psychophys. **28**, 381–389 (1980)
11. Deutsch, D., Feroe, J.: The internal representation of pitch sequences in tonal music. Psychol. Rev. **88**(6), 503–522 (1981)
12. Edexcel: listening and appraising: past paper for GCSE music unit 3. Pearson Education Ltd., London, UK (2012). Accessed 13 Jan 2014. www.edexcel.com/
13. Grachten, M., Gasser, M., Arzt, A., Widmer, G.: Automatic alignment of music performances with structural differences. In: Proceedings of the International Society for Music Information Retrieval Conference, pp. 607–612. Curitiba, Brazil (2013)
14. Hmelo-Silver, C.E., Pfeffer, M.G.: Comparing expert and novice understanding of a complex system from the perspective of structures, behaviors, and functions. Cogn. Sci. **28**, 127–138 (2004)
15. Katsiavalos, A., Collins, T., Battey, B.: An initial computational model for musical schemata theory. In: Proceedings of the International Society for Music Information Retrieval Conference, pp. 166–172. Delft, The Netherlands (2019)
16. Kraus, N., Martin, M.: Biological impact of musical training in at-risk children. In: Proceedings of the American Psychological Association's 122nd Annual Convention. APA, Washington, DC (2014). Accessed 8 Aug 2014. www.apa.org/news/press/releases/2014/08/musical-training.aspx
17. Krumhansl, C.L.: Cognitive foundations of musical pitch. Oxford University Press (1990)
18. Krumhansl, C.L., Kessler, E.J.: Tracing the dynamic changes in perceived tonal organization in a spatial representation of musical keys. Psychol. Rev. **89**(4), 334–368 (1982)
19. Malinowski, S.A.: Time-line of the music animation machine (and related experiments) (1985). Accessed 23 May 2014. www.musanim.com/mam/mamhist.htm
20. Newton, I.: Opticks. Dover (1952). (Original work published 1704)
21. OCR: listening: past paper for GCSE music unit 4. OCR, Coventry, UK (2012). Accessed 13 Jan 2014. www.ocr.org.uk/
22. Owen, A.M., et al.: Putting brain training to the test. Nature **465**(7299), 775–778 (2010)
23. Rauscher, F.H., Shaw, G.L., Ky, K.N.: Music and spatial task performance. Nature **365**(64478), 611 (1999)
24. Saffran, J.R., Johnson, E.K., Aslin, R.N., Newport, E.L.: Statistical learning of tone sequences by human infants and adults. Cognition **1**(70), 27–52 (1999)

25. Sutcliffe, R., Hovy, E., Collins, T., Wan, S., Crawford, T., Root, D.L.: Searching for musical features using natural language queries: the C@merata evaluations at MediaEval. Lang. Resour. Eval. **53**(1), 87–140 (2019)
26. Tillmann, B., Bharucha, J.J., Bigand, E.: Implicit learning of tonality: a self-organizing approach. Psychol. Rev. **4**(107), 885–913 (2000)
27. WJEC: appraising: past paper for GCSE music unit 3. WJEC CBAC Ltd, Cardiff, UK (2012). Accessed 13 Jan 2014. www.wjec.co.uk/
28. Zhang, W., Luck, S.J.: Discrete fixed-resolution representations in visual working memory. Letters, Nature **453**(7192), 233–235 (2008)
29. Zhang, W., Luck, S.J.: The number and quality of representations in working memory. Psychol. Sci. **22**(11), 1434–1441 (2011)

Serendipitous Book Explorer Using Personalized Associative Dictionaries

Takumi Oikawa and Yasuyuki Sumi(✉)

Future University Hakodate, Hakodate, Hokkaido 0418655, Japan
t-oikawa@sumilab.org, sumi@acm.org

Abstract. This paper proposes a system called AssocSearcher that utilizes associative dictionaries as assistance for exploratory search for books. Users of the system can extend their horizons to explore books by getting subtopic or related words from the other people's associative dictionaries. The associative dictionaries are created as substitutes for individual thoughts. We generated associative dictionaries of individual persons using Word2vec and GloVe from sentences read or written by the individuals. This allows each associative dictionary to respond to related words that are characteristics of each person with a particular topic or keyword. Experimental results obtained by searching books using multiple associative dictionaries showed that participants are more aware of the possibility of exploration. We also found a dictionary familiar to a particular participant improves comprehension.

Keywords: Book retrieval · Associative dictionaries · Serendipitous search · Exploratory search

1 Introduction

This paper proposes AssocSearcher, a system to support exploratory book search. AssocSearcher enables users to broaden their book search horizons by retrieving subthemes and related terms from other people's associative dictionaries. Associative dictionaries are created as a substitute for personal thoughts.

Associative dictionaries of individuals were generated from sentences read and written by individuals using Word2vec and GloVe. This allows each association dictionary to correspond to related words that are characteristic of each person with a particular topic or keyword.

Our intension is to encourage serendipitous discovery with AssocSearcher. In other words, users of the system can obtain new books, find new relevance between specific topics by using multiple diverse associative dictionaries. Our hypothesis is as follows:

- Users can extend the search space by using others' associative dictionaries.
- They encounter unexpected books through the extended exploration.

H. Mori et al. (Eds.): HCII 2023, LNCS 14056, pp. 131–150, 2023.
https://doi.org/10.1007/978-3-031-48044-7_10

This paper describes a method for generating associative dictionaries and the AssocSearcher that uses it, and discusses its effectiveness with experimental results.

The outline of this paper is as follows. First, we discuss related research on exploratory search, query expansion, serendipity, and book retrieval. Second, we present the proposed system and its expected results. Third, we describe the method for creating associative dictionaries and the exploratory search system AssocSearcher. Fourth, we describe comparative experiments and results of a search task using a single large corpus of related words and a search task using multiple associative dictionaries. Finally, we summarize the study by discussing the results, limitations, and future prospects.

2 Related Work

2.1 Exploratory Search

We aim to support exploratory search [22,32] by presenting new viewpoints to expand user's horizon and assisting their continuous exploration.

The main approach to date has been to visualize search results and topics to support exploratory search for user understanding [37]. Studies visualizing search results or topics include visualizing an overview of results (e.g., TileBars [14], Scatter/Gather [27], SenseMaker [4]); supporting broaden search space incrementally using the interactive network of data (e.g., PivotPaths [10], Apolo [8], Exploration Wall [19]); supporting topic search by visualizing text corpora enables users to find diverse perspective (e.g., ParallelTopics [12], Serendip [2], TopicPanorama [20]); and allowing users to manipulate the search result visualization partly (e.g., [1,6]).

The other approaches also aim to keep user's mind the possibility of exploration by showing data. ScentBar [35] show proportion of already viewed information of suggested queries. Also there are studies facilitate exploration using visualized timeline information [3].

The above studies facilitate users to keep extending search space by showing the possibility of finding information. In this paper, we use the association of multiple personalized associative dictionaries to facilitate it. They stimulate not only curiosity about specific topic but also stimulate curiosity about other people's thought: "What kinds of association would that person have?" We consider it makes users more aware of the possibility of exploration.

2.2 Query Expansion

We focus on enriching search results by extending or diversifying search query. There are studies to improve the quality of the search results using expansion base on semantic similarity [13,31,36]. There are several studies about personalization of expansion for search queries [5,9,21,39].

We also interested in that the effectiveness of personalization for query expansion becomes diverse for each keyword. Teevan et al. proposed predictive models to identify queries that can benefit from personalization [33]. In the specific search keyword or user, information necessity becomes diverse in complex. Therefore, we consider the flexibility for such search intents is necessary.

We consider multiple associative dictionaries enable users to fit their intent. For example, they can use their own dictionaries if they need personalized suggestion. If they want to know external words of the specific topic, they can use the dictionaries of whom have much interest in topic.

2.3 Serendipitous Search and Recommendation

We focus on facilitating serendipity, the ability to find value in unexpected information. In recommender system, the word "serendipity" often used for representing "unusualness", "unrecognized" or "surprising".

Many systems related to serendipity focus on helping users to find the information includes the above properties to facilitate serendipity. Iaquinta et al. [15] proposed method to recommend items by the system includes randomness in item choosing method. Auralist [38] attempted to change recommended items balancing accuracy, diversity, novelty and serendipity. Kamahara et al. [16] proposed method to recommend unexpected items from clusters similar to the other user.

The term "serendipity" was first used in the ancient fairy tale "The Three Princes of Serendip" by Horace Walpole [29]. In this story, there is the sentence "*as their Highnesses travelled, they were always making discoveries, by accidents and sagacity, of things which they were not in quest of*". That means making discovery needs accidents and sagacity: the wise to comprehend situation. According to Silvia, the emotion of interest, has two appraisals: "*an appraisal of something as new, unexpected, or complex*" and "*an appraisal of one's ability to comprehend the new, complex thing*" [30].

From the original story of Serendipity and Silvia's mention, we consider that the users would discard the unexpected information without ability for comprehending it. We aim not only providing new information but also facilitating comprehension of new information using human factor of other peoples' personalized associative dictionaries.

2.4 Serendipity for Book Exploration

It is said that a library itself has interest to rise exploration and serendipity [17]. There are also studies facilitate them using interface imitates actual bookshelf [11,18]. WebBook and WebForager uses 3D virtual bookshelf to represent exploration space of Web pages [7]. The other studies also use interactive visualization of information such as book cover, author and keyword [25,34].

The inspiration for this study came from thinking about Japanese-language book search sites such as SO-IMAGINE[1] and WebCat-Plus[2]. These websites have the ability to search for books using associative terms based on large corpora such as Wikipedia and newspaper article collections. These sites allow users to explore information from a variety of perspectives. Our system aims to extend the possibilities of exploration by stimulating curiosity about the thoughts of others.

3 Proposed System

3.1 Searching for Books by Distinctive Use of Multiple Personalized Associative Dictionaries

We propose a method to support exploratory search by using multiple personalized associative dictionaries. Associative dictionaries are created with information about which words are related to a given word. This is created using each individual's text collection. This collection consists of Web browsing history, bookmarks, articles written by users, sentences posted on Twitter[3], Facebook[4], Evernote[5] and WorkFlowy[6]. Each associative dictionary is different because each is composed of different reading and writing experiences and thoughts (Fig. 1).

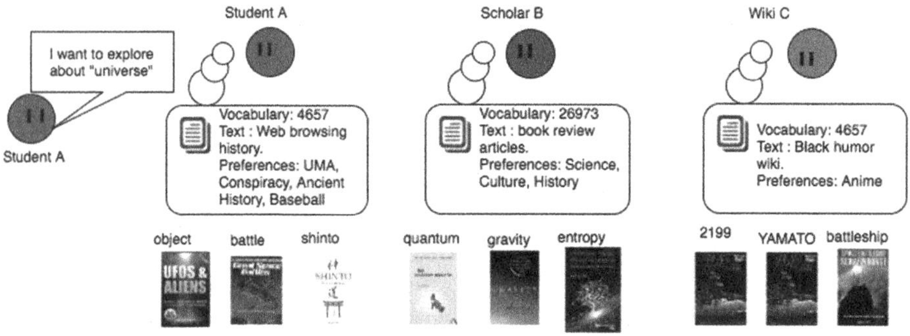

Fig. 1. Usage of the proposed system

When searching for books, users select a dictionary to use from multiple associative dictionaries, including their own dictionary. By performing an AND search or topic change using the associative terms in that associative dictionary,

[1] http://imagine.bookmap.info/index.jsp.
[2] http://webcatplus.nii.ac.jp/.
[3] https://twitter.com.
[4] https://www.facebook.com.
[5] https://www.evernote.com.
[6] https://workflowy.com/.

the user obtains search results that are different from those obtained with a single keyword.

Users are free to change the associative dictionary they use for their search depending on their search intent and interests. For example, if they wanted to look up a mystery novel, they would use the dictionary of someone who is familiar with detective novels. Or, if they want a book recommendation from someone they respect, they would use the dictionary of someone they admire. In this way, the users can flexibly use different associative dictionaries depending on their search purpose and mood.

3.2 Facilitation of Deep Understanding of Search Target Areas

By using the multiple associative dictionaries, the user can easily reach deeper into the information they want to look up. Let us take the case of "Artificial Intelligence" as an example. Word associations by a large single dictionary can only obtain words that have the same level of abstraction as the search keywords, e.g., "AI", "computer", and "robot". With the proposed system, users can obtain associative words such as "Minsky", "connectionism", and "frame problem" through the dictionaries of people who are knowledgeable in the specific field of artificial intelligence. Thus, by using multiple associative dictionaries, it is expected that information specific to the field of interest can be obtained more quickly and easily.

3.3 Discovery of New Books and Topics by Searching for Associative Terms that Users Themselves May Not Have Thought of

Multiple associative dictionaries can expand the search space of books that users can discover. The use of multiple associative dictionaries allows users to search using words that they would not have thought of on their own. Search results that are completely different from the user's expectations, but meaningful to the owner of the associative dictionaries, allow the user to obtain new search results from a different perspective. Thus, this method allows users to acquire unknown books and concepts.

4 Implementation

This section explains how to create a personalized associative dictionary and AssocSearcher which is a book explorer using them (Fig. 2).

4.1 Creation of Personalized Associative Dictionaries

The associative dictionaries are created as substitutes for individual thoughts. They should respond to related words that are characteristics of each person with an input word. We generated associative dictionaries of individual persons using Word2vec and GloVe from collection of sentences read or written by the

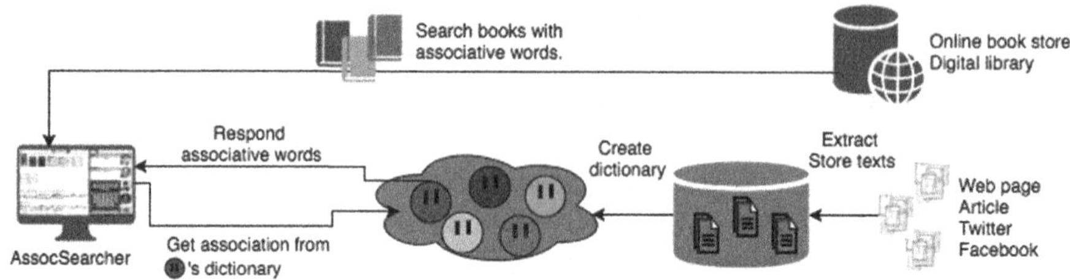

Fig. 2. System Overview

individuals. This collection consist of Web browsing history, bookmarks, articles written by users, sentences posted on twitter, Facebook, Evernote and Work-Flowy.

Word2vec is a tool to represent a language model on a neural network proposed by Mikolov et al. [23,24]. In this method, one word is represented as a vector around 200 dimensions, and the association between words can be obtained by calculating the cosine distance between vectors. Word2vec uses a model called skip-gram model. In the skip-gram model, it is assumed that neighbor of the certain word is related. Parameters of each vector are adjusted for maximizing the occurrence probability of neighbor words. Concretely, the parameters are adjusted to maximize the (1).

$$\frac{1}{T}\sum_{t=1}^{T}\sum_{-c\leq j\leq ,j\neq 0} \log p(w_{t+j}|w_t) \tag{1}$$

where T is the number of words represented in the vector space, c is the width of the neighbor words to examine (e.g. If $c = 1$, only the words before and after are evaluated). wt is the current word and $wt + j$ is the word that is located j word out of there. p is represented by the following (2).

$$p(w_{t+j}|w_t) = \frac{\exp(v'^{T}_{w_{t+j}}\ v_{w_t})}{\sum_{w=1}^{W}\exp(v'^{T}_{w}\ v_{wt})} \tag{2}$$

where v is a vector around 200 dimensions represents one word. By adjusting the parameters of v, (1) is maximized. In order to get a group of words that are related to a certain word, it can be realized by listing top rank word vectors in order of cosine distance from the word vector. Associative dictionaries created in this method was learned with 5 windows and 500 dimensions.

We also used the method called GloVe [26]. In the calculation of the similarity degree, the above method was performed on a probability, but this is a method which creating an overall co-occurrence matrix then converting it to a word vector. In this method, the dimension number is 100, the window is 10, the learning rate is 0.05, and the epoch number is 10.

We used associative words generated by both methods in the system describes later at the same time. We compared which one is used as an associative word for searching, but no difference was found. Therefore, in this paper, we define associative words that there are 10–14 words which combine with the top seven word vectors of cosine distance using each method, removing word duplications.

4.2 Example Association of Associative Dictionaries

The following describes examples of a word associative dictionaries actually created. Each table shows an example of associative words for the keyword "language".

The dictionary shown in Table 1 is a "Student A dictionary" that created from collection of the contents of the web page browsed by him (between two and three months). It can be observed this dictionary responds associative words related to information technology such as "Processing", "programming" and "function". The web browsing history includes Web page about Japanese professional baseball, conspiracy, prehistoric heritage, and programming. Another association example is "Mu" (the continent of legend which was said to exist in ancient times) for "continent". Also, when we enter a place name we get a baseball team name that is base at the place. It is understood that word association related to the information which he inputs.

Table 1. Example of association of Student A dictionary (keyword: language)

Method	Word2vec
Learning data size	11.4 MB
Vocabulary	12201

Word	Similarity
processing	0.8229
natural	0.7438
application	0.7268
speech	0.6903
factoid	0.6876
symposium	0.6564
conventionally	0.6536
word	0.6535

Method	GloVe
Learning data size	11.4 MB
Vocabulary	58120

Word	Similarity
natural	0.9622
type	0.8600
side effect	0.8458
processing	0.8350
functional	0.8336
programming	0.8330
speech	0.8074
Yiddish	0.7704

The dictionary shown in Table 2 is called "Seigo Matsuoka dictionary". Seigo Matsuoka is writer and researcher of Japanese culture. We created this dictionary from Web articles called "Thousand Nights, Thousand Books"[7]. It can be observed Seigo Matsuoka dictionary responds associative words related to

[7] http://1000ya.isis.ne.jp/.

Table 2. Example of association of Seigo Matsuoka dictionary (keyword: language)

Method	Word2vec
Learning data size	19.9MB
Vocabulary	26973

Word	Similarity
mathematical	0.6981
communication	0.6801
recognition	0.6503
eugenic	0.6439
ecology	0.6409
geography	0.6353
physiology	0.6322
symbol	0.6312

Method	GloVe
Learning data size	19.9MB
Vocabulary	77644

Word	Similarity
religion	0.9896
life	0.9772
logic	0.9762
mathematics	0.9722
environment	0.9712
spirit	0.9702
behavior	0.9701
system	0.9687

Table 3. Example of association of Professor A dictionary (keyword: language)

Method	Word2vec
Learning data size	717 KB
Vocabulary	8470

Word	Similarity
occurrence	0.6541
revelation	0.6452
pattern	0.6173
focus	0.5873
co-occurrence	0.5729
total	0.5673
protocol	0.5535
grammar	0.5527

Method	GloVe
Learning data size	717 KB
Vocabulary	14121

Word	Similarity
society	0.9887
target	0.9884
expression	0.9878
realization	0.9875
meaning	0.9874
experience	0.9867
information	0.9850
street	0.9846

communication of human despite previous dictionary. Also, this dictionary has abundant vocabulary about history and cultural history.

The dictionary shown in Table 3 is called "Professor A dictionary", a dictionary created from articles written by him, sentences posted on twitter. Professor A dictionary responds associative words such as "protocol (language protocol analysis)", "co-occurrence (co-occurrence reaction of language)" and "pattern (pattern language)", related to his research interests.

Thus, by using a variety of training data sets, each dictionary can present related terms that are characteristic of each person interested in a particular topic or keyword. Using the dictionaries thus created, we developed a book explorer called AssocSearcher.

4.3 AssocSearcher

We created a system called AssocSearcher that utilizes associative dictionaries as assistance for exploratory search for books. Users of the system can extend their horizons to explore books by getting subtopic or related words from the other peoples' associative dictionaries. This system is able to manage list of associative dictionaries to use, bookmarks and reading list, explore books using dictionaries.

On the exploring view (Fig. 3), search results of books and web pages are displayed on the left, the dictionary list of current user on the right. When a button at the lower left of the dictionary icon is pressed, a list of associative words for the search keyword by the dictionary is displayed. When a specific word is clicked from the list, the result on the left is updated to that search on the search keyword AND the associative word. When a button the right of current associative word, current associative word becomes current keyword, then refresh results into that on next current keyword. When a book image is pressed, a detailed view of the book is displayed, with book title, author name, detailed explanatory note, ISBN. There are "Later" button and close button at the lower right, when "Later" button is pressed, current book is registered for "reading list".

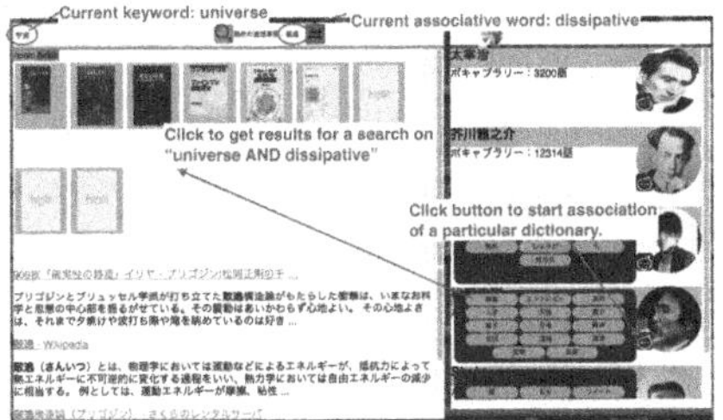

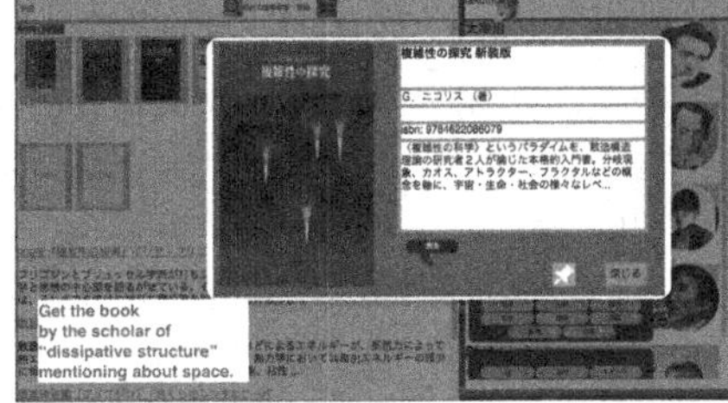

Fig. 3. Exploring view of AssocSearcher

We utilized search results of honto store[8] which is one of the largest Japanese online stores of books. Web search results assist understanding for associative words were obtained from bing[9]. This system is available on the Web, and this system collecting user's usage data.

The system detects the events such as input of a search word, browsing of book information, registration to read later, browsing of Web sites, association of a dictionary, query to get search result. For each event, date, time, search query, bibliographic information, associative word, name of dictionary associated the word.

[8] https://honto.jp/netstore.html.
[9] https://www.bing.com/.

5 Experiment

5.1 Goal

We hypothesize as follows.

- Users of multiple associative dictionaries can obtain more books that will be new discoveries for themselves (more books will be registered for "reading list").
- The exploring space become extended by using multiple associative dictionaries (nouns of detailed explanatory note of books will be diverse).

In order to verify it, a comparative experiment was conducted when using a multiple personalized associative dictionaries and when using a large single related dictionary.

5.2 Participants

6 students aged 21 to 24 (average age: 22) participated in the experiment. Table 4 shows basic information on experiment participants. Both participants are engaged in research activities, at least look through 1 to 2 books per month.

Table 4. Detail of each participant

ID	Gender	Frequency reading books	Keyword	Order
A	female	3–10/month	creature	single->multiple
B	male	1–2/month	gaze	multiple->single
C	male	3–10/month	sense	single->multiple
D	male	3–10/month	robot	multiple->single
E	male	3–10/month	language	multiple->single
F	male	1–2/month	learning	single->multiple

5.3 Task

The participant selected one keyword from 10 prepared keywords. These keywords include the words related to the topics the participants want to explore that were found by hearing in advance. The participant browsed books using the system starting from searching on selected keyword. While exploring, when the participant found a book that he wants to read, he pushed button to register the book for "reading list".

The participants were asked two tasks with AssocSearcher.

Single Dictionary Task. The participants explore books with single large dictionary utilizing Hatena associative words API[10].

Multi Dictionaries Task. The participants explore books with 10 personalized associative dictionaries (Table 5).

The participants performed each task for 15 min with the same keyword (balanced order between participants). We asked the participants to say whatever comes into their mind as much as possible during task.

Table 5. Dictionaries the participants use

dictionary	resources	notes
D1	book reviews	Scholar
D2	literatures	Historically prominent novelist
D3	blog articles	Blogger mentioning about AI
D4	twitter, research articles	University professor
D5	Web browsing history	Colleague of participants
D6	twitter	Colleague of participants
D7	Bookmarks, blog, memo	Colleague of participants
D8	twitter	Colleague of participants
D9	literatures	Historically prominent novelist
D10	official documents	Compendium of laws

5.4 Questionnaire

After completing both tasks, we asked to the participants two kinds of questionnaires. The first is asking the reason why the word was selected for exploring. For each associative word that the participant used for exploration, we asked a question with the following answer in a questionnaire "Please check all of the reasons for choosing this associative word which apply to you".

1. The word presented is relevant to my interests.
2. The word presented surprising to me.
3. The dictionary used to present the word has reliability, familiarity and expectation for me.

The second is a questionnaire on the overall impression evaluation of the task utilizing ResQue framework [28].

---

[10] http://developer.hatena.ne.jp/en/documents/keyword/apis/association/.

6 Results

6.1 Objective Measures

To test our hypothesis, we analyzed usage data of the participants (Table 6). For calculating Variation of books, list of nouns is extracted from a description note of each book registered for "reading list". The value was obtained by dividing the length of lists excluding duplication by that including duplication. Also, from the timestamp for each query history, we calculated topic stay time which is the time the participant keep exploring with the same keyword. Relevance is the rate that the participant checked "The word presented is relevant to my interests" for each questionnaire about associative words. Surprising is the rate that the participant checked "The word presented surprising to me" for that.

In each item, when t-test between two tasks was performed, no significant difference was found for all items ($p > .05$). In number of Associations ($t\ (6) = -2.05$), Topic stay time ($t\ (6) = -2.05$), Relevance ($t\ (6) = -2.53$), marginal differences were observed between the two tasks ($p < .10$).

Table 6. Overall usage data of each participants. Where TM represents multi dictionaries task and TS represents single dictionaries task.

	A		B		C		D		E		F		mean	
	TM	TS	TM	TS	TM	TS	TM	TS	TM	TS	TM	TS	TM	TS
Associations	18	19	8	10	17	19	11	28	3	10	12	14	11.5	16.6
Book views	12	14	33	33	14	18	26	21	33	26	9	14	21.2	21.0
Registrations	8	8	8	6	6	5	7	6	12	13	3	8	7.33	7.66
Variation of books	0.82	0.83	0.80	0.80	0.93	0.81	0.59	0.83	0.65	0.76	0.78	0.83	0.61	0.67
Topic stay time	105.0	109.5	327.5	195.8	141.7	116.4	339.5	139.8	442.4	154.1	147.0	165.4	250.5	143.8
Relevance	0.11	0.52	0.25	0.3	0.41	0.47	0.64	0.64	0.60	0.90	0.25	0.43	0.39	0.55
Surprising	0.44	0.16	0.38	0.40	0.59	0.52	0.18	0.29	0.33	0.30	0.33	0.29	0.38	0.33

6.2 Summary of User Responses Based on Questionnaire

The results of the overall questionnaire are shown in the Table 7. In Q1, Q2, Q3, the answers to each of the questions using the 1–5 likert scales, where 1 indicates "strongly disagree" and 5 is "strongly agree". A t-test performed and we found a significant difference between the two tasks on Q1 ($p < .05$).

We also asked users "The task ended in 15 min. Please choose your feeling of the moment that it ended". The answers to the question are "It ended early", "It ended at just right timing", "It ended late". 5 out of 6 participants answered "It ended early" on multi dictionaries task. 1 out of 6 participants answered "It ended early" on single dictionary task.

Table 7. Summery of overall questionnaire. Where TM represents multi dictionaries task and TS represents single dictionaries task.

Question	TM	TS
Q1 The items recommended to me are novel and interesting	4.0	3.0
Q2 The recommender system helps me discover new products	4.3	3.7
Q3 The items recommended to me are diverse	4.3	3.7

6.3 User Studies

In below, we show user studies about differences in exploration strategies and characteristics between two tasks. We mention them describing the overall usage data (Table 6), the dictionaries list used by participants (Table 5), and the distribution of dictionaries use for each user (Table 8).

Table 8. Distribution of usage of associative dictionaries in multi dictionaries task.

Participant	Distribution(%)
A	D8(33.3),D1(27.8),D5(16.7),D3(11.1),D4(5.6),D6(5.6)
B	D4(37.5),D1(25.0),D6(25.0),D3(12.5)
C	D6(23.5),D4(23.5),D8(17.6),D3(17.6),D5(11.8),D7(5.9)
D	D4(45.5),D7(27.3),D5(18.2),D3(9.1)
E	D1(66.7),D6(33.3)
B	D5(33.3),D2(33.3),D1(25.0),D3(8.3)

Book Exploration from a New Perspective. We will describe the case the user could explore books from new perspectives.

In single dictionary task, participant A started with "creature", explored books by changing current keyword into associative word. However, the participant recognized that new keywords were not lexically far away from start keyword such as "taxonomy", "owls" and "humans". After the task, the participant said, "I have the impression that I have found books related to my favorite topic". In the evaluation on associative words, Relevance was 0.52, Surprising was 0.16, we observed the participant explored books with more relevant associative words.

In the multi dictionary task, we observed the admirations such as "oh", "wow" and "yes" at the more than half time before she registered for "reading list". After the task, the participant said "I found somewhat related to living things with surprising, they seemed like interesting books". In the evaluation on associative words, Relevance was 0.11, Surprising was 0.44, the tendency became opposite to the single dictionary task.

Selection of Dictionaries Based on Known Features. We observed that users use dictionaries depending on the characteristics of dictionaries which they knew in advance.

In multi dictionaries task, we observed selection of dictionaries based on dictionary's characteristics. At the beginning of task, participant C said "Writer or Scholar would associate difficult terms", "I think I can get interesting association from people that is familiar with me". Consequently, participant C did not use D1, D2, D9, D10 which were not familiar with him.

Participant D thought that colleague's dictionaries would associate words related to "robot" because they were interested in such topics. The participant frequently used dictionaries of his supervisor and laboratory members (D4, D5, D7), and D3 based on articles about Artificial Intelligence. Also, we observed when he feels disappointed at D6, his colleague's dictionary that could not respond to keyword on contrary to his expectations.

We observed participant B distinguished the usage of dictionaries. For example, when keyword is the word close to his research field, he used a dictionary of his research supervisor or colleagues. When he wants to broaden the search topic, he used dictionaries of literary giants and scholars. Also, no participants used association of D9 and D10 which were unfamiliar with them.

Selection of Dictionaries Based on Dictionaries Features in the Exploring Process. We observed that users use dictionaries depending on the characteristics of dictionaries which they learned during task.

In multi dictionaries task, we observed selection of dictionaries based on dictionary's characteristic after using particular dictionaries. Participant F looked through the associations of all dictionaries, until he comprehends their characteristic. We observed speeches about tendency of dictionaries such as "D2 will not answer this keyword", "D3 will able to respond such topic infinitely" and "D2 is weak in the keyword consist of European language".

Participant A looked through the associations of all dictionaries like participant F. After she said "association of D8 is interesting", she become positive to use this dictionary. Consequently, D8 marked the highest frequency of use for this participant.

Reactions to Unknown Concepts. We observed behaviors trying to comprehend the meanings of the associative words which are unfamiliar with them.

When participant A could not understand the word associated by the D1, she searches for the word in a single query, attempting to understand the meaning by reading the Web search result. She registered the book found at that process for "reading list". In the questionnaire about that associative word, the item "The dictionary used to present the word has reliability, familiarity and expectation for me" was checked.

Also participant B got unknown word from D4, the dictionary of his supervisor. He searched for that word and opened the detailed information from one book by one book in order to comprehend meaning of it. We also observed the case unknown associative words by personalized associative dictionary were not effective.

Conversely, participant D said, "Although associative words had unexpectedness, I could not find any related books at all, I could not enjoy the search of books". In participant D, the proportion of "relevance" was 0.18, there were no books registered using these unexpected words.

7 Discussion

At beginning of evaluation, we hypothesized as follows.

- Users of multiple associative dictionaries can obtain more books that will be new discoveries for themselves (more books will be registered for "reading list").
- The exploring space become extended by using multiple associative dictionaries (nouns of detailed explanatory note of books will be diverse).

There was no difference in the number of the books registered for "reading list" between two tasks. Also, there was no difference in the variation of the books that were registered for "reading list" between two tasks. We consider that is because the participants took time selecting associative words and browsing association of dictionaries. Our hypothesis was rejected, however, we also consider positively even if the participants took much time to do this, it do not cause decrease of the number of finding books and narrow exploration space.

We also found discussions as follows.

7.1 Search Books Using Words that Do Not Recognize Relevance

In the multiple dictionaries task, there was a tendency to search using associative words with low "relevance". Also in the questionnaire, "the book that came up was surprising and interesting", there was a significant difference between task.

We also found a dictionary familiar to a particular participant improves his comprehension capability. It seems that the user was able to conduct a search using words that are not conscious of the relevance with multiple associative dictionaries.

7.2 Exploration Sustainability

We believe that AssocSearcher helps users continue their book search.

In a single dictionary, keywords changed frequently because there were few options for obtaining associative words. Therefore, the time spent per topic was short. Conversely, in the case of multiple dictionaries, participants often continued AND searches for the same keywords using associative words from various dictionaries. This allowed participants to use multiple associative dictionaries to search for books while creating different perspectives of the search space.

In the single-dictionary task, we observed several "out of ideas" moments. No such moments were observed in the multiple dictionary task. 5 out of 6 participants reported they finished quickly and a marginal difference was observed in relevance of associative words between the two tasks. That means, with multiple associative dictionaries, participants can be more aware of the possibility of exploration. Therefore, we consider AssocSearcher gives users exploration sustainability.

7.3 Intentional Selection of Dictionaries

From the participants' utterances, it was found that participants varied the frequency of dictionary use based on their interest in a particular dictionary and its associations. Some participants limited the dictionaries they used, and unfamiliar dictionaries D9 and D10 were not used by all participants. It was suggested that intentional choice of dictionaries influenced book discovery.

7.4 Recognition of Individual Differences in Associative Dictionaries by Users

We believe that users can recognize the differences and features of multiple personalized dictionaries. In this study, we did not quantitatively evaluate the associative words of the dictionaries themselves. However, we did see predictions of trends in the associative words of certain dictionaries and the selection of dictionaries to use based on dictionary preferences. One participant stated, "It was fun just to see what words were associated with each dictionary, since I could see the characteristics of each dictionary". These results suggest that the AssocSearcher can be used to create a situation in which there is an associative dictionary that matches the personality of the individual user.

8 Limitations

The difference between the two tasks was considered to be the number of books found within the specified time. However, we found that the two tasks differed in terms of the likelihood of exploration perceived by the participants at the end of the task. Therefore, for a more accurate assessment, an experiment comparing the two tasks in terms of task completion time is needed. This can be accomplished by leaving the decision of task completion to the participants in the experiment.

It was also observed that the use of multiple associative dictionaries was counterproductive because if the associative words were too unrelated, no valid search results were obtained. It is necessary to consider how to create associative dictionaries that reflect the individuality of the associative words and have sufficient validity for book searches.

In the experiment, all participants used the same 10 dictionaries. Because the experiment was time-limited, it was not possible to observe in depth the changes in the usage of the dictionaries used by the participants. The experiment suggests that further analysis of the choice of dictionaries by users is needed.

9 Future Directions

We consider possible behavioral changes and social interactions of dictionary owners. During the task, we observed the user speeches such as "I'm wondering what other people think about my favorite word" and "If my dictionary exist, it could respond some associative words to explore for this keyword". People are interested in the information what other people are thinking about a certain word. AssocSearcher allows sharing such information among users. We focus on not only users of dictionaries but also the people who have the dictionary which is used by other people. For example, they might attempt to read or write information that they not usually see to nurture their own dictionary if their dictionaries are not used because of low vocabulary or narrow covering topics.

We believe that AssocSearcher could also recommend the owners of dictionaries which is used by other people discovering books. In this system, the specific user could find the book using the specific user's dictionary. By showing the book to the owner of the dictionary, recommendation to the owner could be realized. In other words, we can recommend the owner of the dictionary which the user get interested in, for the books which the user get interested in. We will analyze the effectiveness of this way of recommendation.

We believe that one person's associative dictionary can be classified into several new dictionaries. A person's interests change over time, and accordingly, the words that come to mind for a given word change. In addition, we can distinguish between private and public writings that a person writes or reads. For example, we believe that a person can create a new dictionary with different characteristics depending on time, purpose of writing, and purpose of reading, such as a dictionary for the year 2014, a dictionary for writing public documents, etc.

10 Conclusions

In this paper, we proposed a method that assists exploratory search by using multiple personalized associative dictionaries. We generated associative dictionaries of individual persons using Word2vec and GloVe from sentences read or written by the individuals. We described a system called AssocSearcher that enables users to extend their horizons to explore books by getting subtopic or related words from the other people's associative dictionaries. A discussion of experimental results comparing the use of multiple personalized associative dictionaries with the use of a large single associative dictionary suggested the following.

- AssocSearcher has enabled users to sustainably search for books.
- Human factor in associative dictionaries could influence book exploration and discovery.
- AssocSearcher could provide users with a situation where they could explore books using multiple perspectives with multiple personalities.

Future directions include discussing user immersion by comparing the execution times of the two conditions; and observing the effectiveness of personalized associative dictionary recommendations to the owners themselves.

References

1. Ahn, J.W., Brusilovsky, P.: Adaptive visualization for exploratory information retrieval. Inf. Process. Manag. **49**(5), 1139–1164 (2013). https://doi.org/10.1016/j.ipm.2013.01.007
2. Alexander, E., Kohlmann, J., Valenza, R., Witmore, M., Gleicher, M.: Serendip: topic model-driven visual exploration of text corpora. In: 2014 IEEE Conference on Visual Analytics Science and Technology (VAST), pp. 173–182 (2014). https://doi.org/10.1109/VAST.2014.7042493
3. Alonso, O., Baeza-Yates, R., Gertz, M.: Exploratory search using timelines. In: SIGCHI 2007 Workshop on Exploratory Search and HCI Workshop, No. 1, pp. 1–4 (2007)
4. Baldonado, M.Q.W., Winograd, T.: SenseMaker: an information-exploration interface supporting the contextual evolution of a user's interests. In: Proceedings of the ACM SIGCHI Conference on Human Factors in Computing Systems, pp. 11–18. ACM (1997). http://dl.acm.org/citation.cfm?id=258563
5. Biancalana, C., Micarelli, A.: Social tagging in query expansion: a new way for personalized web search. In: International Conference on Computational Science and Engineering (CSE 2009), vol. 4, pp. 1060–1065. IEEE (2009)
6. Bostandjiev, S., O'Donovan, J., Höllerer, T.: TasteWeights: A Visual Interactive Hybrid Recommender System, p. 35. ACM Press (2012). https://doi.org/10.1145/2365952.2365964
7. Card, S.K., Robertson, G.G., York, W.: The webbook and the web forager: an information workspace for the World-Wide Web. In: Proceedings of the SIGCHI Conference on Human Factors in Computing Systems, pp. 111–117. ACM (1996)
8. Chau, D.H., Kittur, A., Hong, J.I., Faloutsos, C.: Apolo: making sense of large network data by combining rich user interaction and machine learning. In: Proceedings of the SIGCHI Conference on Human Factors in Computing Systems, pp. 167–176. ACM (2011). http://dl.acm.org/citation.cfm?id=1978967
9. Chirita, P.A., Firan, C.S., Nejdl, W.: Personalized query expansion for the web. In: Proceedings of the 30th Annual International ACM SIGIR Conference on Research and Development in Information Retrieval, pp. 7–14. ACM (2007). http://dl.acm.org/citation.cfm?id=1277746
10. Dörk, M., Riche, N.H., Ramos, G., Dumais, S.: PivotPaths: strolling through faceted information spaces. IEEE Trans. Visual Comput. Graph. **18**(12), 2709–2718 (2012). https://doi.org/10.1109/TVCG.2012.252
11. Detken, K., Martinez, C., Schrader, A.: The search wall: tangible information searching for children in public libraries. In: Proceedings of the 3rd International Conference on Tangible and Embedded Interaction, pp. 289–296. ACM (2009)
12. Dou, W., Wang, X., Chang, R., Ribarsky, W.: Paralleltopics: a probabilistic approach to exploring document collections. In: 2011 IEEE Conference on Visual Analytics Science and Technology (VAST), pp. 231–240. IEEE (2011)
13. Gong, Z., Cheang, C.W., Leong Hou, U.: Web query expansion by WordNet. In: Andersen, K.V., Debenham, J., Wagner, R. (eds.) DEXA 2005. LNCS, vol. 3588, pp. 166–175. Springer, Heidelberg (2005). https://doi.org/10.1007/11546924_17
14. Hearst, M.A.: TileBars: visualization of term distribution information in full text information access. In: 1995 Proceedings of the SIGCHI Conference on Human Factors in Computing Systems, pp. 59–66 (1995) https://doi.org/10.1145/223904.223912

15. Iaquinta, L., de Gemmis, M., Lops, P., Semeraro, G., Filannino, M., Molino, P.: Introducing serendipity in a content-based recommender system. In: 2008 Eighth International Conference on Hybrid Intelligent Systems (HIS 2008), pp. 168–173. IEEE (2008)
16. Kamahara, J., Asakawa, T., Shimojo, S., Miyahara, H.: A community-based recommendation system to reveal unexpected interests. In: 2005 Proceedings of the 11th International Multimedia Modelling Conference (MMM 2005), pp. 433–438. IEEE (2005)
17. Khoo, M., Rozaklis, L., Hall, C.: A survey of the use of ethnographic methods in the study of libraries and library users. Lib. Inf. Sci. Res. **34**(2), 82–91 (2012)
18. Kleiner, E., Rädle, R., and Reiterer, H.,: Blended shelf: reality-based presentation and exploration of library collections. In: CHI 2013 Extended Abstracts on Human Factors in Computing Systems, pp. 577–582 (2013). https://doi.org/10.1145/2468356.2468458
19. Klouche, K., Ruotsalo, T., Cabral, D., Andolina, S., Bellucci, A., Jacucci, G.: Designing for exploratory search on touch devices. In: Proceedings of the 33rd Annual ACM Conference on Human Factors in Computing Systems, pp. 4189–4198. ACM (2015)
20. Liu, S., Wang, X., Chen, J., Zhu, J., Guo, B.: TopicPanorama: a full picture of relevant topics. In: 2014 IEEE Conference on Visual Analytics Science and Technology (VAST), pp. 183–192. IEEE (2014)
21. Liu, S., Liu, F., Yu, C., Meng, W.: An effective approach to document retrieval via utilizing WordNet and recognizing phrases. In: Proceedings of the 27th Annual International ACM SIGIR Conference on Research and Development in Information Retrieval, pp. 266–272. ACM (2004). http://dl.acm.org/citation.cfm?id=1009039
22. Marchionini, G.: Exploratory search: from finding to understanding. Commun. ACM **49**(4), 41–46 (2006). https://doi.org/10.1145/1121949.1121979
23. Mikolov, T., Chen, K., Corrado, G., Dean, J.: Efficient estimation of word representations in vector space. arXiv preprint arXiv:1301.3781 (2013)
24. Mikolov, T., Sutskever, I., Chen, K., Corrado, G.S., Dean, J.: Distributed representations of words and phrases and their compositionality. In: Advances in Neural Information Processing Systems, pp. 3111–3119 (2013). http://papers.nips.cc/paper/5021-distributed-representations
25. Pearce, J., Chang, S.: Exploration Without Keywords: The Bookfish Case, pp. 176–179. ACM Press (2014). https://doi.org/10.1145/2686612.2686639
26. Pennington, J., Socher, R., Manning, C.: GloVe: global vectors for word representation. In: Proceedings of the 2014 Conference on Empirical Methods in Natural Language Processing (EMNLP), pp. 1532–1543 (2014). http://www.aclweb.org/anthology/D14-1162
27. Pirolli, P., Schank, P., Hearst, M., Diehl, C.: Scatter/gather browsing communicates the topic structure of a very large text collection. In: Proceedings of the SIGCHI Conference on Human Factors in Computing Systems, pp. 213–220. ACM (1996)
28. Pu, P., Chen, L., Hu, R.: A user-centric evaluation framework for recommender systems. In: Proceedings of the Fifth ACM Conference on Recommender Systems (RecSys 2011), pp. 157–164. ACM (2011). https://doi.org/10.1145/2043932.2043962
29. Remer, T.G.: Serendipity and the Three Princes. University of Oklahoma Press (1965)

30. Silvia, P.J.: Emotional responses to art: from collation and arousal to cognition and emotion. Rev. Gen. Psychol. **9**(4), 342–357 (2005). https://doi.org/10.1037/1089-2680.9.4.342
31. Song, M., Song, I.Y., Hu, X., Allen, R.B.: Integration of association rules and ontologies for semantic query expansion. Data Knowl. Eng. **63**(1), 63–75 (2007)
32. Teevan, J., Alvarado, C., Ackerman, M.S., Karger, D.R.: The perfect search engine is not enough: a study of orienteering behavior in directed search. In: Proceedings of the SIGCHI Conference on Human Factors in Computing Systems, pp. 415–422. ACM (2004)
33. Teevan, J., Dumais, S.T., Liebling, D.J.: To personalize or not to personalize: modeling queries with variation in user intent. In: Proceedings of the 31st Annual International ACM SIGIR Conference on Research and Development in Information Retrieval, pp. 163–170. ACM (2008)
34. Thudt, A., Hinrichs, U., Carpendale, S.: The bohemian bookshelf: supporting serendipitous book discoveries through information visualization. In: Proceedings of the SIGCHI Conference on Human Factors in Computing Systems, pp. 1461–1470. ACM (2012). http://dl.acm.org/citation.cfm?id=2208607
35. Umemoto, K., Yamamoto, T., Tanaka, K.: ScentBar: a query suggestion interface visualizing the amount of missed relevant information for intrinsically diverse search. In: Proceedings of the 39th International ACM SIGIR Conference on Research and Development in Information Retrieval, pp. 405–414. ACM (2016)
36. Voorhees, E.M.: Query expansion using lexical-semantic relations. In: Croft, B.W., van Rijsbergen, C.J. (eds.) SIGIR 1994, pp. 61–69. Springer, London (1994). https://doi.org/10.1007/978-1-4471-2099-5_7
37. Zhang, J.: Visualization for Information Retrieval, vol. 23. Springer, Heidelberg (2007). https://doi.org/10.1007/978-3-540-75148-9
38. Zhang, Y.C., Séaghdha, D.Ó., Quercia, D., Jambor, T.: Auralist: introducing serendipity into music recommendation. In: Proceedings of the fifth ACM International Conference on Web Search and Data Mining, pp. 13–22. ACM (2012). http://dl.acm.org/citation.cfm?id=2124300
39. Zhou, D., Lawless, S., Wade, V.: Improving search via personalized query expansion using social media. Inf. Retrieval **15**(3–4), 218–242 (2012)

Research on Designing and Evaluating Alarm Signals for Varying Criticality Scenarios

Yeqing Pei(✉)

Beijing Institute of Fashion Technology, No. 2 East Yinghua Road, Beijing, People's Republic of China
caupyq@126.com

Abstract. As an important part of the tractor display interface, the alarm signal plays the role of attracting the driver's attention and pushing important information to the driver under emergency situations. The design level of the alarm signal is related to whether the tractor driver can deal with the abnormal situation effectively, which determines the efficiency and safety of the whole system. Therefore, how to evaluate the alarm signal has become a key issue to be considered in the design of tractor display interface. Based on human situational cognition model, this paper establishes an alarm signal effectiveness evaluation index system for different criticality scenarios, comprehensively evaluates the performance of alarm signals in each stage of situational cognition, explores the effectiveness of multiple alarm signals and combined alarm signals under different criticality scenarios, and proposes alarm signal design strategies applicable to different scenarios. It provides theoretical guidance for the design of alarm signal in display interface.

Keywords: Alarm Signal · High-criticality Scenarios · Medium-criticality Scenarios · Low-criticality Scenarios · Evaluation System

1 Introduction

Due to the development of science and technology, the automation level of intelligent tractors has gradually improved, the amount of information that can be monitored in the cab has increased significantly, and the types of alarm signals have become more and more abundant. In addition to the common auditory signals and visual signals, the use of tactile signals has become more and more common [1, 2]. In the tractor seeding operation, the driver needs to complete the driving task, the seeding task and the anomaly monitoring task at the same time. The parallel mode of multiple tasks requires the driver to recognize the complex and changeable situations timely and accurately. Situational cognitive characteristics refer to the characteristics of tractor driver's cognition of changing situations, which is the key factor affecting the operator's decision-making and operation. In the design stage of the alarm signal, fully considering the tractor driver's situational cognition characteristics is conducive to improving the driver's situational cognition level, so as to improve the efficiency and safety of the whole system.

H. Mori et al. (Eds.): HCII 2023, LNCS 14056, pp. 151–161, 2023.
https://doi.org/10.1007/978-3-031-48044-7_11

For the study of alarm signals, Bazilinskyy et al. [3] studied the driver's preference for different types of takeover request signals in highly automatic driving scenarios. In the test process, the author divided the current takeover scenario into five levels according to different levels of urgency, and the results showed that multi-modal signals were most effective in high-emergency scenarios. In the low emergency situation, the auditory mode is more effective. In the driving simulator test, Maag et al. [4] compared the effect of the tactile alarm signal controlling the steering wheel Angle with that of the visual alarm signal displayed at head-up, and the research results showed that the visual warning would bring greater safety benefits. Hollands et al. [5] studied the impact of signal presentation rate and signal perception channel on people's cognitive load, and the research results showed that faster signal presentation rate and visual signals would increase people's cognitive load. Chi et al. [6] applied structural equation model to analyze the relationship between pitch, loudness, rhythm, timbre and other characteristics, as well as the relationship between them and perceived sound quality. The research results show that for continuous sound, pitch, loudness and timbre all have a direct impact on perceived quality. For intermittent sounds, rhythm and timbre have a direct impact on perceived quality. Yan et al. [7] studied the impact of alarm timing, direction information, driver gender and other factors of voice alarm signals on driving performance, and proposed appropriate alarm timing, which has guiding significance for the design of collision warning system. Murata and Kuroda et al. [8] studied the effects of auditory and tactile alarm signals on drivers' driving behaviors in noisy environments, and the research results showed that vibration and tactile alarm signals were more effective than auditory alarm signals. When the test background was set to the noise of real driving environment, the noise level had no effect on the reaction time of auditory alarm signals.

A comprehensive analysis of the current research status shows that, first of all, the current research on alarm signals is mainly concentrated in the field of automobiles. However, compared with ordinary transportation vehicles, tractors have a harsh operating environment, long continuous operation time, high labor intensity, and need to complete multiple tasks in parallel. Drivers will receive various alarm signals and handle various abnormal situations. The problem of cognitive overload is easily caused by the unreasonable design of alarm signals, so it is necessary to study the effectiveness of tractor alarm signals. Secondly, the current research on alarm signals does not match the severity of the current situation. Most researchers study the effectiveness of various alarm signals by setting a scenario (collision scenario is the most commonly used scenario). However, due to the different severity of the situation, the matching degree of alarm signals with the situation will be different. It is necessary to study the effectiveness of alarm signals according to different emergency levels. Finally, at present, there is no perfect evaluation system for the evaluation of alarm signals, and it is impossible to measure the design level, so it is necessary to study the evaluation system. Based on human situational cognition model, this paper establishes an alarm signal effectiveness evaluation index system for different criticality scenarios, comprehensively evaluates the performance of alarm signals in each stage of situational cognition, explores the effectiveness of multiple alarm signals and combined alarm signals under different criticality scenarios, and proposes alarm signal design strategies applicable to different scenarios. It provides theoretical guidance for the design of alarm signal in display interface.

2 Method

The alarm signal is a kind of alarm notification, which is an information intervention to the driver, and the driver needs to process it through various cognitive abilities such as feeling, perception, memory, judgment and understanding. The different design parameters of alarm signal lead to the different perception characteristics, understanding characteristics and feedback characteristics of the driver in the process of situational cognition. In order to study the effectiveness of alarm signals, it is necessary to start with the characteristics of people's situational cognition and analyze the different effects of different types of alarm signals in different stages of people's situational cognition.

2.1 Situation Awareness Model of Human

Situational cognition refers to the mechanism by which people perceive the elements in the environment within a certain time and space, understand their meaning, and predict their future state. Endsley proposed a widely accepted episodic cognitive model by means of information flow [9]. The process of tractor driver receiving alarm signal for situational cognition can be analyzed by combining this model. The driver uses visual, auditory, tactile, and other sensory organs for sensory processing of alarm signals first, which are temporarily stored in short-term sensory memory. Then, the driver processes the alarm signal perceptively, understands the signal in the early stage, and predicts the future state according to the long-term memory formed by past experience. After that, the driver makes a response choice and takes a certain action accordingly, that is, response execution. Finally, the driver feels the impact of his own response on the tractor, that is, the tractor has a certain feedback on the driver. Each stage during the whole process will create a certain cognitive load on the driver. To evaluate the cognitive load imposed by the alarm signal on the driver during the whole process, the effectiveness of the alarm signal should be assessed from each stage.

2.2 A System to Evaluate Alarm Signal Effectiveness

Evaluation system for the effectiveness of alarm signals is crucial in ensuring that drivers are able to respond appropriately when such signals are activated. The process of situational cognition involved in responding to alarm signals entails several steps. First, the driver perceives the appearance of the signal, followed by perceptual understanding, response selection, and finally performing the corresponding operation and receiving feedback. To design reasonable alarm signals, attention needs to be paid to three aspects. The first is to use signal prompts that enable drivers to quickly perceive the occurrence of abnormal conditions. The second aspect involves ensuring that the driver understands the purpose of the alarm and the present dangerous condition of the system or environment. The third aspect is to avoid negative outcomes such as driver boredom, distrust, and other consequences arising from unreasonable signal design. The following section will illustrate the effectiveness of the alarm signal evaluation indicators in light of the three aspects mentioned above.

(a) Susceptibility. Susceptibility is the premise of the effective alarm signal, and it measures whether the alarm signal is easy to be detected by the driver. To effectively study the susceptibility of different alarm signals, the susceptibility of signals under different scenarios must be considered. In this chapter, the susceptibility of signals will be evaluated using a combination of subjective and objective methods. The subjective aspect will utilize a five-point scale to evaluate the perception of signals, while the objective aspect will use the driver's response time to evaluate.

(b) Intelligibility. Intelligibility measures how easily the current alarm signal is understood by the driver, and it should be designed to minimize the cognitive resources required by the driver to recognize it. The driver's understanding of the alarm signal should be evaluated from two perspectives: whether the driver can understand the meaning of the current alarm signal and whether the current alarm signal is convenient for the driver to recognize the actual danger degree of the current situation. This chapter will evaluate the two aspects of signal intelligibility by combining subjective and objective methods, using a five-point scale to evaluate signal understanding and cognitive matching in the subjective aspect, and the error rate of the driver's response and the number of key corrections in the objective aspect.

(c) Acceptability. Acceptability measures the driver's satisfaction with the current alarm signal, which is closely related to the driver's expectation of the alarm signal, formed by long-term memory and experience with information perception, response selection and execution, and feedback. In this chapter, a five-point scale will be used to measure signal satisfaction. In addition, the balance between the degree of urgency and boredom brought by the alarm signal should be considered when designing alarm signals, as the degree of urgency and annoyance levels vary among different signals. A preliminary trial will study this aspect. These above three evaluations will be used to assess alarm signals in the simulated seeding experiment.

2.3 Experiment

According to the results of previous studies [10], in the high- criticality scenario, suitability is positively correlated with urgency, while in the low- criticality scenario, suitability is negatively correlated with annoyance. Therefore, alternative alarm signals used in the experiment are screened out. For high- criticality scenarios, as shown in Table 1, the six signals with the highest urgency among visual, auditory and tactile alarm signals are selected as alternatives for formal tests. For the medium-criticality scenario, as shown in Table 2, the six signals with the highest suitability among visual, auditory and tactile signals were selected as the alternatives for the formal test. For low- criticality scenarios, as shown in Table 3, the six signals with the lowest annoyance among visual, auditory and tactile signals are selected as alternatives for formal experiments. A total of 54 kinds of alarm signals suitable for different scenarios were selected, and the effectiveness of each alarm signal under different scenarios of tractor seeding operation was studied by using simulated seeding operation scenarios.

Table 1. Alternative alarm signals for high- criticality scenarios.

Visual signals	Auditory signals	Tactile signals
B2YCR(66.09)	TD311/50(72.09)	A311/50(67.45)
B2YSR(65.36)	TM311/50(68.91)	C311/50(65.27)
B2YCY(63.18)	TD261/50(64.55)	C261/50(61.45)
B2YSY(62.91)	TM261/50(63.36)	A261/50(60.91)
B2N(60.45)	TM311/300(61.55)	C311/300(57.82)
B1YCR(58.27)	TD311/300(60.73)	A311/300(56.64)

Note: The mean urgency of this signal is in parentheses. For visual signals, the first digit from left to right is the signal type, where F represents flicker and B represents border. The second represents the flicker frequency, with 1 representing 1 Hz and 2 representing 2 Hz. The third indicates whether there is a text prompt, Y indicates yes, N indicates no. The fourth place represents the location of the text prompt, C is near the center of the field of view, and S is near the instrument. The fifth digit represents the text color, with R representing red and Y representing yellow. For auditory signals, NS represents the tractor starting sound, VF represents the female voice, TD represents the single tone signal, TM represents the chord signal, the number before/represents the signal frequency, and the number after/represents the signal interval. For tactile signals, the letter represents the vibration position, "A" represents the hand, "C" represents the chest, "L" represents the leg, the number before/represents the signal frequency, and the number after/represents the signal interval

Table 2. Alternative alarm signals for medium- criticality scenarios.

Visual signals	Auditory signals	Tactile signals
FYYSY(58.91)	TM220/300(61.73)	A261/300(61.09)
FYYCR(56.45)	TM261/300(59.73)	A311/300(60.55)
FYYSR(55.64)	TD261/300(59.45)	A220/300(57.18)
FYYCY(55.55)	TD220/300(56.91)	L220/300(51.36)
FYN(52.64)	TM311/300(54.36)	C 261/300(50.73)
B1N(52.27)	TM311/550(53.27)	L261/300(49.45)

Note: The mean suitability of this signal is in parentheses. The symbol meaning remains unchanged

Participants and Apparatus. Fifteen male students and five female students aged 22–28 years old with an average driving experience of 1.2 years were invited to participate in a formal experiment with the purpose of simulating a planting operation. Prior to the test, every participant was informed of the test content and process, and only those who willingly participated were selected. In order to ensure the reliability of the results, the subjects were required to be in good health, without color weakness or color blindness, and with normal visual acuity or corrected visual acuity. Furthermore, they were prohibited from taking neurostimulant drugs or drinking alcohol. The test was conducted on a screen that simulated the planting operation, displayed as four meters on the screen

Table 3. Alternative alarm signals for low- criticality scenarios.

Visual signals	Auditory signals	Tactile signals
FYN(30.36)	TD220/550(36.82)	L220/550(34.82)
FRN(31.82)	NS(39.73)	A220/550(36.91)
FYYSY(34.09)	TM220/550(43.27)	L261/550(37.09)
FYYSR(35.91)	VF(43.55)	L311/550(40.55)
FRYSY(37.09)	TD261/550(43.64)	A261/550(42.36)
FYYCY(37.55)	TD220/300(46.55)	C 220/550(43.36)

Note: The mean annoyance of this signal is in parentheses. The symbol meaning remains unchanged

including the speed meter, sowing depth meter, pipe meter and engine water temperature meter from left to right, each meter has an abnormal situation set. The black cross located at the center of the screen served the purpose of attracting the subject's sight and represented the subject's field of vision center. It was placed at a consistent distance from the four meters.

Experiment Design. The experiment began with the subjects being introduced to the experiment before being asked to sit in front of a computer screen in a quiet environment. The experimenter then attached the hollow cup motor to the corresponding position of the subjects' body. During the experiment, the subjects carried out the lane keeping task, using the left and right keys on the keyboard while monitoring four instruments simultaneously. If an instrument became abnormal, a randomly triggered alarm signal required the subjects to respond by pressing the corresponding keys. Upon responding correctly, the scoring interface appeared on the screen, and the subject was required to answer four questions using the five-point scale. These questions measured the cognitive matching degree of the alarm signal, understanding of the alarm signal, susceptibility to the alarm signal and acceptability of the alarm signal. The program automatically recorded the scores of each alarm signal, response time, response accuracy rate, and the number of keystroke corrections during the test. There were a total of 7 groups of tests, with each subject completing 6 groups containing different alarm signals, one control group without alarm signals and each test lasting 8 min on average (excluding rating time). Table 4 shows the evaluation system used in the test, including 9 kinds of alarm signals in high, medium and low criticality scenarios, with each group containing different alarm signals without repetition.

Data Analysis. In order to explore the effectiveness of alarm signals in different sensing channels, one-way ANOVA was performed for the response error rate, response time, and number of keystroke corrections of all alarm signals respectively. Through the analysis, vision, hearing, and touch alarm response error rate showed significant differences ($F(10.400, 187.199) = 2.313$, $p = 0.013$). Nevertheless, the results of multiple comparisons indicated that there was no significant difference in the response error rate among different alarms. Additionally, the results showed that there were significant differences

Table 4. Evaluation system of alarm signals.

Evaluation methodology	Evaluation category	Evaluation index	Description
Objective	Susceptibility	Response time	The time from when the alarm signal appears to when the correct key is pressed
	Intelligibility	Error rate	The ratio of incorrect key presses to the total number of exceptions
		Number of key corrections	The number of times the alarm signal is triggered before the correct button is pressed
Subjective	Susceptibility	Perception	Answer the question "Can I detect warning signs quickly?" using a five-point scale
	Intelligibility	Understanding degree	Answer the question " Do I know which instrument the current warning signal is indicating?" using a five-point scale
		Cognitive matching degree	Answer the question "Do alarm signals help me correctly understand the danger level of the current abnormal situation?" using a five-point scale
		Satisfaction	Answer the question "Am I willing to use the current alert signal to indicate the current abnormal situation in the future" using a five-point scale

in the response time of various alerts, with vision, hearing, and touch alarms showing significant differences ($F(7.679, 138.226) = 4.220$, $p < 0.0001$). Figure 1 presents the response time of each alarm, showing that the response time of the visual signal was basically the shortest, the response time of the auditory signal was basically the second, and the response time of the tactile signal was basically the longest. Through the analysis, vision, hearing, and touch alarm button correct frequency showed significant differences ($F(7.264, 130.747) = 2.269$, $p = 0.031$), but the results of multiple comparisons showed that there was no significant difference in the frequency of keystroke correction among different alarms. Thus, despite the fact that during the experiment, subjects were required to respond quickly and accurately to alarm signals in different criticality scenarios, the analysis of objective indicators does not need to be grouped according to different situational criticality.

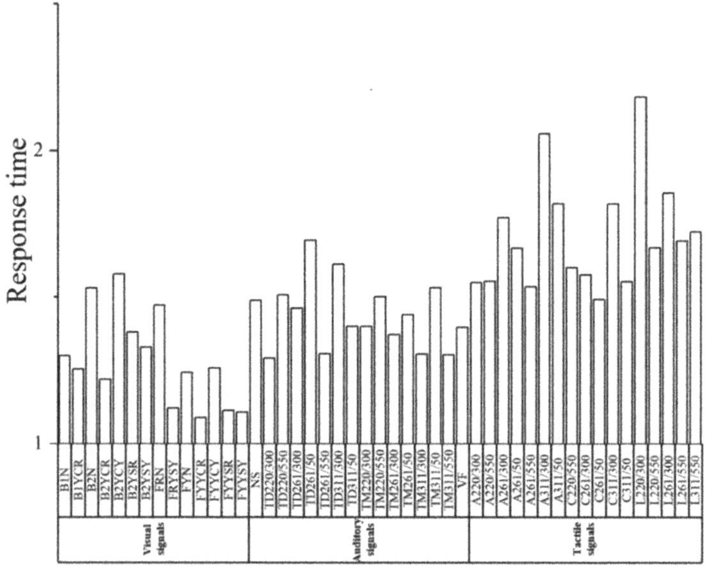

Fig. 1. Response time of alarm signals.

Factor analysis was used to reduce the dimension of different indicators for comprehensively evaluating the effectiveness of each alarm signal under different criticality scenarios.

Each indicator can be represented as the sum of a linear function of common factors and special factors. The five subjective and objective evaluation indices for each alarm signal are: perception, understanding, cognitive matching degrees, satisfaction, and response time. The subjective evaluation indices have a positive correlation with effectiveness, whereas the response time has a negative correlation. Therefore, the objective indicator data needs to be processed forward first by taking the reciprocal of the response time.

A total of 54 signal factor analyses were conducted for 5 kinds of indexes in each key degree scenario. The KMO value being greater than 0.5 and the Bartlett sphericity test showing a correlation between variables confirmed that the data is suitable for factor analysis. The first two common factors, Factor1 and Factor2, were extracted from the principal component results and had eigenvalues of 2.600 and 1.786, respectively, both greater than 1. They explained 51.999% and 35.727% of the variance of total data, respectively, and 87.726% in total. The comprehensive scores of each signal in different criticality situations were obtained based on the variance interpretation rate and scores of each factor. The effectiveness of the alarm signal increases with a higher score, as shown in Figs. 2, 3 and 4.

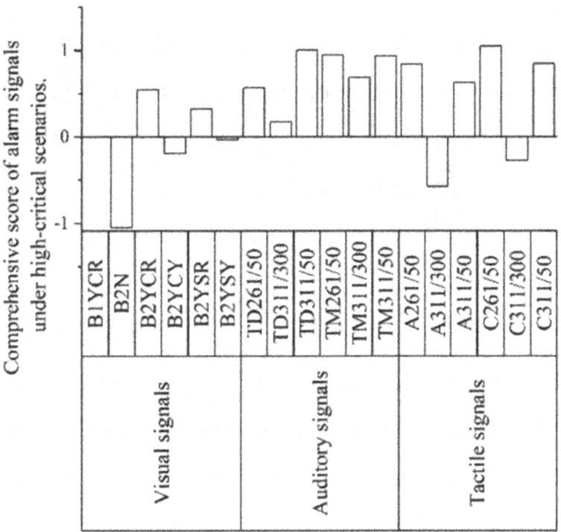

Fig. 2. Comprehensive score of alarm signals under high- criticality scenarios.

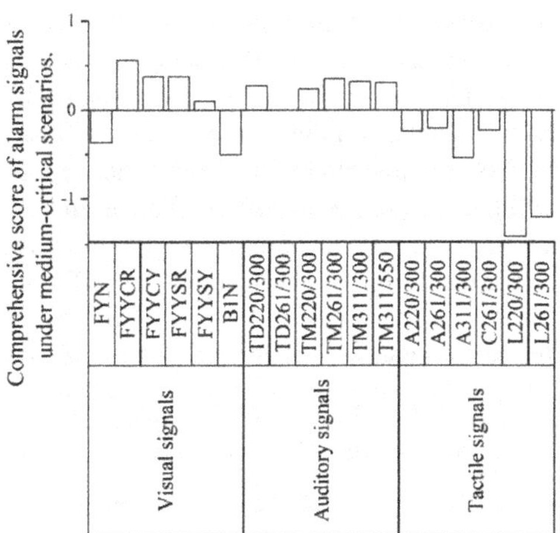

Fig. 3. Comprehensive score of alarm signals under medium- criticality scenarios.

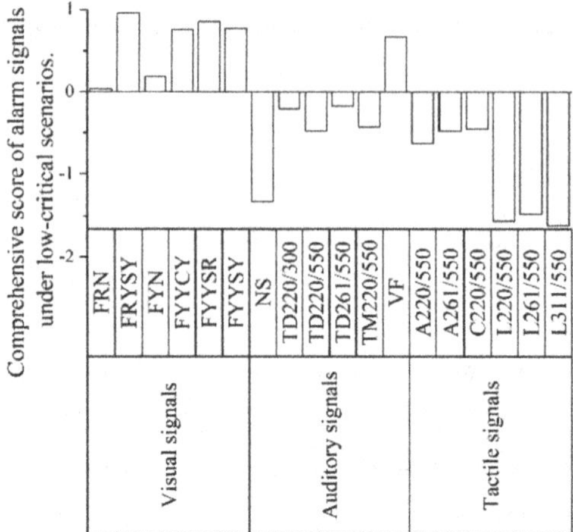

Fig. 4. Comprehensive score of alarm signals under low- criticality scenarios.

3 Conclusion

According to the evaluation system, the formal test reduces 7 indicators to 5 and mainly studies the effectiveness of multiple single alarm signals. The signals are designed based on different perceptual channels under different criticality scenarios. The comprehensive scores of various alarm signals are obtained under different criticality scenarios. The experimental results show that most of the auditory signals, such as chord signals and small interval monophonic signals, and the tactile signals with small interval are more effective in high-criticality scenarios. Under medium-criticality scenarios, auditory signals and visual signals with text prompts are more effective. In low-criticality scenarios, visual signals and clear speech signals are deemed highly effective. These results offer a theoretical foundation for the design of alarm signals in different criticality scenarios.

Acknowledgements. The authors are particularly grateful to all participants in the study. This work was funded by the Special funds for high-level teachers in Beijing Institute of Fashion Technology, with support from Beijing Institute of Fashion Technology, under Grant BIFTXJ202212.

References

1. Lundqvist, L.M., Eriksson, L.: Age, cognitive load, and multimodal effects on driver response to directional warning. Appl. Ergon. **76**, 147–154 (2019)
2. Meng, F., Spence, C.: Tactile warning signals for in-vehicle systems. Accid. Anal. Prev. **75**, 333–346 (2015)
3. Bazilinskyy, P., Petermeijer, S.M., Petrovych, V., Dodou, D., de Winter, J.C.: Take-over requests in highly automated driving: a crowdsourcing survey on auditory, vibrotactile, and visual displays. Transport. Res. F: Traffic Psychol. Behav. **56**, 82–98 (2018)
4. Maag, C., Schneider, N., Lübbeke, T., Weisswange, T.H., Goerick, C.: Car Gestures-Advisory warning using additional steering wheel angles. Accid. Anal. Prev. **83**, 143–153 (2015)

5. Hollands, J.G., Spivak, T., Kramkowski, E.W.: Cognitive load and situation awareness for soldiers: effects of message presentation rate and sensory modality. Hum. Factors **61**(5), 763–773 (2019)
6. Chi, C.F., Dewi, R.S., Surbakti, Y.Y., Hsieh, D.Y.: The perceived quality of in-vehicle auditory signals: a structural equation modelling approach. Ergonomics **60**(11), 1471–1484 (2017)
7. Yan, X., Zhang, Y., Ma, L.: The influence of in-vehicle speech warning timing on drivers' collision avoidance performance at signalized intersections. Transp. Res. Part C: Emerging Technol. **51**, 231–242 (2015)
8. Murata, A., Kuroda, T.: Effects of auditory and tactile warning on drivers' response to hazard under noisy environment. In: Harris, D. (ed.) EPCE 2015. LNCS (LNAI), vol. 9174, pp. 45–53. Springer, Cham (2015). https://doi.org/10.1007/978-3-319-20373-7_5
9. Endsley, M.R.: Toward a theory of situation awareness in dynamic systems. Hum. Factors **37**(1), 32–64 (1995)
10. Pei, Y.: Research on Tractor Human-machine Interface Design and Evaluation Method Based on Cognitive Characteristics. Ph.D. Dissertation, China agricultural university (2020)

Evaluating the Effectiveness of Graph and Timeline-Based Visualizations for Search Engine Results: A Comparative Study

Shahiq Qureshi(✉) and Kerstin Haring

University of Denver, Denver, CO 80208, USA
{shahiq.qureshi,kerstin.haring}@du.edu

Abstract. As the volume of information on the internet continues to expand, search engines play a crucial role in helping users navigate this vast data landscape. While traditional list-based search results enable users to find information efficiently, they often require manual exploration to discover meaningful connections between results. The focus of this research lies in addressing this limitation by proposing and evaluating a prototype that leverages graph-based and timeline-based visualization techniques to highlight temporal and semantic relationships within search results. These visualization methods can potentially enhance user experience and comprehension by minimizing the manual effort required to explore such relationships. Despite the promising potential of combining these two techniques, limited research has been conducted to measure their effectiveness compared to traditional search engine result displays. This research intends to bridge this gap by outlining a comparative study using a prototype that encapsulates the idea of presenting search engine results in these visualizations. The main focus of this work is to present and describe a prototype and shape the background necessary to understand how these visualization techniques can improve search engine design, promote efficient knowledge discovery, and ultimately enhance the user experience.

Keywords: Information Visualization · Search Engine Results · Graphs based Visualizations · Temporal and Semantic Relations

1 Introduction

Search engines are a powerful tool and a part of our daily lives when searching for information. A user enters particular keywords or general ideas as a text prompt on a search engine and is provided with an abundance of information from various sources [13]. It is estimated that what users currently refer to as "the internet" contains around 120 zettabytes in 2023 where A zetabyte is about a trillion gigabytes, an increase of 23 zetabytes from 2022. This accounts to roughly

H. Mori et al. (Eds.): HCII 2023, LNCS 14056, pp. 162–180, 2023.
https://doi.org/10.1007/978-3-031-48044-7_12

328.77 million terabytes of new data are created each day, where around half of that data is videos hosted in over 2700 data centers in the US alone [6]. This data is found on the estimated 6 billion pages (2019). Search Engines enable users to quickly and easily find information of real interest or value without looking at irrelevant web pages, making it easier for users to find the information they are looking for. One of the most used search engines is Google [5]. Using their search engine and their representation of search results as an example, search results are presented as a list containing text with hyperlink to the source, and a panel of information next to the search results titled "About" (see Fig. 1). The panel contains information that is considered most relevant to the text prompt the user entered and Google calls it an *Knowledge graph panel.* This Knowledge graph panel is a representation of various data that comes from a Knowledge Graph [23]. A knowledge graph is a semantic network that represents real-world pieces of information and illustrates the relationship between them. This information is stored in a graph database and visualized as a graph structure that provides various information about a topic in a glance without needing to jump to several sources [7].

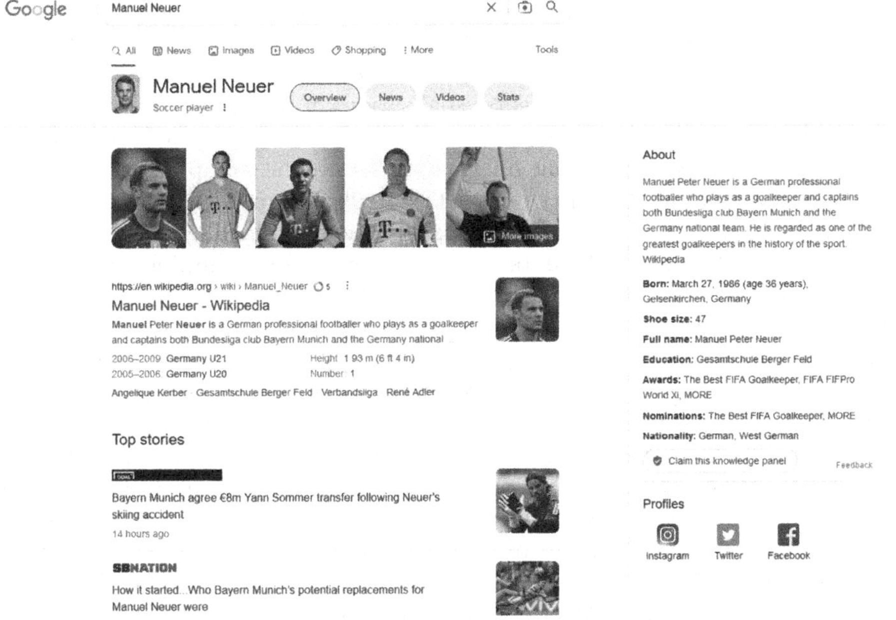

Fig. 1. Screenshot of the user interface using the search engine google and the results it displays when entering a text-based search prompt for "Manuel Neuer". The figure shows the results as obtained on January 18th, 2023.

While highly effective in retrieving information from web pages and displaying that information very similar as shown in Fig. 1, the interfaces in general do not highlight associations between results. So, even if a relation exists between two list-like entries, they are presented as distinct entries with a different information source. Displaying search results as a list is the most common format for search results. There have been some search engines that showed screen shots or interconnected circles, however it seems that for most searches this format is not generally accepted by users [3,16]. It also stands to reason that large companies experimented with different formats but have not yet identified as format that shows significant improvements in user satisfaction and search effectiveness over the most common list-based format of search results [9,24].

Nevertheless, what is missing in how search engine interfaces display information is how the available information links together, as "bigger picture". For example, news articles that cover a story related to a subject, content posted by that subject (i.e., person, entity), and their subsequent reactions on social media are currently not available as a interconnected visualization to the user. While the information itself, the articles or social media posts on the subject are provided as distinct hyperlink, there is no visualization of a connection between them to identify and create a timeline of events, especially when establishing an evolving story [22]. It is left up to the user to browse (i.e., click the provides hyperlinks of a search) different results and platforms to understand the timeline of events themselves. If a timeline is the desired purpose of a user's search, this imposes a higher cognitive load and burden on the user. This work seeks to reduce this cognitive load on the user and explore graph-based timeline visualizations as addition to current visualizations of search results.

Graphs are very common, flexible, and effective visualizers of information. They are effective in organizing information to present complex relationships and highlight patterns within the data [11,14,19]. This paper proposes to measure the effectiveness of graph based visualizations to highlight the temporal and semantic relations in the data that makes up the information from search engine results. We envision two main forms of visualizations: (1) a timeline view that displays information in a chronological order, and (2) a graph-based view that highlights the semantic relation between the search results. This representation of search results uses edges between search results to show relationships and intends to introduce clearly labeled timestamps and ordering to show the chronology of events. We postulate that this graph-based interface eases the burden on a user significantly and is more effective for establishing timelines than to go through the distinct information presented in a list iteratively to establish interconnections. We expect this to be feasible and effective as it preserves some of the structure of current search engine interfaces, showing results (or nodes) similarly to text-based results from search engines. We created a prototype of this visualization to evaluate the effectiveness and to solicit user satisfaction feedback from online participants.

2 Related Work

There is ample evidence that clustering and exploring search results using timeline constructions is highly beneficial for users [1]. One study visualized search engine results as a timeline by using the temporal information associated with each document, with 80% of the participants in their study finding timelines to be a useful tool for daily search activities. However, this representation merely clusters results based on temporal proximity, without considering underlying semantic relationships.

Further innovation in visualizing search engine data was presented by a recent study which replaced the traditional block of text results with an interactive, force-directed graph, incorporating both temporal and semantic information. This visual search representation utilized a dynamic, inertial graph to encode search results as nodes, incorporating elements like color, size, and opacity to represent attributes such as relevance to the query, themes, and publication date. This model notably enhanced user interaction by allowing detailed exploration of each result, while maintaining a static view of the overall search landscape, thus reducing the need to scroll and retrieve unseen results [14]. However, as this approach is still in the early stages, it necessitates further validation and theoretical backing. Despite the need for additional testing, this system's potential in overcoming navigational challenges posed by current text-heavy search methods is promising.

CubanSea proposes a new approach for representing web search results that addresses the limitations of the traditional list-based approach where the order of the documents implies their relevance as determined by the search engine. The new approach uses fuzzy clustering techniques and visual representations to provide additional information to help users when the traditional ranked order of search results is not sufficient. The research is guided by Shneiderman's "overview first, zoom and filter, then details on demand" principle [20]. The visual representation of results provides an overview of the search results space, then allows users to zoom in on clusters that appear relevant to their information seeking goals, and filter the search results using a search field. The system also allows the users to expand and view the details of the search results on demand. The goal is to first present an overview of the search results space, focus on a subset from that space that is relevant, and then access the details of potentially relevant documents as needed. The visualization model used to encode the clusters uses opponent process theory of color to highlight each cluster with lighter shades. Additionally, the top 20 results of each cluster are provided to aid in topic recognition. This approach helps when the queries are "ill-defined, vague, or ambiguous", but give a very mechanical drill down feeling [21].

InfraNodus is an open-source tool for text network analysis that can be used to enhance visual representation of ideas, their consequent analysis, and to generate insight. It uses graph theory instead of probability distribution to identify the related words and assign them into topical clusters. The search results are visualized as an interactive graph that highlights the parts of the text having most relevance to the searched topic. Each node in the graph highlights this specific part of text to which a user can select and be taken directly to that document. As mentioned in their paper, researchers, students, and content writers are using their system to identify structural gaps and generate new ideas [15].

Hearst's "Search User Interfaces" book discusses several innovative visualization approaches for search interfaces [9], including TileBars, a visualization method that displays search results as a series of colored bars, allowing users to quickly identify documents that contain multiple query terms in close proximity [8], and Cat-a-Cone which is an interactive interface for categorizing and visualizing search results, using a conical layout to hierarchically arrange and navigate through categories of information [10]. However, these methods do not explicitly highlight temporal and semantic relationships, and can struggle to present large amounts of information in an easily digestible format.

Addressing these gaps, this paper proposes graph-based timeline visualizations to highlight temporal and semantic relations between search engine results. Our approach aims to keep the visualizations as simple as possible, using only necessary elements like simple undirected graphs and nodes that preserve the structure of traditional search engine results, thereby making it easy to adopt and extend the concept. Evaluations of the design through online surveys help establish user perception and the validity of this concept, in comparison with traditional search interfaces like Google's. By focusing on the chronology and interrelation of events, we believe our visualizations can significantly enhance the user experience in information seeking.

3 Graph Based Visualizations

Different visualizations have their own distinct capacity to represent information, highlighting different kinds of relationships in the data [2]. Traditional search engines are designed to be very generic and represent results in a simple manner, typically as a list of results ordered according to some ranking algorithm. This intentional simplicity is to cater to a wide range of audience having a diverse set of queries [13]. Since search results can have information that is very multi-dimensional it would be hard for current search engines to use visualizations that highlight specific relations which will essentially make it harder if not impossible to find other relations, thus a redefinition of the current paradigm would significantly disrupt user experiences [18].

Therefore, an independent platform which emphasizes visualizing the temporal and semantic aspects of information seems like a more pragmatic approach. This solution can supplement current search engines without disturbing their core functionalities. For this purpose, we introduce two distinct visualizations: 1. *The Timeline view* and 2. *The Graph view*. Each visualization offers unique advantages and are explained in detail in the following subsections.

3.1 Timeline View

The Timeline View, as its name suggests, is designed to represent search results chronologically, creating a visual narrative of events that evolves over time. Organized as a vertical list, this view presents the most recent events first, allowing users to track the development of a story, subject, or theme from the latest developments back to its inception. This unique approach provides an effective way to spotlight significant events, drawing users' attention to key points in the timeline.

Figure 2a illustrates the concept of the timeline view. Here, the search results unfold in a downward sequence, appearing in left-and-right alternating event boxes aligned on a central timeline axis. Each of these event boxes serves as a compact summary of a particular result, featuring a hyperlink title that connects to the original source.

The inside of the event box hosts a brief extract from the content and could also include other elements such as thumbnails, previews, or tags, providing a rich, at-a-glance understanding of the content. The specific arrangement of information within the box is depicted in Fig. 2b. This approach to visualizing data encourages users to engage with the flow of events and better understand the sequence and interplay of occurrences related to their search query.

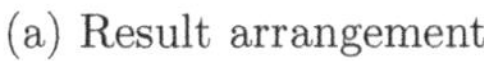

(a) Result arrangement

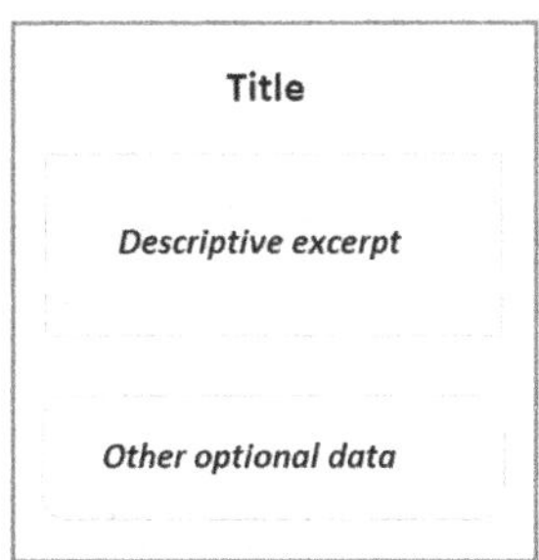

(b) Structure of a result

Fig. 2. Abstract structure of the timeline view describing how data is organized and its contents

3.2 Graph View

For highlighting relationship between results, the graph view is proposed. This visualization maps search results into a graph-like structure, wherein each result (vertex), is connected to others by links (edges). Refer to Fig. 3 for an illustrative example of this configuration. Each vertex in the graph is guaranteed to have at least one link to another, indicating a relation of some kind. These relations can span a range of associations, from semantic similarities and thematic overlap, to explicit responses or continuations. Each vertex in this network can be expanded to reveal additional related results, emphasizing the interconnected nature of information. To demonstrate a potential connection, consider the following example: a company announces a new TV series. One result might be the official announcement from the company's website. This could be linked to another result - a tweet from a cast member sharing their excitement about the new show. Following this chain of information, you might find another result connected to this tweet, like a blog post where fans express their reactions to the cast member's statement. All these results - the announcement, the tweet, and the blog post - are linked together on the graph, showing you how one piece of news can ripple out and generate various responses across different platforms.

The nature of the graph is undirected, which signifies the mutual relevance between the connected vertices. The initial central node does not necessarily represent the search term but the most relevant result which is constantly replaced with the node in focus. The primary purpose here is not to revolve around a central theme or keyword but to illustrate that all the results bear some relevance to each other, forming an intricate web of interconnected information. This is to enable not just finding individual pieces of information, but also about seeing the broader picture - how different facts, ideas, or events are interlinked and influence each other. This aids in the comprehension of interconnected information and the discovery of new, unexpected connections.

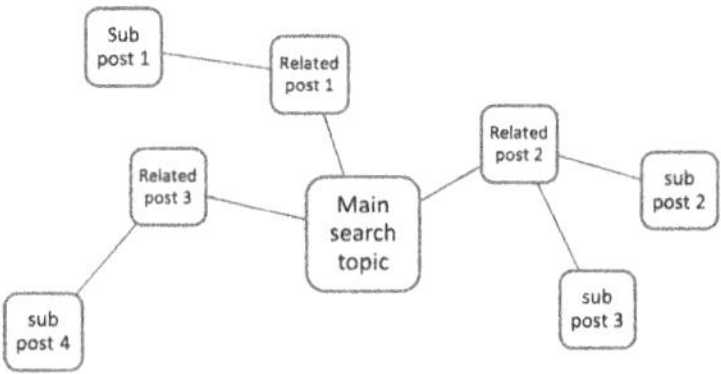

Fig. 3. Abstract representation of the Graph view presenting results displayed in the form of a graph to highlight similarity

4 Visualization Concept Evaluation

To evaluate the visualization concepts, online surveys were conducted to see user perception. A total of 50 responses were recorded. Participants were given a brief explanation about the concept of each visualization and were shown a wireframe designed in *Adobe XD* (as shown in Fig. 4). It shows results for the query "Imran Khan", visualized in both a timeline and graph view. After going through it, participants are then asked questions pertaining the overall concept, ease of use, and comparison to services like Google. Following are some of the metrics that were asked to evaluate the validity of the visualizations.

4.1 User Perception of Design Purposes

After going through the wireframe, the participants were asked to choose out of the 4 main reasons of what they thought to be the purpose of visualizing results in such a manner. The reasons are display events regarding a subject in a chronological order, visualize context between related posts, act as a search

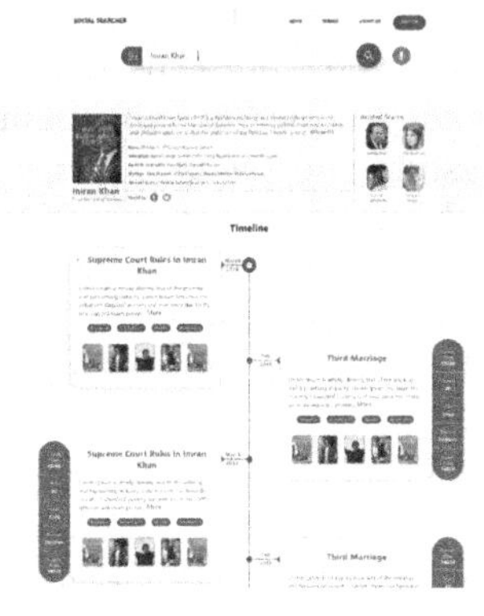

(a) Timeline wireframe

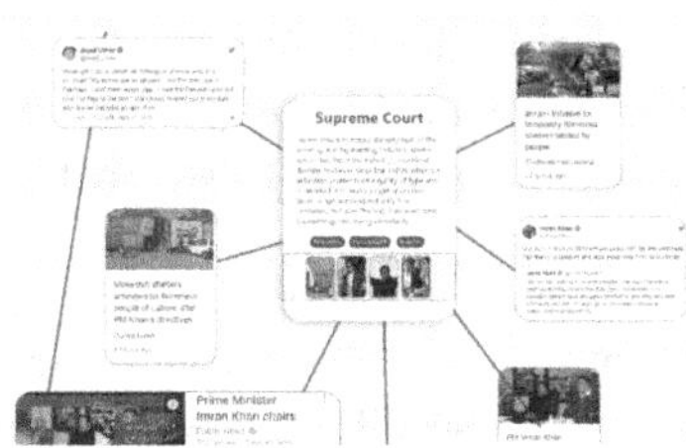

(b) Graph view wireframe

Fig. 4. Wireframes showcasing results displayed in the two forms of visualizations for the search query "Imran Khan"

Table 1. Percentage of Users who identified the following as the primary use or purpose of the design

Purpose	Response
Display events regarding a subject in a chronological order	83.61%
Visualize context between related posts	83.61%
Act as a search engine for different social media platforms	37.7%
Learn facts about a subject of interest	83.61%
Other(s)	0%

engine for different social media platforms, learn facts about a subject of interest, or any other self described reason. Table 1 shows that majority of the participants agreed with the fact that it was mainly to visualize results in a timeline and highlight relations. Interestingly they also found it to be a source of learning new facts about a subject. A minority was of the opinion that it was a search engine specific to social media platforms.

4.2 Pagination and Number of Results

Table 2. Sufficiency for the number of results in the visualizations

Visualization	Needs more results	Results were sufficient	Interface was cluttered
Timeline view	35%	61%	4%
Graph view	16%	57%	27%

Table 2 represents the results from 50 participants (recruited via M-Turk) on the number of results in each view. We see that about 60% of the users found the number of posts to be sufficient. However, this is not an overwhelming number as reviews regarding timeline view needing more results and the graph view being cluttered were recorded. The study was approved by the University of Denver's Institutional review board no participant was excluded from the analysis. Of the 50 participants in the study, there was no demographic information (age, gender, nationality etc.) was collected as it does not hold any significant meaning for the analysis.

Search engines generally have about 7–10 results per page [12] or in a single view before a user needs to move on to another page or the platform loads more like an infinite scroll [4]. The timeline view is also of that nature, having results in an infinite scroll fashion or until the inception of an event is reached. The placement of the result nodes also matters as some participants in the survey said that view was too sparse. An estimated of 4–7 results can be grouped in a single screen view before users needs to scroll down.

For graph view, the survey results how that some participants considered it to be cluttered. A good number of results for this view would be for a result or node to be placed in the center and it has around at most 7 sub nodes or results connected to. This is to reference to the fact that many psychology experiments have shown that our short-term memory can hold only a limited number of separate items. The average is about 7 items, plus or minus 2, varying from each individual [17]. To view more results in this view, a user can click on a node which will then become the central node and have results relevant to it loaded. The new results will still have the previous node that was it came from as part of the cluster which allows to back track to the previous results. This mechanism replicates the functionality of going back and forth in pages. There is no limit to how far a user can go, and is only limited to the amount of results available.

4.3 Relation to Search Engines

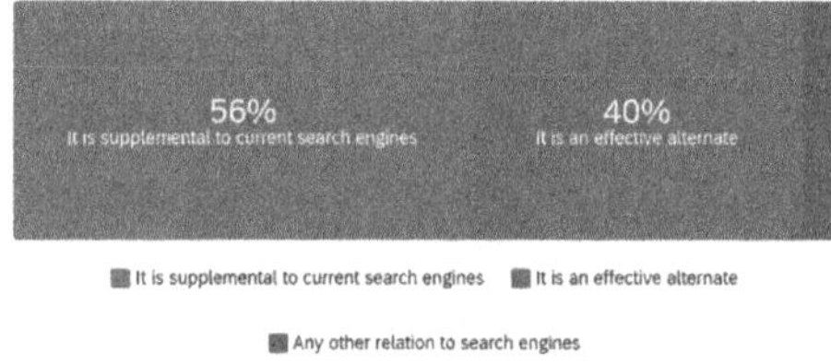

Fig. 5. Chart showing the distribution of users on how they perceive these designs in relation to search engines

Figure 5 shows that out of 50 respondents, a majority of 56% considered it to be a supplement to current search engines rather than an alternate. A minority of 4% said its too early to describe a relation but considered it a supplement as well. The remaining 40% found it to be an alternative and would consider using this as their main search engine. Considering that these visualizations are intended to be used in a new platform which is aimed at being a supplement to enhance searching capabilities, this is a reasonable outcome that can be shaped overtime.

4.4 Identification of Features

Table 3. Table showing results of whether users were able to find the five main features

Feature	Yes, I found it	Didn't notice it	No, I couldn't find it
1	85%	15%	0%
2	46%	52%	2%
3	80%	20%	0%
4	89%	11%	0%
5	79%	20%	2%

A list of features essential to conceptualizing the visualizations. They are as follows:

- Feature 1: "Search bar" for querying search information
- Feature 2: "Metadata" for certain results such as likes, shares etc.
- Feature 3: "Date" or the timestamp of a result on timeline view
- Feature 4: "Links" indicating a relation between two results in graph view
- Feature 5: "Information panel" about the search term, similar to Google's Knowledge graph panel

Table 3 shows the percentage of how many participants were able to identify them given the fact that they had no prior knowledge of how it looked like. From the results we can see that participants were able to find or understand what they meant about 80% of time with the exception of the metadata. In another question, where participants were asked on how useful they found the metadata to be, around 56% of participants did not find it to be useful. This finding tells us that meta information about a result such as sentiments, shares, likes etc. is something that users don't usually care about at first and would rather have it be revealed as an additional detail after specifically asking for it. Overall, participants were able to identify the main features in a convincing way.

5 Prototype Testing

To evaluate the effectiveness of our proposed graph-based visualizations, we developed a prototype that encapsulates our idea of representing search engine results. It was designed to mirror concepts discussed in Sect. 3 to enable a realistic representation of how information would look if visualized in our proposed framework. The prototype layout was structured to adhere to the wireframe design as seen in Fig. 4. Users upon arrival on the landing page, are presented with the knowledge graph information panel along with the timeline view. The graph view is given it's own space separately as it requires more space and allows users to engage in a more exploratory experience. For navigation, a toggle button is incorporated at the right between the information panel and the timeline view, which allows users to switch between the timeline and graph views.

To ensure consistency during the experiment, the search result pages used in the study were offline copies and saved beforehand. This was done to eliminate possible variability in search results due to Google's dynamic search algorithm and personalized results. Similarly, the data in the prototype was not live, but taken from the same Google results and manually embedded. This controlled setup ensured that all participants interacted with the same set of data across all tasks.

5.1 Methodology

To assess the user experience and effectiveness of our visualizations in comparison with list-based result representations by traditional search engines, specifically Google. The evaluation was conducted as an online survey through a series of structured tasks, questionnaire, and open ended feedback, considering the potential learning effect, and by measuring interaction metrics.

Task Structure. The experiment included three tasks, each designed around the theme of finding specific information regarding a person, an event, and a related object. Participants were asked to search for this information using both Google and our prototype. The completion of each task was triggered when the participant successfully located and clicked on the relevant information. The information for each task was distributed among the three main information visualization components namely the Knowledge Graph panel, the Timeline view and the Graph view to demonstrate to participants and evaluate each visualization's capabilities. Following is the description of the tasks:

- In Task 1, participants had to find the city where Queen Elizabeth II was born on Google. On the prototype, the task was to find out who her spouse is. Both pieces of information could be found in the Knowledge Graph panel of both platforms.
- For Task 2, participants were tasked to discover the transition period of Brexit on Google. On the prototype, the task was to identify when the UK and EU

extended Brexit talks. The information was available in the timeline view of the prototype and in the Wikipedia page for Google.
- In Task 3, the goal was to find the celebrity that Anthony Hopkins met in Florence on Google. On the prototype, the task was to look up Hopkins' reaction to his casting in the drama 'Those About to Die'. The required information was present in the graph view of the prototype and in the form of a tweet in Google's search results.

Survey Questions. Following the completion of the tasks, participants were asked to respond to a nine-question survey. The survey was designed to gather participants' thoughts on the interface after using it alongside Google. Questions ranged from rating the timeline and graph views on a scale of 1 to 5, descriptive queries on their potential usage of the system and their experiences navigating it. Open feedback was particularly focused on elements that participants found tricky, hard to use, or less appealing.

Accounting for Learning Effect. The learning effect refers to the phenomenon where repeated exposure to a task or information can make subsequent interactions easier and faster due to the acquired familiarity. In this experiment, the learning effect could occur if the participants were tasked to find the same information on both platforms. To account for this, tasks were designed such that the information to find on platform differed slightly while remaining within the same context. For instance, there is a task revolving around Queen Elizabeth, where participants were asked to find the Queen's birth city on Google, while on the prototype, they had to identify her spouse.

Measured Metrics. Two primary metrics were recorded during the experiment: time and number of clicks. Time was measured from the moment the participant landed on the page until they completed the task by locating and clicking on the required information. The number of clicks, were recorded to track the navigation efforts required by the participant. However, clicks were only counted when a participant navigated clicked on a result hyperlink. These metrics were chosen to provide insights into the efficiency of the prototype as compared to Google, specifically in terms of redirection needs and their impact on search time.

6 Results

6.1 Statistical Analysis

The experiment was conducted on a total of 25 participants. During data analysis, it was observed that the data distribution was not normal, and not all tasks were completed by every participant, leading to differences in sample sizes for some tasks. The maximum difference observed in the sample sizes of at task

Table 4. Mann-Whitney U test results for number of clicks and time taken

Task	p-value (Clicks)	p-value (Time)
1	0.9509	0.01058
2	0.3027	0.0202
3	0.1487	0.007184

was five. Despite the slight imbalance, the decision was taken to proceed with the given dataset, and not reduce responses, as the overall sample size was relatively small. To analyze the non-normally distributed data, the Mann-Whitney U test was chosen, a nonparametric statistical significance test for determining whether two independent samples were drawn from a population with the same distribution.

The Mann-Whitney U test results for the number of clicks and the time taken across three tasks are summarized in Table 4. For all tasks, the p-values for the number of clicks exceed the threshold of 0.05, implying no significant difference between the use of Google and the prototype. However, a contrasting scenario arises when observing the time taken to complete the tasks. Each of these p-values is below 0.05, pointing to a significant distinction between the time duration on Google and the prototype. The interpretation of these outcomes suggests that while the number of clicks required to accomplish each task was comparable across both platforms, the time efficiency to locate the required information exhibited noteworthy variation.

To further explore the relation, the results were visualized as box plots, as seen in Fig. 6, for both the time taken and the number of clicks across each task on both Google and the prototype. The following discussion elaborates on the insights obtained from these plots.

Figure 6a, shows that our prototype typically requires equal or fewer clicks than Google, particularly noticeable in Task 2, where Google demonstrates greater variability in clicks needed. The prototype, while sometimes requiring more clicks, shows consistent values suggesting users may find information more readily. However, the Mann-Whitney U test revealed no significant statistical relation, indicating the need for more samples.

Figure 6b, presents the comparison of task completion time between the interfaces. For Tasks 1 and 2, our prototype outperforms Google, but the trend reverses for Task 3, possibly due to the Graph view being a separate page where the task's information resided. Low variability in the prototype's completion time contrasts with Google's high variability, pointing towards the prototype's efficiency. However, Task 3's high time with the prototype might be attributed to the initial time spent on exploring the Knowledge panel and Timeline first. The presence of a statistically significant relation between completion time from the Mann-Whitney U test supports our prototype's overall time efficiency. Outliers were left included as potential indicators of factors beyond time and number of clicks, requiring for further participant testing and controlled measures.

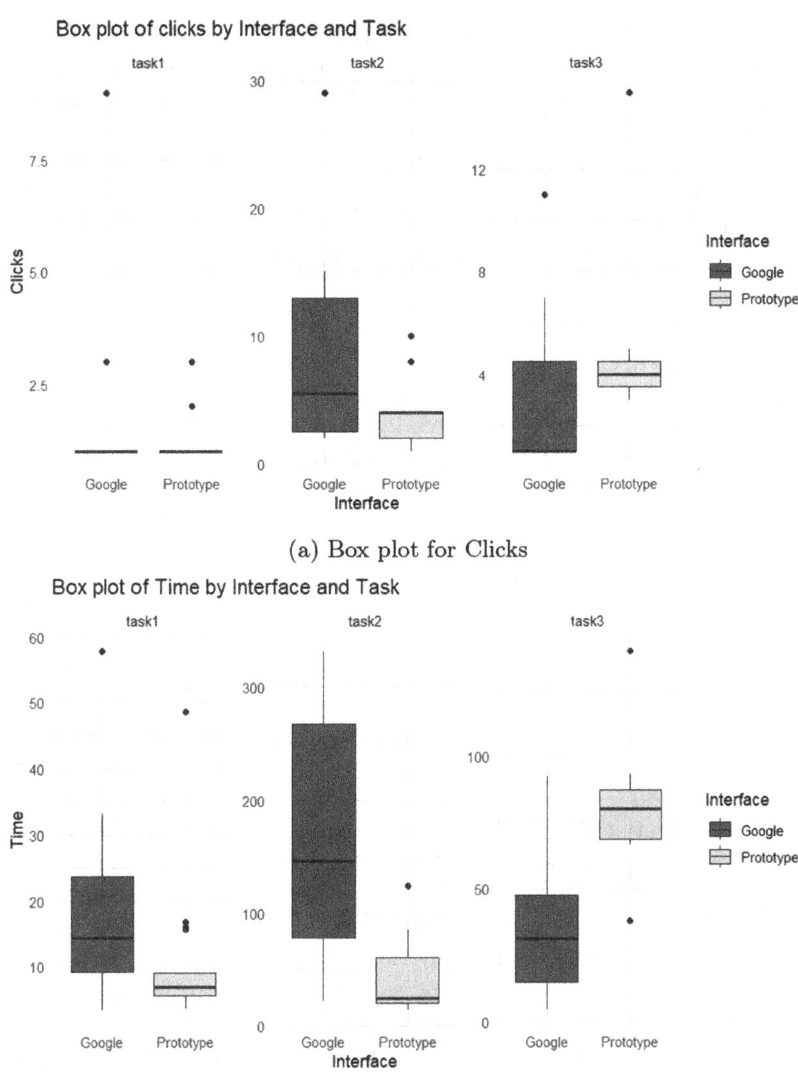

(a) Box plot for Clicks

(b) Box plot for Time

Fig. 6. Comparison of Task Completion Metrics Across Interfaces

Participants were also able to mention if they were unable to complete a task. In Task 1, a notable difference was observed with 8 participants unable to complete the task on Google, as opposed to only 2 on our prototype. For Task 2, which revolved around an event, we noted that the task completion rate was lower on both platforms, but markedly more participants (14) struggled with Google compared to our prototype (7). This might be indicative of the complex nature of finding such information on traditional search interfaces and the potentially enhanced comprehensibility of the timeline view of our prototype. The third task, relating to finding a related object, presented similar challenges on both platforms, with 10 participants unable to find the requested information on both interfaces. This could be attributed to the unfamiliarity of the participants with the graph view, or the need to navigate through different information pieces to arrive at the answer. These observations, alongside our quantitative analysis from the box plots, underpin the necessity of continued user testing and prototype refinement, while simultaneously highlighting the potential merits of our visualization approach.

6.2 Survey Results

The post-task survey aimed to collect participant experience after using the prototype and its features. The responses were gathered on a scale of 1–5 where 1 indicated difficulty or dissatisfaction, and 5 signaled ease or satisfaction. Here's a concise breakdown of the responses:

- Approximately 76% of participants found learning and adapting to the visualizations in the new design and its features fairly easy, giving a score of 3 or above.
- For the Timeline view's effectiveness in illustrating chronological events, a majority (92%) found it somewhat useful to very effective. This shows it was very much successful in its goal at highlighting chronology of events.
- In terms of the Graph view's efficiency in portraying relationships between search results, 80% found it somewhat useful or highly effective. This highlighted its potential in visualizing relationships between search results
- A mixed response was seen regarding the usage of a search engine incorporating these visualization techniques for regular internet searches, with no consensus leaning strongly towards either end.
- Repeating the same question from the preliminary survey, and still most participants (60%) see the prototype as a supplement to their current search engines rather than an outright replacement.
- Lastly, the overall experience with the prototype was generally positive, with approximately 84% of participants rating their experience as good or excellent (4 or 5 on the scale).

6.3 User Feedback

Participants were asked to describe potential use cases for our prototype and to identify any aspects they found challenging or areas they believe could be improved.

For the first question, participants provided varied responses with some finding potential in the prototype for conducting specific searches and understanding chronologically ordered events. One participant noted that the interface would be particularly useful when looking for information that cannot be easily located within a large text body like a Wikipedia article. Another participant appreciated the prominence of the info panel and the reduced clutter compared to standard search results. The timeline view received positive feedback, with participants noting its usefulness in tracking events over time. Some participants liked the feeling of using the graph view which facilitated an exploratory search experience rather than a targeted search.

On the question about the interface's confusing aspects or potential areas for improvement, there were some interesting responses. One participants said the interface felt "bare bones" and could use more content. Some found the graph view and timeline tricky to navigate, suggesting the inclusion of usage instructions could be beneficial. Notably, participants also expressed concerns about the interface's sparse design, saying it could use more content, but not as much as Google or Bing. This point highlighted the shortcomings of current search engines designs and an argument for the usefulness of our proposed designs. The potential delay due to the loading of transition effects in the timeline and graph view was also mentioned. Overall, these responses indicate areas where further design refinement could enhance the usability and adoption of our interface.

7 Limitations and Future Work

Our study unveils some encouraging findings about our search interface prototype. The visualization techniques, notably the timeline and graph views, show promising efficiency and user satisfaction rates. The prototype particularly outshines traditional models in tasks demanding an understanding of the temporal context or relationships between entities. It's worth noting, however, that while these visualizations appear beneficial, none of the traditional search engines such as Bing or Google have fully incorporated them into their search interfaces. This could be due to multiple reasons, such as concerns about information overload, preserving simplicity for varied user demographics, maintaining the performance speed, and the additional computational resources that might be required.

Nonetheless, the study is not without its limitations. The experiment's controlled nature necessitated the use of static search results, which while crucial for maintaining consistency across trials, may not be fully representative of a real-world scenario where search results are dynamically generated. Further, the participants' demographic may not fully capture the diversity of global internet users, potentially limiting the generalizability of the findings. Additionally, the novelty of the interface could have swayed user perceptions, with their performance and responses possibly changing with more frequent use.

Looking ahead, there are multiple avenues to explore. Future work could involve comprehensive user testing to refine the interface design further. In particular, the components that participants found challenging could be the focus of these refinements. Developing a dynamic search result model incorporating these visualization techniques could also be an exciting direction, potentially providing more insights into the real-world applicability and usability of this approach. Finally, expanding the range of search tasks that the prototype can handle could offer additional insights into its effectiveness and versatility.

8 Conclusion

In Conclusion, the research aimed to evaluate the effectiveness of two graph based visualizations that aimed to assist users in discovering relationships in information where there was some aspect of temporal or semantic relevancy. Search engines being the primary source for people to search for information would have a hard time catering to these individualistic, case-by -ase needs as they have to ensure there platforms remain general enough for the global audience. This was reflected in our survey results as well, when participants considered our prototype to be a supplement to current search engines and to be used in specific use cases. Some of these situations highlighted by participants included cases where they had to do a lot of research. Many participants even shared in their feedback that they'd like to use this tool specifically for research. This shows us that these alternative visualizations could really enhance the user experience, especially for people like researchers, journalists, writers, and students who need to explore timelines and relationships in their data.

Moreover, it would be intriguing to approach these visualization techniques from an algorithmic perspective, assessing their feasibility from a computational standpoint. This would involve evaluating the resources required for their implementation and understanding if they pose any additional load on the system. The conclusive aim would be to develop user-friendly, intuitive visualizations that add value without compromising system efficiency. Thus, our research suggests the potential of these graph-based visualizations, providing decent evidence for further exploration and refinement in approaches to enhance the web search experience.

Acknowledgements. I am immensely grateful to my family, especially my Mother, and teachers, whose unwavering love and support have been the backbone of my journey. Their belief in me and my work has always been a source of strength and inspiration.

My sincerest gratitude to my friend, Urvashi Kishnani for her insightful review of my initial work which played a pivotal role in shaping this paper. A shoutout to Naheem Noah for helping me get into latex writing.

Special thanks to my friend, Grant Wischer, whose enthusiasm could spark a wildfire! His help in testing the prototype identified critical areas for improvement and his constructive feedback was instrumental in the development of the project. I am grateful for his unflinching support and his willingness to roll up his sleeves and dive into the work alongside me.

Last but certainly not least, I would like to express my heartfelt gratitude to Yousuf Khan. More than a friend, he has been a brother to me throughout this journey. During challenging times, he provided not only moral support but also constant motivation, pushing me to strive for excellence. His unwavering belief in my potential carried me through, and for that, I am forever grateful.

This acknowledgment is a humble tribute to all these individuals whose contributions have made this paper possible.

References

1. Alonso, O., Gertz, M., Baeza-Yates, R.: Clustering and exploring search results using timeline constructions. In: Proceedings of the 18th ACM Conference on Information and Knowledge Management, pp. 97–106. Association for Computing Machinery, New York (2009). https://doi.org/10.1145/1645953.1645968
2. Card, S., Mackinlay, J., Shneiderman, B.: Readings in Information Visualization: Using Vision to Think (1999)
3. Card, S.K., Robertson, G.G., York, W.: The webbook and the web forager: an information workspace for the world-wide web. In: Proceedings of the SIGCHI Conference on Human Factors in Computing Systems (CHI '96), p. 111-ff. Association for Computing Machinery, New York (1996). https://doi.org/10.1145/238386.238446
4. Chen, D., Chen, W., Wang, H., Chen, Z., Yang, Q.: Beyond ten blue links: enabling user click modeling in federated web search. In: Proceedings of the Fifth ACM International Conference on Web Search and Data Mining, pp. 463–472 (2012)
5. Chris, A.: Top 10 search engines in the world (2023 update) (2023). https://www.reliablesoft.net/top-10-search-engines-in-the-world/
6. Duarte, F.: Web data generated per day (2023). https://explodingtopics.com/blog/data-generated-per-day. Accessed 2023
7. Fensel, D., et al.: Introduction: what is a knowledge graph? In: Knowledge Graphs, pp. 1–10. Springer, Cham (2020). https://doi.org/10.1007/978-3-030-37439-6_1
8. Hearst, M.: Tilebars: visualization of term distribution information in full text information access. In: Proceedings of the Conference on Human Factors in Computing Systems, vol. 1 (2000)
9. Hearst, M.A.: Presentation of Search Results, pp. 120–140. Cambridge University Press (2009). https://doi.org/10.1017/CBO9781139644082.006
10. Hearst, M.A., Karadi, C.: Cat-a-cone: an interactive interface for specifying searches and viewing retrieval results using a large category hierarchy. In: Proceedings of the 20th Annual International ACM SIGIR Conference on Research and Development in Information Retrieval (SIGIR '97), pp. 246–255. Association for Computing Machinery, New York (1997). https://doi.org/10.1145/258525.258582
11. Herman, I., Melancon, G., Marshall, M.: Graph visualization and navigation in information visualization: a survey. IEEE Trans. Visual Comput. Graph. **6**(1), 24–43 (2000). https://doi.org/10.1109/2945.841119
12. Kameni, J.S., Batchakui, B., Nkambou, R.: Search engines in learning contexts: a literature review. Int. J. Emerg. Technol. Learn. **17**(2) (2022)
13. Levene, M.: An Introduction to Search Engines and Web Navigation. John Wiley & Sons (2011)
14. Panagis, Y., Spence, R.: An inertial representation of search results. In: Proceedings of the 15th International Symposium on Visual Information Communication and Interaction (VINCI '22). Association for Computing Machinery, New York (2022). https://doi.org/10.1145/3554944.3554963
15. Paranyushkin, D.: Infranodus: generating insight using text network analysis. In: The World Wide Web Conference, pp. 3584–3589 (2019)
16. Rennison, E.: Galaxy of news: an approach to visualizing and understanding expansive news landscapes. In: Proceedings of the 7th Annual ACM Symposium on User Interface Software and Technology (UIST '94), pp. 3–12. Association for Computing Machinery, New York (1994). https://doi.org/10.1145/192426.192429

17. Saaty, T.L., Ozdemir, M.S.: Why the magic number seven plus or minus two. Math. Comput. Model. **38**(3–4), 233–244 (2003)
18. Sampere, J.V.: Why platform disruption is so much bigger than product disruption. Harv. Bus. Rev. **4**(08), 2–5 (2016)
19. Saraiya, P., Lee, P., North, C.: Visualization of graphs with associated timeseries data. In: IEEE Symposium on Information Visualization (INFOVIS 2005), pp. 225–232 (2005). https://doi.org/10.1109/INFVIS.2005.1532151
20. Shneiderman, B.: The eyes have it: a task by data type taxonomy for information visualizations. In: The Craft of Information Visualization, pp. 364–371. Elsevier (2003)
21. Tilsner, M., Hoeber, O., Fiech, A.: Cubansea: cluster-based visualization of search results. In: 2009 IEEE/WIC/ACM International Joint Conference on Web Intelligence and Intelligent Agent Technology, vol. 3, pp. 108–112. IEEE (2009). https://doi.org/10.1109/WI-IAT.2009.242
22. Uyar, A., Aliyu, F.M.: Evaluating search features of google knowledge graph and bing satori: entity types, list searches and query interfaces. In: Online Information Review (2015)
23. Vincent, N., Hecht, B.: A deeper investigation of the importance of Wikipedia links to search engine results. Proc. ACM Hum. Comput. Interact. **5**(CSCW1), 1–15 (2021)
24. White, R.W., Dumais, S.T., Teevan, J.: Characterizing the influence of domain expertise on web search behavior. In: Proceedings of the Second ACM International Conference on Web Search and Data Mining (WSDM '09), pp. 132–141. Association for Computing Machinery, New York (2009). https://doi.org/10.1145/1498759.1498819

SIMBA: An Interactive Sketch-Based Tool for Motion Visualization

Kalyan Ramana Gattoz(✉), Sumedh Simha, and Prasad S. Onkar

Department of Design, Indian Institute of Technology Hyderabad, Kandi, India
md18resch11002@iith.ac.in, sumedhsimha2410@gmail.com,
psonkar@des.iith.ac.in

Abstract. Articulated products are those where components of the product have relative motion with each other. The relative motion is possible due to interconnections between the components. During the conceptual design of articulated product concepts, designers explore different types of interconnections so as to meet the design requirements. It has been observed that there is a significant amount of effort is involved in such types of explorations. Although, designers are not sure whether the concepts will satisfy the design criteria because there is a lack of information on the nature of relative motion of interconnected components. For this, an interactive tool is developed to trace the concept and to validate the motion of different components so that it meets design requirements. The software is evaluated for subjective satisfaction in terms of ease of use, intuitiveness, and desireness to use. Overall, the participants reported a positive feeback and the user study shows that there is reasonable level of satisfaction while usage of the software application.

Keywords: Articulated product concepts · Tracing over machine · Motion visulization

1 Introduction

Design is one of the profound activities of humans. The design process is categorized into phases [9]. Sketching is one of the most important activities in the design and development of new products. The early phases of product development play a significant role in the success of a product and the prevention of consumption of time and money in late phases. Designers produce sketches, from concept design ideas to highly detailed representations of product artifacts, product sub-assemblies, and so on, to communicate with themselves and with others. For example, the functionality of the carrier mechanism shown in Fig. 1 is difficult to judge directly from the figure. Here the design requirement was

Supported by Department of Science and Technology (DST), Science and Engineering Research Board (SERB) (File no. CRG/2020/005334).

H. Mori et al. (Eds.): HCII 2023, LNCS 14056, pp. 181–195, 2023.
https://doi.org/10.1007/978-3-031-48044-7_13

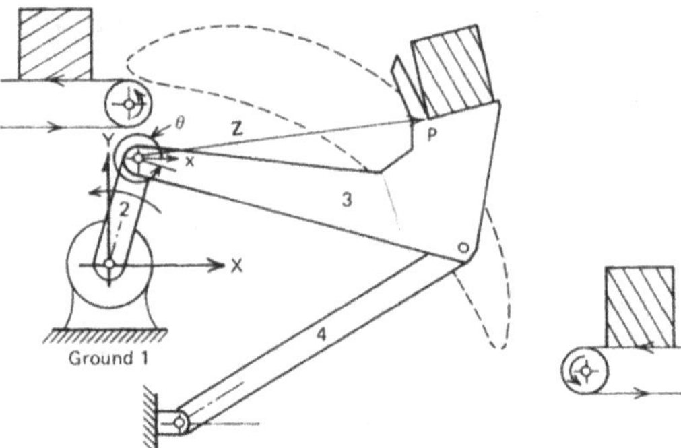

Fig. 1. Carrier mechanism [22].

to shift the box from the right conveyor belt to the left one. But there are constraints for the path traversed by the box. The motion of the box here is complex (neither rotatory nor translatory). In such cases, the designer is challenged to use gestures and annotations to describe motion. Once a mechanism (as shown in the same Fig. 1) is decided, it is not easy to predict whether it will meet the motion (design) requirement. The current study here presents one of the methods to decrease the effort in communicating the functionality of the articulated product concepts.

2 Background

Conceptual design is an important phase in the overall design process because of its influence on the performance parameters of the final outcome [10]. Typically, designers use sketching as a medium to explore concepts in the early stages of design because of its inherent advantages [11]. Starting from Sutherland's SketchPad [12] many applications have been developed to support conceptual design activities in different domains like product design, Architecture, Graphic Design, Interaction design, etc. One such early application developed for creating 3D shapes directly from 2D sketch strokes created on a digital interface is Teddy [13]. Similarly, in the domain of architecture, Electronic Cocktail Napkin [14] is proposed which supports conceptual design activities like editing, critiquing, and simulation of concepts. A dynamic simulation application for product concepts is demonstrated in [16]. Another similar work is a sketching interface for finite element analysis [17] which derives the details like geometry, force interactions, and boundary conditions with the specified material model from the sketch strokes and simulates the strength behavior using Finite Element Analysis (FEA) software. Similarly, Mechanix [18] is another application for solving free-body diagrams of truss problems. A rule-based visualization of how mechanical things work is also demonstrated in [19]. Behavior simulation of product concepts through an intuitive sketching interface is shown in [20]. Thus many of these computer-based sketching support tools for conceptual design are predominantly focused on the geometric/shape information and neglect other information like gestures and annotations.

Chase [22] et al. reviews software packages available for motion generation of rigid bodies. A recent development is by Anurag et al. [23] in motion generation as an Android and iOS application. In the current literature, there is a mention of difficulty in conveying the functionality of the sketch by the designers to themselves and others in [24]. Such difficulty has been quantified in [1]. From the literature review, the study on reducing such difficulty in communicating the functionality of the designers has not been thorough. There is a mention of, in [25], uncertainty or mismatch of information between structurally-oriented sketching (e.g., depicting design elements) and functionally-oriented sketching (e.g., reflecting connectivity between elements and their integrated behavior). [15,21,27,28] are some of the recent works that use machine learning algorithms to predict articulations or relative motion of parts inside a given 3D model.

The present work deals with this aspect of understanding the motion behavior of articulated product concepts. In the rest of the paper, the closest analogy to the articulated product concepts are the linkage mechanisms (in terms of motion behavior). Hence, the articulated product concepts and mechanisms are used synonymously. Similarly, the subcomponents of the articulated products are referred to links/rigid bodies, and their interconnections/motion constraints as joints. This understanding is obtained with the help of the software the authors developed. The main goal of the authors was to reduce the effort in understanding motion behavior at the conceptual stage. The effort is introduced in the next section in terms of a number of actions.

3 Problem Definition

A design experiment was conducted in [1] to measure the percentage of actions that are involved in communicating the functionality of the articulated product sketch. The percentage of actions was directly proportional to the effort made in communicating the functionality with some assumptions. The present work aims to find ways to reduce this effort. There was an error in the equation interpretation, the correct ones are shown below.

$$E_i = E_1 + E_2 + E_3 + ... + E_{ni} \tag{1}$$

$$E_i = E_1 = E_2 = E_3 = ... = E_{ni} \tag{2}$$

$$E_i = n_i E_1 \tag{3}$$

$$E_i \alpha n_i \tag{4}$$

$$E_p = n_p E_1 \tag{5}$$

$$E_t = n_t E_1 \tag{6}$$

$$\frac{E_p}{E_t} = \frac{n_p}{n_t} \tag{7}$$

Table 1. Mental effort in communicating the functionality of the articulated product concept sketches [1]

Subject	Time	Percentage of Effort
1	213	69.33
2	319	55.55
3	363	51.4
4	439	59.26

where, E_i = Effort applied by the designer in i^{th} the design actions,
E_p = Effort applied by the designer to communicate the functionality of the product sketch through the design actions,
n_p = Number of design actions required to communicate the functionality of the product sketch,
E_t = Total effort applied by the designer to communicate the functionality of the product sketch through the design actions throughout the sketching duration. The total time taken by the designer wherein to generate the concept using the product sketch is called sketching duration (t),
n_t = Number of design actions required to communicate the functionality of the product sketch throughout the sketching duration. Here, in equation (7), the left-hand side gives the fraction of effort applied by the designer to communicate the functionality and the right-hand side gives the fraction of design actions required to communicate to the functionality of the product. The estimated effort is tabulated as follows:

It was concluded in the article [1] that more than 50% of effort is going in communicating the functionality of the articulated product sketch.

3.1 Significance of Effort

There was no scale defined to actually measure the effort in communicating the functionality. Obviously, if the percentage of actions to communicate the functionality is 0% then the effort put in is also zero. This implies that the designer did not explain the functionality of the articulated product sketch rather, kept all his/her efforts in the sketching activity only. To the other extreme, if 100% is the percentage of actions to communicate the functionality, then the effort is full. This implies that the designer tried to explain the functionality of the articulated product concept sketch without actually drawing anything on the paper. It was established in [2] that sketching is not a necessary activity for experts. For the current design experiment, the statistical significance was not established. For this, a scale is needed to obtain an approximate measure of the effort. Let the scale, 0–100% of effort be divided into ranges that define as very easy, easy, difficult, and very difficult. This can be tabulated in the form as follows:

Table 2. Mental effort scale in communicating the functionality of the articulated product concept sketches [1]

S. No.	Percentage of Effort	Meaning
1	0	No effort at all
2	0–20	Very easy
3	20–40	Easy
4	40–60	Moderately easy/difficult
5	60–80	Difficult
6	80–100	Very difficult
7	100	Full effort

As shown in the Table 2 0–20% shows the range where the effort to communicate the functionality is very easy. Similarly, other ranges are quantified as shown. A critical range 40–60% is the range where the effort for functionality is moderately easy/difficult. This shows that the easy part has already ended at 20%. This could be understood in such a way that an effort estimate below 50% could be more easy but difficulty still exists. The effort more than 50% could be understood such that the effort is more difficult but the element of easiness is still not yet lost. For the data in Table 1, statistical analysis was performed. The null and alternate hypotheses are described as follows:

1. Null hypothesis (H_0): It is absolutely easy or there is no difficulty to explain the functionality of the product concept sketches during a sketching activity.
2. Alternate hypothesis (H_a): It is not easy or it is difficult to explain the functionality of the product concept sketches during a sketching activity.

By applying the 2-tailed test to data in Table 1. The statistical analysis data is obtained as shown in Table 3. Here, one can see that p-value using the t-statistic method is 0.017 (< 0.05). This gives sufficient evidence to reject the null hypothesis and look for an alternate hypothesis. Therefore, it can be concluded that the effort put in by the designers to explain the functionality of the articulated product sketches is absolutely not an easy one and there is an element of difficulty in the process. The percentage of effort lies in the range of 58.885 ± 12.41 95% of the time.

Table 3. Test for statistical significance

S. No.	Parameter	Value
1	Mean	58.885
2	Median	57.405
3	Standard deviation	7.667814
4	Minimum	51.44
5	Maximum	69.33
6	Range	18.33
7	Hypothesized mean	40
8	p-value using t-statistic	0.017
9	Confidence level (95%)	12.41
10	Standard error	3.833

4 Methodology

The main issue that was observed is that the articulated product concepts that have been generated during the experiment [1] are ambiguous. Unless and until these are virtually/physically prototyped one does not have a single idea whether the designs meet the requirement or not. The designers have sketched the concepts with the idea that they will meet the design requirement, but there is no tool available to quickly verify or validate the sketch.

4.1 Tracing over a Sketch for Motion Visualization

To address this problem of uncertainty a software application was needed because directly going to prototyping includes a lot of resources and time consuming. Even in virtual prototyping, commercial modeling and analysis software need to be used including the human resource. This whole process is time-consuming and resource-intensive.

From the design experiment in [1], it was observed that the relative motion representation of different parts in the concept sketch had a pattern. For example, all the rotation and linear motion where represented as circles and straight lines respectively. These relative motions were possible by revolute and prismatic joints. So, these modes of annotations has been used to represent the relative motion between different components. All such gestures and annotation representation have been used to develop a software application where a designer will not deviate much from the sketching activity and also the mental simulation is offloaded to a computer program. Based on this, a computer application, Sketching Interface for Mechanism Behavior Analysis (SIMBA) was developed using Unity.

The software application works for those product designs where multiple components are in relative motion with each other in parallel planes. In technical terms, the product sketches should be planar mechanisms [26]. The tool was developed in Unity™2021.3.7f1 and Microsoft™Visual Studio 2022. There are no other external inputs to the software application. The sketching is done using dragging the mouse in left-click mode. All other options are initiated using the right click.

SIMBA is an interactive software application that enables users to freely sketch and simulate the motion of an articulated product concept by recognizing its parts and their connections, thereby, helping the designer to visualize the motion. One of the features developed for this work was to trace over an already existing concept and try to visualize motion between its parts. For example, if an articulated product concept is already available in the form of an image, the user can import it into the software application. Then, the user can trace over the important parts of the image that represent links and later the connections between them. This allows the application to recognize links and joint connections. Once, the links and their joint connections are established the relative motion between the parts can be visualized. This visualization can be used to validate the product concept whether it is meeting the design requirements or not.

The main features of the software application are:

1. **Trace Mechanism**: The button trace image is clicked and a window pops which gives an option to choose any image. Once the image is added, it can be resized and repositioned. The image is slightly transparent and can be drawn on using the sketch function.
2. **Adding Joints**: Using the Hinge Joint button, a rotary joint can be added to any of the links. The joints can be between two links or between a link and the ground. A rough circle is drawn (while dragging right-click on the mouse), intersecting the links, at the position where the joint is required. The Slider joint button generates a prismatic joint between the links. A line is drawn intersecting the link/links where the joint is needed. Along with these joints, a spring can be added to the links using the same procedure as the slider joint.
3. **Path Tracing**: A point on a link can be tracked using the path drawing function. A trail is created showing the path taken by the specific point on a link. The point can be chosen by drawing a line over the specific point, which needs to be traced. Once the feature is activated then, the point of interest on a particular link should be intersected by the mouse cursor so that a point is found at the intersection.
4. **Joint Manipulation**: Using the joint manipulation function, the joint position can be changed, thereby increasing the length of the link. When selected, small colored circles appear. The blue circle signifies a rotary joint. Purple circles signify prismatic joints and green circles signify spring. Moving these circles changes the joint position.

4.2 Hypothesis

The software application has been developed from the inputs of the work from [1]. The inputs being the nature of cues (gestures and annotations) in [1] to explain the functionality of articulated product concepts have been incorporated in SIMBA. These digital cues, as part of the interaction, have to be evaluated for subjective satisfaction which is also an important aspect. It is necessary to check whether the software application is functional as per the design criteria. For this, the software application was tested by participants in a design experiment. The following is the hypothesis that was to be tested during the experiment, especially for the tracing feature.

1. Null hypothesis (H_0): There is a negative or neutral effect on the users concerning subjective satisfaction.
2. Alternate hypothesis (H_a): The users are satisfied with the SIMBA.

To test the hypothesis a design experiment was conducted which is explained in the next section.

5 Design Experiments

5.1 Experimental Setup

A total of 10 participants (8 male and 2 females) participated in the design experiment in the range of age group 20–41 years. All of them were part of the workshop. The participants had a background in engineering or/and design at the master's level. The design experiment was set up in a lab where each participant was given a computer/laptop to perform the task. The participants were briefed about the task in a detailed way before beginning the experiment. The software application was installed on each of the computers/laptops. All the participants were given the same product concept to eliminate any bias. If the participants had any questions before the experiment they were clarified. After the task was completed the participants were instructed to take a screenshot of their sketch. In addition, the participants were asked not to worry about the correctness of the outcome of the concept. After the experiment is done, the participants had to fill their feedback in Google forms sent to their respective email ids. The task that was listed as follows

1. Insert a (given) image of a mechanism
2. sketch over the mechanism/articulated product.
3. Apply motion constraints between the parts of the product.
4. Simulate the articulation for motion visualization
5. Choose a point on any rigid link/body/part that matches the prescribed path given in Fig. 1.

5.2 Data Collection

The Google™form contains feedback on each of the tasks mentioned in the above section. Here, each question was about the important features of the SIMBA. The features to be evaluated against subjective satisfaction were image selection and insertion, tracing over the image, applying the joint constraints, and simulation for motion visualization. Correspondingly, these are abbreviated as F1, F2, F3, and F4. Each feature was rated about its ease of use, intuitiveness, and desires to use. Correspondingly, these were abbreviated as EU, INT, and WU. So each task has these three parameters against which they are measured. Each parameter is measured on a scale of 1–5, where 1 and 5 indicate the lowest and the highest subjective feeling about the feature respectively. Each participant has to give his/her rating about their subjective feeling about each feature. There were no duplicates in the data collection. The questionnaire was set per Likert's scale [6]. The authors have taken approval from the ethics committee for the experimentation and data collection method.

5.3 Data Analysis

The data collected has been analyzed to check whether the participants are liking the software in terms of ease of use, intuitiveness, and desireness to use. For this, at first, the data is checked for its reliability and it is tested for its statistical significance.

Data Reliability-Cronbach's Alpha: The internal reliability check has been conducted on the survey for consistency among the questions. The test was conducted by evaluating the Cronbach-alpha [3] using the formula mentioned in [5]. The acceptable numerical value of the alpha range from 0.7 to 0.95 [4]. A low alpha value indicates a poor correlation between items. A high value indicates some of the questions may be redundant. The Cronbach-alpha obtained for the current questionnaire is 0.881. The questionnaire is reliable as the estimated Cronbach-alpha is in the acceptable range.

Test for Statistical Significance: The reliable data can be analyzed in two ways.

1. For every parameter and each feature can be analyzed across all the participants.
2. For every parameter and each participant can be analyzed across all the features.

In this work, the author intends to study how each parameter varies for each feature across all the participants but not to study the participants' variability in their subjective satisfaction across all the features.

The study's main objective was to measure the subjective satisfaction of the participants for each feature in terms of parameters. The author intended to

Table 4. Interval scale for the subjective measure of satisfaction

Interval scale	Subjective measure of satisfaction
1.00–1.80	Strongly dissatisfied (SD)
1.80–2.60	Dissatisfied (D)
2.60–3.40	Neutral (N)
3.40–4.20	Satisfied (S)
4.20–5.00	Strongly satisfied (SS)

make sure the features developed in the application do not make them unsatisfactory. Hence, they can have a neutral or satisfactory experience while using the application. The hypothesis was designed based on this requirement. So to have a non-unsatisfactory measure of the participant's subjective experience, the Likert scale was converted to an interval scale for easy understanding. For this, a rating from 1 to 5 was used as a measurement scale. The means of each subjective feeling score are tested against this scale. The lowest score implies that all the participants were totally dissatisfied with the tool. The highest score of 5 implies that all the participants were strongly satisfied with the tool. So, the scale 1–5 of subjective satisfaction was converted to an interval scale, as shown in Table 4. All the means, standard deviations, standard error means, etc. have been calculated using Microsoft Excel. For example, the EU mean for F2 was 3.4. This implies that the EU mean falls in the category of "Satisfied (S)" as per the Table 4. Hence it can be concluded that the participants consider the subjective measure of satisfaction in agreement. Here, the endpoint convention is used for the intervals as per [7].

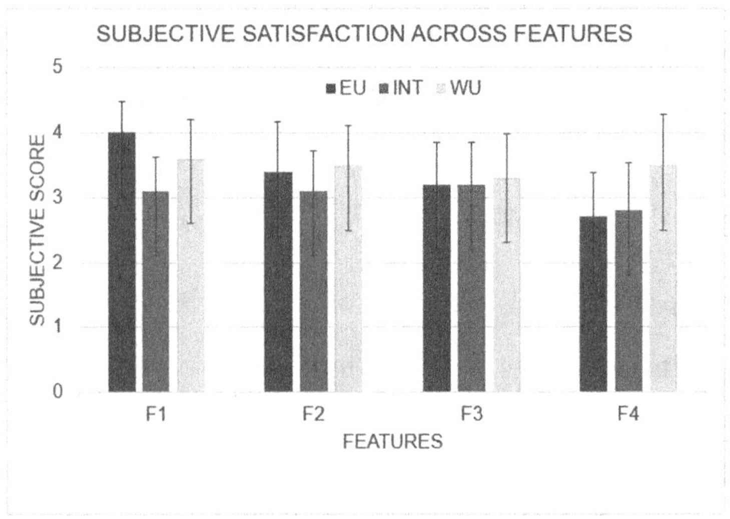

Fig. 2. Score distribution across all the features by the participants

To test for statistical significance, the subjective score for each feature against each parameter was considered. A two-tailed t-test has been performed to get the p-value. Using the estimated p-value confidence interval was calculated for a 95% confidence level. For example, the usage of the feature F2 (relating to image insertion), was tested against ease of use EU. Its mean subjective score was estimated to be 3.4. The p-value for F2 came around 0.0215 (rounded off to three decimals). As the p-value is less than 0.05, it can be concluded that there is no evidence to support the null hypothesis. Hence, it can be concluded that F1 ease of use is statistically significant. Moreover, one can ensure that the confidence interval for the mean subjective score is 3.4 ± 0.769 (rounded off to three decimals) for a 95% confidence level. The means and their confidence intervals for 95% confidence levels are shown in Fig. 2. All the other p-values were found to be less than 0.05 except for the following features and parameters.

1. **EU vs F4**: Overall mean subjective satisfaction score was 2.7 which is above hypothesized mean (2.6). The participants had neither positive nor negative but neutral subjective feelings while simulating the motion of the product. But the p-value was 0.373 (>0.05) which tells us that there is evidence to support the null hypothesis. The participants will face difficulty while simulating the motion of the product 95% of the time.
2. **INT vs F2**: Overall mean subjective satisfaction score was 3.1 which is above hypothesized mean (2.6). The participants had neither positive nor negative but neutral subjective feelings while sketching strokes over the images. But the p-value was 0.522 (>0.05) which tells us that there is evidence to support the null hypothesis. The participants will face difficulty while tracing over the image of the product 95% of the time.
3. **INT vs F4**: Overall mean subjective satisfaction score was 2.8 which is above hypothesized mean (2.6). The participants had neither positive nor negative but neutral subjective feelings while simulating the motion of the product. But the p-value was 0.277 (>0.05) which tells us that there is evidence to support the null hypothesis. The participants will face difficulty while simulating the motion of the product 95% of the time.

6 Results

Some of the mechanisms were tried from the textbook [26] to test their utility apart from the design experiment problem statement. All the models exhibited motion as per the solutions mentioned.

6.1 Example 1: Harvey Mechanism

In the first example, the Harvey Mechanism is tested using SIMBA. The image of the mechanism is spawned using the trace mechanism function. Black lines are drawn which represent the link. Once the links are drawn, the system automatically recognizes different parts. Then rotary joints are added to each of the links

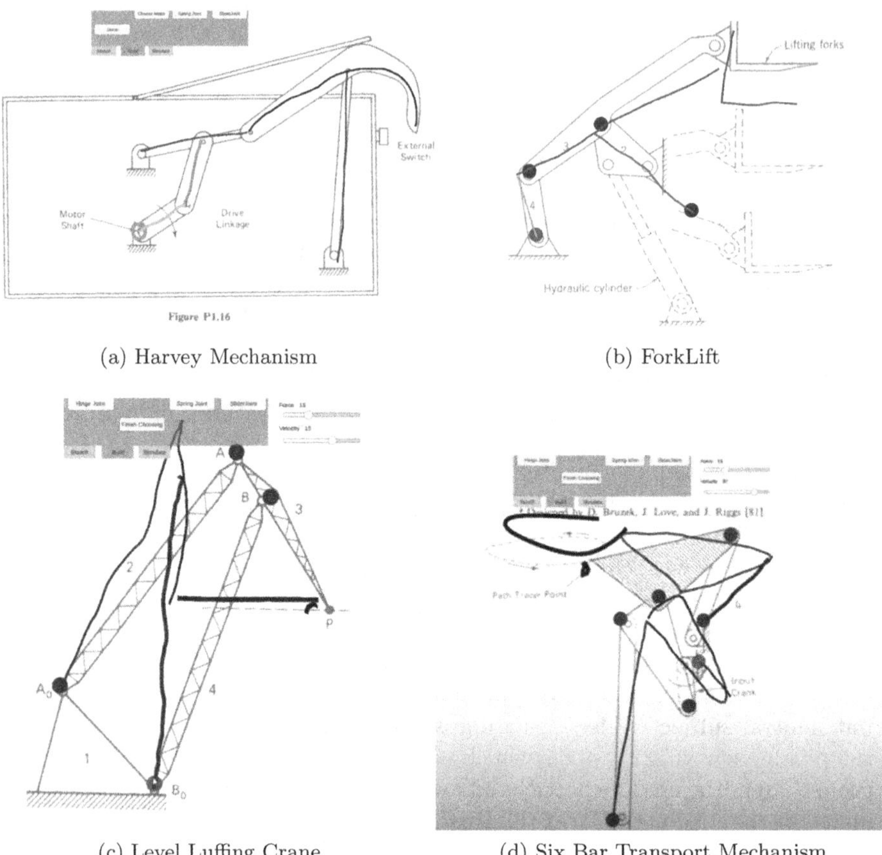

(a) Harvey Mechanism

(b) ForkLift

(c) Level Luffing Crane

(d) Six Bar Transport Mechanism

Fig. 3. The colored strokes are the ones drawn by the user. The background images representing mechanisms are taken from [26]

starting with the ground links (Fig. 3(a)). When a circle is drawn between one link and the white background, it is considered as the ground link. The rotary joint acts as a motor when given the force and velocity.

6.2 Example 2: Forklift

In this example, the Forklift mechanism is tested. The trace mechanism function is used to draw the mechanism. Using the add object feature, the forklift link is attached to link 3 (Fig. 3(b)). The necessary rotary joints are added to the links. When the motor force and velocity are applied, the mechanism works as intended.

6.3 Example 3: Level Luffing Crane

In this example, the Level Luffing Crane mechanism is tested. The trace mechanism function is used to draw the mechanism. The ground joints are applied at link A0 and link B0. The necessary rotary joints are added to the links. The feature to trace a path is used to see how the link moves. The point is selected and the path is traced as shown in Fig. 3(c).

6.4 Example 4: Six Bar Transport Mechanism

In this example, the Six Bar Transport Mechanism is tested. The trace mechanism function is used to trace the links. The ground joints are applied as shown in the image. The necessary rotary joints are added to the links. The highest link is traced using the path trace functionality. A point on the link is used to see the trajectory of the link as shown in Fig. 3(d).

7 Discussion

The applications accurately work with links that are connected by simple joints (two links joined together). Any multiple links joined are susceptible to error. As most of the machines/mechanisms have simple joints this application is useful for the majority of the situations.

From the statistical significance test, it can be clearly seen that the features F4 had issues with ease of use and intuitiveness. It is a good opportunity for the authors to work on the same. The interaction part where regarding the simulations has to be refined. Similarly, tracing over the image was not intuitive. This may be because, in a traditional way of tracing on paper, the users can remove the tracing paper and check whether the drawing is correct or not. Here, that facility is not obvious. The tracing over the image could have blocked the image below. The intuitiveness of subjective feelings about feature F4 also needs to be refined. This could be because of the distinction between holding a rigid body/link physically and by mouse.

The bright side of the experiment is that their desireness to use the software application is statistically significant. This is one of the key findings in the design experiment. The applications mentioned in [22,23] use primitive geometries to represent links and joints. This affects the designer's creative thinking. The naturalness of the sketch with all the ambiguity is not used in these methods. It has been mentioned in [11]. This work integrates the functionality and ambiguity of the sketch so that the designer is still in the zone of creativity without leaving the conceptual stage of design. Tracing over the image is one such feature developed for this application.

8 Conclusion

In this work, a traditional tracing activity over images was implemented on a computer program, to help construct, assemble, and simulate the articulated products for their motion visualizations. The issue faced in the [1], difficulty in visualizing the motion of articulated product concepts has been addressed by using the method of digital tracing over product concepts. The designers will have a quick understanding of motion that is visualized in different parts without digressing from their creative activity at the conceptual stage itself. This is very important because the traditional way of modeling the concept in software is resource intensive. Time and cost can be saved. Moreover, there is an advantage of obtaining motion visualization according to the design requirements in the conceptual stage itself. This software can be used as an educational tool to quickly show the motion behavior of articulated product concepts.

Acknowledgement. It is acknowledged that the work presented in this paper is part of the research funded by Core Research Grant (CRG), Science and Engineering Research Board (SERB), Department of Science and Technology (DST), Govt. of India (File no.: CRG/2020/005334). The authors thank the funding agency for their generous support.

References

1. Ramana, G., Onkar, P.: On how designers communicate the functionality of articulated product concepts in Sketches. In: Proceedings of NordDesign 2020 (DS 101), Lyngby, 12th–14th August 2020, pp. 1–12 (2020)
2. Bilda, Z., Gero, J., Purcell, T.: To sketch or not to sketch? That is the question. Des. Stud. **27**, 587–613 (2006). http://www.sciencedirect.com/science/article/pii/S0142694X06000317
3. Cronbach, L.: Coefficient alpha and the internal structure of tests. Psychometrika **16**, 297–334 (1951)
4. DeVellis, R.: Scale Development: Theory and Applications. SAGE Publications (2012). https://books.google.co.in/books?id=Rye31saVXmAC
5. Miller, M.: Classical Test Theory Reliability. Elsevier (2010)
6. Likert, R.: A technique for the measurement of attitudes. Archiv. Psychol. (1932)
7. Freedman, D., Pisani, R., Purves, R.: Statistics: Fourth International Student Edition. W.W. Norton & Company (2007)
8. Ralph, P., Wand, Y.: A proposal for a formal definition of the design concept. In: Lyytinen, K., Loucopoulos, P., Mylopoulos, J., Robinson, B. (eds.) Design Requirements Engineering: A Ten-Year Perspective. LNBIP, vol. 14, pp. 103–136. Springer, Heidelberg (2009). https://doi.org/10.1007/978-3-540-92966-6_6
9. Pahl, G., Beitz, W.: Engineering Design: A Systematic Approach. Springer, Berlin (1996). https://doi.org/10.1007/978-1-4471-3581-4
10. Boothroyd, G., Dewhurst, P.: Product Design for Manufacture and Assembly. CRC Press (2010)
11. Fish, J., Scrivener, S.: Amplifying the mind's eye: sketching and visual cognition. Leonardo **23**(1), 117–126 (1990). https://www.jstor.org/stable/1578475
12. Sutherland, I.V.: Sketchpad, a man-machine graphical communication system, Ph. D. dissertation. Massachusetts Institute of Technology (1963)
13. Igarashi, T., et al.: Teddy: A Sketching Interface for 3D Freeform Design (SIGGRAPH 99), pp. 409–416. ACM, Los Angeles (1999)
14. Gross, M.D.: The electronic cocktail napkin - a computational environment for working with design diagrams. Des. Stud. **17**(1), 53–69 (1996)

15. Li, X., Wang, H., Yi, L., Guibas, L., Abbott, A., Song, S.: Category-level articulated object pose estimation. In: Proceedings of the IEEE/CVF Conference on Computer Vision and Pattern Recognition (CVPR) (2020)
16. Davis, R.: Sketch understanding in design: overview of work at the MIT AI lab. In: Papers from the 2002 AAAI Spring Symposium on Sketch Understanding (2002)
17. Masry, M., Lipson, H.: A sketch-based interface for iterative design and analysis of 3D objects. In: Eurographics Workshop on Sketch-Based Interfaces and Modeling (2005)
18. Valentine, S., et al.: Mechanix: a sketch-based tutoring system for statics courses. In: Proceedings of the Twenty-Fourth Innovative Applications of Artificial Intelligence Conference (2012)
19. Mitra, N.J., et al.: Illustrating how mechanical assemblies work. ACM Trans. Graph. **29**(4), 58:1–58:12 (2010)
20. Onkar, P.S., Sen, D.: Behaviour simulation in computer aided product concept sketching. In: CIRP Design 2012, pp. 181–191. Springer, London (2012). https://doi.org/10.1007/978-1-4471-4507-3_18
21. Mo, K., Guibas, L., Mukadam, M., Gupta, A., Tulsiani, S.: Where2Act: from pixels to actions for articulated 3D objects. In: Proceedings of the IEEE/CVF International Conference on Computer Vision (ICCV), pp. 6813–6823 (2021)
22. Chase, T., Kinzel, G., Erdman, A.: Computer aided mechanism synthesis: a historical perspective. In: Advances in Mechanisms, Robotics and Design Education and Research, pp. 17–33 (2013)
23. Purwar, A., Deshpande, S., Ge, Q.: MotionGen: interactive design and editing of planar four-bar motions for generating pose and geometric constraints. ASME J. Mechan. Robot. **9**, 024504 (2017). https://asmedigitalcollection.asme.org/mechanismsrobotics/article-abstract/9/2/024504/473124/MotionGen-Interactive-Design-and-Editing-of-Planar?redirectedFrom=fulltext
24. Wetzel, J., Forbus, K.: Automated critique of sketched designs in engineering. In: Proceedings of the 23rd International Workshop on Qualitative Reasoning (2009)
25. Ball, L., Christensen, B.: Advancing an understanding of design cognition and design metacognition: progress and prospects. Des. Stud. **65**, 35–59 (2019)
26. Erdam, A., Sandor, G.: Mechanism Design: Analysis and Synthesis. Prentice-Hall (1998)
27. Liu, G., et al.: Semi-Weakly Supervised Object Kinematic Motion Prediction (2023)
28. Xu, X., Ruan, Y., Sridhar, S., Ritchie, D.: Unsupervised kinematic motion detection for part-segmented 3D shape collections. In: ACM SIGGRAPH 2022 Conference Proceedings, pp. 1–9 (2022)

Investigating the Enhancement of Reading Immersion Experience Through the Integration of Interactive E-Books and Augmented Reality

Pei-Shan Teng(✉)

Providence University, Taichung 43301, Taiwan, Republic of China
psteng@pu.edu.tw

Abstract. In the post-epidemic era, the adoption of isolation measures, remote care, and remote learning and work has become the new norm. These significant changes and the accompanying stresses have led to a rise in psychological issues among individuals in modern society. Consequently, the objective of this study was to design an interactive e-book focused on mental health education. The research methodology employed involved referencing the immersive experience scale and conducting pre-test and post-test questionnaires to evaluate the participants' experiential perceptions. The primary aim of this study was to investigate the impact of immersive experiences in interactive electronic picture books. Additionally, the feasibility of incorporating interactive electronic graphics into the realm of medical and health education was explored.

This research highlights the significance of enhancing public awareness and understanding of depression among adolescents. The development of an interactive e-book has proven to be an effective tool for individuals to acquire knowledge about depression and cultivate empathy and support. The inclusion of interactive reading elements enhances the sense of immersion. Further research can delve into the broader implications of interactive e-books and similar interventions in the field of mental health education. The findings of this study also offer valuable insights into the application of interactive electronic graphics and digital tools in the context of medical and health education.

Keywords: Immersion Experience · Reading Comprehension · Augmented Reality · Interactive Electronic Picture Books

1 Introduction

In recent years, depression has become a younger phenomenon, and in this era of Internet development, peer, relationship, and financial problems are factors that contribute to depression among teenagers. More and more young people are putting a lot of time and effort into using the Internet, and these stressful issues are beginning to manifest themselves in social media. In recent years, depression has become a younger phenomenon, but this symptom is easily ignored by elders and even ostracized by peers. As a result, young people are overly stressed and miss the best opportunity for diagnosis and treatment (Schrobsdorff 2016). This causes a social and economic burden, a decrease in productivity, and a problem that deserves the highest priority in society.

H. Mori et al. (Eds.): HCII 2023, LNCS 14056, pp. 196–202, 2023.
https://doi.org/10.1007/978-3-031-48044-7_14

1.1 Electronic Picture Books Combined with Augmented Reality

With the changing times, books have undergone a gradual transformation from their traditional paper form to digital format, allowing readers to experience the joy of reading through electronic devices. This shift not only enhances entertainment value but also leaves a deeper impression of the content. Moreover, in today's consumer-oriented marketing landscape, keeping pace with trends and prioritizing consumer experience have become paramount. Consequently, many products in the market are incorporating interactive design to engage consumers actively, thus fostering a stronger brand connection. Augmented Reality (AR) serves as a powerful and convenient tool to bring virtual objects to life in the real world. By leveraging the interactive, transparent, disassembled, and animated features of AR, e-books can captivate the public's attention while enriching their content. Text or pictures alone may not be able to convey complex concepts. However, the use of animation and sound can help the reader understand the book's ideas easily.

1.2 Teenage Depression

A survey conducted by the John Tung Foundation (2019), targeting national and high school vocational students in Greater Taipei, found that 12.4% of the more than 2,000 respondents had obvious symptoms of depression and needed professional help, 13.5% felt lonely and easily fell into a sense of hopelessness, and the level of depression was directly proportional to the level of loneliness. The survey further revealed that 48% of teenagers spend more than 6 h a day on the Internet on average, and 41.6% of them have "mood swings", mostly because they feel unhappy in real life and go online to chat and interact with others. Depression is a disease that can affect all ages and can be broadly categorized by symptoms as follows.

Major Depressive Disorder (MDD): This form of depression significantly impacts an individual's daily functioning and activities (Jaycox et al. 2009). It is characterized by a persistent depressed mood, often accompanied by feelings of anxiety and irritability. Physical symptoms may include significant weight loss or gain, loss of energy, fatigue, slow movements, and disruptions in sleep patterns. Cognitive symptoms may manifest as difficulties in concentration, decision-making, and a decrease in self-confidence. Individuals with MDD may have a pessimistic outlook on life, feel inferior or worthless, and constantly question the meaning of their existence. In some cases, they may experience unexplained feelings of guilt, engage in self-harm or harm others, and have recurrent thoughts of suicide (Johnstone & Johnstone 2012).

Dysthymia is a milder form of depression characterized by long-term, chronic symptoms that do not incapacitate the individual (Johnstone & Johnstone 2006). Common symptoms include irritability, insomnia, loss of appetite, and other similar manifestations that persist for at least one year. While individuals with dysthymia may experience symptoms similar to depression, they often maintain a generally good mood. They may be capable of feeling happiness but are often hesitant to fully embrace this positive emotional state.

It is important to note that many individuals with mild depression first experience symptoms during childhood, adolescence, or early adulthood. As a result, these manifestations are sometimes mistaken for typical rebellious behavior or attributed to the natural development of one's personality. Depression is a serious mental illness that requires proper recognition and treatment.

1.3 Purpose of the Study

This study focuses on enhancing the public's understanding of adolescent depression by designing an interactive picture book story. Through the characters facing different events and picture books, the public can understand the psychological state of people with depression. The purpose of this study is to understand the readers' understanding of the interactive picture book. By combining story graphics and animation with augmented reality (AR) technology, the study aims to increase reading interest, interactivity, and comprehension of story themes.

This study designed a textless interactive e-book for the young generation. The picture book follows the story in context with AR musical animations and touch screen interaction. The interactive picture book adds AR to a specific screen in the book, allowing the user to scan the screen to watch an animation of the main character's story. The book includes three different types of interaction: gyroscope, light sensor. Users are expected to maintain a high level of concentration and interest during the experience.

2 Methodology

The study investigates the underappreciated aspect of depression among teenagers, focusing on enhancing reader immersion through the use of interactive e-books combined with augmented reality (AR). The research process for designing interactive e-books is outlined as follows:

(1) Literature Review: A comprehensive review of the literature is conducted to gain insights into the prevalence, causes, and psychological status of depressed adolescents.
(2) Publication Analysis: The current landscape of publications, including books, picture books, and manuals, related to adolescent depression is surveyed. This includes examining news articles, case reports, and statistical data on depression in young people in recent years.
(3) Theme Development for Picture Books: Based on the findings from the literature review, the study aims to identify the difficulties faced by young people and their sources of stress. These insights are used to guide the development of the picture book's theme.
(4) Interactive Design of Picture Books: The decision is made to present the story as a wordless picture book with metaphorical transformations. The study includes designing a script for story segments and planning the incorporation of augmented reality and animation. Interactive testing is conducted using mobile devices such as tablets and phones.

The research adopts a survey method, targeting general users. Pre-test and post-test questionnaires are used to collect survey data and feedback on users' experience with the interactive e-graphic book. The survey results are analyzed to investigate readers' perceptions and understanding of the study's message, enabling adjustments and improvements to be made in the presentation of the study.

The interactive e-book is specifically designed for the general public to foster understanding and empathy toward adolescents with depression by exploring their psychological conditions. It relies solely on visual elements, employing graphics, sound effects, music, and other auditory sensations to deliver the reading experience. The user interface incorporates intuitive symbols to guide the interactive functions, allowing users to navigate the content at their own pace, thereby enhancing interactivity and immersion. Alongside the conventional touch-screen interaction, the interactive e-book offers various engaging methods such as a gyroscope, light sensor, and AR animation to captivate the user's interest. Moreover, the device design is tailored to accommodate a range of user devices, and the interactive e-book is available in both IOS and Android versions.

3 Research Process

In the test, a total of 30 participants were invited to engage with the interactive e-book. Among them, 17 participants (56%) were females, while 13 participants (44%) were males. The majority of participants fell within the age range of 18 to 25. Before the game, all 30 participants were required to complete a pre-survey to assess their knowledge of depression before being influenced by the electronic picture book.

During the game, the investigator refrained from providing instructions on operation and plot explanations. Participants were encouraged to think and understand the content on their own. Following the game, the participants were asked to complete a post-survey. The objective of the survey was to determine whether the interactive e-book helped users gain a better understanding of depression, comprehend the plot and interactions effectively, and evaluate their overall experience during and after the activity.

The survey results revealed the participants' understanding and awareness of "depression" before and after engaging with the interactive e-book. Before the activity, 86.6% of the participants acknowledged depression as a disease. This percentage remained consistent after the activity. When asked about the factors contributing to depression, there was an increase in the percentage of participants who recognized long-term suppression of emotions (from 90% to 93.3%), the influence of the upbringing environment (from 76.6% to 90%), and sudden major life changes (from 73.3% to 83.3%). The understanding of depression is influenced by family genetics also increased from 33.3% initially to 56.6% (refer to Fig. 1).

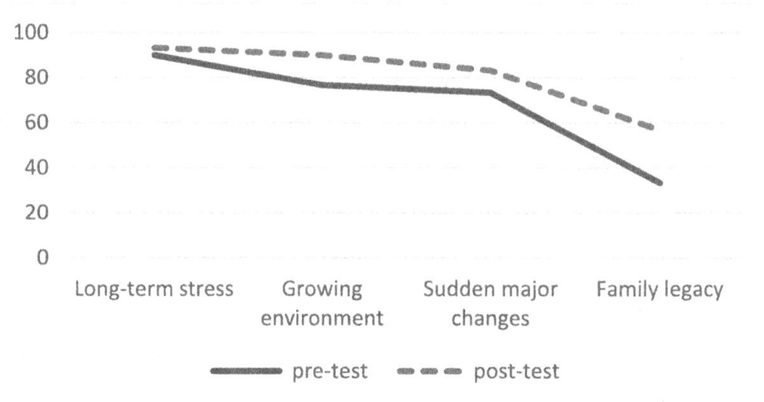

Fig. 1. Illustrates the participants' level of understanding regarding factors related to "depression" before and after the test. The red lines represent the pre-test responses, while the blue lines represent the post-test responses.

Regarding the question of whether depression should be discussed openly in front of individuals with depression, the majority of participants held the view that it should be discussed, with the percentage rising from 33.3% to 40% after the activity. In terms of how to perceive individuals with depression, there was an increase in the percentage of participants who considered themselves as ordinary individuals with heightened emotional sensitivity (from 46.6% to 63.3%), while those who identified individuals with depression solely as patients decreased from 33.3% to 23.3% (refer to Fig. 2).

Other statistics show that 73.3% of the testers in the level where the gyroscope interaction was carried out in the interactive e-book thought that the interaction symbolized a yearning to run to the good. Forty per cent strongly agreed that the gyroscope interaction provided them with a better immersive experience. In the level where the Light Sensor interaction was performed, 73.3% of the testers were able to understand the metaphorical concept of the picture book. 53.3% felt that the Light Sensor interaction provided them with a better immersive experience. In the AR animation section, 76.6% of the testers felt that the interaction symbolized understanding the protagonist's situation. 66.6% felt that the AR animation provided them with a better immersive experience and 63.3% felt that they acted as a facilitator in the game.

Over 50% of those who experienced the interactive electronic picture book did not feel particularly emotional when someone interrupted the experience. 63.3% of those who experienced the interactive electronic picture book did not feel particularly emotional when someone interrupted the experience. The percentage of those who were nervous or excited about the content of the picture book was also 63.3%. In addition, 43.3% of those who did not feel happy when a character completed a task in a graphic game also found it average. In contrast, about 40% of those who played the general game were able to feel the changes around them and the passage of time as usual, without being affected or forgetting what they were supposed to do.

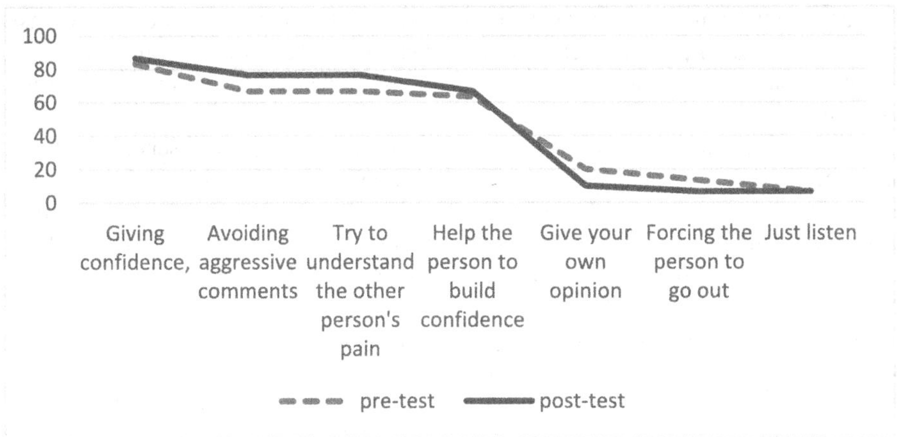

Fig. 2. Displays the participants' level of understanding regarding strategies for accompanying individuals with depression before and after the test. The red lines represent the responses before the test experience, and the blue lines represent the responses after the test.

At the end of using the interactive e-book, 56.6% of the testers said that the work made them very willing to spend time playing it. Fifty percent of the participants liked the design and style of the game and found the experience very interesting. In terms of ease of use, most users found it very easy to follow and 53.3% agreed that the interface of the game made them feel comfortable, but only 33.3% were willing to wait for the game to be downloaded or read out.

Regarding the question of how to effectively engage with individuals experiencing depression, the options of providing sufficient confidence, avoiding aggressive comments, empathizing with their pain, and supporting their self-confidence displayed a slight increase. Conversely, the attitudes of constantly imposing one's own opinion, pressuring individuals to overcome their struggles, and simply listening without offering support showed a decrease or remained stagnant. The integration of health education and medical information within this interactive e-book significantly contributed to the effectiveness of promoting the health education theme.

4 Conclusion

The primary objective of this study is to raise awareness of "adolescent depression" among the general public and facilitate learning on how to confront the pain and become supportive individuals through the interactive game. Regarding the interactive operation methods, users generally affirmed the utilization of interactive features such as the "light sensor" and "AR animation." However, the less commonly used "gyroscope" interaction method in e-books or plot-based games caused slight confusion during operation.

In terms of perception, most participants appreciated the immersion created by the interactive settings and the overall atmosphere of the game's story. However, the level of immersion between the users themselves and the avatars within the game remained relatively neutral. Participants acknowledged the ideas conveyed in the picture book but did not fully immerse themselves in the virtual embodiment. Enhancing the sense of immersion would provide a clearer understanding of the entire storyline, allowing for better conveyance of the character's emotional states within the enclosed virtual environment.

Feedback from the test subjects indicated that the graphic interface served as a helpful prompt, and the inclusion of sound effects and interactive elements further engaged them in the story. The plot of the interactive e-book effectively improved users' understanding of depression-related information, and the interactive design enhanced their comprehension of how to assist. The actual outcomes of the e-book aligned with the anticipated results of this study.

In conclusion, this study has shed light on the importance of raising awareness and understanding of "adolescent depression" among the general public. The development of an interactive game has proven to be an effective tool for educating individuals about depression and fostering empathy and support. The findings highlight the need for continuous improvement in terms of enhancing immersion and user engagement. Future studies can further explore the impact of interactive e-books and similar interventions on mental health education and promote the well-being of adolescents experiencing depression.

Acknowledgements. The work was supported by the Research Support Scheme of the National Science and Technology Council (NSTC), grant no NSTC-111-2410-H-126-020.

References

Chan, L.-J., Lee, C.-C.: Fun Reading with AR stories. Taiwan Public Lib. J. **6**(2), 7–14 (2017)

Dünser, A., Hornecker, E.: Lessons from an AR book study. In: Paper presented at the first international conference on tangible and embedded interaction, Baton Rouge (2007)

Grasset, R., Dünser, A., Billinghurst, M., Seichter, H.: The mixed reality book a new multimedia reading experience. In: Paper presented at the CHI, San Jose (2007)

Schrobsdorff, S.: Teen depression and anxiety: why the kids are not alright. Time Mag. **188**(19), 188–195 (2016)

Jaycox, L.H., et al.: Impact of teen depression on academic, social, and physical functioning. Pediatrics **124**(4), e596–e605 (2009)

Wilson, J.S.: Sensor Technology Handbook. Newnes, USA (2005)

News. https://udn.com/news/amp/story/6885/5110120. Accessed 21 Dec 2020

News. https://www.children.org.tw/research/detail/69/1733. Accessed 01 Apr 2022

AR e-books. https://5-gu.blogspot.com/2012/11/ar.html?m=1. Accessed 11 Feb 2022

Johnstone, M., Johnstone, A.: Living with a black dog: His name is depression. Andrews McMeel (2006)

Johnstone, M., Johnstone, A.: Living with a black dog. Hachette UK (2012)

Brookfield, S.: When the black dog barks: an autoethnography of adult learning in and on clinical depression. New Directions Adult Cont. Educ. **2011**(132), 35–42 (2011)

Perceived Urgency of Asynchronous Audiovisual Alerts

Vivian Tran(✉) and Thomas Z. Strybel

Department of Psychology, California State University Long Beach, Long Beach, CA 90840, USA

vivian.tran1@outlook.com, thomas.strybel@csulb.edu

Abstract. While automated technology continues to evolve and has great potential to reduce accidents and fatalities, drivers are unaware that most cars still require human input in automated mode. Multimodal alarms play a critical role in takeover requests by warning drivers of potential hazards and helping drivers stay-in-the-loop. We measured perceived urgency of audiovisual alerts that varied in timing, frequency and color, and with timing combinations that produced asynchronous audiovisual stimuli. The audio components had the greatest effect on urgency.

Keywords: Urgency · Alerting · Multimodal alerts · Inter-pulse interval (IPI)

1 Introduction

Automation and autonomous technologies are currently being introduced into most transportation systems, to reduce the effects of increasing complexity on user performance. Both ground and air-based systems have benefitted from these improvements, but presently most of these tools are imperfect, meaning that when automation fails, the operator must be able to intervene and assume manual control, often at a moment's notice. Consequently, effective human-automation performance depends on alerts and alarms to warn the operator of such events. For surface transportation, the introduction of new automated tools has increased the number of alerts.

Therefore, designing effective alerts and warnings has become even more critical. Although a considerable literature exists on the effectiveness of alerts, most of the work has focused on unimodal visual, auditory and sometimes tactual signals and the characteristics within each modality that affect perceived urgency and performance.

One method for evaluating the effectiveness of alerts is perceived urgency. Perceived urgency is a construct that refers to the subjective experience of time pressure and the sense of importance associated with a task. Operational definitions of perceived urgency typically involve self-reported measures of time pressure or importance, such as Likert scales or visual analog scales. Perceived urgency is measured by having participants rate their perception of the urgency of signals that vary in one or more signal parameters. Research has identified many factors that contributes to the urgency of unimodal alerts.

H. Mori et al. (Eds.): HCII 2023, LNCS 14056, pp. 203–210, 2023.
https://doi.org/10.1007/978-3-031-48044-7_15

1.1 Unimodal Alerts

Visual alerts are commonly used in vehicles. Drivers may encounter numerous visual warnings both within and outside the vehicle regarding other vehicles, road hazards, and vehicle performance. One important characteristic of visual alerts is color because it can be used to attract the attention of drivers and specific colors are commonly associated with different levels of urgency. It is usually recommended that no more than four colors be used for alerts, each with a specific meaning that conveys the urgency level (Chapanis 1994). The standardization of color on traffic signals and signs has made it easy for drivers to distinguish road conditions based on sign color. According to the Federal Highway Administration (FHA 2020), red is used to communicate stop while yellow is used to convey cautionary messages.

Color is also used in various instances outside of traffic signals to attract attention and convey different levels of urgency. These findings are also applicable to multimodal alarms in automation. When testing the urgency rating of a LED notification light, people rated the notification more urgent when it was presented with a red color and high blinking frequency (Kim, Lee, Lee, Kim, Jung, Han, 2014). It was concluded that red had a longer wavelength than green and therefore, produced greater arousal effects. The wavelength of color has been theorized to influence perceived urgency such that as the wavelength of visible light increases so will perceived urgency (Elliot et al. 2007; Kim et al. 2014). In addition to color, flashing signals increases urgency, based on flash rate.

The effectiveness of auditory alerts can be attributed to the characteristics of the human auditory system. Although the visual system is vastly superior to the auditory system on spatial acuity tasks, the human auditory system can detect and localize sounds from any direction around the listener without any movement of the sensory apparatus (e.g., Middlebrooks and Green 1991). Moreover, the auditory system is superior to vision in temporal acuity. The perceived urgency of unimodal auditory alerts depends on signal frequency, intensity, harmonicity and pulse rate with high-frequency, high-intensity, inharmonic and rapidly pulsed signals being rated the most urgent (e.g., Edworthy et al. 1991; Baldwin and Lewis 2014). Intensity can be a double-edged sword, however, because if intensity is too high, startle effects may be produced, which increase the response time to the alert (Reed and Strybel 2004).

The perceived urgency of both audio and visual alerts is affected by the temporal characteristics of alerts. In vision, flash rate can affect conspicuity and urgency; in audition, pulse rate can affect perceived urgency. For both modalities perceived urgency is inversely related to signal presentation rate. Note that the temporal pattern of any signal can be described in terms of flash/pulse rate but rate measures combine both signal duration and the intervening blank/quiet interval. Therefore, in this report, we characterize the duration and interpulse interval (IPI) separately. Baldwin and Lewis (2014) evaluated several characteristics of audio, visual and tactual alerts on perceived urgency. IPI significantly affected perceived urgency in each modality, but the greatest effect was shown for audio alerts.

1.2 Multimodal Alerts

Urgency can be increased when alerts contain combinations of signals from more than one modality. Several investigations (e.g., Erp et al. 2015; Biondi et al. 2017) have shown that urgency ratings of multimodal alerts are higher than the corresponding unimodal alerts from each modality. Erp et al. (2015) studied the effect of temporal signal characteristics within and across modalities on perceived urgency. Participants rated the perceived urgency of unimodal visual, auditory and tactile alerts, and bimodal and trimodal alerts across a wide range of pulse durations and IPIs. The effects of pulse duration and IPI were consistent across modalities in that IPI was inversely related to urgency. Multimodal signals were perceived as more urgent than unimodal signals, suggesting that temporal parameters can be deployed to construct integrated, multisensory warning signals with a pre-specified degree of perceived urgency.

Biondi et al. (2017) examined the perceived urgency of auditory, visual, tactile, and multimodal audiotactile warnings while participants were multitasking. Multimodal audio-tactile signals were rated higher in urgency, but this effect decreased with increases in work-load. Finally, Lewis et al. (2013) investigated whether multimodal alerting might be more effective than unimodal alerting for drivers who engaged in a secondary, working-memory task. The multimodal stimuli included low and high urgency audio-visual and visuo-tactile combinations with urgency determined by IPI (9 vs 475 ms). Visual signals and visual components were static green or red boxes with the word "Warning" in the center. The results showed that multimodal signals had faster response times than unimodal signals. In general, the higher urgency modalities also had faster response times. However, drivers were less likely to distinguish between high and low urgency signals when working memory demands were high.

In summary, several characteristics of audio and visual unimodal alerts have been shown to affect urgency. Multimodal audiovisual alerts produce higher urgency ratings than unimodal auditory, visual and even tactual alerts. The urgency of unimodal auditory and visual alerts is inversely affected by IPI, and the effect of IPI is more pronounced for audio alerts. Although IPI also affects multimodal alerts in previous work, the IPIs in each modality were equivalent, thus producing synchronous multimodal events. Given the greater sensitivity of the auditory system to temporal changes, and the stronger effect of IPI on unimodal auditory alerts, possibly urgency can be enhanced with asynchronous audiovisual multimodal alerts having IPI values that are optimized for each modality. This was the purpose of the present investigation: determine perceived urgency of multimodal audio-visual alerts for both synchronous and asynchronous IPIs in each modality. We determined combinations of IPI, audio frequency, and visual color of audiovisual alarms that affect perceived urgency and response time.

2 Method

2.1 Participants

Sixty-three participants (14 Males, 47 Females, 2 Non-Binary) were recruited through the CSULB SONA recruitment system and received 1 course credit for participation. Participants' age ranged from 18 to 36 years (M = 19.35 yrs., SD = 2.91 yrs). Three participants reported abnormal vision and were excluded from subsequent analysis, and 4 participants were removed because they exceeded the 90-min time limit. All participants reported not having any hearing deficits.

2.2 Materials/Apparatus

The software PsyToolKit was used for online experimental implementation and data collection (Stoet 2010, 2017). For all stimuli the pulse duration was constant at 200 ms. Audiovisual stimuli were created by presenting a combined alert that varied in Audio Frequency, and Visual Color. The audio stimuli were sine waves with frequencies of 350 Hz or 700 Hz, and these were presented with small one-inch squares of red or yellow. Synchronous and asynchronous Visual and Audio IPIs were created by combining 50, 100, 150, or 200 ms. Table 1 shows all combinations of unimodal characteristics that made up the audiovisual alerts. Some combinations of IPIs, for example 50 ms audio IPI and 50 ms visual IPI, produced synchronous alerts. When IPIs were different between modalities asynchronous alerts were produced with one component being presented at a faster rate (e.g., 50 ms Audio IPI and 100 ms Visual IPI). Figure 1 illustrates one possible alarm combination with a Visual IPI = 50 ms, and Audio IPI = 100 ms, Audio frequency = 350 Hz and Visual color = red. All alerts lasted for 2000 ms as shown in Fig. 1.

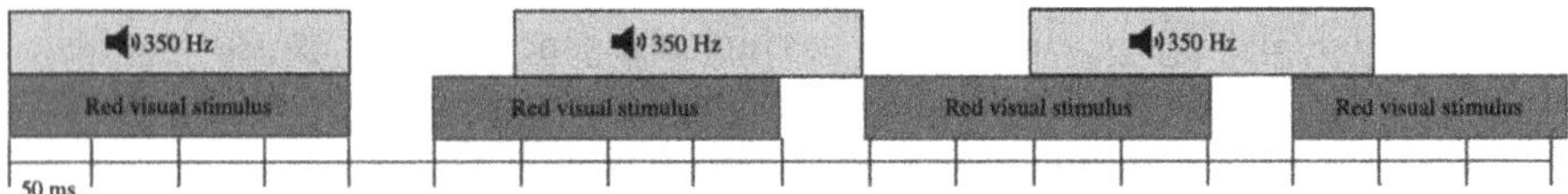

Fig. 1. Illustration of an audiovisual alarm with an audio IPI of 100 ms and a visual IPI of 50 ms. Each stimulus had a 200 ms pulse duration and was presented for approximately 2000 ms.

Table 1 shows the combinations of audio and visual parameters that produced 36 unique stimuli for evaluating perceived urgency and measuring response time. Each combination was presented three times within a trial block (108 trials per block), and two trial blocks were run. In the first block response-time was measured. In the second block urgency ratings were collected.

2.3 Procedure

Participants were instructed to imagine they were driving on a two-lane highway when a car changed lanes in front of them that was signaled by an alert. A braking response consisted of pressing on the spacebar when an alert was presented (see Fig. 2). For response time blocks, participants pressed the spacebar to stimulate braking when an alert was presented. For the rating trial blocks, alarms were presented in random order, and participants rated their level of perceived urgency on a 1–10 scale with one being the lowest urgency and ten being the highest urgency. Participants were instructed to adjust their volume to a comfortable listening level and to keep the volume at the same level throughout the experiment.

Table 1. All combinations of audio and visual stimuli that were tested in this experiment.

Audio IPI (ms)	Visual IPI (ms)	Frequency (Hz)	Color
50	50	700 350	Red Yellow
50	100	700 350	Red Yellow
50	150	700 350	Red Yellow
50	200	700 350	Red Yellow
100	50	700 350	Red Yellow
100	100	700 350	Red Yellow
150	50	700 350	Red Yellow
150	150	700 350	Red Yellow
200	50	700 350	Red Yellow

Fig. 2. Example of the front view windshield presented to the participants during the experiment. The red square is the position of the visual component of the alarm.

3 Results

To determine the effectiveness of each signal characteristic on perceived urgency and response times, two regression analyses were run. The first analysis examined urgency ratings as a function of Visual Color (red vs. green), Audio Frequency (350 vs 700 Hz.),

Visual IPI (50,100,150, 200 ms) and Audio IPI (50,100,150, 200 ms). For urgency ratings the overall regression equation was significant ($F(4,2267) = 376.03$, $p < .0001$; $r^2 = .40$) A summary table of the effectiveness of each factor is presented in Table 2.

Table 2. Summary Table of Regression Analysis Perceived Urgency Ratings

Variable	Parameter estimate	Standard Error	Standardized estimate	t value	p
Intercept	7.16	.13	0	54.33	<.0001
Audio IPI	−.019	.0007	−.48	−27.23	<.0001
Visual IPI	−.001	.0007	−.03	−1.56	.1189
Audio Frequency	1.69	.068	.41	24.95	<.0001
Visual Color	.41	.068	.10	6.07	<.0001

All factors except Visual IPI were significant predictors of urgency ratings. Audio IPI and Audio Frequency were the strongest predictors of urgency, based on standardized coefficients. The Audio IPI coefficient is negative, meaning that lower IPI values are associated with higher urgency ratings. Audio Frequency is a positive predictor of urgency, as the higher frequency produced higher urgency ratings. Visual Color did significantly predict urgency, with red producing higher urgency ratings, but Visual IPI did not significantly predict urgency. To further illustrate the differential effect of IPI in each modality, Fig. 3 shows the mean urgency rating as function of Audio and Visual IPI. Mean urgency ratings were on the average highest for Audio IPI = 50 ms, and decreased

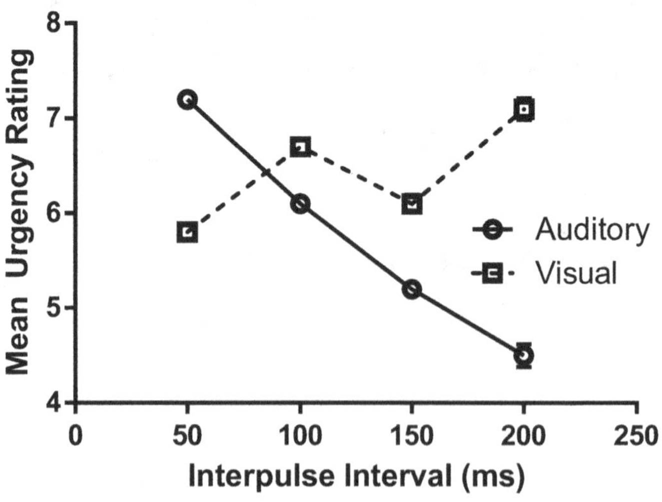

Fig. 3. Urgency ratings as a function of Audio and Visual IPI

linearly with longer Audio IPIs. Urgency ratings were essentially unaffected by Visual IPIs.

A second regression analysis was performed evaluating the effectiveness of each factor on response time. The overall regression equation was not significant ($F(4,2267) = 1.13$, $p = .34$).

4 Discussion

The finding on urgency ratings of multimodal audiovisual alerts were consistent with previous research on unimodal alerts. Auditory IPI had the highest influence on perceived urgency compared with visual IPI, high frequencies and red alerts were highest in urgency (Baldwin et al. 2014). Findings from this study demonstrated that audiovisual alerts do not have to be synchronous to convey high urgency. In fact, alarms that have a faster audio component than the visual component will produce the highest perceived urgency. We obtained the highest mean ratings of urgency ($M = 8.36$, $Std = .16$) for red signals at 700 Hz and Auditory IPI of 50 ms regardless of visual IPI. The mean ratings for yellow signals at 700 Hz and Auditory IPI = 50 ms were only slightly lower ($M = 7.9$, $Std = .05$), regardless of visual IPI. One possible explanation for these results is work in multisensory integration showing that audio temporal signals can capture visual events (e.g., Shams et al. 2000). This would mean that the faster pulse rate of the audio component would make the flashing rate appear faster.

Moreover, the effects of frequency and color shown here are consistent with work on unimodal urgency. Audiovisual alerts that were red in color and contained with high frequencies were perceived as more urgent. Note however, that visual color was not a strong predictor of urgency. Taken together, the visual component of these alerts may not have to flash at all, and a multimodal alert consisting of a stationary visual alert combined with a pulsing audio alert may produce high levels of urgency and be more informative to the user.

However, the audiovisual alerts used here did not affect response time. We believe this is due to the simple response task, which may have produce ceiling effects and limiting the sensitivity of this measure. A more appropriate measure might require driving in a simulator with either braking or steering wheel motions as a response to an alert.

4.1 Summary and Conclusions

Multimodal alarms are becoming more important for notifying users of critical events, and the results from this study might facilitate alarm designs in automated vehicles. The urgency of audiovisual alerts can be achieved with adjustments to the audio components, and provide more information via the visual channel. In fact, as shown by Biondi et al (2017), the visual component of the alert can be stationary thus enabling more information to be presented on the visual component of the alert. Of course, additional research is needed to verify our findings and to examine additional parameters known to affect urgency of unimodal audio and visual alerts.

References

Baldwin, C.L., Lewis, B.A.: Perceived urgency mapping across modalities within a driving context. Appl. Ergon. **45**(5), 1270–1277 (2014)

Biondi, F., Leo, M., Gastaldi, M., Rossi, R., Mulatti, C.: How to drive drivers nuts: effect of auditory, vibrotactile, and multimodal warnings on perceived urgency, annoyance, and acceptability. Transp. Res. Record, **2663**(1), 34–39 (2017)

Chan, A.H., Ng, A.W.: Perceptions of implied hazard for visual and auditory alerting signals. Safety Sci. **47**(3), 346–352 (2009)

Chapanis, A.: Hazards associated with three signal words and four colours on warning signs. Ergonomics **37**(2), 265–275 (1994)

Edworthy, J., Loxley, S., Dennis, I.: Improving auditory warning design: relationship between warning sound parameters and perceived urgency. Hum. Factors **33**(2), 205–231 (1991)

Elliot, A.J., Maier, M.A., Moller, A.C., Friedman, R., Meinhardt, J.: Color and psychological functioning: the effect of red on performance attainment. J. Exp. Psychol. Gen. **136**(1), 154 (2007)

Erp, J.B., Toet, A., Janssen, J.B.: Uni-, bi-, and tri-modal warning signals: effects of temporal parameters and sensory modality on perceived urgency. Saf. Sci. **72**, 1–8 (2015)

Federal Highway Administration. United States Road Symbol Signs (2020). https://mutcd.fhwa.dot.gov/services/publications/fhwaop02084/index.html

Kim, M., Lee, J., Lee, H., Kim, S., Jung, H., Han, K.H.: The color and blink frequency of LED notification lights and smartphone users' urgency perception. In: International Conference on Human-Computer Interaction, pp. 621–625 (2014)

Lewis, B.A., Penaranda, B.N., Roberts, D.M., Baldwin, C.L.: Max brake force as a measure of perceived urgency in a driving context. In: Proceedings of the Human Factors and Ergonomics Society Annual Meeting, vol. 57, no. 1, pp. 2162–2166 (2013)

Middlebrooks, J.C., Green, D.M.: Sound localization by human listeners. Annu. Rev. Psychol. **42**, 135–159 (1991)

Reed, D., Strybel, T.Z.: Does the perceived urgency of auditory signals affect auditory spatial cueing in visual search tasks? In: Proceedings of The Human Factors and Ergonomics Society 48th Annual Meeting, pp. 1853–1858 (2004)

Selcon, S.J., Taylor, R.M., McKenna, F.P.: Integrating multiple information sources: using redundancy in the design of warnings. Ergonomics **38**(11), 2362–2370 (1995)

Stoet, G.: PsyToolkit - A software package for programming psychological experiments using Linux. Behav. Res. Methods **42**(4), 1096–1104 (2010)

Stoet, G.: PsyToolkit: a novel web-based method for running online questionnaires and reaction-time experiments. Teach. Psychol. **44**(1), 24–31 (2017)

Tomkinson, E.J., Stammers, R.B.: The perceived hazardousness, urgency, and attention-gettingness of fluorescent and non-fluorescent colours. Contemp. Ergon. 443–447 (2000)

Van Erp, J.B., Van Veen, H.A.: Vibrotactile in-vehicle navigation system. Transport. Res. F: Traffic Psychol. Behav. **7**(4–5), 247–256 (2004)

Van Erp, J.B., Toet, A., Janssen, J.B.: Uni-, bi-and tri-modal warning signals: effects of temporal parameters and sensory modality on perceived urgency. Saf. Sci. **72**, 1–8 (2015)

Wogalter, M.S., Godfrey, S.S., Fontenelle, G.A., Desaulniers, D.R., Rothstein, P.R., Laughery, K.R.: Effectiveness of warnings. Hum. Factors **29**(5), 599–612 (1987)

SGDraw: Scene Graph Drawing Interface Using Object-Oriented Representation

Tianyu Zhang[1], Xusheng Du[1], Chia-Ming Chang[2], Xi Yang[3], and Haoran Xie[1](✉)

[1] Japan Advanced Institute of Science and Technology, Ishikawa, Japan
s2110414@jaist.ac.jp
[2] The University of Tokyo, Tokyo, Japan
[3] Jilin University, Jilin, China

Abstract. Scene understanding is an essential and challenging task in computer vision. To provide the visually- grounded graphical structure of an image, the scene graph has received increased attention due to offering explicit grounding of visual concepts. Previous works commonly get scene graphs by using ground-truth annotations or generating from the target images. However, drawing a proper scene graph for image retrieval, image generation, and multi-modal applications is difficult. The conventional scene graph annotation interface is not easy to use and hard to revise the results. The automatic scene graph generation methods using deep neural networks only focus on the objects and relationships while disregarding attributes. In this work, we propose SGDraw, a scene graph drawing interface that uses object- oriented representation to help users interactively draw and edit scene graphs. SGDraw provides a web-based scene graph annotation and creation tool for scene understanding applications. To verify the effectiveness of the proposed interface, we conducted a comparison study with the conventional tool and the user experience study. The results show that SGDraw can help create scene graphs with richer details and describe the images more accurately than traditional bounding box annotations. We believe the proposed SGDraw can be useful in various vision tasks, such as image generation and retrieval. The project source code is available at https://github.com/zty0304/SGDraw.

Keywords: Scene graph · Image representation · Object-oriented representation · User interface

1 Introduction

Scene graph is a common and popular way to describe scene understanding, first proposed for image retrieval tasks to search for images with similar descriptions in image datasets [8]. In addition, scene graphs are used for a wide range of vision applications, such as image retrieval [8,18], image captioning [3], visual reasoning [19], visual answering [5], and robotics [1]. The conventional approaches for scene graph creation have been mainly based on a manually annotated image

H. Mori et al. (Eds.): HCII 2023, LNCS 14056, pp. 211–226, 2023.
https://doi.org/10.1007/978-3-031-48044-7_16

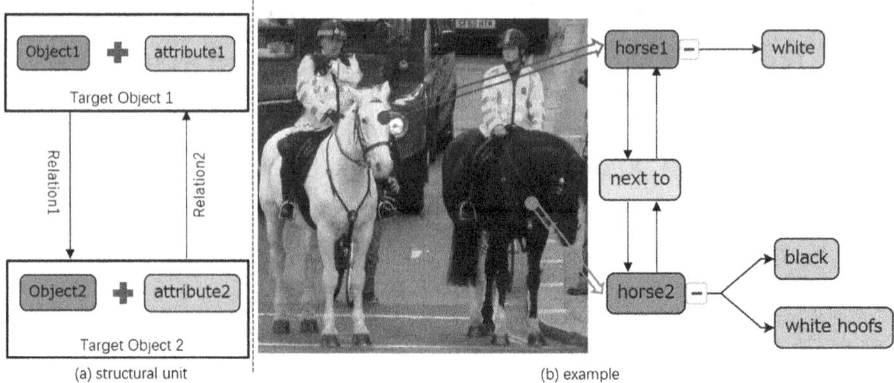

Fig. 1. Illustration of the structural unit (a) as an object-oriented representation and (b) its example in this work. Taking two objects as an example, the attributes as objects can be directly manipulated, and attached to the objects with user operations. The relationships can then be constructed among the objects.

detection dataset, and the annotation tasks are usually time-consuming and laborious. The visual genome dataset [12] is the most common and popular dataset for scene graphs, with around 10^5 annotated images. However, the annotated scene graphs have challenging issues, such as sparse image annotation, repeated labels, and unreasonable annotation. In addition, these scene graphs are difficult to be modified and produced in conventional computer vision tasks.

To solve these issues, one possible solution is the automatic generation of scene graph generation with deep learning approaches. The task of scene graph generation is to generate a corresponding graph-structure representation from an image, and abstract the objects and object relationships from the images. The automatic generation approaches can only generate limited scene graphs on commonly used object categories and predicates, and have difficulty for rare and previously unseen compositions [9,10]. In addition, these automatic approaches can complete the generation of objects and relationships but lack the description of attributes, which makes the generated scene graph incomplete. Therefore, we aim to provide a novel scene graph drawing interface with users in the loop.

In this work, we propose an interactive drawing user interface, SGDraw for creating scene graphs using object-oriented representation, as shown in Fig. 1. The proposed system can achieve more comprehensive and detailed results than the conventional annotation interfaces. SGDraw adopts object-oriented representation for scene graph annotation by considering objects, object relationships, and object attributes. SGDraw can take advantage of the user's cognitive ability in the drawing process from target images. We verified the proposed interface in the image dataset and conducted a comparison study between the conventional annotation method using bounding boxes and our proposed approach. The evaluation results demonstrated the superiority of the proposed approach in drawing comprehensive and detailed scene graphs.

We list our main contributions as follows:

- We propose an object-oriented annotation approach of scene graphs, which adopts the structural unit of the object, its attributes, and the relationships among objects. In this way, we can describe the image in detail and create a comprehensive and detailed scene graph.
- We design a web-based lightweight annotation tool that is easy to deploy and operate so that the proposed SGDraw can draw scene graphs interactively.
- We conduct user experiments to verify the performance of our proposed object-oriented annotation approach for annotation, especially the effectiveness of annotation on complex images.

2 Realted Woek

2.1 Scene Graph Generation

As the expansion of VRD, many methods have been proposed for SGG to detect objects and their relationships [4,14,15,27]. Subsequent works significantly improved performance on all-shot recall [26,28,29] and actively explored the zero-shot generalization problem [21,22]. These methods generated scene graphs in two different approaches [13]. The conventional methods of scene graph generation adopt both object detection and pairwise predicate estimation. The objects are first detected given a bounding box, and then the predicates are predicted using conditional random fields [4,8] or a classification approach [11,17]. The other approach is to jointly infer the objects and their relationships based on the suggestions of object regions [32]. However, these approaches focus on objects and their relations without attention to object attributes that significantly weigh the image description. We consider that equalizing attributes over objects and their relations can improve the quality of scene graphs.

2.2 User Interface for Scene Graph

Visual Genome dataset [12] provided an annotation tool and used Amazon's Mechanical Turk (AMT) to collect scene graph data [8]. This tool can obtain instances of objects and their relationships by users drawing bounding boxes to identify objects and describing relationships between pairs of objects through text box input. However, this interface has no intuitive, real-time visual output and is difficult to modify. GeneAnnotator [31] provided a semi-automatic annotation tool for scene graphs, which provides rule-based relationship recommendation algorithms that can reduce the annotation effort. But this tool only focuses on the traffic images and outputs scene graphs without attributes and suitable layout. An interactive interface was presented for scene graph drawing [30], which recommended attributes for users to reduce the drawing time cost. However, this work lacked image visualization and extensive evaluations of the proposed functions. In this work, we aim to provide an interactive drawing interface for scene graphs by the object-oriented method.

2.3 Object-Oriented Interface

Object-oriented methods have been widely used in design tasks. An object-oriented interface [16] was proposed to generate and manipulate polyhedral data flow graphs. An integrated set of object-oriented pixel-based vectorization algorithms [20] was then presented for various classes of graphic objects in engineering drawings. These interfaces performed interactions that were previously tedious or even impossible with a coherent and consistent interaction experience throughout the entire interface. Next, an object-oriented drawing approach [24] was proposed to represent attributes as objects that can be manipulated directly. Considering the basic components of the scene graph, the objects, object attributes, and their relationships could be manipulated directly by the user in this work.

3 Scene Graph Drawing

In this work, we aim to propose a drawing interface for scene graph annotation and creation. The basic structural unit of the proposed approach is represented in Fig. 1.

3.1 Scene Graph

Since the location relationships between objects, rather than coordinate information, are more used in most of the follow-up research. In this work, scene graph creation is achieved by objects without bounding boxes, and we provide the open-ended and free-form manipulation of scene graph nodes. The scene graph from an image is defined as follows by a tuple of (O', R) with object attributes O' and relations R:

$$P(G|I) = P(O', R|I), \tag{1}$$

where P stands for probability, I represents the input image, and G is the desired target scene graph containing object attributes and relations. Specifically, the image is partitioned into a set of objects $O' = \{o'_1, ..., o'_n\}$ corresponding to each of the n objects with attributes in the image. $R = \{r_1, ..., r_l\}$ is the set of relations between pairs of objects.

$$P(o') = P(o, A), \tag{2}$$

where o' is the target object with attributes to be generated, containing the input target object o and its attribute set A. Each object comes with its unique set of attributes $A = \{a_1, ..., a_m\}$ corresponding to the m attributes of the target object.

In this work, we handle the object and its attributes as a manipulable object unit. By linking the pairwise relationships between different object units, we can perform the task of drawing the original image to the scene graph. In contrast

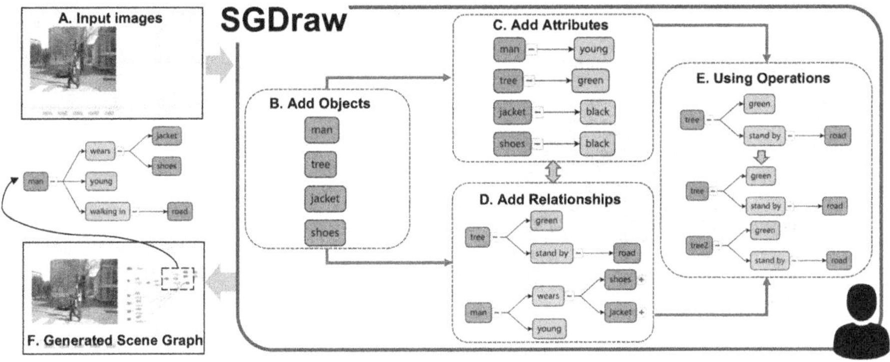

Fig. 2. Workflow of the proposed interface. (A) With a task image inputted to the SGDraw, the user starts (B) adding objects, and then they can (C) add attributes or (D) relationships. After that, they can choose to (E) use the auxiliary operations (like cloning, as shown in the figure) to change the structure of the graph. Repeat these steps until (F) obtains the desired scene graph.

to the conventional scene graph annotation task that focuses on the objects and their relationships, we also focus on the object attributes that are easily ignored and that account for a large proportion of the images. The drawn scene graph can be more consistent with the image content and represent the image scene in more detail.

3.2 Object-Oriented Representation

Inspired by the object-oriented drawing approach [24], we aim to propose an object-oriented representation of scene graphs for image annotation and graph editing tasks. In this representation, we can extend attributes to objects directly for manipulation, as shown in Fig. 2. Specifically, the proposed object-oriented approach has the following features:

Abstraction. The input images may contain repetitive contents, such as many horses and trees (Fig. 1, Fig. 2(A)). For repetitive objects, concrete objects may contain similar attributes. Therefore, we can abstract them into a class, such as the class of horse. Through the process of class abstraction, we can reuse the scene graph data to enhance the versatility and scalability of the proposed system.

Uniqueness. As shown in Fig. 2(B), each object has its unique identifier by which the corresponding object can be located. The identity of the annotated objects will not change during the whole task. Different objects in the same category are given different identifiers, such as "horse1" and "horse2" in Fig. 1. By assigning the identifiers to objects (Fig. 2(D)), we can correspond scene graph nodes to unique objects in the image to create detailed and higher-quality scene graphs.

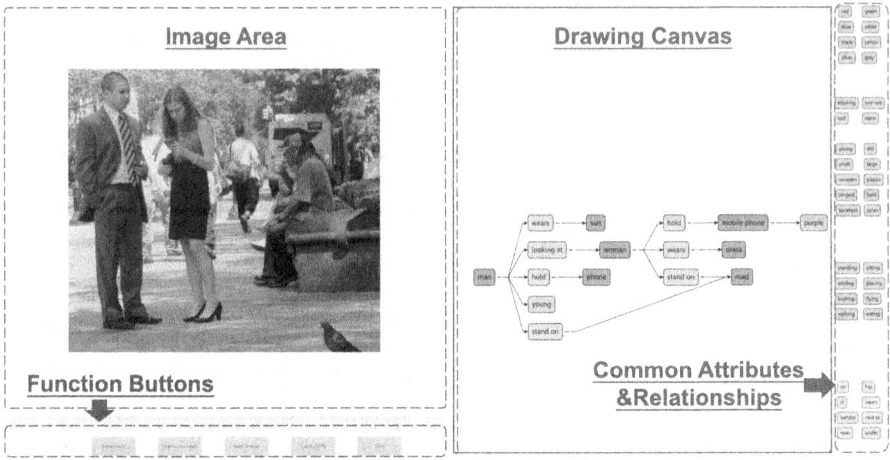

Fig. 3. Screenshot of the SGDraw interface. On the left is the input image display area, and on the right is the scene graph operation and real-time generation area. Meanwhile, on the right side of the interactive interface, we provide some common attributes and relationships for users to choose and reference.

Polymorphism. Polymorphism refers to the fact that objects have diverse attributes. Multiple different attributes can be assigned to the same object simultaneously, and the same attribute can be assigned to multiple different objects simultaneously. For example, in Fig. 1, in the case of several people and horses, different attributes like black color for fur and white color for hoofs can be assigned to "horse2". In addition, as shown in Fig. 2(C), attributes like black can be assigned to the "jacket" and the "shoes". The diversity of attributes allows each object to correspond to the same or different attributes, which enhances the flexibility and reusability of the system.

Inheritance. Inheritance refers to the ability to define and implement objects on the basis of objects that already exist. The attributes and relationships associated with existing objects can be used as their own content, and new attributes and relationships can be added. Specifically, the user can select objects to store after drawing the scene graph. As shown in Fig. 3, all attributes and relationships of the selected object can be stored in the drop-down box in the left corner of the interactive interface. The user can select the object at any time to inherit all previously stored attributes and relationships in subsequent operations (Fig. 2(E)). The use of inheritance provides a hierarchical structure between objects, attributes, and relationships. Inheritance makes it possible to share common features and increase the reusability of the system.

3.3 SGDraw Interface

In order to explore the effectiveness of the proposed SGDraw, we developed a web-based user interface, as shown in Fig. 3. The objects, attributes, and pairwise

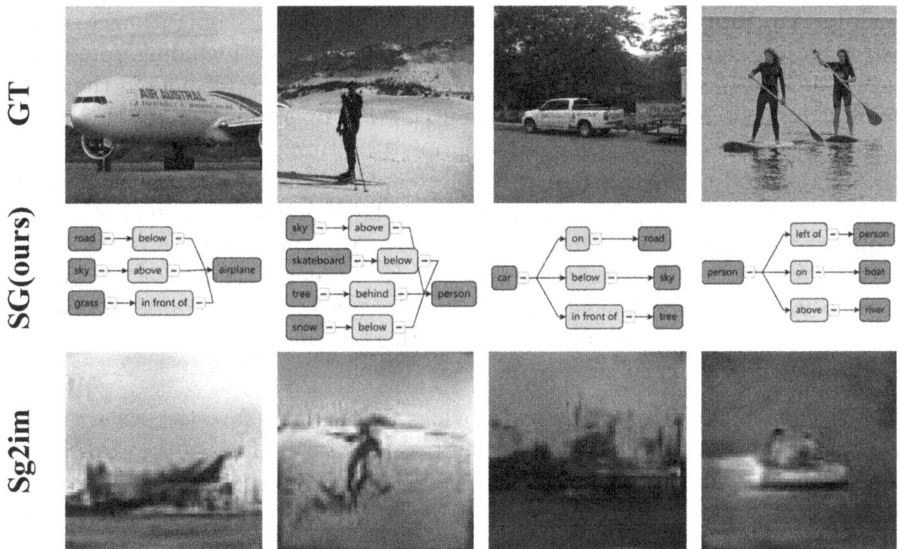

Fig. 4. Example of image generation tasks with the drawn scene graphs with ground truth images from the VG dataset (1st row), the drawn scene graphs (2nd row), and the generated images (3rd row).

relationships between objects are considered as objects that can be manipulated directly. We provide an open and fully accessible annotation tool that takes full advantage of the user's cognitive ability to perform the task of annotating any kind of image and creating their corresponding scene graphs in real time. In contrast to the previous approach that requires drawing the bounding box on the image first and then describing the objects inside the box, SGDraw can help users easily add/delete and drag nodes depending on their knowledge of the image content until a satisfactory scene graph is drawn. Specifically, we provide the SGDraw with the following interaction features:

Direct Operation of the Scene Graph. In previous interfaces [8,31], the users cannot observe the visualized scene graphs in real time and modify the input content. To solve this issue, we consider the input of the scene graph as a drawing. We provide three kinds of nodes: red nodes for objects; yellow nodes for relationships; blue nodes for attributes. The user can add a new object and attribute by simply right-clicking on the background and object. A relationship node can be generated when clicking two different objects. We also provided common attributes and relationships for reference, which were derived from the common ranking in the scene dataset [25]. The common part is not displayed on the screen initially to avoid giving hints to the user and making the drawn scene graph monotonous. It will be shown by pressing the key when the user needs it and will be automatically closed after use. We believe that common attributes and relationships can simplify users' input and facilitate creative thinking.

Various Auxiliary Operations. We designed the auxiliary operations to modify the graph structure and simplify the input process, including removing, cloning, undoing, zooming, collapsing, and dragging. We implemented the undo function to reduce the loss caused by user error operations, and the removing function to help users change the graph structure freely. We implemented the zooming and collapsing functions for complex scene graph drawing to help users understand the overall graph structure. The dragging function allows users to optimize the layout to achieve visual results that are easier to operate and observe. We also added the cloning function for similar attributes and relationships to increase the efficiency of the drawing process. These operations are directly conducted on the scene graphs with real-time feedback to help users clearly understand the changes in the scene graphs.

Flexible Data Archive. SGDraw provides two ways to save the scene graph: JSON files to facilitate subsequent vision tasks, and SVG files so that the visual scene graphs become available to study and understand the scene images more intuitively. For JSON files, as shown in Fig. 4, the created scene graph results can be adapted to various vision tasks, such as image generation. In particular, we suggested the user write objects and relationships due to the limitations of the generation algorithm (sg2im [7]). For SVG files, users can draw the images directly and make the image interactive by changing part of the code, and then inserting it into HTML while viewing through the browser. SGDraw allows the users to load the graph and modify it for further usage, which can improve the reusability and maintainability of the scene graph data.

4 User Study

In the user study, we confirmed SGDraw for scene graph drawing and collected feedback from potential users about the effectiveness and usability of the interface. We asked 14 participants (aged 25 to 30, eight males and six females) who are graduate students with knowledge of machine learning. Especially, we designed two experiments: a comparison study and a user experience study. We reproduced the previous interface for scene graphs [8] in the comparison study, and the task images used in the experiments were selected from the Visual Genome dataset [12]. The evaluation process consisted of three stages:
1) Introduction and Training (10–15 min). We first introduced the background of the scene graphs. The experimenter then guided the participants to explore the functions and workflow of the previous interface and SGDraw, and we intentionally provided a simple image for participants as an example. This was done for two reasons: First, it ensured that participants had a full understanding of the interfaces, and second, it allowed participants the opportunity to explore and demonstrate understanding.
2) Experience and Usage (20–30 min). To avoid the proficiency effect caused by the interface order for usage, participants were divided into two groups. One group used the previous interface first and then used SGDraw. The other group used SGDraw first and then used the previous interface. Each participant

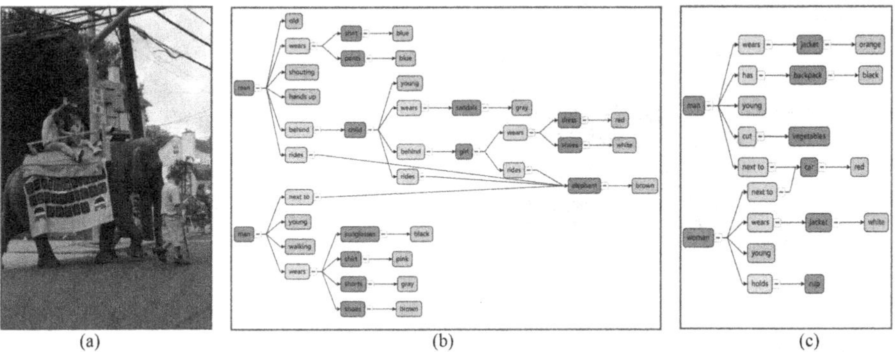

Fig. 5. Examples of scene graphs completed by SGDraw with (a) an image input from the VG dataset, and (b) a completed scene graph. (c) shows the scene graph freely designed from the text input "a couples drive to the forest to have a picnic".

was asked to draw the scene graphs in two interfaces based on two different images. The system automatically counted time without user knowledge. When the participants thought they had finished describing the content of the images, the experimenter collected the results.

We obtained seven task results from the experimenters finally. Each task included four results for an image, two results from the SGDraw, and two results from the previous interface. We collected the objects, attributes, and relationships that participants described on the scene graphs. After collecting the data, we calculated the instances (including objects, attributes, and relationships) per minute for each interface to compare the efficiency of the two interfaces.

3) Questionnaire and Interview (10–15 min). The participants next completed questionnaires about the system. The questionnaires were composed of a 5-point Likert scale (1 for strongly disagree and 5 for strongly agree) to collect the participants' experience of SGDraw. The questions on the first questionnaire, based on the System Usability Scale (SUS), were used for the usability measurement of an interface. The second questionnaire collected usability feedback on every function. The interview then consisted of open-ended questions that were asked to gain the users' feedback on workflow, utility, and usability.

5 Results

5.1 Drawn Scene Graph

Figure 5 shows that SGDraw could help users complete the scene graph drawing task. Without the given ground truth image, the users would use SGDraw to express the image they desired. Users will not be limited to using the scene graphs in the dataset for subsequent tasks such as generation and retrieval. In addition, compared with the results of previous research that did not visualize [8] or whose layout was messy [31], the drawn scene graphs in SGDraw are constructed based

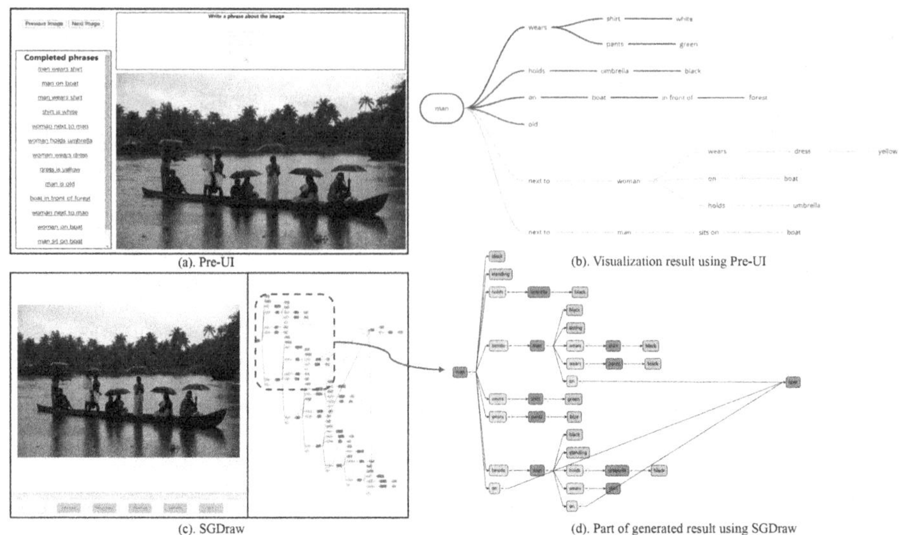

Fig. 6. We conducted the comparison study on Pre-UI [8] and the propsed SGDraw. (a) shows the Pre-UI that we reproduced, and (b) shows the visualization result of the graph. (c) is the screenshot of SGDraw, and (d) is the drawn result.

on an automatic tree layout, which enhances the readability and aesthetic of the users' results. The automatic tree layout helps but does not limit users. The results will be expanded automatically and hierarchically, and users are allowed to change the graph structure with any node or link. In the results, red nodes represent objects, blue nodes represent attributes, and yellow nodes represent relationships. The nodes classified by colors strengthen the user's understanding of specific details and further enhance the comprehensibility of the results on top of the clear layout. The joint storage of the visual scene graphs and the textual results are more conducive to the user's subsequent use and modification.

5.2 Comparison Study

In the comparison study, participants are asked to draw scene graphs with the previous interface (pre-UI) and SGDraw respectively, with two random images, as shown in Fig. 6. We recorded the number of objects, attributes, relationships, and time cost. As shown in Fig. 7(a), SGDraw does not achieve a time advantage on all drawings, but it does achieve the advantage of instance quantity (including objects, attributes, and relationships.) as shown in Fig. 7(b). To verify efficiency, we calculated the number of instances that could be completed for each task per minute. In all experiments, SGDraw achieved the advantage of efficiency.

For Task 1, SGDraw had a larger time cost but better performance in instances quantity (4.9 instances per minute, and 2.1 instances per minute for pre-UI). As shown in Fig. 8, the objects of the task have the same attributes and

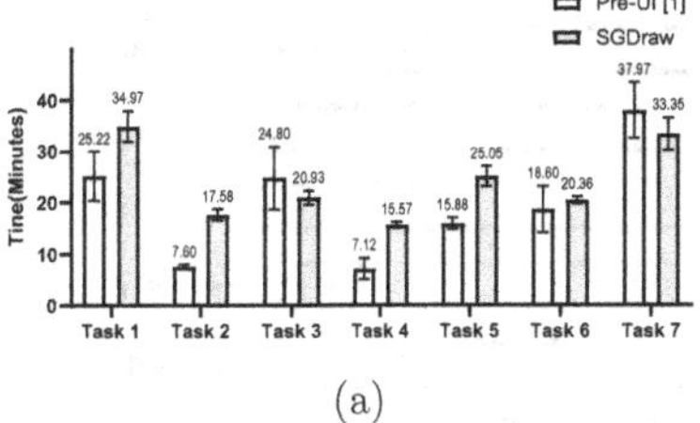

(a)

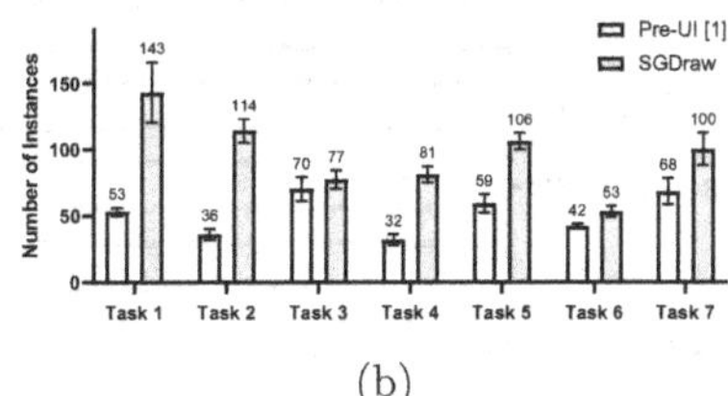

(b)

Fig. 7. (a) The time cost of tasks. The system counts time automatically and implicitly. (b) For each task, experimenters calculated the instances (including objects, attributes, and relationships) in two interfaces. The number of instances that are completed by the SGDraw is more than pre-UI [8].

Fig. 8. Scene graph drawing results from the user study. One participant used SGDraw to complete the complex scene graph for the task image by the auxiliary tool. The similar attributes and relationships of objects in the image made our interface facilitate the scene graph drawing process.

relationships. After completing the scene graph of one person, the participants only needed to use the cloning function with a few modifications using SGDraw to complete the whole task. For Task 7, SGDraw achieved higher scores in both time cost and instance quantity than pre-UI. After the interview and analysis, we found that the recommendation part played a significant role. For complex images with blurry objects, participants had to think about and describe the scene for a long time. The common part helped participants facilitate the input by the given attributes and relationships. In addition, the common part better cued them about attribute and relationship categories that could be considered when participants were out of ideas. For example, the "wooden" given in the common part, users can quickly associate "metallic" and "plastic", even though these attributes are not commonly used compared to color gestures. This part enlightened the participants' minds and reduced their thinking pressure. Task 6 had the smallest difference in the efficiency of the two interfaces. In this task, the image composition was simple and clear; thus, the participants understood

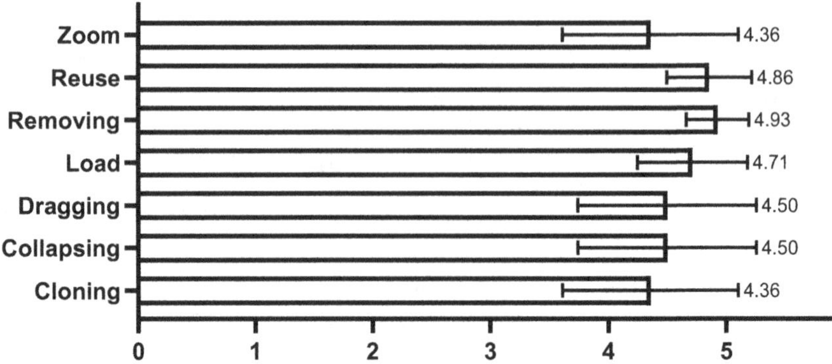

Fig. 9. Result of five-point Likert-scale responses to "Do you agree that function is useful for your scene graph drawing tasks?"

the main objects explicitly in the image. Based on less similar attributes and relationships, the scene graph was completely dependent on the participants to finish it, so SGDraw achieved fair efficiency for this task.

5.3 User Experience Study

Workflow. Participants were interviewed about how the SGDraw integrated with their workflow. Almost all responded positively; the specific feedback from the participants included the following: *"After learning the simple operations, my workflow in this interface was fluid."* (P2). *"In traditional painting, the overall composition of the picture is firstly carried out to determine the position of the objects. In addition, some people have the habit of proceeding to the next object after describing one object. Either of these two workflows can be well implemented in this interface, and both have specific functional assistance."* (P5). Participants also pointed out that there is some disadvantage to the SGDraw. *"The system is smooth and can complete tasks well, but a lot of use of the right click will be unfriendly to people who are used to the left click."* (P10).

According to the interviews, SGDraw obtained a good performance in the workflow. The participants agreed that SGDraw is smooth and helpful for users with different backgrounds. We also found that few function operations may cause discomfort for users with specific computer habits.

Utility. Participants were also asked to rate the usefulness of each of the functions. The functions of SGDraw received a high agreement, as shown in Fig. 9. All of the functions obtained more than four points, which verified that the proposed functions could achieve simple operation and good user experience. Among the various functions, SGDraw's ability to delete the link and node with their subtrees was strongly praised by participants. In addition, the scores of some functions were underrated due to the limitations of usage fields. For example, in scenes with complex and repetitive objects (such as stadiums, and parking), the cloning function always brought a good experience to users. However, in other simple scenes, cloning was not so important.

Based on the various functions, SGDraw could save and reuse scene graphs was strongly favored by participants. Users could thus build their datasets in turn to facilitate later operations. Some specific feedback included the following: *"I like the Cloning function; it frees me from repetitive typing work. Being able to replicate attributes and relationships together is simply awesome."* (P5). *"The Removing function combines delete and rollback, which is a sensible approach. I can easily do what I want, and reduce the cost of my mistakes."* (P7). The functions in SGDraw have high approval which indicates that the various functions are valued and desired. Users can achieve the desired results through the functions we provided in SGDraw, which makes the input process more convenient and quick.

Table 1. The result of the SUS questionnaire. ⇑ indicates that higher scores are better; ⇓ for the other case.

	Questions	Mean
1	I would like to use this system frequently. ⇑	3.86
2	I found this system unnecessarily complex. ⇓	2.21
3	This system was easy to use. ⇑	4.36
4	I would need the support of a technical person to be able to use this system. ⇓	2.14
5	I found the various functions in this system were well integrated. ⇑	4.21
6	I thought there was too much inconsistency in this system. ⇓	1.29
7	I would imagine that most people would learn to use this system very quickly. ⇑	4.57
8	I found this system very cumbersome to use. ⇓	2.00
9	I felt very confident in using this system. ⇑	4.14
10	I needed to learn a lot of things before I could get going with this system. ⇓	1.57

Usability. Participants were asked to complete questionnaires about interface usability. The questionnaire was designed with the question items using SUS, which provides an overall usability assessment measure consisting of 10 items. We use a five-point Likert scale (one for strongly disagree and five for strongly agree).

As shown in Table 1, SGDraw achieved good performance with high scores in positive items and low scores in negative items. Almost all participants agreed that SGDraw is easy to use (Scored 4.36) and that most people learned to use it quickly (Scored 4.57). They strongly disagreed that there were too many inconsistencies in SGDraw (Scored 1.29) and many things to learn before usage (Scored 1.57). The total SUS availability score of SGDraw was 78.9 out of 100. Based on the results of previous research [2], this total score shows that SGDraw should be judged to be acceptable, and the Adjective Rating should be "excellent."

All participants commented that the interface is intuitive and easy to learn. The participants noted the following: *"The common attributes part is great! It helps me spread my mind when I don't know what to write, and it's usually hidden without making me rely on it."* (P11). *"No need for more knowledge, it seems friendly for most people."* (P1). *"It is interesting to operate directly on the results. You can intuitively see the changes in the graphs. Compared with the textual results, the graphs are always easier to understand."* (P4). Several participants pointed out that more functions are needed, such as selecting the common attributes by themselves: *"Quite smart and consistent functions it has created. For people with different tasks, the common attributes required are also different. Perhaps it is a better way to let users set the common attributes themselves."* (P6).

Based on the interviews, the visualization results and direct operations on the graphs have received favorable reviews. We noted that the common area on the right side of SGDraw sparked discussion. Participants agreed that it can simplify operations and inspire users' minds, but it should also be able to be smarter. At the moment, we only display some common attributes fixedly. However, different users need different common attributes. Allowing users to change the common area by themselves will improve the interface's interactivity.

6 Conclusion

This work presented SGDraw, a scene graph drawing interface based on the object-oriented method, to help users draw scene graphs succinctly and conveniently. We designed a set of complete functions and presented common tools to ease user operations. Finally, we conducted a user study to verify our proposed interface. We found that the proposed interface can especially work well with complex scene graphs.

For limitations of this work, the frequent right clicks may make users who are accustomed to left clicks uncomfortable. In addition, the function design can be improved to help users obtain free and better experiences. As future work, we envision combining SGDraw with the scene graph generation algorithms, which can help users semi-automatically complete the scene graph drawing. Beside of scene graph, we also plan to apply the object-oriented method in other domains, such as illustration drawing [6] and layout design [23]. To facilitate the subsequent work using SGDraw, we released the source code of this work in an open source platform.

Acknowledgements. We thank all the participants in our user study. This work was supported by JAIST Research Grant, and JSPS KAKENHI JP20K19845, Japan.

References

1. Amiri, S., Chandan, K., Zhang, S.: Reasoning with scene graphs for robot planning under partial observability. IEEE Robot. Automat. Lett. **7**(2), 5560–5567 (2022)
2. Bangor, A., Kortum, P.T., Miller, J.T.: An empirical evaluation of the system usability scale. Int. J. Hum. Comput. Interact. **24**(6), 574–594 (2008)

3. Chen, S., Jin, Q., Wang, P., Wu, Q.: Say as you wish: fine-grained control of image caption generation with abstract scene graphs. In: Proceedings of the IEEE/CVF Conference on Computer Vision and Pattern Recognition, pp. 9962–9971 (2020)
4. Dai, B., Zhang, Y., Lin, D.: Detecting visual relationships with deep relational networks. In: Proceedings of the IEEE Conference on Computer Vision and Pattern Recognition, pp. 3076–3086 (2017)
5. Hildebrandt, M., Li, H., Koner, R., Tresp, V., Günnemann, S.: Scene graph reasoning for visual question answering. arXiv preprint arXiv:2007.01072 (2020)
6. Huang, Z., et al.: dualface: two-stage drawing guidance for freehand portrait sketching. Comput. Vis. Media **8**(1), 63–77 (2022)
7. Johnson, J., Gupta, A., Fei-Fei, L.: Image generation from scene graphs. In: Proceedings of the IEEE Conference on Computer Vision and Pattern Recognition, pp. 1219–1228 (2018)
8. Johnson, J., et al.: Image retrieval using scene graphs. In: Proceedings of the IEEE Conference on Computer Vision and Pattern Recognition, pp. 3668–3678 (2015)
9. Knyazev, B., De Vries, H., Cangea, C., Taylor, G.W., Courville, A., Belilovsky, E.: Graph density-aware losses for novel compositions in scene graph generation. arXiv preprint arXiv:2005.08230 (2020)
10. Knyazev, B., de Vries, H., Cangea, C., Taylor, G.W., Courville, A., Belilovsky, E.: Generative compositional augmentations for scene graph prediction. In: Proceedings of the IEEE/CVF International Conference on Computer Vision, pp. 15827–15837 (2021)
11. Kolesnikov, A., Kuznetsova, A., Lampert, C., Ferrari, V.: Detecting visual relationships using box attention. In: Proceedings of the IEEE/CVF International Conference on Computer Vision Workshops (2019)
12. Krishna, R., et al.: Visual genome: connecting language and vision using crowdsourced dense image annotations. Int. J. Comput. Vision **123**(1), 32–73 (2017)
13. Li, Y., Ouyang, W., Zhou, B., Shi, J., Zhang, C., Wang, X.: Factorizable net: an efficient subgraph-based framework for scene graph generation. In: Proceedings of the European Conference on Computer Vision (ECCV), pp. 335–351 (2018)
14. Li, Y., Ouyang, W., Zhou, B., Wang, K., Wang, X.: Scene graph generation from objects, phrases and region captions. In: Proceedings of the IEEE International Conference on Computer Vision, pp. 1261–1270 (2017)
15. Liang, X., Lee, L., Xing, E.P.: Deep variation-structured reinforcement learning for visual relationship and attribute detection. In: Proceedings of the IEEE Conference on Computer Vision and Pattern Recognition, pp. 848–857 (2017)
16. Popoola, T., et al.: An object-oriented interface to the sparse polyhedral library. In: 2021 IEEE 45th Annual Computers, Software, and Applications Conference (COMPSAC), pp. 1825–1831. IEEE (2021)
17. Qi, M., Li, W., Yang, Z., Wang, Y., Luo, J.: Attentive relational networks for mapping images to scene graphs. In: Proceedings of the IEEE/CVF Conference on Computer Vision and Pattern Recognition, pp. 3957–3966 (2019)
18. Qi, M., Wang, Y., Li, A.: Online cross-modal scene retrieval by binary representation and semantic graph. In: Proceedings of the 25th ACM International Conference on Multimedia, pp. 744–752 (2017)
19. Shi, J., Zhang, H., Li, J.: Explainable and explicit visual reasoning over scene graphs. In: Proceedings of the IEEE/CVF Conference on Computer Vision and Pattern Recognition, pp. 8376–8384 (2019)
20. Song, J., Su, F., Tai, C.L., Cai, S.: An object-oriented progressive-simplification-based vectorization system for engineering drawings: model, algorithm, and performance. IEEE Trans. Pattern Anal. Mach. Intell. **24**(8), 1048–1060 (2002)

21. Suhail, M., et al.: Energy-based learning for scene graph generation. In: Proceedings of the IEEE/CVF Conference on Computer Vision and Pattern Recognition, pp. 13936–13945 (2021)
22. Tang, K., Niu, Y., Huang, J., Shi, J., Zhang, H.: Unbiased scene graph generation from biased training. In: Proceedings of the IEEE/CVF Conference on Computer Vision and Pattern Recognition, pp. 3716–3725 (2020)
23. Weng, J., Du, X., Xie, H.: Dualslide: global-to-local sketching interface for slide content and layout design. arXiv preprint arXiv:2304.12506 (2023)
24. Xia, H., Araujo, B., Grossman, T., Wigdor, D.: Object-oriented drawing. In: Proceedings of the 2016 CHI Conference on Human Factors in Computing Systems, pp. 4610–4621 (2016)
25. Xu, D., Zhu, Y., Choy, C.B., Fei-Fei, L.: Scene graph generation by iterative message passing. In: Proceedings of the IEEE Conference on Computer Vision and Pattern Recognition, pp. 5410–5419 (2017)
26. Yang, J., Lu, J., Lee, S., Batra, D., Parikh, D.: Graph r-cnn for scene graph generation. In: Proceedings of the European Conference on Computer Vision (ECCV), pp. 670–685 (2018)
27. Yikang, L., Ouyang, W., Wang, X.: Vip-cnn: a visual phrase reasoning convolutional neural network for visual relationship detection
28. Zellers, R., Yatskar, M., Thomson, S., Choi, Y.: Neural motifs: scene graph parsing with global context. In: Proceedings of the IEEE Conference on Computer Vision and Pattern Recognition, pp. 5831–5840 (2018)
29. Zhang, J., Shih, K.J., Elgammal, A., Tao, A., Catanzaro, B.: Graphical contrastive losses for scene graph parsing. In: Proceedings of the IEEE/CVF Conference on Computer Vision and Pattern Recognition, pp. 11535–11543 (2019)
30. Zhang, T., Du, X., Chang, C.M., Yang, X., Xie, H.: Interactive drawing interface for editing scene graph. In: 2022 International Conference on Cyberworlds (CW), pp. 171–172. IEEE (2022)
31. Zhang, Z., Zhang, C., Niu, Z., Wang, L., Liu, Y.: Geneannotator: a semi-automatic annotation tool for visual scene graph. arXiv preprint arXiv:2109.02226 (2021)
32. Zhu, G., et al.: Scene graph generation: a comprehensive survey. arXiv preprint arXiv:2201.00443 (2022)

Social Media, Creative Industries and Cultural Digital Experiences

Ghostlee: A Location-Based Social Augmented Reality Application

Abdullah Alzeer[1,2](✉), Felwah Alhudaithi[2], and Abdulrahman Alshimemeri[2]

[1] Outbound Interactive, Riyadh, Saudi Arabia
abdullahzeer27@gmail.com
[2] Table Knight Games, Riyadh, Saudi Arabia

Abstract. Ghostlee is a location-based pervasive social game in which players use mobile devices with location-based capabilities to create, share and reply to comments posted by others. Feedback from initial user testing involving 18 players over 2 weeks reveals patterns of play, preferred settings for play, and the limitations of location-based play. Social AR sessions are frequently short, conducted in between, around, and sometimes in conjunction with the many activities of people's daily lives. In this study we reflect on the AR design patterns and their alignment with Ghostlee's socio-cultural design considerations. Future directions for location-based social games are described.

Keywords: Location-based games · augmented reality · social games · locative games

1 Introduction

Location technologies, such as global positioning systems (GPS) have facilitated the accelerated growth of location-based games [1, 2]. Location-based games have emerged in fields ranging from leisure [3–5], education [6], entertainment [7], cultural heritage [8], marketing [9] to social networking [10], events [11] and health [12]. Social location-based games (or locative social games) are a genre of games that facilitate social connection within the gameplay. Augmented reality (AR) location-based games involve overlaying information such as text and/or multimedia over the physical interaction space. In the present study, we examine the efficacy of "Ghostlee", a location-based augmented reality (AR) application designed to engage users via overlaying messages in the spaces visited by users, while allowing users to contribute towards the shared user-generated narrative. The "Ghostlee" game is an AR game that provides a glimpse into the messages and narrative posted by others in specific locations. In clear contrast to applications that are used to facilitate multimedia layers overlaid in the physical spaces of interaction, our application focuses on textual content. It was exclusively designed for short narratives designed to spark the curiosity of users to explore further. Users can publish their own content through Ghostlee's AR platform aligned with a 3D model which is associated with real-world coordinates, and interact with content published by others. Our research focuses on the question, to what extent our application is considered applicable towards the purpose of location-based social gameplay.

H. Mori et al. (Eds.): HCII 2023, LNCS 14056, pp. 229–238, 2023.
https://doi.org/10.1007/978-3-031-48044-7_17

The remainder of this paper is organized as follows. Section 2 presents an overview of AR the applied areas for AR. Section 3 describes the design considerations for Ghostlee's location-based Social AR. Section 4 describes the playtesting for the location-based social AR. Finally, we conclude in Sect. 5 with presenting a summary of the design considerations and lines of future work.

2 Related Work

In this section, we present a brief literature review of location-based interaction design, followed by extended reality (XR) applications that include social interaction.

2.1 Location-Based Interaction Design in Games

Location-based games seek to move interaction from desktop machines to the "real world" of cities, streets, parks, restaurants, and other locations such as Pokemon Go's design considerations that are described in [9] and [13]. Previous research has investigated how location-based games can be designed to overcome the challenges of scalability, interaction design, connectivity and accessibility [14–20]. Several studies examined users' motivations for creating content in location based games. The motivations varied from self expression and knowledge creation as noted in [21] and [22] to competition or social link creation as highlighted in [7] and [10].

2.2 Social Extended Reality (XR) Games

A taxonomy for social VR applications was introduced by Jonas et al. in [22] which highlighted the areas in the applied computation domains and future designs of social VR applications, The three main categories in [22] were features related to the "self", "interacting with others" and the environment. The communication privileges were particularly relevant to asynchronous XR to ways that a user can control the mode of interaction and the users who are granted access to the interaction spaces in the virtual realm. The interaction design in [14] and [15] highlighted the design considerations for interacting with others in the virtual realm, such as scaffolding types and modes of interaction (textual, visual, haptic, audio).

3 Design Considerations for Ghostlee's AR Social Game

Ghostlee was designed to add a programmed layer over actual reality to create a third, dynamic level of augmented experience based on geo-locations of mobile devices.

3.1 Spatial Design Considerations

The mobile application gives users a clear understanding of the amount of space they will need to experience the AR. The application's visual cues such as 3D modeled avatars and onscreen arrows and guidelines that are spatially aware help users understand how their

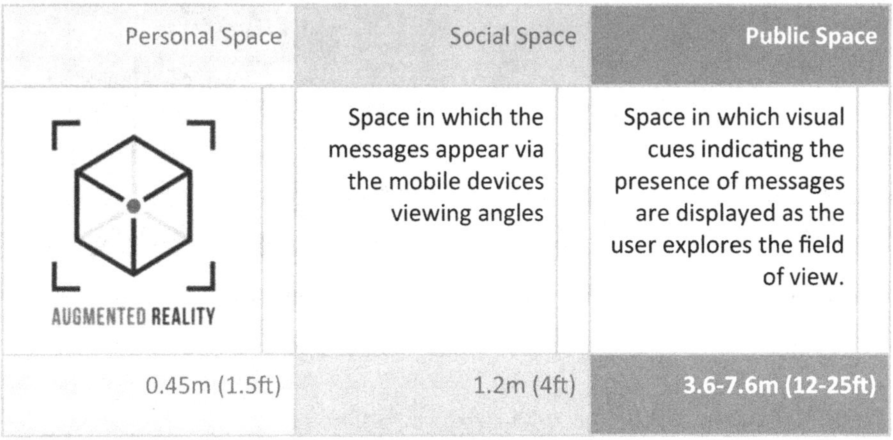

Personal Space	Social Space	Public Space
AUGMENTED REALITY	Space in which the messages appear via the mobile devices viewing angles	Space in which visual cues indicating the presence of messages are displayed as the user explores the field of view.
0.45m (1.5ft)	1.2m (4ft)	3.6-7.6m (12-25ft)

Fig. 1. Ghostlee's spatial design considerations for location-based social AR interaction design.

physical environment can affect their AR experience. Since the AR design will be integrated into the users' environment, the designers considered the spatial context (which is described in Fig. 1) to help users align the user's experience with the surroundings.

In contrast to AR experiences in private settings (e.g. home, work environments), designing for public environments (e.g., outdoors) requires special attention to the duration of the interaction. Designers focused on short user sessions with Ghostlee because regardless of how much people might enjoy Ghostlee's AR experience, they are not expected to walk around with their hands up, holding a device for an extended period of time.

3.2 Design for Safety and Continuous System Feedback

Given that users often get too immersed in an AR experience, designers need to consider that users may ignore physical objects around them during the use of the AR application. As a result, users might bump into objects or people. To prevent such behavior, the designers addressed the safety issue in two ways: built in reminders for users to check their surroundings and made the surroundings visible during the interaction as depicted in the screenshot in Fig. 2.

3.3 Physical Constraints

Since users will hold mobile devices while interacting with Ghostlee, comfortable designs were considered to prevent physical strains. For example, holding a device at a certain distance or angle for longer periods was avoided because it can be fatiguing. To prevent fatigue, the interaction was designed to keep sessions short. Moreover, the AR experience was designed to make it easy to resume an experience where they left off, even if they switch their physical location. An example of how sessions are saved and resumed in Ghostlee are depicted in Fig. 3.

Visual cues to notify users of messages

Location accuracy is visible upon launch

Fig. 2. Safety and system feedback design considerations for AR in Ghostlee.

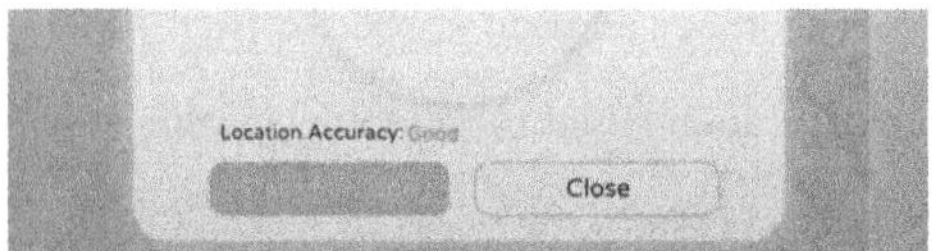

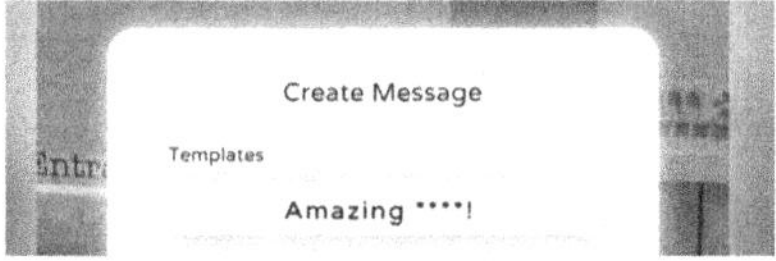

Fig. 3. The UI controls were kept simple, and enabled users to save and resume sessions.

3.4 Minimizing Input

The AR experiences in Ghostlee were designed to require as little physical input from users as possible. When users are looking through the mobile device screen at an augmented picture which shows the message, it's recognized that it would be difficult to expect users to input data at the same time. The input modalities in Ghostlee involved selection rather than typing such as utilizing templates and word selection rather than typing or recall. These examples demonstrate how alternative modes of entering information contribute towards an enhanced UX as shown in Fig. 4.

3.5 Immersive UX Design Considerations

Aligned with the principle of "good AR experiences need to immerse users into interactions" [23], Ghostlee devoted as much of the screen as possible to display the physical space in which the interaction is taking place because immersive AR can only happen when people believe that what they see on the screen is real. In addition to the surroundings, the Ghostlee AR application displays the app's virtual objects. Cluttering the screen was avoided with visible UI controls and information such as location accuracy and preview areas as shown in Fig. 5 because dense information would diminish the immersive experience.

Audio is also a multipurpose tool that is considered to enhance the immersive AR experience. Sound effects can improve the usability of social AR application. For example, the Ghostlee experience includes sound effects to confirm that a user selected a category or is inclose proximity to a virtual object. Background music can also help envelop users in the virtual world by creating the right mood.

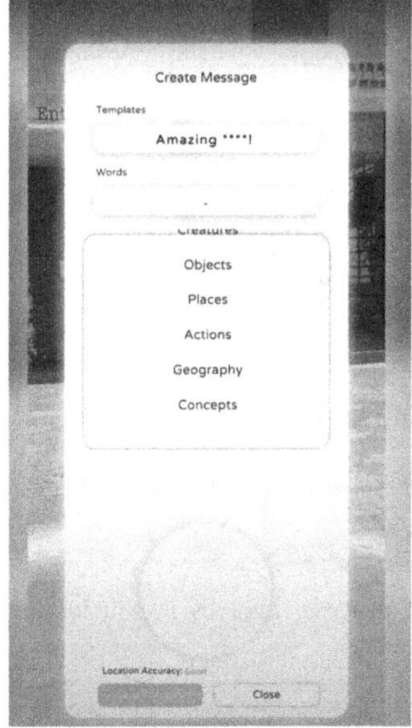

Fig. 4. Data scroll in AR to facilitate selection from a predefined vocabulary.

→ Visibility of physical location
→ Location accuracy is salient
→ Visual cues aligned with relevance
→ Contextual information
→ AR in discovery mode of interaction
→ Task variability remains limited
→ Leveraging camera-based anchors

Example of UI Elements in Ghostlee — Core Elements of AR in Ghostlee

Fig. 5. The UI in Ghostlee leverages the camera-view and overlays would emerge when content is relevant for the context of social interaction.

3.6 Onboarding Kept Simple

The Ghostlee onboarding process is intuitive and kept simple. It shows instructions or tips on how to perform specific things in the context of actual interactions. By doing that, the designers avoided overloading users with information that is not essential to the social AR interaction that is sought by the Ghostlee application, and users would be able to get all the important information at hand.

The swipe-through type of onboarding would not work in the social AR context. This type of onboarding won't work well for AR experience because the interactions are described out of the actual context. Instead, Ghostlee reveals the instructions gradually to the user as depicted in Fig. 6.

Fig. 6. The onboarding approach in the social AR process involves in-situ instructions that gradually reveal the instructions to the user.

3.7 Guiding the Users Visually to Sustain Presence

To sustain presence and awareness of self and others, the designers use a combination of visual cues, motion, and animation to keep users engaged. That illustrates and uses in-app experiences such as lively 3D avatars that show emotes and animations based on the user's proximity. Since a majority of mobile users know how to tap, drag and swipe objects, these interaction patterns were considered in the UI as shown in Table 1.

Table 1. UI Patterns for the AR in Ghostlee

UI Pattern	Example	Ghostlee's Approach
Launching the Hologram (message)	Launching on default or custom distance or Launching as tag along	Launching on default distance
Positioning Holograms	Rotation (Y, X, Z axis) and altitude	Initial rotation
Distance Responsiveness	Default view vs distant view vs wireframe view	Default view
Interactions	Pick, point, pull, push, select	Point and select
Magnetism	Attraction and repulsion forces	Both

Users can launch holograms in order to start their AR experience interacting with them in three different ways, Launching on default distance, custom distance or launching as tag along. The way the user launches the holograms (i.e. message) indicates how they want to interact with them, fitting different needs during their AR experience. The illustration in Fig. 7 shows the launching of the holographic message in the design of the AR application.

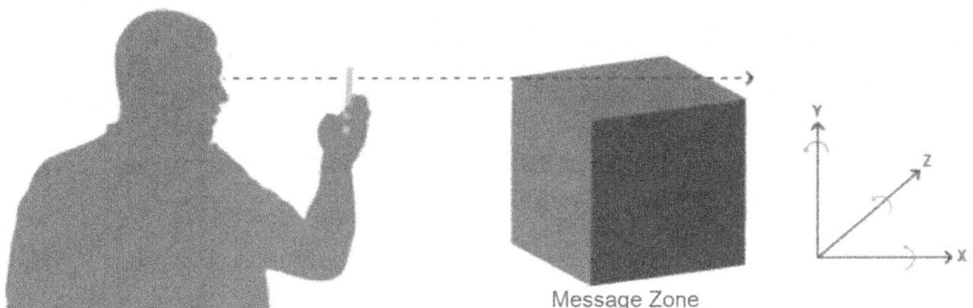

Fig. 7. UI patterns for positioning or manipulating the messages in the Ghostlee application

The distance responsiveness UI pattern is a hologram's ability to change their visualization according to the user's distance. In Ghostlee's design, if the user is too close (less than 20 cm) to the virtual messages, only their wireframe views are displayed and no interaction is supported. If the user is within 20 cm to 3 m the hologram displays its default view. If the user is beyond 3 m, interaction and readability are poor, so the hologram displays its distant view, which its content is replaced by its identifier (icon or equivalent) and interactions are limited.

As holograms interact with the real world or other holograms, it's often recommended they have an attractive force as soon as they get closer to surfaces with a distance of 10 cm and a repulsive force if they get closer (such as 2 cm) to another hologram in the virtual space. This magnetic behavior was applied on Ghostlee's hologram messages to improve user experiences especially in geo-locations which have a relatively large amount of messages.

4 Player Testing

Methodologically, we focused on the players' UX in Ghostlee to assess the usability and viability of using the application in the local context. Recognizing the importance of a new game release optimally performing in real-world situations, Alpha and Beta testing was conducted in two iterations to examine the onboarding and message composing and geolocation system respectively. Beta testing involved 18 users and was conducted via discord (link) with recruitment via an online form as shown in Fig. 8. The playtesting provided valuable user experience feedback as well as identifying functionality, connectivity and performance issues under real-world networking conditions.

The Ghostlee community participated in private betas via their own personal consoles and ISPs in their home environments, thoroughly testing the Android version of the social AR game in a controlled manner and 'in the wild' before the game goes live. The testing ranged from objective performance testing to subjective user feedback.

The alpha and beta testing included, but was not limited to, server load testing and concurrency scaling, geolocation and cross-region connectivity testing, synchronous

Fig. 8. Iterative playtesting was considered to determine Ghostlee's readiness for release.

gameplay and performance handling, subjective satisfaction surveys to elicit user feedback, and end-user experience simulation through retail hardware and personal networks. Recommendations from these testing iterations were considered for the final version of the game.

5 Conclusion

Using augmented reality, we described how Ghostlee provides a shared immersive narrative and asynchronous collaborative gameplay in a shared physical space which consequently offers an opportunity for meaningful engagement using user-generated narratives. Through the AR journey, the user experiences an exploratory narrative of messages posted by others in a location-based trail. Reflecting on Ghostlee's alignment with AR design patterns, it was evident that because of its relatively high level of immersion, Ghostlee has the potential to make asynchronous communication more engaging and therefore more effective in attracting and sustaining user engagement in this social gameplay context.

In this paper, we provide the scope of our AR application and reflect on the design considerations for location-based social AR applications, along with preliminary results of Ghostlee's ongoing usability and usefulness evaluation process. Future work would explore the relationship between the session motivations in Ghostlee and the physical settings in which they took place (e.g. contexts of leisure, learning, tourism).

Acknowledgments. The authors acknowledge the support of the Saudi eSport Federation for the ideation phase and initial design of Ghostlee through the Gamers 8 season's event (Gameathon) held in August 2022, and the Game Innovation Lab at Alfaisal University for extending the invitation to showcase Ghostlee in 2023.

References

1. Low, A., Turner, J., Foth, M.: Pla (y) cemaking With Care: Locative Mobile Games as Agents of Place Cultivation. In: Proceedings of the 25th International Academic Mindtrek Conference, pp. 135–146 (2022)

2. Yue, Y., Ding, J., Kang, Y., Wang, Y., Wu, K., Fei, T.: A location-based social network system integrating mobile augmented reality and user generated content. In: Proceedings of the 3rd ACM SIGSPATIAL International Workshop on Location-based Recommendations, Geosocial Networks and Geoadvertising, pp. 1–4 (2019)
3. Bell, M., et al.: Eyespy: supporting navigation through play. In: Proceedings of the SIGCHI Conference on Human Factors in Computing Systems, pp. 123–132 (2009)
4. La Salandra, A., Fraternali, P., Frajberg, D.:. A location-based virtual reality application for mountain peak detection. In: Companion Proceedings of the Web Conference 2018, pp. 1206–1214 (2018)
5. Lochrie, M., Pucihar, K.C., Gradinar, A., Coulton, P.: Designing seamless mobile augmented reality location based game interfaces. In: Proceedings of International Conference on Advances in Mobile Computing & Multimedia, pp. 412–415 (2013)
6. Avouris, N.M., Yiannoutsou, N.: A review of mobile location-based games for learning across physical and virtual spaces. J. Univers. Comput. Sci. **18**(15), 2120–2142 (2012)
7. Chen, L., Chen, G., Benford, S.: Your way your missions: a location-aware pervasive game exploiting the routes of players. Int. J. Hum.-Comput. Interact. **29**(2), 110–128 (2013)
8. Koutsabasis, P., et al.: Location-based games for cultural heritage: applying the design thinking process. In: CHI Greece 2021: 1st International Conference of the ACM Greek SIGCHI Chapter, pp. 1–8 (2021)
9. Dunham, J., Xu, J., Papangelis, K., & Schwartz, D. I. (2022, April). Advertising in Location-Based Games: An Exploration in Pokémon GO. In CHI Conference on Human Factors in Computing Systems Extended Abstracts (pp. 1–6)
10. Grant, L., Daanen, H., Benford, S., Hampshire, A., Drozd, A., Greenhalgh, C.: MobiMissions: the game of missions for mobile phones. In: ACM SIGGRAPH 2007 Educators Program, pp. 12-es (2007)
11. Markopoulos, P., Pyae, A., Khakurel, J., Markopoulos, E., Saarnio, R., Luimula, M.: Understanding how users engage in an immersive virtual reality-based live event. In: Proceedings of the 12th IEEE International Conference on Cognitive Infocommunications (CogInfoCom), pp. 881–899. Institute of Electrical and Electronics Engineers (IEEE) (2021)
12. Lan, R., Adelfio, M.D., Samet, H.: Spatio-temporal disease tracking using news articles. In: Proceedings of the Third ACM SIGSPATIAL International Workshop on the Use of GIS in Public Health, pp. 31–38 (2014)
13. Saaty, M., Haqq, D., Toms, D. B., Eltahir, I., McCrickard, D.S.: A study on Pokémon GO: exploring the potential of location-based mobile exergames in connecting players with nature. In: Extended Abstracts of the 2021 Annual Symposium on Computer-Human Interaction in Play, pp. 128–132 (2021)
14. Laato, S., Fernández Galeote, D., Altarriba Bertran, F., Hamari, J.: Balancing the augmented experience: design tensions in the location-based game Pikmin Bloom. In: CHI Conference on Human Factors in Computing Systems Extended Abstracts, pp. 1–7 (2022)
15. Xu, J.: From augmented reality location-based games to the real-world metaverse. In: Extended Abstracts of the 2022 Annual Symposium on Computer-Human Interaction in Play, pp. 364–366 (2022)
16. Gunkel, S., Stokking, H., Prins, M., Niamut, O., Siahaan, E., Cesar, P.: Experiencing virtual reality together: Social VR use case study. In: Proceedings of the 2018 ACM International Conference on Interactive Experiences for TV and Online Video, pp. 233–238 (2018)
17. Greuter, S., Mueller, F.F., Hoang, T.: Designing public VR installations. In: Designing Interactive Systems Conference, pp. 792–806 (2022)
18. Karre, S. A., Mittal, R., Reddy, R.: Requirements elicitation for virtual reality products-a mapping study. In: 16th Innovations in Software Engineering Conference, pp. 1–11 (2023)

19. Gunkel, S.N., Stokking, H.M., Hindriks, R., de Koninck, T.: VR Conferencing: communicating and collaborating in photo-realistic social immersive environments. Int. J. Virtual Real. (2019)
20. Liu, Q.: Contextual group walkthrough: social VR platform comparison and evaluation. HCI-E MSc Final project report (2020)
21. Goh, D.H.-L., Lee, C.S., Low, G.: Who, what, why: examining annotations in mobile content sharing games. In: Xing, C., Crestani, F., Rauber, A. (eds.) ICADL 2011. LNCS, vol. 7008, pp. 247–256. Springer, Heidelberg (2011). https://doi.org/10.1007/978-3-642-24826-9_31
22. Jonas, M., Said, S., Yu, D., Aiello, C., Furlo, N., Zytko, D.: Towards a taxonomy of social vr application design. In: Extended Abstracts of the Annual Symposium on Computer-Human Interaction in Play Companion Extended Abstracts, pp. 437–444 (2019)
23. Song, H.K., Baek, E., Choo, H.J.: Try-on experience with augmented reality comforts your decision: focusing on the roles of immersion and psychological ownership. Inf. Technol. People **33**(4), 1214–1234 (2020)

Virtual Platforms for the Asian Religious Deities in the Era of Pandemic

Wu-Wei Chen(✉)

Arts and Science School at New York, Affiliated Faculty of Center for Global Asia, Core Faculty of Shanghai Key, Laboratory of Urban Design and Urban Science, University Shanghai, 567 Yangsi W. Rd., Pudong New District, Shanghai, China
wc54@nyu.edu, dawuwei23@icloud.com

Abstract. Under the surge of COVID 19, the dire situation goes back and forth and does not seem to cease today. Like the rest of the world, similar scenarios attack Asia and profoundly affect the progression of research, collaborations, and exchanges of heritage sites. With the restriction of onsite visits and limited access, the sustainability of tangible and intangible heritage confronts challenges from multiple aspects. The paper starts from the perspective of individual research on religious heritage sites in Asia. Through the studies and collaborations, the paper examines the pre-pandemic developments of selected sites, and how they cope with the challenges during the pandemic. Through the joint efforts of practitioners and institutions from different geolocations of Asia, the paper provides observations and reflections on how virtual platforms assist to cope with the challenges and reactivate the research, exchange, and studies of Asian heritage.

Keywords: Pandemic Digital Heritage · religious heritage · virtual platform · live-streaming · open data · crowdsourcing

1 Digital Heritage Archive: A Virtual Platform Toward Heritage of Asia in the Pre-Pandemic Era

1.1 Context and Progress

The origin of Digital Heritage Archive (DHA) starts from the self-initiated project of the author entitled Body As Echoes. The aim is to document the religious deities through digital methods. The first collection is the Gandhara statues from private collectors. During the documentation process, research questions emerge: what is the definition of authenticity when it comes to the digital double of real-world objects? What can get further connected with the scanned data of religious deities? How can we utilize the scanned assets for academic exchange, public access, and global dissemination? What is the diversity of the iconology of religious deities in the other geolocations of Asia?

In China, the efforts of Liang Sicheng and Lin Huiyin have inspired scholars to step into the study of surveying wooden carpentry architecture and cave temples. It is also the reason for the author to initiate the Digital Heritage Archive (DHA) - to systematically

H. Mori et al. (Eds.): HCII 2023, LNCS 14056, pp. 239–253, 2023.
https://doi.org/10.1007/978-3-031-48044-7_18

organize the documented data and provide to the public for research. The first site survey of DHA starts from Dazu Rock Carvings of Chongqing, Sichuan province of China. Then the route is toward the north from Anyue, Guangyuan, Luoyang (Henan), Datong (Shanxi), and Ding County (Hebei) to Beijing. To further understand the full spectrum of Asian religious iconography, the DHA project sets foot in Japan (Nara), Korea (Daegu), Indonesia (Surakarta and Yogyakarta) and Thailand (Sukhothai).

1.2 Structure

DHA consists of text, images, videos, point cloud and polygonal models of the sites, interactive VR/AR asset browsing, and immersive experience through the game engine. The near-future goal of the archive is to equip with search, filter, tag, and GIS mapping so that the audience gets to efficiently spot the sites and contents. The prototype of the DHA virtual museum aims for curatorial approaches toward the collections of virtual sites and relics. The following paragraphs will focus on the efforts of DHA toward the documentation, collaborations, and networking for the digital heritage. (Fig. 1).

Fig. 1. Digital Heritage Archive. https://www.bodyasechoes.com/dha. Figure painting of Sudhana searching for enlightenment by Piao Shi.

2 Southeast Asia

2.1 Indonesia: Relief, Performance and Hand-Craft Art

In the DHA, Candi Sukuh is the first site documented in Surakarta of Central Java. The Garuda sculpture with the inscription at the back of the pedestal kicks off this digital documentation and the following ones in Central Java. Lokapala and Apsara reliefs in the Prambanan Temple mark the follow-up documentation. Finally, among 360 square feet of space with stepped terraces and staircases (no interior space)[1], the selected narrative reliefs of Borobudur get documented to echo the intangible heritage such as Gamelan music, Kris and Wayang performances, and Batik textile making. (Fig. 2).

2.2 Thailand: Sukhothai

Bangkok, Chiangmai, and Sukhothai are the major destinations in Thailand. In DHA, the focus lies on Sukhothai. The idea of "stupa as Buddha" can be easily identified by the juxtapositions of the architecture and the deity sculptures. With the excavations and restored conditions of the architecture, structures, and sites, Sukhothai makes a significant site to explore the religious iconography: The spindle shaped, flame like Ushnisha (assimilation of the stupa pinnacle)[2], tender smile of facial expression, elongated body, walking-like posture with Vitarka or Abhaya mudra (or sitting posture with Bhumisparsha mudra of the right hand such as Phra Achana) compose the core appearances of the deities in Sukhothai and also reflects the influences Hindu iconography.

Fig. 2. Digitization s of tangible and intangible heritage of Central Java.

3 East Asia

3.1 Korea

The main focus of Korea in the DHA is on Gyeongju, specifically the World Heritage Site of Namsan Mountain. The Namsan expedition of the author with colleagues of the Institute of Fine Arts in 2018 inspires research interests in the follow-up explorations of petroglyphs, high reliefs, and rock carvings spreading all over Namsan Mountain. The relics and sites represent the religious iconography developed in Korea. The challenges

[1] P.362, Snodgrass.

[2] P.181, Leidy.

also lie within the accessibility to the various spots following different valley routes. The abundant data collected by the local institution and the Cultural Heritage Administration (CHA) gets distributed to the public openly. The open data benefits global researchers who need access to excavation and conservation data.

3.2 Japan

Through the academic exchange seminar "Resonance of Wisdom" moderated by the author in Shanghai, the preservation of cultural relics, and the digital restoration process of religious heritage in Japan get introduced to the audiences. From the printed versions of annual reports to the case studies of hand-craft deity restorations, Mr. Satoshi Yabuuchi, the former Director of the conservation studio of Tokyo University of the Arts Graduate School and the present Director of Nara Prefectural Museum of Art, dedicates his work on deity conservation. The conservation studio applies optical imaging (X-ray/CT scan) and AR technology to examine the deterioration of the statues, and also create artwork inspired by Buddhism Art (Fig. 3).

4 China

4.1 Sichuan

Dazu Rock carvings mark the first site documentation in China of the DHA database. Dazu Institute is the local authority which provides the supports to scholars. The documentations go smoothly for the Charming Bodhisattva niche, Avalokiteshvara and Ksitigarbha niches in Beishan Mountain, and also the Peacock Radiant Wisdom King niche at the Shimen Mountain. Dazu Rock Carvings is known for the religious iconography back in the Song Dynasty. It also represents the last large-scale cave temple site in China. The fusions of Buddhism, Confucian and Daoism depicted among caves and niches represent the variety of the site.

The second site documented in Sichuan province is the outdoor Bodhisattva deity sculpture in Anyue. Located among the valley, the sitting posture and the tranquil appearance of the Potalaka Bodhisattva gets surrounded by the other niches around. Further up north in Guangyuan City, Da Yun Cave of Thousand Buddha Grotto and the Big Buddha Cave of Huang Ze Temple get documented. The reason for choosing the above is to follow the transitional style of Chinese Buddhist iconography. (Fig. 4).

4.2 Shanxi

For the province full of various types of tangible heritage (timber-framed structure, deities, mural paintings…, etc.), Yungang Grottoes in the Shanxi province is the quintessential cave temple to represent the colossal, volumetric aura of the royal style back in the Northern Wei dynasty of China. Among all the caves of Yungang Grottoes, Tan Yau Five Caves represent the public image of the site and raise academic debates about the year, order, and form. (Fig. 5) In the Datong City of Shanxi, Wooden Pagoda of Fogong Temple in the Ying County represents the iconic work of monastery structure in China. (Fig. 6).

Fig. 3. Moments of the presentations from Director Satoshi Yabuuchi and Prof. Osamu Yamada in the Resonance of Wisdom symposium.

Fig. 4. Video archive of cave-temple surveys in Sichuan.

The ongoing project of the Prefectural Governor's Residence Garden and Jiang Zhou Government Office excavation site marks the joint exploration between DHA and the local authority toward the digital narrative and revitalization of the government building compound including the main hall and prefectural garden.

Fig. 5. Point Cloud view of the Cave No. 20 of Yungang Grottoes.

Fig. 6. Point Cloud view of the timber-framed pagoda in Shanxi.

4.3 Henan

In the book A Record of Buddhist Monasteries in Luoyang, the ancient city with religious icons everywhere during the Northern Wei dynasty gets documented by the literature work.[3] Fengxiansi, the biggest cave in the Longmen Grottoes, got accomplished much

3 洛陽伽藍記.

later in the early Tang dynasty. The colossal scale and the Avatamsaka cosmo are significant elements of the Fengxiansi. Challenges also increase when documenting the full scale of the site with photogrammetry approach. (Fig. 7) Right next to the Fengxiansi, the Guyang Cave symbolizes the great collections of Wei-Bei calligraphy writing in the Inscription of 20 Longmen Statues. (Fig. 8).

Fig. 7. Point Cloud view of the Fengxiansi, Longmen Grottoes.

Fig. 8. Point Cloud view of the Guyang Cave, Longmen Grottoes.

4.4 Hebei

Longxing Monastery is the first destination when researching with the delegation led by the Archaeology and Museology College of Peking University from 2020 to 2021. During the studies of Buddhist heritage and monastery architecture, the collection of religious iconography reflects on the timber-framed structure, deity sculptures (Buddha, Avalokiteshvara) (Fig. 9) and mural paintings of the Mani Hall.[4] The historical, Dougong-based form is derived from the Yingzhao Fashi and regarded as the style from Song dynasty. The Avalokiteshvara deity at the back of the main hall gets documented and converted into digital form.

Fig. 9. Avalokiteshvara of Longxing Monastery.

4.5 Shanghai

Yu Garden is the first collaboration between DHA and the local university in Shanghai (College of Architecture and Urban Planning, CAUP). The site is known for its traditional Chinese garden aesthetics. Through the joint vision to revitalize the documented data, the point cloud model of the garden becomes a way to reimagine the dynamic aesthetics for Chinese garden appreciation. The virtual camera gets applied to the point cloud visualization of the garden, and the expression of the Chinese ink-painting style emerges while strolling through the virtual garden in the digital realm.

The ongoing project of Zhenru Monastery digitization in the Putuo District of Shanghai strives to document its main hall of the Yuan-dynasty Dougong structure. In the process of documentation, the name of the monastery inspires alternative thought: Bhutatathata (真如) symbolizes the concept of dharma nature in Buddhist thought. (Fig. 10).

[4] 摩尼殿.

Fig. 10. Working progress of developments for the Zhenru Monastery research project.

5 Pandemic Impacts on the Heritage Sites in Asia

5.1 Live-Streaming: Central Java as Example

The initial goals of the Indonesian project aim for the world heritage sites of Borobudur and Prambanan. The research gets even further and pushes toward collaboration with local institutions, academia, musicians, and performers. The research period spans from the pre-pandemic period of 2019 till now. It is meaningful to witness how the drastic change impacts the sites, researchers, performers, and artisans. The way they survive the challenges and the devotion to the tangible and intangible heritage dissemination is a precious experience for coping with similar incidents in the future. Kraton palaces in Central Java, for example, live streaming gets utilized for the performers at multiple palace sites of Surakarta and Yogyakarta. The senior performers' pre-recorded narrations become invaluable oral history asserts to kick off the live streaming performances of young artists onsite.

5.2 Crowdsourcing: Deity Restoration Projects in Japan

During the early impact of COVID 19 global wide in 2020, Prof. Yabuuchi led the crowdfunding project to restore the standing statue of Shukongōshin, the Japanese national treasure at Lotus Hall of Tōdaiji temple in Nara, Japan. Despite the challenges of the pandemic, Yabuuchi and his team take the crowdfunding project online, successfully obtain the budget to kick off the project, and return the favor to the donators and general public with splendid results. Through the sculpted work and digital visualizations, the outlook of the statue including the restored color, accessories, textures, and patterns gets resurrected by the conservation efforts. The statue represents the influence of the Silk Road culture that formed the basis of the Tenpyō era, and the further inspiration of DHA to network with conservators global-wide.

5.3 Open Data: Cultural Heritage Administration of Korea

The collaborations with the Borobudur Conservation Office of Indonesia and the Cultural Heritage Administration of Korea represent the strategic transformation under the challenge of the pandemic. Borobudur Conservation Office offers online training toward the traditional conservation by utilizing essential oil and local materials. Under the global lockdowns during the surge of COVID 19, live streaming of Borobudur conservation workshop brings together practitioners and keeps the knowledge exchange going. In Korea, CHA and KAIST co-hosted the international symposium toward the discussions of digital transformation in the post-pandemic scenarios of Asia. The multilateral exchange among the government, academia, and industry initiates further chances to collaborate on digital twins, crowdsourcing, archiving, cultural data sculpting, and curatorial approaches for museums. The documentation and open data platform established by the Cultural Heritage Administration expand the learned knowledge of ground-truth data. The accessibility of data benefits the researchers in need and continues the momentum of joint research in the long run.

5.4 Virtual Museum Visit: WeChat Mini Programs of China

Before the pandemic, a physical museum visit in China before accessing the caves and niches is the standard process. During the lockdown period, an in-person visit to the museum is not an option. Virtual tours become the standard package for remote visits of museum. WeChat mini programs offer easy, hands-on access to province-level museums.

The package includes an audio guide tour, 360° VR panoramic views, text and image introductions, and hotspot navigations to zoom in or enhance the virtual collections. The accessibility of the mini programs ensures the remote visits of the museum exhibitions in different domestic locations by the terminal devices.

6 Revitalization of the Documented Data of DHA

6.1 Annotation, Juxtaposition and Comparison

Current solutions of DHA to utilize the documented data include compiling dense point-cloud models, free access and embedding from the 3D website, and web-based VR/AR experiences. The annotation function is not open to the public but to the administrator and collaborators. The VR/AR viewing function further enables the usage of the content for curatorial approaches and museum content. Through the wearable devices, audiences can experience the immersive narrative in the VR goggle or AR spectacle. The augmented information and motion contents will expand the digital narration through spatial computing.

6.2 Pedagogical Approaches

The practical use of the annotations gets applied to the pedagogical approaches of the selected sites. In the research assignments of monasteries in Shanxi and Sichuan, students get to browse online the 3D models of interiors in the main halls and caves. Then they pin-pint the short paragraph and images of research results onto the spots of the 3D models. The interactive functions enable students to either auto play the annotations around the 3D models following the order of pinpoints or randomly click on the selected ones for presentations. Since the perspective view also gets defined after setting the pinpoints, the virtual camera gets smoothly and seamlessly from pin to pin.

The author delivers the course teaching by using the DHA data. It enables students to apply to field-trip studies, visual creations, and capstone research. The quintessential cases are documented works from Bazhong Grottoes and Mingshan Monastery of Sichuan, China. The Avalokiteshvara niche documentation of Bazhong Grottoes by students gets applied to miniature 3D printing and projection mapping in the student work showcase. The deity niche of Mingshan Temple documented by Li Yifei gets utilized in her research on the feminized transformation of the Chinese region's deity (Fig. 11) and serious-game development in the visual work Mingshan Temple: A Digital Tour. (Fig. 12) Li conducts field research at the Mingshan Temple and documents the ground-truth data directly from the selected niche. Li then compiles the data into polygonal models and imports it into the game engine for authoring, annotation, and guide tour design. The captured data merges with the virtual topography and landscape in the game environment.

6.3 Cross-Disciplinary Collaborations

Academia. In New York, the collaboration with the Institute of Fine Arts of New York University toward the time-based media conservation is diverse from the rest of the

Fig. 11. Poster design of the student project: Mingshan Temple: A Digital Tour. (Image courtesy of Li Yifei)

approaches of cultural heritage conservation of DHA. The born digital heritage conservation (software art, time-based media art) might be different, but there is still a mutual concern when referring to the museum contents, exhibited works, and restorations. The

Fig. 12. Game play demonstration of the student project: Mingshan Temple: A Digital Tour. (Image courtesy of Li Yifei)

museums embracing time-based media works in the collection will need practitioners in the files for preservations.

In Indonesia, ISI Surakarta of Central Java is the principal collaborator. Its full coverage of intangible heritage art making (Wayang theater, Kris making, batik textile) inspires the tangible and intangible heritage integration in the DHA content.

Korea Advanced Institute of Science and Technology (KAIST) of Korea and New York University co-announced the collaboration in 2022. The KAIST-NYU partnership embarks on opportunities for innovative collaborations. The author won the NYU research grant around the same time to continue the Namsan Mountain research and keep communicating with the Digital Heritage Lab of KAIST for the possible direction of the heritage conservation stream in the KAIST-NYU partnership.

Conservation Academies. Research of Dazu Rock Carvings kicks off the DHA data collections in China, and the support from the Dazu Rock Carvings Institute and Sichuan Art Museum is always appreciated. Yungang Grottoes is the follow-up of the research in China to distinguish the royal cave temples from the ones with civilian style down south. The digitization of Tan Yau caves, actual scale 3D printing, big data revitalization, and the traditional conservation studio for Yungang Grottoes' mural paintings inspire further thoughts of efficient dissemination of heritage narrative nationwide and overseas. Through the invitation as a review committee member of Cave No. 12 digitization, the approaches of Yungang Grottoes using digital twins to reactivate the documented data also intrigue research interests to follow up on future progress.

Digital Cultural Data Sculpting for Museums and Galleries. The first application of the DHA cultural data sculpting is the private collections of Gandhara statues exhibited in Hong Kong and the ground-truth documentations of niches and caves in the site of Dazu Rock Carvings. The two projects examine the diversity of the digitization process in the controlled studio environment and the field documentation. Challenges are diverse, and the integrated results get applied to exhibitions and workshops in the museums. The workshop demonstration in the conservation studio of Freer Sackler Gallery focuses on the Cosmic Buddha statue. The Cosmic Buddha collection of the Smithsonian Museum gets scanned into 3D models by its Digitization Program Office (The statue's significance lies in the six realms of samsara delicately depicted on the Kasaya-like sculpture. The author utilizes the model in the workshop to demonstrate the further application of collecting the narrative relief with ease by a digital sculpting tool. The introduction also includes the use of collected information for collaborative research from cross-disciplinary areas.

Bibliography

1. Gallery, A.M.S.: Body of devotion: the cosmic buddha in 3D. https://www.si.edu/newsdesk/releases/cosmic-buddha-3d-exhibition-open-jan-30
2. Cultural Heritage Administration of Republic of Korea. http://www.cha.go.kr/main.html
3. Digitization Program Office. Washington D.C.: Smithsonian museum. https://ncp.si.edu/collections-digitization
4. KAIST Digital Heritage Lab. https://www.dhlab.kaist.ac.kr

5. Leidy, D.P.: The Art of Buddhism. Boston: Shambhala Publications, Inc., 181 (2008)
6. Nara Prefectural Museum of Art. https://www.tokyoartbeat.com/en/venues/-/A8873FA2
7. Prospectus: The Tenpyō Period Reborn in Reiwa! A Project to Reproduce the Standing Statue of Shukongōshin [Skt. Vajrapāṇ] Belonging to Tōdaiji Temple's Hokkedō [Lotus Hall]. https://readyfor.jp/projects/hozonchoukoku-shukongoujin
8. Snodgrass, A.: The Symbolism of the Stupa, p. 362. Motilal Banarsidass Publishers Private Limited, Delhi (2007)
9. SSu-ch'eng, L.: A pictorial history of Chinese architecture: a study of the development of its structural system and the evolution of its types. Hong Kong: Joint Publishing (H.K.) Co., Ltd., pp. 56–66 (2001)
10. Tokyogeidai-Hozon conservation studio. Tokyo: Tokyo University of Arts. https://www.tokyogeidai-hozon.com

Social Network Analysis-Based Evaluation on Carbon Neutrality Acceptance of Weibo Users

Yuan Fu, Peihan Wen(✉), and Junlin Wu

School of Management Science and Real Estate, Chongqing University, Chongqing 400045, China
wen@cqu.edu.cn

Abstract. Public perception and opinion have an important influence on tackling carbon emission and climate. Since the introduction of the carbon neutrality target in China, there has been widespread debate and action by various stakeholders. Weibo is an effective tool for gaining a timely and comprehensive understanding of public acceptance of carbon neutrality policy in China. Based on text data crawled on the Weibo platform, this paper combines improved sentiment analysis and network analysis methods to innovatively propose a multidimensional feature research framework that integrates time, space, sentiment, behavior and content to explore the single and multiple types of interactive behaviors, fine-grained emotions and differences in opinions of different types of users on the national policy of carbon neutrality target. The results show that the rise in popularity of carbon neutrality is related to the occurrence of important carbon events, and the public in economically developed regions such as Beijing and Shanghai are more concerned about carbon neutrality. Positive public sentiment towards carbon neutrality dominates, with the proportion of neutral sentiment increasing when major carbon events occur. Governments and celebrities are more influential than other types of users, and the core content of public concern is consistent, with marginal content varying by identity. This study provides a comprehensive analysis and support for the effective implementation of carbon neutrality related policies as well as the improvement of public awareness and acceptance.

Keywords: Carbon peaking and carbon neutrality · Social media · Public opinion · Network analysis · Sentiment analysis

1 Introduction

On 22 September 2020, China solemnly pledged to reach peak carbon by 2030 and carbon neutrality by 2060 (Zhang et al., 2023; Xiang et al., 2021; Li et al., 2022). This policy target has provoked a dramatic reaction in our country and abroad. A growing body of ex-post evidence suggests that policies to address climate change require strong public engagement and support (T. Bernauer and McGrath, 2016). Public participation in the development and implementation of climate policy contributes to the transparency

H. Mori et al. (Eds.): HCII 2023, LNCS 14056, pp. 254–272, 2023.
https://doi.org/10.1007/978-3-031-48044-7_19

of policy governance (Thomas Bernauer and Gampfer, 2013). There are currently many divergent views among the public on China's carbon neutrality (Xiang et al., 2021; Stroik et al., 2019; Wei et al., 2021). Examining public awareness, opinions and emotions towards the carbon neutrality and the clear commitment of some stakeholder companies to carbon reduction is essential to achieving the policy target. (Wei et al., 2021; Bennett et al., 2021; Li et al., 2022; Qazi et al., 2023).

The traditional method of measuring public perceptions of carbon reduction is through questionnaires and in-depth interviews, which are limited by insufficient data sample size, inconsistent evaluation criteria, cumbersome statistical process and high acquisition costs, which inevitably make the analysis results questionable in terms of comprehensiveness, timeliness and credibility (Stroik et al., 2019; Kantenbacher et al., 2018; Bennett et al., 2021; Cebeci et al., 2023). With the popularity of the Internet and the emergence of various social media platforms, people have become more vocal and expressive, and are increasingly enthusiastic about participating in public affairs, expressing their views and experiences on carbon emissions and environment-related issues and participating in online discussions (Wei et al., 2021; Fownes et al., 2018; Cebeci et al., 2023; Yang, 2019; Dahal et al., 2019). Social media enables a two-way connection between the public and decision makers rather than a one-way communication, which has a wider audience and better interactivity than traditional media (Simonofski et al., 2021; Gao et al., 2017). The use of social media by different social groups has collectively expanded the scope and content of policy communication (Panagiotopoulos et al., 2014), and can have an immediate and profound impact on the audience (Mah et al., 2014). In contrast, traditional media and government websites convey messages that are mostly official and educational, but do not quite match public expectations, resulting in a lack of depth of public understanding (Linde, 2017). Therefore, social media plays a crucial role in quickly disseminating voices from various stakeholders at different stages of policy release, implementation, and monitoring feedback, which can be used to assess public acceptance with the carbon neutrality policy.

In recent years, scholars have begun to analyze corporate and public opinions and attitudes on environmental-related topics through online comments on the Internet, for example, unearthing the influence of China's official Twitter account on global views of China's carbon policy by analyzing sentimental high-frequency words (Xiang et al., 2021), analyzing public attention and influence combining the strengths of social network analysis and textual thematic analysis to construct a framework for research on climate policy perceptions (Wei et al., 2021), identifying different topics that influence climate opinion through statistical learning theory and NLP (Bennett et al., 2021), analyzing geotagged tweets for keywords related to climate change using volume analysis, LDA, and sentiment analysis (Dahal et al., 2019), using sentiment analysis to uncover the changing attitudes of China's Public Firms towards environmental protection (Li et al., 2022). However, research exploring public opinion on environmental and climate-related policies through online public opinion is still in its exploratory stage. Existing public attitudes and opinions on climate policy have been studied from a single perspective, lack of integrated systematic analysis. Moreover, the clarity of the carbon neutrality target immediately triggered a heated public debate and a new perspective. There are few studies on public acceptance toward this specific policy target.

Therefore, this study uses Weibo (the most active and influential social media among the many social networking platforms in China) as a data source for carbon neutrality, from the perspective of multi-dimensional feature fusion, to illustrate the public participation and dynamic trends as well as the geographical distribution of participants; to explore public sentiment combining emotional dictionaries and semantic rules; to construct social networks based on users' retweeting, liking and commenting behaviors to explore the forms of dissemination of carbon neutrality information among the public; and to identify the key contents of public attention by co-word network analysis. This study is important for the effective implementation of carbon neutrality policy, the improvement of public participation and awareness of carbon neutrality target, and the early realization of the target.

This study contributes to existing research in three ways. Firstly, an innovative research framework for policy topics based on Weibo social media was constructed, incorporating multiple features such as time, space, content, user sentiment and behavior, in order to explore the Chinese public's acceptance of carbon neutrality, with a more comprehensive analytical perspective compared to existing studies, and this framework lays the foundation for the continued analysis of carbon neutrality public opinion in future updates. Secondly, the existing emotion dictionary is extended and different grammatical rules are designed in view of the content of public discussion on carbon neutrality, so that a sentiment analysis model is constructed to analyze the different emotional characteristics of the public towards carbon neutrality at a fine-grained level. Thirdly, the carbon neutrality information dissemination social network with multiple interactive behaviors is constructed by taking into account the 'like', 'retweet' and 'comment' behaviors of users and assigning different edge weights to these three behaviors according to their degree of importance, which breaks the tradition of single-user behavior as an edge in the network, and analyzing and comparing the overall index characteristics of multi-behavioral and single-behavioral networks.

The rest of this article is structured as follows: The second part introduces the source, acquisition method, and preprocessing process of data. The third part describes the research methods used in this article. The fourth part analyzes and discusses the research results. The fifth part summarizes the main research findings. The research framework of this paper is shown in Fig. 1.

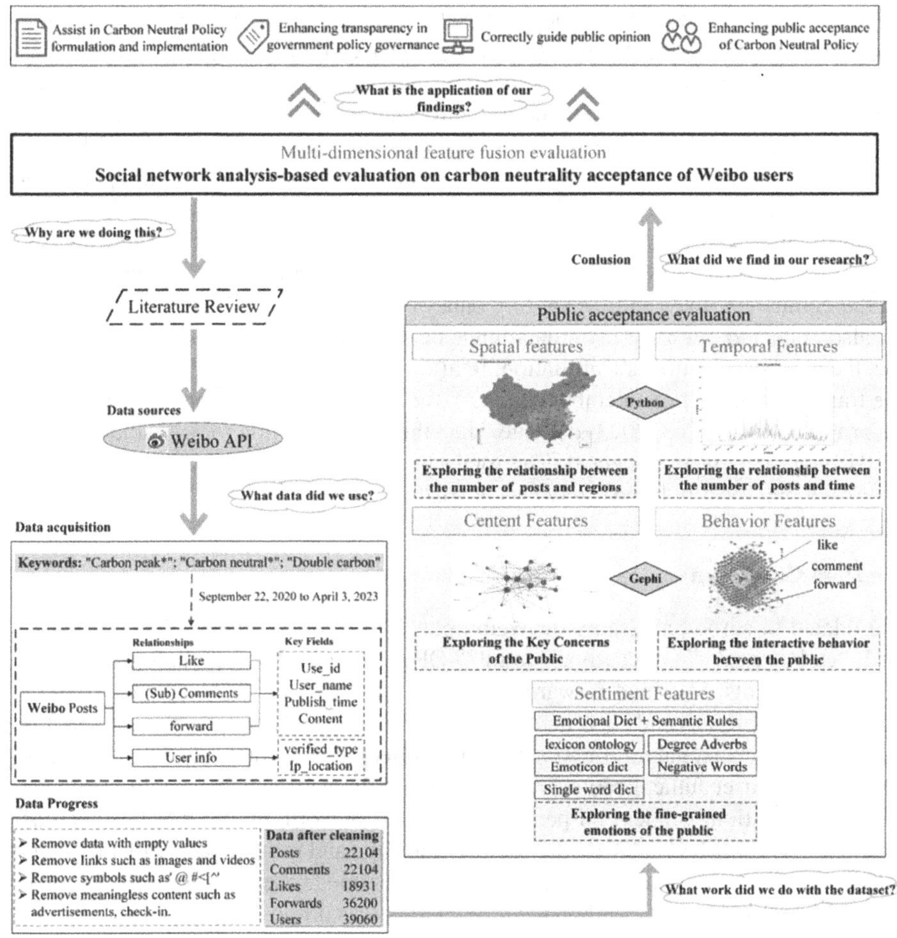

Fig. 1. Research Framework

2 Dataset

2.1 Data Sources

Weibo, a microblogging social media site that functions similarly to Twitter and Facebook, has become an indispensable communication platform for Chinese people (Chen et al., 2011). Because of its large number of users and real-time status updates, Weibo has a huge amount of data that is easy to access and analyze, making it a major way for people to post, obtain, and share news in their daily lives, and influential celebrities, governments, and enterprises have also registered official microblogs, making it an important channel for the Chinese public to participate in politics. The Chinese public can register accounts on Weibo and express their views by posting short texts, emoticons, pictures and even videos. Users can pass information to each other through actions such as liking, commenting and retweeting. Weibo discloses non-private information about each user, such as occupation, birthday, affiliation, and geographic location. In addition, Weibo also provides authentication for users with special identities, such as celebrities, government, enterprises, media, and social groups, to verify the authenticity and reliability of the information posted, and this information provides more possibilities for cross-analysis of results in our study. Therefore, this paper selects Weibo, a social media platform, as the data source for this paper to study the Chinese public acceptance on carbon neutrality.

Data related to carbon neutrality on Weibo platform were retrieved by using the keywords "carbon peak*" OR "carbon neutral*" OR "double carbon", including blog posts and the comments, likes and forwarding data of each blog post. Personal information was also collected, with the main data fields being user nickname, user authentication type, the number of followers, affiliation, IP affiliation, gender and personal profile. The time frame was set from September 22, 2020 (the date when the carbon neutrality target was proposed) to April 3, 2023 (the date when the data collection for this study began). 22,104 blog posts were collected. The total number of comments and sub-comments under each blog post is 19,661, retweets is 36,200 and likes is 18,931.

2.2 Data Collection

Data related to carbon neutrality on Weibo platform were retrieved by using the keywords "carbon peak*" OR "carbon neutral*" OR "double carbon", including blog posts and the comments, likes and forwarding data of each blog post. In order to study the differences in opinions and sentiments towards carbon neutrality among users with different identities, personal information was also collected, with the main data fields being user nickname, user authentication type, number of followers, number of followers, affiliation, IP affiliation, gender and personal profile. It is worth noting that this personal information is set to be visible on the user's home page and is made public by the Weibo platform, and is not a matter of personal privacy. The time frame was set from September 22, 2020 (the date when the carbon neutrality target was proposed) to April 3, 2023 (the date when the data collection for this study began) to ensure the validity and comprehensiveness of data. Specifically, the third-party python library "requests" was used to simulate user login behavior to request advanced search pages on Weibo, and a web crawler was used to perform keyword-based data crawling.

Through the above data collection method and process, 22,104 blog posts were collected on carbon neutrality topics, with the main data fields being unique blog post identifier, posting time, publisher nickname, posting location, blog post content and link, number of retweets, number of likes, and number of comments. The total number of comments and subcomments under each blog post is 19,661, retweets is 36,200 and likes is 18,931. In particular, this paper forms a carbon neutrality topic ecosystem of all the users who post, comment, and retweet carbon neutrality topics, and the like behavior should be generated among these users.

2.3 Data Preprocessing

To ensure the reliability of the study results, the data obtained above were further preprocessed by: 1) Removal of some null-valued data. The rows of data with empty values in the body of the tweet, comments and retweets due to network or Weibo API limitations were removed; 2) Removal of a large amount of noisy data. Under the hot blog posts, there are users who take the opportunity to post advertisements, lucky draws and other content with commercial nature. For the retweet data, some of them only contain content such as "retweeted tweet" and "quickly retweeted tweet". For comments, the data includes links to web pages, images, videos and animations, as well as combinations of symbols such as "@ + username" and "#topic#". All of the above are not relevant to the topic of this paper, and were cleaned using regular expressions and keyword matching; 3) Unity of text expression language. Traditional Chinese characters and other languages such as English in the text were translated into Chinese using the Baidu translation tool. After data cleaning, a total of 19,352 posts, 18,693 comments, 34,201 retweets and 18,931 likes were retained as data for subsequent research. Complementally, this is only a preliminary data processing process, and in exploring the different dimensions of public acceptance of carbon neutral policies, we will further process the data to match the format of the input data required by our different research methods.

3 Methods

3.1 Sentiment Analysis

Text sentiment analysis, also known as opinion mining, tendency analysis, etc., is the process of analyzing, processing, generalizing and reasoning about subjective texts with emotional overtones. The existing sentiment analysis for Weibo text data is generally coarse-grained analysis, only analyzing sentiment tendency, without fine-grained sentiment classification (Wang et al., 2014). However, coarse-grained sentiment analysis does not provide insight into the specific emotional categories of the reviewers, and the accuracy rate is low to provide useful references for decision making. In particular, building emotion lexicon based on emotion knowledge can identify fine-grained emotions by matching with words in the text and then calculating the emotion type of the text, which is suitable for mining emotion-rich data like Weibo texts.

Therefore, based on the simplified Chinese social media sentiment lexicon published by the Information Retrieval Research Laboratory of Dalian University of Technology (Xu et al., 2008) as a benchmark, the relevant lexicon was expanded, and a sentiment analysis model was constructed by synthesizing the influence of semantic rules to realize fine-grained sentiment classification of Weibo comments, and the specific work done is as follows:

Emotional lexicon construction: 1) Select a basic emotion dictionary. The Chinese emotion lexicon of Dalian University of Technology divides emotions into 7 major categories and 21 sub-categories, the major categories being happy, good, sad, disgust, fear, angry, and surprise. Each word has a polarity value, with 0 being neutral, 1 being positive, 2 being negative, and 3 being both positive and negative. The emotional intensity labels of the lexicon are divided into levels 1, 3, 5, 7 and 9. Level 1 indicates the lowest intensity and level 9 indicates the highest intensity. The lexicon contains 27466 emotional words. 2) Add Emoticon Dictionary. Emoticons are an important way for the public to express their emotions, and it is extremely important to identify them in short texts of Weibo. Emoticons will be displayed in the form of "[]" after extracting the text of Weibo comments, Such as "[smile]" and "[sad]". Therefore, a total of 126 emoticons appearing in the corpus were identified using python regular expression rules. 3) Add a dictionary of Internet terms. The expression of online language has the characteristics of colloquialism and informality, which leads to many internet terms being unable to be included in a universal emotional dictionary in a timely manner. For example, the internet term "breaking defense" indicates a breakthrough in psychological defense, while "lying flat" indicates no longer participating in competition. A dictionary of new Internet terms provided by Sogou (Sui, 2021) was extracted, and a part of popular Internet terms (Zhi, 2020) was collected to obtain a total of 53 new Internet words.

Semantic rules construction: Chinese often uses degree adverbs to deepen or diminish the emotion being expressed. Degree adverbs can change the intensity of the emotion or even change the emotional tendency. Negative words are a special type of degree adverb that can change emotional tendencies if used to modify emotional words, such as "not liking" no longer indicating emotional "good", but rather indicating emotional "disgust". If used to modify degree adverbs, it plays a role in reducing degree. The combination patterns between emotional words, degree adverbs, and negative words can produce different expressive effects. 219 adverbs of degree provided by HowNet are used, which are divided into six grades in total. The six grades of emotional words are weighted as 1.5, 1.25, 1.0, 0.75, 0.5, 0.25 respectively. The negative dictionary provided by CSDN was used (CSDN, 2019). Table 1 shows the different sentiment weight values assigned to different combination patterns between sentiment words, degree adverbs, and negation words in the microblog text.

Table 1. Different Sentimental word combinations and weights

Combination	Weight
Only Sentimental Words	1
Degree Adverbs and Sentimental Words	*ad*
Negative Words and Sentimental Words	-1
Degree Adverbs and Negative Words and Sentimental words	-1**ad*
Negative Words and Degree Adverbs and Sentimental words	0.5**ad*
Negative Words and Negative Words and Sentimental words	1

Combined Emotional Score Calculation:

1) Calculate the emotional value of a single word in the comment text, the emotional value v_i of the i-th emotional word in the text:

$$v_i = \omega * p * (-1)^m * ad$$

where ω denotes the strength of the emotion word, taking values of 1, 3, 5, 7 and 9; p denotes the polarity of the emotion word, taking values of 1 for positive, 0 for neutral and -1 for negative; m denotes the number of negative words; and ad denotes the weight of the degree adverb appearing before the emotion word.

2) The sentiment value of the comment text is calculated by adding up the sentiment values of all words. Then S_j denotes the sentiment value of the j th text. S_j is calculated by:

$$S_j = \sum_{1}^{n} v_i$$

where n is the number of emotional words in the comment text. If $S_j > 0$ means the comment text has positive sentiment; if $S_j < 0$ means the comment text has negative sentiment; if $S_j = 0$ means the comment text has neutral sentiment.

3.2 Social Network Analysis

A social network is a collection of points (actors) and links (relationships) between the points. Any social unit or entity can be seen as a 'point' or actor, and the 'links' can be various relationships such as friends, superiors and subordinates, trade between countries, etc. (Bhagwan et al., 2004). Weibo users and their interrelationships (following, being followed, commenting, retweeting, and liking) have led to the formation of a large social network structure between users as they explore a common topic. This study takes users who participate in carbon neutrality discussions as nodes, and the interactions between users, including likes, comments and retweets, as edges between nodes. In the process of browsing microblogs, users are not only "spectators", but also imagine themselves in the process, when the content of microblogs is in the same frequency with their own demands, "liking" is a faster way to reflect their attitude, while the time to post comments is much longer than the time to "like". Retweets can be seen as a combination of "likes" and "comments" (Zhao, 2019). Therefore, for the study of user interactions, side weights of 1.0, 2.0 and 3.0 were assigned to the likes, comments and retweets in order to construct a public social network of carbon neutral circles, which was visualized using Gephi software (Bastian et al., 2009). The overall network characteristics are explored by calculating the average distance and network diameter of the network. The Pagerank values of the nodes in each network are calculated to find out the influential user nodes in the network and their identity information to explore the behavioral characteristics of users.

3.3 Co-Word Network Analysis

A co-word network is a special kind of complex network, which is a traditional bibliometric method of content characterization at the 'word' level. Co-word analysis is essentially a content analysis method that reflects the association between hot words by calculating the strength of relationships between high-frequency theme words (Feng and Leng, 2006).

Using the ROST Content Mining software written by Dr. Shen Yang's research team at Wuhan University, the co-word matrix was extracted from the posts, comments and retweets of different types of users, and imported into the Gephi software to obtain the co-word network. Eigenvector centrality considers the centrality of a node to be a function of the centrality of neighboring nodes, unlike degree centrality, where a node with high point centrality, i.e. with many connected nodes, does not necessarily have high eigenvector centrality, as all of its connectors may have low eigenvector centrality. Similarly, a high eigenvector centrality does not mean that it has a high degree centrality; it can have a high eigenvector centrality even if it has few but important connectors. Point degree centrality assumes that all neighbors contribute equally, but in co-word networks the importance of neighboring word nodes themselves is different due to different semantic links in the context, and therefore they have different effects on the central node. Words with higher feature vector centrality can be considered to be in an important position in the co-word network. The size of the node is used to characterize the magnitude of the feature vector centrality of the words in the co-word network, so that the graph can visualize the level of importance of the content that different users focus on.

4 Results and Discussion

4.1 Temporal and Spatial Features

Carbon neutrality related blog post trend was plotted on a day-by-day basis, as shown in Fig. 2. Since the introduction of the carbon neutrality target to date, the topic has remained high and the number of user posts can see a sudden increase due to important events. We have reviewed the top five dates and events for the number of posts. The highest number of user posts was found on December 8 and 9, 2021. In particular, on 8 December, the editorial board of "Bite the bullet" released the top 10 buzzwords of 2021, and "carbon peaking, carbon neutrality" was one of them. Meanwhile, the Central Economic Work Conference, held in Beijing from 8 to 10 December, clearly emphasized the need to properly understand and grasp carbon peaking and carbon neutrality. On January 24, 2022, General Secretary Xi stressed at the 36th collective study of the Political Bureau of the CPC Central Committee that the situation and tasks facing the promotion of carbon peaking and carbon neutrality should be deeply analyzed, and the decision-making and deployment of the Party Central Committee should be implemented in a solid way. At the same time, the CPC Central Committee and The State Council issued "the 14th Five-Year Comprehensive Work Plan for Energy Conservation and Emission Reduction". June 13 to 19, 2022 is the National Energy conservation Publicity Week, the theme is "green and low carbon, energy saving first", June 15 is the 10th "National Low Carbon Day", the theme is "implement the 'double carbon' action, build a beautiful home", the relevant users in various provinces and cities expressed their determination to save energy and reduce carbon, and carried out related activities. On 16 October 2022, the 20th Party Congress was held, and the report proposed to actively and steadily promote carbon peaking and carbon neutrality. 24 October 2021, the Central Committee of the Communist Party of China and the State Council issued "the Opinions on Completely and Accurately Implementing the New Development Concept and Doing a Good Job of Carbon Peaking and Carbon Neutral Work", and on 26 October, the State Council issued "the Action Plan for Carbon Peaking by 2030", the top-level design was introduced, which caused extensive discussion and interpretation among major enterprises and the public widely discussed and interpreted. Overall, the discussion heat of carbon neutrality has remained high since its inception and is closely linked to national calls, low carbon activities and the introduction of relevant policies.

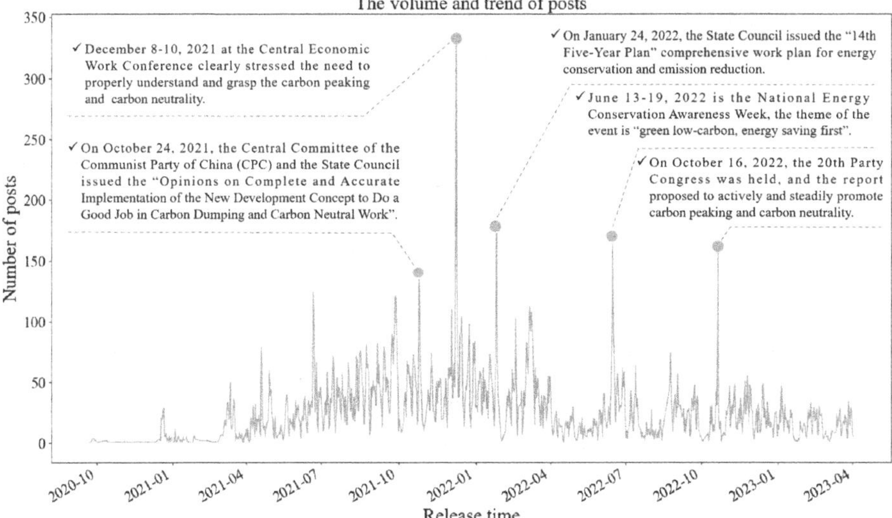

Fig. 2. The volume and trend of posts

The regional distribution of the total number of carbon-neutral related posts and comments is shown on a heat map, as shown in Fig. 3. Regionally, 34 provinces, municipalities, autonomous regions and Hong Kong, Macau and Taiwan are covered, indicating that the carbon neutrality target has sparked widespread debate across the country. Although carbon neutrality related posts and comments were posted across the country, there were significant differences in the distribution of numbers, with Guangdong Province, Beijing and Shandong Province having the highest number of discussions, with 5445, 5217 and 4807 respectively. This was followed by Shanghai, Jiangsu and Zhejiang with 3316, 2841 and 2557 respectively. Beijing and Shanghai are the two major economic centers of China with extremely high population densities, while Guangdong, Shandong, Jiangsu and Zhejiang are all coastal cities with the highest GDPs. It can be seen that the level of economic development has a strong influence on whether people from all walks of life in each region are concerned about carbon peaking and carbon neutrality, reflecting sideways the close relationship between following a low carbon path and economic growth. On the contrary, except for Hong Kong, Macau and Taiwan, which have paid less attention, Tibet, Qinghai and Ningxia in the Mainland have significantly less enthusiasm for carbon neutrality discussions and insufficient call for publicity.

Fig. 3. Geographical distribution

4.2 Sentiment Features

Figure 4 illustrates the characteristics of the public's temporal distribution of the three emotions regarding carbon neutrality. Overall, the green line is much higher than the blue and red for most of the time, indicating the dominance of positive public sentiment on the topic since the introduction of the carbon neutrality target. However, when the comment lines crest, there is a clear trend towards a higher increase in the blue line, suggesting that more public comments occur when carbon-neutral hotspots emerge, and that the proportion of these public comments that do not carry any affective tendencies (i.e. neutral sentiment) is increasing. Specifically, on 30 September 2021, the topic of "double control of energy consumption" sparked a public debate, with high energy-consuming and high-polluting companies and public facilities in some areas being subject to power cuts and restrictions as a result of the double control of energy consumption policy. While the positive sentiment of the public was still dominant at 52.2%, the neutral sentiment of the public reached 34.7%.

The red line has been present throughout the carbon neutrality debate, but the vast majority is covered by the green and blue lines, suggesting that there are still some concerns and worries about the carbon neutrality target among a minority of the public. It is worth mentioning that on 26 June 2022, the user "HW Ex-HR" published an article titled "Hong Kong Media: Europe's Restart of Coal Power Plants Goes Backwards in Carbon Emissions", which pointed out that European and American countries have set stringent environmental standards and carbon emission thresholds for developing countries in addressing the issue of climate change, without regard to the stage of economic development of developing countries and the pressure of employment of their respective large populations. This blog post triggered strong negative public sentiment in China, amounting to 45.5%. Therefore, it is necessary for the government and the relevant media to take measures to guide the public's correct perception of the controversial issues, to avoid excessive negative emotions and to ensure the smooth implementation of the guidelines and strategies at the national level.

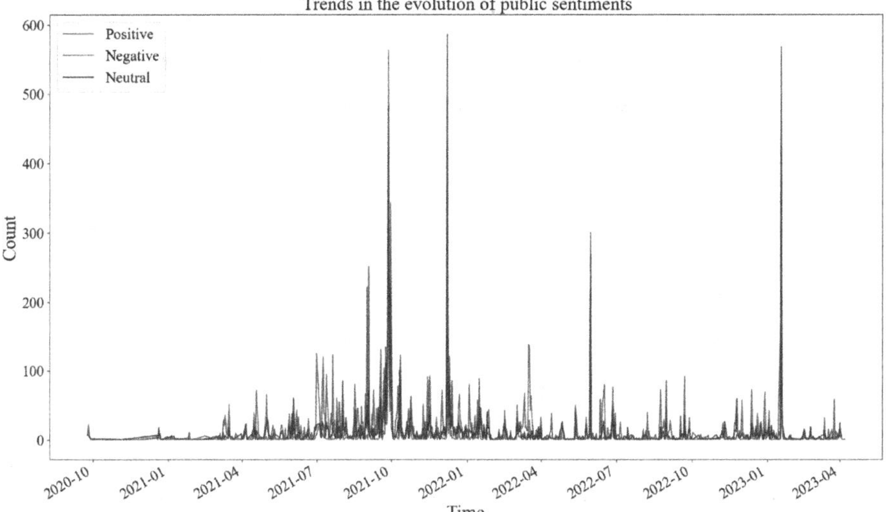

Fig. 4. Trends in the evolution of public sentiments

4.3 User Behavioral Features

Figure 5 illustrates the network made up of the different interactive behaviors generated by the public. The color of the node indicates the authenticated identity of the different users, and Table 2 lists the identity corresponding to each color and the proportion of users with different identities. Ordinary users make up the vast majority of the network diagram, indicating that public participation in carbon neutrality discussions is still dominated by ordinary Chinese citizens. Although the number of celebrities involved in the discussion is less than that of ordinary users, the red edges stand out in all subplots, indicating that celebrities receive more attention as target nodes and trigger more interactive behavior from other users. The blue nodes and edges account for a certain proportion of all the subgraphs, indicating that government departments play an important role in both publishing carbon-neutrality related content and generating user discussion.

Table 3 shows the overall metric characteristics of the four user behavior networks. In terms of the number of nodes and edges, the number of user nodes generating liking behavior is about 25% of the number of user nodes with commenting and retweeting behavior, but the frequency of liking behavior is comparable to that of commenting and liking. This suggests that liking occurs on a smaller scale in carbon neutrality related topics, but that users within the scope are prone to liking each other, while comments and retweets are more widespread and one-way in character.

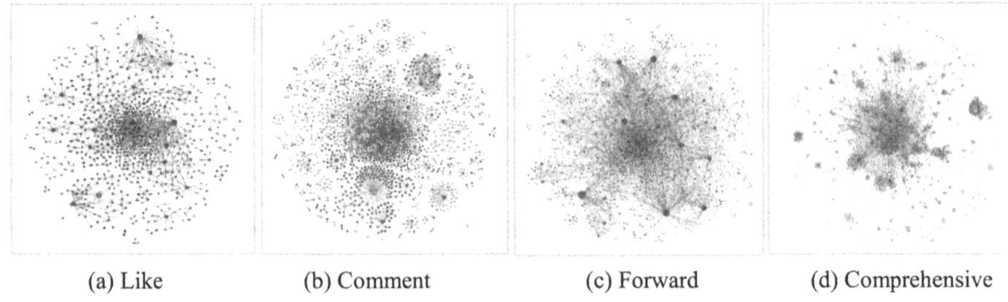

(a) Like (b) Comment (c) Forward (d) Comprehensive

Fig. 5. User interaction behavior network

Table 2. Authentication identity represented by the color of user nodes

Color	Identity	Proportion of user identities
# green	Ordinary users	74.58%
# red	Celebrity	9.3%
# blue	Government	8.58%
# orange	Enterprise	4.06%
# brown	Media	2.46%
# pink	Group(Institution)	0.58%
#dark green	Campus	0.45%

The average distance of the network can be used to measure the efficiency of information transfer between users. The shorter the average distance of the network, the more efficient the transfer of information and the less likely it is to be contaminated. The average network distances for individual behaviors were maintained at a low level between [2, 4], which indicates that the messaging of individual behaviors is high and that users can identify the messages conveyed by homogeneous behaviors more accurately. However, the average distance of the combined networks is 6.459, which is high, suggesting that after multiple retweets, likes and comments, a message is prone to distortion, which can lead to "rumors" and incorrect discussion directions. The traceability of carbon neutrality information under multiple acts is therefore essential to ensure the accuracy and reliability of the information.

The size of the network diameter indicates the length of the information dissemination chain; the larger the network diameter, the longer the chain and the more users are involved in the content discussion. The network diameter of the commenting behavior is 13, twice as large as that of the liking and retweeting behavior, and the diameter of the combined multi-behavior network is 17, suggesting that the commenting behavior is more likely to transmit information about the carbon neutrality topic. The size of the network diameter of the combined multi-behavior state does not surprise us, as the combination of multiple behaviors can act as a catalyst for the transmission of information, extending the chain of transmission of information through multi-behavior interaction. Therefore, directing positive user comments and multi-behavioral interactions can effectively promote the dissemination of carbon-neutrality information.

Table 3. Overall indicator characteristics of user behavior network

Diagram Type	Number of nodes	Number of edges	Average distance	Network diameter	Graph density
Like	854	1527	2.028	7	0.0002
Comment	3541	1796	3.764	13	0.001
Forward	3523	1721	2.029	7	0.001
Comprehensive	11467	5249	6.459	17	0.00005

Table 4 shows the top 20 user nodes in the weighted degree centrality ranking of the combined user behavior network along with their authentication identities and PageRank values. The ranking results show that 12 users have "Government" as their authentication type, and most of these government departments are from Shandong Province, China, which is consistent with the heat map results in the spatial analysis section. This shows that the content released by government departments is the focus of public debate and high-frequency interactive behavior, and is at the forefront of the messaging and opinion-led process. It is also noted that the Pagerank value of "Shandong Environment" is as high as 0.021151, which indicates the outstanding contribution of Shandong's environment department to the promotion of carbon neutrality and the correct orientation of the public on social media. In addition, a significant number of celebrity nodes have also gained high weighted centrality and PageRank, such as the veteran media personality "Wang Qing", the Internet human resources expert "HW ex-HR", and the economic and investment blogger "Cai Lian Gu Hai", etc. These bloggers are keen to express their opinions and views on hot topics and have accumulated a high number of followers, and posting related topics about carbon neutrality has also caused more public interaction, we call these users "opinion leaders", and they are also at the core of the discussion. As mentioned in the above analysis, there are individual media users who are also in an important position in the network, such as "Xinhua News Agency", which is the main key news website in China, publishing authoritative, accurate and punctual content, and playing an important role in the dissemination of information on carbon neutrality.

Therefore, giving full play to the publicity and guidance role of government departments, guiding the influence of "opinion leaders" on the public, as well as strengthening media publicity and coverage, is important in drawing on public opinion, gaining public support and participation, and achieving the carbon neutrality target on time and with high quality.

4.4 Content Features

Figure 6 shows the co-word network formed by the topic content of carbon neutrality that users with different identities pay attention to. The colors of the nodes in the network are consistent with the identity colors shown in Table 2, but the shade of color varies according to the size of the node degree. The size of the node indicates the magnitude of the centrality of the node's feature vector, and the core content of the user's attention can be identified based on the color and size of the node. As can be seen in Fig. 7, there is

Table 4. Top 20 user nodes with weighted centrality ranking

User name	Identity	weighted degree	PageRank
山东环境	Government	13828	0.021151
临沂生态环境	Government	4503	0.007883
德州环境	Government	3495	0.004322
刍二不呆	Ordinary users	1903	0.004262
济南生态环境	Government	1823	0.001976
齐河环境	Government	1597	0.001641
济宁生态环境	Government	1548	0.001493
王磬	Celebrity	1190	0.01207
财联股海	Celebrity	987	0.015397
潍坊环保	Government	956	0.001375
生态环境部	Government	934	0.009454
HW前HR	Celebrity	858	0.019147
郯城生态环境	Government	845	0.000351
太白湖环境保护	Government	843	0.000149
青岛环保	Government	830	0.002598
新华社	Media	812	0.006603
商河生态环境	Government	778	0.000299
墨香书坊	Celebrity	667	0.00068
七叔东山再起	Celebrity	636	0.006115
价值投资日志	Celebrity	630	0.003286

a high degree of overlap between the larger and darker nodes, such as "Develop", "Carbon Neutrality", "Target", "High Quality Development" and "Green and low-Carbon", which fully demonstrates the importance that all sectors of Chinese society attach to the Chinese government's implementation of "Green and Low Carbon" and actively promote the "High Quality Development" of various industries, as well as its unanimous determination to achieve the carbon neutrality target.

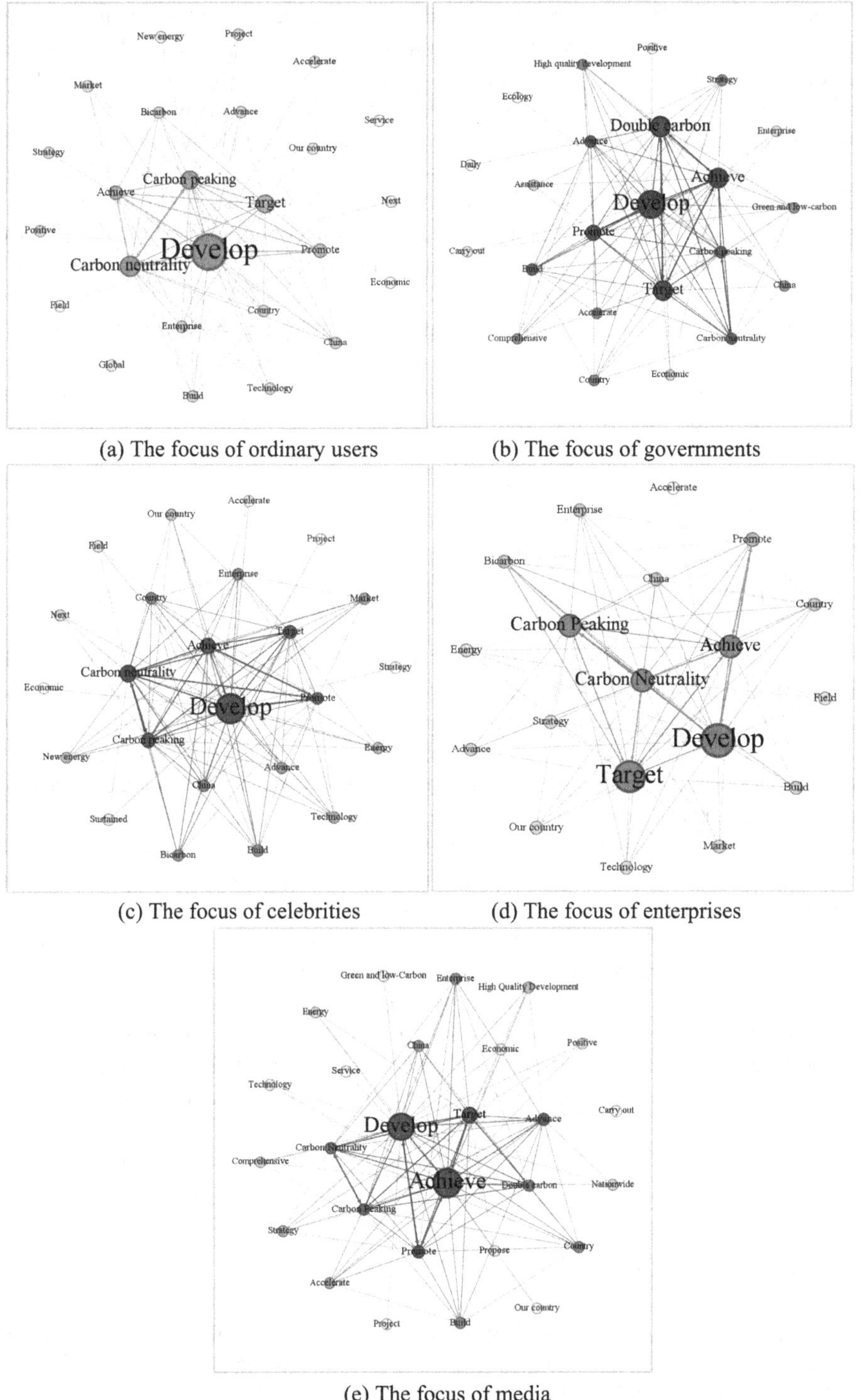

(a) The focus of ordinary users

(b) The focus of governments

(c) The focus of celebrities

(d) The focus of enterprises

(e) The focus of media

Fig. 6. Co-word network of key content focused on by users with different identities

In addition, the words that are central in the co-word network, while highly overlapping, differ in terms of their marginal position and lighter color. It is worth noting that the words that appear in the constructed co-word network are already the focus of the user's attention on the theme, and even though these marginal position words are not prominent in the co-word network, it is still not possible to ignore its importance in all the content of attention. By looking at the marginal and lighter colored words in the different co-word networks, it is clear that government are more concerned with the control of overall goal of carbon neutrality, and that most of the content published and focused on is related to long-term strategies at the national level. Companies mention "energy", "technology" and "market" more often, which is related to the fact that since the introduction of the carbon neutrality target, the government has set carbon emission limits for the relevant enterprises, and enterprises have undertaken technological innovation and industrial green transformation. The media is more concerned with the promotion and implementation of carbon neutral policies, celebrities are mainly concerned with the future of sustainable development, and ordinary users are a cross between the other four types of users. The ordinary user is more of a "participant" than a "speaker" on the topic of carbon neutrality.

5 Conclusions

This paper explores the public's acceptance of carbon neutrality in China from a multidimensional feature fusion perspective by collecting posts, retweets, comments and likes on Weibo on the topic of carbon neutrality. The results of the study show that, firstly, the number and trend of posts over time show that the discussion of carbon neutral topics increases significantly at the time when low-carbon events are held by related enterprises, major conferences are held by the government and relevant policies are introduced. Secondly, the spatial distribution characteristics of users show that the public in all regions of the country have participated in discussions related to the topic of carbon neutrality, but there are differences in the number. Thirdly, in terms of the public's emotional characteristics, the Chinese public's positive emotions have dominated since the introduction of the carbon neutrality target; when hot topics emerge, the proportion of neutral sentiment increases; when guided by incorrect content, the public is more likely to have negative sentiment. Fourth, the main participants in the discussion are ordinary Chinese citizens, with the government and celebrities playing an important role in both publishing carbon-neutrality content and generating discussion among users. Fifth, in terms of the characteristics of the content of public concern, the focus of the content is relatively consistent across all types of users, focusing closely on the issue of carbon neutrality, while, other content of concern differs between user types.

References

1. Bastian, M., Heymann, S., Jacomy, M.: Gephi: an open source software for exploring and manipulating networks. In: Proceedings of the Third International Conference on Weblogs and Social Media, ICWSM 2009, vol. 3, issue 1, pp. 361-362 (2009)

2. Bennett, J., Rachunok, B., Flage, R., Nateghi, R.: Mapping climate discourse to climate opinion: an approach for augmenting surveys with social media to enhance understandings of climate opinion in the United States. PLoS ONE **16**(1), e0245319 (2021)
3. Bernauer, T., Gampfer, R.: Effects of civil society involvement on popular legitimacy of global environmental governance. Glob. Environ. Chang. **23**(2), 439–449 (2013)
4. Bernauer, T., McGrath, L.F.: Simple re-framing unlikely to boost public support for climate policy. Nat. Clim. Chang. **6**(7), 680–683 (2016)
5. Bhagwan, R., Tati, K., Cheng, Y.C., Savage, S., Voelker, G.M.: Total recall: system support for automated availability management. In: Usenix Association Proceedings of the First Symposium on Networked Systems Design and Implementation (Nsdi'04), pp. 337–350 (2004)
6. Cebeci, H.İ, Güner, S., Arslan, Y., Aydemir, E.: Barriers and drivers for biking: what can policymakers learn from social media analytics? J. Transp. Health **28**, 101542 (2023)
7. Chen, S., Zhang, H., Lin, M., Lv, S.: Comparison of microblogging service between Sina Weibo and Twitter. In: International Conference on Computer Science and Network Technology, Harbin, China, pp. 2259–2263 (2011)
8. CSDN. Negative Word Dictionary. https://download.csdn.net/download/u012464467/10546895. Accessed (2019)
9. Dahal, B., Kumar, S.A.P., Li, Z.: Topic modeling and sentiment analysis of global climate change tweets. Soc. Netw. Anal. Min. **9**(1), 1–20 (2019)
10. Feng, L., Leng, F.H.: Theoretical development of co word analysis methods. J. Library Sci. China **32**(2), 5 (2006)
11. Fownes, J.R., Yu, C., Margolin, D.B.: Twitter and climate change (Article). Sociol. Compass **12**(6), 12 (2018)
12. Gao, L., Wang, S., Li, J., Li, H.: Application of the extended theory of planned behavior to understand individual's energy saving behavior in workplaces. Resour. Conserv. Recycl. **127**, 107–113 (2017)
13. Kantenbacher, J., Hanna, P., Cohen, S., Miller, G., Scarles, C.: Public attitudes about climate policy options for aviation (Article). Environ Sci Policy **81**, 46–53 (2018)
14. Li, C., Li, L., Zheng, J., Wang, J., Yuan, Y., Lv, Z., et al.: China's public firms' attitudes towards environmental protection based on sentiment analysis and random forest models. Sustainability **14**(9), 5046 (2022)
15. Linde, S.: Political communication and public support for climate mitigation policies: a country-comparative perspective. Climate Policy **18**(5), 543–555 (2017)
16. Mah, D.N.-Y., Hills, P., Tao, J.: Risk perception, trust and public engagement in nuclear decision-making in Hong Kong. Energy Policy **73**, 368–390 (2014)
17. Panagiotopoulos, P., Bigdeli, A.Z., Sams, S.: Citizen–government collaboration on social media: the case of Twitter in the 2011 riots in England. Gov. Inf. Q. **31**(3), 349–357 (2014)
18. Qazi, A., Bhowmik, C., Hussain, F., Yang, S., Naseem, U., Adebayo, A.-A., et al.: Analyzing the public opinion as a guide for renewable-energy status in Malaysia: a case study. IEEE Trans. Eng. Manage. **70**(2), 371–385 (2023)
19. Simonofski, A., Fink, J., Burnay, C.: Supporting policy-making with social media and e-participation platforms data: a policy analytics framework. Gov. Inf. Q. **38**(3), 101590 (2021)
20. Stroik, P., Chakraborty, D., Ge, W., Boulter, J., Jamelske, E.: Effect of reciprocity on public opinion of international climate treaties: experimental evidence from the US and China. Climate Policy **19**(8), 959–973 (2019)
21. Sui, x. 2021 List Released: Top 10 Popular Words and Top 10 Internet Phenomena. https://news.mydrivers.com/1/800/800830.htm. Accessed (2021)
22. Wang, M., Liu, M., Feng, S., Wang, D., Zhang, Y.: A novel calibrated label ranking based method for multiple emotions detection in Chinese microblogs. Commun. Comput. Inf. Sci. **496**, 238–250 (2014)

23. Wei, Y.G., Gong, P., Zhang, J.H., Wang, L.: Exploring public opinions on climate change policy in "Big Data Era"-A case study of the European Union Emission Trading System (EU-ETS) based on Twitter. Energy Policy **158**, 112559 (2021)
24. Xiang, N., Wang, L., Zhong, S., Zheng, C., Wang, B., Qiushi, Q.: How does the world view China's carbon policy? A sentiment analysis on twitter data. Energies **14**(22), 7782 (2021). https://doi.org/10.3390/en14227782
25. Xu, L., Lin, H., Pan, Y., Ren, H., Chen, J.: Constructing the affective lexicon ontology. J. China Soc. Sci. Tech. Inf. **27**(2), 180–185 (2008)
26. Yang, S.: The impact and risk of new media on public policy making—based on the perspective of "Technology and Civilization". Nanchang Univ., **50**, 64–71 (2019)
27. Zhang, J. S., Shen, J. L., Xu, L. S., Zhang, Q.: The CO2 emission reduction path towards carbon neutrality in the Chinese steel industry: a review. Environ. Impact Assess. Rev., 99 (2023)
28. Zhao, X.J.: Further Analysis of Weibo's "Like" Behavior. News Research Guide (10), 2, 107017 (2019)
29. Zhi, H.: A brief analysis of internet terminology in recent years. https://zhuanlan.zhihu.com/p/339805257. Accessed (2020)

The Social Life of Algorithms: Tracing Notions of Algorithms Beyond Human-Algorithm Interactions

Ignacio Garnham(✉) and Rachel C. Smith

Aarhus University, Aarhus, Denmark
igarnham@cc.au.dk

Abstract. This paper examines how the social meaning, agency and potentials of algorithms in everyday life are challenging the technical notions of algorithms that are embedded in their design. Although tensions between social and technical aspects of algorithms have been explored in critical algorithm studies, there remains a research gap regarding the integration of algorithms into social discourse, material culture, local practices, and imaginaries. Building on the concept of *social life* the paper traces how notions of algorithms are negotiated, imagined and re-interpreted within the context of social interactions as the Bitcoin Beach project is integrated into everyday life of people in the Salvadorian town of El Zonte. The findings presented in this paper contribute to extending ethnographies of algorithms beyond human-algorithm interactions by exploring the various contexts in which algorithms are constructed and scrutinising what is at stake when notions of algorithms become social by design.

Keywords: HCI · Human-algorithm · Design anthropology

1 Introduction

In recent years, HCI researchers aligned with the emergent field of critical algorithm studies have increasingly adopted anthropological lenses to position the interactions between humans and algorithm-driven technologies as the sites where the concept of an algorithm becomes appropriated [Kitchin, 2017]. The move from human-computer interactions to human-algorithm interactions seeks to pay closer attention to how bottom-up notions of the meaning, agency and potential of algorithms can inform a more contextual understanding of the everyday impact of algorithmic technologies, interfaces and services [Gran et al., 2021; Seaver, 2018, 2017]. To support this transition, a growing number of researchers are demonstrating how people construct diverse notions of the meaning, agency and potential of the concept of *an algorithm* through gossip, folk theories, diverse forms of anthropomorphization and imaginaries that emerge from everyday uses of algorithm-driven technologies rather than from knowledge of their technical properties.

While ethnographic approaches in critical algorithm studies contribute to broadening how the concept of an algorithm can be understood, they rely on the perceived duration,

H. Mori et al. (Eds.): HCII 2023, LNCS 14056, pp. 273–289, 2023.
https://doi.org/10.1007/978-3-031-48044-7_20

quality and outcome of specific human-algorithm interactions. In doing so, emerging notions of algorithms become entangled with the technologies that allow humans and algorithms to interact. In contrast, scarce attention has been placed on developing methods to examine how people make sense of algorithms outside the spatial and temporal boundaries where humans and algorithms interact. By relying on samples made from those who (can afford to) experience human-algorithm interactions, current approaches in critical algorithm studies risk limiting the analysis to a one-dimensional understanding of how the concept of an algorithm becomes appropriated, and to what consequences.

To address this gap in research towards an ethnography of algorithms in everyday life, we examine the transition from technical to social understandings of the meaning, agency and potential of algorithms through the lens of the social life of things: a conceit proposed by Appadurai [1988] to place attention on the diverse situations and practices that imbue meaning to things that inherently have none. Through this lens, we extend the reach of critical algorithm approaches and examine how notions of algorithms are discussed, negotiated and adopted outside interactions with technology, focusing instead on interactions with other notions of algorithms and the ideals and values attached to them. In doing so, we shift attention to the everyday situations and practices where, even though algorithm-driven technologies are not in sight, notions of algorithms continue to be discussed, imagined and re-interpreted, and ask:

- How are everyday practices shaping notions of algorithms?
- How are notions of algorithms transforming everyday practices?
- How are notions of algorithms mediating the perception and adoption of algorithm-driven technologies?

This late-breaking paper presents findings from field research in the Salvadorian town of El Zonte, where the foreign-led Bitcoin Beach project aims to transition the local population into a sustainable Bitcoin economic ecosystem by promoting the adoption of, as the project frames it, the *Bitcoin algorithm.* Building on multi-sited theory [Marcus, 1995] and methods from design anthropology [Smith et al., 2016; Gunn et al., 2013], we traced how, when and where notions of the *Bitcoin algorithm* are becoming embedded with different–often opposing–ideals and potentials as the Bitcoin Beach project continues to be implemented and contested.

The following sections provide empirical accounts detailing how notions of the *Bitcoin algorithm* became social, and opens a conversation regarding the feedback-loop between the construction of these notions and the transformation of the practices where notions emerge. We begin by positioning the social life of algorithms in relation to current approaches in HCI and critical algorithm studies. After a brief introduction to El Zonte and the ambitions of the Bitcoin Beach project, we follow how notions of the *Bitcoin algorithm* become social by connecting the experiences of different members of the community. We end with a discussion of the opportunities for approaching algorithms through the lens of *social life*, the tensions that arise when notions of algorithms are constructed alongside everyday practices, and the implications of purposefully curating top-down notions of algorithms.

2 HCI and the Social Life of Algorithms

Emerging critical approaches in the broader field of HCI were characterised by challenging the dominant narratives and discourses around the impact of algorithm-driven technologies, paying close attention to the broader political and economic implications and unintended outcomes of algorithmic systems. In doing so, early research shaping the field of critical algorithm studies often overlapped with critical data and critical media studies [Kitchin and Lauriault, 2014] as the three areas studied the impact of algorithms at a systemic scale by quantifying the results of unintended outcomes rather than by understanding how the behaviour of algorithms is perceived and experienced contextually. Some of this early research includes the themes of algorithmic bias and discrimination [Noble, 2018; Eubanks, 2016], the politics of algorithmic transparency, accountability, explainability and interpretability [Mittelstadt et al., 2019; Pasquale, 2015; Diakopolus, 2015], how algorithms reinforce and amplify existing social inequalities, particularly concerning race, gender, and class [Ruha, 2020], how algorithms can systematically discriminate against marginalised communities [Kleinberg, 2018; Sandvig et. al., 2014], as well as a more critical approach to the use of machine learning algorithms that focus attention on their social and political implications [Crawford and Calo, 2016].

To distance themselves from critical data and critical media studies, researchers in critical algorithm studies began to adopt ethnographic methods to engage with the everyday experiences of people with algorithm-driven technologies [Gillespie, 2014]. Kitchin and Dodge [2014] first hinted at studying the lives of algorithms by proposing a research agenda that looks at the feedback loop between algorithmic systems and their users, raising concerns about the capacity of algorithms to mediate information and shape everyday practices. Similarly, around the time when critical approaches to algorithms were becoming established in HCI research, Dourish, although not directly, pointed out to Appadurai's approach by stating that *"the limits of the term algorithm are determined by social engagements rather than by technological or material constraints"* [Dourish, 2016]. By placing the focus on the social and cultural contexts where algorithmic systems are deployed [Seaver, 2018], researchers have begun to pay closer attention to how these systems are implemented and experienced by both professionals [Ruckenstein and Granroth, 2020] and laypeople [Gillespie, 2018].

As the move towards understanding and documenting public perceptions of algorithms grows stronger, researchers increasingly shift attention away from code and into human-algorithm interactions where people make sense of code. The move from technical to cultural notions of algorithms is relevant because, although from a technical perspective, the term algorithm has historically referred to a rigorous set of (mathematical) instructions used for calculations and problem-solving, research in social sciences and humanities has shown that, over time, the concept of *an algorithm* has been subject to varied interpretations–from the magical and mythical to the anthropomorphic–that are continually transformed alongside the contexts and purposes in which algorithms are deployed [Cave et al., 2020].

To encounter emerging notions of algorithms, research in critical algorithm studies has relied primarily on building from people's experiences while using algorithms-driven services and technologies to reverse engineer how their notions of algorithms became constructed. In doing so, researchers aim to provide empirical accounts of how people build relationships with algorithmic systems and how these relationships can shape how users approach algorithm-driven technologies. Some of these approaches include algorithmic folk theories as a method to collect lay understandings of algorithms that are constructed due to negative or positive experiences with algorithmic platforms [Eslami et al., 2016], stories about algorithms [Schellewald, 2022] and algorithmic gossip [Bishop, 2019] as methods to document shared ideas of algorithms by users of the same platform, algorithmic personas as a method to visualise algorithmic functions through stereotypical human characters [Büchi, 2021], a 'decoding' of algorithms as an approach to studying the relationships that people experience with algorithms [Lomborg and Kapsch, 2020], and algorithmic imaginaries as an approach to capture what algorithms mean for people in the intersection of use, gossip and reflection [Bucher, 2017].

The ethnographic turn in critical algorithm studies has been central to highlighting the relevance of context both for researching how notions of algorithms are constructed and for broadening how the impact of algorithms can be understood and studied. Nevertheless, while providing rich accounts of emergent notions of algorithms, the reliance on human-algorithm interactions as the sites where humans become aware of algorithms leaves out of sight the myriad social and cultural practices where notions of algorithms are socialised, negotiated and adopted. To approach these practices as research sites, the analysis needs to account for how the ideals and values embedded in (the design of) algorithms influence how people talk about, explain, introduce, and imagine algorithms as part of everyday life.

The view that things–such as stones, trees, trinkets and algorithms–have a social life aims to place attention on the diverse situations and practices that imbue meaning to things that inherently have none. Kopytoff [1986] first proposed the concept of *object biographies* to emphasise the need to examine the entire life cycle of objects–through production, exchange and consumption–as a method for understanding that the meanings attached to an object are dependent on the people and events to which it is connected. The social life of things [Appadurai, 1988] is a conceit to further the notion that the transactions that enable the exchange of things are invested with the ideals and values of social relations. By focusing on how relationships between objects and people are constructed over time, the essays collected by Appadurai show that objects are not static, inert things. Instead, they are part of dynamic social and cultural networks where things can be used to express and reinforce cultural values, traditions and social hierarchies. As a result, *things* can be used to maintain or shift power relations and create new cultural practices and identities.

The term *algorithm*, therefore, can be said to have a social life, collecting and shedding varied ideals and values as the term is appropriated and scrutinised across diverse practices of everyday life. In the following sections, we provide an overview of the theory and methods we used to operationalise the lens of *social life* as a framework for extending critical algorithm approaches outside the spatial and temporal boundaries of human-computer interactions, expanding the sites where notions of algorithms are constructed, and scrutinising what is at stake when notions of algorithms become social by design.

3 Research Design

This late-breaking research discusses early findings from an eight weeks ethnographic study of the social life of the Bitcoin algorithm in the Salvadorian town of El Zonte. To research the social life of the Bitcoin algorithm empirically, we prototyped ethnographic methods based on design anthropology and multi-sited theory. Multi-sited theory [Marcus, 1995] is an approach for researching social phenomena that cannot be accounted for by focusing on a single site, such as following the construction of a metaphor or a story and the cultural transformations taking place as they become socialised and adopted. It is relevant to highlight that, In a multi-sited research approach, the concept of the site is understood as the object of study, not the context of study. From this perspective, the negotiations that take place as notions of algorithms are socialised and scrutinised become the sites of research.

To encounter these sites, we prototyped ethnographic methods through the lens of design anthropology. Design anthropology is a theoretical and methodological approach that explores the cultural phenomena that emerge in everyday life by moving beyond traditional ethnographic methods, which rely primarily on observation and reflection, to actively involve research participants in co-creating knowledge [Smith and Kjærsgaard, 2015; Rabinow, 2008]. Design anthropology is relevant to support the study of the social life of things as it provides an interdisciplinary, future-oriented approach to studying, documenting, and understanding the beliefs, tensions, power relations and feedback loops that hold together the relationships between people and *things* and how these relationships are shaped by social, cultural, and historical contexts [Tunstall, 2020].

By combining design anthropology and multi-sited theory, we engaged 20 residents from El Zonte with different affiliations and positions towards the Bitcoin Beach project. More specifically, these accounts belong to participants from two age groups that are indicative of the positionality of participants. One group corresponds to the 20 to 35 years old members of the community socialising a singular notion of the Bitcoin algorithm. The second group represents the 45 and over segment of the population who are going through the process of negotiating multiple notions of the Bitcoin algorithm. Some of these methods included participants mapping where gossip [Dunbar, 2004] concerning the meaning, agency and potential of the Bitcoin algorithm emerges across the town and its surroundings, positioning the influence and positionality of different notions of the Bitcoin algorithm in relation to social learning strategies [Bandura, 1977], and graphing reciprocity [Mauss, 2005] in relation to shared expectations regarding adopting the ideals embedded in the Bitcoin algorithm.

We also relied on traditional methods such as graphic elicitation [Varga-Atkins and O'Brien, 2009] and directed storytelling [Thomson, 1999] to access concepts, feelings, and imaginaries that are hard to put into words. This interdisciplinary approach allowed us to position the participant's recollections of memories and anecdotes as research sites for unpacking individual and shared notions of the Bitcoin algorithm and the practices being transformed alongside them.

In the following sections, we introduce accounts of ideals and notions of the *Bitcoin algorithm* collected during mapping sessions in the town of El Zonte and during the Adopting Bitcoin Conference held in San Salvador in November of 2022. We use these accounts to trace the social life of the *Bitcoin algorithm* from its inception by the hand of the Bitcoin Beach project leadership to its adoption and contestation by different members of the community in El Zonte. The accounts are pseudonymised to preserve the age range of participants as indicative of positionality.

4 El Zonte as a Test Site for the *Bitcoin Algorithm*

El Zonte is a small coastal town in the country of El Salvador–just a few unpaved roads wide on both sides of a small stream–about one hour away from the capital city. For many decades, people in El Zonte–like most other communities in El Salvador–lived in relative isolation from foreign interests due to the country's political, economic and social insecurities. However, In the early 2000s, before El Salvador began to reform its image and invest in attracting foreign tourism and investment, El Zonte had already begun to make a name for itself thanks to the surfing conditions that can be found around the town. This resulted in foreign tourism slowly coming to El Zonte, gradually introducing the community to ideas and ideals of what a different life could or should look like. By 2010, the community started seeing Salvadorian investors coming into town to build accommodations to support local tourism, which in the last years has been doubled by foreign developers as a result of a growing sense of security in living and investing in the country. These days, the people of El Zonte interact daily with foreigners. Most of its residents between 18 and 35 speak English fluently–with many working hospitality jobs–and a growing number of expats are residing in the area.

Nonetheless, until 2019 the town had a precarious physical and digital infrastructure, and it was far from having a thriving tourism industry. Things rapidly changed with the arrival of the Bitcoin Beach project, the first of a growing number of initiatives worldwide aimed at transforming small communities, mostly in developing countries, into Bitcoin circular economies. El Zonte was chosen as the context to explore the adoption of Bitcoin because it offered both a local community with a lack of economic, technological and educational opportunities and a growing foreign community interested in investing in the town because of its tourism potential. During its first years, the project was mainly discussed amongst Bitcoin enthusiasts. However, the ambitions of the Bitcoin Beach project became internationally known seemingly overnight as El Salvador's president announced that the country would be adopting Bitcoin as a legal tender at the end of 2021. The news sparked worldwide interest, an influx of tourism and the necessary momentum to hold the first Bitcoin conference in El Salvador.

While attending the 2022 Adopting Bitcoin Conference in San Salvador, it became apparent that the Bitcoin Beach project is more than just allowing people in El Zonte to have digital currency and pay for services and subscriptions that otherwise they could not access: *"Bitcoin is a way of life,"* as speakers and participants, most of which are in their late 20s and early 30s, are quick to share. The approach to Bitcoin–a blockchain-supported cryptocurrency–as an analogy to discuss how people approach everyday life is scaffolded by the diverse principles and ideals that have been associated with Bitcoin and blockchain technology since the appearance of the white paper anonymously written in 2008 under the pseudonym of Satoshi Nakamoto [2008]. However, the anonymity of the key figure behind Bitcoin, as well as the decentralised nature of the technology–where there is no legally recognised authority that can say which principles and ideals align better with Satoshi's vision–has resulted in the use and potential of Bitcoin to be open for interpretation. As a conference speaker puts it: "*The only way to control the narrative is by becoming a relevant voice in the community.*"

5 Tracing the Social Life of the *Bitcoin Algorithm*

The following subsections examine four stages in the social life of the Bitcoin algorithm. We begin by tracing the ideals that became attached to the concept and continue by scrutinising the strategy behind their socialisation. Once we have identified how these ideals are curated and socialised, we focus on the tensions and transformation that arise as notions of the Bitcoin algorithm are negotiated alongside everyday practices. We end by unpacking how members of the community contest top-down ideals by reflecting on potential changes to their everyday practices.

5.1 Curating the Ideals of the Bitcoin Algorithm

Bitcoin Beach aims to become a relevant voice in guiding how the potential and purpose of Bitcoin are understood and implemented, and El Zonte was the first step in prototyping how to talk about Bitcoin in order to encourage adoption; now, there are dozens of similar projects aiming to transition entire communities into adopting Bitcoin as a currency and a way of life. A member of the Bitcoin Beach leadership explains that:

> *We are an ideology, a way of living life through the ideals that Bitcoin represents, but the technical side of things is too...well, technical! No one sells these [algorithm-driven] services to regular folks by explaining how their maths work, but what we can do is take leverage how algorithms are perceived in mainstream media, like smart, sleek, connected, modern and so on, and use those ideals to paint a picture of the Bitcoin algorithm that people in El Zonte can relate to.*

For the Bitcoin Beach project, the *Bitcoin algorithm* embodies ideals of efficiency, inclusivity and modernity. These values were picked amongst other popular ones within the Bitcoin community–such as trustworthy, clean, incorruptible and truthful–because of their higher chance to resonate with the community of El Zonte. Another member of the Bitcoin Beach leadership adds that:

> *If I have to explain the Bitcoin algorithm to some wealthy guy back home [in Canada], I will probably have to use other values because he won't be so excited about efficiency and modernity because he probably experiences those anyway. Instead, he probably is more excited about concepts like trustworthy and incorruptible...My point is that the Bitcoin algorithm can do many things, but we need to be strategic about the ones we highlight based on the context and people we are working with.*

Although using ideals and values in the design of algorithms has become a common practice, such as in popular frameworks like fairness accountability and transparency (FAT), responsible AI, and human-centred AI, the ideals imbued to the *Bitcoin algorithm* were chosen based on their likeness to become adopted and promoted by the people of El Zonte. Consequently, the early success of the Bitcoin Beach project depends largely on the community of El Zonte adopting these ideals.

The ideals of the *Bitcoin algorithm* are first introduced to the community of El Zonte within the walls of Hope House, the headquarters of Bitcoin Beach. There, Bitcoin Beach offers free education and capacitation about Bitcoin and how to *evangelise*–as the practice is referred to by Bitcoiners–others in the community. The target demographic consists mainly of the 20 to 30 years old native residents of El Zonte who, in recent years, have become exponentially exposed to the worldviews of tourists and expats, many of whom support the vision of the Bitcoin Beach project. The recruiting of Bitcoin promoters is done by core members of the project. Alan, a native of El Zonte in his mid-30s who has been working as a recruiter since the early days of Bitcoin Beach, explains that:

> *The younger generations of El Zonte are much more aligned with the values we believe in than the older ones. They want the kind of lifestyle that has become associated with algorithms, you know, fast, sleek, clean, shiny, efficient...they might not know what algorithms are or how they work, but they are aware of the hype around them, and they want to be a part of it...everyone wants to live in the future, and we are bringing that future to El Zonte.*

People who complete training at Hope House become Bitcoin promoters, tasked with encouraging both business owners and the community at large to embrace the social and cultural transformations that Bitcoin Beach seeks to achieve. Recruiting business owners is necessary to support a circular Bitcoin economy through Bitcoin Beach services and takes place mostly at their place of business, such as restaurants, hotels, and convenience stores. On the other hand, recruiting other community members is a strategy to spread the ideals of the Bitcoin algorithm outside the relational, spatial and temporal boundaries where humans and algorithms interact.

5.2 Socialising the Ideals of the Bitcoin Algorithm

While the Bitcoin Beach project socialises ideals of efficiency, inclusivity and modernity to drive adoption of the Bitcoin algorithm, modernity and efficiency resonate the most amongst Bitcoin promoters and their peers. El Zonte–despite the influx of money and tourism in the last five years–is mostly run-down houses and restaurants, poorly-kept dirt roads, and not much to do for the local residents in their 20s. The new hotels and restaurants that cater to foreign Bitcoin and surf enthusiasts stand in contrast with what the town had offered until recently, and Bitcoin advertisements, stickers and graffiti have become part of the fabric of the town, turning otherwise unremarkable spaces, like trash cans and electricity poles, into postcards of the Bitcoin Beach project.

When asked about the sudden appearance of Bitcoin (Beach) propaganda, promoters agree that they appreciate seeing signs of Bitcoin everywhere because it reminds them of the ideals they are working hard to instil in the everyday life of people. Yet, the contrast between these ideals and the everyday reality of El Zonte has led to promoters becoming more critical of what they see and encounter as they go about their daily life in El Zonte.

Yenny, a 25 years old resident of El Zonte and one of the first to become a promoter, shares that:

We [the promoters] are more perceptive now, to…you know, things that need to change. Before, we would just see things and be like [shrugging]; it's just how things are. But now, when we are waiting in line because the old guy [the shop owner] is counting pennies and doing maths to give change, we know it doesn't have to be that way. That he could be more efficient, that we could have more time to do our things if others were more efficient.

These reflections are common amongst promoters as they discuss ideals like efficiency and modernity in relation to changing daily practices and behaviours that, in their views, would benefit the community. Promoters share that they often find themselves discussing the potential of the *Bitcoin algorithm* and its values when doing things *the old way*, such as collecting wood and cooking with fire, taking the bus for 30 min to pay for basic services, or doing laundry by hand. Jerson, a recently trained promoter in his early 20s, shares:

I see a different version of myself when I think through these values–a sort of algorithmic version of myself that encourages me to be more efficient, smarter, sophisticated. And we [the promoters] feel a responsibility to help others realise how things can change for the best if they apply the ideals of the Bitcoin algorithm to the things they do.

While embodying the ideals embedded in the Bitcoin algorithm might sound abstract, for promoters, it is no different to embodying ideals such as solidarity and humility as part of embracing the teachings of the local church. Maura, one of the few promoters over 30, explains that:

The community in El Zonte is very religious, and when people are discussing a challenge or wrongdoing, it is common to encourage others to see themselves in the light of scripture, like, making those ideals part of how you approach life and all that stuff. So we are doing the same thing, except we want them to see themselves in the light of the Bitcoin algorithm.

Evangelising the community is widely seen as part of the social contract of being part of the Bitcoin (Beach) community, and promoters are encouraged to use any opportunity to nudge the community into associating the ideals of Bitcoin Beach with positive changes in their day-to-day life. Mateo, a 30 years old recruiter, describes that:

The job of the promoters is to convert the community. You know, the 'orange pilling' thing, and they do it by telling others that adopting Bitcoin is not only about digital payments or having access to more services or whatever, but that the Bitcoin algorithm embodies the ideals needed to become a modern, digital and future-thinking community. If the community adopts our ideals first, they will not question adopting our services later…so spreading our ideals is a priority. We need the community to be aligned with the kind of transformation we want to see.

While promoters are eager to embrace new ideals as a means to trigger changes to everyday practices, those in the community who are new to the concept of *an algorithm* are faced with negotiating change against little information. To encourage the older generations to visualise the person they can become if they apply the principles of the *Bitcoin algorithm* to everyday decisions, behaviours and practices, promoters often approach them while performing everyday tasks that could be transformed through the services and ideals of Bitcoin. These tasks range from paying bills and shopping for groceries, cooking and cleaning in their homes, or taking walks to collect wood and shells. As a result, people are beginning to make sense of the meaning, agency and potential of the *Bitcoin algorithm* based on how they imagine these practices transforming if they were to embrace the ideals of efficiency and modernity.

5.3 Negotiating the Ideals of the Bitcoin Algorithm

To unpack how different members of the community make sense of the meaning, agency and potential of the Bitcoin algorithm, this subsection provides extended accounts of three ongoing negotiations unfolding alongside everyday practices.

The first negotiation is between Mila, a promoter in her early 20s, and her 65 years old uncle, Antonio, who owns and runs a small stall in town.

> *Mila: My uncle has a little stall on one of the side roads. He sells just a few things, cheap stuff for kids and some grains and flour, pencils, and things like that. But he is also the only one that sells sim cards, so tourists are always going there to top-up their phones...oh and he also has a few old slot machines on the side and sells beer...cheap beer! So it can get busy at times! It sounds good, but there is often a long line, and locals are used to it, but you can see tourists get frustrated, and sometimes they just leave or will not come back to buy beer from him because they know it's slow. You see, he [the uncle] likes to talk to people, which is good for him perhaps but not good for business. So I am pushing hard to get him to stop chatting and focus on giving better service to tourists. A Bitcoin terminal will not be enough to keep tourists coming, he needs to embrace efficiency.*
>
> *Antonio: She [her niece] is so concerned with time and money since these [Bitcoin Beach] people started coming. Efficiency here and there all the time! That my shelves don't look modern, sell this instead of that, don't chat at work, chat later, bla bla. I know she wants to help, but I have a stall to talk to people, not to make money. They [the promoters] talk about efficiency as if we didn't know the concept [laughing], but I am an old man, and talking to my friends all day feels like an efficient use of the time I have left!...So their ideas of efficiency are definitely not the same as mine.*

As the ideals of the *Bitcoin algorithm* become subject to scrutiny, different understandings of efficiency and modernity begin to be formed and attached to new interpretations of the meaning, agency and potential of the *Bitcoin algorithm.* Such is the outcome between the negotiations of Gladys, a convenience store owner in her early 60s who adopted Bitcoin in 2021 and remains one of the few active Bitcoin users over 50, and Laura, a close friend of hers who remains sceptical of the benefits of adopting Bitcoin.

Gladys: I have had this [convenience] store for more than 15 years now. People trust me; I have fair prices and good products. Business is good, I like being a shop owner, but I never liked handling cash. It's messy, it's scary...you know, things were different [less safe] just until a few years ago, so having cash lying around was never to my liking. So when the kids [the promoters] started telling me about this Bitcoin thing and that people would pay with their phones and I would not have to deal with cash, I was intrigued! They said it would be more efficient and quick, instant...like magic! And that the shop would look nicer and modern if I have these terminals and screens and stuff, so it would attract more tourists. So I gave it a try, and it took me some time to get used to it, but I love it now! So now I barely accept cash anymore, only from people I trust, but [laughing] I am still trying to get my friends to sign up so they stop bringing me cash!

Laura: Oh, you spoke with Gladys? Let me tell you something, we are good friends, but we almost got into a big fight over this Bitcoin algorithm crap because we [Laura and her friends] don't think she thought this [adopting Bitcoin] through. Our whole thing was sending the kids in the morning to buy some candy to get them out of the house and give us some space. But now she [Gladys] is not accepting cash, so now none of us can get the kids out of the house anymore! So I'm sitting at home taking care of my grandchildren, and I'm just thinking, damn, this Bitcoin thing!... I'm not mad at her anymore, but I'm mad at those Bitcoin people because they don't seem to understand how things work here. They just think their ways are more efficient because they come from [air quotes] more developed countries? This Bitcoin algorithm is just like the gringos that come looking to take things away from us and pretend they are helping...you tell me, modernity for whom are we talking about?

A similar situation occurs as Maria, a promoter in her late 20s, tries to onboard 50 years old Teresa, who runs one of the few remaining locally-owned restaurants in town, which is also one of the last restaurants using wood for cooking meals.

Maria: I explained to her that I understood why they cook with an open fire and that I know that gas is expensive and wood is freely available. But I also explained to her that if she switched to gas, she could serve more customers because she could cook faster because gas is more efficient than fire. I also said I knew that waiting for the [gas] truck can be inconvenient, but that with Bitcoin she can now buy gas online and get it delivered without any hassle. I explained to her that the Bitcoin algorithm makes these things possible, that it allows you to be more efficient and take less time doing chores so that you can have more time to do other things. I also pointed out that the restaurant would look nicer and more modern with a nice gas stove, Bitcoin terminals, etc. And that the only thing that would change for her is that her life would be easier. She was not interested...I mean! [shrugging in disbelief] I think it's just because they want to go against things they don't understand as old people do.

Teresa: Well, I didn't think much about [the Bitcoin algorithm] before. I am not interested in those things, and I don't entertain gossip, so all I can say is that I don't know how it works, but it makes me nervous that they talk so much about

> *becoming something we are not by adopting these [air quotes] ideals as they call them...And that is a problem because what Maria doesn't want to understand or even believe is that I like cooking with fire. It is how my mother taught me, and it makes food more tasty. And it keeps me engaged with what I am doing; fire is unpredictable, it tests you as a cook...anyone can cook with gas! People come to my restaurant because I cook with care, not with time in mind. I also enjoy looking for wood. It is my private time for thinking, and sometimes I invite people to join me, and we chat and gossip. Switching to gas would take all these experiences and memories away! I wish they [the promoters] were more in tune with our ideals, like, what happens to tradition when everything has to become modern?*

As the ideals attached to the *Bitcoin algorithm* become increasingly negotiated alongside everyday practices, a growing number of people in the community are resenting the pressure to change that is socialised as part of adopting the ideals of efficiency and modernity. These tensions are giving rise to notions of the *Bitcoin algorithm* that stand in opposition to those first set into a social path inside the rooms of Hope House.

5.4 Contesting the Ideals of the Bitcoin Algorithm

The inclination towards contestation emerges from two converging factors. On the one hand, many members of the community, particularly those over the age of 40, are growing wary of promoters constantly approaching them during routine chores and everyday practices to encourage them to adopt the ideals of the Bitcoin algorithm. On the other hand, the same segment of the population–as a result of growing up more deprived of technology and infrastructure–has a stronger connection to the backdrop of El Zonte: the Pacific Ocean, rough waves, volcanic sand, rocky cliffs and thick vegetation. This convergence has led to a growing number of people weighing the ideals of the Bitcoin algorithm against the values and memories that being close to nature evokes in them.

Mayte, a childhood friend of Teresa, shares that when being by themselves with nature, they are inspired to share memories and anecdotes of growing up in El Zonte and reflect on how quickly things have changed in the last ten years. While the community generally appreciates the influx of tourism, there are issues of displacement, water scarcity and inflation that have transformed and, in many ways, affected how they live. Consequently, the sudden arrival of the Bitcoin Beach project and the rapid transformations taking place as a result make many in the community uneasy. Raul, a local surf instructor in his mid-40s, describes how he came to challenge the ideal of efficiency by thinking about how the sand on the beach is constantly in motion, being renewed by the tides and shaping the waves in turn. This reflection led him to conclude that nature is not efficient, it is consistent, and if you study the cycles, you can engage nature meaningfully instead of efficiently.

Lynda and Juan, who have been fishing in the area since childhood, are suspicious of ideas of efficiency and what it can do to their way of life. Juan explains he wishes he could sit down with the algorithm, have a beer and understand why efficiency and modernity are so important to "it". Lynda complains that people in El Zonte do not even know what the *Bitcoin algorithm* looks like and that people cannot negotiate with something they can't touch or see. Juan argues:

> Juan argues: *We can touch the sand, the ocean, we can feel the rain, we can connect to the sensations and memories that these experiences generate and put them in the balance against those that this algorithm is supposed to give us...[gesticulating, looking around and making pfft sound] nothing!*
>
> Lynda ends with an analogy: *If you stay too long in the fishing boat you'll forget how to swim, so when you rod brakes you'll starve because you've forgotten how to dive and spear. I understand that fishing with a rod is more efficient, but what about the things you lose in exchange?*

Others in the community are relying on similar experiences and memories of different times to make sense of how they feel about the ideals being socialised by promoters. It is during these moments of reflection in nature that, increasingly, members of the community find themselves scrutinising the meaning, agency and potential of algorithms and constructing alternative notions of the Bitcoin algorithm. As the pressure to adopt the ideals and services of Bitcoin Beach grow, these experiences give members of the community a safe space to contextualise, imagine, and, if needed, contest the ideals and transformations that the *Bitcoin algorithm* might bring, not only to their everyday practices but to how they approach the present and think about the future.

While promoters were prompted to reflect on the *Bitcoin beach* algorithm when performing practices directly associated with the perceived benefits of Bitcoin, such as paying for goods and services, older members of the community are triggered by practices that are further removed from the physical infrastructure of Bitcoin, such as collecting wood or fishing, as these practices remind them of what is at stake if they embrace the ideals of the *Bitcoin algorithm.* Consequently, promoters are more likely to attach positive implications to adopting Bitcoin as a currency and way of life, while the older generations are more prone to attach negative ones.

6 Discussion

Through the lens of social life, we traced how notions of algorithms are constructed in El Zonte, from being curated and strategically socialised, to being negotiated and contested in relation to the practices that the ideals embedded in the *Bitcoin algorithm* aim to transform. We discuss our findings in the following subsections.

6.1 The Social Life of Algorithms

Approaching notions of algorithms through the lens of *social life* allowed us to demonstrate that both notions of algorithms and positions towards algorithm-driven technologies can be constructed alongside daily practices that transcend the relational, spatial and temporal boundaries of human-algorithm interactions. More so, our findings indicate that emerging notions of algorithms are largely defined by the practices that trigger reflection about the meaning, agency and potential of algorithms. A design anthropological account of the social life of algorithms provided us with a framework to identify new sites of research where we documented tensions, negotiations and transformations that would have remained hidden if we had conducted our research in traditional sites such as Hope House and the business being onboarded.

These findings suggest that current approaches in critical algorithm studies could benefit from tracing the origins and spreading patterns of algorithmic gossip, folk theories and imaginaries as a means to extend how we understand what classifies as an everyday experience of people with algorithm-driven technologies. Positioning ethnographic methods in these new sites can shorten the gap in critical algorithms studies concerning the everyday social and cultural factors that pressure notions of algorithms into being, such as the distance that notions of algorithms can travel, which everyday practices lead to higher rates of adoption or rejection, and the role of ideals and values in shaping how people make sense of algorithms.

6.2 Notions of Algorithms and Changing Practices

In addition, by relying on multi-sited theory to follow how the concept of the *Bitcoin algorithm* is curated, socialised, negotiated and contested, we show how everyday practices and notions of algorithms continually shape each other, leading to the embedding of new meanings, agency and potentials not only to emerging notions of algorithms but to everyday practices.

On the one hand, these findings contribute to research in critical algorithm studies showing how the social, cultural and political context must be accounted for when scrutinising public notions of the impact and potential of algorithms. On the other hand, the capacity of algorithmic gossip, folk theories and imaginaries to pressure change raises new questions concerning how emerging notions of algorithms are given agency by those who construct or adopt them and how these shape the power dynamics of human-algorithm relationships.

While studying the social life of algorithms allows to empirically study the theoretical approaches of Kitchin and Dodge [2014] and Dourish [2016], additional research concerning the coevolutionary dynamics between everyday practices and emerging notions of algorithms would benefit from engaging participants during a longer timeframe and limiting the study to a single practice undergoing transformations. In the context of El Zonte, this could be the transition from cooking with fire to cooking with gas or the fading out of cash as payment in a local business. A more focused approach would still benefit from a social life approach as a strategy to identify stakeholders, narratives and adjacent sites that pressure the feedback loop.

6.3 Floating Narratives

In the context of El Zonte, rationalising the concept of an algorithm through a set of curated ideals resulted in people developing different and often contrasting notions of the agency and potential of algorithms. These notions rapidly led to members of the community transforming their practices and beliefs to accommodate the potentials and fears imbued in the Bitcoin algorithm, many of which were transformed to embrace the use of the services provided by Bitcoin Beach. These transformations suggest that purposefully curating and mobilising a specific set of ideals alongside the deployment of algorithm-driven technologies provides a strategy to mediate the negotiation, contestation and appropriation not only of these technologies but of the concept of an algorithm and the benefits or harms it can bring to people, regardless of their interactions with these technologies.

Although we need to replicate our methods in contexts that include the practices taking place as algorithms are envisioned and designed to map the entire social life of *an algorithm*, these early findings indicate that embedding ideals and values to algorithms disguise algorithmic potentials and limitations as sensible rather than logical, which helps control the narratives of appropriation and adoption. This raises concerns about how the ideals and values that are used to guide the design of principled algorithms can be easily replaced as soon as the technologies are deployed. Therefore, focusing on how algorithms are imbued and removed of ideals and values is relevant not only for scrutinising the ways in which researchers race to replace technical ideals with moral ones as a strategy to enable a more humane use of algorithmic technologies [Morley et al., 2021]. In addition, more attention needs to be placed on examining how the ideals and values which we rely upon to talk about, explain, introduce, and imagine algorithms can lead to changes in social and cultural practices that unfold outside the relational, spatial and temporal boundaries where humans and algorithms interact.

7 Conclusion

Through an empirical account of the social life of the *Bitcoin algorithm*, this late-breaking research contributes a novel approach to extend ethnographies of algorithms beyond the spatial and temporal boundaries where humans and algorithms interact. Our findings show that notions of algorithms and positions towards algorithm-driven technologies are shaped not only by human-algorithm interactions but also by engagements with the embedded ideals and values within algorithms. These negotiations are influenced by the contextual factors and situations in which they occur, wherein the values and ideals inherent in practices and algorithms continually shape one another.

Consequently, the deliberate socialisation of a carefully curated understanding of *an algorithm* led the residents of El Zonte to adopt a position towards Bitcoin technology based on their perception of its transformative potential rather than solely on the technical attributes of Bitcoin services. This research underscores the need to examine further how the principles, ideals, and values underpinning algorithm design can influence individuals' comprehension and adoption of algorithm-driven technologies.

Acknowledgments. This work is part of the DCODE project. The project has received funding from the European Union's Horizon 2020 research and innovation programme under the Marie Skłodowska-Curie grant agreement No 955990.

References

1. Appadurai, A., (ed.) The social life of things: Commodities in cultural perspective. Cambridge University Press (1988)

2. Benjamin, R.: Race after technology: abolitionist tools for the new Jim code, 1–3 (2020)
3. Bandura, A., Walters, R.H.: Social Learning Theory, vol. 1. Prentice Hall, Englewood Cliffs (1977)
4. Bishop, S.: Managing visibility on YouTube through algorithmic gossip. New Media Soc. **21**(11–12), 2589–2606 (2019)
5. Bucher, T.: The algorithmic imaginary: Exploring the ordinary affects of Facebook algorithms. Inf. Commun. Soc. **20**(1), 30–44 (2017)
6. Büchi, M., et al.: Making sense of algorithmic profiling: user perceptions on Facebook Inf. Commun. Soc., 1–17 (2021)
7. Cave, S., Dihal, K., Dillon, S., (eds.) AI narratives: a history of imaginative thinking about intelligent machines. Oxford University Press, Oxford (2020)
8. Crawford, K., Calo, R.: There is a blind spot in AI research. Nature **538**(7625), 311–313 (2016)
9. Diakopoulos, N.: Algorithmic accountability: journalistic investigation of computational power structures. Digit. J. **3**(3), 398–415 (2015)
10. Dourish, P.: Algorithms and their others: algorithmic culture in context. Big Data Soc. **3**(2), 2053951716665128 (2016)
11. Dunbar, R.I.M.: Gossip in evolutionary perspective. Rev. General Psychol. **8**(2), 100–110 (2004)
12. Eslami, M., et al.: First I like it, then I hide it: Folk Theories of Social Feeds. In: Proceedings of the 2016 cHI Conference on Human Factors in Computing Systems (2016)
13. Eubanks, V.: Automating inequality: how high-tech tools profile, police, and punish the poor. St. Martin's Press (2018)
14. Fournier, M.: Marcel Mauss. Princeton University Press (2005)
15. Gillespie, T.: The relevance of algorithms. Media technologies: essays on communication, materiality, and society 167.2014, 167 (2014)
16. Gillespie, T.: Custodians of the internet: platforms, content moderation, and the hidden decisions that shape social media. Yale University Press (2018)
17. Gran, A.-B., Booth, P., Bucher, T.: To be or not to be algorithm aware: a question of a new digital divide? Inf. Commun. Soc. **24**(12), 1779–1796 (2021)
18. Gunn, W., Otto, T., Smith, R.C., (eds.) Design Anthropology: Theory and Practice. Taylor & Francis (2013)
19. Kitchin, R., Lauriault, T.: Towards critical data studies: charting and unpacking data assemblages and their work (2014)
20. Kitchin, R., Dodge, M.: Code/Space: Software and Everyday Life. MIT Press (2014)
21. Kleinberg, J., et al.: Human decisions and machine predictions. Q. J. Econ. **133**(1), 237–293 (2018)
22. Kitchin, R.: Thinking critically about and researching algorithms. Inf. Commun. Soc. **20**(1), 14–29 (2017)
23. Kopytoff, I.: The cultural biography of things: commoditization as process. Soc. Life Things: Commodities Cultural Perspect. **68**, 70–73 (1986)
24. Lomborg, S., Kapsch, P.H.: Decoding algorithms. Media, Culture & Society **42**(5), 745–761 (2020)
25. Marcus, G.E.: Ethnography in/of the world system: the emergence of multi-sited ethnography. Annu. Rev. Anthropol. **24**(1), 95–117 (1995)
26. Mehlman, J.: The floating signifier: from Lévi-Strauss to Lacan. Yale French Studies, 10–37 (1972)
27. Mittelstadt, B., Russell, C., Wachter, S.: Explaining explanations in AI. In: Proceedings of the Conference on Fairness, Accountability, and Transparency (2019)
28. Morley, J., et al.: Operationalising AI ethics: barriers, enablers and next steps. AI Soc., 1–13 (2021)

29. Nakamoto, S.: Bitcoin: a peer-to-peer electronic cash system. Decentralized Bus. Rev., 21260 (2008)
30. Noble, S.U.: Algorithms of oppression. Algorithms of oppression. New York University Press (2018)
31. Pasquale, F.: The Black Box Society: The Secret Algorithms that Control Money and Information. Harvard University Press (2015)
32. Rabinow, P., et al.: Designs for an Anthropology of the Contemporary. Designs for an Anthropology of the Contemporary. Duke University Press (2008)
33. Ruckenstein, M., Granroth, J.: Algorithms, advertising and the intimacy of surveillance. J. Cultural Econ. **13**(1), 12–24 (2020)
34. Sandvig, C., et al.: Auditing algorithms: research methods for detecting discrimination on internet platforms. Data Discrimin.: Convert. Critical Concerns Product. Inquiry 22.2014, 4349–4357 (2014)
35. Schellewald, A.: Theorizing "stories about algorithms" as a mechanism in the formation and maintenance of algorithmic imaginaries. Soc. Media+ Soc. **8**(1), 20563051221077025 (2022)
36. Seaver, N.: Algorithms as culture: Some tactics for the ethnography of algorithmic systems. Big Data Soc. **4**(2), 2053951717738104 (2017)
37. Seaver, N.: What should an anthropology of algorithms do? Cult. Anthropol. **33**(3), 375–385 (2018)
38. Smith, R.C., Kjærsgaard, M.G.: Design anthropology in participatory design. ID&A Interaction Design Architect. **26**, 73–80 (2015)
39. Smith, R.C., et al.: Design Anthropological Futures (2016)
40. Thomson, A.: Making the most of memories: the empirical and subjective value of oral history. Trans. R. Hist. Soc. **9**, 291–301 (1999)
41. Tunstall, E.D.: Decolonizing design innovation: design anthropology, critical anthropology, and indigenous knowledge. In: Design Anthropology, Routledge, pp. 232–250 (2020)
42. Varga-Atkins, T., O'Brien, M.: From drawings to diagrams: maintaining researcher control during graphic elicitation in qualitative interviews. Int. J. Res. Method Educ. **32**(1), 53–67 (2009)

Workshop of the Automatiers: A Digital Database of Historical Automata and Contemporary Automaton-Making in an Immersive Environment

Yihao Li[1,2](✉) and Wu-Wei Chen[1]

[1] New York University Shanghai, 567 West Yangsi Road, Shanghai, China
{yl5429,wc54}@nyu.edu
[2] Washington University in St. Louis, 1 Brookings Drive, St. Louis, MO 63130, USA
l.rayna@wustl.edu

Abstract. In art history, an "automaton" (plural: "automata") generally refers to a non-electric robot made to mimic a living creature. Popular in Europe since the eighteenth century, historical automata have a multi-faceted legacy that makes them important subjects for scholarly research in the arts and humanities. The timeless charm of the "self-moving machine" has also inspired contemporary scholars and artists to utilize digital technology to better preserve and promote both extant historical artifacts and the intangible practice of automaton-making. There is not yet, however, a transdisciplinary online resource on this subject. Considering the high potential of this research topic and the gaps in existing practice, we propose a digital database entitled *Workshop of the Automatiers*. Inspired by the key considerations of scenic design in immersive theater practice, *Workshop of the Automatiers* experiments with alternative ways of organizing scholarly knowledge and community contribution from a variety of automaton experts and enthusiasts in the format of an immersive digital environment.

Keywords: Automaton · Digital Art History · Interactive Digital Museums · Object Studies · Culture-Based Media Art · Extended Reality (XR)

[A]mong others was a little *Automaton* (here "Boy of wood" has been crossed out) who drew perfectly well *the Prince of Wales leaning on his horse* and a *Dog* at the same time moving his head and eyes / in another was a little *automaton* that danced and made divers odd attitudes upon the tight rope / in another was a large pile of fruit with a dog near it, and if you took away a loose piece of the fruit the dog began to Bark…

— George Thomas Staunton (1781 – 1859 CE) [1],
page to Lord George Macartney, first British Ambassador to China,
in an unpublished "Journal of a Voyage to China",
August 30, 1793, to February 1, 1794

H. Mori et al. (Eds.): HCII 2023, LNCS 14056, pp. 290–304, 2023.
https://doi.org/10.1007/978-3-031-48044-7_21

1 Introduction

1.1 The Timeless Charm of the Self-moving Machine

On December 30, 1793, the 12-year-old George Thomas Staunton described in his diary a strange yet marvellous sight he witnessed in one of many European-run shops located in Guangzhou, China. Having accompanied the Macartney Embassy (1792 – 1794 CE) on its mission to the Qing (1644 – 1912 CE) court, young Staunton would have encountered many "automata" on his trip, including those in Chinese Emperor Qianlong's extensive personal collection of European musical clocks and other luxury mechanical devices [1].

Etymologically, the word "automaton" (plural: "automata") refers broadly to any "self-mover"—an entity capable of movement without the assistance or intervention of an outside force [2]. Beginning in the latter half of the eighteenth century, and especially in the fields of European art history, philosophy, and literature, the automaton was vested with a more specific image and definition: a mechanical construction made to mimic a living creature [2], such as the drawing "boy," rope-walking acrobat, and barking dog described by young Staunton in his diary [1]. Compared to a machine made solely for a utilitarian purpose, the automaton as an object and concept has sparked artistic imagination and philosophical debates alike since its inception, challenging its makers and viewers to consider and confront the possibility of artificial life and the ethics of metaphorical "life-giving" [2].

It would not be difficult to glimpse young Staunton's overwhelming sense of wonder and excitement in the face of these self-moving machines from his childish writing. Yet, at that time, he likely had little knowledge of the multi-faceted significance of these automata both in his era and the centuries beyond.

Automaton-making is practiced across the globe and throughout history [2, 3]. In this paper, we will focus specifically on the craft of automaton-making as formalized in eighteenth-century Europe. We begin by discussing an important historical significance of this highly specialized art practice—the European automata as a facilitator of interregional and intercultural communication and exchange between Europe and Asia during the eighteenth century. Having established the automata as a valuable subject in the study of global art history, we will illustrate why and how this subject could benefit immensely from tools in the digital humanities. We will then introduce our ongoing work in creating a digital database of historical automata and contemporary automaton-making in an immersive environment—a project entitled *Workshop of the Automatiers*. Inspired by the key considerations of scenic design in immersive theater practice, *Workshop of the Automatiers* experiments with alternative ways of organizing scholarly knowledge and community contribution from a variety of automaton experts and enthusiasts in a database format.

1.2 Historical Automata and Its Multi-faceted Legacy

Before young Staunton accompanied the first British diplomatic mission to the Chinese court in 1793 CE, European automata and automaton-clocks have already entered the

Chinese palace in large numbers, serving as material gateways that allowed its Chinese clientele to access and understand European artistic tastes and technology [1, 4].

Since Italian Jesuit missionary Matteo Ricci introduced the first European mechanical clocks to the Ming (1368–1644 CE) court, many subsequent Chinese rulers of the Ming and Qing dynasties showed considerable interest in these spring-driven devices from Europe [5]. One particularly fervent collector of European automata was Emperor Qianlong (1736–1795 CE), who not only received numerous imported automata through tribute and procurement, but also commissioned specific designs from Jesuit missionaries at his service [1, 4, 6]. Considering the commercial potential of the Chinese market, automaton-makers in Europe designed highly creative and luxurious works that catered to the Chinese elites, and sometimes directly to the Chinese emperor himself [1]. As young Staunton's diary reveals, some European makers and tradesman even set up agencies directly in Guangzhou to ensure first-hand access to the Chinese market. In sum, these automata could be key in understanding long-distance trade, intercultural contact, and gifting in the political context between eighteenth-century Europe and China.

Unfortunately, as automata are essentially delicate machines, many historical automata have been lost or fallen into disrepair. There is, however, one surviving eighteenth-century European automaton at the Palace Museum, Beijing, that stands witness to this historical legacy [6]. Named "The Writing Person" (*Xieziren*) in the museum catalog, this automaton is in the form of kneeling gentleman in European dress writing Chinese calligraphy with a brush (see Fig. 1). Previous research has attributed this automaton to Swiss workmanship, and there is also evidence to suggest a connection to the Jaquet-Droz workshop—one of the most famous manufacturers of drawing and writing automata in history [7, 8]. From this extant example, we can observe multiple aspects worthy of scholarly discussions.

Structurally, a writing automaton like this is a masterpiece of precision mechanics. As automata are non-electric robots, all their movements are controlled by a series of brass discs known as cams [9]. The edges of the cams are carved into irregular shapes, which encoded action commands [9]. When these cams are turned by a clockwork motor, steel fingers known as cam followers would run along the hills and valleys of the cams and trigger further movements in the mechanical structures attaching to the automaton's body parts, enabling the desired movement [9]. In an automaton that could write with pressured strokes and coordinate its eyes and head in a vivid performance, the levels of technical ingenuity and engineering expertise are self-evident.

Historical automata tend to be naturalistic to give the most convincing impression of life. Similarly, humanoid automata from this period are often carefully sculpted and dressed. In addition, as automata are work-intensive and mostly decorative mechanical devices, their makers often adorned their works with high-quality materials such as velvet to further accentuate the luxury status of these automata. It is thus possible to argue that a single automaton can reflect input from multiple fields of artistic and artisanal practice, including textiles, dressmaking, wig making, sculpting, painting (makeup), metal smithing, and jewelry design.

The above mentioned historical, technical, and aesthetic significances of the automaton are only a glimpse of these astonishing machines' full potential. Yet, we have moved

Fig. 1. "The Writing Person" (*Xieziren*) automaton on display at the Clocks and Watches Gallery at the Palace Museum, Beijing. When activated, this automaton writes eight Chinese characters in two vertical lines: *ba fang xiang hua / jiu tu lai wang*— "The eight quarters of the world look hither for enlightenment; from nine continents they come to crown you as the ruler." Photo by Yihao Li, August 7, 2021.

far beyond a world where the spring-driven clock represents the cutting edge of technological innovation. In the age of digital technology—of AI humanoid robots and virtual personal assistants—would the self-moving machine eventually lose its charm?

2 Review of Related Work

2.1 Digital Technology in Aid of "Analog" Automata

Thankfully, there is never a shortage of interest in things vintage and mysterious; there is only detachment and unawareness deriving from gradual oblivion. Digital technology, without doubt, can be a powerful solution to the dilemma of lack of public exposure. In recent years, practitioners in mass entertainment and public education alike have used digital technology to conserve or promote the automaton, and many have achieved notable results. Contemporary artists and restorers focusing on the spring-driven automaton have also actively employed videos and social media as primary means to promote their work.

Film and Entertainment. In 2011, American director Martin Scorsese's cinematic adaptation of Brian Selznick's 2007 book *The Invention of Hugo Cabret* featured a five-minute sequence of a drawing automaton in motion [10]. The automaton used in filming was a fully functional model that required no special effects, allowing the audience to observe the real movements and innerworkings of an automaton on the big screen [11].

Museum and Exhibition. In museums, curators have also employed high-quality audio and video recording to capture their precious collections in motion. As it is not feasible or sustainable to continuously wind up an antique automaton on display, and yet automata are designed to be appreciated for their movement, digital recordings can help resolve this dilemma of conservation versus consumption. For example, the Metropolitan Museum of Art's 2019–20 exhibition *Making Marvels: Science and Splendor at the Courts of Europe* included 12 meticulously produced and professionally narrated videos of mechanical artworks, all freely available on the Internet [12]. In Switzerland, the Neuchâtel Museum of Art and History have prepared a twenty-minute audio-visual presentation in various languages for their most renowned collection—the original Draughtsman, Writer, and Musician automata made by the Jaquet-Droz [13].

Practicing Contemporary Artists. Nowadays, both professional and amateur automaton-makers use videos and the Internet to document and promote their work, as well as to connect with other enthusiasts and potential clients. In Switzerland, automaton-maker and sculptor François Junod (to whom the word "*automatier*" is most frequently associated) runs a portfolio website that features professional documentations of his entire oeuvre [14]. In Britain, Cabaret Mechanical Theatre is a one-stop site for automata enthusiasts, featuring on-demand video tutorials, free downloadable activity kits, and both vintage and original automata for sale [15]. Inspired by the Cabaret Mechanical Theatre, American arts professor Michael Croft compiled and published automata-related bibliography and audio-visual resources on his website "Contemporary Automata" [16]. In China, a younger generation of automaton-makers have moved their portfolios and promotional content onto mobile-based social media platforms, such as WeChat, Douyin (TikTok), and Bilibili. On the latter, a video platform oriented towards the anime, comics, and games community, Chinese *automatier* Zhanlong Li's reimagining of Studio Ghibli's moving castle has received more than 1.38 million views to date [17]. Another *automatier* Jiawei Du, a self-described "amateur," has transformed scenes and characters from video games into automata and launched his original design into mass production, maintaining nearly 120k subscribers to date [18].

2.2 Locating the Missing Gears

From the above examples, we have seen how institutions and individuals have contributed to the conservation and promotion of the legacy of the "analog" automaton using digital technology, chief among them audio-visual documentation and web-based storage and transmission platforms. We have also witnessed a breadth in their work. From the scholarly to the entertaining, from the professional to the grassroot, each contributor in the community has devised a viable way to document and share their interactions with the fascinating automaton and/or the craft of automaton-making.

Yet, these contributions—fragmentary in nature—are not yet capable of addressing several pressing concerns facing automaton scholars and enthusiasts. Based on our previous experience researching eighteenth-century automata, we have identified the following gaps in the digital infrastructure surrounding work on this subject. We will follow each point with a brief discussion on how different stakeholders might work towards mitigating these issues.

Bibliographic Resource and Digital Accessibility. Most of the automaton-related resources in print that are commonly available on the market are "how-to-make-your-own" instruction manuals, such as those developed by Cabaret Mechanical Theatre [15, 19]. For art historians and researchers, however, references can be much harder to acquire. Many foundational texts and comprehensive studies have not had reprints or new editions since their publication in the 1920s–1950s. For example, Alfred Chapuis and Edmond Droz's seminal work in the field, *Automata: A Historical and Technological Study*, was published nearly 70 years ago [3]. The book's first iteration in French was published nearly a century ago [20]. As a result, scholars can find it difficult to access this title as all copies except one listed on the catalog service WorldCat are housed in Euro-American institutions [21].

Libraries, archives, and publishers may consider digitizing these older references and making them available through a database service. On the one hand, maintaining an annotated online research guide of important works in this field with detailed instructions on how to access each title can also help significantly streamline the literature review process. On the other hand, digitization can enable better instant machine translation. As researchers of automata in interregional trade frequently need to process sources in French, English, (Classical) Chinese, and Japanese, they can benefit immensely from machine translations in early stages of their work.

Objects in Motion and Faithful Documentation. While The Metropolitan Museum of Art has set an example in integrating audio-video documentation in every stage of their exhibition on automata [12], most museums continue to treat their automata collection as static works of art, overlooking their original beauty in movement. For the "The Writing Person" (*Xieziren*) in the Palace Museum, Beijing, the only available video documentation of the automaton in motion was from a 1979 film [22]. Thus, it would be important for curators and conservators to collect high-resolution audio-video footage of these works in motion to faithfully convey the objects' original functions. Additional tools such as photogrammetry and digital sculpting can greatly expand possibilities in exhibition design and museum education, allowing visitors rotate a 3D model, touch a 3D-printed replica, or even digitally dismantle an automaton's mechanism. This is an important direction of our current investigation, see Sect. 3.

Diversified Expertise and Connecting-Making. Both in the literary imagination and in real life, the *automatier* is often conceptualized as a clockmaker, technician, or metalsmith, which are occupations traditionally held by men. In fact, as noted above, the realization of an automaton takes more than one field of expertise, which underscores the often-collaborative nature of automaton-making. Thus, public educators are tasked with presenting the automaton as a composite and complex, but not inaccessible art form. In the same vein, researchers need to engage in interdisciplinary work and synthesize art historical knowledge across different media. However, there is not yet a curated resource that can, for example, discuss an eighteenth-century writing automaton vis-à-vis the decorative scheme of the figure's rococo writing desk, or his dressing gown inspired by the contemporary vogue of chinoiserie.

3 *Workshop of the Automatiers*: Between Archive and *Atelier*

The challenges enumerated above inspired us to propose *Workshop of the Automatiers*, an online resource database with the objective of rendering the automaton more legible and accessible in the full support of its historical, social, and material contexts.

In this section, we will begin by illustrating how scenic design practice in contemporary immersive theater productions has inspired us to reconceptualize the format and function of the database and the research site. We will follow our design choices with discussions of their potential implications for both the site producers and audiences. Next, we will present our work in-progress. Finally, we will summarize major foreseeable challenges and directions for further research.

3.1 Project Overview

A definition of Digital Humanities provided by Anne Burdick posits that Digital Humanities "[treats] design as an integral component of research" and places "an intensified focus on the building of transferrable tools, environments, and platforms for collaborative scholarly work and … an emphasis upon curation as a defining feature of scholarly practice." [23]. We have distilled a key theme from Burdick's theoretical argument to serve as the guiding principle of our work: meaningfully designed presentation of scholarly information is just as important as collecting and correlating such knowledge.

Workshop of the Automatiers is a digitally rendered environment that serves the function of both an archive and an *atelier* (workshop). We use these two words to index the project's record-keeping function and experimental aspect, respectively.

Archive. The online platform provides storage and presentation of curated bibliographies, images, videos, sounds, such as photo essays on historical automata, references by subject and language, and oral history and interviews with contemporary makers.

Atelier. The online platform is a place to publish and showcase new work, both textual and non-textual, such as educational activities, new writings, finished products and concepts, and announcements of real-life events.

3.2 Project Concept and Design

Site Structure and Browse Functionality. Traditional databases and research websites for digital art history are often meant to be read in a linear and hierarchical sequence. Upon landing on the home page, which introduces the project objectives and scope, visitors are led to click on one of the parallelly listed tabs that connect to subtopics or projects on the second level.

While this classic site structure is advantageous in clarity and user familiarity, it is not well-suited to the subject of automata. As illustrated above, we aim to accentuate the multi-media and transdisciplinary nature of automaton-making, which means that we need to organize and connect a true kaleidoscope of knowledge in various digital formats. It would be confusing to a general audience if we simply arrange topics from "biographies of notable makers" to "a map of eighteenth-century workshops in the Swiss Jura" in a horizontal manner as tabs on the landing page, causing them to mistake fragmentedness for triviality (See Fig. 2, top).

Fig. 2. Mockups for a traditional database and research site on the automaton. The top example has a shallow structure that fails to make the connections between topics self-evident. The bottom example is organized along disciplinary divides, making the interface appear too rigid and the browsing experience too tedious.

Alternatively, if we keep only essential categories on the landing page along perceived disciplinary divides, we would be unwillingly perpetrating the existing segregation of different expertise and forms of knowledge. Given the convenience of categories and hierarchies, visitors may find themselves in information cocoons, evading unexpected encounters of unfamiliar topics (See Fig. 2, bottom). In essence, we are tasked with finding an effective system of cueing a wide array of subtly related topics and staging an experience of constant discovery and active sense-making for our audience.

A Lesson from Immersive Theater. In pondering this metaphor, we naturally arrived at an important inspiration from immersive theater practice. The term "immersive theater" is used to describe a style of "contemporary performance practice involving a visceral and participatory audience experience with an all-encompassing, sensual style of production aesthetic" [24]. Instead of watching a series of events unfold in front of them under a proscenium arch, the audience is permitted to inhabit a theatrical environment alongside the actors and choose their own vantage point of spectatorship [25]. To provoke further curiosity in the audience and facilitate this process of active sense-making, the built theatrical environment often doubles as a hands-on art installation that is not only capable of illustrating the fictional setting, but also of conveying implicit messages on character and story through symbolisms hidden in set decoration.

Methodology and Realization. Similarly, *Workshop of the Automatiers* re-envisions the database landing page as the furnished interior of an automaton-making workshop. We left the identity of the workshop owners deliberately ambiguous to suggest to the audience the very possibility that the workshop is their own.

In this digital environment, the indexing role of traditional subpage dividers is performed by meaningfully placed objects (See Fig. 3). Available portals for interaction are highlighted with a marker, clicking on which will open an on-screen window (See Fig. 4). New content added in future updates will be highlighted with a different marker to draw the attention of repeat visitors.

The workshop environment will be digitally composited in Unreal Engine, which allows the user to be immersed in the hand-crafting space via an interactive VR walk-through. Individual automata used in case studies will be created through a hybrid method using both modelling and digital sculpting tools (Maya and ZBrush). We have experimented with creating a realistic 3D model of the Palace Museum "Writing Person" from reference photos taken during field visits (See Fig. 5). Digital sculpting affords a higher degree of precision, which is ideal for modelling the automaton's naturalistic facial expressions and wardrobe. More importantly, as the physical object has already fallen into disrepair, our attempt to digitally recreate the automaton in motion could serve as an important resource both for the museum curators and the general audience.

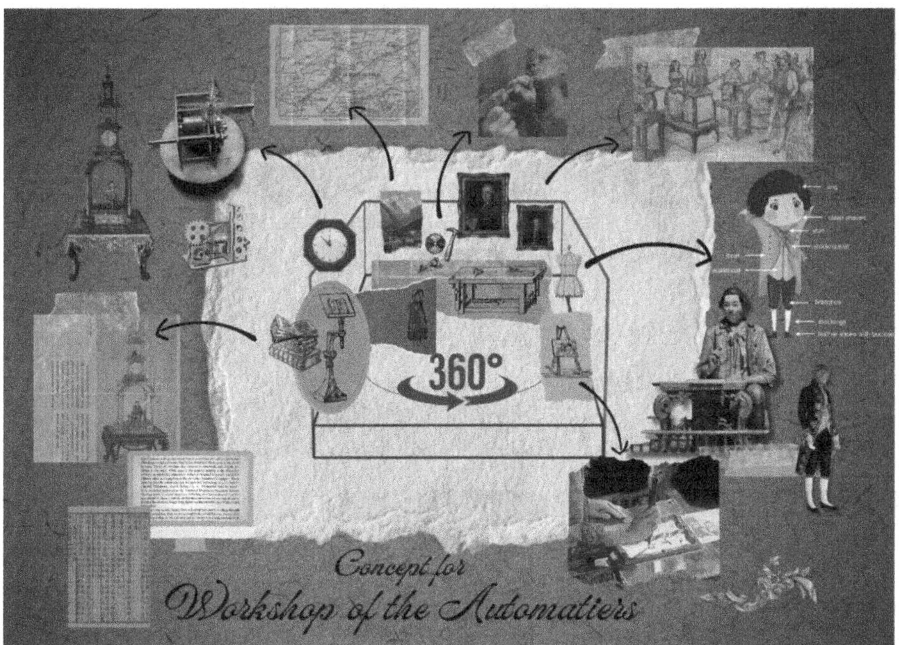

Fig. 3. A concept art showing how individual objects in the digital environment can serve as indexes to detailed discussions on an automaton's historical, social, and material contexts.

4 Discussion and Conclusion

4.1 Conceptual and Practical Implications

We propose the re-imagining of a database as an immersive digital environment with the interests of both developers and audiences in mind.

For developers, this design makes it possible to insert additional content directly to the indexing page without significantly altering its appearance or site structure. The site has the potential to grow organically, and it would be easy for new pieces of automaton-related information or contribution to find its logical place.

For the audience, the metaphor of a workshop allows them to directly visualize how different sources of knowledge come together in practice. The general atmosphere also highlights the spirit of collaboration and exploration. When not using the site search tool, the audience can self-curate a non-linear and individualized path of reading and discovery, reducing the feeling of unease commonly associated with overly didactic research sites.

4.2 Foreseeable Challenges and Limitations

As a project based in research and enabled by digital technology, *Workshop of the Automatiers* is faced with several technical and administrative challenges.

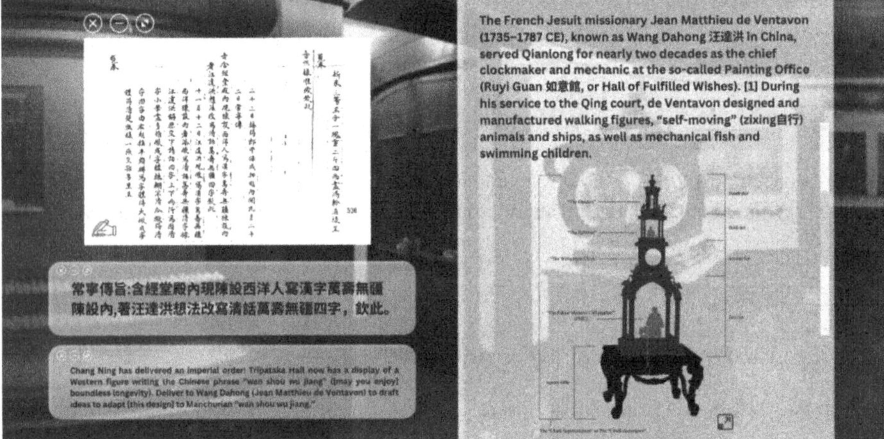

Fig. 4. Preliminary rendering of the exhibition room of the Workshop (top) and a sample activity exploring the biography and work of Jesuit missionary Jean Matthieu de Ventavon (bottom). This activity allows the viewer to read a Qing-dynasty primary source (bottom image, top left) with the aid of a transcription (bottom image, middle left) and a translation (bottom image, bottom left).

Technical Challenges. Currently, the most significant challenge faced by the digital sculpting team is the lack of visual references and technical advising. A wealth of high-quality photos is needed to create a realistic replication of any given automaton, yet it is often difficult to photograph a historical artifact up-close due to conservation concerns. It is notably more difficult to access an automaton's inner mechanism or document its precise movement. Although it is sometimes possible to acquire and reference published footage of a historical automaton in motion, the team would require professional advising to ensure that the digital replication is technically sound and structurally correct.

Administrative Challenges. On the fronts of human resources, we rely on a wide range of expertise and would require the concerted effort from the stakeholders enumerated

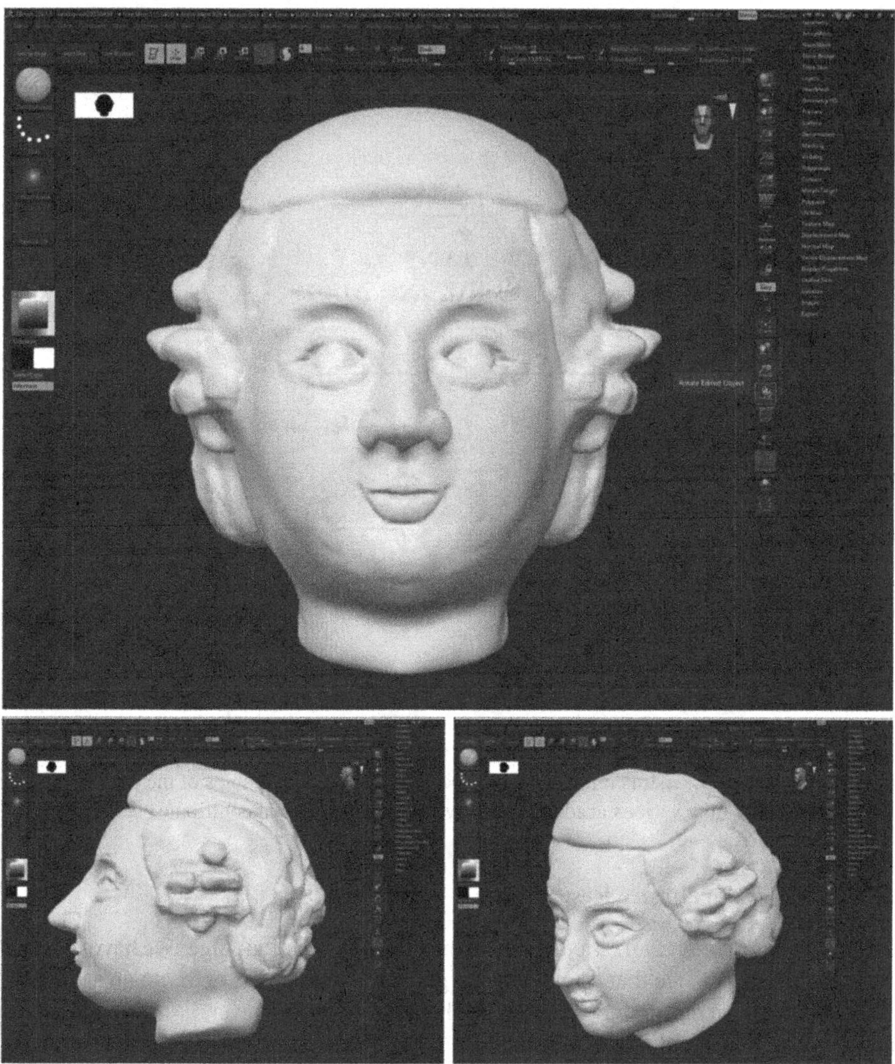

Fig. 5. Digitally sculpting the head of the "Writing Person" automaton from the Palace Museum, Beijing. Courtesy of Xinyu Liu.

above (See Fig. 6). For the digitization of historical automata and archival sources, we would need the permission and support of partner institutions to be able to soundly access, document, and disseminate the data collected. For contemporary automata, some makers may not wish to disclose their designs online out of intellectual property concerns. In these situations, it would be important to make full use of what is already publicly available and consider hyperlinking instead of embedding. Furthermore, as the project involves actors from multiple sectors and countries, all the issues inherent in interdisciplinary and cross-cultural work are immediately present.

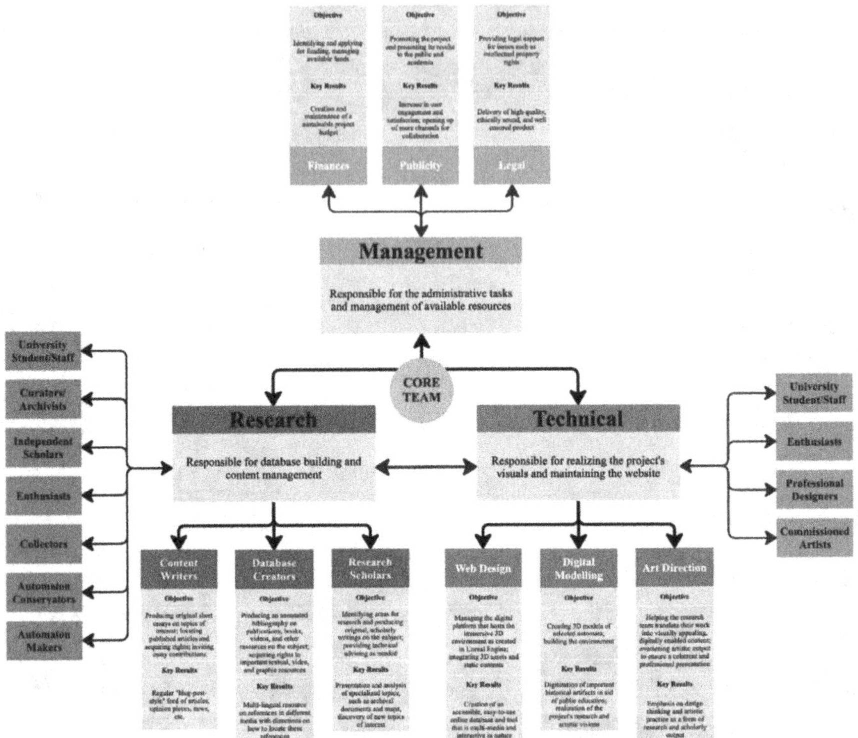

Fig. 6. Summary of the main components, key objectives, and deliverables of the current project with indications of how various academic and civil society actors can contribute.

4.3 Directions for Future Research

Workshop of the Automatiers is currently at the pilot and ideation stage. We have focused on the branch of practice that originated in eighteenth-century Europe with an art historical focus based on our previous research. The automaton, however, presents a timeless and universal fascination, and we aspire to expand the scope of our project to eventually include automata from other periods and locations. It would also be beneficial to consider automata beyond the scope of material culture and physical objects—in philosophy, literature, and imagination—as there has also been a strong foundation of research in these fields [2].

4.4 Conclusion

More than two centuries after the heyday of the spring-driven automaton in Europe, we can still resonate with young Staunton's sense of excitement and astonishment in the face of these ingenious mechanical artworks. In addition to providing entertainment and sensory experiences, these automata are also important subjects in scholarly research, having historically served as status symbols and diplomatic gifts alike. Similarly, the automaton as a unique medium continues to fascinate contemporary artists, who helped rejuvenate and safeguard this century-old art form.

With the rise of digital technology, scholars, artists, and the interested public did not hesitate to use digital tools to further their engagement with automata and automaton-making. While there have been increasing efforts to produce audio-video documentations and promotional materials of historical and contemporary automata, there has not yet been any transdisciplinary online resource on this subject.

In response, we have proposed *Workshop of the Automatiers* and discussed our vision for a digital database in the format of a virtual and immersive environment. In experimenting with design as a critical component of research [23], we became increasingly certain that the study of automata relies fundamentally on transdisciplinary collaborations. We hope to continue unlocking the magic of the automaton with the keys entrusted to us by contributors with a diverse range of expertise.

References

1. Pagani, C.: Eastern Magnificence & European Ingenuity: Clocks of Late Imperial China. University of Michigan Press, Ann Arbor (2001)
2. Kang, M.: Sublime Dreams of Living Machines: The Automaton in the European Imagination. Harvard University Press, Cambridge, MA (2011)
3. Chapuis, A., Droz, E.: Automata: A Historical and Technological Study. Editions du Griffon, Neuchâtel (1958)
4. Guo, F.: Shijian de Lishi Yingxiang: Zhongguo Zhongbiao Shilun Ji (Imprints of Time on History: Miscellaneous Writings on the Historiography of Chinese Clocks and Watches). Gugong Chubanshe (The Forbidden City Publishing House), Beijing (2013)
5. Li, S.: Qingchao Huangdi yu Xiyang Zhongbiao (Qing Emperors and Western Clocks and Watches). Zijincheng (The Forbidden City) **2**, 100–104 (2004)
6. Guan, X.: Niaoyinlong, Xieziren, Moshuren: Qing Gong de Jixie Wanju (Bird Cages, Writing Figures and Magician Figures: Mechanical Toys in the Qing Palace). Zijincheng (The Forbidden City) **2**, 104–113 (2014)
7. Lei, Y., Wang, J.: Gugong de "Xieziren Zhong" Shi Shei Zhizuo de? (Who Made the "Calligrapher Automaton Clock" in the Palace Museum?). Zijincheng (The Forbidden City) **2**, 105–107 (2006)
8. Li, Y.: One Mechanical Man, Two Connected Contexts: A New Transcultural Biography of the Eighteenth-Century "Calligrapher Automaton Clock" In The Palace Museum, Beijing (un-published thesis) (2022)
9. Maillardet's Automaton. https://www.fi.edu/history-resources/automaton. Accessed 04 June 2023
10. Scorsese, M., Logan, J.: Hugo (film). Paramount Pictures, United States (2011)
11. Hugo Automaton Behind the Scenes. https://www.youtube.com/watch?v=fnzCXsjvWDs. Accessed 20 June 2023
12. Art in Motion. https://www.metmuseum.org/exhibitions/listings/2019/making-marvels-science-splendor/art-in-motion. Accessed 20 June 2023
13. Automates Jaquet-Droz. Nouvelle Salle. (The Jaquet-Droz-Droz Automata. New Room.). https://www.mahn.ch/fr/expositions/automates-jaquet-droz. Accessed 20 June 2023
14. François Junod. http://www.francoisjunod.com. Accessed 20 June 2023
15. Cabaret Mechanical Theatre: Video. https://cabaret.co.uk/product-category/video/. Accessed 20 June 2023

16. Contemporary Automata. http://www.contemporaryautomata.com/index.html. Accessed 20 June 2023
17. Handmade 50-kg Wooden Automaton Inspired by Howl's Moving Castle. https://b23.tv/oHfYMTk. Accessed 20 June 2023
18. Fei Shou Gong's Personal Channel. https://b23.tv/8RCl7GF. Accessed 20 June 2023
19. Alexander, G., Onn, A.L.: Cabaret mechanical movement: understanding movement and making automata. Cabaret Mechanical Theatre, United Kingdom (2013)
20. Chapuis, A.: Le monde des automates; étude historique et technique (The world of the automata: a historical and technical study). Gélis, Édouard, Paris (1928)
21. Find a Copy in a Library: Automata: A Historical and Technological Study. https://worldcat.org/title/1928394, Accessed 20 June 2023
22. Deng, B.: Gugong Zhongbiao (Clocks and Watches of the Palace Museum) (film). Beijing Kexue Jiaoyu Dianying Zhipianchang (Beijing Science Education Film Studio), China (1979)
23. Burdick, A., Drucker, J., Lunenfeld, P., Presner, T., Schnapp, J.: Digital_Humanities. The MIT Press, Cambridge, MA (2016)
24. Machon, J.: Watching, attending, sense-making spectatorship in immersive theatres. J. Contemp. Drama English **4**, 34–48 (2016). https://doi.org/10.1515/JCDE-2016-0004
25. Biggin, R.: Immersive theatre and audience experience: space, game and story in the work of Punchdrunk. Palgrave Macmillan, Cham, Switzerland (2017). https://doi.org/10.1007/978-3-319-62039-8

Creative Design of Interactive Platform for Ethnic Embroidery in the Web 3.0 Era - Take the Sanjiang Dong Embroidery Culture for Example

Yinyin Lu[1(✉)], Chen Wei[1], and Jing Huang[2]

[1] GXNU School of Design, Guangxi Normal University, Guilin 541000, China
1533570605@qq.com

[2] GDTC Arts Department, Guangdong Technology College, Zhaoqing 526100, China

Abstract. Web 3.0 is the third-generation internet which integrates multiple information technologies. It has intelligent interaction function and provides an innovative form of digital interaction for cultural production and communication. Dong minority is an ethnic minority in China. Dong embroidery, as a traditional handicraft of the Dong people, has been listed as an intangible cultural heritage. Based on the background of the Web 3.0 era of information technology such as blockchain and virtual-real interaction, this paper takes traditional ethnic embroidery as the research object, this paper takes traditional national embroidery as the research object, and puts forward the new forms of cultural interaction of ethnic embroidery in cultural cognition, entertainment experience, digital collection and so on through the research on the cultural transmission path and cultural cognitive characteristics of ethnic embroidery in the Web 3.0 era. Finally, the "Wenqu" creative interaction platform takes Sanjiang Dong Embroidery culture as the case to design, which construction of interactive mode is based on the embroidery pattern, embroidery stitches and colour assortment. It highlights the cultural design, sportful design and innovative design, so as to realize the new mode of "Embroider to Earn" in Sanjiang Dong embroidery in the Web 3.0 era. The research shows that the inheritance and development of ethnic embroidery should conform to the transformation of media mode in the Web 3.0 era. The technical advantages of interactive platforms should be adequately utilized to promote the spread and innovate the cognitive way of ethnic embroidery culture, so that we can inject new vitality into the traditional ethnic culture in the inheritance and development.

Keywords: Web 3.0 · Sanjiang Dong Embroidery · Interactive platform · Creative Designs

1 Introduction

Ethnic embroidery culture is a treasure of traditional Chinese culture, a crystallization of national beliefs and wisdom of life. It embodies the spiritual qualities of the people's respect for nature, their love of life and their strength. Dong embroidery is an important

H. Mori et al. (Eds.): HCII 2023, LNCS 14056, pp. 305–315, 2023.
https://doi.org/10.1007/978-3-031-48044-7_22

branch of Chinese minority embroidery. Among them, the Dong embroidery of Sanjiang in Guangxi was listed as a regional intangible cultural heritage in 2009, and its high artistic and technical value has been noticed by humanities scholars. However, as modern civilisation invades the inherited land, there are fewer and fewer inheritors of the Sanjiang Dong embroidery craft, and the current state of development of ethnic embroidery is in jeopardy.

With the continuous development of virtual-real interaction technology and blockchain technology, the era of Web 3.0 is approaching. Digital interactive platforms are widely used, and the cross-fertilisation of Intangible Cultural Heritage and interactive technologies continues, bringing new opportunities for the preservation, transmission and innovation of Intangible Cultural Heritage. In May 2021, the Ministry of Culture and Tourism proposed the "New Media Communication Plan for Intangible Cultural Heritage" in the "14th Five-Year Plan for the Protection of Intangible Cultural Heritage" to support the comprehensive and in-depth participation of various new media in the communication and development of intangible cultural heritage [1]. Therefore, it is important to give full play to the advantages of intelligent interaction technology in the Web 3.0 era, adhere to the principle of "keeping the righteousness and innovation", and study the deep integration of interaction and culture to empower the experience of ethnic embroidery culture, innovate the dissemination of ethnic embroidery culture, and stimulate the contemporary value of intangible cultural heritage.

2 The Current Situation and Dilemmas of Ethnic Embroidery Heritage in the Web 3.0 Era

With the deepening influence of industrial civilisation and the Internet, the natural environment on which ethnic embroidery depends has been eroded and compressed, and the transmission of the cultural heritage of ethnic embroidery skills has been seriously hampered, even at the risk of extinction. Take Sanjiang Dong embroidery as an example, its development status is worrying, mainly in the following two aspects.

2.1 Industrial Civilization Squeezes the Living Space of Dong Embroidery and the Lack of Inheritance of Embroidery Skills

Dong embroidery is an important part of the Dong culture and is closely related to the life of the Dong people. With the development of modern civilization and the acceleration of the integration of modern life with Dong culture, resulting in a sharp decline in the heirs of traditional Dong culture in Sanjiang, there is less and less room for the development of traditional Dong embroideries. At the same time, industrial mass production has taken away the competitive edge of traditional hand embroidery, making it difficult for those skilled in the art of ethnic embroidery to make a living [2]. The new generation of Dong children have been influenced by the idea of going out to earn a living, and fewer and fewer young people are able to learn the craft of Dong embroidery patiently, which seriously affects the inheritance and development of Dong embroidery in Sanjiang.

2.2 The Form of Communication Limits the Scope of Dong Embroidery and Makes it Difficult to Effectively Promote the Embroidery Culture

Currently, the dissemination of Sanjiang Dong embroidery culture still relies on interpersonal and group communication [3], In today's Internet era, where information is transmitted rapidly, it is difficult to obtain good communication effects with the traditional publicity model. In recent years, people are gradually trying to use various media and internet platforms to adopt new communication methods to spread the Dong embroidery culture, and at the same time increase their efforts to promote the Dong embroidery culture [4]. However, the lack of clarity in the target audience and the difficulty in choosing the channel of communication makes it difficult to effectively promote the Dong embroidery culture. The data in the New Economy Consumption Report 2019 [5] even reveals the low number of channels and ways for communication audiences to learn about Intangible Cultural Heritage: the majority of those who choose online methods choose graphic presentations and videos, fewer listen to audio and learn about it through games, and offline methods are mainly seeing exhibitions and travelling to local areas.

In terms of heritage and dissemination, the existing methods of dissemination of Dong embroidery do not meet the needs of the public. In the era of Web 3.0, both the heritage of Dong embroidery and the dissemination of Dong embroidery culture need to be combined with the development of Internet technology and the characteristics of the information received by the target audience to push the heritage of Dong embroidery to new forms of dissemination. The interactive platform is a modern and enjoyable way to experience the culture of Sanjiang Dong embroidery, and as a new medium for the dissemination of the culture, it may effectively achieve the digital heritage and innovative dissemination of Sanjiang Dong embroidery.

3 Web3.0 basic Technology and its Impact on Cultural Industry

3.1 The Technical Support of Web3.0

At present, Web 3.0 represents a wealth of technology and content, including: three-dimensional holographic Internet, safe and reliable value Internet, and intelligent interactive Internet [6], so it is necessary to integrate various new technologies to create.

Network Technique. 5G technology with high performance, low latency and high capacity is an important infrastructure for Web 3.0. In the 4G network era, virtual reality technology (AR technology) and augmented reality technology (AR technology) are mostly personal and local experiences. Realizing remote virtual interaction is still a technical challenge.Vega proposed to combine the ultra-reliable low-latency communication (URLLC) technology in 5G to design an AR / VR end-to-end architecture to solve the vertigo caused by network delay [7]. At present, with the rapid maturity of 5G technology, more and more researchers begin to make prospects for 6G technology. Qiao describes the future 6G network: 6G is envisaged as a distributed, decentralized and intelligent innovation network [8], in which the new feature of decentralization is particularly important for the development of Web 3.0.

Virtual-Real Interaction Technology. The underlying logic of virtual-real interaction technology is three-dimensional expression, including VR, AR, naked eye 3D, brain-computer interface and other technologies. Through these technologies, users are no longer the coordinate points in the two-dimensional quadrant in the Web3.0 era, but the presenters and experiencers in the three-dimensional world, which provide strong support for the realization of the interactive experience of ethnic embroidery.

VR Technology. VR is the abbreviation of VirturalReality, which means virtual reality. It is a computer system that can create and experience a virtual world. It mainly includes four aspects: simulated environment, perception, natural skills and sensing equipment(see Fig. 1).

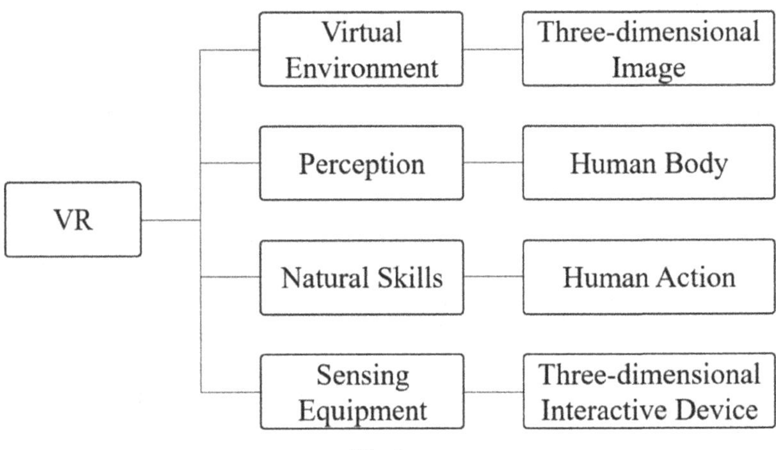

Fig. 1. .

VR technology has the characteristics of immersion and interactivity. The first is the sense of immersion. Users using VR products can use VR products to see realistic three-dimensional images generated by computers [9], as if immersed in a virtual scene. When the user moves, the scene will change accordingly, so it will give people an immersive feeling. Secondly, interactivity. When users use products based on VR technology, it is essentially human-computer interaction in a virtual system. The way of interaction is not only to watch and feel, but also to participate in virtual situations and realize virtual operations. If VR technology can be applied to ethnic embroidery, the immersion and interactivity it brings will greatly promote the experience of ethnic embroidery culture.

AR Technology. AugmentedReality, or AR for short. It is a new technology that seamlessly integrates real-world information and virtual world information. Augmented reality technology takes the information that is difficult to experience in the real world, such as vision, hearing, touch, taste, etc., through computer simulation to generate virtual information, and then integrates it into the real world [10]. It is perceived by human senses, so as to achieve a sensory experience beyond reality.

Similarly, AR interaction is to realize the interaction between users and virtual superimposed information in the real environment, which mainly includes two kinds: Firstly, hardware-based interaction, such as digital gloves, sensor device interaction, intelligent terminal device interaction [11], etc. Secondly, based on computer vision processing methods, such as generating buttons, menus, etc. on markers and interacting with gesture recognition. The role of AR interaction in improving efficiency in the cognitive learning of popular science knowledge [12] has been verified. It is of great significance to further explore AR interaction to promote users ' cognition of ethnic embroidery culture in museums.

Blockchain Technology. Blockchain technology is the underlying driving force for the credibility of Web 3.0. Blockchain technology is a fusion technology, including distributed ledger, consensus algorithm, cryptography technology, smart contracts, etc. (see Fig. 2). These technologies are the key to breaking through the bottleneck of Web 2.0.

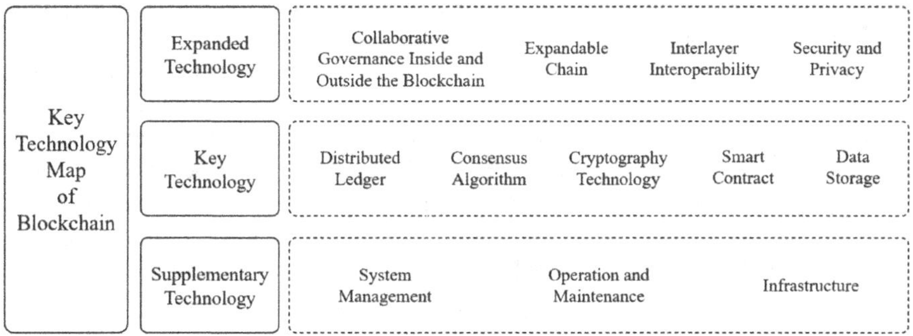

Fig. 2. .

In the Web3.0 era, users are not only experiencers, but also content creators. NFT is a technology to determine the property rights of digital assets. Because of the existence of blockchain, content is the creator 's asset (forming NFT), stimulating users ' enthusiasm for creation and participation. As mentioned above, the importance of decentralization for the development of Web3.0. And as a trusted infrastructure, the main role of blockchain is to glue the various technical systems in Web3.0 and provide de-intermediation trust guarantee for value exchange [13]. Blockchain technology provides a decentralized clearing and settlement platform, which records the "digital copyright (NFT)" of users' virtual items in Web 3.0 to the blockchain, ensuring the rights and interests of users' assets and circulation.

In recent years, the blockchain NFT in the Internet has entered the art field with its rapid posture. NFT has been widely used in digital products in the fields of pictures, music, film and television, games [14] and so on. Correspondingly, different types of NFT art trading platforms have also been established around the world, and digital collections of NFT art have formed huge liquidity in the meta-universe. This provides a practical basis and experience for the integration of intangible cultural heritage and blockchain technology.

3.2 The Impact of Web3.0 Interactive Technology on Cultural Industry

Empower Cultural Experience and Innovate Cultural Cognitive Form. To enhance cultural experience in the form of "technology + culture". For example, the dance "Tang Palace Night Banquet", which is popular on the Internet, uses new technologies such as 5G and AR to "awaken" historical relics and turn "history in the window" into "participatory, experiential and interactive history". And like the cultural tourism project launched in Quanzhou, Fujian Province in January 2022, it is planned to show the 22 local world heritage classics to the public through AR cultural tourism. In the past, ethnic embroidery culture focused on the exhibition of handicrafts in museums, presenting cultural memories to the audience through text introduction. Nowadays, the development of Internet information technology has expanded the display form of online graphics and video for national embroidery culture. However, at present, these two forms can only meet people's "plane" cognition of national embroidery culture, and can not realize people's interactive experience of national embroidery skills and three-dimensional perception of national embroidery culture.

The development of national embroidery culture should conform to the requirements of the times, and take the immersive interactive experience of "technology + culture" as a new attempt to the cognitive experience of embroidery culture. Taking the virtual and real interaction technology as an example, in terms of immersive experience, VR technology can highly restore the cultural environment, shape the virtual form of culture, and make cultural experiencers have a sense of substitution and realism. In terms of cognitive learning, Zhang Shupeng and others believe that the AR virtual-real interactive cognitive learning method is more efficient. It can meet users ' more attention to the interaction between learning content and users, and can further strengthen the understanding and memory of detailed content [12]. With the help of virtual and real interaction technology, the offline museum vividly interprets the process of national embroidery skills by using technology to make up for the shortcomings of static display, so that users can feel the beauty of embroidery and strengthen the cultural cognition of participants. As off online, interactive technology makes the user 's cultural cognition from the Internet one-way text, pictures, video output to the user 's initiative to explore the interaction, through cultural, entertainment, innovative interactive experience process, step by step to deepen the user 's cultural cognition.

Acculturation of Cultural Values, Broaden the Path of Cultural Transmission. In the Web3.0 era, in addition to using VR / AR technology to enhance the experience of tourists when visiting museums, Web3.0 provides protection for the rights and interests of art works and creative users through payment, intellectual property management, contract and governance, digital storage [15], etc., which will greatly promote the protection of cultural heritage and the development of cultural industries. As a representative of dematerialization in the Web3.0 era, NFT constitutes a new art form and shoulders the responsibility of creating new cultural values [16]. Since 2021, there has been a wave of digital collections. Compared with the museum 's collection of cultural relics or paintings, digital collections allow buyers to buy, watch and collect online at a low price, without worrying about the storage and storage of collections, counterfeit imitation and other problems that plague physical collectors. This provides a new idea and reference for the transformation of national embroidery culture into digital collections.

The cultural value of the national embroidery collection in the museum is mainly to convey the wisdom, beauty and diversity of the national culture; because ethnic embroidery skills are only mastered by a few people, the cultural value of the skills is mainly reflected in the collection of embroidery handicrafts. Therefore, on the one hand, through the intelligent interactive technology of Web3.0 (including Semantic Web, Internet of Things, Blockchain), the formal transformation of national embroidery from offline physical collection to online digital collection is realized, and the digital collection shortens the distance between the public and museums and cultural and artistic appreciation. It is positioned as self-entertainment, increasing cultural and artistic knowledge, cultivating social aesthetic taste and cultural self-confidence, and enriching the cultural value of national embroidery at the social level. On the other hand, in the wave of decentralized finance (Decentralized finance, DeFi), Web 3.0 presents DeFi products in the form of games, turning NFT into game props to form financial gamification (GameFi), that is, GameFi = DeFi + NFT + game, with the mode of "Game to Earn" as the representative feature. For example, Axie Infinity, the head product of blockchain games, also provides an innovative idea of "Embroider to Earn" for the cultural interaction of ethnic embroidery, broadening the path of cultural communication and enhancing the cultural value of culture at the economic level.

4 The Construction of Interactive Platform of Ethnic Embroidery Culture in the Web3.0 Era

Based on the analysis, the interactive platform of national embroidery culture in Web3.0 era has two major sections: one is the interactive section of embroidery cultural experience based on virtual and real interactive technology, and the other is the interactive section of storage, collection and transaction of embroidery digital works based on intelligent interactive technology.Facing the development dilemma of Sanjiang Dong embroidery, this paper takes Sanjiang Dong embroidery as an example to explore the construction of national embroidery culture interaction platform based on Web3.0 technology.

4.1 AR Interactive Experience Model of Sanjiang Dong Embroidery Culture Based on Experiential Learning Theory

Before carrying out the AR interactive platform design of Sanjiang Dong embroidery culture, an intangible cultural heritage, it is necessary to pay attention to the in-depth experience and meaningful interaction behavior, that is, to construct an interactive experience model of Sanjiang Dong embroidery culture based on experiential learning theory, and to realize the experience-centered AR interactive platform design to promote user learning and cognition of Sanjiang Dong embroidery culture(see Fig. 3.). Based on experiential learning theory, the model integrates users, objects (Sanjiang Dong embroidery) and equipment (AR interactive platform), highlights cultural interactive experience, includes four stages of learning Sanjiang Dong embroidery culture, and forms an experiential closed loop.

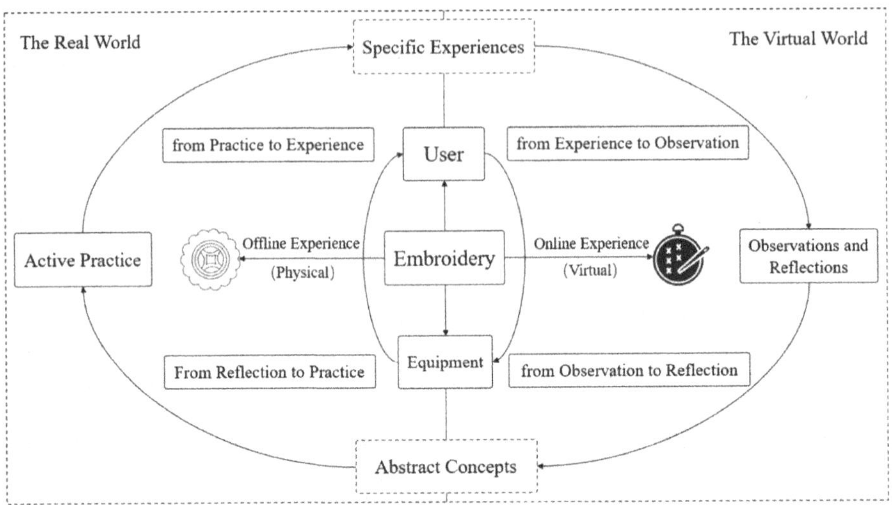

Fig. 3. .

Experience Stage. Emphasize the user's existing cognition and social experience to experience Sanjiang Dong embroidery. The user's perception of embroidery includes the user's understanding and perception of the basic patterns of learning content (short-term memory), and the intervention of AR enables the digitisation of embroidery content, including the graphical representation of embroidery content (decomposition and combination) and the interface design of embroidery (dynamic display, gestural interaction).

Observation Stage. By observing and understanding the patterns, colors, stitches and other contents of Sanjiang Dong embroidery, users can deepen their understanding of embroidery by combining existing knowledge. The involvement of AR mainly enables users to further acquire knowledge through online virtual dynamic display interaction.

Reflection Stage. Users mainly gain cognition through the interactive experience with Sanjiang Dong embroidery. In this process, users gain more knowledge through thinking and practice, and further strengthen memory (long-term memory). The intervention of AR can guide users to complete natural and efficient learning, so that users can construct behavioral memory independently.

Practice Stage. Users gain cognition through the creative practice process of existing experience and re-creation. The intervention of AR can be based on the user 's previous learning data, open innovative online and offline mixed, comprehensive interactive experience, allowing users to freely operate colors and stitches, etc., to achieve the user 's deep understanding of Sanjiang Dong embroidery.

4.2 Sanjiang Dong Embroidery AR Interactive Gesture Design

According to the natural characteristics of gestures, we define seven command gestures, which only involve one-handed movements, including palm movements and hand shape changes. The defined command gesture is divided into static and dynamic gestures, in which the palm position and hand shape of the static gesture do not change, the palm position of the dynamic gesture changes. The specific definition is shown in Table 1.

Table 1 .

Gesture Number	Hand Gestures	Gesture Meaning	Gesture Graphics	Gesture Categories
G1	Open palm of right hand	Start		Static
G2	Right hand palm to the left	Select to the left		Dynamic
G3	Right hand palm to the right	Select to the right		Dynamic
G4	Drawing a rectangle with the index finger of the right hand	Launch pattern drawing		Dynamic
G5	Patterned tracing on the right index finger	Cut out patterned paper		Dynamic
G6	Right thumb and index finger pressed against the circle	Embroidery thread on wrapped patterned paper		Dynamic
G7	Right hand in a fist with index and middle fingers spread out	Determine your choice / End		Static

(G1) Five fingers stretching motionless means a state open; (G2) Five fingers stretch to the left, indicating the choice of pattern and color to the left; (G3) The five fingers stretch to the right, indicating the right to choose the pattern and color; (G4) the index finger stretches the remaining four fingers to hold the drawing rectangle, indicating the drawing of the starting pattern; (G5) the index finger stretches the remaining four fingers to hold, and the edge is traced according to the pattern shape, indicating that the pattern paper is cut off with scissors; (G6) The thumb index finger is tightly attached, and the remaining three fingers stretch and circle repeatedly, indicating that the hand-held needle and thread are embroidered around the pattern paper (paper-cut embroidery); (G7) The middle finger of the index finger extends and holds the other three fingers at the same time, indicating the end of the current state (Table 1).

4.3 Sanjiang Dong Embroidery Digital art NFT Creation and Transaction

In order to let more people understand and collect Sanjiang Dong embroidery cultural works, it is an important way to reflect its influence and value to enter the market display

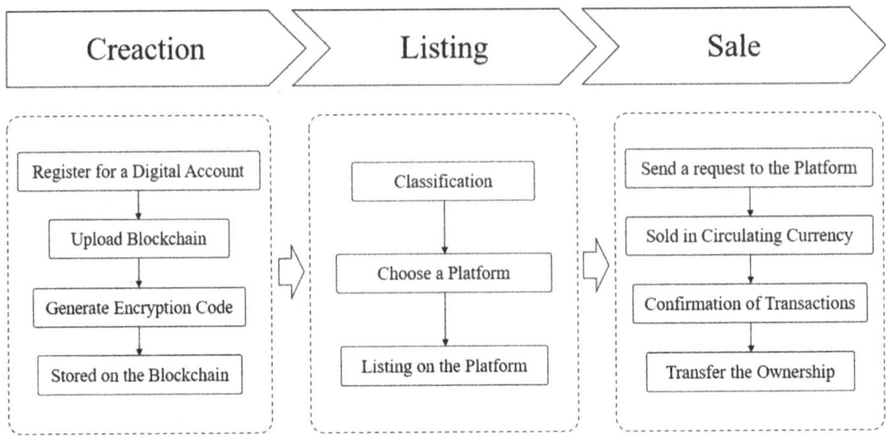

Fig. 4. .

and circulation of Sanjiang Dong embroidery cultural digital works. At the same time, the irreplaceable currency (NFT) in the Web3.0 protocol is a way to provide proof of ownership and authenticity of digital assets. Through the low threshold of NFT market, the popular digital art trading platform is more conducive to cultivating the public 's awareness of traditional culture in the new form. There are three stages in the NFT transaction of Sanjiang Dong embroidery digital art, NFT creation stage, NFT listing stage and NFT sale stage (see Fig. 4).

Creating NFT Stage. Sanjiang Dong Embroidery digital art creators need to register a digital account and upload digital artworks to a designated blockchain through a specific website or program (this process is usually called casting). When casting, the website program will generate a unique encryption code for Sanjiang Dong Embroidery digital artworks through the algorithm, and store it in the blockchain through the rules of distributed accounting. Sanjiang Dong Embroidery digital artworks enter the blockchain and become unique and unchangeable NFT.

Listing NFT Stage. The application for hanging order stage requires NFT holders to classify the produced NFT.For example, the NFT of Sanjiang Dong embroidery digital art can be divided into three types: picture, model and video. NFT holders are free to choose the listing platform, such as Bigverse, Opensea and KnownOrigin, to complete the NFT listing.

Selling NFT Stage. When the buyer looks at an NFT and applies for purchase, the buyer and the NFT holder apply to the platform, and the platform completes the transaction between the digital accounts, and then pays the NFT holder in the circulation currency. The NFT holder needs to visit the NFT auction page and click the collection button to complete the transaction of the platform, and the buyer obtains the limited ownership of the NFT in the platform.

In the era of Web3.0, the transformation of media mode, virtual and real interaction technology and NFT digital collection transaction have become an important way to inherit and promote intangible cultural heritage. As an important medium for popular public experience and learning, AR interactive platform plays an important role in strengthening people 's cognition of ethnic embroidery. The characteristics of NFT 's storage, collection and transaction of digital products enrich the economic value of national embroidery and spread the national embroidery culture.

References

1. China government. http://www.gov.cn. Accessed 3 Feb 2021
2. Zhang, Q.: Research on the innovative development of ethnic hand embroidery crafts under the background of "internet+"--taking Guizhou Miao embroidery as an example. Marketing Community **26**, 39–40 (2020)
3. Yuan, H., Qin, L.: Exploring the dissemination path of Guangxi Liuzhou embroidery culture. Tiangong **36**(6), 12–15 (2020)
4. Lu, T.: Research on the Dissemination of Guangxi Zhuang Embroidery Crafts in the New Media Era. Shanghai Normal University, Shanghai (2021)
5. China Economic Information. http://www.cinic.org.cn. Accessed 3 Feb 2021
6. Xu, L., Li, S., Ning, H.: The concept, connotation, technology and development status of Web 3.0. J. Engineering Science **45**(05), 774–786 (2023)
7. Vega, M.T., Liaskos, C., Abadal, S., et al.: Immersive interconnected virtual and augmented reality: A 5G and IoT perspective. J. Netw Syst Manage **28**(4), 796 (2020)
8. Qiao, X.Q., Huang, Y.K., Dustdar, S.: 6G vision: An AI-driven decentralized network and service architecture. IEEE Internet Comput. **24**(4), 33 (2020)
9. Zhao, Y.: The application of VR technology in marketing from the perspective of customer experience. Business Economics Res. **17**, 53-55 (2017)
10. Zheng, C.: Design and Implementation of Mobile Augmented Reality Navigation Software Client Based on iOS. Beijing University of Posts and Telecommunications, Beijing (2017)
11. Kaneto, Y., Komuro, T.: Space Sharing AR Interaction on Multiple Mobile Devices with a Depth Camera (2009)
12. Zhang, S., Hou, W., Wang, X.: Research on the design of popular science knowledge learning method based on augmented reality virtual and real interaction. Package Engineering **38**(20), 48-55(2017)
13. Dong, Y.: Digital collections open the wave of 'encryption art' - Research on the digital collection industry. Big Data Era **6**, 65-80 (2022)
14. Lu, W., Jiang, Y.: Open the original era of contemporary art. Research on National Art **35**(02), 96-101 (2022)
15. Meng, Q., Li, J.: A Study on the Change of Music Copyright Protection Path from the Perspective of Blockchain. Technology and Law 06, pp. 17-24 (2018)
16. Li, Y., Wu, W., Jiang, M.: Awareness and associativity in design for all. Package Engineering **39**(06), 29-33 (2018)

Investigating the Factors to Improve Discrimination of the Desire for Approval in Tweets by Incorporating Dependency Analysis

Erina Murata[1], Kiichi Tago[2], and Qun Jin[3](✉)

[1] School of Human Sciences, Waseda University, Tokorozawa, Japan
erinamurata@ruri.waseda.jp

[2] Department of Information and Network Science, Chiba Institute of Technology, Narashino, Japan
tago@net.it-chiba.ac.jp

[3] Faculty of Human Sciences, Waseda University, Tokorozawa, Japan
jin@waseda.jp

Abstract. In our previous study, we used Naive Bayes to discriminate and quantify approval desire in tweets based on words. To correctly understand a sentence, it is important to consider not only words but also word relationships and grammar. In this study, we investigate the possibility of improving the accuracy of discrimination and quantification of the desire of approval in tweets by weighting word using dependency analysis results and examine and clarify the factors that may lead to improvement. The results of the experiment showed that the correlation coefficients between the classification results with weighting and the evaluators' ratings increased compared to the correlation coefficients between the classification results without weighting and the evaluators' ratings.

Keywords: Approval Desire · SNS · Naive Bayes · Text Mining · Dependency Analysis

1 Introduction

In a study by Murata et al. [1], word-based Naive Bayes was used to discriminate and quantify the desire of approval in tweets. However, the results of five cross-validation between human evaluation and machine learning classification results are only about 60%. To correctly understand a sentence, it is important to consider not only words but also word relationships and grammar. Incorporating the way humans read sentences into machine learning is expected to improve its accuracy.

This study examines the possibility of improving the accuracy of classification by Naive Bayes and further performing morphological analysis and dependency analysis and weighting the words determined by the analysis results and clarifies the factors that may lead to improvement.

H. Mori et al. (Eds.): HCII 2023, LNCS 14056, pp. 316–325, 2023.
https://doi.org/10.1007/978-3-031-48044-7_23

The paper is organized as follows. Section 2 overviews related work. Section 3 describes how to adjust the values of approval desire by incorporating dependency analysis. Section 4 shows the experiment results and discusses on the results. Finally, in Sect. 5, the conclusions of this study and future work are given.

2 Related Work

2.1 Analysis Using SNS

Various studies have been conducted on SNSs. Kim et al. [2] hypothesized that dependence on SNSs is positively related to community participation and conducted an analysis using SNSs. The results showed that closed SNSs such as KakaoTalk were more likely to promote community participation than open SNSs such as twitter. Marouf et al. [3] used user-generated social media content, such as Facebook statuses, and explored the possibility of reflecting personality in social media. The results showed that the Pearson correlation coefficient-based model for extraversion, one of the big-five-factor models, was 72.13% accurate. Swartz et al. [4] used social media data to analyze diversity and identified patterns of user behavior with similar diversity characteristics. The results showed that both social media content and user profiles need to be considered.

Yoshida et al. [5] proposed a new approach to sentiment analysis using a Naive Bayes classifier that selects features of tweets and comments and captures negative expressions. The results showed that the proposed model of the Naive Bayes classifier works well with semi-supervised learning for long comments on SNSs. Yamaoka et al. [6] used Naive Bayes to identify hobbies from posts on personal Twitter accounts. The results showed that Naive Bayes had a classification accuracy of about 80%. However, it was found that when the amount of data was small, it tended to be less responsive to unknown words.

2.2 Dependency Analysis

According to Koo et al. [7], experiments using the dependency analysis showed significant performance gains under a variety of conditions. The method was able to improve performance even with small amounts of training data. In a study by Tago et al. [8], some words were weighted using dependency analysis results. As a result, they stated that emotions could be more accurately discriminated by Naive Bayes in a certain extent. However, the accuracy of Naive Bayes was not greatly improved. One of the reasons for this is that they were not able to set appropriate weighting on the target words. Miwa et al. [9] performed morphological analysis on the collected tweets and then created their dictionary to incorporate the strong and weak expressions of sentences into the analysis. Groupings were set up in the dictionary to classify the tweets, and weighting was applied to each grouping. As a result, they were able to improve the rate of correct classification.

In this study, we investigate whether Naive Bayes accuracy can be improved by considering relationships between words. We weight word according to the result of dependency analysis and compare the results without and with incorporating dependency analysis to examine the possibility of improving the accuracy of approval desire discrimination and quantification in tweets.

3 Adjusting Quantification of Approval Desire by Dependency Analysis

3.1 Weighting Based on the Dependency Analysis Result

In this study, we conduct dependency analysis based on the approach used in Tago et al. [8]. Firstly, the DAWScore, NDAWScore, and NCUWScore are calculated for all words in a tweet. For example, the word "fun" is quantified with DAWScore = 1.0, NDAWScore = 0.5, NCUWScore = 0.8. Next, DAScore, NDAScore and NCUScore defined in Eqs. (1)-(3) are calculated for all tweets.

$$DAScore = \sum\nolimits_{i=1}^{n} DAWScore_i \tag{1}$$

$$NDAScore = \sum\nolimits_{i=1}^{n} NDAWScore_i \tag{2}$$

$$NCUScore = \sum\nolimits_{i=1}^{n} NCUWScore_i \tag{3}$$

where n is the number of morphemes in one tweet.

A label DA, NDA or NCU is assigned to a tweet if its corresponding value DAScore, NDAScore or NCUScore is the biggest, as shown in Eq. (4).

$$\text{A label of} \begin{cases} DA \\ NDA \\ NCU \end{cases} \text{is assigned to a tweet,}$$

$$\text{if Max\{DAScore, NDAScore, NCUScore\}} = \begin{cases} DAScore \\ NDAScore \\ NCUScore \end{cases} \tag{4}$$

For example, a tweet "I'm having so much fun today!" is given three scores "DAScore = 6.0, NDAScore = 4.0, NCUScore = 3.5". Since DAScore is the biggest, DA is assigned as the label to the tweet.

The above method did not consider the relationship between words. However, when a word such as "very" is included in a sentence, the words associated with that word are considered to have a stronger meaning than those without. For example, when we say "very funny", the word "funny" is emphasized more than "funny" only, it should be given a higher score. Therefore, words that strengthen or weaken the meaning, such as "very", are grouped and weighted against the words with which they are associated. The adjusted DAScore, NDAScore and NCUScore are defined in Eqs. (5)-(7).

$$DAScore' = DAScore + \sum\nolimits_{i=1}^{n} DAWScore_i(W_i - 1) \tag{5}$$

$$NDAScore' = NDAScore + \sum\nolimits_{i=1}^{n} NDAWScore_i(W_i - 1) \tag{6}$$

$$NCUScore' = NCUScore + \sum\nolimits_{i=1}^{n} NCUWScore_i(W_i - 1) \tag{7}$$

where W_i indicates the weight for each word in a category corresponding to the dependency analysis result, and n is the number of morphemes in one tweet.

In addition, the following four rules are applied to make the evaluation method closer to the human evaluation method.

1. If there is more than one word included in the grouping, add them in the same way. For example, if there is a tweet "It was very, very beautiful," add the $WScore_i$ of "very" twice.
2. If there is no word to be engaged, no weighting is given. For example, tweet like "Yeah! Especially!!!!", "Especially" does not modify any words.
3. When two or more words have an engaged target, no weighting is applied. As an example, tweet like "Great, I feel so much better", "Great" modifies the sentence "I feel so much better."
4. If none of the DAWScore, NDAWScore, or NCUWScore is assigned to the word to be engaged with, i.e., the word was not included in the training data among the tweets in the test data, no weighting is applied.

3.2 Adjusted Quantification of Approval Desire

We describe how to adjust quantification of approval desire per tweet. As described in 3.1, DAScore, NDAScore and NCUScore are calculated for each tweet. The degree of approval desire per tweet is defined in Eqs. (8) for the original method without weighting.

$$\text{FScore} = \text{DAScore}/(\text{DAScore} + \text{NDAScore}) \tag{8}$$

In this study, we adjusted the degree of approval desire by applying weighting based on the dependency analysis result, which is defined in Eq. (9).

$$\text{FScore}' = \text{DAScore}'/(\text{DAScore}' + \text{NDAScore}') \tag{9}$$

3.3 Experiment Design

The detail of experiment is given as follows.

1. Tweets are collected, and a part of tweets are classified by the evaluators into three categories: "Desire for Approval (DA)", "No Desire for Approval (NDA)", or "Not Clear/Unknown (NCU)." A majority vote is taken on the evaluated tweets to determine the category.
2. Create a Naive Bayes classifier to categorize tweets. DAWScore, NDAWScore and NCUWScore are calculated for all words in a tweet. Then, DA, NDA or NCU is assigned to the tweet as described in 3.1, by applying Eqs. (1)-(4).
3. Morphological analysis and dependency analysis is performed on the collected tweets to examine word relationships. The results of the dependency analysis are used to group the words that are influencing the sentences.
4. Weight the tweets according to the weighting method described in 3.1, using Eqs. (5)-(7).
5. Adjust the degree of approval desire for each tweet according to 3.2, using Eq. (9).
6. Perform five cross-validation to verify whether the weighting improves the accuracy of Naive Bayes.

4 Experiment Results and Discussion

4.1 Dataset

In this study, we used the dataset used in [1]. First, we collected 7116 tweets from 20 Twitter users. From these, 1200 tweets were randomly selected and rated by four evaluators in three categories: DA, NDA or NCU. The evaluators were four native Japanese-speaking students of 20s. If the evaluations resulted in a majority tie, no judgment could be made on the discrimination of the desire for approval. Therefore, it was removed from the results. In addition, tweets with duplicated content or tweets with only URLs were removed. As a result, the number of tweets used as training data was 904.

4.2 Morphological Analysis and Weighting Results

Morphological analysis and dependency analysis were performed on the 904 tweets collected, using Yahoo Dependency Analysis [10]. The results of the morphological analysis are shown in Table 1.

Next, we used the results of the dependency analysis to group the words that influenced the sentences and set a weight for each group. In this study, emphasizing and weakening were used as groups, following the method proposed by Tago et al. [8]. An associative thesaurus [11] was used to find words for emphasizing and weakening. Emphasizing is a word that strengthens the extent on another word it modifies. As a result, there were 29 words determined, such as "very" and "very much". Weakening is a word that obscures or understates the extent on another word it modifies, and there were three words specified, such as "a little" and "somewhat". For each group, a weight of 2.0 for emphasizing and 0.5 for weakening are applied in this experiment, as proposed in [8].

Table 1. Results of morphological analysis

Part of speech	Number concerned	Part of speech	Number concerned	Part of speech	Number concerned
Nouns	4190	Conjunctions	28	Auxiliary verbs	422
Verbs	2405	Prefixes	206	Undefined words	5155
Adjectives	962	Suffixes	1821	Determiners	247
Adverbs	460	Emotions	176	Directives	194
Couplets	16	Adjuncts	3641	Specials	1792

The number of tweets subject to weighting is shown in Table 2. Of the total of 904 tweets, 103 tweets were subject to weighting. In addition, 86 tweets were subject to emphasizing only, 13 tweets were subject to weakening only, and four tweets were subject to both emphasizing and weakening.

Table 2. Number of tweets subject to weighting

Fold	Emphasizing only	Weakening only	Both Emphasizing and weakening	Total
1st	19	5	0	24
2nd	18	0	1	19
3rd	11	4	1	16
4th	16	3	0	19
5th	22	1	2	25
Total	86	13	4	103

4.3 Verification of Naive Bayes Accuracy

Five cross-validations were performed to investigate whether the adjustment on the degree of approval desire using weighting based on the dependency analysis result improves the accuracy of Naive Bayes, in terms of correlation coefficients and determination coefficients between the human evaluation result and FScore and between the human evaluation result and FScore'.

If FScore' is closer to the human evaluation result than FScore, the accuracy of Naive Bayes can be considered improved by incorporating dependency analysis. In other words, the correlation coefficient and determination coefficient get greater after weighting. For the evaluator's ratings, DA is taken as 1, NDA as -1, and NCU as 0. The sample number was 904 tweets after cleaning. The average of five folds is the average value for five cross-validations, and the overall is the value obtained for the entire sample. The correlation coefficients and determination coefficients are shown in Table 3. The absolute values of the difference between the DAScore and NDAScore for each fold in Table 3 are shown in Table 4.

Table 3. Results of correlation and determination coefficients for 904 tweets

Fold	Between the human evaluation result and FScore		Between the human evaluation result and FScore'	
	Correlation coefficient	Determination coefficient	Correlation coefficient	Determination coefficient
1st	0.370	0.137	0.373	0.139
2nd	0.303	0.092	0.305	0.093
3rd	0.317	0.101	0.317	0.101
4th	0.483	0.233	0.482	0.233
5th	0.428	0.183	0.437	0.191
Average of five folds	0.380	0.149	0.383	0.151
Overall	0.380	0.145	0.382	0.146

Table 4. Absolute differences between DAScore and NDAScore for each fold in Table 3

Fold	ABS (DAScore- NDAScore)
1st	3.494
2nd	3.105
3rd	3.423
4th	4.087
5th	3.596

With weighting, the correlation coefficient and determination coefficient increased slightly. Table 4 shows that it has the largest difference for the fourth fold, and it has the smallest difference for the second fold. This result indicates that the larger the difference in absolute value, the more clearly it can be evaluated as DA or NDA.

Next, the correlation coefficient and determination coefficient were obtained only for the 103 tweets that were subject to weighting. The correlation and determination coefficient are shown in Table 5. The absolute values of the difference between the DAScore and NDAScore for each fold in Table 5 are shown in Table 6.

Table 5. Results of correlation coefficient and determination coefficient for 103 tweets

Fold	Between the human evaluation result and FScore		Between the human evaluation result and FScore'	
	Correlation coefficient	Determination coefficient	Correlation coefficient	Determination coefficient
1st	0.098	0.010	0.154	0.024
2nd	0.362	0.131	0.408	0.167
3rd	0.420	0.176	0.376	0.141
4th	0.675	0.456	0.638	0.407
5th	0.247	0.061	0.287	0.082
Average of five folds	0.360	0.167	0.373	0.164
Overall	0.308	0.095	0.335	0.112

When weighting is applied, the correlation coefficients increased. On the other hand, the determination coefficients for the overall increased, but the determination coefficient for the average of five folds decreased slightly. Table 6 is almost the same as Table 4, and it has the largest difference for the fourth fold and the smallest difference for the second fold. Compared to Table 4, the absolute values have increased for all folds. Moreover, the

Table 6. Absolute differences between DAScore and NDAScore for each fold in Table 5

Fold	Abs (DAScore- NDAScore)
1st	4.755
2nd	3.185
3rd	4.641
4th	5.676
5th	5.474

difference between DA and NDA tends to be bigger for the weighted results compared to the unweighted ones.

4.4 Discussion

The correlation coefficients and determination coefficients obtained for the 904 tweets showed almost no change without and with weighting. One of the reasons for the lack of improvement was the small number of tweets subject to weighting in relation to the total number of tweets. As shown in Table 2, the number of tweets subject to weighting in this experiment was 103, which is only about one ninth of the total number of tweets. Therefore, to determine whether the accuracy of Naive Bayes improved with weighting, it is better to compare only the tweets subject to weighting according to the dependency analysis results. Therefore, we calculated the correlation coefficients using the 103 tweets that were subject to weighting and found that the correlation coefficients increased. In other words, the results of Naive Bayes classification came closer to the evaluator's assessment by weighting the tweets using the dependency analysis results.

However, there is a large variation in the correlation and determination coefficients among the five data sets. Table 3 shows that the correlation coefficient for the fourth fold is the largest at 0.483, while for the second fold it is the smallest at only 0.303. The reason for this difference may be that the fourth fold with the highest correlation coefficient had fewer tweets whose evaluation was determined by a small difference, and they had more DA or NDA overwhelmingly. We can see that the fourth fold in both Table 4 and Table 6 have the largest absolute value of the difference between DAScore and NDAScore. On the other hand, the second fold with the smallest correlation coefficient may have had many tweets that could not be clearly evaluated because of the close difference between the highest value and the second highest value. This is based on the fact that the absolute value of the difference between the DAScore and NDAScore for the second fold in Table 4 is the smallest. In this study, we adopt the determination rule based on the largest value regardless of the difference between the first and second largest values. Therefore, it is expected that the accuracy of discrimination may be improved by incorporating dependency analysis when the difference is very close.

In a study by Murata et al. [1], they stated that the human evaluation changed by about 14% on average with the passage of time. Evaluators seem to become unsure of their ratings for some tweets, and evaluation of such tweets may change over time. In other words, tweets that have a close difference in the Naive Bayes classification may be difficult for humans to evaluate. By using the dependency analysis, it is possible to capture ambiguous evaluations, and it can become closer to the way that humans evaluate.

5 Conclusion

To correctly understand a sentence, it is important to consider not only words but also word relationships and grammar. In this study, we investigated the possibility of improving the accuracy of approval desire discrimination and quantification in tweets by weighting word based on the dependency analysis results and examine and clarify the factors that may lead to improvement. By weighting, the correlation and determination coefficients increased slightly. Especially, using only the tweets subject to weighting, the correlation coefficients increased compared to the results without weighing. It implies that dependency analysis may have the effect of increasing accuracy for tweets whose ratings were determined by a narrow margin. In other words, it is approaching to the way that humans evaluate.

There are some limitations in this study. First, the weighted FScores for some tweets could not be obtained due to lack of DAWScore, NDAWScore, and NCUWScore for the words. Second, weighting could not be adopted when two or more words have an engaged target. Third, the dependency analysis we used could be improved.

As for our future work, we will solve the problems involved with the above limitations. We will explore the weighting factors to optimize the adjustment for quantification of approval desire in tweets. Furthermore, we plan to improve the discrimination accuracy by applying more advanced machine learning methods other than Naive Bayes and using larger data sets for the experiment.

References

1. Murata, E., Tago, K., Jin, Q.: Linguistic and contextual analysis of SNS posts for approval desire, social computing and social media: design, user experience and impact. 14th International Conference (SCSM 2022), 24th HCI International Conference (HCII 2022), Proceedings, Part I, Lecture Notes in Computer Science (Springer), 13315, pp. 332–344 (2022)
2. Kim, Y.C., Shin, E., Cho, A., Jung, E., Shon, K., Shim, H.: SNS dependency and community engagement in urban neighborhoods: the moderating role of integrated connectedness to a community storytelling network. Commun. Res. **46**(1), 7–32 (2019)
3. Marouf, A.A., Hasan, M., Mahmud, H.: Comparative analysis of feature selection algorithms for computational personality prediction from social media. IEEE Transactions on Computational Social Systems **7**(3), 587–599 (2020)

4. Swartz, M., Crooks, A., Kennedy, W.G.: Diversity from emojis and keywords in social media. Proc. SMSociety'20: International Conference Proceeding Series, ACM, pp. 92–100 (2020)
5. Yoshida, S., Kitazono, J., Ozawa, S., Sugawara, T., Haga, T., Nakamura, S.: Sentiment analysis for various SNS media using Naïve Bayes classifier and its application to flaming detection. Proceedings 2014 IEEE Symposium on Computational Intelligence in Big Data, pp. 1–6 (2014)
6. Yamaoka, H., Sano, M.: Persona estimation using SNS based on naive bayes method. Proceedings the 32nd Annual Conference of the Japanese Society for Artificial Intelligence, JSAI2018 (2018). https://doi.org/10.11517/pjsai.JSAI2018.0_4Pin120 (In Japanese)
7. Koo, T., Carreras, X., Collins, M.: Simple semi-supervised dependency parsing. 46th Annual Meeting of the Association for Computational Linguistics: Human Language Technologies, Proceedings of the Conference, pp. 595–603 (2008)
8. Tago, K., Takagi, K., Kasuya, S., Jin, Q.: Analyzing influence of emotional tweets on user relationships using Naive Bayes and dependency parsing. World Wide Web **22**(3), 1263–1278 (2019)
9. Miwa, M., Tatsuma, A., Aono, M.: Sentiment analysis of tweets focusing on the position of polarity words and on the emphasized and de-emphasized expressions. Forum on Information Technology **2**, 227–228 (2014). (In Japanese)
10. Yahoo Ditransitive Analysis. https://developer.yahoo.co.jp/webapi/jlp/da/v2/parse.html. Accessed 19 June 2023
11. Japanese Thesaurus Associated Thesaurus. https://renso-ruigo.com. Accessed 19 June 2023

YouNDigital: A Multidisciplinary Co-creation Strategy to Define Audiences, Users, and Contexts of Use of a Digital Newsroom

Andreia Pinto de Sousa[1(✉)], Margarida Maneta[2], Teresa Sofia Castro[2], Mafalda Marinho[3], and Maria José Brites[2]

[1] HEI-Lab: Digital Human-Environment Interaction Lab, Lusófona University, Lisbon, Portugal
andreia.pinto.sousa@ulusofona.pt
[2] Lusófona University, CICANT, Lisbon, Portugal
[3] Lusófona University, Lisboa, Portugal

Abstract. Aiming to engage young people in critical social matters, the project YouNDigital- Youth, News and Digital Citizenship (PTDC/COM-OUT/0243/2021) is developing a digital newsroom to understand young people's interests and engagement with news. This paper discusses the methodological process of designing a Web application to host a digital newsroom that can also be attractive and user-friendly. This process was guided by a bottom-up approach with the user at its centre. It began with co-creation sessions involving a multidisciplinary team and interviews with young people from different life contexts. These inputs were valuable for the design of the Web app. Next, we will conduct user usability tests and heuristic validation with experts. The challenge was gathering all the knowledge and information and meeting project expectations. The co-creation sessions and the interviews were central to producing meaning and enlightenment about the Web app, its users and its contexts. The co-creation sessions enabled the creation of three different Personas and context scenarios, and the interviews with young people validated the outputs of the design thinking process and offered additional information to meet young people's expectations and needs.

Keywords: Co-creation · Design Thinking · User-Centred Design

1 YouthNDigital Project

YouNDigital - Youth, News and Digital Citizenship (PTDC/COM-OUT/0243/2021) is a Portuguese-funded project that aims to capture young people's (aged 15–24) socialisation, attitudes, practices, and relationships towards news and digital citizenship. The project follows participatory approaches involving young people in different stages of the project's lifecycle, namely designing and testing the YouNDigital digital newsroom. Considering the plethora of digital means, social platforms young people access daily, and the amount of content that comes to them, we regard the construction of a digital newsroom as a powerful hub to engage young people in important social matters. Young

H. Mori et al. (Eds.): HCII 2023, LNCS 14056, pp. 326–336, 2023.
https://doi.org/10.1007/978-3-031-48044-7_24

people are expected to participate in the YouNDigital newsroom to interact and produce content on topics related to the 2030 Agenda and in matters that interest them in a safe and inclusive atmosphere. In this paper, we will discuss the methodological process that entailed the project's challenging task: designing a Web application to host a digital newsroom to understand young people's interests and engagement with news. This process was developed using a bottom-up approach in which the user is at the centre of the process. The project has a multidisciplinary team of researchers from communication, education, psychology, sociology, technology, and youth and media studies.

2 Methodological Approach to Understanding the Context

Being the focus of this project, the relationship of young people with news, shaping the experience, which constitutes a complex problem concerning the multiple dimensions of engagement, is the most challenging purpose of the Web application. To do that, we opt to conduct our methodological process under the Design Thinking (DT) User-Centred Design (UCD) umbrella [1, 2].

This article focuses on the Emphasise and Define phases of the DT process; the approach adopted comprises desk research and state-of-the-art analysis, team co-creation sessions to Personas and Context Scenarios development.

2.1 State of the Art

The first stage of this process was a state-of-the-art analysis of other related solutions: Scrivener; Pocket; Instapaper; News with Friends; Momento; Penzu; FlipBoard, and Apple News. The analysis comprised interface elements, layout, colours, alignment and typography, navigation models, information and media, technical issues, functionalities, main objective, and characteristics.

This examination and some desk research about similar projects allowed us to get valuable insights concerning the project strategies to adopt and mainly to raise questions that helped define our product strengths. One of the main questions surrounding this analysis was what would differentiate us from other platforms and how to engage users. At the end of this phase, along with team expectations, the primary purpose of the project web app was defined: to provide youth with a personalised space to share ideas and express on different topics with a participatory approach to create and consume news in a dedicated platform that could gather content from other platforms as TikTok, Instagram, Facebook, Blogs and so on using engagement strategies as a recommendation and that could be used for personal or scholar contexts.

This solution is intended to promote knowledge transfer at the national and international levels, improve critical digital literacy and engagement between participants and promote participation rights.

2.2 User Research and Personas Development

After the project's first meetings, the design team quickly understood that the phase to collect user information had been made by the team members for years. Therefore, more than conducting user research, it was necessary to gather all this knowledge and this expertise [3–5] and develop Personas that represent project users.

In the DT or even in the UCD methodologies, it is crucial to discover "the underlying thoughts and emotions that guide someone's decisions and behaviours" [6, p. 25]. To do so, developing user models has been widely adopted in the context of design technologies. These models, called Personas, use abstraction to represent complex phenomena as humans' behaviours regarding other humans, their context, and the artefact we are designing [7]. This technique which emphasises the user's goals, tasks, environments, and needs relating to the focus area, could be a powerful tool for a multidisciplinary team.

One of the primary purposes of Personas is to complement and gather information collected during user research and build a common ground for team communication and inform design decisions. The process of developing the personas should include the whole team that is working on this task. It can contribute to creating an empathetic mindset about users and not relying on preconceived individual ideas of team members. This empathetic mindset is paramount in guiding the team throughout the process and modelling the user experience [8].

However, it is well known that Personas can also represent a trap in the design process, which is why it has been under criticism [9]; regarding our multidisciplinary team that has been developing research in the focus area, it was believed that this technique could be the foundation to share knowledge and built the fundamental common ground to effective communication among the research team and mainly as "a process of ensuring user-focused design in all phases of the project" [10, p. 10].

Including as many project participants in team members had been making the developing personas is widely recommended to mitigate the main criticised aspect of using them; they are only used by the ones who create them [9–11]. Creating personas with an engaging perspective can also surpass this criticism as it becomes easier for the team to effectively involve them in the lives of personas [10].

After the data collection, three different profiles were defined. It was also defined that two are primary and one secondary persona [7]. The definition of what information would be needed to describe our personas, not only to inform the design process but also to achieve the project team's expectations and keep a user-centric vision and focus on user engagement. Therefore, in addition to the usual demographic information and to meet consumer profiles, Personas were built focusing on biography, personal interests, personality traits, skills, goals, frustrations, inspirations, devices they are familiar with, social networks which they use and need from the point of view of experience and expectations of use over time. For each Persona, a description of one day was also developed.

A first version of the project's Personas was submitted for team members' approval in a co-creation session, where it was possible to refine the roles, motivations, behaviours, and attitudes. After this iteration, it was consensual that the Personas represent the project's target and that we can move further to the next phase, the context scenarios.

2.3 Framework to Scenarios Co-creation Session

Context scenarios allow us to define the ideal user experience; they "establish the primary touch points that each primary and secondary persona has with the system (and possibly with other personas) for a day or some other meaningful length of time… focusing on high-level actions from the user's perspective" [7, p. 113].

To collect as much information as possible from the team of researchers in defining the contexts of use and user experience, a framework was prepared to explain and illustrate the user scenarios (see Fig. 1).

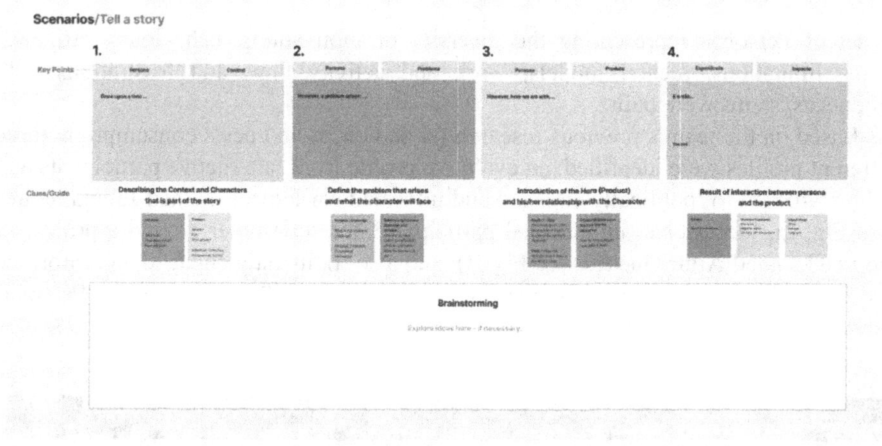

Fig. 1. Scenario framework created for the co-creation sessions

This structure consists of a template that guides the team to write a story based on the classic narrative in which one starts by describing the context and the characters of the story (Personas and, if necessary, other stakeholders), defining the problem that arises and that the character will face, the appearance of the hero (the product/solution) and his relationship with the character (Persona), and, finally, the result of the story in which the outcome of the interaction is described (Persona and solution). This exercise was conducted during two remote co-creation sessions in January 2023.

The first session occurred on the 6th of January with 9 participants. The first part of the session was dedicated to revisiting the personas, creating groups of work, and presenting the scenario framework and what scenarios are in the context of user-centred design. After that, each group started the development of the scenario for a specific persona. At the end of the session, each group presented the scenario and this moment of sharing and discussing some of the themes and issues raised in this activity. After the session, a summary was sent to the team.

The second session occurred one week after, on the 13th of January. The session script was the same, but different groups were created to explore different perspectives.

These sessions allowed the team to engage with the personas, understand the motivations and actions, and immerse in the world surrounding them. Additionally, it was possible to identify specific and sensitive issues of the project that needed to be deepened, as well as an alignment with priorities regarding the digital newsroom.

3 YouthNDigital Personas and Scenarios

3.1 Personas

A set of Personas representing the diversity of motivations, behaviours, attitudes, skills, limitations, mental models, work and activity flow, and frustrations with products/systems were built.

Based on the team's previous research on audiences and news consumption, three different profiles were identified: an evolutive profile from 'alternative participants and online citizens' to 'politically engaged and informed participant' named Julieta Soares (see Fig. 2), 'occasional, uninformed participant' and 'consumer around a project of the Self' named Artur Guedes (see Fig. 3); and also 'politically engaged and informed participant' named José Martins (see Fig. 4) [12, p.180–192], each of these Personas validated by previous studies [13–20].

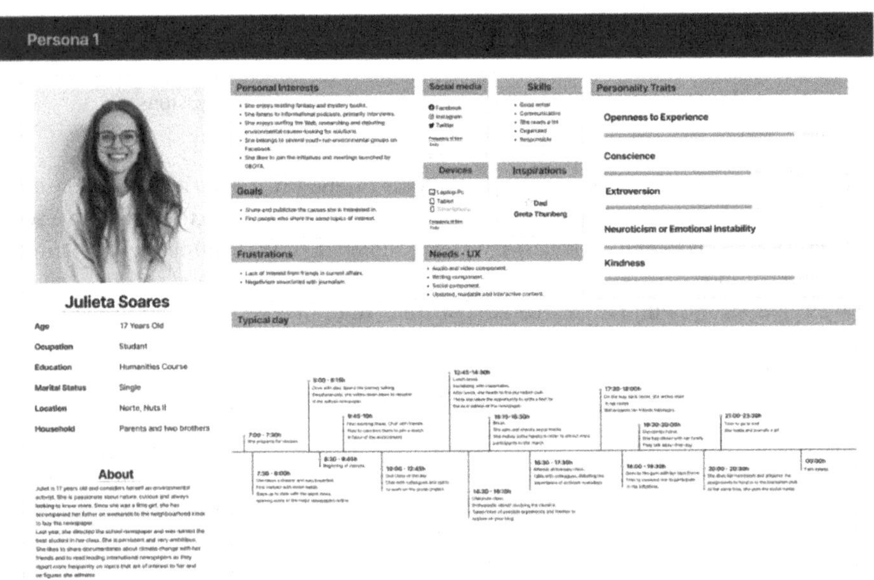

Fig. 2. Persona: Julieta Soares

Julieta is 17 years old and considers herself an environmental activist. Ever since she was little, she has accompanied her father on weekends to buy the newspaper. She's curious and passionate about nature and always looking to learn more. Last year, she headed the school newspaper and was voted the best student in her class. Julieta likes to share climate change documentaries with her friends and read international reference newspapers. She is frustrated with her friend's lack of interest in current affairs and wants to find a space to spread and share the causes she cares about. This genuine interest and the need to create impact may make her a candidate for prolonged app use.

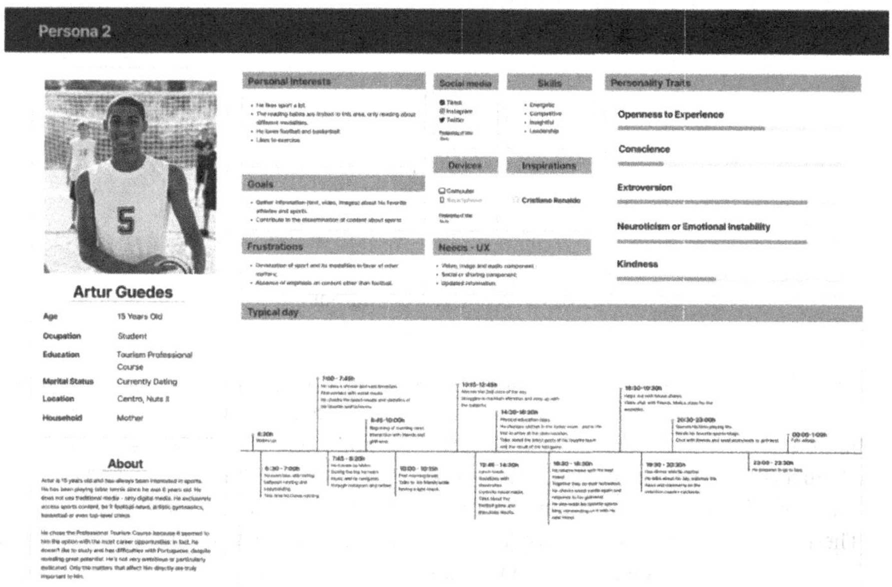

Fig. 3. Persona: Artur Guedes

Artur Guedes (see Fig. 3) is 15 years old and has always been interested in sports. He has been playing table tennis since he was six years old. He does not use traditional media, only digital media and only accesses sports content, be it football news, artistic gymnastics, basketball, or even high-competition chess. He chose the Tourism Professional Course because it appeared to him to have the best career opportunities: he does not like to study. He has difficulties in Portuguese, despite showing great potential. He could be more ambitious and exceptionally dedicated. Only the issues that affect him directly are essential. An app could spark his interest to share the content he enjoys and encourage more people to enjoy the sport.

Although our target group is young, one of our hypotheses to promote the app usage is to use that as a tool in a scholarly context. To do that, a persona representing teachers' motivations was developed.

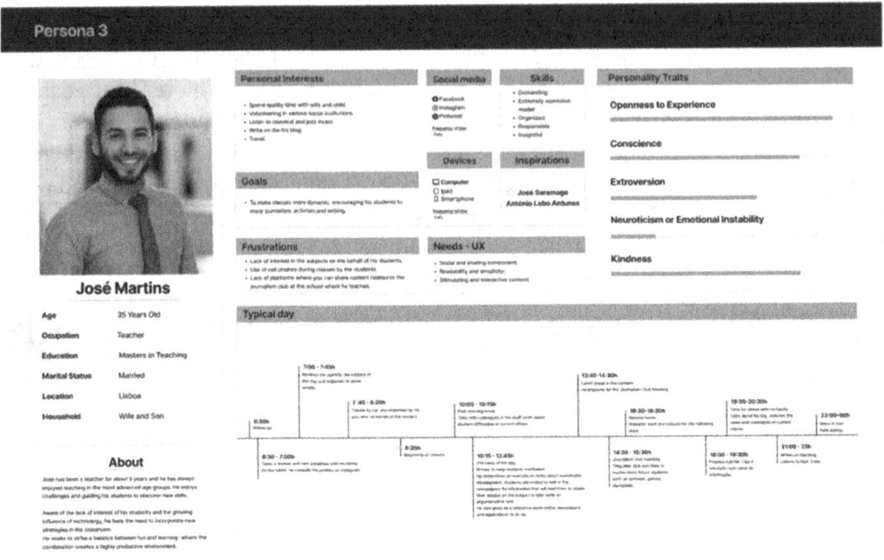

Fig. 4. Persona: José Martins

José Martins (see Fig. 4) is a teacher and has always enjoyed teaching young people. He wants challenges and to guide his students to discover new skills. Aware of the declining interest of his students and the growing influence of technology, he feels the need to incorporate new strategies in the classroom. He seeks to balance fun and learning - considering that this combination generates a highly productive environment.

The Personas definition supports the definition of a product so that we can project the product usage for a specific person for a specific need in a specific context of use.

3.2 Scenarios

The narrative has been seen as a powerful tool to design [4, 7]; they are the foundation for project materialisation since this is where the solution starts to be imagined in context, action and relation with the user (Persona).

The two co-creations sessions have resulted in seven different scenarios, two from Julieta and Artur and three from José.

Table 1 contains one of the scenarios developed for Julieta. As mentioned before, after the co-creation sessions, a moment of sharing and discussion with all the groups was made. At that moment, scenarios were presented, and ideas and concerns were shared. At the end of the sessions, a summary of these moments was made to develop the main ideas and functionalities. In this scenario, Julieta is presented as a promoter.

Julieta presented as Promoter, and that idea raises some questions regarding the evolution of digital sharing vs face-to-face sharing.

Gamification was identified as a feature among the launch of challenges for different teams, the possibility to activate timers, and the attribution of points for carrying out the activities developed.

Table 1. Scenario for Julieta Soares, one of the primary Persona

Julieta's Scenario, Co-creation session #2. Team 1
While having lunch with her colleagues, Julieta starts reviewing her plans for the afternoon. Today is Journalism Club Day, and in last week's session, the teacher told the students that they could bring ideas and suggestions for tools that they thought could be useful for the club's activities. Julieta recently discovered a new application for young people in an article published on the Portuguese newspaper-based platform Público na Escola (Public at the School) website. Julieta thinks that the introduction of a new tool in the journalism club can be an interesting way to create more dynamic and to stimulate the sharing and exchange of ideas among the members. Sometimes, Julieta feels that, even with her friends, it's easier to chat or exchange ideas through Instagram or WhatsApp than in person. When she finishes lunch, Julieta goes to the Journalism club and meets the teacher there with whom she shares her discovery of the App. The teacher thinks it's a good idea and suggests that she present the application and propose an activity with it to her colleagues. Julieta presents the application to her colleagues. Although initially, they are a little sceptical, after freely browsing the application, they can understand how this can be a good way of being up to date on topics of interest to them. In addition, they find this application's features interesting - it allows highlighting, saving news, and sharing with groups and people outside the application (by email, WhatsApp, and airdrop). Julieta then suggests that they create groups and accept the invitation to the challenge: select three pieces of news, identify the different parts of a piece of news (title, lead and body of the text) and use the underline function and the different colours to find the answers to these questions: Who? What? Where? When? As? Why? Julieta sets a timer for the challenge, making the activity more fun and challenging. Whenever a group completes one of these tasks, points are added to the team (group created by club members). Whoever finishes the challenge with more points - wins, being able to choose the theme of the next challenge. At the end of the activity, colleagues share their experiences. They mentioned that they enjoyed using the application and found it a fun way to read the news. The teacher was also happy with the result of the experience and proposed that in one of the next sessions, they repeat the activity At dinner time, Julieta shares with her father the activity she did at the journalism club. The father is very interested in the application and asks Julieta to show him how it works. He even suggests that they create a group between the two to share news about their common interests

Another idea that came out was the possibility of allowing the user to create activities to remove pressure from being limited to those suggested by the app and relieve problems related to inhibition or unhealthy competition.

It was also noted that it would be helpful to share the contents with family and teams would be helpful.

The analysis of each scenario and the discussion with the team members was a crucial moment to engage the team in the design process and gather more information about users' behaviours concerning news consumption, and also to move forward for more technical issues regarding web application development (Fig. 5).

This phase of definition of what capabilities and information the web application should have, led us to a more concise and enlightened idea of what our audiences will need to engage with the YouNDigital digital newsroom.

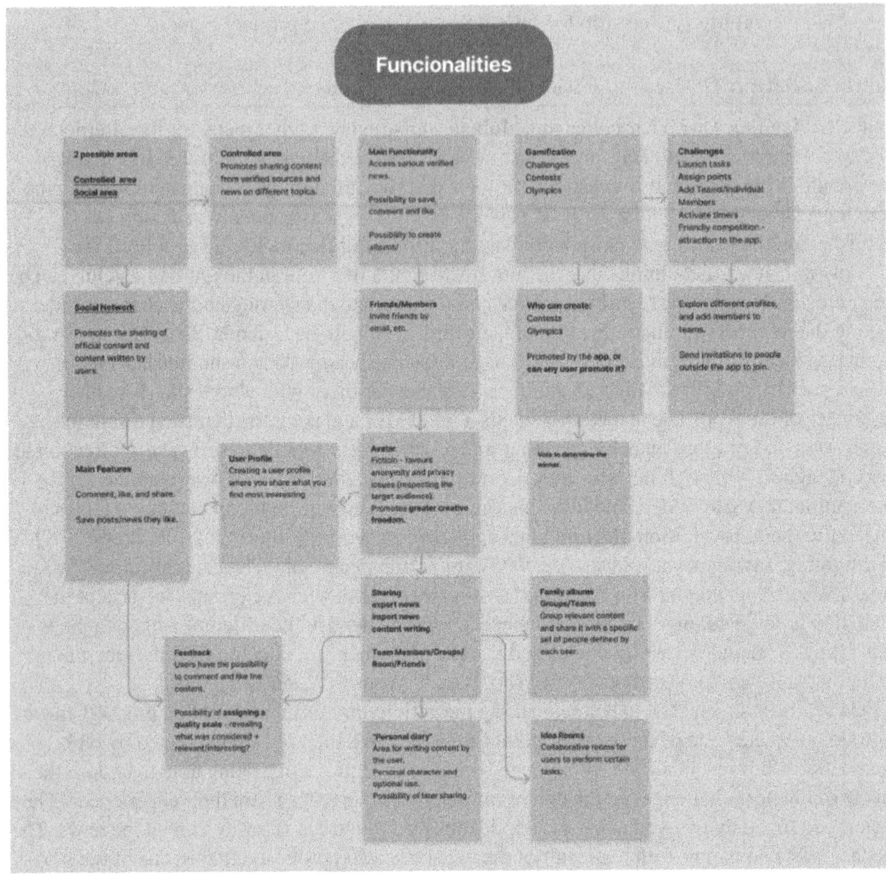

Fig. 5. Functionalities gathered from the context scenarios

4 Final Considerations

The definition of user-profiles and contexts of use in co-creation sessions with different project researchers allowed the alignment of objectives and expectations, knowledge-sharing between various researchers, and crossing areas of expertise. Personas and scenarios are solid tools for a human-centred design approach. In this context, they also prove to be robust instruments of co-creation and scientific and empiric knowledge collection among a research team.

Furthermore, after these co-creation sessions, the team interviewed young people (from different socio-demographic backgrounds) and focused on their views of the digital newsroom. The data collected shows that the young respondents attach importance to the themes, functionalities (such as multimedia tools) and formats. Some aspects they valued were already thought out in the design thinking process, which validates the work done by the research team during the co-creation moments and is in tune with the project and platform objectives. This user-centred approach values the active involvement of the target group from an early stage of the project, recognising their expertise and giving them a voice and a platform to exercise their right to participation as field collaborators. Regarding the project team, the hands-on approach added value to the researchers involved in these sessions, of which most of them are not acquainted with design thinking methodology. Their participation in the co-creation sessions enabled them to immerse in the process through a different lens, broadening their expertise and knowledge transfer by creating team-building opportunities and sharing.

The following steps under this user-centred design approach, to learn and validate solutions with users, will be besides submitting the solution to heuristic expert reviews and conducting usability tests on the digital newsroom with young people.

Overall, at the end of this task, the YouNDigital project will contribute to the studies focusing on information production by young people, adding a participatory dimension considering learning by doing and, in this case, the educational dimensions of journalism.

References

1. Gibbons, S.: Design Thinking 101. Nielsen Norman Group (2016)
2. Buchanan, R.: Wicked Problems in Design Thinking Author (s): Richard Buchanan Published by: The MIT Press Stable: http://www.jstor.org/stable/1511637. vol. 8, no. 2, pp. 5–21 (2016)
3. Brites, M.J., Santos, S.C., Jorge, A., Catalão, D.: Ferramentas jornalísticas na educação: Uma rádio online para jovens. Sociologia, Problemas e Práticas **84**, 81–100 (2017). https://doi.org/10.7458/SPP2017846102
4. Ravenscroft, A., Dellow, J., Brites, M.J., Jorge, A., Catalão, D.: RadioActive101-Learning through radio, learning for life: an international approach to the inclusion and non-formal learning of socially excluded young people. International Journal of Inclusive Educational Review **24**(9), 997–1018 (2020). https://doi.org/10.1080/13603116.2018.1503739
5. Brites, M.J., Castro, T.S., (edts.),: DiCi-Educa: Experiências e reflexões sobre cidadania digital. Edições Universitárias Lusófonas, Lisboa (2020)
6. Martin, D.: Practical Empathy (2015). https://doi.org/10.5848/amacom.978-0-814417-53-9_23
7. Cooper, A., Reimann, R., Cronnin, D., Noessel, C., Csizmadi, J., LeMoine, D.: About Face. 4th Editio. John Wiley & Sons. Inc (2014)
8. Constantine, L., Hayes, B.: Users , Roles, and Personas. Constantine&Lockwood, Ltd. (2005)
9. Howard, T.W.: Are personas really usable? Communication Design Quarterly Review **3**(2), 20–26 (2015). https://doi.org/10.1145/2752853.2752856
10. Nielsen, L.: Personas - User Focused Design. Second Edition, Second. Springer (2019)
11. Kim, S.: "Why Personas Fail," *Nielsen Norman Group* (2018). https://www.nngroup.com/articles/why-personas-fail/. Accessed 17 Apr 2023
12. Brites: O papel das notícias na construção da participação cívica e política dos jovens em Portugal: Estudo de caso longitudinal (2010–2011). [Tese de Doutoramento, Universidade Nova de Lisboa]. Repositório da Universidade Nova de Lisboa (2013)
13. Jenkins, H., Shresthova, S., Gamber- Thompson, L., Kligler- Vilenchik, N., Zimmerman, A.: *By Any Media Necessary: The New Youth Activism.* NEW YORK UNIVERSITY PRESS. ISBN: 978-1-4798-9998-2 (2016)
14. Van Damme, K., Kobbernagel, C., Schrøder, K.C.: Comparing European citizens' news media repertoires across nations: a second-order factor analysis approach to explore crossnational patterns. Participations-Journal of Audience & Receptions Studies **14**(2), 437–463 (2017)

15. Kõuts-Klemm, R., Brites, M.J.: How digital converges cross-media news typologies across countries: a comparative study of news consumption in Estonia and Portugal. Participations-Journal of Audience & Receptions Studies **14**(2), 464–483 (2017)
16. Silva, M.T., et al.: Audiências e cross-media: estudo de padrões de consumo de notícias em Portugal. Estudos em Comunicação **25**(1), 177–199 (2017). https://doi.org/10.20287/ec.n25.v1.a11
17. Schrøder, K.C.: Antigas e novas notícias: Audiências flutuantes, repertórios noticiosos e locais de consumo. Parágrafo **2**(3), 125–139 (2015)
18. Hobbs, R., Tuzel, S.: Teacher motivations for digital and media literacy: an examination of Turkish educators. British Journal of Educational Technology, pp. 1–16 (2015)
19. Hobbs, R.: Approaches to Instruction and Teacher Education in Media Literacy. United Nations Literacy Decade: Research paper prepared for the UNESCO Regional Conferences in Support of Global Literacy (Doha, 12 – 14 March 2007) (2007)
20. Pozas, M., Letzel, V.: "Do you think you have what it takes?" – exploring predictors of pre-service teachers' prospective ICT use. Tech Know Learn (2021). https://doi.org/10.1007/s10758-021-09551-0

Understanding Major Topics and Attitudes Toward Deepfakes: An Analysis of News Articles

Zhong Tang(✉), Stella Xin Yin, and Dion Hoe-Lian Goh

Wee Kim Wee School of Communication and Information, Nanyang Technological University, Singapore, Singapore
{zhong005,xin013}@e.ntu.edu.sg, ashlgoh@ntu.edu.sg

Abstract. Deepfakes, highly realistic fake videos or images created using deep learning algorithms, have raised concerns due to their potential for malicious use and the dissemination of false information. This paper aims to analyze news articles related to deepfakes, focusing on the major topics discussed and the attitudes expressed toward this emerging technology. Understanding the public's awareness, concerns, and reactions toward deepfakes is crucial in shaping informed responses. This study conducted exploratory data analysis, topic modeling analysis, and sentiment analysis by examining 4,920 news articles from the Nexis Uni database between 2000 and 2022. The topics discussed encompass various domains, including politics, business, entertainment, and more. We uncovered how deepfakes can be used for manipulation, the risks they pose to industries, and their potential impact on public trust and society. Furthermore, sentiment analysis of the news articles allowed us to gauge the overall public perception of deepfakes. We examined the emotional tone and attitudes conveyed in the articles to determine whether deepfakes were portrayed as a threat, a tool for mischief, or a harmless form of entertainment. This analysis provides insights into the prevailing sentiments surrounding deepfakes and their potential implications. This study addresses the research gap on the evolution of deepfake topics and sentiments over time and across diverse contexts.

Keywords: Deepfakes · misinformation · news articles · topic analysis · sentiment analysis

1 Introduction

Deepfakes, a form of digital forgery, have recently gained significant attention due to their increasing prevalence. This phenomenon involves using deep learning algorithms to create remarkably realistic fake videos or images [1]. Individuals can manipulate visual content to make it appear like someone is saying or doing something they never actually did in real life by employing this technology. Although deepfakes can serve as a means of entertainment, there is a growing concern regarding their potential malicious use for purposes such as political sabotage, market manipulation, and the dissemination of false information [2, 3].

H. Mori et al. (Eds.): HCII 2023, LNCS 14056, pp. 337–355, 2023.
https://doi.org/10.1007/978-3-031-48044-7_25

As the primary source of information for many individuals, online news plays a vital role in shaping attitudes and public perceptions [4, 5]. Notably, news articles discussing deepfakes have witnessed a significant rise in recent years. Consequently, analyzing news articles related to deepfakes is imperative as they reflect the public's awareness, concerns, and reactions toward this emerging technology [3]. We can gain valuable insights into the prevalence, frequency, and diverse range of deepfake-related issues and their potential implications for society and public opinion by examining news articles.

Analyzing news articles is a tool to gauge the current state of deepfake awareness among the general public [6]. News outlets often act as intermediaries between technology advancements and the wider society, offering insights, explanations, and opinions on various topics. News articles allow journalists and writers to convey information regarding deepfake technology's capabilities, potential risks, and societal impact. Therefore, understanding the major topics discussed within news articles allows us to identify the key concerns and areas of focus about deepfakes.

Moreover, news articles provide rich data on the public's attitudes and perceptions toward deepfakes [7]. Through analysis, we can gain an understanding of how the general public perceives and responds to this technology. Do they consider deepfakes a serious threat or a harmless tool for entertainment? Are they aware of the potential dangers associated with malicious use? By examining the tone, sentiment, and rhetoric employed in news articles, we can uncover the range of attitudes, concerns, and even public policy proposals that have emerged in response to deepfakes.

News articles also offer insights into the broader implications of deepfakes for society and public opinion. We can identify the emerging themes regarding deepfakes by examining the context in which deepfakes are discussed within news articles [8]. Political discourse, market dynamics, and public trust in media are a few examples of areas mentioned in news articles. Analyzing news articles allows us to explore the potential consequences and challenges that arise from the proliferation of deepfakes, aiding policymakers, researchers, and the public in formulating informed responses.

However, a research gap exists in understanding how deepfake topics and sentiments have evolved over time and across different sources and themes. While some studies have focused on specific aspects of deepfakes, such as detection methods [9] and social implications [10], to our knowledge, there is a lack of work that examines trends and patterns of deepfake news coverage over an extended period and across diverse contexts. This is important to address since it can help researchers and practitioners to understand the societal and historical factors influencing the public discourse and perceptions of deepfake technology. Therefore, this study aims to fill the above gap by analyzing 4920 new articles about deepfakes from the Nexis Uni database between 2000 and 2022.

The objectives of this paper are twofold. Firstly, we aim to identify the main topics and trends that emerge from news articles concerning deepfakes. We uncover the predominant themes, issues, and debates surrounding this technology by conducting a topic modeling analysis to understand the critical areas of focus within the public discourse on deepfakes. We also identify shifting narratives and emerging concerns or perspectives by tracking trends over time.

Secondly, we investigate the sentiments expressed in news articles related to deepfakes. Sentiment analysis allows us to explore the emotional tone and attitudes conveyed within the articles, providing insights into the public's perception of deepfakes. Examining emotions - positive, negative or neutral, allows us to gain a nuanced understanding of how news outlets and journalists frame deepfakes. This analysis will shed light on whether deepfakes are predominantly portrayed as a threat, a tool for mischief, or a harmless form of entertainment.

2 Literature Review

2.1 Deepfakes Introduction and Their Societal Impacts

Deepfakes have emerged as a significant technological phenomenon with profound societal implications [11]. Deepfakes are artificial intelligence image synthesis technologies that produce videos that may imitate actual videos [12]. The term "deepfake" is derived from "deep learning" and "fake," highlighting the role of deep learning algorithms in generating deceptive media. These fabricated media assets make it possible to manipulate visual content to convincingly portray individuals saying or doing things they never actually did in real life [13].

The societal impact of deepfakes stems from their potential to undermine truth, trust, and authenticity. One of the most concerning aspects of deepfakes is their ability to deceive viewers, blurring the line between real and fake [14]. The hyper-realistic nature of deepfakes makes it increasingly difficult for people to discern genuine content from manipulated or fabricated ones. This erosion of trust can have wide-ranging consequences, from damaging the credibility of individuals and public figures to fueling misinformation campaigns. Misinformation can violate one's right to privacy by harming that person's reputation under specific conditions [15], and by disregarding the privacy of others who are part of its target audience.

Political sabotage and manipulating public opinion are one of the most significant societal risks associated with deepfakes [16]. Deepfakes are misinformation campaigns that are weaponized to influence elections and cause unrest [3]. These campaigns create false or misleading videos of political leaders or candidates, making them appear to engage in compromising or unethical behavior. For instance, a deepfake video might depict a candidate accepting bribes, making inflammatory statements, or engaging in illicit activities [17]. The intention is to damage reputation, credibility, and public image, thereby influencing public perception and potentially swaying electoral outcomes. The potential impact of such malicious use of deepfakes on political stability and public trust in institutions is a cause for grave concern.

Deepfakes are often associated with negative implications and concerns about their potential misuse. However, it is essential to recognize that deepfakes also have the potential for positive societal impact in certain contexts. One of the positive applications of deepfakes lies in the realm of entertainment and creative expression. Deepfake technology allows for seamless face-swapping, enabling filmmakers and visual effects artists to bring characters to life in previously unimaginable ways [18]. This technology opens up possibilities for enhanced storytelling, enabling filmmakers to resurrect deceased actors or seamlessly blend real and fictional elements [19]. This creative application of deepfakes has the potential to captivate audiences and enhance the cinematic experience.

Deepfakes can also enhance learning experiences in educational settings [20]. Educators can create immersive simulations and interactive experiences that help people visualize historical events and enable art education using deepfake technology [21, 22]. For example, traditional methods of teaching history often rely on textbooks, images, or recorded audio to convey information about historical events and figures. However, deepfake technology can recreate historical figures or bring famous speeches to life, allowing individuals to engage with the material more vividly and memorably. These educational applications can potentially foster more profound understanding and engagement among learners.

2.2 News Articles and Deepfakes

News coverage of deepfakes has garnered significant attention as technology continues to evolve and impact various aspects of society. Journalists and news outlets are crucial in informing the public about the emergence, implications, and risks associated with deepfakes [21]. These articles often cover the latest advancements in deepfake technology, exploring the technical processes behind their creation, the challenges associated with detecting them, and the strategies to combat them [3]. These news articles have expressed worry that deepfakes would sabotage the democratic process, jeopardize national security, and continue the persistent problem of fake news and misinformation [7]. However, such news articles also help the general public understand the complexity of deepfakes and their potential consequences by presenting these technical aspects in accessible language.

News articles on deepfakes cover various topics, providing readers with different understandings of this emerging technology and its implications. These articles delve into multiple domains, including politics, business, entertainment, and more, to explore the multifaceted nature of deepfakes. In politics, news articles examine how deepfakes can be used for political manipulation and misinformation campaigns, threatening the basic information security of democratic polities [24]. They analyze the potential impact of deepfakes on elections, public perception of political leaders, and the erosion of trust in democratic processes [25]. These news articles contribute to the discussion on the vulnerability of political systems to deepfake threats and the need for safeguards and awareness among the public by highlighting these concerns.

In the business sector, news articles highlight the risks deepfakes pose to industries such as advertising, marketing, and brand reputation [26, 27]. They discuss the challenges media organizations face in verifying the authenticity of video content and the potential reputational risks associated with the spread of deepfakes. Entertainment is another area covered by news articles on deepfakes. While deepfakes can enhance storytelling and create stunning visual experiences, the potential for deepfakes to be utilized for misleading intentions is demonstrated in news articles, such as creating explicit or non-consensual content using people's likenesses without their permission [28]. These articles emphasize the need for businesses to stay informed and be proactive in addressing the risks posed by deepfakes, whether through technology-driven solutions, legal frameworks, or public awareness campaigns.

These news articles aim to raise individuals' awareness of the impacts and dangers of deepfakes in various contexts and explore the influence of deepfakes on individual credibility assessments of articles [6, 7]. Deepfake-related content and public service announcements like Jordan Peele's Obama deepfake aim to heighten viewer skepticism about political videos [29]. News articles also attempt to educate readers on deepfakes' potential for deception and how they might be used to mislead. Readers are encouraged to engage in scrutiny, actively assessing the credibility and potential manipulations present within media artifacts. These critical analyses extend beyond deepfakes, spurring a broader examination of media literacy and how information is consumed and shared [30].

3 Methodology

In this section, we elaborate on our dataset, followed by a brief description of text preprocessing. We then introduce exploratory data analysis, topic modeling analysis, and sentiment analysis as our research methods applied in this study.

3.1 Dataset and Text Preprocessing

We retrieved deepfake news articles from the Nexis Uni database using the search term "deepfake". We focused exclusively on newspapers with English content. The preliminary search resulted in 5,569 news articles published by 569 different sources, with dates ranging from April 27, 2000, to October 8, 2022. We extracted various data elements for analysis, including the news article's title, publication source, publication date, and content. Additionally, we gathered geographical information to gain insights into the relevant geographical regions associated with the content.

After eliminating duplicates, non-English content, and incomplete items, we narrowed our dataset to 4,920 news articles. Next, we preprocessed the news content by removing emojis, URL links, punctuations, numbers, and special tokens (e.g., "&"). We also converted the terms into single words and lowercase. Further, we removed standard stopwords from the NLTK library. Finally, we conducted a stemming process to enhance interpretability. After preprocessing, 43,792 valid English terms were prepared for further analyses described next.

3.2 Exploratory Data Analysis (EDA)

EDA is a fundamental step in data analysis that involves summarizing the main characteristics of a dataset. The main objective of EDA is to better understand the underlying data structure, identify patterns and relationships, and uncover hidden insights [31]. EDA uses various statistical and visualization techniques to explore the data, such as histograms, scatterplots, and word clouds. By performing EDA, researchers can make more informed decisions about further analyses, develop hypotheses, and refine models. In this study, we used histograms, frequency counting, and word clouds to explore the meaning of the data and inform our further analyses.

3.3 Topic Modelling Analysis

Latent Dirichlet allocation (LDA) is a popular and widely used machine learning method for text analysis. It is an unsupervised clustering technique to identify latent topics from a corpus and then calculate topic distributions [32]. In our study, we map all the documents to the classified topics and calculate the representatives of each topic. To make each document and each word as monochromatic as possible, we used the Gibbs sampling algorithm to increase the statistical inference [32]. Next, we apply Cao et al.'s [33] and Deveaud et al.'s [34] metrics to identify the optimal number of topics. Since the best topics number shows low values for Cao et al. [33] and high values for Deveaud et al. [34], we find the point that best fits the criteria. According to the metrics, we generated 11 topics in this study.

3.4 Sentiment Analysis

To address RQ2, we conducted sentiment analysis. Sentiment analysis is a broad term encompassing various approaches that extract emotion or opinion-related information from natural language [35]. This analytical technique has been applied in multiple disciplines, including psychology, economics, education, and political and social science [36]. Sentiment analysis provides information about positive, negative, or neutral attitudes, allowing us to investigate the author's attitude toward the topics. To obtain the sentiment of each news article, we first applied the VADER (Valence Aware Dictionary for Sentiment Reasoning) model to generate sentiment scores for each document [37]. Next, we categorized each document into three classifications according to the sentiment scores ($-0.5 <$ neutral < 0.5, negative ≤ -0.5, positive ≥ 0.5).

4 Findings

Our findings are presented from three aspects. Section 4.1 provided an overview of our dataset from 2000 to 2022, including the distribution of publication sources and geographic information. Section 4.2 delves into a detailed description of the 11 topics generated through LDA analysis. Moreover, we demonstrate how these topics have evolved and diversified over the years, offering valuable insights into the changing landscape of deepfake news. Section 4.3 shifts our focus to illustrating sentiment distribution across both years and topics.

4.1 EDA

The emergence of deepfake news articles can be traced back to 2000, although it remained relatively scarce from 2000 to 2017, with an average of only two news articles per year. However, a significant shift occurred in 2018, marking a turning point in the landscape of deepfake news, as shown in Fig. 1. In 2018 and 2019, the number of news articles experienced a dramatic surge, reaching an unprecedented peak of 1,217. This surge can be attributed to various factors, including advancements in technology, increased accessibility to deepfake creation tools, and growing concerns surrounding the potential consequences of this technology [2, 38, 39]. The years 2020 and 2021 witnessed a slight decline in deepfake news articles, potentially influenced by the COVID-19 pandemic and its impact on media coverage. Nevertheless, deepfake-related content regained momentum and reached a new pinnacle in 2022, with 1,486 news articles. These fluctuations in deepfake news reflect the development of deepfake and the public's increasing awareness of its implications.

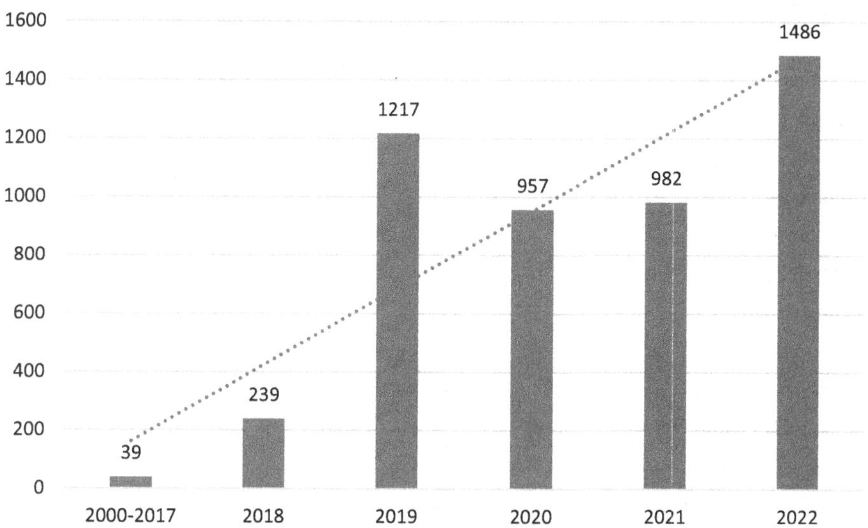

Fig. 1. News publishing trend over years

Over 500 news sources have published articles related to deepfake technology during 2000–2022. Table 1 shows the list of the top 20 sources and how these news publishers are distributed. Here, CE Noticias Financieras emerged as the most prolific publisher, account for 14.6% (720 news articles) of the total coverage. CE Noticias Financieras is renowned for its extensive daily coverage of Latin America, including Central, and South America, Mexico, with over 9,000 news stories published daily. The New York Times and The Independent have made similar contributions to deepfake-related news, accounting for approximately 4.3% and 4.2% of the articles, respectively. Notably, 12 are based in the United Kingdom among the top 20 sources. This concentration of sources from the UK could be attributed to the country's robust justice system [40].

We utilized word clouds to depict the significance of keywords based on frequency analysis visually. In the word cloud, the font size represents the frequency of each keyword's occurrence in the news content. Figure 2 presents the top 50 keywords ranked by their frequency. The keyword "say" holds the highest rank with a frequency of 24,205. Additionally, other highly recurring keywords include "video" (15,167), "use" (14,336), "make" (11,556), and "people" (10,598). These keywords unequivocally suggest that the primary application of deepfake technology lies in video production.

Table 1. Top 20 news sources

News source	No. of news
CE Noticias Financieras English	720
The New York Times	213
The Independent (United Kingdom)	207
The Guardian (London)	181
MailOnline	174
The Times (London)	140
Financial Times (London)	97
The Daily Telegraph (London)	77
thesun.co.uk	77
Hindustan Times	69
The Straits Times (Singapore)	63
The Sun (England)	63
thetimes.co.uk	58
Indian Express	56
Postmedia Breaking News	50
The Sunday Times (London)	46
National Post (f/k/a The Financial Post) (Canada)	46
The Times of India	43
mirror.co.uk	39
i-Independent Print Ltd	38

In the same way, we visually represent the geographic information that appeared most frequently in the news content. Figure 3 illustrates the frequencies of places mentioned in the news articles. The United States (USA) had the highest occurrence, with 2,648 mentions, followed by the United Kingdom (UK), with 1,263 mentions. China (541), India (463), Australia (371), and Canada (348) were also frequently referenced countries. It can thus be seen that news content related to deepfakes is mainly concentrated in the United States.

Fig. 2. Top 50 most frequently occurring terms

Fig. 3. Top 50 Geographic information mentioned in news content

4.2 Major Topics and Trends

As shown in Table 2, topics 1, 2, 3, 9, and 11 showcases the diverse applications of deepfake technology in areas such as marketing, politics, entertainment, military, and digital life. The utilization of deepfake technology has had a positive impact, opening up numerous possibilities and opportunities within society (Topic 5). However, it also raises concerns, including issues related to victimization and crime (Topic 6), the spread of mis/disinformation on social media (Topic 7), and cyber security (Topic 8). Despite being a double-edged sword, researchers and companies are dedicated to improving this technology while exploring ethical safeguards (Topic 10).

Table 2. 11 topics generated by topic modeling analysis

Topic label	Top 10 words	Rate	No. of Doc	Description
Topic 1: Marketing	company, user, app, channel, sell, message, service, tech, launch, brand	9.90%	287(5.83%)	Companies use deepfake technology to create immersive user experience
Topic 2: Political campaign	political, election, campaign, government, trump, candidate, party, vote, democracy, law	9.10%	398(8.09%)	Deepfake videos and audios persuade voters and threat to election
Topic 3: Entertainment usage	film, make, character, play, music, artist, fan, story, live, song	9.80%	500(10.16%)	Deepfakes in film and entertainment are common. It includes realistic-looking videos and images
Topic 4: Deepfake voice	video, face, voice, speak, actor, real, person, audio, clip, footage	8.00%	633(12.87%)	Deepfake voice refers to synthetic voice that closely mimics a real person's voice
Topic 5: Positive influence	world, good, work, change, society, student, future, idea, power, understand	8.70%	316(6.42%)	Deepfakes can create numerous possibilities and opportunities in society. For example, it increase efficiency and accessibility of work
Topic 6: Victim and crime	image, woman, online, victim, child, photo, police, abuse, crime, report	8.40%	475(9.65%)	A lot of women are victims of deepfake porn
Topic 7: Social media information	medium, social, news, content, facebook, twitter, disinformation, misinformation, spread,	9.20%	597(12.13%)	Deepfake are used to spread mid/disinformation on social media platforms
Topic 8: Cyber security	security, datum, threat, attack, cyber, information, risk, business, digital, increase	9.20%	460(9.35%)	Deepfake technology threat to cybersecurity. It can be applied to biometric authentication

(*continued*)

Table 2. (*continued*)

Topic label	Top 10 words	Rate	No. of Doc	Description
Topic 9: War and military	russian, country, war, force, claim, military, block, state, ukrainian, report	10.70%	322(6.54%)	Deepfake video used for propaganda and disinformation during Russia and Ukraine conflict
Topic 10: Technology development	human, image, create, system, generate, tool, develop, word, model, researcher	7.30%	377(7.66%)	Researchers endeavoured to develop research model and tools to fight deepfakes
Topic 11: digital life	life, series, good, deep, watch, leave, give, capture, family, episode	9.60%	555(11.28%)	Deepfake technology is used to resurrect deceased people

The line graph below demonstrates how deepfake topics have evolved and diversified over the years, and how specific topics gained more attention than others (see Fig. 4). For example, the sixth topic about victims and crime was the third least popular topic in 2019 but rapidly gained attention and rose to second place in 2022. Furthermore, Topic 7, which focuses on social media information, emerged as the most prominent topic in 2020, probably influenced by the pandemic and the widespread dissemination of mis/disinformation on social media platforms. Nevertheless, this topic experienced a significant decline and dropped to the fifth rank in 2022.

4.3 Sentiment Distribution

The results showed that the majority of deepfake news articles are positive in sentiment (50%), followed by negative (43%) and neutral (7%). The sentiment trends and distributions across year and topic were also examined, as shown in Fig. 5 and Fig. 6. In Fig. 5a, the distribution of news across three sentiments follows a similar trend as the total amount of news from 2000 to 2022. However, it is challenging to discern sentiment fluctuations over the years from this data alone. To address this, we calculated the percentage of sentiments for each month by dividing the number of articles in each sentiment category by the total number of news in that month. Our analysis revealed a slight rise in negative and neutral sentiments, accompanied by a corresponding decrease in positive sentiment over the years (see Fig. 5b).

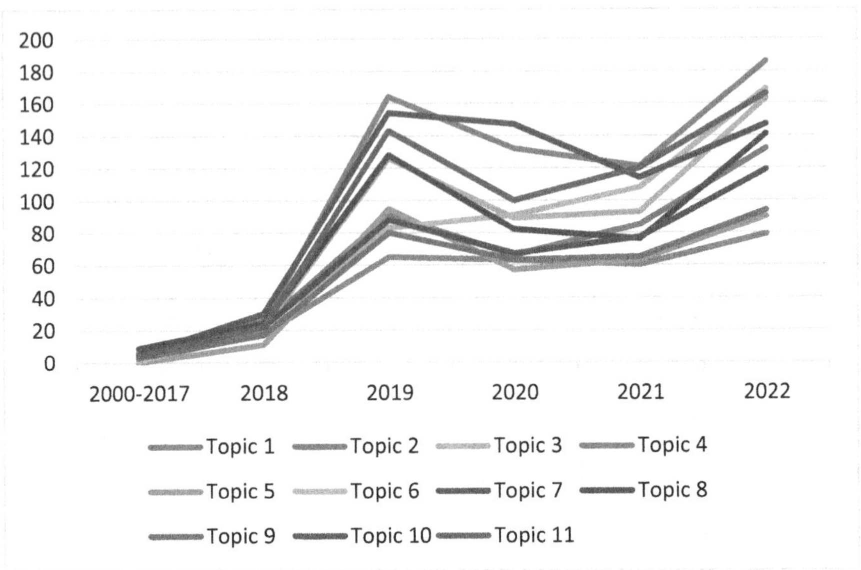

Fig. 4. Topic distribution over years

This finding suggests that deepfake-related content tends to exhibit an inclination towards negative or neutral sentiments, highlighting the potential concerns and challenges associated with this technology. Figure 6 reveals significant variations in sentiment distributions across different topics. Figure 6a demonstrates the amount of news in each sentiment category across topics. Our findings revealed that the top three positive news observed in Topic 3, 4 and 11, while the top three negative news observed in Topic 4, 6 and 7. To gain further insights, we calculated the percentage of sentiments in each topic by dividing the number of news pertaining to each topic by the total number of articles in that topic (see Fig. 6b). In Topic 6, Topic 7, and Topic 9, negative sentiment prevails over positive sentiment. On the other hand, in Topic 2, Topic 4, and Topic 8, the weightage of negative and positive sentiments is relatively balanced. In contrast, positive sentiment dominates in Topic 1, Topic 3, Topic 5, Topic 10, and Topic 11. These differences in sentiment distribution across topics highlight the diverse perspectives and attitudes associated with deepfake technology.

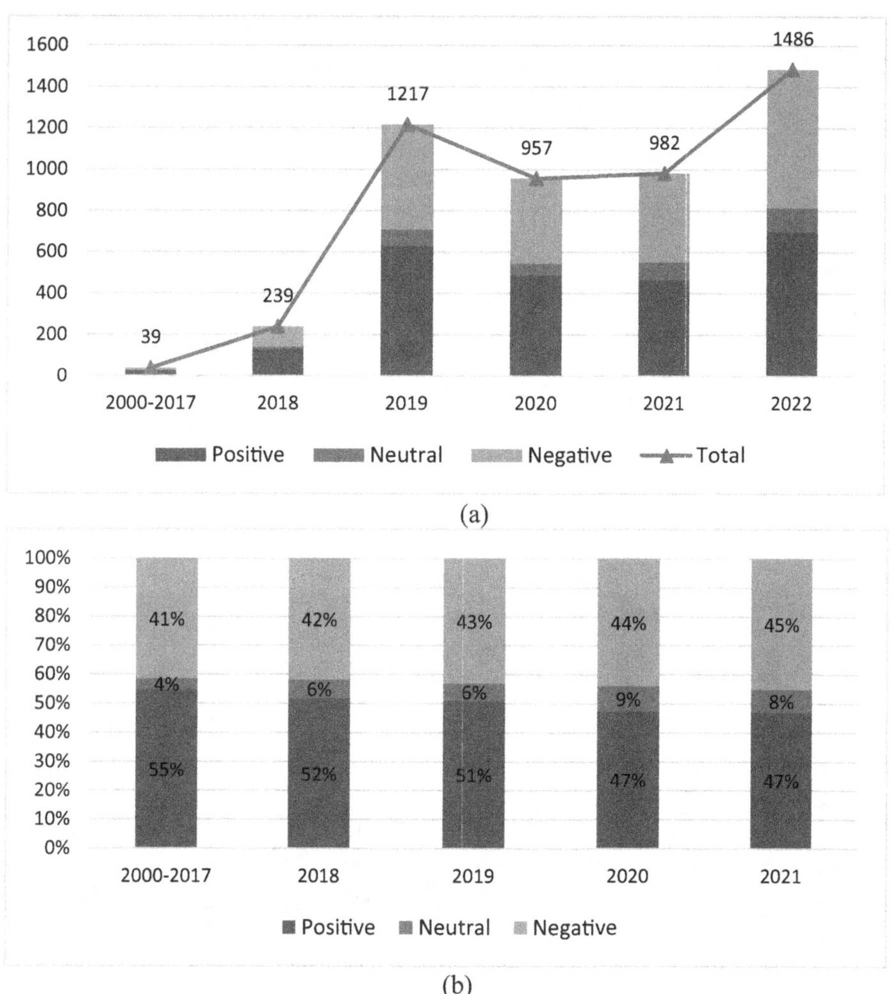

(a)

(b)

Fig. 5. Sentiment distribution by (a) No. of news (b) % of news

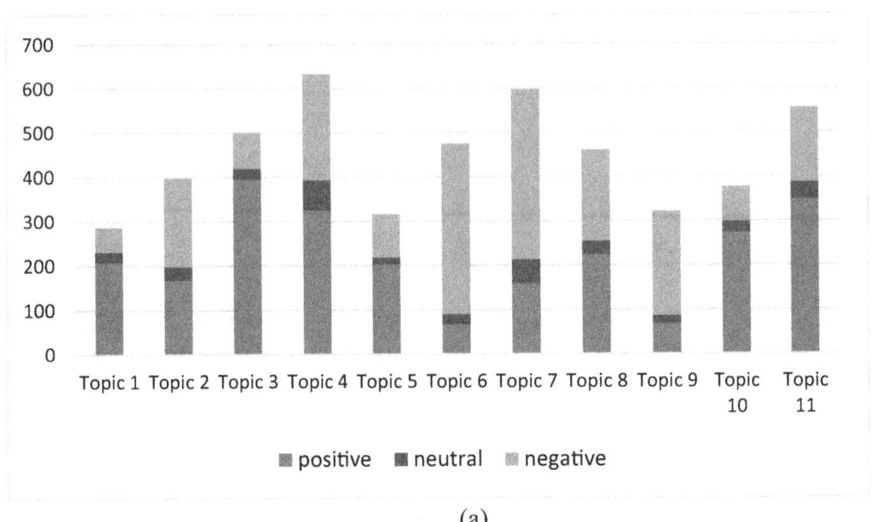

(a)

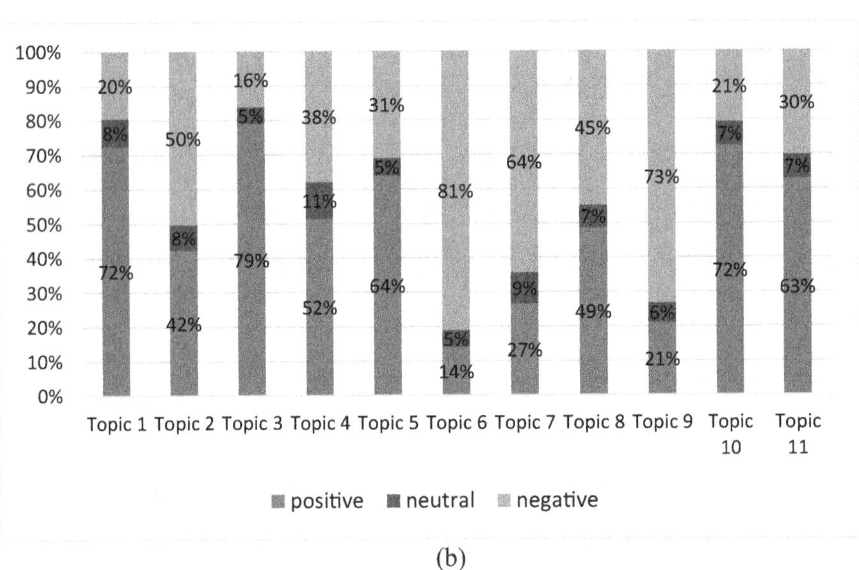

(b)

Fig. 6. Sentiment distribution by (a) No. of news (b) % of news in each topic

5 Discussion

The major topics identified through the topic modeling analysis encompass applications and concerns associated with deepfake technology. This study found that deepfake technology has been applied in different domains, as described in the news articles. Topics such as marketing, military, victimization and crime, cyber security, and digital life explore the wide-ranging uses of deepfakes. Deepfake technology can be leveraged in marketing to create compelling and persuasive advertisements. The military topic suggests the potential of deepfakes for training simulations and strategic operations. While deepfake technology offers opportunities, there are concerns and ethical considerations. Topics such as victimization and crime draw attention to the possibility of using deepfakes for harmful purposes, including revenge porn, harassment, and extortion. The issue of cyber security also arises, as deepfakes can be utilized as a tool for cyber-attacks and identity theft.

Another finding is that deepfake topics change in focus over the years. For instance, victimization and crime gained prominence in 2022, indicating an increasing awareness of the potential harm caused by deepfakes. As deepfake technology becomes more sophisticated and accessible, there is a heightened risk of individuals being victimized by creating and disseminating manipulated videos [41]. Another significant shift in deepfake topics occurred in 2020, with a notable increase in the focus on social media misinformation. Deepfakes, with their ability to create realistic but fabricated videos, have the potential to amplify and spread false information at an alarming rate [42]. The rise of this topic in 2020 indicates the growing recognition of deepfakes' role in fueling misinformation campaigns and the urgent need for effective strategies to detect and combat them.

Moreover, our analysis of the distribution of publication sources provide insights into the extensive coverage of deepfake technology across the globe. With over 500 news sources publishing articles related to deepfakes, it is evident that this phenomenon has captured the attention of media outlets worldwide. Also, our geographic information analysis highlights the countries most frequently mentioned in deepfake news articles. The United Kingdom and the United States are the most referenced countries, and China, India, Australia, and Canada also receive notable mentions. These findings highlight the global reach and impact of deepfake news because its use and misuse have extended beyond national borders and resonated with media outlets globally. Our findings underscore the interconnection of deepfakes and emphasizes the need for international collaboration to develop strategies to mitigate the potential harms and promote the responsible use of this technology [43].

Furthermore, previous research has shown that deepfake technology has positively impacted society and daily life. It has been utilized in various areas, such as marketing campaigns, entertainment content, and increasing work efficiency [19, 27]. These benefits align with the findings of our study, which reveal a prevailing positive attitude towards this emerging technology in a large portion of news articles. In addition, much news content contained expectations for deepfake applications to enrich our society and enhance various aspects of our lives. For instance, an article published by The Sunday Herald sheds light on the capabilities of deepfake software and its potential for creating highly realistic face swaps in both images and videos, thereby driving advancements in the entertainment field.

In addition to the aforementioned advantages, our study revealed that the topic of digital life emerged prominently in recent deepfake news content. Many individuals have welcomed the integration of this technology and its potential applications. For instance, CE Noticias Financieras English reviewed deepfake application in avatar creation. The articles show that deepfakes have been used to generate realistic digital avatars that can be employed in virtual reality environments, allowing users to better immerse themselves and interact with others more realistically online.

While there are generally positive attitudes towards deepfake technologies in Topics 1, 3, 5, 10, and 11, concerns have been growing regarding their potential for malicious use. These concerns include using deepfakes for political sabotage, market manipulation, and disseminating misinformation [2, 3]. Our findings in Topics 6, 7, and 9 also reflected similar concerns. For instance, an article released on April 22, 2019, in The New York Times expressed concerns about the spread of misinformation, offensive content, and disturbing videos as some of the challenges faced by YouTube. It also discussed controversies surrounding the platform, such as running ads alongside anti-vaccine content, enabling child suicide, and hosting videos with inappropriate content. These examples illustrate the potential negative consequences associated with the misuse of deepfake. It is thus crucial for platforms and policymakers to develop robust strategies for addressing these concerns and ensuring responsible use of the technology.

Lastly, the war between Ukraine and Russia has sparked heated discussions regarding deepfake technology in warfare and military operations. Undoubtedly, people have expressed negative opinions on its potential risks in such a context. The fake video or audio recordings could be employed to manipulate public opinion, deceive military forces, and spread disinformation during the conflict. One of the examples in our dataset stated, "Would Facebook allow distribution of a deepfaked video if it were shared by the president as the rationale for the bombing of Iran? What if the president shared a less manipulated "shallow fake" video like the Pelosi video of a potential 2020 opponent?" This example raises important questions about the extent to which platforms should permit the dissemination of manipulated media, particularly in high-stakes situations such as international conflicts and elections. The potential consequences and ethical implications of allowing such content to circulate freely necessitate careful consideration and robust policies to protect the public interest and prevent harmful outcomes.

6 Conclusion

This study analyzed news articles to gain insights into major topics and attitudes toward deepfakes. We aimed to understand the prevalence, frequency, and diverse range of deepfake-related issues discussed in news articles and the public's perceptions and attitudes toward this emerging technology through the analysis. Our findings have implications for both theoretical understanding and practical applications. From a theoretical perspective, this study contributes to the existing literature by offering insights into the evolving landscape of deepfake-related news coverage. The significant increase in the number of deepfake news articles in recent years indicates a growing recognition of the consequences and risks of deepfakes. The findings align with previous research on the prevalence and impact of deepfakes in society.

The study's topic modeling analysis uncovers the main themes and concerns discussed in news articles, providing a comprehensive overview of deepfake technology's implications. This contributes to a nuanced understanding of its societal impacts. Additionally, our sentiment analysis offers insights into the emotional tone and attitudes conveyed in news articles, aiding in understanding public opinion as well as informing future research on the social and psychological effects of deepfake technology. From a practical standpoint, the findings have implications for various stakeholders. Policymakers can benefit from the insights provided by our analysis of news articles, facilitating the development of appropriate regulations, guidelines, and awareness campaigns to mitigate the negative impacts of deepfakes. Media organizations and journalists can utilize our analysis to understand prevailing topics, narratives, and attitudes surrounding deepfakes. This understanding enables the development of informed and responsible reporting practices, ensuring accurate and balanced coverage of deepfake-related issues, thereby fostering media literacy among the general public.

However, our study has some limitations. The analysis was based solely on news articles, which may not capture the full range of public opinion and attitudes toward deepfakes. Other sources, such as social media or public forums, could provide additional insights. Also, the analysis focused on English-language news articles, which may limit the generalizability of the findings to other languages and regions. Future work in this area could expand the study to include a broader range of sources, such as online forums, to capture a more comprehensive understanding of public perceptions and attitudes toward deepfakes. Additionally, conducting comparative studies across different languages and cultures would provide insight into the cultural variations in attitudes toward deepfakes.

Acknowledgements. We would like to acknowledge the financial support provided by the Ministry of Education (Singapore) through the Tier 2 grant (MOE-T2EP40122–0004).

References

1. Katarya, R., Lal, A.: A study on combating emerging threat of deepfake weaponization. Proc. 4th Int. Conf. IoT Soc. Mobile, Anal. Cloud, ISMAC 2020, pp. 485–490 (2020). https://doi.org/10.1109/I-SMAC49090.2020.9243588
2. Kwok, A.O.J., Koh, S.G.M.: Deepfake: a social construction of technology perspective. Curr. Issues Tour. **24**, 1798–1802 (2021). https://doi.org/10.1080/13683500.2020.1738357
3. Westerlund, M.: The emergence of Deepfake technology: a review. Technology Innovation Management Rev. **9**(11), 39–52 (2019). https://doi.org/10.22215/timreview/1282
4. Jiang, T., Li, J.P., Haq, A.U., Saboor, A., Ali, A.: A novel stacking approach for accurate detection of fake news. IEEE Access. **9**, 22626–22639 (2021). https://doi.org/10.1109/ACCESS.2021.3056079
5. Sude, D.J., Knobloch-Westerwick, S., Robinson, M.J., Westerwick, A.: "Pick and choose" opinion climate: How browsing of political messages shapes public opinion perceptions and attitudes. Commun. Monogr. **86**, 457–478 (2019). https://doi.org/10.1080/03637751.2019.1612528
6. Shin, S.Y., Lee, J.: The effect of deepfake video on news credibility and corrective influence of cost-based knowledge about deepfakes. Digit. Journal. **10**(3), 412–432 (2022). https://doi.org/10.1080/21670811.2022.2026797
7. Gosse, C.E., Burkell, J.: Politics and porn: how news media characterizes problems presented by deepfakes. Crit. Stud. Media Commun. **37**(5), 497–511 (2020). https://doi.org/10.1080/15295036.2020.1832697
8. Lee, Y., Huang, K., Blom, R., Schriner, R., Ciccarelli, C.A.: To believe or not to believe: framing analysis of content and audience response of top 10 deepfake videos on YouTube. Cyberpsychol. Behav. Soc. Netw. **24**(3), 153–158 (2021). https://doi.org/10.1089/cyber.2020.0176

9. Lyu, S.: Deepfake detection: current challenges and next steps. 2020 IEEE Int. Conf. Multimed. Expo Work. ICMEW (2020). https://doi.org/10.1109/ICMEW46912.2020.9105991
10. Gamage, D., Ghasiya, P., Bonagiri, V.K., Whiting, M.E., Sasahara, K.: Are Deepfakes Concerning? Analyzing Conversations of Deepfakes on Reddit and Exploring Societal Implications (2022). https://doi.org/10.1145/3491102.3517446
11. Karnouskos, S.: Artificial intelligence in digital media: the era of deepfakes. IEEE Trans. Technology and Society **1**(3), 138–147 (2020). https://doi.org/10.1109/tts.2020.3001312
12. Vaccari, C., Chadwick, A.: Deepfakes and disinformation: exploring the impact of synthetic political video on deception, uncertainty, and trust in news. Social Media + Society **6**(1), 205630512090340 (2020). https://doi.org/10.1177/2056305120903408
13. Nagothu, D., Xu, R., Chen, Y., Blasch, E., Aved, A.: DeFake: Decentralized ENF-consensus based DeepFake detection in video conferencing. 2021 IEEE 23rd International Workshop on Multimedia Signal Processing (MMSP) (2021). https://doi.org/10.1109/mmsp53017.2021.9733503
14. Yadlin-Segal, A., Oppenheim, Y.: Whose dystopia is it anyway? deepfakes and social media regulation. convergence: The International J. Research into New Media Technologies **27**(1), 36–51 (2020). https://doi.org/10.1177/1354856520923963
15. Eigbedion, A.: Deepfakes: legal & regulatory considerations in Nigeria. SSRN Electronic Journal (2020). https://doi.org/10.2139/ssrn.3670644
16. Afanasyeva, T., Yumasheva, I.: Research on the effects of "DeepFake" technology for the modern digital space. Challenges and Solutions in the Digital Economy and Finance: Proceedings of the 5th International Scientific Conference on Digital Economy and Finances (DEFIN 2022), pp. 5765 (2022). https://doi.org/10.1007/978-3-031-14410-3_7
17. Chesney, R., Citron, D.K.: Deep fakes: a looming challenge for privacy, democracy, and national security. Social Science Research Network (2018). https://doi.org/10.2139/ssrn.3213954.
18. Holliday, C.: Rewriting the stars: Surface tensions and gender Troubles in the online media production of digital deepfakes. Convergence: The International J. Research into New Media Technologies **27**(4), 899918 (2021). https://doi.org/10.1177/13548565211029412
19. Whittaker, L., Kietzmann, T.C., Kietzmann, J., Dabirian, A.: "All around me are synthetic faces": the mad world of AI-generated media. IT Professional **22**(5), 90–99 (2020). https://doi.org/10.1109/mitp.2020.2985492
20. Aliman, N., Kester, L.: VR, Deepfakes and epistemic security. IEEE International Conference on Artificial Intelligence and Virtual Reality (AIVR) (2022). https://doi.org/10.1109/aivr56993.2022.00019
21. Pandey, C.K., Mishra, V.K., Tiwari, N.K.: Deepfakes: When to use it. International Conference on System Modeling & Advancement in Research Trends (SMART) (2021). https://doi.org/10.1109/smart52563.2021.9676297
22. Ramachandra, N., Ahuja, M., Rao, R. M., Dubash, N.: Human centered computing in digital persona generation. Lecture Notes of the Institute for Computer Sciences, Social Informatics and Telecommunications Engineering, pp. 385401 (2021). https://doi.org/10.1007/978-3-030-82565-2_32
23. Wahl-Jorgensen, K., Carlson, M.: Conjecturing fearful futures: journalistic discourses on Deepfakes. Journal. Pract. **15**(6), 803–820 (2021). https://doi.org/10.1080/17512786.2021.1908838
24. Whyte, C.: Deepfake news: AI-enabled disinformation as a multi-level public policy challenge. J. Cyber Policy **5**(2), 199–217 (2020). https://doi.org/10.1080/23738871.2020.1797135
25. Ray, A.: Disinformation, Deepfakes and democracies: The need for legislative reform. University of New South Wales Law J. **44**(3) (2021). https://doi.org/10.53637/dels2700

26. Kietzmann, J., Mills, A.J., Plangger, K.: Deepfakes: perspectives on the future "reality" of advertising and branding. Int. J. Advert. **40**(3), 473–485 (2020). https://doi.org/10.1080/02650487.2020.1834211
27. Whittaker, L., Letheren, K., Mulcahy, R.: The rise of deepfakes: a conceptual framework and research agenda for marketing. Australas. Mark. J. **29**(3), 204–214 (2021). https://doi.org/10.1177/1839334921999479
28. Maddocks, S.: A Deepfake porn plot intended to silence me': exploring continuities between pornographic and 'political' deep fakes. Porn Studies **7**(4), 415–423 (2020). https://doi.org/10.1080/23268743.2020.1757499
29. Ternovski, J., Kalla, J., Aronow, P.: Negative consequences of informing voters about Deepfakes: evidence from two survey experiments. J. Online Trust and Safety **1**(2) (2022). https://doi.org/10.54501/jots.v1i2.28
30. Hwang, Y., Ryu, J.Y., Jeong, S.: Effects of disinformation using Deepfake: the protective effect of media literacy education. Cyberpsychol. Behav. Soc. Netw. **24**(3), 188–193 (2021). https://doi.org/10.1089/cyber.2020.0174
31. Morgenthaler, S.: Exploratory data analysis. WIREs Comput. Stat. **1**, 33–44 (2009). https://doi.org/10.1002/wics.2
32. Blei, D.M.: Probabilistic topic models. Commun. ACM **55**, 77–84 (2012). https://doi.org/10.1145/2133806.2133826
33. Cao, J., Xia, T., Li, J., Zhang, Y., Tang, S.: A density-based method for adaptive LDA model selection. Neurocomputing **72**, 1775–1781 (2009). https://doi.org/10.1016/J.NEUCOM.2008.06.011
34. Deveaud, R., SanJuan, E., Bellot, P.: Accurate and effective latent concept modeling for ad hoc information retrieval. Doc. Numer. **17**, 61–84 (2014). https://doi.org/10.3166/DN.17.1.61-84
35. Silge, J., Robinson, D.: Text Mining with R: A Tidy Approach. O'Reilly Media, Inc. (2017)
36. Zhang, L., Wang, S., Liu, B.: Deep learning for sentiment analysis: a survey. WIREs Data Min. Knowl. Discov. **8** (2018). https://doi.org/10.1002/widm.1253
37. Hutto, C.J., Gilbert, E.: VADER: A parsimonious rule-based model for. Eighth Int. AAAI Conf. Weblogs Soc. Media. **18** (2014)
38. Kietzmann, J., Lee, L.W., McCarthy, I.P., Kietzmann, T.C.: Deepfakes: trick or treat? Bus. Horiz. **63**(2), 135–146 (2020). https://doi.org/10.1016/j.bushor.2019.11.006
39. Albahar, M., Almalki, J.: Deepfakes: threats and countermeasures systematic review. J. Theor. Appl. Inf. Technol. **97**(22), 3242–3250 (2019)
40. Jones, K., Jones, B.: How robust is the United Kingdom justice system against the advance of deepfake audio and video?. In Proceedings of the 36th International Conference on Information Technologies IEEE Conference, pp. 13–24 (2022)
41. Lucas, K.T.: Deepfakes and domestic violence: perpetrating intimate partner abuse using video technology. Victims & Offenders **17**(5), 647–659 (2022). https://doi.org/10.1080/15564886.2022.2036656
42. Perot, E., Mostert, F.: Fake it till you make it: an examination of the US and English approaches to persona protection as applied to deepfakes on social media. J. Intellectual Property Law & Practice **15**(1), 32–39 (2020). https://doi.org/10.1093/jiplp/jpz164
43. Velasco, C.: Cybercrime and artificial intelligence. an overview of the work of international organizations on criminal justice and the international applicable instruments. ERA Forum **23**(1), 109–126 (2022). https://doi.org/10.1007/s12027-022-00702-z

Leveraging Large Language Models and Weak Supervision for Social Media Data Annotation: An Evaluation Using COVID-19 Self-reported Vaccination Tweets

Ramya Tekumalla and Juan M. Banda(✉)

Georgia State University, Atlanta, GA 30328, USA
{rtekumalla1,jbanda}@gsu.edu

Abstract. The COVID-19 pandemic has presented significant challenges to the healthcare industry and society as a whole. With the rapid development of COVID-19 vaccines, social media platforms have become a popular medium for discussions on vaccine-related topics. Identifying vaccine-related tweets and analyzing them can provide valuable insights for public health researchers and policymakers. However, manual annotation of a large number of tweets is time-consuming and expensive. In this study, we evaluate the usage of Large Language Models, in this case GPT-4 (March 23 version), and weak supervision, to identify COVID-19 vaccine-related tweets, with the purpose of comparing performance against human annotators. We leveraged a manually curated gold-standard dataset and used GPT-4 to provide labels without any additional fine-tuning or instructing, in a single-shot mode (no additional prompting).

Keywords: Large language models · GPT · weak supervision · social media data

1 Introduction

The widespread adoption of social media platforms has led to an explosion of user-generated content, making them valuable sources of real-time information [1]. Social media platforms have become a valuable resource for studying public health issues [2], including the COVID-19 pandemic. Social media platforms like Twitter have a vast user base, representing diverse demographics and geographic locations. Analyzing vaccination sentiment data from such platforms allows for a more comprehensive understanding of public opinion, as it encompasses a wide range of perspectives. Twitter, in particular, has emerged as a platform where individuals share their personal experiences, including vaccination updates [3]. By analyzing the data, public health officials, policymakers, and researchers can gauge the overall sentiment towards vaccines, identify trends, and make informed decisions to address concerns or misconceptions. Analyzing self-reported vaccination tweets can provide valuable insights into vaccine sentiment, vaccine uptake, and vaccine-related concerns among the general population. However, manually annotating large volumes of social media data is labor-intensive and time-consuming, requiring domain experts to label the data.

H. Mori et al. (Eds.): HCII 2023, LNCS 14056, pp. 356–366, 2023.
https://doi.org/10.1007/978-3-031-48044-7_26

Weak supervision [4] techniques have emerged as a powerful approach for data annotation, offering significant advantages in terms of scalability [5], cost-effectiveness [6], and flexibility [7]. Traditional methods of data annotation often rely on manual labeling, which can be time-consuming, expensive, and limited in terms of the volume of labeled data that can be produced. In contrast, weak supervision techniques leverage various sources of supervision to automatically generate labeled data, reducing the manual effort required while maintaining reasonable accuracy. Scalability is one of the primary advantages of weak supervision. With the exponential growth of data, manually labeling vast amounts of data becomes impractical and expensive. Weak supervision allows for the rapid annotation of large datasets by leveraging existing resources such as heuristics, rules, or readily available weak labels [8]. These weak signals can be automatically applied to unlabeled data, effectively increasing the amount of labeled data available for training and development of robust machine learning models. Cost-effectiveness is another key benefit of weak supervision techniques. Manual data annotation often requires skilled human annotators, which can be costly and time-consuming. In contrast, weak supervision reduces the reliance on manual annotation efforts, thus reducing costs. Although weakly supervised labels may not be as accurate as manually annotated labels, they can still provide valuable insights and improve the performance of machine learning models. By combining weakly supervised labels with a smaller amount of manually labeled data, comparable results can be achieved at a fraction of the cost [9]. Additionally, traditional data annotation methods often require significant upfront effort to design annotation schemas, guidelines, and quality control processes. These rigid procedures can be challenging to adapt as new data sources or requirements emerge [10]. In contrast, weak supervision provides a more agile and adaptable approach to data annotation. Weakly supervised labels can be easily generated or modified based on changing needs, enabling rapid iteration and refinement of models in response to evolving data or domain-specific requirements.

Large language models (LLMs), such as GPT-3 [11], have revolutionized natural language processing and transformed various applications across multiple domains. These models employ deep learning techniques to generate coherent and contextually relevant text, making them invaluable for tasks like language translation, text summarization, and conversational agents. Their effectiveness is attributed to the vast amount of pre-training data and the ability to capture complex linguistic patterns. This work assesses the effectiveness of LLMs (GPT-3.5 and GPT-4 (March 23 version)), in conjunction with weak supervision, for the identification of COVID-19 vaccine-related tweets. The primary objective is to compare the performance of LLMs against human annotators. To achieve this, we utilized an expertly curated gold-standard dataset and employed GPT3.5 and GPT-4 to generate labels in a single-shot mode, without resorting to additional fine-tuning or explicit instructions.

2 Related Works

In the past weak supervision has demonstrated successful results in clinical text classification [12], multi-language sentiment classification [13], generating training sets for phenotype models [14], information retrieval [15], identifying drugs from Twitter [16–18], classifying different kinds of epidemics [19], natural disasters [20, 21] and several health applications [22–24]. In this aspect, LLMs have been effectively utilized to leverage weak supervision techniques, automating data annotation processes by generating or modifying labels based on the model's pre-trained knowledge and heuristics. LLMs, such as BERT [25] and GPT [26], have shown impressive performance in various natural language processing tasks, including sentiment analysis, named entity recognition, and text classification. These models can be fine-tuned on domain-specific datasets, enabling them to learn specific patterns and characteristics of the data. By leveraging pre-trained LLMs, researchers can automate or assist in the annotation process, significantly reducing the human effort required for data labeling. The evolution of LLMs has been marked by significant milestones, with BERT acting as a groundbreaking advancement. BERT introduced the concept of pretraining and fine-tuning, revolutionizing the field of NLP. By pretraining models on large corpora of text data and fine-tuning them on specific downstream tasks, BERT achieved state-of-the-art performance on a wide range of NLP benchmarks. BERT served as a foundation and inspiration for the development of numerous pre-trained models like GPT [26], AlBERT [27], RoBERTa [28], DistilBERT [29], ELECTRA [30], XLNet [31], T5 [32], MegatronLM [33], BART [34], CamemBERT [35]. These models have leveraged the success of BERT's architecture and training techniques to and improved the model by tackling various limitations like performance, optimization, reduction in training size. As a result, several other domain specific pre-trained models like Covid-Twitter-BERT [36], BioBERT [37], SciBERT [38], ClinicalBERT [39], LegalBERT [40], FinBERT [41–43] emerged. Building upon the success of BERT, subsequent models such as GPT-2 [44] and GPT-3 [11] further pushed the boundaries of LLM capabilities. GPT-3.5 is a transitional model, which further refines the AI's capabilities of GPT-3 and is known for nuanced understanding and contextual response generation. GPT-4 introduces a major leap with significant improvements in model size, training data, and comprehension abilities. GPT-4 is designed to better handle ambiguities and complexities in natural language, generating more coherent, relevant, and detailed responses.In the aspect of data labeling, LLMs have emerged as a promising solution to address these challenges by automating or assisting in the data annotation process. With their language understanding capabilities, LLMs can be employed to generate annotations or suggest labels for a given input, a technique known as active learning [45]. This approach allows human annotators to focus their efforts on more challenging or uncertain instances, thereby improving the efficiency and quality of the annotation process. Previous research has demonstrated that 35–40% of the crowd workers widely use LLMs for text related data annotation tasks [46]. In a study conducted by Gilardi et.al, Chat-GPT outperformed Crowd-Workers for text annotation tasks [47]. To improve the precision of ChatGPT as the hallucination is one of the limitations of LLMs, He et.al. Designed a two-step approach to explain why the text was labeled [48]. LLMs have demonstrated success in various data annotation tasks [49], sentiment analysis [50], text categorization, linguistic annotations [51], multi-linguistic data annotation [52] and social computing [53].

This work examines the role of LLMs in data annotation, discussing the benefits, limitations, and potential future directions. The advancements in LLMs have not only transformed NLP tasks but have also had a profound impact on human tasks that involve language understanding and generation. LLMs have been integrated into various applications, ranging from chatbots and virtual assistants to language translation and content generation. In human-computer interaction scenarios, LLM-based systems have enabled more natural and effective communication, bridging the gap between machines and humans. However, the increasing reliance on LLMs also raises important ethical and societal considerations, such as potential biases and the responsible deployment of AI technologies [54]. LLMs exhibit non-deterministic behavior, similar to human coders, where identical input can produce varying outputs [55, 56]. Hence, it is crucial to exercise caution when utilizing LLMs to ensure consistent and reliable results.

3 Methods

3.1 Datasets Used

Gold Standard Dataset. We collected a dataset of tweets related to COVID-19 vaccines by filtering related keywords, from one of the largest COVID-19 Twitter datasets [57] available. After filtering, this dataset consists of 2,454 self-reported vaccination confirmation tweets and 19,946 vaccine chatter tweets. The complete dataset was manually curated by two medical students, having a Cohen Kappa score inter annotator agreement of 0.82 with a third annotator resolving all conflicts. This dataset was used in the Social Media Mining for Health 2022 shared tasks [58]. With the annotation task consuming over 200 human hours, it is vital to try to identify additional techniques to attempt to streamline this process.

Silver Standard Dataset. While weak supervision has shown promise in social media mining [17, 59], we extracted an additional dataset, not manually curated, which consists of tweets selected by a weak labeling heuristic consisting of expressions like "vaccine causes", "I was vaccinated", "I got Moderna", and similar. This weakly-supervised, or 'silver standard', consists of 750,000 randomly sampled (from a larger set of 12 million) tweets with an unidentifiable mixture of both classes. The rationale for doing so is that researchers have shown that data augmentation using weak supervision leads to better and more generalizable models, than when only using gold standard data [60, 61]. Note that none of the 750,000 randomly sampled tweets used in this dataset do not have any overlap with the gold standard data.

3.2 Additional Language Models Used

Besides the previously mentioned GPT-4 and GPT-3.5, we fine-tuned COVID-Twitter-BERT [36] and BERTweet [62] with the GPT-labeled silver-standard data, for downstream tweet classification. Note that the class imbalance from the gold-standard dataset is roughly 1 to 8, between self-reported vaccination tweets and vaccine chatter tweets. This was also found to be similarly the same in the GPT-labeled silver-standard data, making the fine-tuning and evaluation comparable.

3.3 Evaluation Set-Up

LLM Performance in Annotating Data. We evaluate the performance of GPT-4 and GPT-3.5 on the labeling of the gold-standard data. This evaluation will assess how good are LLMs in labeling data when compared to a set of medical professionals. As one of the most resource-expensive parts of generating datasets, if human annotation/labeling can be aided or streamlined, there is great value in leveraging LLMs in these types of tasks. Leveraging the Open AI API for both GPT-3.5 and GPT-4, we used the following prompt: "Categorize the following text: XXXXXXXXXXXX into vaccine self-reports or vaccine chatter. Figure 1 shows a sample output of the GPT-4 prompting on the chat.openai.com website. This evaluation made 22,400 API calls to each GPT-4 and GPT-3.5 models.

LLM to Improve Weakly Supervised Dataset Creation. In these evaluations, we leverage GPT-4/GPT-3.5 to attempt to 'properly' label the silver-standard data and then fine-tune BERT-like models to classify the gold-standard data. The creation of silver-standard datasets has gained popularity in the field of NLP with many groups building systems that leverage silver-standard data to enhance their training sets and achieve state-of-the-art results in a variety of NLP shared tasks [58, 63]. Using the same prompt for the first evaluation, we made a total of 750,000 API calls to each GPT model to label this silver-standard dataset.

With these evaluations we aim to answer two questions: a) is GPT-4/GPT-3.5 enough to annotate data with similar quality than a human expert, b) could we leverage both weak supervision and GPT-4/GPT-3.5 to quickly and scalably annotate large amounts of

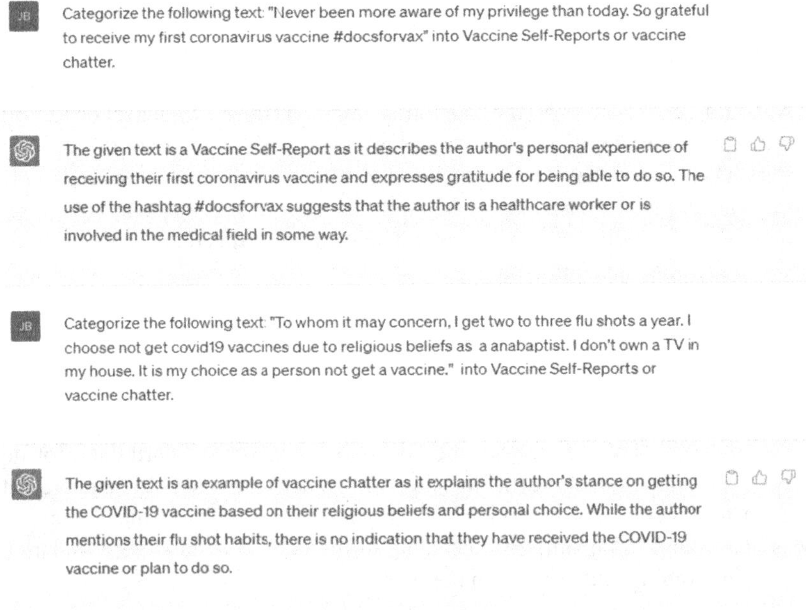

Fig. 1. Sample GPT-4 prompts to evaluate the created datasets.

data with near-expert level performance. We would call these datasets: electrum datasets, which are a mixture of gold and silver standard-data.

4 Results

Before we introduce the actual results of our analysis, we would like to present a cost analysis of how much it would cost to run the data annotation tasks leveraging the GPT models and other traditional sources. We sent a total of 1,544,800 API calls, with a total cost of $2,743.40 USD. While this price might seem high, note that we annotated a total of 1,544,800 tweets, which would be time and cost prohibitive to do hiring humans and paying them a fair wage. Even using a service like Amazon SageMaker Ground Truth, would cost around $52,896.00 USD for the same task. Leveraging Amazon Mechanical Turk would cost $37,075.20 USD for the same number of text classification tasks [64]. There is clear value in evaluating if we can leverage such a resource for data annotation, this would particularly help resource constrained researchers that cannot afford to pay expert annotators. The second aspect is scale, while ~ 1.5 million API calls are done quickly, nobody to our knowledge has manually annotated any dataset this large.

Results for LLM Performance in Annotating Data. In Table 1 we showcase the annotating performance of both GPT-4 and GPT-3.5. It is not surprising that GPT-4 outperformed GPT-3.5 by nearly 10% for the self-reported vaccination tweets category, the more interesting one, and marginally for vaccine chatter. While vaccine chatter is more easily identified, nearly 90% for both models, GPT-3.5's 71.11% performance on the self-reported class, and 80.81% for GPT-4 are promising numbers. However, once larger amounts of data are annotated this way, this would lead to a considerable amount of noise to be added. These results are still promising as there was no additional prompting or fine-tuning performed, so the zero-shot results are solid.

Table 1. Correct tweet labeling results for GPT models.

Label	GPT-4	%	GPT-3.5	%
Self-reported vaccination	1,983	80.81%	1,745	71.11%
Vaccine chatter	18,541	92.96%	17,842	89.45%

We look at the inter-annotator agreement between both GPT models using Cohen Kappa coefficient [65] and the human annotators. We evaluate this to get insights into how much the correctly labeled tweets diverge between models. The inter annotator agreement between GPT models was 0.79 (p-value < 0.0001), which is considered substantial [66]. In comparison, the human Cohen Kappa score inter annotator agreement was of 0.82, with a p-value < 0.0001, which is considered near perfect agreement. Objectively, the difference is not much, 0.03, however it does show that humans agree slightly better than the GPT models. Note that our human annotators worked independently and did not know or communicated with each other.

Results for LLM to Improve Weakly Supervised Dataset Creation. In the second evaluation, GPT-4 labeled 68,561 tweets as vaccine self-reports and 681,439 tweets as vaccine chatter. GPT-3.5 labeled 66,288 tweets as vaccine self-reports and 683,712 as vaccine chatter. While it might seem that GPT-4 labels more tweets, we are not sure they are correctly labeled, and they have not been annotated by a human. Due to this fact, there are no comments on accuracy, the idea behind this exercise is to then feed this data as part of the fine-tuning step for the previously identified BERT-like models.

After fine-tuning COVID-Twitter-BERT and BERTweet, Table 2 shows the correct tweet labeling results achieved. It is very interesting to see that a fine-tuned COVID-Twitter-BERT performs marginally better than GPT-4 (and GPT-3.5) at labeling both tweet classes. While the improvement is marginal, it goes to show that a properly fine-tuned model does outperform a more complex model, at least in this scenario. Another interesting finding is that BERTweet performs slightly worse than GPT-4, but better than GPT-3.5. This is most likely due to the training data for BERTweet not being focused on COVID-related tweets.

Table 2. Correct tweet labeling results for BERT models.

Label	COVID-Twitter-BERT	%	BERTweet	%
Self-reported vaccination	2,045	83.33%	1,897	77.30%
Vaccine chatter	19,012	95.32%	18,457	92.53%

In order to assess the actual labeling agreement between our top two models (GPT-4 and COVID-Twitter-BERT) we measured the Cohen Kappa score, which was quite surprising to learn that it was 0.85 with a p-value < 0.0001. This means that both models have a high level of agreement in which tweets they labeled, even more so than humans. Additionally, we calculated the Fleiss Kappa statistic [67] between all annotators, showing that we have a score of 0.76 with a p-value < 0.0001. This showcases that both the models and the humans mostly agree on what class the tweets should be labeled.

5 Conclusion

In conclusion, our study has several important findings:

GPT models perform well, in a zero-shot, task of properly labeling social media data, tweets in this case. However, at larger scales the number of incorrect classifications might start becoming problematic, particularly depending on the downstream task that said data will be used for.

- When leveraging GPT models alongside weak supervision techniques to identify 'silver-standard' data, we can use data augmentation with higher confidence. These resulting 'electrum datasets' could be leveraged for further fine-tuning with potentially a considerable amount of less noise than just using weak supervision alone.

- Fine-tuned BERT models are still not obsolete, as we showed them outperforming GPT-4 for labeling social media data, self-reported vaccine tweets in this case. While this comparison might be unfair, the point we show is that combining approaches leads to better results.
- Lastly, we show with our cost analysis that it is very cost effective to label data using GPT models, and that the results data is usable for downstream tasks. While we would continue to use human annotators to label data for our NER tasks, we can consider labeling less data to have equally or better performant systems in downstream tasks.

While we show that GPT models perform well, this work does not advocate for the replacing of human labeled data with GPT-annotated data. Our argument is to show that leveraging multiple approaches together, and fine-tuning, leads to potentially better and more generalizable results. The limitations of our work are clear: we only used one task - self reported vaccine tweet labeling, we only fine-tuned two different BERT models, and we did not evaluate how large our 'electrum dataset' should be to fine-tune a model enough to achieve solid performance. All these are future research directions that would greatly inform the community.

References

1. Agichtein, E., Castillo, C., Donato, D., Gionis, A., Mishne, G.: Finding high-quality content in social media. In: Proceedings of the 2008 International Conference on Web Search and Data Mining, pp. 183–194. Association for Computing Machinery, New York, NY, USA (2008). https://doi.org/10.1145/1341531.1341557
2. Pershad, Y., Hangge, P.T., Albadawi, H., Oklu, R.: Social Medicine: twitter in healthcare. J. Clin. Med. Res. **7** (2018). https://doi.org/10.3390/jcm7060121
3. Xue, J., et al.: Twitter discussions and emotions about the COVID-19 pandemic: machine learning approach. J. Med. Internet Res. **22**, e20550 (2020). https://doi.org/10.2196/20550
4. Ratner, A., Bach, S., Varma, P., Ré, C.: Weak Supervision: the New Programming Paradigm for Machine Learning. Hazy Research. https://dawn.cs (2019)
5. Cutler, J., Culotta, A.: Using weak supervision to scale the development of machine-learning models for social media-based marketing research. Applied Marketing Analytics. **5**, 159–169 (2019)
6. Chandra, A.L., Desai, S.V., Balasubramanian, V.N., Ninomiya, S., Guo, W.: Active learning with point supervision for cost-effective panicle detection in cereal crops. Plant Methods **16**, 34 (2020). https://doi.org/10.1186/s13007-020-00575-8
7. Shin, C., Li, W., Vishwakarma, H., Roberts, N., Sala, F.: Universalizing Weak Supervision. http://arxiv.org/abs/2112.03865 (2021)
8. Ratner, A., De Sa, C., Wu, S., Selsam, D., Ré, C.: Data programming: creating large training sets. Quickly. Adv. Neural Inf. Process. Syst. **29**, 3567–3575 (2016)
9. Zhang, J., Hsieh, C.-Y., Yu, Y., Zhang, C., Ratner, A.: A Survey on Programmatic Weak Supervision. http://arxiv.org/abs/2202.05433 (2022)
10. Munro, R., Monarch, R.: Human-in-the-Loop Machine Learning: Active Learning and Annotation for Human-centered AI. Simon and Schuster (2021)
11. Brown, T., et al.: Others: language models are few-shot learners. Adv. Neural. Inf. Process. Syst. **33**, 1877–1901 (2020)
12. Wang, Y., et al.: A clinical text classification paradigm using weak supervision and deep representation. BMC Med. Inform. Decis. Mak. **19**, 1 (2019). https://doi.org/10.1186/s12911-018-0723-6

13. Deriu, J., et al.: Leveraging large amounts of weakly supervised data for multi-language sentiment classification. In: Proceedings of the 26th International Conference on World Wide Web, pp. 1045–1052. International World Wide Web Conferences Steering Committee, Republic and Canton of Geneva, CHE (2017). https://doi.org/10.1145/3038912.3052611
14. Agarwal, V., et al.: Learning statistical models of phenotypes using noisy labeled training data. J. Am. Med. Inform. Assoc. **23**, 1166–1173 (2016). https://doi.org/10.1093/jamia/ocw028
15. Zamani, H., Bruce Croft, W.: On the Theory of Weak Supervision for Information Retrieval (2018). https://doi.org/10.1145/3234944.3234968
16. Tekumalla, R., Asl, J.R., Banda, J.M.: Mining archive. org's twitter stream grab for pharmacovigilance research gold. In: Proceedings of the International AAAI Conference on Web and Social Media, pp. 909–917 (2020)
17. Tekumalla, R., Banda, J.M.: Using weak supervision to generate training datasets from social media data: a proof of concept to identify drug mentions. Neural Comput. Appl. (2021). https://doi.org/10.1007/s00521-021-06614-2
18. Tekumalla, R., Banda, J.M.: An enhanced approach to identify and extract medication mentions in tweets via weak supervision. In: Proceedings of the BioCreative VII Challenge Evaluation Workshop (2021)
19. Tekumalla, R., Banda, J.M.: Identifying epidemic related Tweets using noisy learning. In: Proceedings of LatinX in NLP Research Workshop at NAACL 2022
20. Tekumalla, R., Banda, J.M.: TweetDIS: A large twitter dataset for natural disasters built using weak supervision. In: 2022 IEEE International Conference on Big Data (Big Data), pp. 4816–4823 (2022). https://doi.org/10.1109/BigData55660.2022.10020214
21. Tekumalla, R., Banda, J.M.: An empirical study on characterizing natural disasters in class imbalanced social media data using weak supervision. In: 2022 IEEE International Conference on Big Data (Big Data), pp. 4824–4832 (2022). https://doi.org/10.1109/BigData55660.2022.10020594
22. Saab, K., Dunnmon, J., Ré, C., Rubin, D., Lee-Messer, C.: Weak supervision as an efficient approach for automated seizure detection in electroencephalography. NPJ Digit Med. **3**, 59 (2020). https://doi.org/10.1038/s41746-020-0264-0
23. Fries, J.A., et al.: Weakly supervised classification of aortic valve malformations using unlabeled cardiac MRI sequences. Nat. Commun. (2019). https://doi.org/10.1101/339630
24. Saab, K., et al.: Doubly weak supervision of deep learning models for head CT. In: Medical Image Computing and Computer Assisted Intervention – MICCAI 2019, pp. 811–819. Springer International Publishing (2019). https://doi.org/10.1007/978-3-030-32248-9_90
25. Devlin, J., Chang, M.-W., Lee, K., Toutanova, K.: BERT: Pre-training of Deep Bidirectional Transformers for Language Understanding. http://arxiv.org/abs/1810.04805, (2018)
26. Radford, A., Narasimhan, K., Salimans, T., Sutskever, I.: Improving Language Understanding by Generative Pre-Training (2018). Accessed 17 June 2023
27. Lan, Z., Chen, M., Goodman, S., Gimpel, K., Sharma, P., Soricut, R.: ALBERT: A Lite BERT for Self-supervised Learning of Language Representations. http://arxiv.org/abs/1909.11942 (2019)
28. Liu, Y., et al.: RoBERTa: A Robustly Optimized BERT Pretraining Approach. http://arxiv.org/abs/1907.11692 (2019)
29. Sanh, V., Debut, L., Chaumond, J., Wolf, T.: DistilBERT, a Distilled Version of BERT: Smaller, Faster, Cheaper and Lighter. http://arxiv.org/abs/1910.01108 (2019)
30. Clark, K., Luong, M.-T., Le, Q.V., Manning, C.D.: ELECTRA: Pre-training Text Encoders as Discriminators Rather Than Generators. http://arxiv.org/abs/2003.10555 (2020)
31. Yang, Z., Dai, Z., Yang, Y., Carbonell, J., Salakhutdinov, R.R., Le, Q.V.: Xlnet: Generalized autoregressive pretraining for language understanding. Adv. Neural Inf. Process. Syst. **32** (2019)

32. Raffel, C., et al.: Exploring the limits of transfer learning with a unified text-to-text transformer. J. Mach. Learn. Res. **21**, 5485–5551 (2020)
33. Shoeybi, M., et al.: Training Multi-Billion Parameter Language Models Using Model Parallelism. http://arxiv.org/abs/1909.08053 (2019)
34. Lewis, M., et al.: BART: Denoising Sequence-to-Sequence Pre-training for Natural Language Generation, Translation, and Comprehension. http://arxiv.org/abs/1910.13461
35. Martin, L., et al.: CamemBERT: a Tasty French Language Model. http://arxiv.org/abs/1911.03894 (2019)
36. Müller, M., Salathé, M., Kummervold, P.E.: COVID-Twitter-BERT: A Natural Language Processing Model to Analyse COVID-19 Content on Twitter. http://arxiv.org/abs/2005.07503 (2020)
37. Lee, J., et al.: BioBERT: a pre-trained biomedical language representation model for biomedical text mining. Bioinformatics **36**, 1234–1240 (2020). https://doi.org/10.1093/bioinformatics/btz682
38. Beltagy, I., Lo, K., Cohan, A.: SciBERT: A Pretrained Language Model for Scientific Text. http://arxiv.org/abs/1903.10676 (2019)
39. Huang, K., Altosaar, J., Ranganath, R.: ClinicalBERT: Modeling Clinical Notes and Predicting Hospital Readmission. http://arxiv.org/abs/1904.05342 (2019)
40. Chalkidis, I., Fergadiotis, M., Malakasiotis, P., Aletras, N., Androutsopoulos, I.: LEGAL-BERT: The Muppets straight out of Law School. http://arxiv.org/abs/2010.02559 (2020)
41. Liu, Z., Huang, D., Huang, K., Li, Z., Zhao, J.: Finbert: A pre-trained financial language representation model for financial text mining. In: Proceedings of the twenty-ninth international conference on international joint conferences on artificial intelligence, pp. 4513–4519 (2021)
42. Yang, Y., Uy, M.C.S., Huang, A.: FinBERT: A Pretrained Language Model for Financial Communications. http://arxiv.org/abs/2006.08097 (2020)
43. Araci, D.: FinBERT: Financial Sentiment Analysis with Pre-trained Language Models. http://arxiv.org/abs/1908.10063 (2019)
44. Radford, A., Wu, J., Child, R., Luan, D., Amodei, D., Sutskever, I.: Language Models are Unsupervised Multitask Learners. https://d4mucfpksywv.cloudfront.net/better-language-models/language_models_are_unsupervised_multitask_learners.pdf (2023)
45. Settles, B.: Active Learning Literature Survey. University of Wisconsin-Madison Department of Computer Sciences (2009)
46. Veselovsky, V., Ribeiro, M.H., West, R.: Artificial Artificial Artificial Intelligence: Crowd Workers Widely Use Large Language Models for Text Production Tasks. http://arxiv.org/abs/2306.07899 (2023)
47. Gilardi, F., Alizadeh, M., Kubli, M.: ChatGPT Outperforms Crowd-Workers for Text-Annotation Tasks. http://arxiv.org/abs/2303.15056 (2023)
48. He, X., et al.: AnnoLLM: Making Large Language Models to Be Better Crowdsourced Annotators. http://arxiv.org/abs/2303.16854 (2023)
49. Møller, A.G., Dalsgaard, J.A., Pera, A., Aiello, L.M.: Is a Prompt and a Few Samples All You Need? Using GPT-4 for Data Augmentation in Low-Resource Classification Tasks. http://arxiv.org/abs/2304.13861 (2023)
50. Huang, F., Kwak, H., An, J.: Is ChatGPT better than Human Annotators? Potential and Limitations of ChatGPT in Explaining Implicit Hate Speech. http://arxiv.org/abs/2302.07736
51. Yu, D., Li, L., Su, H., Fuoli, M.: Using LLM-Assisted Annotation for Corpus Linguistics: A Case Study of Local Grammar Analysis, http://arxiv.org/abs/2305.08339 (2023)
52. Kuzman, T., Mozetic, I., Ljubešic, N.: Chatgpt: Beginning of an End of Manual Linguistic Data Annotation? Use Case of Automatic Genre Identification. arXiv e-prints, arXiv--2303 (2023)
53. Zhu, Y., Zhang, P., Haq, E.-U., Hui, P., Tyson, G.: Can ChatGPT Reproduce Human-Generated Labels? A Study of Social Computing Tasks. http://arxiv.org/abs/2304.10145 (2023)

54. Bender, E.M., Gebru, T., McMillan-Major, A., Shmitchell, S.: On the dangers of stochastic parrots: can language models be too big? 🦜. In: Proceedings of the 2021 ACM Conference on Fairness, Accountability, and Transparency, pp. 610–623. Association for Computing Machinery, New York, NY, USA (2021). https://doi.org/10.1145/3442188.3445922
55. Reiss, M.V.: Testing the Reliability of ChatGPT for Text Annotation and Classification: A Cautionary Remark. http://arxiv.org/abs/2304.11085 (2023)
56. Beware the Hype: ChatGPT didn't Replace Human Data Annotators. https://news.techworkerscoalition.org/2023/04/04/issue-5/. Accessed 17 June 2023
57. Banda, J.M., et al.: A large-scale COVID-19 twitter chatter dataset for open scientific research—an international collaboration. Epidemiologia. **2**, 315–324 (2021). https://doi.org/10.3390/epidemiologia2030024
58. Weissenbacher, D., Banda, J., Davydova, V., et al.: Overview of the seventh social media mining for health applications (#SMM4H) shared tasks at COLING 2022. In: Proceedings of The Seventh Workshop on Social Media Mining for Health Applications, Workshop & Shared Task, pp. 221–241. Association for Computational Linguistics, Gyeongju, Republic of Korea (2022)
59. Tekumalla, R., Asl, J.R., Banda, J.M.: Mining archive.org's twitter stream grab for pharmacovigilance research gold. ICWSM. **14**, 909–917 (2020). https://doi.org/10.1609/icwsm.v14i1.7357
60. Solmaz, G., Cirillo, F., Maresca, F., Kumar, A.G.A.: Label Augmentation with Reinforced Labeling for Weak Supervision. http://arxiv.org/abs/2204.06436 (2022)
61. Robinson, J., Jegelka, S., Sra, S.: Strength from weakness: fast learning using weak supervision. In: Iii, H.D., Singh, A. (eds.) Proceedings of the 37th International Conference on Machine Learning, pp. 8127–8136. PMLR (13--18 Jul 2020)
62. Nguyen, D.Q., Vu, T., Tuan Nguyen, A.: BERTweet: a pre-trained language model for english tweets. In: Proceedings of the 2020 Conference on Empirical Methods in Natural Language Processing: System Demonstrations, pp. 9–14. Association for Computational Linguistics, Online (2020). https://doi.org/10.18653/v1/2020.emnlp-demos.2
63. Magge, A., et al.: Overview of the sixth social media mining for health applications (#SMM4H) shared tasks at NAACL 2021. In: Proceedings of the Sixth Social Media Mining for Health (#SMM4H) Workshop and Shared Task, pp. 21–32. Association for Computational Linguistics, Mexico City, Mexico (2021). https://doi.org/10.18653/v1/2021.smm4h-1.4
64. AWS Pricing Calculator. https://calculator.aws/#/addService/SageMakerGroundTruth. Accessed 22 June 2023
65. Cohen, J.: A coefficient of agreement for nominal scales. Educ. Psychol. Meas. **20**, 37–46 (1960). https://doi.org/10.1177/001316446002000104
66. McHugh, M.L.: Interrater reliability: the kappa statistic. Biochem. Med.. Med. **22**, 276–282 (2012). https://doi.org/10.1016/j.jocd.2012.03.005
67. Fleiss, J.L.: Measuring nominal scale agreement among many raters. Psychol. Bull. **76**, 378–382 (1971). https://doi.org/10.1037/h0031619

Analysis of User Diversity-Based Patterns of Public Discourse on Twitter About Mental Health in the Context of Online Learning During COVID-19

Nirmalya Thakur(✉), Hazel Cho, Haokun Cheng, and Hyunji Lee

Department of Computer Science, Emory University, Atlanta, GA 30322, USA
{nirmalya.thakur,hazel.cho,haokun.cheng,hyunji.lee}@emory.edu

Abstract. This work focuses on the analysis of user diversity-based patterns of the public discourse on Twitter about mental health in the context of online learning during COVID-19. Two aspects of user diversity – gender and location are the focus of this work. A dataset comprising 52,984 Tweets about online learning during COVID-19, posted on Twitter between November 9, 2021, and July 13, 2022, was used for this analysis. A Bag of Words model comprising 218 keywords related to mental health was developed and used to categorize the Tweets into two topics – Tweets that focused on mental health in the context of online learning during COVID-19 (Topic 1) and Tweets that did not focus on mental health in the context of online learning during COVID-19 (Topic 2). Thereafter, two algorithms were developed to infer the gender and location of a Twitter user based on their Twitter username and the location listed on their Twitter account, respectively. The results of this work present several novel findings. First, for Topic 1, a higher percentage of the Tweets were posted by females as compared to males. However, for Topic 2, a higher percentage of the Tweets were posted by males as compared to females. Second, Twitter users from 193 countries posted about Topic 1, and Twitter users from 228 countries posted about Topic 2. Third, the highest number of Tweets on Topic 1 and Topic 2 were posted by Twitter users from the United States. Finally, the work also reports the gender-based Tweeting patterns on Topic 1 and Topic 2 from different countries. For instance, in the United States, for Topic 1, a higher percentage of the Tweets were posted by females as compared to males. However, for Topic 2, males posted a higher percentage of Tweets as compared to females.

Keywords: COVID-19 · Online Learning · Twitter · Big Data · Data Analysis

1 Introduction

According to the Mental Health Action Plan proposed by the World Health Organization (WHO), it is the need of the hour to strengthen "*information systems, evidence, and research*" for supporting, monitoring, and assisting mental health [1]. Some of the common mental disorders include – Anxiety Disorders, Depression, Bipolar Disorder,

H. Mori et al. (Eds.): HCII 2023, LNCS 14056, pp. 367–389, 2023.
https://doi.org/10.1007/978-3-031-48044-7_27

Schizophrenia, Eating Disorders (nervosa and bulimia nervosa), Disruptive Behavior, and Dissocial Disorders. By 2030 the worldwide cost of providing care to individuals with mental disorders is expected to reach $6 trillion annually [2]. Mental disorders may be broadly categorized as Any Mental Illness (AMI) and Serious Mental Illness (SMI). Prior works in this field have focused on studying two major characteristics of user diversity in this context – gender and location. The findings of a recent study showed that AMI and SMI were found to be higher in females than in males. This study also showed that the prevalence of AMI and SMI were lowest among Asian adults [3, 4].

As a result of the rapid spread of the SARS-CoV-2 virus since the initial outbreak in December 2019 [5], many countries declared a lockdown to reduce the spread of the virus. Therefore, several universities, colleges, and schools across the world were required to transition to online learning to continue education. This rapid transition to online learning was associated with stress, depression, frustration, anxiety, and insomnia in students as well as educators [6]. Therefore, understanding and analyzing the extent to which various sectors of the population experienced mental disorders or communicated about mental health problems in the context of online learning during COVID-19 becomes crucial to investigate. The ubiquitousness of social media platforms, specifically Twitter, makes it a rich resource for sharing and seeking information on diverse topics such as ChatGPT [7], the Russia–Ukraine war [8], cryptocurrency markets [9], virtual assistants [10], loneliness in the elderly [11], housing needs of low-income families [12], fake news [13], abortion [14], religion [15], cognitive impairment [16], gender identity [17], elections [18], fall detection [19, 20], drug safety [21], pregnancy [22], food insufficiency [23], indoor localization [24], education [25], exoskeletons [26], MPox outbreak [27], and COVID-19 outbreak [28–33], just to name a few. In addition to being a resource for sharing and seeking information on diverse topics, Twitter has also been referred to as an *"online community"* [34] that provides *"helping hands"* [35] to people seeking help related to mental health. Mining and analysis of such conversations on Twitter have been of significant interest to researchers in this field in the last few years, as can be seen from the recent works that analyzed Tweets containing specific hashtags such as #depression [36], #schizophrenia [37], #mydepressionlookslike [38], #dearmentalhealthprofessionals [39], and #WhyWeTweetMH [40]. However, these works have two major limitations. First, these specific hashtags represent only a limited number of mental disorders. Second, these works did not focus on Tweets about mental health in the context of online learning during COVID-19. The interdisciplinary work proposed in this paper at the intersections of Big Data, Data Analysis, Natural Language Processing, and Data Science aims to address these limitations. The rest of this paper is organized as follows. A review of recent works in this field is presented in Sect. 2. Section 3 presents the methodology that was followed. The results are presented and discussed in Sect. 4. Section 5 presents the conclusions and outlines the scope for future work. It is followed by references.

2 Literature Review

The outbreak of COVID-19 served as a "catalyst" for Twitter usage for seeking and sharing information, news, views, opinions, perspectives, ideas, awareness, comments, and experiences on various topics related to the outbreak. This resulted in the generation of tremendous amounts of Big Data. Mining and analysis of this Big Data have been of significant interest to data scientists, computer science researchers, healthcare researchers, epidemiologists, and medical practitioners, as is evident from the recent works in this field. This review of recent works in this context is divided into two sections. Section 2.1 outlines the recent works in this field that focused on the analysis of Tweets about mental health in the context of COVID-19. Section 2.2 outlines the recent works in this field that focused on the analysis of Tweets about online learning during COVID-19.

2.1 Recent Works that Focused on the Analysis of Tweets about Mental Health in the Context of COVID-19

Valdez et al. [41] analyzed a total of 86,581,237 Tweets from a dataset. The results from topic modeling by the Latent Dirichlet Allocation (LDA) approach showed that the Tweets that were mined early in the dataset had topics that were directly linked to specific COVID-19 occurrences. However, when state and local governments began issuing stay-at-home orders, underlying topics changed from worldwide pandemic-related occurrences to US-related lifestyle adjustments. Zhang et al. [42] collected COVID-19-related tweets from March 5, 2020, to January 31, 2021. Thereafter the authors applied data filters to filter Tweets that contained one of these keywords - "depress", "failure", and "hopeless". The results showed that there was a positive correlation between mental health concerns on Twitter and the COVID-19 pandemic in the US. In the work by Jansli et al. [43], a total of 2,700 tweets related to seven mental health conditions: schizophrenia, depression, anxiety, autism, eating disorders, OCD, and addiction, were collected by the authors. The authors aimed to investigate how COVID-19 affected mental health-related conversations on Twitter. The results showed that 40.8% of the Tweets were stigmatizing. Sadasivuni et al. [44] collected 3,18,847 Tweets about COVID-19. The findings showed that the rate of growth of the number of Tweets that communicated depression and the number of Tweets that did not communicate depression was similar till March 11, 2020. El-Gayar et al. [45] analyzed 273 million Tweets on mental health in the context of COVID-19. The findings revealed a substantial shift in the trend of the number of Tweets on mental health over time. The findings also showed that there was a significant rise in the number of Tweets related to depression, anxiety, stress, and suicide.

Massel et al. [46] analyzed Tweets by 4735 Twitter users related to mental health and COVID-19. The authors applied mixed negative binomial regression models to estimate monthly word counts prior to and during the pandemic. The findings showed that there was a significant increase in grief, worry, anger, and concerns about home and health at that time. The work by Jones et al. [47] focused on understanding the emotional response to COVID-19 information in news and social media. Cohrdes et al. [48] focused on performing two types of analysis in their study. These included studying the temporal progression of depressive symptoms in the context of COVID-19 as expressed on Twitter and the consistency of the results from Tweets and survey-based self-reports of depressive symptoms during the same timeline. The findings showed that fatigue or loss of energy were the most frequently reported depressive symptoms, and feelings of worthlessness were the least reported depressive symptoms. Zhang et al. [49] designed a regular expression-based search method and created a Twitter depression data set containing 2575 distinct identified users with depression and their past tweets. They trained 3 transformer-based depression classification models on the data set, evaluated their performance with increasingly larger training sizes, and then analyzed the model's Tweet chunk-level and user-level results. Koh et al. [50] studied Tweets that focused on loneliness during the outbreak of COVID-19. Ghosh et al. [51] proposed a methodology based on long-short term memory (LSTM) and convolutional neural networks (CNN) that could recognize Tweets that focused on depression during COVID-19 with an accuracy of 99.42%. Levanti et al. [52] collected 18 million Tweets from 7 US cities: Atlanta, Chicago, Houston, Los Angeles, Miami, New York, and Phoenix, and performed a comprehensive analysis of the same. The findings showed that the degree of depression and anxiety was elevated in all these cities during the outbreak. The study by Leung et al. [53] focused on the analysis of anxiety related to panic buying during the pandemic, as expressed on Twitter. Zhong et al.'s work [54] was aimed at studying depression and any secondary trauma as expressed by the residents of Wuhan during the pandemic. Akhther et al. [55] performed a cross-sectional online survey to explore self-ratings of anxiety and depression, perceived peer support, and perceived health advantages of social media during the pandemic. The works of Blair et al. [56] and Ye et al. [57] focused on the analysis of Tweets to investigate the mental well-being of essential workers and college students, respectively, during the COVID-19 pandemic. The work done by Ueda et al. [58] showed that the emotional distress in Twitter users in Japan (in the age group of 18 to 49) increased when the closure of schools took place in March 2020, and the emotional distress peaked in April 2020 when a state of emergency in the context of COVID-19 was declared in Japan.

2.2 Recent Works that Focused on the Analysis of Tweets About Online Learning During COVID-19

Asare et al. [59] performed sentiment analysis and topic modeling of Tweets about online learning during COVID-19, posted between March 10, 2020, and July 25, 2020. The findings showed that there were more positive and negative sentiments expressed in the Tweets as compared to neutral sentiments. The findings also showed that the topics these Tweets focused on were learning support, COVID-19, online learning, schools, distance learning, e-learning, students, and education. The work of Alwafi et al. [60] focused on analyzing the structure and content of conversation by educators on Twitter both before and during the pandemic. Trust et al. [61] collected 10,444 Tweets posted between March 15, 2020, and April 15, 2020, comprising the hashtags #RemoteTeaching and #RemoteLearning, and performed sentiment analysis of the same. The results indicated that 58% of these Tweets were neutral, 36% were positive, and 5% were negative. The authors also performed various forms of text analysis of these Tweets. The work of Almossa et al. [62] analyzed Tweets about online learning posted by students from Saudi Arabia. The study involved the analysis of 124,810 Tweets posted between March 2020 and May 2020. The findings of this study showed that the degree of engagement of students towards online learning and online assessments was affected on account of COVID-19.

Alswedani et al. [63] performed topic modeling of Tweets about online learning posted by individuals from Saudi Arabia. A total of 128,805 Tweets posted between

October 1, 2020, and December 6, 2020, were analyzed in this study. The authors used LDA and identified 10 topics related to urban governance parameters in the Tweets. The work of Al-Obeidat et al. [64] involved a sentiment analysis-based approach to understand the perceptions of students about online learning during the COVID-19 pandemic. The sentiments detected from the Tweets were categorized into positive, negative, and neutral. In addition to this, the authors also used the term frequency-inverse document frequency (TF-IDF) techniques to examine the attitudes toward online learning as expressed in the Tweets. Senadhira et al. [65] performed sentiment analysis of Tweets about online learning during COVID-19. A total of 8976 Tweets were analyzed by the authors. The findings showed that 4486 Tweets had a positive sentiment, and 4490 Tweets had a negative sentiment. A similar sentiment analysis-based study was performed by Patil et al. [66]. Zhou et al. [67] studied the opinion of Chinese students towards online learning at three different timelines, as expressed on Sina Weibo Microblogs (the Chinese equivalent of Twitter). The three timelines, as stated in this study, were July 1, 2019, to January 9, 2020 (before the pandemic), January 10, 2020, to April 30, 2020 (during the pandemic), and May 1, 2020, to November 30, 2020 (after the pandemic). Based on this analysis, the study reported the perceptions and opinions towards online learning during these timelines. The work by Ali [68] focused on performing sentiment analysis of Tweets that were posted in the Arabic language where the theme of conversations was online learning during COVID-19. The authors used 2 datasets for their study. The datasets contained Tweets about online learning and COVID-19, which were posted between September 20, 2020, and October 15, 2020. The study reported the number of positive and negative Tweets in each of these datasets. The author also performed text analysis of these Tweets and reported the number of words, unique words, average number of words, and average number of characters in each Tweet. The work by Jogezai et al. [69] focused on studying the attitudes of educators toward social media usage in online learning during the COVID-19 pandemic. Ewing et al.'s work [70] focused on identifying themes of conversation on Twitter related to online learning in Australia during the COVID-19 pandemic. A total of 10,421 tweets posted between April 2020 and May 2020 were studied in this work. A total of 9 themes were identified by the authors.

As can be seen from the recent works reviewed in Sect. 2.1 and Sect. 2.2, there hasn't been any study conducted in this field thus far that focuses on analyzing conversations on Twitter about mental health in the context of online learning during COVID-19. The work presented in this paper aims to address this research gap. The methodology that was followed for this work is described in Sect. 3.

3 Methodology

The section is divided into two parts. Section 3.1 describes the dataset that was used for this work. This section also states the steps that were followed for the hydration of the Tweet IDs that are present in this dataset. Section 3.2 presents the step-by-step methodology that was followed after the Tweet IDs were hydrated.

3.1 Description of the Dataset, Hydration of Tweet IDs, and Data Filtering

The dataset that was used in this work was proposed in a recent work [71] in this field. This dataset contains a total of 52,984 Tweet IDs of the same number of Tweets that focused on online learning and COVID-19 at the same time. The Tweets in this dataset were posted on Twitter between November 9, 2021, and July 13, 2022. The development of this dataset involved searching for Tweets on Twitter in this time range based on the presence of at least one synonym of COVID-19 and one synonym of online learning in the Tweets. As this dataset contains only Tweet IDs, the Tweet IDs had to be hydrated. The process of retrieving a Tweet's complete information using its ID is known as the hydration of a Tweet ID. To hydrate these Tweet IDs, the Hydrator app [72] was used. The Hydrator app operates by adhering to the Twitter API regulations as well as the rate constraints for accessing the Twitter API. The Tweet IDs in this dataset are present as 9.txt files. These.txt files were merged and provided as input to the Hydrator app. The output, upon completion of the hydration of all these Tweet IDs, was a.csv file that contained the text of these respective Tweets along with specific information related to these Tweets, such as created_at, hashtags, URLs, favorite_count, place, user_location, etc. A total of 49,408 Tweets were obtained after the hydration of these Tweet IDs. It is worth stating here that Twitter introduced multiple updates to the Twitter API in April 2023. On account of these updates, the Hydrator app is no longer functional for the hydration of Tweet IDs. However, the hydration of these Tweet IDs from this dataset

Table 1. List of 218 keywords related to mental health that were used for filtering the relevant Tweets.

List of Keywords
alone, helpless, heartbroken, cries, mental illness, bipolar, depressing, emptiness fail, tears, mourn, damaging, sorrow, disillusion, sad, whining, solemn, defeating, isolation, suicidal, inferiority, losing, unhappy, tired of living, lone, hurting, not worth living, mental disorder, depressed, disillusioned, panic, stress, whine, wept, longing, inadequate, anxiety, depression, don't want to be here, sobbing, isolate, depress, indecisive, grief, deprive, yearn, gloom, discouraging, sleep forever, useless, fear, pessimistic, lost, neglect, medications, self-harm, suicide pact, failure, dull, homesick, abuse, cremation, groggy, disheartening, tragic, devastation, medication, ready to jump, agonizing, disadvantage, dazed, shock, pain, damage, loser, reject, restless, suicide plan, flunk, miser, melancholy, grim, weep, agony, dissatisfaction, doom, resign, hallucination, go to sleep forever, overwhelm, inferior, mental health, hopeless, empty, kill myself, death, isolation, sobbed, tired, guilt, dishearten, fatigue, grieved, disheartened, divorce, lame, pity, woe, , discourage, longingness, loss, be dead, heartbreaking, die, grieving, disappointing, broke, jitter, deprivation, my suicide note, end my life, funeral, discouraged, Emotion, mental disorders, devastated, broken me, sobs, better off dead, cried, heartbreak, emotions, burden, loses, want to die, ruin, hallucinations, pitiful, suicide, my suicide letter, tragedy, insomnia, die alone, remorse, damaged defeat, defeated, grave, doctor, dissatisfied, worthless, cry, appetite, lonely, unsuccessful, deprived despair, pathetic, regret, disappointed, never wake up, ache, better off without me, indecisiveness, crushed, can't go on, lose, hurt, abandon, unhappiness, aching, end life, unimportant, hurtful, suffer

was performed in February 2023. So, the recent updates to the Twitter API did not have any effect on this study.

After hydrating these Tweet IDs, the next step was to identify those Tweets that focused on mental health based on keywords. To develop this list of keywords, recent works in this field [41–58, 73–77] that focused on keyword-based mining or keyword-based analysis of Tweets related to mental health were studied, and a list of 218 keywords related to mental health was compiled to develop a Bag of Words. This list of 218 keywords is presented in Table 1.

Using this Bag of Words, the Tweets were divided into two topics - Tweets that focused on mental health in the context of online learning during COVID-19 (Topic 1) and Tweets that did not focus on mental health in the context of online learning during COVID-19 (Topic 2). A total of 14443 Tweets were categorized as Topic 1, and 34965 Tweets were categorized as Topic 2. Thereafter, the Tweets in these respective categories were analyzed to infer the diversity-based (gender and location) patterns of the public discourse related to each of these topics. The associated methodology that was followed in this context is described in Sect. 3.2.

3.2 Methodology for Diversity-Based (Gender and Location) Analysis of Tweets that Focused on Topic 1 and Topic 2

The result of the hydration of these Tweet IDs provided the publicly available usernames of each Twitter user who posted the Tweets. This information was retained during the categorization of the Tweets into Topic 1 and Topic 2, respectively. The usernames of Twitter users were used to detect their genders. To perform the same, an algorithm was developed by using the GenderPerformr package in Python [78]. The GenderPerformr package is a methodology that predicts gender from names based on an LSTM model built in PyTorch. The working of this algorithm involved classifying Twitter usernames into 4 categories – male, female, none, and maybe. The algorithm was developed and implemented in Python 3.10 installed on a computer with a Microsoft Windows 10 Pro operating system (Version 10.0.19043 Build 19043) comprising Intel(R) Core (TM) i7-7600U CPU @ 2.80 GHz, 2904 MHz, 2 Core(s) and 4 Logical Processor(s). The algorithm classified a username as ‘male’ if that username matched a male name from the list of male names accessible to this Python package. Similarly, the algorithm classified a username as ‘female’ if that username matched a female name from the list of female names accessible to this Python package. The algorithm classified a username as ‘none’ if that username was a word in the English dictionary that cannot be a person’s name. Finally, the algorithm classified a username as ‘maybe’ if the username was a word absent in the list of male and female names accessible to this Python package and the username was also not an English word. A total of 30,553 usernames from Topic 1 and Topic 2 combined were classified as ‘maybe’ by this algorithm. This list of 30,553 usernames was then manually labeled and classified as ‘male’, ‘female’, or ‘none’ by the authors of this paper. A recent work in this field [79] stated the process of agreement between annotators during data labeling. So, the classification of these usernames was performed by the authors of this paper based on mutual agreement of the classification labels. The sequence of steps that were followed in this regard is outlined in the flowchart presented in Fig. 1.

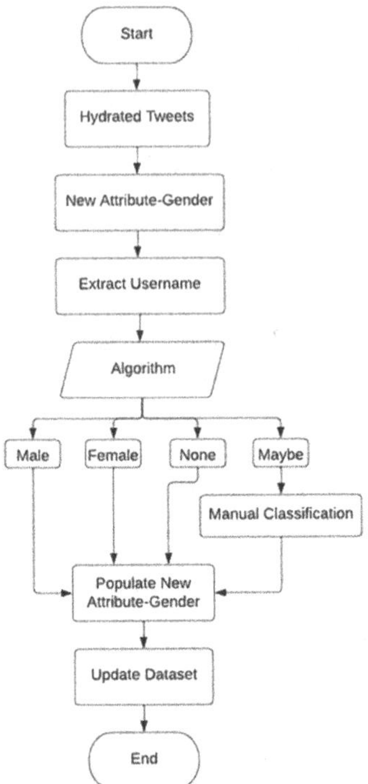

Fig. 1. Flowchart of the methodology that was followed for detecting the gender of a user from their Twitter username.

The results of gender detection from both these topics are presented and discussed in Sect. 4. After completing the steps for gender detection, location detection was performed. This involved analysis of the attribute – user_location, which was obtained upon hydration of the Tweet IDs. This attribute was also retained during the categorization of the Tweets into Topic 1 and Topic 2. This attribute represented the publicly listed location of each Twitter user who posted the Tweets in the dataset. To detect the location (country) based on the city, state, county, region, or country information that was publicly listed on a user's Twitter profile as their location, the PyCountry package in Python was used. A program was written in Python 3.10 that used PyCountry 22.3.5.

The PyCountry package uses ISO 3166 to detect a country based on the city, state, county, and region. If the value of the user_location was None, null, NaN, or an empty string, the result of country detection was "none". If the value of the user_location was not None, null, NaN, or an empty string, the program removed all non-word characters from the value of this variable using a regular expression. Thereafter, the data was analyzed using the search fuzzy method to deduce if the user_location comprised the name of a country or comprised the names of a city, state, county, or region of a country. For the former scenario, the presence of a country name directly provided information on the user's location (country). For the latter scenario, the methods of this package were used to deduce the user's location (country). After deducing the location of all the Twitter

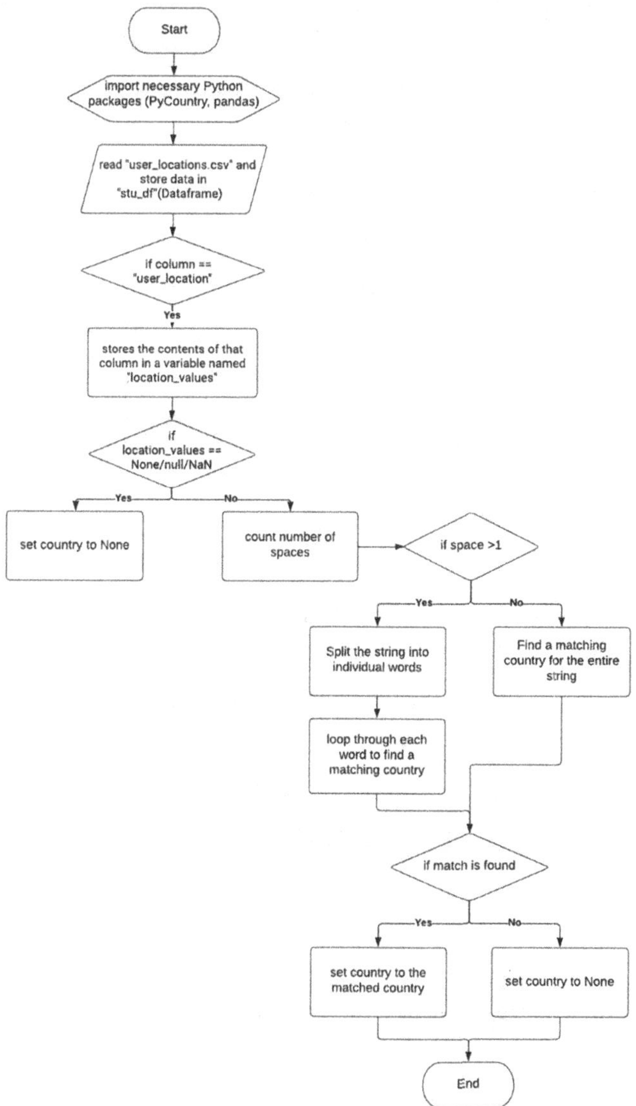

Fig. 2. Flowchart of the methodology that was followed for detecting the location (country) of a user from the publicly listed location information on their Twitter account.

users associated with these Tweets, the authors of this paper manually reviewed all the locations and corrected any inaccuracies. This step-by-step methodology is represented as a flowchart in Fig. 2. The results of applying this approach to the Tweets in both topics – Topic 1 and Topic 2 are discussed and presented in Sect. 4. Figure 3 summarizes the entire methodology of the work of this paper as described in this section.

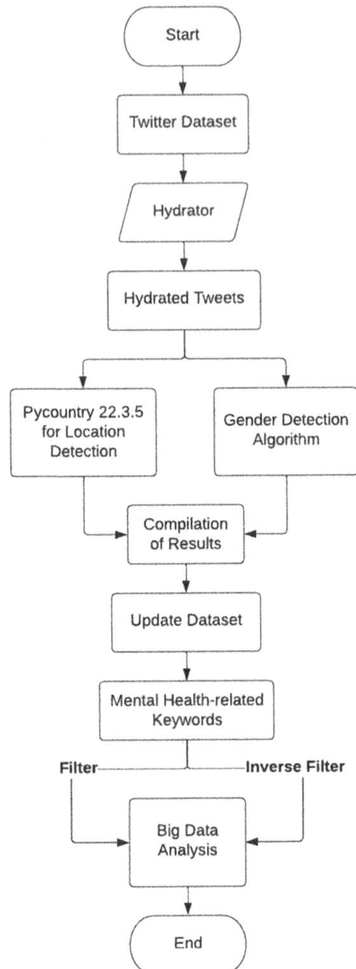

Fig. 3. Flowchart of the overall methodology that was followed in this research work.

4 Results and Discussions

The section presents the results of this research work. In Topic 1, there were a total of 14443 Tweets. Out of these Tweets, males posted 3308 Tweets, and females posted 3454 Tweets, respectively. The remaining 7681 Tweets were posted from Twitter accounts (such as a company, university, school, etc.) to which gender could not be attributed. This is represented in Fig. 4. In Topic 2, there were a total of 34965 Tweets. Out of these Tweets, males posted 8638 Tweets, and females posted 6308 Tweets, respectively. The remaining 20019 Tweets were posted from Twitter accounts (such as a company, university, school, etc.) to which gender could not be attributed. This is represented in Fig. 5.

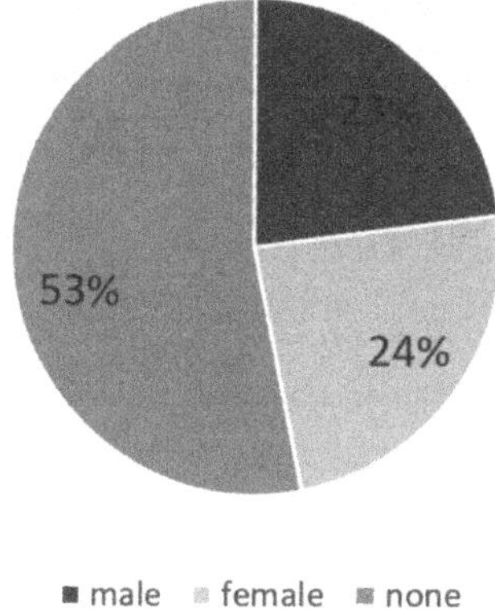

Fig. 4. Percentage of Tweets on Topic 1 posted by different genders. Here, the percentage values were rounded off to the next integer.

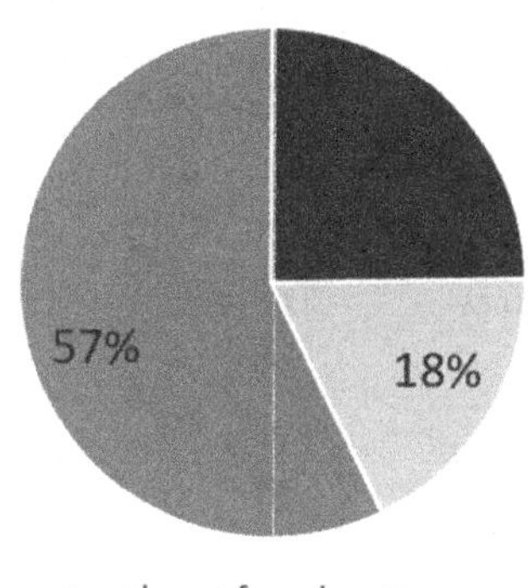

Fig. 5. Percentage of Tweets on Topic 1 posted by different genders. Here, the percentage values were rounded off to the next integer.

As can be seen from Figs. 4 and 5, for Topic 1, a higher percentage of the Tweets were posted by females as compared to males. However, for Topic 2, a higher percentage of the Tweets were posted by males as compared to females. In terms of the location of the Twitter users, who posted Tweets that were categorized as Topic 1, the results are shown in Table 2. In this Table, the names of different countries and the number of Twitter users from each of these countries who posted Tweets that were categorized as Topic 1 are presented. Tweets that were categorized as Topic 1 were posted by Twitter users from a total of 193 countries. For the paucity of space, the top 50 countries (in terms of the number of Tweets) are listed in Table 2.

Table 2. Results of location detection for the Tweets in Topic 1.

Country	Number of Tweets	Country	Number of Tweets
United States	3404	Netherlands	37
United Kingdom	1032	France	36
India	884	Austria	34
Canada	827	Bulgaria	33
Australia	311	Dominican Republic	31
Eritrea	102	Fiji	31
Cameroon	100	New Zealand	30
Ireland	96	Cabo Verde	29

(continued)

Table 2. (*continued*)

Country	Number of Tweets	Country	Number of Tweets
Germany	95	Chile	29
Bangladesh	77	Comoros	28
Philippines	68	Latvia	27
Iceland	65	Malaysia	27
Kenya	62	Slovenia	23
Uganda	57	United Arab Emirates	23
Italy	53	Argentina	22
South Africa	49	Nigeria	22
Switzerland	48	Bahamas	21
Pakistan	47	Morocco	21
Botswana	43	Belgium	20
China	42	Japan	20
Ghana	42	Indonesia	19
Spain	42	Norway	19
Sweden	41	Thailand	19
Panama	39	Sao Tome and Principe	18
Jamaica	37	Czechia	17

In a similar manner, the locations of the Twitter users who posted Tweets that were categorized as Topic 2 were detected. A total of 228 countries were represented in the locations of Twitter users who posted these Tweets. Once again, for the paucity of space, the top 50 countries (in terms of the number of Tweets) are shown in Table 3.

Table 3. Results of location detection for all the Tweets in Topic 2.

Country	Number of Tweets	Country	Number of Tweets
United States	8212	Kazakhstan	86
India	2688	Singapore	86
United Kingdom	1863	Chile	84
Canada	1782	Botswana	83
Australia	421	United Arab Emirates	81
Spain	290	Bulgaria	80
Philippines	287	Dominican Republic	76
Cameroon	282	Comoros	70

(*continued*)

Table 3. *(continued)*

Country	Number of Tweets	Country	Number of Tweets
Bangladesh	253	Indonesia	68
Eritrea	241	Slovenia	68
Germany	177	Jamaica	64
Uganda	158	New Zealand	63
Ireland	150	Netherlands	62
South Africa	149	China	61
Pakistan	143	Thailand	60
Malaysia	137	Argentina	55
Kenya	131	Bahamas	55
Iceland	121	Estonia	55
France	118	Norway	54
Italy	116	Sao Tome and Principe	53
Cabo Verde	115	Latvia	51
Sweden	100	Fiji	50
Switzerland	98	Nigeria	50
Ghana	92	Austria	49
Panama	87	Slovakia	49

As can be seen from Tables 2 and 3, Twitter users from the United States posted the highest number of Tweets on Topic 1 as well as Topic 2. However, there were differences in these Tweeting patterns for both topics from several other countries. Thereafter, the country-specific Tweeting patterns for both these topics were analyzed. This is presented in Table 4. As mentioned earlier in this section, a total of 193 countries and 228 countries were represented in the user locations of Tweets, which were categorized as Topic 1 and Topic 2, respectively. So, for the paucity of space, Table 4 presents the data of 87 countries that were represented in Topic 1 as well as in Topic 2. For each of these countries, the percentage of Tweets posted by males and by females are listed in this Table. Before performing this analysis for each country, the number of Tweets for which the usernames were assigned a gender – 'none' were subtracted from the total number of Tweets. This was performed to infer what percentage of the total number of Tweets posted by males and females, were posted by either gender, for both these topics. As can be seen from this Table, the Tweeting patterns from males and females varied for different countries. For instance, in the United States, for Topic 1, a higher percentage of the Tweets were posted by females as compared to males. However, for Topic 2, males posted a higher percentage of Tweets as compared to females. A similar pattern was observed in the United Kingdom. However, in Australia, females posted a higher percentage of Tweets for both these Topics as compared to males. A different pattern was observed in Malaysia. For Topic 1, the percentage of Tweets posted by males and females was the same. However, for Topic 2, males posted more Tweets as compared to females. Another pattern of Tweeting was observed in India. The results showed that for both topics, in India, males posted more Tweets as compared to females. In this context, the authors would like to clarify that the work of this paper presents the results of a comprehensive analysis performed on these Tweets. These results are presented in "as-is" form and are not presented with the intention to comment on any gender directly or indirectly. Furthermore, the authors respect the gender identity of every individual and do not intend to comment on the same in any manner by presenting these results.

Table 4. Results of gender-based Tweeting patterns from different countries for Topic 1 and Topic 2.

Country	Topic 1		Topic 2	
	Percentage of Tweets by Males	Percentage of Tweets by Females	Percentage of Tweets by Males	Percentage of Tweets by Females
India	75.21368	24.78632	78.40376	21.59624
United States	47.27389	52.72611	50.43304	49.56696
Spain	56.25	43.75	64.58333	35.41667
Pakistan	81.48148	18.51852	65.71429	34.28571
France	30	70	55.88235	44.11765
Indonesia	33.33333	66.66667	59.25926	40.74074
Cameroon	50	50	57.00935	42.99065
Estonia	50	50	33.33333	66.66667
Philippines	58.33333	41.66667	61.44578	38.55422
South Africa	45.45455	54.54545	50	50
Austria	33.33333	66.66667	50	50
Canada	42.79661	57.20339	47.75726	52.24274
Fiji	53.33333	46.66667	77.27273	22.72727
Australia	33.08824	66.91176	40.72165	59.27835
United Kingdom	45.39615	54.60385	53.60825	46.39175
China	53.33333	46.66667	76.47059	23.52941
Malaysia	50	50	56	44
Somalia	44.44444	55.55556	47.05882	52.94118
New Zealand	33.33333	66.66667	61.76471	38.23529
Nigeria	50	50	50	50
Belgium	81.81818	18.18182	65.38462	34.61538

(*continued*)

Table 4. (*continued*)

Country	Topic 1		Topic 2	
	Percentage of Tweets by Males	Percentage of Tweets by Females	Percentage of Tweets by Males	Percentage of Tweets by Females
Germany	38.59649	61.40351	55.38462	44.61538
Uganda	55.17241	44.82759	61.53846	38.46154
Sao Tome and Principe	50	50	56.66667	43.33333
Switzerland	71.42857	28.57143	52.17391	47.82609
Brazil	80	20	72.72727	27.27273
Japan	42.85714	57.14286	52.94118	47.05882
Ireland	59.52381	40.47619	43.85965	56.14035
Marshall Islands	50	50	66.66667	33.33333
Jamaica	72.22222	27.77778	50	50
Trinidad and Tobago	40	60	87.5	12.5
Taiwan	80	20	44.44444	55.55556
Croatia	80	20	80	20
Eritrea	41.02564	58.97436	52.68817	47.31183
Cabo Verde	57.14286	42.85714	44.44444	55.55556
Saint Kitts and Nevis	50	50	75	25
Ghana	44.44444	55.55556	51.6129	48.3871
Slovenia	30.76923	69.23077	34.48276	65.51724
Norway	77.77778	22.22222	72.22222	27.77778
Lebanon	50	50	75	25
Kenya	52.38095	47.61905	65.11628	34.88372
Korea Republic of	33.33333	66.66667	33.33333	66.66667
Singapore	50	50	95.45455	4.545455
Greece	28.57143	71.42857	62.5	37.5
Bangladesh	48.64865	51.35135	52.32558	47.67442
Malta	66.66667	33.33333	46.15385	53.84615
Italy	63.63636	36.36364	58.13953	41.86047

(*continued*)

Table 4. (*continued*)

Country	Topic 1		Topic 2	
	Percentage of Tweets by Males	Percentage of Tweets by Females	Percentage of Tweets by Males	Percentage of Tweets by Females
Zimbabwe	33.33333	66.66667	77.77778	22.22222
Finland	42.85714	57.14286	41.66667	58.33333
Netherlands	34.78261	65.21739	46.66667	53.33333
Panama	50	50	70.58824	29.41176
Latvia	40	60	47.36842	52.63158
Morocco	57.14286	42.85714	38.46154	61.53846
Kazakhstan	33.33333	66.66667	51.72414	48.27586
Iceland	48	52	45.71429	54.28571
Georgia	20	80	42.85714	57.14286
Dominican Republic	58.82353	41.17647	51.51515	48.48485
Chile	57.14286	42.85714	60	40
Czechia	16.66667	83.33333	23.52941	76.47059
Colombia	37.5	62.5	42.85714	57.14286
Belize	50	50	20	80
Sweden	35.71429	64.28571	39.53488	60.46512
Argentina	40	60	40	60
Bahamas	33.33333	66.66667	40	60
Bulgaria	55.55556	44.44444	68	32
Comoros	35.71429	64.28571	40	60
Portugal	25	75	92.30769	7.692308
Sri Lanka	25	75	44.44444	55.55556
Botswana	33.33333	66.66667	60.86957	39.13043
Russia	60	40	55.55556	44.44444
Sierra Leone	50	50	28	72
Sudan	25	75	12.5	87.5
Mexico	83.33333	16.66667	85.71429	14.28571
Denmark	66.66667	33.33333	85.71429	14.28571
Viet Nam	66.66667	33.33333	30.76923	69.23077

(*continued*)

Table 4. (*continued*)

Country	Topic 1		Topic 2	
	Percentage of Tweets by Males	Percentage of Tweets by Females	Percentage of Tweets by Males	Percentage of Tweets by Females
Jersey	28.57143	71.42857	14.28571	85.71429
Luxembourg	66.66667	33.33333	61.53846	38.46154
South Sudan	14.28571	85.71429	50	50
Azerbaijan	20	80	80	20
United Arab Emirates	44.44444	55.55556	59.09091	40.90909
Serbia	25	75	60	40
Israel	50	50	66.66667	33.33333
Tanzania	60	40	62.5	37.5
Tunisia	33.33333	66.66667	75	25
Montenegro	50	50	16.66667	83.33333
Turks and Caicos Islands	66.66667	33.33333	25	75
Greenland	50	50	50	50

5 Conclusion and Future Work

To reduce the rapid spread of the SARS-CoV-2 virus, several universities, colleges, and schools across the world transitioned to online learning. This was associated with stress, depression, frustration, anxiety, and insomnia in students as well as educators who used social media platforms such as Twitter during this time to share and exchange information, views, and perspectives related to mental health in the context of online learning. Twitter has been a rich information resource for analyzing conversations related to mental health problems, as evidenced by several prior works in this field. However, those works did not focus on the analysis of mental health-related conversations in the context of online learning during COVID-19. This work aims to address this research gap. A dataset comprising 52,984 Tweets about online learning during COVID-19, posted on Twitter between November 9, 2021, and July 13, 2022, was used for this study. A Bag of Words containing 218 distinct keywords related to mental health was developed after reviewing several recent works in this field. By using this Bag of Words, these Tweets were categorized into two topics – Tweets that focused on mental health in the context of online learning during COVID-19 (Topic 1) and Tweets that did not focus on mental health in the context of online learning during COVID-19 (Topic 2), to infer the user diversity-based paradigms of public discourse related to both these topics. This work specifically focused on two aspects of user diversity – gender and location. Two algorithms were developed that used existing Python packages to infer the gender (from Twitter usernames) and location of the Twitter users (from the location listed on Twitter profiles) who posted about mental health in the context of online learning during COVID-19. The results of gender detection and user location detection for Topic 1 and Topic 2 are presented and discussed. The results of gender detection show that for Topic 1, a higher percentage of the Tweets were posted by females as compared to males. However, for Topic 2, a higher percentage of the Tweets were posted by males as compared to females. The results of location detection show that Twitter users from 193 countries posted about Topic 1, and Twitter users from 228 countries posted about Topic 2. The results also reveal that the highest number of Tweets on Topic 1 and Topic 2 were posted by Twitter users from the United States. The paper also presents the gender-based Tweeting patterns on Topic 1 and Topic 2 for different countries. For instance, in the United States, for Topic 1, a higher percentage of the Tweets were posted by females as compared to males. However, for Topic 2, males posted a higher percentage of Tweets as compared to females. As per the best knowledge of the authors, no similar work has been done in this field thus far. As stated in the methodology section, for the detection of gender and location, manual labeling was necessary for several Tweets. As there may be human error in such manual labeling tasks, this is one of the limitations of this work. Future work would involve collecting more data and repeating this study to infer any patterns of user diversity-based public discourse on Twitter related to Topic 1 and Topic 2 since the beginning of COVID-19.

References

1. Mental health action plan 2013 – 2020. https://www.who.int/publications-detail-redirect/9789241506021. Accessed 11 June 2023
2. Bloom, D.E., et al .: The global economic burden of noncommunicable diseases. PGDA Working Papers (2012)
3. Mental illness. https://www.nimh.nih.gov/health/statistics/mental-illness. Accessed 11 June 2023
4. Mental health. https://www.who.int/health-topics/mental-health. Accessed 11 June 2023
5. Fauci, A.S., Lane, H.C., Redfield, R.R.: Covid-19 - navigating the uncharted. N. Engl. J. Med. **382**, 1268–1269 (2020). https://doi.org/10.1056/NEJMe2002387
6. Tortella, G.R., Seabra, A.B., Padrão, J., Díaz-San Juan, R.: Mindfulness and other simple neuroscience-based proposals to promote the learning performance and mental health of students during the COVID-19 pandemic. Brain Sci. **11**, 552 (2021). https://doi.org/10.3390/brainsci11050552
7. Taecharungroj, V.: What can ChatGPT do? analyzing early reactions to the innovative AI chatbot on twitter. Big Data Cogn. Comput. **7**, 35 (2023). https://doi.org/10.3390/bdcc7010035
8. Tao, W., Peng, Y.: Differentiation and unity: A cross-platform comparison analysis of online posts' semantics of the Russian–Ukrainian War based on Weibo and Twitter. Commun. Public. 205704732311655 (2023). https://doi.org/10.1177/20570473231165563
9. Ante, L.: How Elon Musk's Twitter activity moves cryptocurrency markets. Technol. Forecast. Soc. Change. **186**, 122112 (2023). https://doi.org/10.1016/j.techfore.2022.122112
10. Thakur, N., Han, C.Y.: An approach to analyze the social acceptance of virtual assistants by elderly people. In: Proceedings of the 8th International Conference on the Internet of Things. ACM, New York, NY, USA (2018)

11. Thakur, N., Han, C.Y.: A framework for facilitating human-human interactions to mitigate loneliness in elderly. In: Human Interaction. Emerging Technologies and Future Applications III, pp. 322–327. Springer International Publishing, Cham (2021)
12. Thakur, N., Han, C.Y.: A human-human interaction-driven framework to address societal issues. In: Human Interaction. Emerging Technologies and Future Systems V, pp. 563–571. Springer International Publishing, Cham (2022)
13. Bodaghi, A., Oliveira, J.: The theater of fake news spreading, who plays which role? a study on real graphs of spreading on Twitter. Expert Syst. Appl. **189**, 116110 (2022). https://doi.org/10.1016/j.eswa.2021.116110
14. Chang, R.-C., Rao, A., Zhong, Q., Wojcieszak, M., Lerman, K.: #RoeOverturned: Twitter dataset on the abortion rights controversy. https://ojs.aaai.org/index.php/ICWSM/article/view/22207 (2023)
15. Bhatia, K.V.: Hindu nationalism online: Twitter as discourse and interface. Religions (Basel). **13**, 739 (2022). https://doi.org/10.3390/rel13080739
16. Thakur, N., Han, C.Y.: A multimodal approach for early detection of cognitive impairment from tweets. In: Human Interaction. Emerging Technologies and Future Systems V, pp. 11–19. Springer International Publishing, Cham (2022)
17. Peña-Fernández, S., Larrondo-Ureta, A., Morales-i-Gras, J.: Feminism, gender identity and polarization in TikTok and Twitter. Comunicar. **31** (2023). https://doi.org/10.3916/c75-2023-04
18. Berrocal-Gonzalo, S., Zamora-Martínez, P., González-Neira, A.: Politainment on Twitter: engagement in the Spanish legislative elections of April 2019. Media Commun. **11**(2), 163-175 (2023). https://doi.org/10.17645/mac.v11i2.6292
19. Thakur, N., Hall, I., Han, C.Y.: A comprehensive study to analyze trends in web search interests related to fall detection before and after COVID-19. In: 2022 5th International Conference on Computer Science and Software Engineering (CSSE 2022). ACM, New York, NY, USA (2022)
20. Thakur, N., Han, C.Y.: Country-specific interests towards fall detection from 2004–2021: an open access dataset and research questions. Data (Basel). **6**, 92 (2021). https://doi.org/10.3390/data6080092
21. Klein, A.Z., O'Connor, K., Levine, L.D., Gonzalez-Hernandez, G.: Using twitter data for cohort studies of drug safety in pregnancy: proof-of-concept with β-blockers. JMIR Form. Res. **6**, e36771 (2022). https://doi.org/10.2196/36771
22. Klein, A.Z., Kunatharaju, S., O'Connor, K., Gonzalez-Hernandez, G.: Pregex: rule-based detection and extraction of twitter data in pregnancy. J. Med. Internet Res. **25**, e40569 (2023). https://doi.org/10.2196/40569
23. Goetz, S.J., et al.: Food insufficiency and twitter emotions during a pandemic. Appl. Econ. Perspect. Policy **45**, 1189–1210 (2022). https://doi.org/10.1002/aepp.13258
24. Thakur, N., Han, C.Y.: Google trends to investigate the degree of global interest related to indoor location detection. In: Human Interaction. Emerging Technologies and Future Systems V, pp. 580–588. Springer International Publishing, Cham (2022)
25. Mouronte-López, M.L., Ceres, J.S., Columbrans, A.M.: Analysing the sentiments about the education system trough Twitter. Educ. Inf. Technol. 1–30 (2023). https://doi.org/10.1007/s10639-022-11493-8
26. Thakur, N.: Twitter big data as a resource for exoskeleton research: a large-scale dataset of about 140,000 tweets from 2017–2022 and 100 research questions. Analytics. **1**, 72–97 (2022). https://doi.org/10.3390/analytics1020007
27. Thakur, N.: MonkeyPox2022Tweets: a large-scale twitter dataset on the 2022 monkeypox outbreak, findings from analysis of tweets, and open research questions. Infect. Dis. Rep. **14**, 855–883 (2022). https://doi.org/10.3390/idr14060087

28. Müller, M., Salathé, M., Kummervold, P.E.: COVID-Twitter-BERT: A natural language processing model to Analyse COVID-19 content on Twitter (2020). http://arxiv.org/abs/2005.07503
29. Banda, J.M., et al.: A large-scale COVID-19 Twitter chatter dataset for open scientific research – an international collaboration. ArXiv. **2**, 315–324 (2020). https://doi.org/10.3390/epidemiologia2030024
30. Rufai, S.R., Bunce, C.: World leaders' usage of Twitter in response to the COVID-19 pandemic: a content analysis. J. Public Health (Oxf.) **42**, 510–516 (2020). https://doi.org/10.1093/pubmed/fdaa049
31. Haman, M.: The use of Twitter by state leaders and its impact on the public during the COVID-19 pandemic. Heliyon. **6**, e05540 (2020). https://doi.org/10.1016/j.heliyon.2020.e05540
32. Thakur, N.: Sentiment analysis and text analysis of the public discourse on Twitter about COVID-19 and MPox. Big Data Cogn. Comput. **7**, 116 (2023). https://doi.org/10.3390/bdcc7020116
33. Thakur, N., Han, C.Y.: An exploratory study of tweets about the SARS-CoV-2 Omicron variant: Insights from sentiment analysis, language interpretation, source tracking, type classification, and embedded URL detection. COVID. **2**, 1026–1049 (2022). https://doi.org/10.3390/covid2080076
34. Lee, H.E., Cho, J.: Social media use and well-being in people with physical disabilities: Influence of SNS and online community uses on social support, depression, and psychological disposition. Health Commun. **34**, 1043–1052 (2019). https://doi.org/10.1080/10410236.2018.1455138
35. Knightsmith, P.: Twitter saved my life - why social media isn't all bad. http://www.huffingtonpost.co.uk/dr-pooky-knightsmith/social-media-mental-health_b_8943202.html. Accessed 11 June 2023
36. Tsugawa, S., Kikuchi, Y., Kishino, F., Nakajima, K., Itoh, Y., Ohsaki, H.: Recognizing depression from twitter activity. In: Proceedings of the 33rd Annual ACM Conference on Human Factors in Computing Systems, pp. 3187–3196. ACM, New York, NY, USA (2015)
37. Joseph, A.J., et al.: #schizophrenia: use and misuse on Twitter. Schizophr. Res. **165**, 111–115 (2015). https://doi.org/10.1016/j.schres.2015.04.009
38. Lachmar, E.M., Wittenborn, A.K., Bogen, K.W., McCauley, H.L.: #MyDepressionLooksLike: examining public discourse about depression on Twitter. JMIR Ment. Health. **4**, e43 (2017). https://doi.org/10.2196/mental.8141
39. Shepherd, A., Sanders, C., Doyle, M., Shaw, J.: Using social media for support and feedback by mental health service users: thematic analysis of a twitter conversation. BMC Psychiatry **15**, 29 (2015). https://doi.org/10.1186/s12888-015-0408-y
40. Berry, N., Lobban, F., Belousov, M., Emsley, R., Nenadic, G., Bucci, S.: #WhyWeTweetMH: understanding why people use twitter to discuss mental health problems. J. Med. Internet Res. **19**, e107 (2017). https://doi.org/10.2196/jmir.6173
41. Valdez, D., Ten Thij, M., Bathina, K., Rutter, L.A., Bollen, J.: Social media insights into US mental health during the COVID-19 pandemic: longitudinal analysis of Twitter data. J. Med. Internet Res. **22**, e21418 (2020). https://doi.org/10.2196/21418
42. Zhang, S., et al.: The COVID-19 pandemic and mental health concerns on Twitter in the United States. Health Data Sci. 9758408 (2022). https://doi.org/10.34133/2022/9758408
43. Jansli, S.M., Hudson, G., Negbenose, E., Erturk, S., Wykes, T., Jilka, S.: Investigating mental health service user views of stigma on Twitter during COVID-19: a mixed-methods study. J. Ment. Health **31**, 576–584 (2022). https://doi.org/10.1080/09638237.2022.2091763
44. Sadasivuni, S.T., Zhang, Y.: Using gradient methods to predict twitter users' mental health with both COVID-19 growth patterns and tweets. In: 2020 IEEE International Conference on Humanized Computing and Communication with Artificial Intelligence (HCCAI), pp. 65–66. IEEE (2020)

45. El-Gayar, O., Wahbeh, A., Mohammad, A.-R.: Mental health and the COVID-19 pandemic: Analysis of twitter mental health and the COVID-19 pandemic: Analysis of twitter discourse discourse. https://scholar.dsu.edu/cgi/viewcontent.cgi?article=1287&context=bispapers/. Accessed 11 June 2023
46. Massell, J., Lieb, R., Meyer, A., Mayor, E.: Fluctuations of psychological states on Twitter before and during COVID-19. PLoS ONE **17**, e0278018 (2022). https://doi.org/10.1371/journal.pone.0278018
47. Jones, R., Mougouei, D., Evans, S.L.: Understanding the emotional response to COVID-19 information in news and social media: a mental health perspective. Hum. Behav. Emerg. Technol. **3**, 832–842 (2021). https://doi.org/10.1002/hbe2.304
48. Cohrdes, C., Yenikent, S., Wu, J., Ghanem, B., Franco-Salvador, M., Vogelgesang, F.: Indications of depressive symptoms during the COVID-19 pandemic in Germany: comparison of national survey and Twitter data. JMIR Ment. Health. **8**, e27140 (2021). https://doi.org/10.2196/27140
49. Zhang, Y., Lyu, H., Liu, Y., Zhang, X., Wang, Y., Luo, J.: Monitoring depression trends on Twitter during the COVID-19 pandemic: observational study. JMIR Infodemiology. **1**, e26769 (2021). https://doi.org/10.2196/26769
50. Koh, J.X., Liew, T.M.: How loneliness is talked about in social media during COVID-19 pandemic: text mining of 4,492 Twitter feeds. J. Psychiatr. Res. **145**, 317–324 (2022). https://doi.org/10.1016/j.jpsychires.2020.11.015
51. Ghosh, T., Banna, M.H.A., Nahian, M.J.A., Taher, K.A., Kaiser, M.S., Mahmud, M.: A hybrid deep learning model to predict the impact of COVID-19 on mental health form social media big data. https://www.preprints.org/manuscript/202106.0654/v1, (2021). https://doi.org/10.20944/preprints202106.0654.v1
52. Levanti, D., et al.: Depression and anxiety on Twitter during the COVID-19 stay-at-home period in 7 major U.s. cities. AJPM Focus. **2**, 100062 (2023). https://doi.org/10.1016/j.focus.2022.100062
53. Leung, J., Chung, J.Y.C., Tisdale, C., Chiu, V., Lim, C.C.W., Chan, G.: Anxiety and panic buying behaviour during COVID-19 pandemic-a qualitative analysis of toilet paper hoarding contents on Twitter. Int. J. Environ. Res. Public Health **18**, 1127 (2021). https://doi.org/10.3390/ijerph18031127
54. Zhong, B., Huang, Y., Liu, Q.: Mental health toll from the coronavirus: Social media usage reveals Wuhan residents' depression and secondary trauma in the COVID-19 outbreak. Comput. Human Behav. **114**, 106524 (2021). https://doi.org/10.1016/j.chb.2020.106524
55. Akhther, N., Sopory, P.: Seeking and sharing mental health information on social media during COVID-19: Role of depression and anxiety, peer support, and health benefits. J. Technol. Behav. Sci. **7**, 211–226 (2022). https://doi.org/10.1007/s41347-021-00239-x
56. Blair, J., Hsu, C.-Y., Qiu, L., Huang, S.-H., Huang, T.-H.K., Abdullah, S.: Using tweets to assess mental well-being of essential workers during the COVID-19 pandemic. In: Extended Abstracts of the 2021 CHI Conference on Human Factors in Computing Systems, pp. 1-6. ACM, New York, NY, USA (2021)
57. Ye, S.: Ho, KKW: College students' Twitter usage and psychological well-being from the perspective of generalised trust: comparing changes before and during the COVID-19 pandemic. Libr. Hi Tech. **41**, 152–173 (2023). https://doi.org/10.1108/lht-06-2021-0178
58. Ueda, M., Watanabe, K., Sueki, H.: Emotional distress during COVID-19 by mental health conditions and economic vulnerability: retrospective analysis of survey-linked Twitter data with a semisupervised machine learning algorithm. J. Med. Internet Res. **25**, e44965 (2023). https://doi.org/10.2196/44965
59. Asare, A.O., Yap, R., Truong, N.: Sarpong, EO: the pandemic semesters: examining public opinion regarding online learning amidst COVID-19. J. Comput. Assist. Learn. **37**, 1591–1605 (2021). https://doi.org/10.1111/jcal.12574

60. Alwafi, E.: Tracing changes in teachers' professional learning network on Twitter: Comparison of teachers' social network structure and content of interaction before and during the COVID-19 pandemic. J. Comput. Assist. Learn. **37**, 1653–1665 (2021). https://doi.org/10.1111/jcal.12607
61. Torrey, T., Carpenter, J.P., Krutka, D.G., Kimmons, R.: #RemoteTeaching & #RemoteLearning: educator tweeting during the COVID-19 pandemic. J. Technol. Teach. Educ. **28**, 151–159 (2020)
62. Almossa, S.Y.: University students' perspectives toward learning and assessment during COVID-19. Educ. Inf. Technol. **26**(6), 7163–7181 (2021). https://doi.org/10.1007/s10639-021-10554-8
63. Alswedani, S., Katib, I., Abozinadah, E., Mehmood, R.: Discovering urban governance parameters for online learning in Saudi Arabia during COVID-19 using topic modeling of Twitter data. Front. Sustain. Cities. **4**, (2022). https://doi.org/10.3389/frsc.2022.751681
64. Al-Obeidat, F., Ishaq, M., Shuhaiber, A., Amin, A.: Twitter sentiment analysis to understand students' perceptions about online learning during the Covid'19. In: 2022 International Conference on Computer and Applications (ICCA), pp. 1–7. IEEE (2022)
65. Senadhira, K.I., Rupasingha, R.A.H.M., Kumara, B.T.G.S.: Sentiment analysis on twitter data related to online learning during the covid-19 pandemic. In: 2022 International Research Conference on Smart Computing and Systems Engineering (SCSE), pp. 131–136. IEEE (2022)
66. Patil, V., Mandal, A., Bhavane, H.: Sentimental analysis of twitter data on online learning during unlock phase of COVID-19. In: Applied Computational Technologies, pp. 12–20. Springer Nature Singapore, Singapore (2022)
67. Zhou, M., Mou, H.: Tracking public opinion about online education over COVID-19 in China. Educ. Technol. Res. Dev. **70**, 1083–1104 (2022). https://doi.org/10.1007/s11423-022-10080-5
68. Ali, M.M.: Arabic sentiment analysis about online learning to mitigate covid-19. J. Intell. Syst. **30**, 524–540 (2021). https://doi.org/10.1515/jisys-2020-0115
69. Jogezai, N.A., Baloch, F.A., Jaffar, M., Shah, T., Khilji, G.K., Bashir, S.: Teachers' attitudes towards social media (SM) use in online learning amid the COVID-19 pandemic: the effects of SM use by teachers and religious scholars during physical distancing. Heliyon. **7**, e06781 (2021). https://doi.org/10.1016/j.heliyon.2021.e06781
70. Ewing, L.-A., Vu, HQ: Navigating 'home schooling' during COVID-19: Australian public response on Twitter. Media Int. Aust. **178**, 77–86 (2021). https://doi.org/10.1177/1329878x20956409
71. Thakur, N.: A large-scale dataset of Twitter chatter about online learning during the current COVID-19 Omicron wave. Data (Basel). **7**, 109 (2022). https://doi.org/10.3390/data7080109
72. hydrator: Turn Tweet IDs into Twitter JSON & CSV from your desktop!. Accessed 12 June 2023
73. Mowery, D., et al.: Understanding depressive symptoms and psychosocial stressors on twitter: a corpus-based study. J. Med. Internet Res. **19**, e48 (2017). https://doi.org/10.2196/jmir.6895
74. Makita, M., Mas-Bleda, A., Morris, S., Thelwall, M.: Mental health discourses on twitter during mental health awareness week. Issues Ment. Health Nurs. **42**, 437–450 (2021). https://doi.org/10.1080/01612840.2020.1814914
75. Santos, W., Funabashi, A., Paraboni, I.: Searching Brazilian twitter for signs of mental health issues. In: Proceedings of the Twelfth Language Resources and Evaluation Conference, pp. 6111–6117. European Language Resources Association, Marseille, France (2020)
76. O'Dea, B., Wan, S., Batterham, P.J., Calear, A.L., Paris, C., Christensen, H.: Detecting suicidality on twitter. Internet Interv. **2**, 183–188 (2015). https://doi.org/10.1016/j.invent.2015.03.005

77. Watkins, N.G., Lovell, N.H., Larsen, M.E.: SMCT - an innovative tool for mental health analysis of Twitter data. In: Annual International Conference of the IEEE Engineering in Medicine and Biology Society (EMBC), pp. 4114–4117 (2018). https://doi.org/10.1109/EMBC.2018.8513257
78. Wang, Z., Jurgens, D.: It's going to be okay: measuring access to support in online communities. In: Proceedings of the 2018 Conference on Empirical Methods in Natural Language Processing, pp. 33–45. Association for Computational Linguistics, Stroudsburg, PA, USA
79. To, Q.G., et al.: Anti-vaccination attitude trends during the COVID-19 pandemic: A machine learning-based analysis of tweets. Digit. Health. **9**, 20552076231158030 (2023). https://doi.org/10.1177/20552076231158033
80. Pycountry. https://pypi.org/project/pycountry/. Accessed 12 June 2023

The Relevance of Emotional AI-Generated Painting to the Painting Subject and Main Colors

Yan Wang(✉) and Yifan Sun

College of Art Design and Media, East China University of Science and Technology, 130 Meilong Road, Xuhui District 200237, Shanghai, People's Republic of China
syfdyx@qq.com

Abstract. To solve the current problem of AI-generated paintings requiring too precise physical descriptions, and to explore the association between the original descriptions and emotional perception, the experiment used specific prompts to control two elements of the painting, the main color and the object. The emotional arousal and affective effect of the viewer were observed by setting different preferred colors, blue and yellow, and different preferred animal images, cranes and mice. It was found that the role of the painting object in conveying the emotion was significantly higher than that of the color. Therefore, using objects with certain emotional preferences to express emotions during text-generated painting is more effective than the main color. The results of this study will be beneficial to further explore the creation of AI-generated paintings with more emotional expression.

Keywords: AI-generated · AI painting · Emotional Impact

1 Introduction

The release of ChatGPT, a large language model developed by OpenAI [1], made the whole world seem to experience a baptism of AI technology. These advances in machine learning have facilitated the exploration of research and applications of artificial intelligence in various fields [2]. This has equally stirred a boom in visual arts research and AI art creation, with AI painting being a very typical application. With the advent of generative adversarial networks (GAN) and deep convolutional neural networks (CNN), AI as art creators while analyzing, machine learning, and continuously iterating on the generated content has greatly accelerated the application of AI in art creation [3].

There are still many aspects of today's AI painting that need to be studied and refined. It operates mainly through a mechanism of generating and creating paintings by imitating and reorganizing existing paintings from the past through extensive machine learning. AI generators often require precise physical descriptions to obtain the desired results, and it is difficult for non-experts to use purely emotional statements closer to natural language for AI creation. Several studies have attempted to explore the emotional representation of AI, and it has been proposed that AI can predict the emotions that a painting will evoke in us [4].

H. Mori et al. (Eds.): HCII 2023, LNCS 14056, pp. 390–399, 2023.
https://doi.org/10.1007/978-3-031-48044-7_28

Therefore, we control two painting factors of the picture, namely object, and tone, through prompts, and then explore the correlation between the control factors of AI paintings and emotional expressions. The results will facilitate the study of the affective nature of AI-generated models and stimulate the creative power of AI techniques.

2 Related Works

2.1 The Development of Artificial Intelligence Painting

In 1973, Harold Cohen from the University of California created an artificial intelligence program called AARON, which demonstrated the ability to generate images independently. In 2006, Simon Corton developed the "Paint fall" program.[5] Since the 21st century, artificial intelligence has seen significant advancements in the development of neural networks and deep learning techniques [6]. These advancements have played a crucial role in the field of AI-generated art. In 2016, Google introduced "deepdream," a computer vision program that employed deep convolutional neural networks (CNN) to learn and enhance image models (Google Research, 2016). This program created surreal and stylized images, giving rise to a new art form known as inceptionism. The introduction of generative adversarial networks (GANs) further accelerated the development of AI-generated paintings. The Creative Adversarial Network (CAN) emerged in 2017, which produced artwork that was indistinguishable from contemporary artists' paintings displayed at top art expositions, as evidenced by passing the illustration test.

These advancements in artificial intelligence have marked the beginning of a new era, where AI systems demonstrate remarkable capabilities in generating artistic content [7].

The big event that brought AI-generated artwork into the public arena occurred in 2018, when an AI painting, "Portrait of Edmond de Bellamy," fetched a staggering $43.25 million at an auction [8]. Since then, there has been a surge of research and applications in the field of AI-generated artwork, particularly text-to-image generation techniques based on Clip + GAN and Clip + diffusion models. These advances have led to the development of popular models such as disco diffusion, stable diffusion, midjourney, and DALL-E 2 that enable artists to generate images quickly and with high quality using AI tools.

In this experiment, we use the disco diffusion program to generate images, and the conditions that can be adjusted in the formation process include descriptive phrases, which include elements such as color, composition, painting style, and image in the picture. We select two elements of color and image in this research process.

2.2 The Lack of Emotion in Artificial Intelligence Painting

The controversial point of artificial intelligence painting is that it is not considered to meet the criteria proposed by some scholars. Firstly, the painting must have the free will of the creative subject; secondly, the painting must have the aesthetic value of reflecting the objective world. Artificial intelligence painting is carried out by computer in the form of program and algorithm, which is full of randomness in the creation process, and even the creator or user of the program cannot predict the final result. And after all, AI is only data algorithm and mapping mechanism, although it can precisely imitate the response of human brain, but it cannot completely replicate the complex life experience that has evolved through billions of years [9]. Ai-Da, the world's first surreal humanoid robot artist, will present a solo exhibition of her artwork as an artist at the Venice Biennale on April 23, 2022. Although her form takes on a surreal human appearance, the work is done by a robot arm controlled by a machine under the command of a program, without the involvement of a specific person during the specific painting period, just like the imaging process of a camera or a video camera [10].

At the current level of technology, artificial intelligence is not able to create relatively subjective works like human beings, and the so-called "creation" process is entirely based on data integration and machine learning. This makes painting, an art form that aims to convey a special emotional expression of the spirit, reduce the emotional influence of the traditional painting author on the viewer when the subject of creation is transformed into an AI.

This investigation into the emotional expression of AI painting provides a different machine perspective to verify the connection between the emotional experience brought by painting and the elements of painting, on the one hand, and on the other hand, the research results can be used to optimize the emotional expression as a human or machine in design creation.

2.3 The Descriptors and Emotional Expressions

This experiment uses a model for generating paintings with the help of text input, so it is necessary to define and classify the vocabulary for describing the objects of paintings according to their relevance to feelings.

Language is the most important communication tool for human beings, and human beings are emotional creatures, so words are often used in the process of application and communication with emotional colors, and these words are called emotional words. Xu (1978) believes that the emotional color of words contains people's evaluation and attitude towards certain things, phenomena and behaviors, which is an objective phenomenon formed in the process of long-term use of language" [9]. Due to the difference of national and regional cultures, the emotional color of words can reflect the collective good and bad of a nation, reflecting a nation's moral and ethical thinking, value judgment and abandonment, in this article focuses on the association and connection within the Chinese cultural language.

In terms of color, people's liking or disliking of a certain color essentially stems from their liking or disliking of things that are primarily a certain color. Two scholars, Zhang Tengxiao and Han Buxin, used 1814 adults from 27 provinces and 4 municipalities to test their preferences and psychological perceptions of eight basic colors. The results were that "Chinese people's preferences for the five basic colors were blue, red, green, purple, and yellow in descending order" [10]. Cheng, Xue et al. (2017) also tested in a healthy population and obtained the abstract color preferences in the order of blue, red, green, yellow, orange, gray, purple, white, and black from highest to lowest [11]. Blue, which has a higher preference, and yellow, which has a lower preference, were selected as the primary colors in the experiment.

In terms of depicting objects, relatively specific imagery was chosen for selection, so texts about animals were selected for description. From the situation reflected by the sentiment color words, people prefer animals such as cranes, dragons, phoenixes and tigers, which are mostly found in positive words. From the situation reflected by emotionally colored words, the Han people have negative feelings such as aversion to those animals that are ugly, of little value and pose a threat to people's productive life, mainly showing that the words composed of these animals as morphemes are mostly derogatory, such as dog, wolf, fox, insect, rat, snake [12]. In the experiment, cranes with higher preference and rats with lower preference were chosen to be depicted.

3 Materials and Methods

3.1 Apparatus and Stimuli

The stimuli were four paintings generated by artificial intelligence software Disco Diffusion based on the keywords of the aforementioned independent variables. The prompt corresponding to a crane is "a crane flying in the sky", while the prompt corresponding to a mouse is "a mouse wandering in the garden". The main color of the painting can also be set to blue and yellow respectively. Each combination of hue and painted subject produced at least three paintings to minimize chance error. Four eligible experimental materials were screened by balancing the effects of control variables such as color, size, emotional validity, and arousal on the experiment. (see Fig. 1).

Fig. 1. AI-generate painting stimuli.

3.2 Experimental Equipment

The experimental device was a Legion Y7000P IAH7 laptop with a 15.6-inch screen size, 2560 × 1440 resolution, 165 Hz refresh rate, 300nit brightness, 100% sRGB color gamut. The subject was seated in a quiet, soundproof room with both eyes approximately 70 cm from the display (2.4 × 4.5°viewing angle) [13].

3.3 Participants

We recruited thirteen volunteers to participate in this experiment (7 females; mean age = 27.35 years, SD = 13.42; range 13–52 years-old). All participants had normal or corrected-to-normal vision and reported not being color-blind or color weakness. All subjects were not professionally trained in drawing or working in art-related jobs. Informed consent was obtained from all participants prior to the start of the experimental session.

3.4 Procedure

All subjects were first invited individually to the laboratory, where each subject was briefly introduced to the experimental procedure and invited to fill out an information sheet. Prior to the start of the formal experiment, subjects were not informed that the images presented were paintings automatically generated by artificial intelligence, and the experiment was well set up and prepared so that the experimenter was seated in front of the display and the distance between the display and the subject was adjusted to approximately 70 cm, allowing the experimenter to maintain a horizontal view of the screen. The experimental material was presented on the computer screen in full-screen format.

Once adjusted, the formal experimental procedure began. The experiment starts with a presentation description with the background set to white (RGB: 255, 255, 255) and the font set to black (RGB: 0, 0, 0) to avoid eye strain on the subject, and the drawings are presented in a banner format in the middle of a uniform black (RGB: 0, 0, 0) background. An introduction to the experiment appears on the monitor. Next three pictures will appear on the screen, and after enjoying them, please fill in the contents according to the form provided. After filling in the form press the space to proceed to the next set of experiments. If you understand the experiment procedure, press the space bar to start the experiment. When the participants understood all the instructions and did not have any questions, the experiment continued.

After the experiment starts, the screen will present a 3000 ms picture of the experiment material. Immediately afterwards, questions about the degree of emotional arousal and emotional potency judgment would appear one after another, and participants were instructed to answer a 5-point Likert scale via the provided paper form. A score of 1 represented the lowest score (very low arousal/unpleasant emotions) and a score of 5 represented the highest score (very high arousal/pleasant emotions). When the participant has finished answering, a black buffer screen of 800 ms appears. Then a new judgment will start. To avoid interactions between the ratings of the different tonal groups, subjects were required to complete the blue-toned pictures before moving on to the yellow-toned pictures in the next group.

The experiment ended when each participant completed four groups of tasks. The participants saw the same target icon for all four groups of pictures. Finally, a short interview was conducted with the participants about the emotional details after viewing, which allowed to learn more and to review the accuracy of the data filled in the form. Considering that participants may forget the experimental materials, all experimental materials are replayed aside for the experimental participants during the interview phase to reconfirm the accuracy of the results. The average experiment duration was approximately 15 min.

3.5 Data Processing

To ensure the validity of the data, the results were reviewed in conjunction with the interviews of all participants at the end of the experiment prior to data analysis. If a participant showed diametrically opposed performance in the interview and form completion, then that participant's data would be considered invalid. After verification of the data, it was found that all participants' data were valid.

4 Result

We conducted data analysis on 12 AI-generated paintings, using painting tone (blue tone, yellow tone) and painting subject (crane, mouse) as independent variables, and emotional arousal and emotional valence ratings as dependent variables. The paintings were divided into four groups based on their painting tone and painting subject, and we used a two-way ANOVA to compare the data.

Table 1 shows the descriptive results of task emotional arousal and emotional valence rating of different interfaces.

Table 1. The mean and standard deviation of the dependent variables (N = 13).

Dependent variables		Crane		Mouse	
		B	Y	B	Y
Emotional arousal	M	4.08	4.23	3.31	3.23
	SD	0.95	0.73	1.03	0.73
Emotional valence rating	M	4.31	4.31	2.39	3.46
	SD	0.75	0.63	1.04	0.78

Note: B means blue-toned. Y means yellow-toned

The results showed that for emotional arousal, the main effect of painting primary color was not significant [F (1, 13) = 0.03, p = 0.87, η2 = 0.001]. Contrary to experimental expectations, the emotional arousal of blue hue (M = 3.69, SD = 1.04) and yellow hue (M = 3.73, SD = 0.87) was not much different, and even the yellow color is even more intense.

The main effect of the subject of the painting content was significant, with the rating of emotional arousal significantly higher for the painting with the crane as the subject (M = 4.15, SD = 0.83) than for the rat as the subject (M = 3.27, SD = 0.87), [F (1, 13) = 12.74, $p < 0.05$, $\eta 2 = 0.219$].

Further simple effects analysis revealed (Fig. 2) that subject one (crane) had a significantly higher emotional arousal score, while the color factor did not have a significant effect.

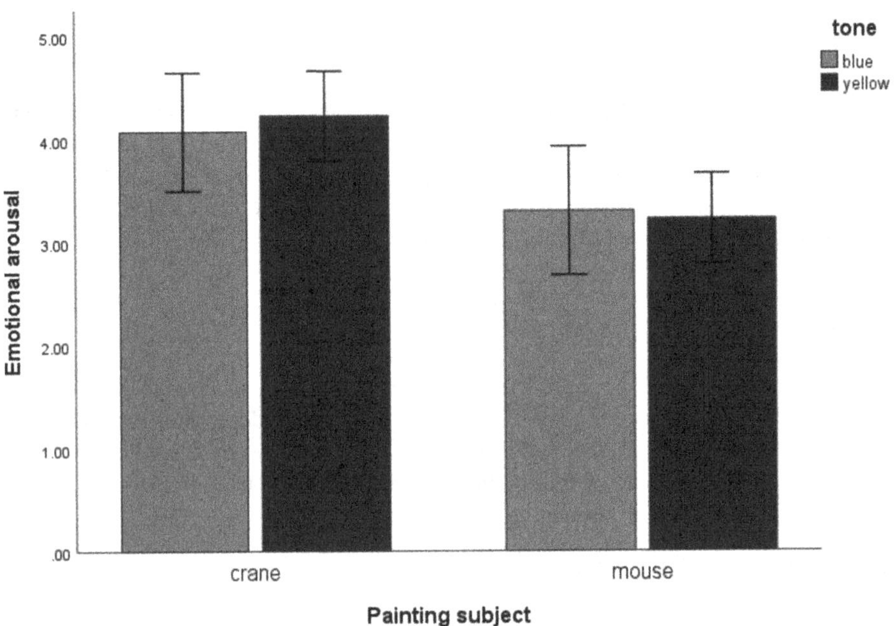

Fig. 2. The interaction of painting subject and tone on the emotion arousal. Error bars represent ± 1 standard error of the mean.

The main effect of the main color of the painting was more significant in terms of emotional valence [F (1, 13) = 5.68, p = 0.02, $\eta^2 = 0.11$). And there was no significant difference between the emotional valence of the blue hue (M = 3.34, SD = 1.32) and the yellow hue (M = 3.88, SD = 0.82).

The main effect of painting content subject was significant [F (1, 13) = 37.57, $p < 0.01$, $\eta^2 = 0.44$]. The rating of emotional valence was significantly higher for the painting with crane as the subject (M = 4.31, SD = 0.67) than for the painting with mouse as the subject (M = 2.92, SD = 1.01).

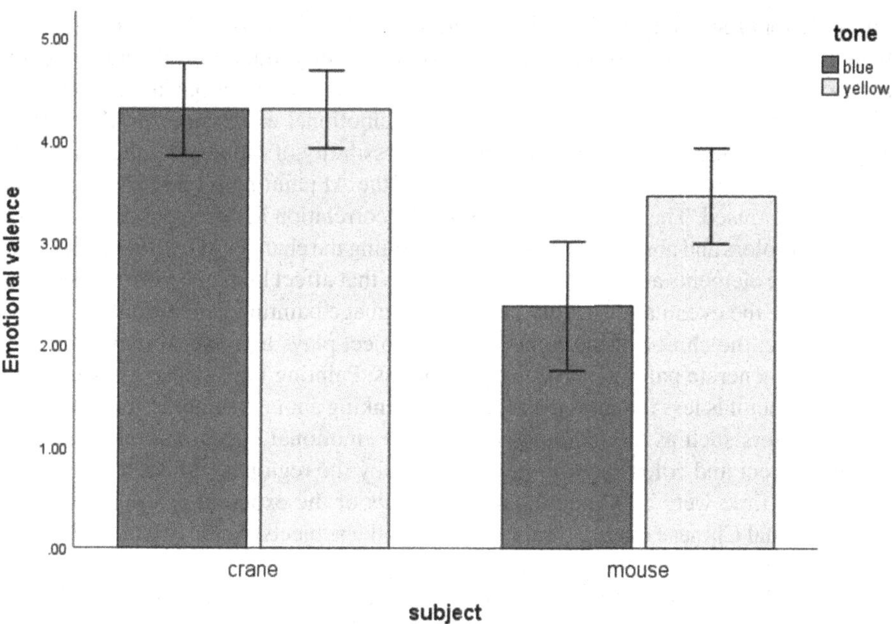

Fig. 3. The interaction of painting subject and tone on the emotion valence. Error bars represent ± 1 standard error of the mean.

5 Conclusion

In the experimental task of emotional efficacy, the main effect of the main color of the painting and the painting subject were significant, and there was an interaction effect between the two. The effect of the painting subject was stronger when intersected with the main color of the painting. The significant main effect of the painting subject was evident in both the blue-toned paintings and the yellow-toned paintings, where the emotional effect scores of the paintings with the crane as the subject were significantly higher than those of the paintings with the mouse as the subject.

Interestingly, the main effect was significant when the painting subject was a crane, but as shown in Fig. 3, it was not so significantly affected by color, and the scores for blue-toned and yellow-toned paintings were not very different from each other.

For the painting with mouse as the theme, the public's favorite blue color instead got more negative emotional ratings. Color does not play an absolute influence in painting, but will be influenced by the interaction of factors such as the painting object. Therefore, if we want to control color to express emotion, we need to consider not only the public's emotional preference, but also the combination of various painting factors and deeper emotional factors.

In the emotional evocation task, the main effect of the painting subject was significant, with paintings featuring cranes rated significantly higher than paintings featuring rats among the different paintings. The emotional potency and emotional arousal of the crane imagery was always rated significantly higher than that of the rat imagery, regardless of the variation of the painting's main color conditions. This result is consistent with the preference for crane imagery in Chinese culture, which in Tang poetry is a very positive object for painting, as it can be a symbol of high morality, immortality, and longevity [16]. In contrast, the image of the rat tends to evoke negative emotions in the viewer.

It will enrich the theoretical research on the emotional expression of AI painting. Based on the splitting of painting elements, the possibility of influencing the emotional changes of the viewer by controlling the color of the AI painting picture and the painting subject is raised. The experiments explore the correlation between concrete objects, images and colors and abstract emotions by controlling the changes of cue words. Exploring the image elements and corresponding weights that affect human emotional feelings will facilitate the eventual direction of natural language painting generation for AI.

Therefore, the choice of the right painting subject plays a greater role when trying to use AI to generate paintings to convey emotions. Painting tone is also an issue to be considered, but it is less influential and requires thinking about the interaction with other painting factors such as the painting subject. The emotional impact stimulated by the painting subject and color can also be influenced by the regional culture. The subjects targeted this time were all Chinese, and the results of the experiment were consistent with traditional Chinese culture. In the next study, the subjects can be expanded to other countries and regions to verify the findings.

None of the subjects in this study had any experience with painting, and the influence of the meaning knowledge system on the experimental results can be excluded. However, in the picture selection process, the random nature of AI painting resulted in an uneven degree of aesthetics in the paintings, some of which were influenced by other factors such as composition and brushstroke. And in the current experience, using AI to draw people or animals may cause the "Valley of Terror effect"[17], so we can try to use some abstract words to generate images. Further experiments are needed to prove this.

Numerous ERP (event-related potential) studies have found that the emotional nature of words enhances the activity response of the cerebral cortex, involving all stages of visual word processing. [18] Therefore, in the next study, we will try to apply specialized research instruments, such as oculomotor and EEG, to more comprehensively measure and assess the physiological activity of the viewer. At the same time, we will try to describe more abstract words to explore and discover the potential of artificial intelligence to understand and express emotional words.

References

1. Kirmani, A.R.: Artificial intelligence-enabled science poetry. ACS Energy Lett. **8**, 574–576 (2022)
2. Cetinic, E., She, J.: Understanding and creating art with AI: review and outlook. ACM Trans. Multimedia Comput. Commun. Appl. (TOMM), **18**(2), 1–22 (2022)
3. Goodfellow, I., Pouget-Abadie, J., Mirza, M., Xu, B., Warde-Farley, D., Ozair, S., Bengio, Y.: Generative adversarial nets Advances in neural information processing systems (2014). arXiv preprint arXiv:1406.2661
4. Gent, E.: AI can predict the emotions a painting will evoke in us (2021)
5. Dietrich, F.: Visual intelligence: the first decade of computer art (1965–1975). Leonardo **19**(2), 159–169 (1986)
6. Feng, T.: Research on artificial intelligence visual art. Liter. Artistic Controversy No. 300. 07(2019), 73–81 (2019)

7. Elgammal, A., Liu, B., Elhoseiny, M., Mazzone, M.: Can: creative adversarial networks, generating art by learning about styles and deviating from style norms (2017)
8. Epstein, Z., Levine, S., Rand, D.G., Rahwan, I.: Who gets credit for AI-generated art? Iscience **23**(9), 101515 (2020)
9. Zhao, Y.: On the two-way limit of artificial intelligence and the return of aesthetic theory to sensibility. J. Southwest Univ. Nationalit. (Humanit. Soc. Sci. Ed.) **05**, 184–189 (2020)
10. Chen, H.: Analysis of the creative field of artificial intelligence painting and its value in the new ecological context of literature and art. Chongqing Soc. Sci. **08**, 45–52 (2020). https://doi.org/10.19631/j.cnki.css.2020.008.004
11. Xu, Z.: The positive and negative colors of the words. Lang. Learn. **07**, 108–112 (1978)
12. Zhang, T., Han, B.: Chinese people's psychological perception and preference for basic colors. In: (eds.) Psychology and Innovation Enhancement - Proceedings of the 16th National Psychology Conference, pp. 123–124 (2013)
13. Xue, C., et al.: A study on abstract color preference and its influencing factors in healthy population. Lab. Med. Clin. (20), 3003–3005+3008 (2017)
14. Wang, M.: A study of emotionally colored words in Modern Chinese Dictionary (6th ed.) (Master's thesis, Wenzhou University) (2021). https://kns.cnki.net/KCMS/detail/detail.aspx?dbname=CMFD202202&filename=1021115501.nh
15. Luo, W., Feng, W., He, W., Wang, N.Y., Luo, Y.J.: Three stages of facial expression processing: ERP study with rapid serial visual presentation. Neuroimage **49**(2), 1857–1867 (2010)
16. Sun, H.: The formation of crane imagery and its characteristics in Chinese culture-from Zhaoming Wenxuan and Quan Tang Poems. J. Changchun Normal Coll. **11**, 64–70 (2011)
17. MacDorman, K.F.: Androids as an experimental apparatus: why is there an uncanny valley and can we exploit it. In: CogSci-2005 Workshop: Toward Social Mechanisms of Android Science, vol. 3, pp. 106–118 (2005)
18. Kissler, J., Assadollahi, R., Herbert, C.: Emotional and semantic networks in visual word processing: Insights from ERP studies. Prog. Brain Res. **156**, 147–183 (2006)

Re-feminizing Beauty in the Multimodal Storytelling Practices of Chinese Social Media Influencers on Xiaohongshu (RED)

Wei Wei(✉)

King's College London, London, UK
viviweiwei@kcl.ac.uk

Abstract. Influencers are a prominent group of content creators and opinion leaders on social media. In China, influencers are referred to as "wanghong" (internet red) or "bozhu" (bloggers), whose practices are deeply interwoven with the development of the digital market economy and the creative and cultural industry. Wanghong is also a gendered profession, notably consisting of young women engaging in discussions of beauty and fashion who manifest postfeminist sensibilities of beauty as personal choice and empowerment, with consumerism serving as a subtext. Taking a transnational perspective on postfeminist media culture, this study examines the multimodal storytelling practices of nine micro- and mid-tier influencers in the beauty and fashion domains on Xiaohongshu (RED), a highly popular Chinese social media platform that remains largely unexplored in digital communication research. Using a small stories approach and social semiotic multimodal analysis, this study shows how storytelling, particularly in the influencers' discourse practices of OOTD (Outfit of the Day) and product review, imbues beauty with ordinariness and communicability. The results shed light on the construction of Chinese femininities on social media in the post-socialist context on the one hand, and the linguistic-semiotic features of influencer marketing and Electronic Word of Mouth (eWOM) on the other hand.

Keywords: Social media influencer · Social commerce · Narrative analysis · Multimodality · Postfeminism · China

1 Introduction

Social media influencers (SMIs), micro-celebrities, or internet celebrities, have received considerable critical attention in digital media and communication research in recent years. Influencers accumulate followers through their sharing of personal lives and amateur-professional content on sites such as Facebook, Twitter, YouTube, Instagram, and TikTok [3,4]. Scholars in media and culture studies have underlined influencers' performance of a likeable and monetizable identity (i.e., self-branding) [5,36]. Moreover, they have examined how

Funded by the China Scholarship Council.

H. Mori et al. (Eds.): HCII 2023, LNCS 14056, pp. 400–419, 2023.
https://doi.org/10.1007/978-3-031-48044-7_29

influencers manage an intimate, parasocial relationship with their followers [7]. Authenticity, relatability, and visibility labor are prominent topics of discussion against the backdrop of attention economies [2]. Linguistic and discursive studies are also well-placed to investigate influencers' social media communication by unravelling the pragmatic, linguistic-semiotic features of their identity work, content creation, and audience interaction [8,11].

However, amid the current discussion, a gender perspective is called for. Social media influencers are overwhelmingly comprised of young women working in the domains of beauty and fashion [1,16,44]. Their popularity is grounded in the development of postfeminist media culture, consumerism, and the sociocultural negotiation of feminine beauty ideals. In feminist studies, the linkage between femininity and beauty has long been problematized. The gendered and commercialized beauty practices are oppressive in that they often perpetuate restrictive aesthetic standards and reinforce "lookism" for women (i.e., judging women by their appearances), limiting women's role to that of consumers [34]. But postfeminist media culture has reframed beauty practices as pleasurable and self-chosen [27]. The liberating or empowerment discourse of beauty is particularly conveyed through young female influencers, in their construction of entrepreneurial femininity-being "agentive cute" [1] and "having it all" [17]. Underneath their glam lives, the regulatory aspect of the beauty practices remains, evidenced in influencers' aesthetic labors for conforming to patriarchal norms [6,17]. In the context of mainland China specifically, beauty and femininity in influencer research also concern the intersection between the development of "her economy" or "beauty economy" and the development of the wanghong industry in the post-socialist, digitized market [13,54].

Moreover, to understand how influencers share their personal lives whilst commercializing such content, there is still much scope for studying their storytelling practices. Storytelling is central to influencers' "authentic" identity performances, the presentation of a self that is genuine, real and relatable (e.g., via "imperfect sharing" on Instagram Stories [24]). The strategic curation of daily life (personal) in combination with product/service consumption (commercial) also heavily relies on storytelling, which serves to mitigate sponsorship disclosure and encourage viewer engagement [18,42]. Multimodality is a key aspect to be addressed, which has received a growing interest not only in influencer research but also in social media narrative research [26].

To pursue these lines of enquiry, this study zooms in on multimodal storytelling practices of young female beauty and fashion influencers on the Chinese social media platform, Xiaohongshu (RED). It aims to shed light on influencer communication from a practice-based, narrative, and linguistic-semiotic perspective. Situating the study in the context of Chinese beauty and femininity practices and social media communication, the study also supports Dosekun's [15] call for a transnational approach to researching postfeminism, with a sensitivity to the different material and historical conditions of women across the globe. Specifically, this study addresses the following research questions: (1) What types of stories are told in beauty and fashion influencers' Xiaohongshu posts as well as in the interactions with other users? (2) What are the communicative functions and linguistic-semiotic features of their storytelling practices? (3) What do these storytelling practices reflect on the negotiation of sociocultural meanings about beauty and femininity in contemporary China?

In the following, I will first provide a historical overview of the relationships between beauty and femininity in the Chinese context, review the related linguistic and discursive work on Chinese social media influencers, and introduce the platform of Xiaohongshu. I will then discuss the overarching framework for analysis, the small stories approach and social semiotic multimodal analysis. Using data of photo-text and video posts by nine beauty and fashion influencers on Xiaohongshu, the analysis will specifically examine two storytelling practices, minimal telling in OOTD (Outfit of the Day) and co-telling in product review. Minimal telling involves mobilizing verbal and visual resources to an elliptical narration of mundane daily life occurrences, which serves as a contextualization to street style fashion, its textually-mediated consumption and aesthetic negotiation. Co-telling highlights the interactive features of product-centered stories, which shows how Electronic Word of Mouth (eWOM) operates on social media and how it is mediated by influencers' practices, intertwining beauty with a sense of sociality and communicability. Finally, I will discuss the implications for social media communication and feminist approaches to beauty and femininity.

2 Beauty, Chinese Femininities and Social Media Influencers (Wanghong)

Prior to the establishment of the People's Republic of China (PRC), beauty practices as oppressive for women were particularly shown in the descriptions of feudalist femininity, a case in point being the thousand-year-long practice of "footbinding": Women bound their feet at a very young age, enduring pain and rotten skin and life-long mobility limitation, in pursuit of an ideal known as the "golden lotus" (three-itch feet) [47]. In the 1930s, however, under Western imperialism and influxes of consumer goods, the development of the "New Woman" established the idea of beauty as agentive and pleasurable [45]. The "New Woman" at that time signposted a positive move to modernity and featured an urban ideal of femininity: sexually liberated, educated, and having a public presence in the dance halls and coffee houses [19]. A characteristic costume was the feminized "qipao," a one-piece dress tailored to highlight the feminine bodyline [20]. Between the establishment of the PRC in 1949 and the Cultural Revolution in the 1960s, the Mao era, beauty for women was neither oppressive nor agentive, but was rather absent or silenced. A dominant discourse at that time was that beauty and fashion are decadent capitalist practices, and that women should participate in the state-allocated labor force, same as men, for going through national economic hardships: "Women hold up half the sky" [49]. The de-coupling between beauty and femininity generated a socialist ideal: the "Iron Girls" [49], who were wearing male and militant costumes and were expected to be strong and productive in physical labor.

Since the reform and opening up in 1978 and the beginning of the market economy in the 1980s, the post-Mao era, beauty has been revitalized for rebuilding Chinese femininity. This began with the criticism of the unadorned "Iron Girls" as negative relics of the Mao era and exploration of "modern" Chinese femininities [32]. In the nationwide magazine, *Chinese Women*, a lengthy discussion was conducted in 1991 and 1992 under the heading of "What is the Beauty of Modern Women?] [32]. The intense interest in rebuilding femininity via beauty and fashion was also pushed by the development of consumer culture. This shift is now evidenced in the burgeoning beauty industry as well as the wanghong industry. By 2020, China had become the second-largest beauty and personal care product market in the world after the United States [12]. In 2021, the total retail sales of cosmetics in China reached 402.6 billion yuan (c. 63.3 billion US dollars), with an annual growth rate of 14.0%, exceeding the growth rate of the total retail sales of consumer goods (12.5%) [37]. On the other hand, wanghong ("wangluo hongren," "internet red," "people who have gone viral on the internet"), the Chinese social media influencers, have established themselves as crucial figures not only in the cultural and creative industry but also in the digital economy, becoming a distinctive industry of its own-the wanghong industry/economy [13,30].

Wanghong are also referred to as content creators or bozhu (bloggers) when foregrounding their creative work, KOLs (key opinion leaders) or KOCs (key opinion consumers) when discussing their roles in marketing, and daren (gurus) when emphasizing their expertise in such fields as beauty. As Craig et al. [13] argue, what separates the Chinese wanghong industry from social media influencer practices in the West is that Chinese social media platforms have deeply integrated sociality and e-commerce (i.e., social commerce, with a variety of interactive, monetizing and purchasing affordances). Governments have also developed policies in regulating and promoting wanghong (e.g., "Internet+," "Mass Entrepreneurship and Innovation," and "Operation Qinglang") [13]. In 2022, the investment on wanghong (i.e., advertising, public relations, and livestreaming) reached 86 million yuan (c.12 million US dollars) [46]. Wanghong, notably consisting of young females, have now become the new opinion leaders in consumption and in the re-construction of Chinese femininities.

There has been a growing group of linguistic-semiotic research, though still very few at this stage, investigating the discourse practices of wanghong. Li [35] analyzed the most prominent example of young female Chinese influencers (top-tier, with tens of millions of followers), Papi Jiang, using a grounded theory approach and showed how she reached virality with her unadorned beauty and ludicrous discussion of issues relatable to Chinese young urban generation. Also studying Papi Jiang, Weninger and Li [51] combined corpus linguistic and qualitative discourse analytic methods to unpack her satirical linguistic-semiotic style, such as her use of stance markers for negativity, intensity, and urgency. Drawing on a multimodal approach, Wang and Feng [48] analyzed the identity performance and self-branding strategies of 6 top-tier female wanghong on TikTok. They demonstrated how the influencers managed three major identity aspects, including the celebrity self, the entrepreneur self, and the ordinary woman self. Sandel and Wang [43] examined the multimodal communicative practices of three influencers, two women and a man, on three separate platforms, namely, Weibo, Douyin (Chinese TikTok) and Bilibili. They highlighted the influencers' construction of personal stories in creating intimacy with their followers, telling ordinary life struggles while drawing on discourses such as feminine empowerment, "leftover" woman, and satirical parody. However, these studies have focused on top-tier wanghong as illustrative examples, whereas we have very limited knowledge about the practices of a large group of micro- or mid-tier wanghong. They have also mainly adopted the thematic frames in media culture research such as identity performance and self-branding, with less attention paid to such aspects as genre and interaction. Moreover, practices on Xiaohongshu (RED), one of the major Chinese social media platforms, have not yet been investigated.

2.1 The Rise of Xiaohongshu (RED)

Xiaohongshu (also known as RED or Little Red Book) was founded in 2013 in Shanghai, China, now branded as "a lifestyle platform that inspires people to discover and connect with a range of diverse lifestyles" [53]. The notion of a "book" can be traced back to its debut as a PDF named "Overseas Shopping Guide," written by the founders and uploaded online, before developed into version 1.0 of the Xiaohongshu app named "Hong Kong Shopping Guide," where users can share their personal shopping experience (with product photos and information about prices and locations) as "shopping notes" [52]. By the end of 2021, Xiaohongshu had over 200 million active users, 70% being females under the age of 32 [41,53]. Its rise to popularity and demographically-specific user base (i.e., Chinese young females) have now attracted growing attention in postfeminist media culture research [29]. In Western media, Xiaohongshu is often taken up as China's Instagram with a blend of ecommerce (Amazon) and Pinterest. The agenda of sharing beauty and fashion products among young women with both photo-text and short video formats distinguishes Xiaohongshu from other Chinese platforms such as Weibo (microblogging, predominantly for sharing social, political, celebrity news), Bilibili (video-sharing with subculture appeals such as AGC and K-pop), Douyu (livestreaming), and Kwai and Douyin (short-video sharing).

Figure 1 shows Xiaohongshu's homepage [53]. Xiaohongshu posts, in default, are presented in an algorithmically generated stream under the "Discover" section, with an asymmetrical four-grid layout. Each post is presented with its first photo or video thumbnail, title, author profile picture and username, and like count. The bottom navigation bar presents functionalities of "Shop" for in-app product purchases, "Messages" for private communication and interaction notification, and "Me" for user profiling. The plus icon at the bottom centre is for making a new post. Xiaohongshu posts have two formats, photo-text and video, with three main interactive affordances, namely, like, collect, and com-

Fig. 1. Xiaohongshu homepage

Fig. 2. Xiaohongshu posts

ment. Figure 2(a) and (b) respectively show screenshots of a photo-text post and a video post.

3 Methodology

3.1 Small Stories Research

This study uses small stories as the overarching approach for analysis. The development of small stories research by Georgakopoulou [21] opens an important analytical space for exploring diverse storytelling activities in daily life. The notion of "small" carries both literal and metaphorical meanings: 1) storytelling can occupy a much-limited length in an interaction, and 2) "telling of mundane, ordinary, everyday events, not world-disruption and narration of complications" [23]. The initial research has identified three major types of small stories: breaking news (telling of very recent, just-now, or still happening events), projections (telling of events to take place in the near future), and shared stories (stories known by the interlocutors and oriented to in the interaction) [21]. These types of small stories have shown how storytelling in everyday life can involve non- or multi-linear sequencing, world-making, detachment and recontextualization, and multi-tellership. While small stories research in face-to-face contexts started out as a "counter-move" to the structural canon in sociolinguistic research (Labov's model) [23], small stories are widely present in social media communication, such as status update for telling "breaking news" about daily happenings [39], profile archival for creating an extended personal narrative [14], and networked posting for telling "shared stories" about macro social events [25]. This study draws on the small stories heuristic to map out the storytelling practices involved in the influencers' Xiaohongshu posts, including 1) *ways of telling* (the communicative how), 2) *sites* (situational context factors, where the storytelling and stories take place), and 3) *tellers* (participants in the communicative activity) [21,23].

Social Semiotic Multimodal Analysis as a Supplementary Approach. To integrate a multimodal perspective into the narrative analysis, this study also draws on social semiotic multimodal analysis as a supplementary method. For example, Page [40] has also combined small stories approach with social semiotics to study how social media images capture different tellable moments for different tellers. This study uses Kress and Van Leeuwen's [33] *grammar of visual design* to interpret visual meaning-making in storytelling. They have detailed how narrative processes can be represented in images, such as an action (conceptualized as a vector) directed from one participant to the other. Moreover, they have proposed ways of interpreting interpersonal meanings achieved by visual resources, such as the use of a direct gaze to establish an imagined, on-demand contact between the represented participant and the viewer or a close shot to indicate intimacy. The textual meanings can also be examined, such as the use of a foreground placement for enhancing salience, framing for separating elements, or left-right placement for differing given and new information.

3.2 Data Collection, Transcription and Analysis

This study is part of a longitudinal project on the construction of young female identities on Xiaohongshu. The project has used methods of digital ethnography, small stories and positioning analysis, and social semiotic multimodal analysis. We focused on nine beauty and fashion micro- and mid-tier influencers who were recruited on a basis of a 4-month ethnographic observation on Xiaohongshu (September-December 2022). According to Weiboyi [50], over 75% of the popular Xiaohongshu posts in 2020 were produced by micro- and mid-tier influencers. Among Xiaohongshu's active users, 46.39% are in the age range of 18 to 24 and 50% are living in the cities in China, and cosmetics, outfits and skincare are the top three popular topics on the site [41]. With the aim to construct a representative group with variations, we recruited nine influencers as participants, who were, at that time, between the age of 20 to 22, living in different cities in mainland China and with a follower size ranged from 41k (thousand) to 277k. Table 1 gives a summary of information about the participants. The names reflect how they address themselves as well as how they are addressed by other users in the comments on Xiaohongshu. Informed consent has been obtained from the participants for semi-structured interviews and collection as well as presentation of their Xiaohongshu data either with explicit attribution or pseudonymity (based on their choices). The primary dataset comprises a total of 602 Xiaohongshu posts (i.e., 20 most-liked and 50 most recent posts at the time of collection for each influencer, top 10 publicly visible comment threads for each post), their Xiaohongshu profile pages, and fieldnotes.

Table 1. Information of the participants

Name	Domain	Age	Location	Profession	Followers on Xiaohongshu
Miaoyan	Fashion	22	Hunan	Student	41k
Xue'er	Fashion	21	Guizhou	Student	102k
Lulu	Fashion	20	Sichuan	Student	138k
Pax	Fashion, beauty	22	Shanghai	Office worker	41k
Jiban	Beauty	21	Beijing	Student	63k
Rourou	Beauty	21	Hunan	Student	84k
Taotao	Beauty	20	Zhejiang	Student	97k
A'tian	Beauty	22	Guangdong	Student	181k
Huanhuan	Beauty	20	Guangdong	Influencer	277k

To transcribe the videos in the posts, we adopted a multi-column format separating the verbal content (overlaying text and speech) and non-verbal content (video screenshots) [38]. The speech was transcribed using the "Auto Captions" function on CapCut. The data were analyzed through qualitative, inductive manual coding using NVivo. Specifically, the posts were first categorized into different types of beauty and fashion content (as discourse practices) such as

OOTD, OOTW, vlog, makeup tutorial, unboxing, product review, lip swatch, outfit collection, and makeup transformation. To identify stories in the posts, we drew on the notion of narrative stancetaking in small stories research [22]. This involved considering elements of time, place, reported action or speech and characters, told or shown, as well as framings of a story to tell. We then analysed the storytelling features vis-à-vis three interconnected levels: ways of telling (linguistic-semiotic features of emplotment), sites (where the reported events as well as storytelling events were located), and tellers (who they are, their roles in contributing to story-making). In the following sections, I will discuss the analytical results derived from a subset of data, including 48 stories within 89 OOTD (Outfit of the Day) posts and 61 stories within 85 product review posts. OOTD (Outfit of the Day) and product review are two prominent discourse practices among the influencers.

4 Results

4.1 Minimal Telling in OOTD (Outfit of the Day)

OOTD (Outfit of the Day) is a genre of social media posts where the users share the clothes, shoes, and even accessories worn on a particular day [2]. On Xiaohongshu, an OOTD post can be presented in a photo-text format: the photos show a user in an outfit from various angles, such as full-body and close-up shots taken by others or mirror selfies with different poses (i.e., holding a camera/mobile phone to capture one's own reflection in the mirror). An OOTD post can also be in a video format. In a video, a user can present multiple sets of outfits, also in motion. The notion of "the day" thus can have a metaphorical meaning, in that OOTD does not necessarily mean sharing an outfit worn "today" in the here and now but outfits for daily occasions or worn across multiple days. A user might film an OOTD video in their bedroom, fixing a camera to a mid-body level and walking towards and away from it like doing a catwalk on a stage. In editing the video, they may add transition effects, changing from showing an outfit to wearing it or from wearing one outfit to another. They may also use background music to evoke specific moods (e.g., casualness, lightheartedness, or nostalgia) or apply stickers as well as overlaying images to convey specific themes (e.g., K-pop girl group style, China-Chic, or Y2K). For both photo-text and video posts, there is a caption (a title and a main text) section where a user can describe the outfit and sometimes talk about their day. Hashtags such as "OOTD" or the Chinese equivalent terms of "Daily outfit," "Everyday outfit," and "Today's outfit" are also often used to enhance a post's searchability and connectivity to other related posts.

OOTD is an important discourse practice for fashion influencers to showcase their personal styles. It is also a practice of social commerce. It is typical for an influencer to list the brands or shops where an outfit is from in the caption or overlaying text in the video or for viewers to ask about the shops in the comments if such information is not provided. Although Xiaohongshu does not allow posting any external links (e.g., not being able to offer a hyperlink directly to any shops outside of Xiaohongshu), an influencer can still profit from just wearing and mentioning an item from a shop as a form of endorsement. The viewers who are interested can get to the item by cross-platforming (switching to the platform where the shop is located). In the current project, OOTD posting is a prominent practice among two fashion influencers, Miaoyan and Lulu, with the former focusing on photo-text posts and the latter on videos. Miaoyan was a first-year postgraduate student and Lulu was an undergraduate at the time of data collection. The outfits they shared are mainly from online shops on Taobao, with each item falling within a price range of ¥50 (c.$7) to ¥200 (c.$28). As Taobao is the most widely used online shopping platform in mainland China, in their posts, they often do not explicitly mention Taobao but simply provide the names of the shops, which can be understood by their followers.

Instead of gaining followership through an extended, detailed narration of their personal lives with anything celebrity-like (e.g., being in exclusive, glamorous events or collaborating with luxury brands), Miaoyan and Lulu post their OOTDs every two or three days, with a very limited telling of their daily life occurrences. Rather, storytelling is a contextualization strategy for showcasing their fashion styles, that is, situationalizing the outfit within a specific time, place, and activity. Figure 3 shows an OOTD post by Miaoyan, which received 5,585 likes. It has 6 photos. Photo 1 features her sitting on the floor, looking directly at the camera and smiling, while making a wink (one eye closed) and a V sign. The V sign, that is, raising the index and middle fingers, with the palm facing outward, is a popular photo gesture among young East Asians or Chinese, which is also noted to be associated with a visual cuteness culture, a technique to make one's face looking smaller while being lively [10]. Photo 2 shows her leaning against a fence, head-tilted. Photo 3 depicts her taking a selfie with another girl. Photo 4, in a similar background with trees, features her in some action with her head lowered, not directing her attention to the camera when doing what she was doing. Photo 5 shows her kissing a calf while facing away from the camera, which further indicates some distance from the photographing activity. Photo 6 shows her sitting in a car in a relaxing pose. In all the photos, she is wearing the same outfit.

This post tells and shows a small story: she had a day off "today" and went to a ranch with good friends. The gist of the story is given in the first line of the main text, with her excitement expressed through an exclamation mark and the people involved characterized as "good friends." The photos provide glimpses of the location and the activities involved (e.g., taking selfies together, hanging out under the trees, playing with a calf, and being on the move in a car). An orientation to the settings is also conveyed through the text (sunny days, summer). However, the post does not detail what happened on that day, and the photos might not reflect actions in their actual order of occurrence. In this as well as other photo-text OOTD posts, the key point is to show an outfit in different contexts of situation: As highlighted in the title, the outfit is perfect as a summer wear. The story then demonstrates what it looks like (a casual look) in such a situation as going out with friends on a sunny summer day. The

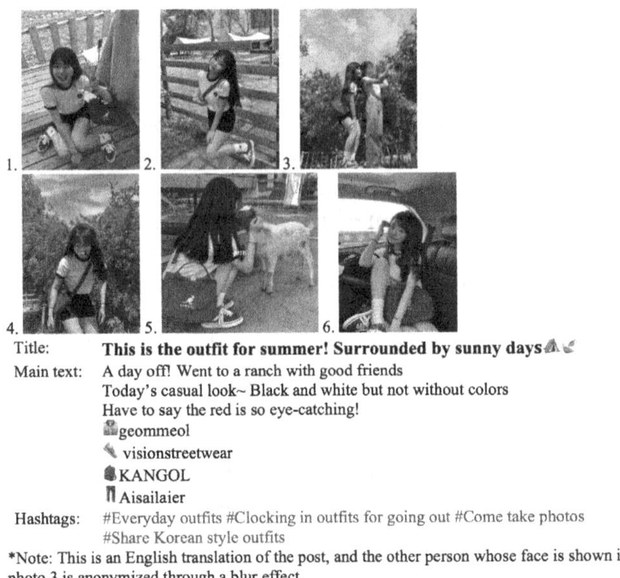

Fig. 3. Storytelling in a photo-text OOTD post

hashtags not only link this post to other OOTD posts (e.g., #Everyday outfits) but also categorize the style (#Share Korean style outfits). OOTD posts also use a lot of emojis to represent items in an outfit such as a shirt, a pair of shoes or a backpack as well as the actions and environment of the stories told, as shown in this post. The emojis, compared to the use of descriptive language, make a post more concise and playful, also with some textual functions (e.g., separating the lines or acting as a punctuation mark).

In other photo-text OOTD posts, the main plots of the stories, also typically summarized in a sentence or two in the text, are about going to a restaurant (e.g., "let's have McDonald's!" "Went to a retro, American style café" "Yea! Today I had a durian pizza") or simply going out somewhere (e.g., "Wearing this doggy [shirt] to a date" "Today's going out"). In the comments, these stories are not oriented to by other users. For example, a commenter will not normally ask "Where the ranch is" and "What have you done" but express appreciation towards the look in general (e.g., "So pretty!") or towards specific items in the outfit (e.g., "Really love this backpack"), similar to commenting on posts without storytelling. In this sense, the stories are minimalized not only by the influencers but also by the audience who are more concerned about the fashion styles shared through the OOTD posts. In the video posts, the contextualization function and minimal features of storytelling are also evident. Figure 4 shows an extract (screenshots and translated overlaying texts) of an OOTD video post by Lulu.

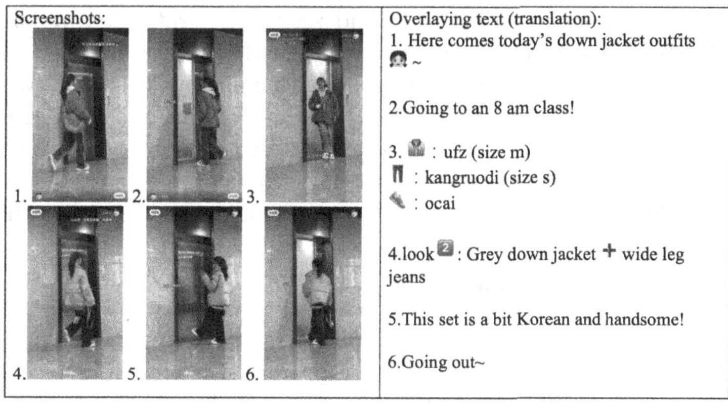

Fig. 4. Storytelling in a video OOTD post

Most of Lulu's video OOTD posts are in the same setting, with her walking in and out of an elevator. This elevator, according to her, is located in one of the teaching buildings at the university where she studied. Lulu's OOTDs do not feature her in any extraordinary, highly tellable fashion events but consistently depict her arriving and leaving class in various outfits on different days, often featuring scenes around that elevator. For example, as shown in Fig. 4, she adds the texts, "Going to an 8 am class" and "Going out," to the left-center of the shots of her entering the elevator (screenshots 2 & 6), which gives salience to her actions framed as taking part in particular events. In screenshot 3, the outfit's shop details are provided at the top-left margin alongside the default Xiaohongshu platform logo, signaling them to be supplementary, known information.

The temporal display of the actions and her verbalizing them as events thus create a small story of her mundane daily life. The use of brief portions of a process, typified images, and informative titles to compress a series of actions and the temporal progression into a few moments is a common narrative filmmaking technique for ellipsis known as *montage sequences* [9]. Her telling is similarly minimal as that in the photo-text posts, with one non-subject sentence offering the gist, but the ways of mobilizing the visual resources are different. While in a photo-text post, the photos and the text are displayed on a page as a relatively static multimodal text, in a video post, the telling and showing come together and unfold in time. Furthermore, in Miaoyan's example, the showing of a story involves multiple scenes depicting different aspects of the reported experience, whereas in Lulu's example, the telling is more performative or figurative, as a way to reframe her actions of walking in and out of an elevator not so much as a fashion catwalk as an influencer but as part of her daily activities as a student.

Instead of constructing a "sexy" body as a source of femininity or operating a makeover paradigm that highlights beauty as the solution to self-betterment as in Western postfeminist media culture [27], the OOTD posts rather convey the idea that beauty is an integral part of ordinary life. This is particularly shown through a minimal telling of mundane and relatable events (e.g., having a day off with friends or going to a morning class) coupled with a linguistic-semiotic presentation of aspirational fashion styles (e.g., being "eye-catching" with a red backpack in Miaoyan's example, or being "a bit Korean and handsome" in a grey down jacket and a pair of wide leg jeans in Lulu's example)-a selling of "lifestyles" to Chinese young girls like themselves who are also college students and who can afford and access the same items through the Taobao online shops.

4.2 Co-Telling in Product Review

In genres such as makeup tutorial or GRWM (Get Ready with Me) that involve documenting uses of cosmetics or skincare products, beauty influencers might, in the process of application, suddenly go into detail about a specific product, its effect and even ingredients, highlighting its selling points and telling while illustrating how it should be properly used from their "personal" and "professional" viewpoints [8]. Such product talk sometimes runs the risk of being criticized by their viewers as advertising. On Xiaohongshu, the platform has required users to register their advertising activities on a "Brand Collaboration Platform," where Xiaohongshu can gain commission fees from such activities and disclose the paid nature of the posts with an "ad" label, but as reflected in the dataset of this project, the influencers, more often than not, do not necessarily go along with this procedure. For them, doing the right thing is not so much about adherence to formal rules but about mitigating the detrimental impact of soft selling on the trust they have built with their followers. One mitigating technique is to do giveaways or price draws, through which they can share the financial gains from product promotion with some of their followers. Another technique is to tell stories to authenticate their product usage, indicating that even though the post may be sponsored, they have personally used the product before recommending it to their audience [42].

The analysis of the storied posts shows that they might recount the twists and turns of getting recommendation from somewhere or someone and previous uses of related products, showing proof of purchase (e.g., presenting a screenshot in a video as a pop-up overlaying image), or recording a day in life with the product applied to demonstrate its effect. However, for the genre of product review, in which product talk is expected and centered, storytelling becomes less of an influencer monologue to avoid blatant selling in between a discussion of "how to" but more of an interaction, in which other users in the comments are important co-tellers for product experience sharing and negotiation. On Xiaohongshu, the activity of giving and receiving product recommendations also has an idiomatic term: "zhongcao" (seeding, or planting grass), which expresses the intention to purchase the product shared by others or the sharing of one's own experience in order to cultivate similar intentions in others.

Figure 5 presents the video thumbnail and a storytelling extract of a product review post by Huanhuan. All product review posts in the dataset are video posts, typically lasting for 3 min or less. The video thumbnails of these posts prominently showcase the influencers in a talking head mode, holding all the products to be discussed together, with one or two lines of overlaying texts (i.e., short phrases in relatively large fonts and bright, eye-catching colors) underlining the theme and marking the genre of the posts. For positive product reviews in particular, these posts can be labelled as "goodies/good things to share," "product recommendation," "my favorites," "monthly/yearly favorites" (periodized posts), or "double eleven/618/38 goodness festival must-buys" (posts temporally anchored to online shopping festivals). As illustrated in Fig. 5, in the video thumbnail, Huanhuan holds three products in her hands, which are exactly the ones she reviews in the video. The overlaying text at the top highlights the products' shared function as the theme, that is, to stop foundation creasing in autumn and winter. The bottom text categorizes the post as a product review-"skincare goodies to share." With the top and bottom placements, the texts do not block Huanhuan's face. The composition of the scene thus still highlights her eye contact as a form of direct address to the audience and the showing of the actual products.

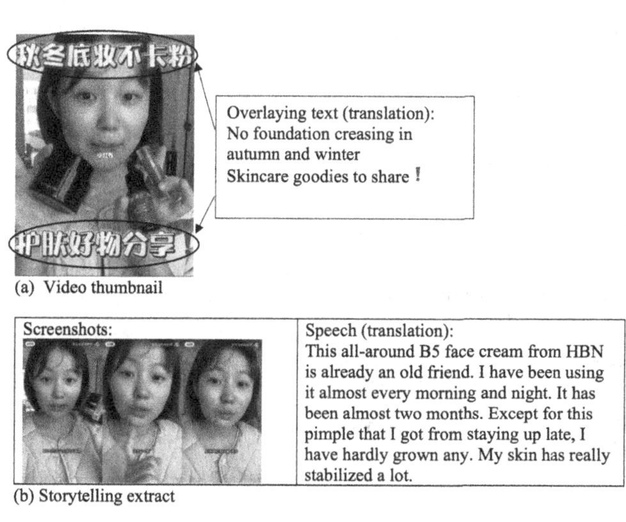

Fig. 5. Storytelling in a product review post

Stories are typically embedded in the talk for illustrating a point about a product (e.g., surprising effect or newness). In this post by Huanhuan for instance, to introduce the HBN all-around B5 face cream, Huanhuan first picks up the product. She then enters into a small story about how the face cream has helped her stabilize her skin in the past two months, while remaining in the talking head mode throughout the talk. As a brief orientation, she introduces the character of the story, the face cream, as "already an old friend," which indicates her familiarity with the product. She then presents the main event: After consistently using the product day and night for two months, she has noticed a significant improvement in her skin, which has now become stable. When stressing the time frame, she makes a pointing finger gesture in front of the camera.

As her skin condition is clearly observable in the upper-half-body shot, she also specifically addresses the remaining acne on her left face, attributing it to herself staying up late.

Notably, unlike the OOTD posts where stories are minimalized by both influencers and their audience, in the product review posts, other users in the comments do orient to the reported experience in various ways. Figure 6 presents extracts of four comment threads from Huanhuan's post. In thread (a), commenter 1 asks where the products can be purchased-a missing component of the story. In the initial telling, Huanhuan does not mention where she purchased the face cream. In response to this question, Huanhuan rather reveals that she is not the customer but the seller. In the video, she does not promote her livestreaming practice at all but takes the position of a peer consumer. It is then this co-telling turn of interaction that facilitates her move from recommending the product to selling it, from the story to future actions, which also leads to commenter 2's further questioning about potential discounts. In other product review posts similarly, the influencers might not disclose the commercial practices involved in the videos but talk about them later on by answering questions such as the way to buy the same products. Commenter 1's response also exemplifies how the listeners of a product story develop and express a purchasing intention.

(a) *Commenter 1:* Where to buy
Huanhuan: Tomorrow's livestream
Commenter 2: Will it be cheaper than the official

(b) *Commenter 3:* I used that hbn one before. It's really nice. The retinol cream from the same brand is literarily my favorite
Huanhuan: Hahaha

(c) *Comment 4:* You called this good?
Huanhuan: If you don't like it, don't watch it

(d) *Comment 5:* Is hbn suitable for dry skin
Huanhuan: Suitable

Fig. 6. Co-telling in the comments of a product review post

In thread (b), commenter 3 supports Huanhuan's assessment of the product's effectiveness by bringing in her own experience of using it and even adding a recommendation for another product of the same brand. The "Hahaha" from Huanhuan is not a reaction to anything funny but a friendly acknowledgement of this comment. In contrast, commenter 4 takes a hostile stance towards Huanhuan's evaluation of her skin condition with a rhetorical question. At the start of the video, Huanhuan proposes that her skin has been looking good recently. This comment raises doubts about her characterization of "good," which destructs her claim that the products have contributed to improving her skin. Instead of dismissing it, Huanhuan puts it in the spotlight by explicitly rejecting the commenter's perspective, also as a way to defeat trolling. Thread (d) represents another type of response, which seeks advice on the suitability of the product, implying a purchasing intention.

In summary, storytelling in the product review posts is notably embedded in the influencers' talk for an initial emplotment (i.e., introducing the key product and the emblematic event) and extended in the comments, with other users acting as co-tellers with negotiation of details, assessments (e.g., trolling or bringing in their own experiences for alignment), and questions indirectly projecting their related future actions. From a critical viewpoint, it can be said that these posts reflect the restrictive or oppressive features of beauty practices, with a display of postfeminist sensitivities: a construction of appearance problems as trivial as having a remaining pimple from staying up late or experiencing foundation creasing in the cold weather, which necessitates ongoing labor for resolving them, such as using a face cream diligently to "stabilize" the skin-a self-discipline, self-monitor discourse [27]. The commitment to continued consumption and devotion of time and effort are implicit but notable. However, rather than simply being "victims" of the beauty industry or "empowered" female entrepreneurs profiting from commercial practices, the young women here are also socializing over the beautification processes, telling as well as reacting to stories in their everyday lives with products as a shared point. Beauty and its related consumption then become communal and communicative rather than individual, as practices associated with relationship building and experience sharing. The predicament for feminist researchers, therefore, lies not in highlighting the disillusionment of pursuing appearance perfection via consumption and body work while revealing the underlying neoliberal, patriarchal ideologies, but rather in disentangling beauty from its communicability and sociality for women.

5 Conclusions: Re-feminizing Beauty as Ordinary and Communicative

Drawing on a small stories approach and social semiotic multimodal analysis, this paper examined the storytelling practices of nine beauty and fashion influencers on the Chinese social media platform, Xiaohongshu (RED). The analysis singled out the salient telling features of two types of posts, namely, OOTD and product review. With a minimal telling of mundane life events coupled with documentation of outfit choices, the OOTD posts facilitate a linking between beauty and everyday life. These posts exemplify the contemporary practices of street style fashion on Chinese social media among young women (i.e., photographing and documenting one's clothing styles in lay, urban locations, with styling coming from the grassroots). The analysis made a case for considering storytelling as an important contextualization strategy as well as an apparatus for conveying ordinariness in such practices. In terms of the product review posts, co-telling points to the various contributions of other users in the comments to the stories about products initiated in the influencers' talk, such as moving from a past story of using the product to a future commercial activity of selling it, validating or refuting the influencers' assessment, or providing additional insight or personal experience related to the product. For instance, the act of challenging-"You called this good?"-deconstructs the influencer's problem-solution discourse about how the product has stabilized her skin.

The findings of this paper provide insights into the construction of post-socialist Chinese femininities on social media. The paper began by discussing the gendered aspect of influencers, the circulation of postfeminist media culture as an empowered, consumerist discourse, and the historical complexities in the (de)coupling between beauty and femininity in China. It also identified Xiaohongshu as a popular site among Chinese young women centering on topics of beauty and fashion. The analysis has enabled us to see the linguistic-semiotic specificities of their discourse practices, such as how the young micro-/mid-tier influencers story their personal styles with ordinariness, which is far from the postfeminist representations of entrepreneurial femininity and expert taste-making. Nevertheless, with the OOTDs, they are directing aesthetic norms (i.e., with aspirational descriptions) and creating consumption desires (i.e., offering shoppable detail) among their audience. This paper has also pinpointed the challenges in approaching the problem of beauty from a feminist critical perspective, highlighting the entanglement of beauty and sociality and how storytelling contributes to constructing the communicability of beauty-appearance work as sharable, communal experiences. The social activity of "seeding" on Xiaohonghsu, a relaying behavior in beauty product consumption, is a case in point. Furthermore, the collaborative engagement in product storytelling sensitizes us to the concurrence of influencer marketing and Electronic Word-of-Mouth on social media, in which the meanings (reputations) of products and brands are co-constructed and negotiated in the sharing of product information and experience [31].

For future research, more work will need to be done in two directions. The first direction concerns the mediating role of the social media platforms. It remains to be explored whether and how a platform's design enables as well as constrains what types of stories to be shared and how [26], including such aspects as its governance of interactive and commercial activities, the pre-formatting of the posts and provision of specific sets of linguistic-semiotic resources that can be value-laden, and the algorithmic distribution of content that shapes tiers of user visibility. The second direction, particularly in relation to feminist media research, involves examining the intersectionality of postfeminist media culture [28]. The influencers this paper has focused on are urban, middle-class, educated young women in China similar to their privileged Western counterparts, epitomizing the neoliberal globalization of beauty and fashion consumption and digital communication practices (e.g., the use of the term "OOTD" on both Instagram and Xiaohongshu). An important next step is to zoom in on a wider variety of feminine subjects across age, class, and ethnicity, from online to offline, which will enrich our understanding of the division structures within the transnational flow and also raise crucial questions about accessibility and targeting of social media practices and cultures. It is equally important not to reduce a feminist critique on beauty to language and discourse as signification and interpretation but to also attend to materiality, matters of actions and practices.

References

1. Abidin, C.: Agentic cute (^.^): pastiching East Asian cute in influencer commerce. East Asian J. Pop. Cult. **2**(1), 33–47 (2016). https://doi.org/10.1386/eapc.2.1.33_1
2. Abidin, C.: Visibility labour: engaging with influencers' fashion brands and# ootd advertorial campaigns on instagram. Media Int. Aust. **161**(1), 86–100 (2016). https://doi.org/10.1177/1329878X16665177
3. Abidin, C.: Mapping internet celebrity on tiktok: exploring attention economies and visibility labours. Cult. Sci. J. **12**(1), 77–103 (2021). https://doi.org/10.5334/csci.140
4. Abidin, C., Brown, M.L.: Microcelebrity Around the Globe: Approaches to Cultures of Internet Fame. Emerald Group Publishing, Bradford (2019)
5. Banet-Weiser, S.: Authentic^{TM}: The Politics of Ambivalence in a Brand Culture. New York University Press, New York (2012). https://doi.org/10.18574/nyu/9780814739372.001.0001
6. Banet-Weiser, S.: "I'm Beautiful the Way I am': Empowerment, Beauty, and Aesthetic Labour, pp. 265–282. Palgrave Macmillan, London (2017). https://doi.org/10.1057/978-1-137-47765-1_15
7. Berryman, R., Kavka, M.: 'I guess a lot of people see me as a big sister or a friend': the role of intimacy in the celebrification of beauty vloggers. J. Gend. Stud. **26**(3), 307–320 (2017). https://doi.org/10.1080/09589236.2017.1288611
8. Bhatia, A.: Interdiscursive performance in digital professions: the case of youtube tutorials. J. Pragmat. **124**, 106–120 (2018). https://doi.org/10.1016/j.pragma.2017.11.001
9. Bordwell, D., Thompson, K., Smith, J.: Film Art: An Introduction, vol. 8. McGraw-Hill, New York (2008)
10. Burnett, S.: Have you ever wondered why East Asians spontaneously make v-signs in photos? (2014). https://time.com/2980357/asia-photos-peace-sign-v-janet-lynn-konica-jun-inoue/
11. Droz-dit Busset, O.: "So-called influencers": stancetaking and (de)legitimation in mediatized discourse about social media influencers. Discour. Cont. Media **49**, 100629 (2022). https://doi.org/10.1016/j.dcm.2022.100629
12. Cosmetics Business: Cosmetics business forecasts 5 global beauty trends of 2020 in new report. Cosmetics Business (2020). https://bit.ly/3yj3IOv
13. Craig, D., Lin, J., Cunningham, S.: Wanghong as Social Media Entertainment in China. Springer, Heidelberg (2021). https://doi.org/10.1007/978-3-030-65376-7
14. Dayter, D.: Small stories and extended narratives on twitter. Discour. Context Media **10**, 19–26 (2015). https://doi.org/10.1016/j.dcm.2015.05.003
15. Dosekun, S.: For western girls only? post-feminism as transnational culture. Fem. Media Stud. **15**(6), 960–975 (2015). https://doi.org/10.1080/14680777.2015.1062991
16. Duffy, B., Hund, E.: Gendered visibility on social media: navigating instagram's authenticity bind. Int. J. Commun. **13**, 20 (2019). https://ijoc.org/index.php/ijoc/article/view/11729
17. Duffy, B.E., Hund, E.: "Having it all" on social media: entrepreneurial femininity and self-branding among fashion bloggers. Social Media Soc. **1**(2), 2056305115604337 (2015). https://doi.org/10.1177/2056305115604337

18. Feng, Y., Chen, H., Kong, Q.: An expert with whom i can identify: the role of narratives in influencer marketing. Int. J. Advert. **40**(7), 972–993 (2021). https://doi.org/10.1080/02650487.2020.1824751
19. Ferry, M.M.: Advertising, consumerism and nostalgia for the new woman in contemporary china. Continuum **17**(3), 277–290 (2003). https://doi.org/10.1080/10304310302738
20. Finnane, A.: What should Chinese women wear?: a national problem. Mod. China **22**(2), 99–131 (1996). http://www.jstor.org/stable/189339
21. Georgakopoulou, A.: Small stories, interaction and identities. John Benjamins (2007)
22. Georgakopoulou, A.: Small stories transposition and social media: a micro-perspective on the 'greek crisis'. Discour. Soc. **25**(4), 519–539 (2014). https://doi.org/10.1177/0957926514536963
23. Georgakopoulou, A.: Small stories research: methods - analysis - outreach. In: The Handbook of Narrative Analysis, pp. 178–193. Wiley Blackwell (2015)
24. Georgakopoulou, A.: Co-opting small stories on social media: a narrative analysis of the directive of authenticity. Poetics Today **43**(2), 265–286 (2022). https://doi.org/10.1215/03335372-9642609
25. Georgalou, M.: Small stories of the greek crisis on facebook. Social Media Soci. **1**(2), 2056305115605859 (2015). https://doi.org/10.1177/2056305115605859
26. Giaxoglou, K., Georgakopoulou, A.: A narrative practice approach to identities: small stories and positioning analysis in digital contexts. In: Cambridge Handbooks in Psychology, pp. 241–261. Cambridge University Press, Cambridge (2021). https://doi.org/10.1017/9781108755146.014
27. Gill, R.: Postfeminist media culture: elements of a sensibility. Eur. J. Cult. Stud. **10**(2), 147–166 (2007). https://doi.org/10.1177/1367549407075898
28. Gill, R.: Post-postfeminism?: new feminist visibilities in postfeminist times. Fem. Media Stud. **16**(4), 610–630 (2016). https://doi.org/10.1080/14680777.2016.1193293
29. Guo, J.: The postfeminist entrepreneurial self and the platformisation of labour: a case study of yesheng female lifestyle bloggers on xiaohongshu. Glob. Media China **7**(3), 303–318 (2022). https://doi.org/10.1177/20594364221095896
30. Han, X.: Historicising wanghong economy: connecting platforms through wanghong and wanghong incubators. Celeb. Stud. **12**(2), 317–325 (2021). https://doi.org/10.1080/19392397.2020.1737196
31. Jiménez-Castillo, D., Sánchez-Fernández, R.: The role of digital influencers in brand recommendation: examining their impact on engagement, expected value and purchase intention. Int. J. Inf. Manag. **49**, 366–376 (2019). https://doi.org/10.1016/j.ijinfomgt.2019.07.009
32. Johansson, P.: Selling the "modern woman": consumer culture and Chinese gender politics. In: Images of the "Modern Woman" in Asia: Global Media, Local Meanings, pp. 94–121 (2001)
33. Kress, G., Van Leeuwen, T.: Reading Images: The Grammar of Visual Design, 3rd edn. Routledge, Abingdon (2020). https://doi.org/10.4324/9781003099857
34. Lazar, M.M.: The Right to be Beautiful: Postfeminist Identity and Consumer Beauty Advertising, pp. 37–51. Palgrave Macmillan, London (2011). https://doi.org/10.1057/9780230294523_3
35. Li, A.K.: Papi jiang and microcelebrity in China: a multilevel analysis. Int. J. Commun. **13**, 19 (2019). https://ijoc.org/index.php/ijoc/article/view/10796
36. Marwick, A.E.: Status Update: Celebrity, Publicity, and Branding in the Social Media Age. Yale University Press, Yale (2013)

37. National Bureau of Statistics of China: Total retail sales of consumer goods in 2021 (2022). http://www.stats.gov.cn/english/PressRelease/202201/t20220118_1826503.html
38. Ochs, E.: Transcriptions as theory. In: Developmental Pragmatics, pp. 43–72. Academic Press (1979)
39. Page, R.: Re-examining narrativity: small stories in status updates. Text Talk **30**(4), 423–444 (2010). https://doi.org/10.1515/text.2010.021
40. Page, R.: Narratives Online: Shared Stories in Social Media. Cambridge University Press, Cambridge (2018)
41. Qian-gua: Qian-gua active user portrait trend report in 2022 (xiaohongshu platform) (2022). https://www.qian-gua.com/blog/detail/1591.html
42. Ringrow, H.: 'This is a Sponsored Post, But All Opinions are My Qwn': Advertising (re)tellings on Social Media, pp. 163–178. Bloomsbury Academic, London (2021). https://doi.org/10.5040/9781350120051.ch-010
43. Sandel, T.L., Wang, Y.: Selling intimacy online: the multi-modal discursive techniques of China's Wanghong. Discour. Cont. Media **47**, 100606 (2022). https://doi.org/10.1016/j.dcm.2022.100606
44. Senft, T.M.: Camgirls: Celebrity and community in the age of social networks, vol. 4. Peter Lang (2008)
45. Stevens, S.E.: Figuring modernity: the new woman and the modern girl in Republican China. NWSA J. **15**(3), 82–103 (2003). http://www.jstor.org/stable/4317011
46. Topklout: 2022–2033 advertiser kol marketing market inventory and trend forecast (2023). https://www.sohu.com/a/670601332_483389
47. Wang, P.: Aching for Beauty: Footbinding in China. University of Minnesota Press, Minneapolis (2000)
48. Wang, Y., (William) Feng, D.: Identity performance and self-branding in social commerce: a multimodal content analysis of Chinese Wanghong women's video-sharing practice on tiktok. Discour. Cont. Media **50**, 100652 (2022). https://doi.org/10.1016/j.dcm.2022.100652
49. Wang, Z.: Gender, employment and women's resistance. In: Chinese Society, pp. 176–204. Routledge (2003)
50. Weiboyi: How to create popularity using the "picks" methodology on xiaohongshu to help brands win xiaohongshu (2021). https://pic.optaim.com/ifans/2021-05/1621577103W4XDQ007Jke39b1F.pdf
51. Weninger, C., Li, D.: Performing microcelebrity: analyzing Papi Jiang's online persona through stance and style. Lang. Soc. **52**(2), 263–294 (2023). https://doi.org/10.1017/S0047404521001020
52. Xiaohongshu: The story of how it all started (2022). https://www.xiaohongshu.com/en/newsroom/detail/xiaohongshu-the-story-of-how-it-all-started
53. Xiaohongshu: Creators. https://www.xiaohongshu.com/en/creators (nd)
54. Xu, G., Feiner, S.: Meinü jingji/China's beauty economy: buying looks, shifting value, and changing place. Fem. Econ. **13**(3–4), 307–323 (2007). https://doi.org/10.1080/13545700701439499

Multi-sensory Interactive Experience Design of Museum Musical Instrument Collections

Yanan Wu[2], Yiyuan Huang[1(✉)], Wenchen Guo[2,3(✉)], Xiao Li[2,5], Zhirui Chen[4], Zheyu Feng[2], Yubin Zhu[2], and Guoyu Sun[2(✉)]

[1] Beijing Institute of Graphic Communication, Beijing, China
yiyuan.huang@bigc.edu.cn
[2] Communication University of China, Beijing, China
beihuanfanchen@sina.com, guoyusun_cuc@126.com
[3] Peking University, Beijing, China
[4] University of Chinese Academy of Social Sciences, Beijing, China
[5] University of Edinburgh, Edinburgh, UK

Abstract. This paper explores museum musical instrument exhibits' current status and development trends. It highlights the importance of multi-sensory interaction for the museum experience, especially for musical instrument exhibits. Based on existing literatures and case studies, the strengths and weaknesses of current musical instrument exhibit interaction forms are analyzed, and the possibility of applying intelligent replicas to museum musical instrument interaction is proposed. This project produced an interactive prototype in which a physical model of chimes is embedded in a digital component that serves as an interface to control the delivery of virtual instrument sounds and animation effects on screen. The aim is to restore the functionality of the chimes as musical instruments by representing their visual, acoustic, and in some cases, tactile characteristics to visitors through physical interaction.

Keywords: Chinese Chimes · Interactive Art and Design · Tangible Interaction · User Experience · Digital Cultural Heritage

1 Introduction

Museums shape how people perceive and see the world [1]. As defined by the International Council of Museums [2], museums are non-profit, permanent institutions at the service of society and its development, preserving, studying and exhibiting the tangible and intangible heritage of humanity and its environment for the purposes of education, studying and enjoyment. In the early days, museums focused on collecting and preserving collections, and the main reason people came to museums was to view these objects. As time passed, people started to have higher expectations of museum visits. Visitors generally perceive museums as setting too strict rules, primarily confined to observing exhibits, and lacking in interactivity and challenge. The museum's glass showcases isolate visitors and objects in separate spaces. Graham [3] describes them as "mausoleums of objects" [4]. In such context, it is difficult to show the function of many functional

H. Mori et al. (Eds.): HCII 2023, LNCS 14056, pp. 420–437, 2023.
https://doi.org/10.1007/978-3-031-48044-7_30

exhibits. Museum musical instrument exhibits, as artefacts with complex structures used to produce sound, also lose their function of creating music and are reduced to silent decorative objects in glass display cases. As a result, the experience of visiting musical instrument exhibits in museums is disappointing for visitors [4]. Chinese chimes, one of the treasures of the National Museum of China, face the same problem. Museums need to re-examine the way they exhibit their musical instrument exhibits and improve the visitor experience. This paper explores the current situation and trends of museum experience based on the available literature. It focuses on the impact of multisensory 4 stimulation on the visitor's experience of the exhibition and its use in the design of museum interactions. It also emphasizes the importance of listening experiences and tactile experiences for designing musical instrument collection experiences in museums and lists possible solutions for realizing these experiences. Based on the case study and analysis, this paper proposes a physical interaction solution for the interaction of museum instrument collections. The interaction scheme embeds replicas of musical instrument collections into digital components that act as interactive interfaces to control the delivery of digital content to compensate for the missing sensory experience of virtual musical instruments. "Chimes" is a physical museum interactive installation based on the Chinese Museum's collection of Zeng Hou Yi chimes. The project created a digital model of the bell and an interactive game based on Unity using real sampled sounds of the chimes. The user triggers sound and animation effects by interacting with the chimes' physical installation. The installation soldered the physical model of the chimes to a cable and connected it to a computer via a circuit board. The physical chimes model acts as the input interface to the game program. The user can interact with the physical chime model in real-time by striking it with a brass hammer to simulate the playing of the chimes. The results show that the solution enables a visual and auditory experience and a partial tactile experience of the musical instrument exhibit, offering a new direction for the design of future museum musical instrument exhibit experiences.

2 Literature Review

2.1 Current Situation and Development Trend of Museums

Passive viewing and walking through the glass showcases no longer satisfy visitors, especially adult visitors, many of whom say the museum experience is not as pleasant as they expected [5, 6]. Building social relationships and anticipating interesting informal learning processes have become why people decide to visit museums [7]. Most museums, however, are still in the stage of preserving and displaying objects note that the first paragraph of a section or subsection is not indented.

Shift from Collection-Centered to Visitor-Centered. Over time, museums are shifting from being collection-centered to being visitor-centered [7]. The function of museums has shifted from preserving objects and displaying them to the public to providing meaningful learning experiences for the public. The concept of the "museum experience" has begun to be discussed frequently, meaning that museums are focusing more on the connection between visitors and exhibits rather than just collecting and preserving items. Liu and Yu [8] identified three trends in the development of modern museums:

first, the environment of exhibitions has become more open and enjoyable. Monotonous environments and a single way of viewing exhibitions can no longer meet the public's cultural consumption needs, and museums need to place more emphasis on creating environments and atmospheres that give visitors a richer and more vivid viewing experience. Secondly, diversified exhibition forms and visiting behaviors. Museums need to reshape the attributes of their exhibitions in new and appropriate ways and no longer limit themselves to static and monotonous displays. Thirdly, the viewing process is becoming more interactive. Museums are encouraging visitors to participate in exhibitions through new forms of display, allowing them to actively explore and trigger information rather than just passively receive it as observers. Creating sufficiently engaging engagement behaviors is, therefore, an essential direction for museums to take in order to enhance the museum visiting experience (see Fig. 1).

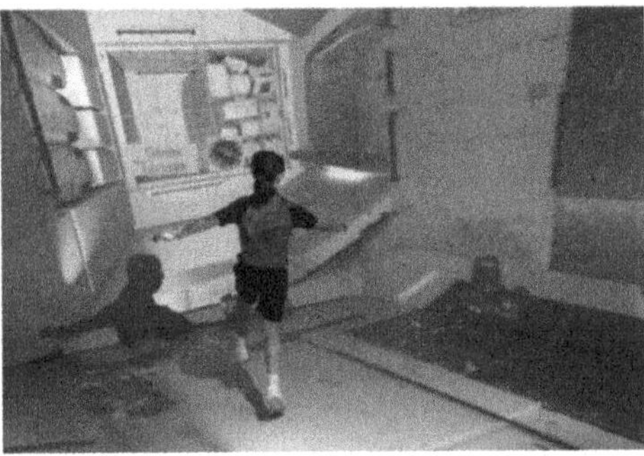

Fig. 1. "Docking in Space" (Left) allows visitors to control the spacecraft to dock with the International Space Station. "Disorientation" (Right) takes visitors into an upside-down space station to experience what it's like to be in a state of weightlessness in space (Hong Kong Space Museum).

Engagement Behaviors Help Enhance the Visitor Experience. The engaging behavior of museum visitors enriches their experience and enhances their learning. Falk and Dierking [9] proposed an interactive experience model of visitor experience factors. The model suggests that visitors' experiences result from personal, social and environmental factors. This paragraph discusses the impact of interactive, participatory behavior on visitors' experience of visiting museums in terms of both individual and environmental aspects.

On the one hand, interactive exhibitions align with visitors' expectations of museums. According to Larsen [10], visitors' expectations of museum visits fall into five main categories: fun and relaxation, cultural entertainment, personal identity, historical learning and escapism. The highest mean values and lowest variances were found for the relaxation and historical learning expectations, indicating that most visitors' expectations of visiting museums are focused on relaxation and historical learning. Studies have noted that, compared with traditional exhibition formats visitors generally show a higher interest in interacting with exhibits in a participatory manner, which is regarded to be more enjoyable [5]. However, there are differences in the ability of visitors with different backgrounds, interests and purposes to digest museum knowledge and information. Few will read the exhibition carefully unless visitors have specific prior knowledge or this learning intention [11, 12]. In such contexts, interactive content plays an active and essential role in visitors' learning processes. A study from the British Audiovisual Society has proved this, which states that people remember only 10% of what they read, but 90% of what is said and done [13]. In addition, interactive exhibitions offer the possibility of deeper learning [14], which means that interactive exhibitions are more responsive to the needs of different levels of learning than traditional exhibitions. On the other hand, digital technology provides a dynamic environment for museums, where the physical form of objects and digital information merge, transforming the museum into a hybrid and complex participatory space, which is a significant shift. Museum visitors are no longer passive recipients but become participants in the museum space [3, 5, 15]. In such an environment, visitors can choose when and in what way they want to receive the information they want, which makes the information they receive more personal and consequently leads to a positive learning experience [5, 16].

The Importance of Multisensory Stimulation. Visiting a museum was primarily a single-sensory visual experience for a long time. Although there has been a shift in focus from collections to visitor experiences over the last 20 years, most of these experiences have remained at the stage of visual and textual displays [7, 17, 18]. Visual touch interaction is currently one of the museums' primary forms of interaction. It is more accessible to the general public when operated through the medium of a screen than traditional forms of interaction with mouse, keyboard or joystick input. However, using all two-dimensional forms of interaction can easily lead to visual fatigue and a lack of immersion for visitors. Research has demonstrated that introducing multisensory stimuli (auditory, olfactory, tactile, etc.) into the design of museum experiences significantly impacts visitor arousal. Contributes to emotional responses and longer-term memory, which can play an essential role in enhancing the museum experience [8, 19, 20]. Pine and Gilmore [21] state that multisensory engagement is one of the critical principles of experience design, which is directly related to the emotional arousal of the user [22]. As early as the 1990s, the American Society for Non-Visual Arts (ABS) began researching how to enable people with visual impairments to experience museum culture in a multisensory way, including studying multiple modes of perception such as tactile, auditory verbal sound. As multisensory research has developed, a growing number of studies have shown that multisensory learning methods are not only suitable for visually impaired groups and children but also play a significant role in ordinary youth and adults [8]. Pine and Gilmore's [21] experience design principles suggest that sensory stimuli in experience design should support and enhance its theme. The more senses an experience engages, the more powerful and memorable it will be. Although museum environments sometimes do not provide all types of sensory stimuli, such as smell and taste, visual, auditory and tactile stimuli can at least be considered to enhance the visitor experience. Jelinčić, Šveb and Stewart [20] investigated the impact of visual and auditory stimuli on the emotions of museum visitors. The results showed that visual and auditory stimuli were equally accurate in inducing specific emotions in visitors. For most emotions, auditory stimuli showed higher arousal levels than visual stimuli. Jelinčić suggested that museums combine visual and auditory stimuli for a better experience. However, current museums with multisensory experiences are still in the minority, and there is less research on multisensory interaction and sensory experience enhancement in museums. Using multisensory stimuli in museums to promote interaction, enhance immersion and learning, and improve visitor experience is an important direction for future museum design.

2.2 Experience Design of Museum Musical Instruments Exhibits

Many museums have collections of musical instruments, often ancient ones that are culturally symbolic or rare, made by remarkable craftsmanship. These instruments were made to produce sound, but it has been difficult for museums to present them to visitors as musical instruments in their sound-making function. This section describes the culture of silence in museums and the current state of musical instrument exhibits and discusses possible solutions for improving the experience of musical instrument exhibits.

Silence in the Museum. The common perception of museums as quiet places where visitors observe exhibits in silence in front of glass display cases has been the dominant image of the museum experience for many years [23]. The silence here does not refer to a state of complete silence but rather to people's active selection and moderation of the presence of sound. There is a variety of sounds in museums, and it is just that in traditional museum exhibitions, the sound is not used as a medium to convey knowledge and information. This culture of silence stems from an early conception of the museum as a space of contemplation, isolated from the world's noise, where only in silence can visitors perceive the essence of an exhibition through contemplation. Museums were held up as the ultimate sanctuary for preserving human civilization [1]. Even today, many museums still implicitly retain such a cultural perspective. In this context, silence seems to be a prerequisite for people to acquire knowledge, and visitors become silent readers in libraries. Everrett [24], an advocate of museum sound design, describes this as a well-known and long-standing prejudice in museums. This prejudice has led to a lack of attention to museum sound design and the acoustic planning of exhibition spaces. The dynamic acoustic character of many exhibits is difficult for visitors to understand and learn. In recent years, some museums have experimented with the use of sound in exhibitions, and audio tours are widely used in a variety of museums as a major form of sound use. However, there is still a lack of attention to the acoustic properties of the exhibits themselves in museums. Museums preserve objects with a primary focus on their visual integrity rather than their function [25], meaning that most museums' sound-based collections do not emit any sound. Furthermore, visitors are not usually able to hear recordings of the sounds of these collections. Archives rather than museums usually collect recordings, and there is little collaboration between the two. As a result, it is difficult for visitors to learn about the acoustic properties of objects during their visit, even if they were produced to create sound [26]. In such context, when the subject matter of an exhibition or the objects on display are related to sound culture (e.g. musical instruments, phonographs), it is particularly important to create a relevant listening experience for museum visitors. The sounds from the exhibit itself can reproduce its acoustic properties and the actual context of its use, thus bridging the gap between reality and the museum's collection [23]. The previous section has discussed the importance of sound as a sense to the museum experience, and sound design has become an integral part of the museum experience. More museums should integrate sound into their exhibitions as a tool and medium for creating meaning, especially for exhibits with a clear sonic identity.

Musical Instrument Collections Require Multi-Sensory Experience. Collections of ancient and rare musical instruments are an important part of museum art collections. Unlike other ancient objects, musical instruments provide not only visual effects but complex sound-making mechanisms, making them exceptional works of art [27, 28]. As early as the mid-20th century, the Victoria and Albert Museum staged live concerts of its instrument collection, successfully shaping public listening habits and reviving visitors' interest in Renaissance and Baroque music [26]. However, in a world where museums are increasingly becoming interactive environments, musical instruments - despite being one of the most interactive objects in museums - are not usually part of the interactive experience. Museums are more concerned with the visual integrity of these instrument collections, which are often housed in glass display cases. In such a context, the decorative nature of the instruments is magnified. At the same time, their acoustic and physical characteristics are often ignored. Visitors find it difficult to gain insights from these collections, such as how they are supposed to be played and the mechanisms by which they sound [29]. Take, for example, the Chinese chimes in the National Museum of China collection (see Fig. 2), which are housed in a massive glass display case, with a board with text below giving its historical context. However, visitors have no access to how they were played as musical instruments, nor can they hear them in any form. This large instrument is simply displayed as an ornament and has lost its soul as a musical instrument. Visitors' experience with the museum's instrument collection has been frustrating [4]. Museums should at least create an essential listening experience for these instrument collections, as listening is instinctive when one sees an instrument [26].

Fig. 2. Chimes in a glass showcase in the National Museum of China

In addition, the sense of touch has an important influence on the experience of museum instrument collections. Bubaris [23] point out that a multi-sensory exhibition can create a dynamic environment for the instruments, allowing experience and meaning to emerge simultaneously. Mansell, De Little and Jamieson [26] suggest that the listening experience associated with museum instrument collections should be interactive. They argue that sound alone is not enough to engage visitors when designing experiences with audible objects in museums. Interactive listening experiences can enrich the way museums listen and encourage visitors to engage with and understand the sonic and physical properties associated with interactive objects, such as the movement of fingers on a fingerboard, the movement of a bow on a string or the sensation of a bell hammer hitting a bell [30]. Mansell et al.'s [26] Sonic Futures project shows that visitors not only want to hear the sounds of these sound-based collections but also to manipulate them and experience their functions. The search for alternatives that visitors can identify with and are interested in is a inevitable trend in the interaction of musical instrument collections in museums.

Possible Alternatives to Original Musical Instrument Collections. The best way to understand and learn about an instrument is to try playing it; museum collections of old and rare instruments are no exception. Playing an instrument reinforces the impression of the visitor's visit and builds a deep memory [29]. However, as these collections need to be protected, it is almost impossible to allow spectators or musicians to play them. Alternatives are needed to mimic the characteristics of these instruments to help visitors experience them as they are played. In museums, creating digital replicas of musical instrument exhibits is one way of allowing visitors to experience the instruments being played. For example, Gardo and Lukasik [27] use virtual reality technology to present an old piano playing. The piano was made by the famous manufacturer JAHsss in the 18th century. Many of its parts have been destroyed and are now kept in the Museum of Musical Instruments in Poznan, Poland. They have created a visual reconstruction of the old piano in virtual reality, combining visual animation and sound representation and allowing the user to interact in real-time via data gloves (see Fig. 3). This virtual reality-based solution gives visitors a sense of immersion and immediate engagement. However, it lacks the haptic feedback to demonstrate the instrument's physical properties, such as its tactile impression and material. To simulate the haptic characteristics of musical instruments, Leonard and Cadoz [31] proposed the GENESIS-RT system, which allows the design of virtual interactable models of musical instruments, simulating these instruments in real-time and interacting with them through force feedback sensors. Different playing forces map different sounds, enabling the reproduction of part of the tactile and mechanical characteristics of the instruments, making the virtual instruments more realistic. The focus of these solutions has been mainly on the digital simulation of musical instruments and has been well implemented. However, the problem with digital virtual musical instruments is their sense of detachment from the physical world; these intangible digital contents are cut off from the visitors of the physical world. Contact interaction in the museum has generally stimulated more emotional solid experiences and memories. Therefore, additional touchable ways of restoring the physical world to its character are needed to build on the digital reconstruction of musical instrument collections.

In order to have a better experience of the physicality of exhibits, museum research has started to focus on the use of tangible interactions in museum interaction. Tangible

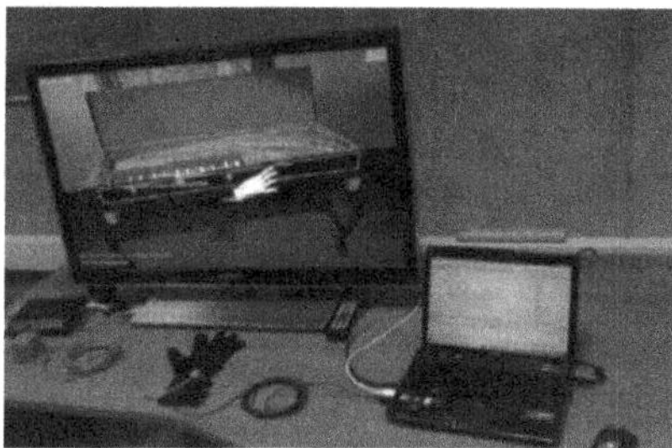
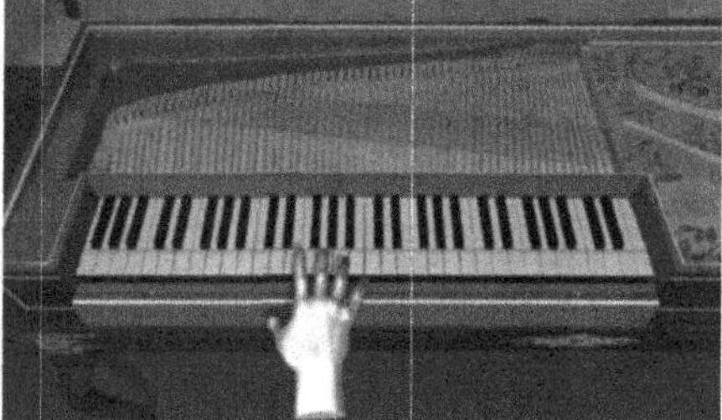

Fig. 3. System for playing 3D virtual copy of a historical clavichord [27]

interaction refers to the manipulation of digital content using physical interaction interfaces, embedding real space into digital content and using digital content as an extension of physical space [32]. Tangible interactions based on smart replicas have provided a direction for research into physical interaction in museums. Smart replicas are interactive physical objects. People activate certain behaviors and reactions (such as animation effects or the playing of sound) through it, often either as original physical objects of cultural heritage or as replicas of them enhanced by digital technologies [33]. Such replicas are gradually beginning to be used in interactive museum experiences, where tangible smart replicas of exhibits or objects associated with them are constructed and embedded in digital assemblies to allow them to become part of the interactive experience. Smart replicas act as an extension of the exhibit's digital content in the physical world, complementing its physical characteristics to overcome the sense of detachment between digital technology and the artefacts on display.

Smart replicas can replace untouchable collections for interactions such as touch, allowing visitors to perceive their full physical detail and explore the knowledge associated with them through digital content such as sound and images. As an interface, the smart replica provides an interesting way for museums to interact with each other. It has proven to be engaging and popular. Smart replicas could therefore be considered for use in the interaction of musical instrument exhibits, where digital components are embedded in replicas of musical instruments as triggers for virtual digital instruments and their images, sounds and other content, complementing their physical characteristics that are missing.

3 Project Background

3.1 The Historical Background and Cultural Value of the Chimes

China was the first country to manufacture and use musical bells. Chimes were large percussion instruments used by the Han aristocracy in ancient China, emerging during the Zhou Dynasty and flourishing during the Spring and Autumn and Warring States periods and the Qin and Han Dynasties. Cast in bronze, it consists of flat round bells of different sizes arranged in order of pitch and suspended from a colossal bell stand. The performers use wooden hammers and long rods to strike the bronze bells to produce different musical notes. Each bell has a different pitch; the player strikes the chimes following a musical score to produce a beautiful piece of music. Generally, a group of bells of different pitches was hung on the wooden stand and played by attendants with small mallets (see Fig. 4).

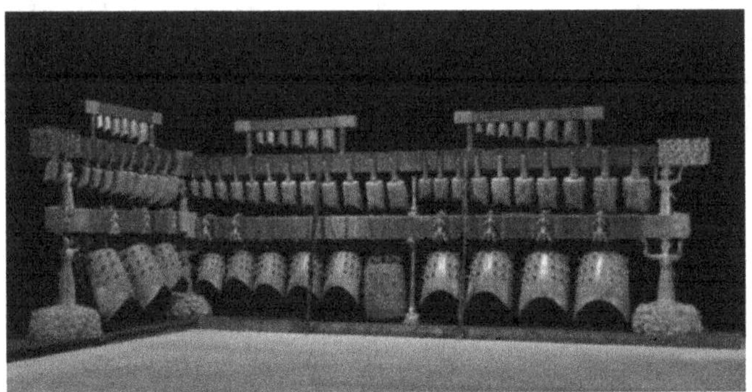

Fig. 4. The Zeng Hou Yi Chimes (Hubei Provincial Museum)

A significant archaeological find that shocking the world was the Zeng Hou Yi Chimes, unearthed in 1978 at the Zeng Hou Yi Tomb in Suizhou, Hubei, China. It has been proven that this set of chimes was buried around 433 BCE. This means that such a large bronze instrument, buried underground for more than 2,400 years, still stands intact, and its material and structural design is astoundingly rational and scientific [34]. The 3755-character inscriptions on the bell form a complete system of rhythms, indicating the tonic order of each bell and clearly indicating the correspondence between these orders and the rhythms of various countries during the Spring and Autumn and Warring States periods. The inscription is particularly valuable as it contains a list of twelve tones and their 28 synonyms, most of which have long been lost. It proves that the concept of the seven-tone scale and absolute pitch already existed in China in the fifth century BC, indicating that culture and technology had reached a high level by that time [35].

3.2 Silent Chimes in the Museum

Since the discovery of the Zeng Hou Yi Chimes, researchers have been most concerned with using this precious instrument to play musical pieces. All conservation around the chimes has been based on comprehensive research into their musical function. Zhang Xiang of the Hubei Provincial Museum Research Institute said, "The Zeng Hou Yi Chimes are the peak of Axial Age musical culture, bringing sounds from more than two thousand years ago to the present" [35]. However, despite researchers having managed to ring these chimes and sample their sounds, it is unfortunate that the wider public is not hearing these sounds from 2,000 years ago. The bells are housed in glass display cases in museums where people can look closely at their appearance but not listen to their sound. Due to the complexity of the production process of chimes, from the 19th century to the present, China has only made five replicas of Zeng Hou Yi chimes, which are also collected in the glass showcases of museums and rarely used for performances [34]. In interviews with visitors to the National Museum of China, the vast majority of visitors showed an interest in the playing and sound of the chimes, which is not offered in the museum's exhibitions. The National Museum of China's approach to the display of chimes is frustrating. It is the potential to create an interactive chime playing experience using digital technologies such as smart replicas.

4 Design Process

4.1 Problem Define

As a precious musical instrument made more than two thousand years ago, the Chinese chimes constitute a significant discovery in the archaeological and musical world. The discovery of the Zeng Hou Yi Chimes has made it possible to listen to the sounds of two thousand years ago. However, until now, chimes have been displayed in museums as mere ornamental objects in glass display cases. This traditional way of presenting the bell has allowed people to observe its physical features through the glass case but not to listen to its sound or experience its performance. This project seeks to enable multi-sensory interaction between visitors and the chimes by embedding chime replicas into digital components and acting as an interface to control the delivery of digital content. Facilitating visitors' understanding and learning about the sound and playing style of the chimes and bringing the sounds of 2,000 years ago back to life in the museum.

4.2 Development

The project can be broadly divided into two parts, the physical part and the digital part, which are the implementation of a tangible replica of the chimes as an interface for interaction and the digital modelling of the chimes and delivery of sound content, respectively. In order to explore the feasibility of the interactive solution, we first carried out prototype building and testing of the physical part (see Fig. 5).

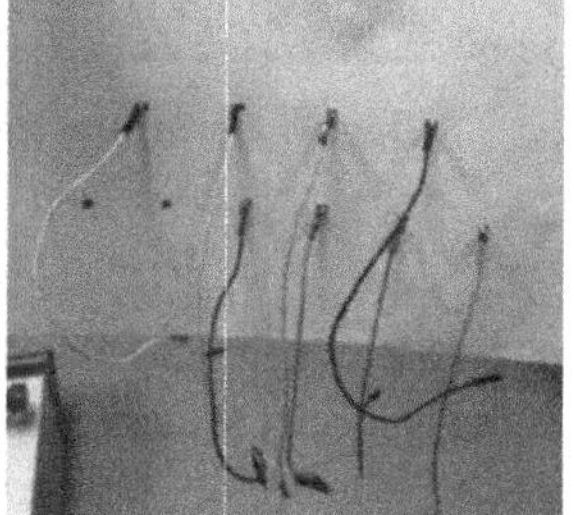

Fig. 5. Preparing materials

We purchased simple chime models in copper from the National Museum of China, which have good electrical conductivity. We soldered them to cables and connected them to a Makey Makey circuit board. The board uses a closed loop electrical signal to send a keyboard tap or mouse click signal to the computer. This feature allows Makey Makey to work with any computer program or web page that accepts keyboard or mouse clicks. We connected the earth wire to a conductive metal hammer. Therefore, when someone strikes the chime model with the hammer, a closed loop will be formed. The circuit board will send an electrical signal to the computer and, in this way, controls the delivery of the corresponding sound and animation effects (see Fig. 6).

Fig. 6. Soldering and connecting the brass chime model to the circuit board.

Based on this, we created a simple, click-to-play application using Unity to test the feasibility of activating sound delivery by striking on a chime model. The prototype was tested to enable different sounds and animation effects to be played in real-time by striking different chime models (see Fig. 7).

Fig. 7. Testing its feasibility by creating a simple program in Unity.

After verifying the feasibility of the interactive approach, we used Maya to digitally model the individual chimes and bell frames separately, based on the chime collection held at the National Museum and put them together to form a complete, playable set of chimes (see Fig. 8, Fig. 9, Fig. 10).

After building the 3D model of the chimes, we used Unity to create a preliminary version of the game program. The program allows the user to strike on the physical chime model to get real-time animation and sound feedback (the sound material is the real Zeng Hou Yi chimes sample purchased from the Chinese sound shop Yipaner). At the same time, historical and cultural knowledge related to the chimes is scrolled on the left side of the screen, aiming to give the user a multi-dimensional understanding of the chimes through both reading and interactivity (see Fig. 11).

Fig. 8. Construction of a single chime model

Fig. 9. Chimes collected by the National Museum of China

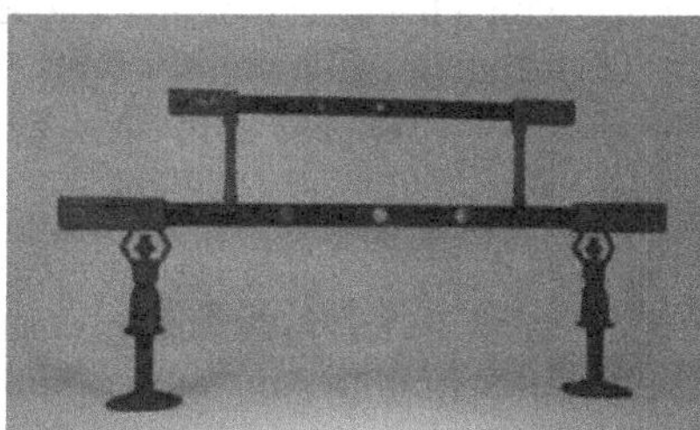

Fig. 10. Model construction of bell stands and a set of chimes

4.3 User Testing and Interaction

User testing aims to discover visitors' problems when using this interactive device and improve those problems. Seven respondents from different age groups who completed the interaction without much guidance participated in the test to test whether museum visitors can understand the interaction method without guidance (see Fig. 12).

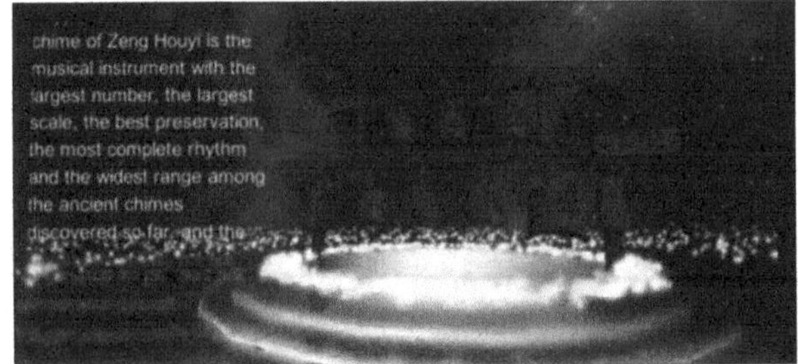

Fig. 11. The game scene of the preliminary version of the program

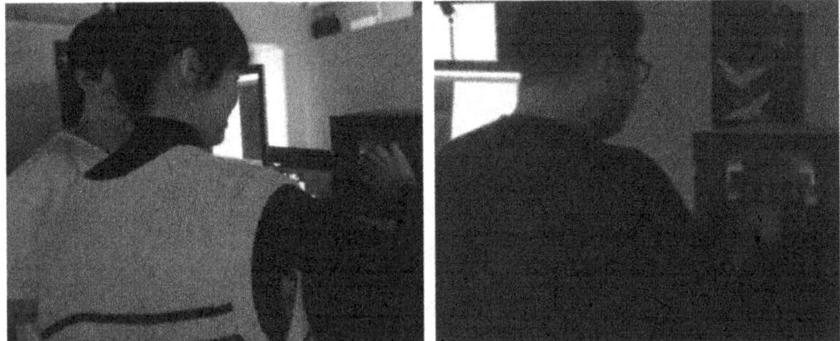

Fig. 12. User testing

The results showed that all respondents completed the interaction without much guidance. The interaction method of striking the bell with a hammer is simple enough and conforms to the common sense and cognition of the public, so the respondents did not encounter too many obstacles. However, some issues that need to be improved have also emerged during the testing process. The issues and solutions are organized based on respondents' feedback.

(1) It is difficult for the user to focus on both the chimes and the text presentation during the interaction. The scrolling text will distract the user from looking at the chimes themselves.

    Solution: Separate the text reading from the interaction with the chimes. When there is no action by the user, the screen scrolls through the text description. When someone strikes the chime model, the text is hidden, and only the digital chime and its animation are displayed on the screen, making the subject of the interaction more prominent and clearer.

2) The color of the chime model and background are too close together, making the swing of the chime imperceptible.

    Solution: Brighten up the chimes' digital model to create a stronger contrast with the background.

3) The feedback effects when struck are too eye-catching and too distracting. It is difficult for users to identify which bell they have struck through such effects.

Solution: Reduce the size of the feedback effects and focus them on the bottom of the chime being struck so that the user can identify which chime is making the sound.

4) A Chinese caption needed to be added to reflect the inscription features of the chimes.

Solution: A Chinese seal script 'Chimes' was added to the standby screen to enhance the theme of the project, which is the ancient Chinese font used for the chimes' inscriptions.

Following the solutions, we have made improvements to the problems users encountered. In the new version, when the user has no operation, the screen will display the text description related to the chimes. When someone strikes the chime's mock-up with a hammer, the digital content of the digital chime will be triggered, and the text disappears. The text will reappear from the paused position when the user does nothing for 5 s. The interaction flow is as follows (see Fig. 13, Fig. 14).

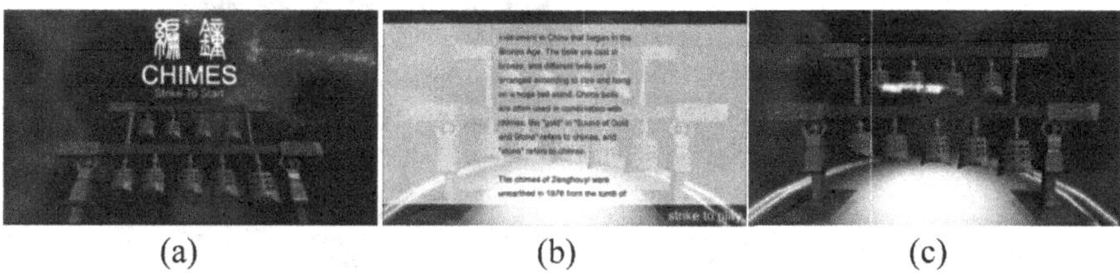

Fig. 13. (a) The start interface; (b) When no one strike the chimes, the text of background knowledge about the chime will be played automatically; (c) When user strikes the physical chime model, it will trigger the shaking animation of the chime at the corresponding position on the screen and deliver the sound effect of the chime being struck. The chime being struck in the picture is the second from the left in the upper row.

Fig. 14. When user stops striking, the text reappears and continues to play, and automatically returns to the start interface after the playback ends.

4.4 Final Design

Through continuous design iterations and user experience optimization, the final output of the interactive installation is shown in the Fig. 15 and Fig. 16.

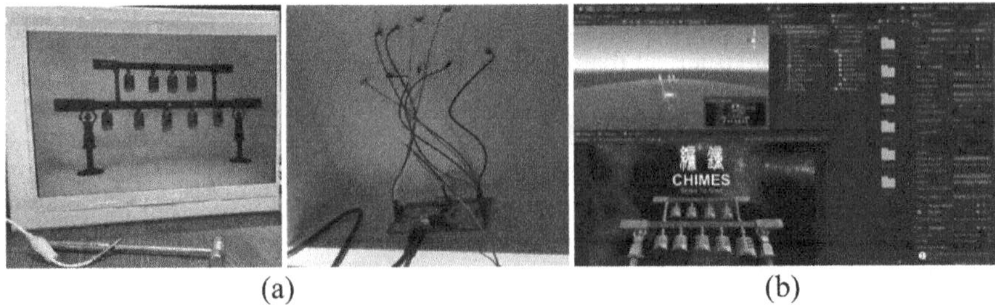

(a) (b)

Fig. 15. (a) Front and back of the physical installation prototype; (b) Unity screenshot of the digital program.

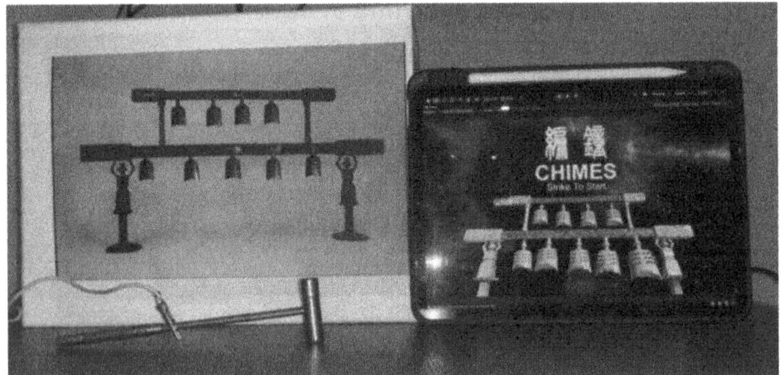

Fig. 16. Digital program connected with the physical installation.

5 Limitations and Future Works

This project attempts to use tangible intelligent replicas as an interactive interface to the museum's musical instrument collection. It attempts to represent the chimes' visual, acoustic and partly tactile characteristics to the visitor through digital modelling and smart replicas. Due to cost issues, this prototype uses small pieces of chime modules as smart replicas. It is difficult for the user to achieve the desired immersion and full tactile experience with such small replicas. However, this prototype demonstrates that the interactive solution is feasible and provides design ideas that can be used to design future experiences for museum instrument collections. Large museums such as the National Museum of China can easily afford to produce detailed replicas of large chimes. Using intelligent replicas that are more realistic in terms of material and size can lead to better multi-sensory interaction and immersion.

Furthermore, using pressure sensors, technology already exists to map the strength of a user's striking to the volume and sound quality of a sound effect [31]. Due to technical limitations, this was not implemented in this prototype. However, in future work, using this technology for physical interaction with musical instruments could make the interactive experience more realistic.

6 Conclusion

In general, museums are changing from institutions that collect and conserve objects to places that provide meaningful informal learning experiences for the public. To achieve this, a growing number of museums are offering interactive exhibitions. The traditional silent museum is becoming a multi-sensory learning environment. The visual, auditory, tactile and other multi-sensory stimuli have been shown to have a significant improvement on the visitor's visit and learning experience. In this context, museums should provide the necessary listening experience and interactive experience for musical instrument exhibits. Traditional glass display cases cannot convey the musicality and physical nature of musical instrument exhibits for visitors. Current interactions with musical instrument collections are often virtual, and these virtual instruments allow visitors to hear and play rare instruments. However, virtual instruments cannot provide visitors with musical instruments' physical properties and tactile sensations. This paper proposes using intelligent replicas of musical instruments embedded with digital components as interactive interfaces for virtual instruments to compensate for the lack of their physical properties. It also uses the National Museum of China chimes collection as an example of interactive experience design. The project connects a bronze chime model to a circuit board as an interface to control the delivery of the virtual chime animation and its sound, allowing the user to interact in real-time and simulate the chime playing process. In terms of results, despite the many limitations, the prototype of this project provides visitors with a visual and aural experience of the chimes, restoring their functionality as musical instruments and enabling a partially tactile experience. The experience would have been better if used a highly realistic and detailed chime model as the smart replica. In future work, pressure sensors can be used to sense the force of the strikes, allowing different feedback on the sound of the chimes when struck with different forces. Using replicas as an interactive interface allows visitors to interact with the instrument in a tactile way without damaging the original instrument. This form of interaction offers a new direction for designing future interactive experiences for museum instrument collections.

Acknowledgements and Funding Information. This research was supported by 2022 Humanities and Social Sciences Youth Fund Program of the Ministry of Education "Research on the innovation of immersive interactive experience mode with the integration of reality and imagination" (No. 22YJC760019).

References

1. Bennett, T.: Civic seeing: museums and the organization of vision. Companion Museum Stud. 263 (2006). https://doi.org/10.1002/9780470996836.ch16
2. International Council of Museums: Museum Definition. https://icom.museum/en/resources/standards-guidelines/museum-definition/. Accessed 15 June 2022
3. Graham, H.C.: The 'co'in co-production: museums, community participation and science and technology studies. Sci. Museum Group J. **5** (2016)
4. de Visscher, E.: Sound in Museums. https://www.vam.ac.uk/blog/news/sound-in-museums-by-eric-de-visscher-vari-visiting-professor. Accessed 13 Jan 2022

5. Dal Falco, F., Vassos, S.: Museum experience design: a modern storytelling methodology. Des. J. **20**, S3975–S3983 (2017). https://doi.org/10.1080/14606925.2017.1352900
6. Simon, N.: The Participatory Museum (Museum 2.0). http://www.participatorymuseum.org
7. Vermeeren, A.P., et al.: Future Museum Experience Design: Crowds, Ecosystems and Novel Technologies. Springer (2018)
8. Liu, M., Yu, X.: Perception and interaction: enhancement of museum interactive experience. Furniture Interiors **29**, 61–65 (2022). https://doi.org/10.16771/j.cn43-1247/ts.2022.03.013
9. Dierking, L.D., Falk, J.H.: Redefining the museum experience: the interactive experience model. Visitor Studies. **4**, 173–176 (1992)
10. Larsen, S.: Aspects of a psychology of the tourist experience. Scand. J. Hosp. Tour. **7**, 7–18 (2007). https://doi.org/10.1080/15022250701226014
11. Falk, J.H.: Identity and the Museum Visitor Experience. Routledge (2016)
12. Wang, Q., Lei, Y.: Minds on for the wise: rethinking the contemporary interactive exhibition. Museum Manag. Curatorship. **31**, 331–348 (2016). https://doi.org/10.1080/09647775.2016.1173575
13. Fahy, A.: New technologies for museum communication. In: Museum, Media, Message, pp. 82–96 (1995)
14. Guo, W., et al.: The rebirth of traditional musical instrument: an interactive installation based on augmented reality and somatosensory technology to empower the exhibition of chimes. Comput. Anim. Virtual Worlds e2171 (2023). https://doi.org/10.1002/cav.2171
15. O'dell, T.: Tourist experiences and academic junctures. Scand. J. Hospitality Tourism. **7**, 34–45 (2007)
16. Guo, W., Li, S., Zhang, Z., Chen, Z., Chang, KH., Wang, S.: A magic world for children: design and development of a serious game to improve spatial ability. Comput. Anim. Virtual Worlds e2181 (2023). https://doi.org/10.1002/cav.2181
17. Edwards, E., Gosden, C., Phillips, R.: Sensible Objects: Colonialism, Museums and Material Culture. Berg (2006)
18. Kannenberg, J.: Towards a more sonically inclusive. Sci. Museum Group J. **8** (2017)
19. Baumgartner, T., Esslen, M., Jäncke, L.: From emotion perception to emotion experience: emotions evoked by pictures and classical music. Int. J. Psychophysiol. **60**, 34–43 (2006). https://doi.org/10.1016/j.ijpsycho.2005.04.007
20. Jelinčić, D.A., Šveb, M., E. Stewart, A.: Designing sensory museum experiences for visitors' emotional responses. Museum Manag. Curatorship. **37**, 513–530 (2022).https://doi.org/10.1080/09647775.2021.1954985
21. Pine, B.J., Gilmore, J.H.: Welcome to the Experience Economy. Harvard Business Review Press (1998)
22. Jelinčić, D.A., Senkić, M.: Creating a heritage tourism experience. the power of the senses. In: Etnološka tribina, pp. 109–126 (2017). https://doi.org/10.15378/1848-9540.2017.40.03
23. Bubaris, N.: Sound in museums–museums in sound. Museum Manag. Curatorship. **29**, 391–402 (2014). https://doi.org/10.1080/09647775.2014.934049
24. Everrett, T.: A curatorial guide to museum sound design. Curator Museum J. **62**, 313–325 (2019). https://doi.org/10.1111/cura.12305
25. Boon, T., Jamieson, A., Kannenberg, J., Kolkowski, A., Mansell, J.: Organising sound: how a research network might help structure an exhibition (2017)
26. Mansell, J., De Little, A., Jamieson, A.: Staging listening. Sci. Museum Group J. **17** (2022). https://doi.org/10.15180/221704
27. Gardo, K., Lukasik, E.: VClav 2.0 – system for playing 3D virtual copy of a historical clavichord. In: Shumaker, R. (ed.) VMR 2011. LNCS, vol. 6774, pp. 141–150. Springer, Heidelberg (2011). https://doi.org/10.1007/978-3-642-22024-1_16
28. Lukasik, E., Materski, M.: Sonification of A Virtual Model of the Old Rare Musical Instrument. Presented at the (2013)

29. Birley, M., Eichler, H., Myers, A.: Voices for the silenced: Guidelines for interpreting musical instruments in museum collections. Edinburgh: CIMCIM (1998)
30. de Visscher, E.: Sound in Museums (2): What About Musical Instruments?. https://www.vam.ac.uk/blog/projects/sound-in-museums-2-what-about-musical-instruments. Accessed 13 Jan 2022
31. Leonard, J., Cadoz, C.: Physical modelling concepts for a collection of multisensory virtual musical instruments. In: New Interfaces for Musical Expression 2015, pp. 150–155 (2015)
32. Hornecker, E., Buur, J.: Getting a grip on tangible interaction: a framework on physical space and social interaction. In: Proceedings of the SIGCHI Conference on Human Factors in Computing Systems, pp. 437–446 (2006). https://doi.org/10.1145/1124772.1124838
33. Marshall, M.T., Dulake, N., Ciolfi, L., Duranti, D., Kockelkorn, H., Petrelli, D.: Using tangible smart replicas as controls for an interactive museum exhibition. In: Proceedings of the TEI'16: Tenth International Conference on Tangible, Embedded, and Embodied Interaction, pp. 159–167 (2016). https://doi.org/10.1145/2839462.2839493
34. Wang, L.: Common Sense of Ancient Chinese Culture, 4th edn. Beijing United Publishing Company, Beijing (2015)
35. Pi, S., Yu, P.: Observation: New discovery of Chu chimes. http://www.xinhuanet.com/politics/2018-06/19/c_1123000865.htm. Accessed 15 June 2022

Knowledge Archaeology of Light Environment Art in the Era of Media Convergence

Hantian Xu and Lin Zhang(✉)

Communication University of China, Beijing, China
zhlin197412@126.com

Abstract. In the era of media convergence, the discipline of light environment art has changed. The development of media and the evolution of urban environment are the two direct factors. Since the 1980s, the concept of "light environment" has gradually matured in the field of architecture and began to extend to the fields of art, drama, communication, etc. in China, and has extended and crossed to the fields of public art, environmental drama, urban social design, digital art, etc. In recent decades, the concept of light environment art has been divided into four main categories: 1. Landscape concept of light environment art with the purpose of beautifying the environment and constructing visual myths; 2. Media concept of light environment art with the purpose of information multiplication and communication; 3. Post-humanism of light environment art with the purpose of constructing humanized environment and realizing environmental experiential expansion. By sorting out the connotation and concept of light environment art, this paper clarifies the path and direction of the construction and research of light environment art in China.

Keywords: light environment art · discipline crossing · knowledge archaeology

1 Light Environment Art in the Changing Ages

In recent years, many cities in eastern China have completed at least one round of lighting transformations, making buildings and scenic areas more colorful and vibrant. The concept of urban lighting has become more prominent in people's minds. Compared to the daytime urban environment, the true significance of urban lighting is not just the increase in the city's night-time brightness, but also the degree of activity in cultural leisure and consumption activities. The more developed a city's business activities and cultural affairs, the greater the proportion of urban lighting quality in the lives of residents. With the promotion of flexible work arrangements and remote work, the proportion of urban lighting in the human work environment is also increasing. As David Harvey pointed out, the development of economic globalization has brought different time zones closer together, with some typical industries, such as the financial market, even maintaining 24-h operation, further compressing time and space, and making urban lighting an important representation of capital control over space [1]. By using DMSP/OLS technology, researchers have obtained detailed information on global continuous time series

H. Mori et al. (Eds.): HCII 2023, LNCS 14056, pp. 438–453, 2023.
https://doi.org/10.1007/978-3-031-48044-7_31

of fires, oil and gas combustion, fishing boat lights, and human settlements through continuous monitoring of the region (see Fig. 1), and have obtained regional average night light intensity data for the study of regional urbanization level, urbanization process, and urban pattern changes [2]. In recent years, with the increasing importance of light environment art, light environment research in China has also been deepening, and light environment art has made breakthroughs in various disciplines. The concept of "light environment" has different understanding and interpretation under different historical, disciplinary, and technical backgrounds, and the connotation of the light environment art discipline has undergone a transformation. Among them, the breakthrough of direct technical tools and the change of urbanization are the two direct influencing factors. The breakthrough of technical tools has brought about the upgrading of light source technology, the development of control systems, and the improvement of reflective materials, which directly affect the lighting presentation of light environment art, and fundamentally affect the ontological development and cognition of the light environment discipline. The development and transformation of cities bring about the location of the environment, the change of market subjects, and the change of social production and living ways in the environment, which are jointly external factors in the transformation of the light environment art concept.

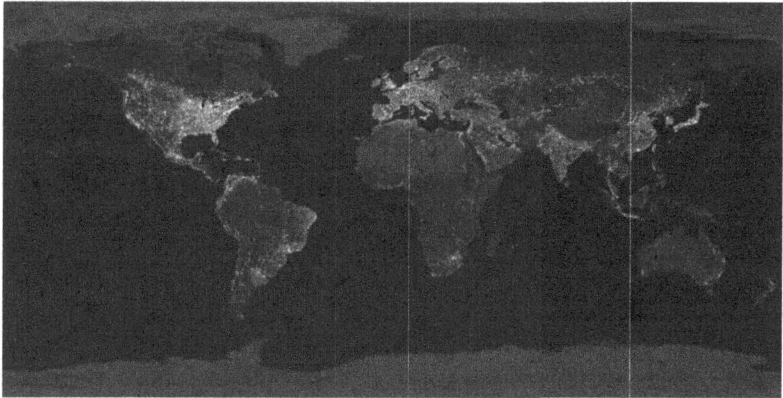

Fig. 1. Average night light intensity data through DMSP/OLS technology © NASA [3].

Since the launch of the "National Semiconductor Lighting Engineering" by the Ministry of Science and Technology of China in 2004, China's semiconductor lighting technology has developed rapidly. Around 2007, semiconductor lighting gradually replaced incandescent lighting, and in 2012 it gradually replaced fluorescent lighting. In addition to the many advantages of semiconductor lighting compared to traditional light sources, such as energy saving, fast response speed, long life, small size, and stable component structure, it can adapt to various adverse conditions [4]. Another important advantage of semiconductor lighting is that its controllability is greatly enhanced compared to traditional light sources. Its mainstream control systems include bus-type intelligent control systems, network lighting control systems, and integrated systems, which can achieve regulation and matching of light source brightness, color temperature, and color at different levels, and even cooperate with the access of smart furniture and smart city systems. In addition to the visual effects, the non-visual effects of the light environment are also being further developed. The application of the light environment in physiological therapy, children's intelligence development, and the promotion of plants and other fields is being further explored [5]. In the foreseeable future, the light environment engineering will present a more intelligent and convenient control means at the environmental lighting level, and will further combine with the Internet and cloud technology to develop in a more complex and diverse direction.

One direction of the extension of photonic environmental technology tools is digital and virtual technology. Virtual technology, including virtual reality (VR) and augmented reality (AR), has been constantly developing since the 1960s and has been widely used in daily life applications, forming the concept of "virtual reality continuous unity" (VR Continuum) [6]. Its core feature is the ability to combine virtual content with the real environment using light as a medium, allowing users to interactively browse and interact with three-dimensional images with high realism. Compared to the urban dimension of photonic environmental engineering, virtual technology has implanted more possibilities for the development of photonic environmental art in the micro interaction environment.

The development of the city's light environment has a high degree of correlation with the level of urbanization. With the deepening of urbanization, the expansion of cities has become an irreversible trend. Both domestically and abroad, there are more and more mega-cities with a permanent population of over 10 million. However, cities not only expand in spatial scale, but also further extend in the temporal dimension. The development of cities as a global issue brings new opportunities, new developments, and new problems to the light environment. In China, the rapid urbanization development in recent decades has also brought about a leapfrog development of the light environment. In recent years, the party and government have also paid increasingly attention to the development of the light environment. In 2019, the State Council Office successively issued guiding documents such as "Opinions on Promoting Cultural and Tourism Consumption Growth" and "Opinions on Accelerating the Development of Circulation to Promote Commercial Consumption", which set off a wave of industry development [7]. "Night Economy" and "Nighttime Tourism" have become the focus of attention of the general public and scholars.

Professor Hao Luoxi from Tongji University divides China's urban light environment development (1992–2012) into three stages [8]. In the first stage (1992–1999) and the second stage (2000–2003), the light environment project gradually expanded from points (landmarks) and lines (urban axes) to surfaces (regions), and the rapid development of cities required the light environment design and other matching projects to follow up in synchrony. For example, the planning and renovation of Beijing's central urban area and Shanghai's Huangpu District were carried out in this stage. In the third stage (2004–2012), the pollution and waste problems in cities made the emergence of "environmental awareness" conscious, and "coordinated development between people and the environment" became a new topic of the light environment. In the past ten years, the new characteristic of today's light environment art is that the city, as a place for people to work, live, relax, and wonder, is separated from the definition of "residential machine" [9], and urban context and regionalism become the topic of concern for local residents and the symbol of urban cohesion. As the concentrated embodiment of the night image of the city, the light environment reflects the contradictions and complexities of the city in a graphic and symbolic way, and is embodied in media buildings with the function of information dissemination. It embodies the dynamic image, graphic, and text media facade that has an impact on the city space [10]. The light environment is not only a visible brightness space, but also becomes an object to be understood as a subject of information.

2 The Development of the Opinion of Light Environment Art

The concept of "light environment" comes from architectural environmental engineering, called "photonic environment" which is a scientific branch that studies the theory and practice of applying air, heat, sound, light, and color factors in architecture. Since the late 1980s, domestic research on photonic environment has been basically divided into two dimensions. On the one hand, based on engineering, some researchers have devoted themselves to studying the impact of photonic environment on agriculture and forestry, exploring the function and utility of photonic environment in areas such as poultry farming and forest management, and making explorations in the research on the non-human body effects of light. In 1989, professor Yang Gongxia from Tongji University summarized the research situation on the non-visual effects of light radiation based on CIE sixth division, and prospected on the future research on the non-visual effects of light, especially on the effects on human subjective sensation, emotion, and health, and on the application in dermatology and ophthalmology lighting environment [11]. Besides scholars such as Gao Lutai, Chen Zhonglin, and Xi Yucheng have studied the effects of parameters such as lighting level, glare, brightness distribution, light and shadow, light color, and color display on the visual environment, and have tried to study the environmental utility of light environment with psychology, human body engineering, and visual environment. They have focused on the physiological and psychological effects of light on the human visual energy efficiency level in the architectural environment. Furthermore, another academic concept as "light environment" has been researched in a new step. It refers to the lighting conditions in a particular space or environment. It includes both natural and artificial light sources, and can affect the visibility, mood, and overall experience of a space. In architectural design, the concept of light environment is often considered in order to create an optimal lighting design that enhances the aesthetic and functional qualities of a building or space [12]. The light environment as a building aesthetic and modeling element is also valued by some scholars, and it is proposed that the light environment as a "addition" of a building has the role of rich spatial content, decorative space art, and atmosphere of space [13]. The overall direction of light environment research in developed countries such as the United States also presents a trend of transition from building lighting engineering to building lighting design, "from illuminance calculation to aesthetic evaluation, from quantity to quality [14]. "On this basis, in 2005, Professor Chang Zhigang from Central Academy of Fine Arts proposed the concept of "integrated design of light and spatial vision", and regarded the light environment as the mechanism of artistic psychology and visual formation, and studied the composition and performance rules of visual art. He believed that the architectural lighting vocabulary of light environment design can learn and learn lighting means from stage lighting [15]. Although the light environment has not been able to get rid of the research framework of architecture, lighting design as an independent discipline has been recognized by architects and lighting designers [16].

Based on the widespread urban light environment construction projects in China, in 1995, Ma Jian and Shen Tianxing proposed their thoughts on urban nightscape planning. Through the study of the nightscape lighting of Tianjin, they proposed that "from the spontaneous lighting of individual buildings, gradually develop to nightscape lighting with planning and overall design [17]". In 1999, Ma Jian and Wang Lixiong further discussed and reflected on the urban nightscape problem, but their main views focused on the study of nightscape brightness, urban image and visual modeling, without departing from the scope of architectural art and engineering management. The research of urban residents' work, life, and leisure behavior presents an absence status. In 2008, Hu Hua proposed the concept of "nocturnal city", believing that urban dimension light environment research is a kind of urban space based on night activities, and incorporates sociological perspectives and research methods into the research scope of light environment disciplines [18]. In 2005, Peng Jun proposed the concept of "environmental lighting art" under the theoretical framework of light environment, and incorporated the forms of light art such as "light painting" and "light sculpture" into the connotation of light environment discipline, and emphasized the concept of "forming a city nightscape environment with cultural foundation" and "forming a unique systematic urban light culture" [19]. With the deepening of cross-disciplinary studies, the concept of light environment has gradually not been limited to the development in the study of architecture and cities. Light environment Art plays an important role in the research of art, urban communication, and even media environment. In 2013, Cao Sanxing integrated relevant domestic and foreign research results and proposed that "media architecture" can include participatory architecture, dynamic media architecture, 3D media architecture, and spatial media art. With light as the medium of digital network media, augmented reality light and shadow art and interactive design have all deeply participated in traditional architectural design, from architectural skin to space experience, deeply imprinted with the brand of light media. Two years later, Chang Zigang further sorted out the connotation definition and historical clues of media architecture development. He regarded "the development of architectural skin technology", "the symbolization of architecture", "the mature application of digital images", and "the development of public art" as the sources of media architecture, and clarified the complexity and cross-nature of light environment in the era of media architecture in terms of knowledge composition and development trends [20]. The research on media architecture both domestically and abroad has greatly expanded the definitions of the concepts of photonic environment to light environment. In 2013, Zhang Lin made an attempt to "re-define" the discipline of light environment studies, proposing that "light environment" be considered as a composite interdisciplinary field and providing sufficient arguments for the establishment of relevant undergraduate majors. In "Conceptual Design of the Subject of light environment Design", Zhang Lin further expands the connotation and extension of the discipline of light environment, and proposes to integrate the concept of "Urban Scenography" into light environment design, "using urban real public space as a stage, with the purpose of information communication and cultural construction, for lighting setting and visual planning. "Light environment design" becomes a public information carrier and public artistic action, an interactive device between man and city, and an interactive landscape between man and city [21]. "The research on light environment is not necessarily limited to the fields of spatial research and environmental research, but is a cultural-driven experience research.

In recent years, research on the light environment based on cultural night-walking and digital media art has continuously supplemented the discipline of light environment. The emergence of concepts such as "Digital Twins" and "Augmented Cities" means that the study of light environment is no longer limited to "light as a visual phenomenon", but is also recognized and studied as "light as an extension of human experiential experience". In the field of night-time tourism and night-time economic consumption research, "perception research", "aesthetic research" and "consumption research" on consumer markets, consumers and experiencers make the construction of the light environment more complete and three-dimensional in the disciplinary system, constantly adjusting to the current domestic development status and environment.

Overall, the connotation of light environment art is constantly enriched. The term light environment originated in optics, physics and engineering, but in the process of development, it gradually broke through the research framework of physics and architecture, and extended to public art, environmental drama, urban social research, digital art and other fields.

3 The Knowledge Taxonomy of Light Environment Art

According to the research purposes and conceptual definitions of researchers and research schools in recent decades, the concept of light environment art can be divided into four parts: 1) landscape concept light environment art with the purpose of beautifying the environment and constructing visual myths; 2) media concept light environment art with the purpose of information proliferation and communication; 3) post-humanism of light environment art concept with the purpose of constructing a humanized environment and realizing the experiential expansion of the environment.

The narrow definition of light environment art can be traced back to the early 18th century, when under the stimulus of the Industrial Revolution, lighting began to serve night markets and provide light sources for night-time transportation. The promotion of gas lamps dissipated people's fear of the night, and the form of light environment art consciously began with the expansion of capital, manifesting as functional illumination and illumination. By the end of the 19th century and the beginning of the 20th century, major cities including Chicago and New York had successfully used arc lights for outdoor lighting. The widespread use of white and colored light in cities led Chicago to be known as the "White City" and the "Colored City," and German architect Walter Gropius compared the buildings of New York at night to "Walt Disney's enchanted castle." At this time, the city's light environment was already saturated in terms of brightness environment, and lighting not only provided spatial visibility but also further entered the mainstream aesthetic value system. There was even a certain degree of "anti-functionality" and "over-illumination," and the landscape concept replaced functionalism as the focus of examination at this time. Then, along with the deepening of urbanization, landscape phenomena appeared in major urban centers including Tokyo, Lyon, Sydney, and Singapore, launching a fierce "City Beautification" movement centered on lighting and beautification. In the 21st century, the maturity and development of semiconductors and projection technology have provided the material basis for the growth of urban screens, from public transportation to building facades, media screens are almost everywhere, and light has become a direct means of image expression and information transmission. In addition to relying on the internet's viral information transmission, media-oriented light environments also provide a more immersive information environment. In recent years, virtual reality and augmented reality technology have brought new concepts to light environment. When virtual images are involved, or even replace real scenes, the ontological significance of light environments is re-examined, and when people are the subjects of light environment experiences or even creators, light environments become pure image experiences, and post-humanism concepts subvert traditional concepts of light environments. In addition to the differences before the concept, In the process of recognizing different light environment art concept, there is actually no right or wrong, and the recognition of light environment art under different concepts is just specific knowledge based on specific disciplinary backgrounds.

(1) *Landscape concept of light environment art*

The transformation to the landscape concept is the inevitable result of the development of the functionalist in light environment art. The second stage (2000–2003) of the development of urban light environment art in China is in the transition stage of the landscape concept, and "landscape beautification as the orientation, brightness as the standard" has become the main feature of the urban lighting planning stage [22]. The word "landscape" has a dual meaning. On the one hand, landscape a synonym for scenery. In urban studies and architecture, the meaning of landscape refers to the concepts of "ShanShui City" and "Ecological City", and landscape becomes a form of "anti-architecture". On the other hand, landscape refers to "Spectacle". In Guy Debord's review of "Hiroshima Mon Amour" in the third issue of "Situationist International" in 1959, he proposed that "landscape" is a non-violent and non-interventional representation and image group. In the concept of light environment art, landscape has a dual meaning in both spatial attributes and cultural attributes. On the one hand, light becomes an important element in the service of architectural space performance, texture presentation, and decorative effects. From the perspective of phenomenology, human visual perception of space and architecture is entirely dependent on the reflection of light, just as Louis Kahn said, "material is consumed light, and light is thus in resonance with space, and designing space is designing light [23]". On the other hand, landscape also refers to the expression of night scenes and night images, which is a political and economic projection of symbols at the visual level. Since the new century, the nightscape lighting of Chinese cities has been composed of two strands. The first is the lighting planning that is based on urban development, urban renewal and repair. The second is the lighting planning of urban nightscape under the influence of major events. The former includes the "135" landscape lighting project in Tianjin in 2008, the lighting planning of Pingyao Ancient City, and the lighting planning of Yingxiu Town after the

Wenchuan earthquake. The latter includes the Beijing Olympic Games, the Shanghai World Expo, the Guangzhou Asian Games and other large cultural and sports events. However, regardless of government behavior or business behavior, in the stage of rapid expansion of urban light environment projects in China, landscape has also gradually exposed many problems. For example, the arbitrary stacking of visual symbols (dragon and phoenix symbol), the "power aesthetic" of the leaders' approval, the copying foreign city templates, and the competition for night visual focus between buildings, the "brightness comparison" has become the embodiment of the blind development of landscape. In the process of the transformation of the light environment art concept, the contradictions between different concepts are becoming increasingly prominent. Some concepts under the landscape concept even go in the opposite direction of functionalism. For example, the abuse of flood lighting not only causes brightness energy efficiency overflow, but also causes glare and waste of electric energy. The standardized use of color, such as blue symbolizing tranquility and green symbolizing ecology, often goes against the expectations of viewers, especially the large-scale and long-term projection of cold colors such as blue, green, and purple on the facade of buildings, which causes discomfort [24].

In the landscape concept, architecture plays an increasingly important role in the art of the light environment. The spatial concept and design method of architecture have had a profound impact on the design and implementation of the light environment. In 2008, the Central Academy of Fine Arts founded the "Architectural Light Environment Laboratory", and in 2014, the China University of Media founded the "Light Environment Design and Application Joint Research Center"; In 2009, Tsinghua Tongheng Light Environment Planning and Design Research Center affiliated with Tsinghua University won the Excellent Nomination Award for Lighting Engineering Design. After the city was lit up by lights, the time of tourism was extended and night consumption was created, which promoted economic development. The market demand also gave birth to a number of design units, including Dongliang Xu's founding of Dongliang International Lighting Design Center and Zheng Jianwei's Beijing Architectural Design Research Institute Lighting Studio and other enterprises and institutions, which have widely participated in the light environment art project guided by the landscape concept, and have had a profound impact on China's urbanization construction since the new century, until today. In recent years, the problems brought by the landscape concept have attracted the full attention of research units and governments, aiming to solve the problems of energy waste and light pollution in the urban economy development. Moreover, the city's excess light can improve the sky background brightness by reflecting the air suspended particles, even affecting the astronomical observation and the ecological habitat of birds and insects, and is not conducive to the ecological sustainable development of the city (see Fig. 2). In December 2019, the Central "Do not forget the original intention and keep the mission" leadership team issued the "Notice on Rectifying Landscape Lighting Engineering" and other "achievement projects" and "face projects". The notice pointed out that necessary lighting engineering can be done, but it should be based on reality. Focus on long-term, based on standards, establish and improve relevant mechanisms around motion, planning, approval, construction, and other aspects to prevent "achievement projects" and "face projects" from the source [25].

Fig. 2. Light pollution from the town of Kaihua dims views of the night skies above Taihui Mountain, Zhejiang province © Dai Jianfeng [26]

In recent years, the landscape concept has also continued to draw on experience from the functionalist. In the early century designers has blindly pursued visual effects to the present while now focus on landscape visual, urban vitality and sustainable development as the three core elements of planning [27]. Among them, lighting landscape and modeling design fully express the visual sensation of material space is the means of light environment expression. Improving the lives of citizens, expressing the characteristics of human geography, and driving the cultural and tourism economy market are the goals of planning. Finally, energy conservation and environmental protection are the guarantee of sustainable development of the project.

(2) *Media Concept of Light Environment Art*

Chinese artist and researcher Qiu Zhijie from Central Academy of Fine Arts summarized in "Total Art Theory" that "any media or style, as a game, always experiences its utopia stage, grammar stage, poetics stage and marginalization stage" [28]. In the functionalist, the aesthetic significance of light environment art is hidden behind the function, while the light environment art under the landscape concept reflects the aesthetic and artistic consciousness. The form expression of light environment art becomes the main driving force. In this stage, the light environment becomes the piling up of lighting equipment, the brightness becomes higher and higher, and the light color becomes more and more. The media concept to a certain extent, the focus of light environment art from visual seizure to content presentation, the perceived object from the presence of light modeling into the "remote presence" through the media. Through the transplantation of images, the combination of digital landscape and architectural environment is realized. The Qianjiang New City Light Show in Hangzhou is the key light environment project in Hangzhou after the Hangzhou G20 Summit in 2016. The light show is composed of 700,000 LED lights, installed on the 30 high-rise building facades along the coast of Qianjiang New City's core area, connecting 30 high-rise buildings along the Qiantang River into a huge painting, presenting natural landscapes, humanities, architecture, and Hangzhou logo elements. The research of the media concept is in a stage of development and growth both in China and other countries. The abuse of media design can be traced back to the early 20th century, when American designer Oscar Nitzschke transformed the external wall of a building from a solid wall into a replaceable image skin supported by cantilevers, transforming the building into a pure media device for the "Maison de la Publicité Project" (1934). The media concept has continuously expanded its influence in environmental design and urban planning, from public art projects such as "Untitled" (Magdalena Jetelová, 1946) by Czech installation artist Magdalena Jetelová (see Fig. 3) to urban night scenes in film and television concept design such as Ridley Scott's science fiction film "Blade Runner" (1982) to urban architecture such as the Kunsthaus Graz in Austria (Colin Fournier, Peter Cook, 2003), where designers integrated BIX system circuits and lighting control, truly realizing the real-time change of light and shadow on the building's facade. As media technology develops, the media constantly transforms people's perception of the world, and this change is also reflected in the development and change of architecture and the environment.

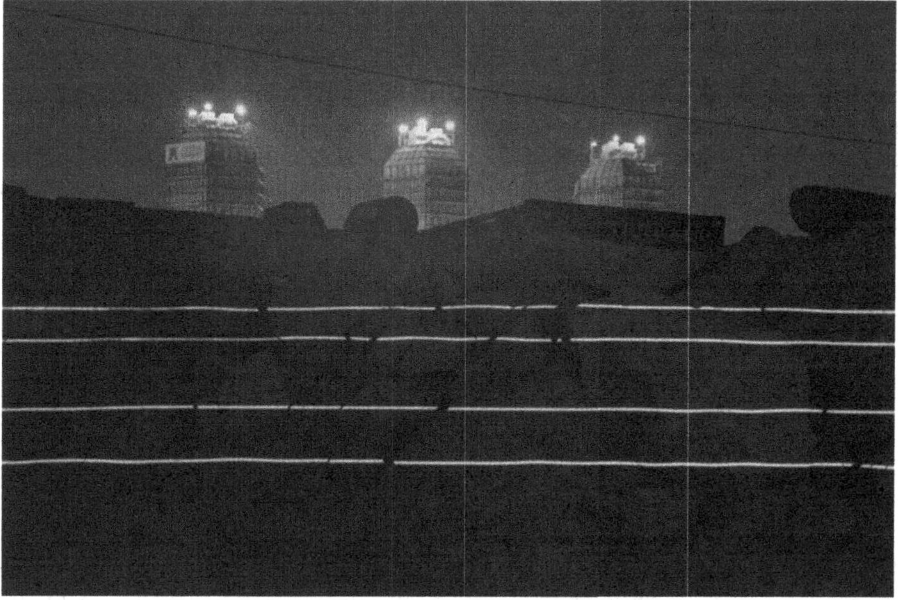

Fig. 3. Untitled © Magdalena Jetelová [29]

On the other hand, media studies and political science are also experiencing a "Spatial Turn" in their research objects, such as David Harvey, Zoan, and Robbins combining light and shadow with space and geography to study the image as a visual way of providing meaning [30]. Guy Debord and Douglas Kellner and other scholars have analyzed the national, national, and power themes in the media landscape [31]. Lefebvre argues that under the capitalist mode of production, the production of space is a socialized product. On the one hand, the Practiced Space exists through the user's perception, and on the other hand, the Conceived Space composed of knowledge and power is constantly guiding and intervening in the Live Space formed by daily life [32]. In the media concept, designers, real estate developers, and government departments often play a crucial role in the coding process of information as sources of information, while the public mainly receives external visual information from buildings. In urban lighting enhancement projects such as the "Changjiang Two Banks Scenic Lighting Improvement and Transformation Project" in Nanchang City, the "Night Scene Lighting Quality Improvement Project in Qingdao City", and the "Wenzhou Oujian Lighting Night Tour Project Design", a large number of symbolic city cultural animations are implanted on the screens of city facades and played in turn. The public is either actively or passively watching, and the problems of glare and excessive blue light caused by the media epidermis are covered by the production and expansion of capital images. As Feuerbach stated, our era is one in which "images surpass reality, copies surpass the original, appearances surpass reality, and appearance surpasses essence [33]." The power of images is even greater than the function and aesthetic of a given object. Therefore, in media architecture, the expression of image content becomes a form of propaganda or advertising. In 2009, famous Chinese lighting designer Zhang Xin was invited to design a linked lighting system for a street in a certain city. He planned to project the image of clouds onto the surface of each building to create a scattered cloud picture, but the plan was ultimately rejected by the client, who wanted the project to be more grandiose and hoped to play animated films on the building's facade. As some scholars have said, "determining a prominent position in the night skyline has become a subtle and powerful form of advertising, and this is exactly what the owners of buildings desire."

In media concept media architecture art becomes a one-way forced viewing under the guise of capital and power. Through the production of the media architecture's spatial environment, capital spreads and reproduces itself through symbols and images. Political celebrities, entertainment idols, and corporate CEOs all use media architecture to ascend to the top of buildings and look down upon the city, creating a dream-like symbol. The media architecture screens, such as the NASDAQ screen on New York's Times Square and the Reuters screen, are all priced clearly and are out of reach for the average person. The public's face, image, and voice are hidden under the glow of celebrities. Under the media concept, the public's opinions and ideas cannot be disseminated and feedback through the media architecture's transmission mechanism, which is one-way. The encoding is a monopolistic power, and the dissemination process ends here. As the main carrier of media architecture art, buildings lose their own characteristics and functionality in the transmission process. Walls, which serve as load-bearing, insulation, and lighting functions, are replaced by other devices and facilities such as frame structures, air conditioning, and daylight lamps. Walls become pure planes that serve the visual. On the other hand, due to the public nature of media architecture art, once created, media buildings are often massive in volume and eye-catching in shape, with an emphasis on visual competition rather than information exchange. As a result, the monumentality they present often overwhelms their mediaticity and becomes a megaphone for the personal ideas of real estate developers or rulers, rather than a truly efficient information exchange platform for the public. The Jiaozi Twin Towers lighting show in Chengdu uses custom LED metal strip screens to form a new building facade, covering the original building facilities. The screens are 16.2 km long and 52,000 square meters in area. When lit up at night, the entire building surface is covered by the LED screens 360 degrees, producing a stunning effect.

(3) *Post-humanism of Light Environment Art*
The concept shift of light environment art presents a trend of transformation from tool to media, that is, the proportion of symbolic representation of light environment in planning and design is increasing. The application scenarios of light environment art are not only in home, office, factory and other places with high visual task requirements, but also in public space, media architecture, real-time performance and other fields. In recent years, under the perspective of network technology and digital virtual technology, light environment art has undergone new changes and trends in concept transformation. In terms of the essence of technology, whether it is network communication or digital virtual technology, both rely on the instantaneity of telecommunication to establish. If the media environment of the media is based on the acceptance and acquisition of people's visual patterns of pixelization of images, then the post-humanism is more prominent in the real-time transmission of optical signals, and the light environment is simulated, feedback, or even intervened into a new stage of human perception and cognition. In terms of technological essence, both network communication and digital signal-based virtual technology rely on the instantaneity of telecommunication to establish themselves. If the media aura is built on the acceptance and acquisition of the visual pattern of pixelized images of human light points, then posthumanism is more prominently displayed through the real-time transmission of optical signals. The light environment enters a new phase through its simulation, feedback, and even intervention in human perception and cognition.

In the concept of media imperialism, light environment art continues the tradition of the panoramic theater inherited from Louis Daguerre, simulating the landscape through images and making remote presence a reality. The light environment works in the symbolic domain through an array of pixels that compose an image, and "all data flow must pass through the bottleneck" to be understood by people [34]. The audience translates the two-dimensional image into a three-dimensional environment through imagination. The breakthrough of virtual reality technology presented by light field images makes this way of viewing, prevalent since the Renaissance, collapse. Digital images are no longer attached to the facade of architecture, and even things like sound and smell that cannot be referred to by medium information can also be perceived by sensory perception through wearable devices [35]. Virtual technology breaks through the symbolic domain of the media imperialism concept and enters reality, allowing people to accurately select, store, and produce things that cannot be squeezed into the bottleneck [36]. Compared to media buildings that stand tall like monuments, virtual reality devices such as the CAVE system based on multi-channel view synchronization technology and 3D display technology, and VR systems such as the Oculus Rift headset, as well as AR devices such as Microsoft HoloLens, all construct a self-consistent simulation environment to a certain extent, rather than a patchwork media imperialism building. In order to achieve high convenience and seamless use, current wearable electronic devices and retina technology are actually constantly invading the body. Even smartphones, a kind of external electronic device, have become an essential part of human social life, becoming an actual "electronic organ". As Australian body behavior artist Stelarc said, "the skin has always been the boundary of the soul, self, and at the same time, the beginning of entering the world. Once the skin is extended and penetrated by technology, its role as a boundary is lost [37]." On the other hand, the simulation environment not only provides a perceptible external environment, but also allows users to interact and modify the virtual environment, trim, edit, and even transform themselves in the environment, forming their own avatar. In 2020, the American social app Snapchat launched an augmented reality application called Local Lens. Users can use this application to do color graffiti on Carnaby Street in London, and in the future, the functions and geographical scope of this application will be further expanded, including advertising, video games, shopping experiences, and map navigation (see Fig. 4). People can visit, leave messages, share photos and videos, etc. in this digital city. In this context, light environmental art is not only the carrier of information and landscape or an extension of human visual function, but when light media becomes internalized as part of the human eye's perception system, the boundaries between people, the environment and technology begin to blur, "post-human" discourse begins to appear, human purity is in crisis, and the exteriority of light environment also collapses.

Fig. 4. Snapchat's augmented reality with Local Lens © Snapchat [38]

From the perspective of research and technical implementation, the post-humanist light environment art concept is still in the development and prospect stage, and many theories are not yet mature. Commercial large-scale promotion is also facing difficulties. Whether it is augmented reality technology, which is more closely combined with the real environment, or virtual reality technology, which has a stronger immersion experience, both face the double bottleneck of technology and business. On the hardware level, it is still unknown when the wearable devices relied on by virtual technology can truly change from "human extension" to "human body enhancement". The distributed computing relied on by virtual technology networks is also limited by the speed of image signal propagation and calculation power, and there is a delay or poor imaging effect, which makes it difficult to achieve large-scale instant virtual experience. Despite the many uncertainties, post-humanist light environmental art still gives people an infinite space for imagination. After breaking free from the constraints of the physical environment, as an experiential environment, what role will light environmental art play in people's future production and life? Only the future can give the answer.

4 Conclusion

From God saying "let there be light", Prometheus stealing fire, Plato's "Allegory of the Cave", to the light and electric revolution and the information revolution brought by the industrial revolution, the development history of light environment in a broad sense has almost run through the entire process of human civilization. However, narrowly speaking, the establishment and development of the discipline of light environment art in China is only less than half a century old. The concept study of light environment art began in engineering, gradually matured in the field of architecture and began to extend its tentacles to fields such as art, drama, and communication. At present, the functionalist concept is still an important foundation for light environment research, while light environment art commercial projects under the guidance of the landscape and media concepts have a large proportion in China, which is also a natural result of the demand for urban residents' nightlife in China. The post-humanism of light environment art is a search for progress in the field of theory and application, and it requires relevant scholars and practitioners to continue working in this soil. Light environment art is a new field and direction, and research on light environmental art under different concepts is also advancing in unison, making corrections and growing. How can landscape light environment art be better combined with daily practice? Will media light environmental art gradually disappear, and is post-humanistic light environment art really just a kind of epistemic experience? These questions will all become part of the future research on luminous art concepts.

References

1. He, X.: Spatial turn: a glimpse of david harvey's dialectical view of time and space. Frontiers **20**, 63–66 (2011)
2. Guo, L.: Analysis of spatial differences in China's urbanization process based on DMSP/OLS image data . MS thesis. Lanzhou University (2011)
3. Average night light intensity data through DMSP/OLS technology by NASA, http://antwrp.gsfc.nasa.gov/apod/ap001127.html. Accessed 25 Dec 2022

4. Guo, H., Zhou, T.: Expected application of LEDS in city landscape lighting. In: International Forum on LED Semiconductor Lighting, pp. 137–139 (2004)
5. Liang, R.: Development status and future prospects of intelligent lighting control technology. J. Illum. Eng. **25**(2), 15–26 (2014)
6. Zhou, Z., Zhou, Y., Xiao, J.: A review of virtual reality augmented technology. Sci. China Inf. Sci. **45**(2), 157–180 (2014)
7. Chu, D., Liao, J., Xu, Y.: Research on the evolution mechanism of China's nighttime economic policy. Consum. Econ. (2021)
8. Hao, L., Yang, X., Zeng, K., Jin, Q.: Exploration and practice of urban lighting planning in China——20 years review of urban lighting planning in China. Chin. J. Light. Eng. **S1**, 17–26 (2012)
9. Corbusier, L.: Toward an architecture. frances lincoln ltd (2008)
10. Hausler, M.H.: Media facade: history, technology and content. Ludwigsburg: Avedition **57** (2009)
11. Yang, G.: Non-visual effects of lighting (introduction of CIE division six). J. Illum. Eng. **2**(2), 9–16 (1989)
12. Chen, Z., Xi, Y.: Evaluation method of architectural light environment. J. Illum. Eng. **3**(4), 26–30 (1992)
13. Lvtai, G.: Discussion on the theory of architectural light environment. J. Beijing Inst. Archit. Eng. **2**, 83–92 (1989)
14. Rea, M.S.: IESNA Lighting Handbook: Reference and Application. New York: The Iluminating Engineering Society of North America, pp. 351–367 (2000)
15. Chang, Z.: The reduction of optical space concept and lighting design. In: Special Report and Proceedings of the Twelfth Cross-Strait Symposium on Lighting Technology and Marketing (2005)
16. Chang, Z.: Reflections on lighting design as a discipline. In: Special Report and Proceedings of the Twelfth Cross-Strait Symposium on Lighting Technology and Marketing (2005)
17. Ma, J., Shen, T.: On night scene lighting planning. J. Illum. Eng. **6**(1), 30–34 (1995)
18. Hu, H.: Night City——Research on Urban Space Based on Night Behavior Activities (Doctoral dissertation. Tianjin University), Tianjin (2008)
19. Peng, J.: Light environment culture and artistic expression. Decoration **1**, 81 (2005)
20. Chang, Z.: Clues to the development of media architecture. Art Res. **1**, 101–107 (2015)
21. Zhang, L., Du, C.: Concept of discipline construction of light environment design. Mod. Commun. J. Commun. Univ. China **12**, 118–121 (2013)
22. Hao, L., et al.: Exploration and practice of urban lighting planning in China—a 20-year review of urban lighting planning in China. J. Light. Eng. **S1**, 17–26 (2012)
23. Kahn, L.I.: Louis I. Kahn from Aspen Conference, 1972, Youtube (1972). https://www.youtube.com/watch?v=ZaUtcKqdL5E
24. Ma, J., Wang, L.: Discussion and reflection on urban nightscape development. Urban Planning **23**(6), 44–46 (1999)
25. Xinhua News Agency: The Central Remembering the Original Aspiration, Keeping in Mind the Mission Theme Education Leading Group issued the Notice on Rectifying the Excessive Transformation of 'Landscape Beautification Projects' and Other 'Performance Projects' and 'Face-saving Projects, The Government of the People's Republic of China (2019). http://www.gov.cn/xinwen/2019-12/02/content_5457679.html
26. Light pollution from the town of Kaihua dims views of the night skies above Taihui Mountain, Zhejiang province by Dai Jianfeng. https://www.sixthtone.com/news/1002662/why-chinas-stargazers-want-to-turn-down-the-lights. Accessed 03 Dec 2022
27. Rong, H.: The value orientation of urban landscape lighting. J. Illum. Eng. **1** (2013)
28. Qiu, Z.: Total Art Theory . Shanghai jin xiu wen zhang chu ban she (2012)

29. Untitle by Magdalena Jetelová. https://www.mutualart.com/Artwork/Untitled/63EED1EFF C1DA04B. Accessed 02 Jan 2022
30. Brownei, R.: Boo review place.: power situation and spectacle a geography of film. J. Popular Cult. Bowling Green **28**(2), 215(1994)
31. Fang, L.: Theory of the Media Space, Publisher of Communication University of China **18** (2011)
32. Zhang, L., Xu, H.: A study of urban space in Jacques Tati's films from the perspective of space triadic dialectics. Contemp. Cinema (2021)
33. Feuerbach, L.: The essence of Christianity. Barnes & Noble Publishing (2004)
34. Kittler, F.A.: Gramophone, Film, Typewriter. CA: Stanford University Press, pp. 40–41 (1999)
35. Choi, Y., Cheok, A.D., Roman, X., et al.: Sound perfume: designing a wearable sound and fragrance media for face-to-face interpersonal interaction. In: Proceedings of the 8th International Conference on Advances in Computer Entertainment Technology, pp. 1–8 (2011)
36. Zhang, Y.: The theory of media technology towards post-humanism——an interpretation of Friedrich Kittler's media thought. Mod. Commun. J. Commun. Univ. China **9**, 22–25 (2014)
37. Atzori, P., Woolford, K.: Extended-body Interview with Stelarc, Ctheory (1972). https://journals.uvic.ca/index.php/ctheory/article/view/14658,
38. Snapchat's augmented reality with Local Lens by Snapchat. https://www.wired.co.uk/article/snapchat-launches-local-lenses. Accessed 11 Dec 2022

The Association Between Academic Clickbait and Impact: From the Perspective of Online Media News

Yifan Zhu[1], Xin Li[2], Jia Zhou[1](✉), and Yunshan Jiang[1]

[1] School of Management Science and Real Estate, Chongqing University, Chongqing, People's Republic of China
jiazhou@cqu.edu.cn

[2] Zhaoqing Xiaopeng New Energy Investment Co Ltd., Guangdong, People's Republic of China

Abstract. Most readers tend to decide whether to click on a news link based on its title, which gives rise to clickbait. Academic research news reporting may be influenced by the accuracy of the titles of the research papers. Our study analyzed the current state and impact of the academic clickbait phenomenon from the perspective of online media news based on the PubMed platform. First, we found the phenomenon of clickbait titles in both the titles of articles on the PubMed platform ($N = 6{,}720$, 2011–2021) and related news articles ($N = 44{,}718$, 2011–2021) has exhibited an increasing trend, and the trend in article titles follows the trend of clickbait titles in news ($Granger\_p < 0.05$). Second, the use of clickbait in academic paper titles did not lead to higher media attention but rather had a negative impact on citation metrics ($t = -2.248$, $p = 0.025$) ("penalty" effect of academic clickbait). Hence, the result of our study suggested academics use professional conventions to standardize the description of article titles within the relevant field and be responsible for their headlines.

Keywords: Academic clickbait · Article title · Online media news

1 Introduction

With the internet development, the primary platform of news shifted from newspapers and television to online media such as news websites, social media, and smartphone apps [1], and the number of online news content has considerably increased. Related investigations showed, 80% of readers tend to skim headlines to help them decide whether to click on a news link [2]. In order to promote click rate, the editors of "Clickbait" (the phenomenon of baiting readers to click the content through a specific title style) exploited people's thirst for unknown information [3] and used a narrative style that evokes readers' emotions to enhance their retention of the information after reading [4]. (such as, "win up to 500$ with 5 min survey";) Previous studies explored clickbait often produced viral transmission, carrying fraud and false information [5, 6].

Clickbait on the internet was not exclusive to media but could also be found in academic article titles to varying degrees, commonly referred to as academic clickbait (For

H. Mori et al. (Eds.): HCII 2023, LNCS 14056, pp. 454–469, 2023.
https://doi.org/10.1007/978-3-031-48044-7_32

example, academic clickbait title "Let's look at leeks! Picture books increase toddlers' willingness to look at, taste and consume unfamiliar vegetables"; academic title "On interpretation and task selection in studies on the effects of noise on cognitive performance") [7]. In academic papers included on PubMed, the frequency of using overly positive affirmation words (such as Amazing, Robust, etc.) greatly increased from 2.0% (1974–1980) to 17.5% (2014), a relative increase of 880% [8]. Over humorous and problematic titles were gradually been used by paper authors. Among the psychological field papers collected and analyzed by the Lockwood team, the proportion of papers with question titles is 8.24% [8]. Some fixed formats that attract attention (such as "X is All You Need") had also become common templates for article titles. Academic clickbait in the title of academic articles in attracting more attention, this action may be more harmful than clickbait in the news. Sumner et al. [9] found that the exaggeration in the news related academic paper was closely linked to the exaggeration in journal press releases. It suggests that clickbait in scientific research may become more skewed in public discourse than it in news.

The majority of previous studies had explored academic clickbait as a correlation with click rates and its citation [8, 9, 21–23], and whether academic clickbait had a positive impact on citations remains controversial. In addition, academic clickbait not only impacted citation but also influent daily life through media. However, there was a lack of examining the clickbait impact from the perspective of online media news.

Therefore, this study mainly explores two questions: (1) What is the current status of clickbait headlines in academic and news on internet platforms? (2) What is the correlation between the use of clickbait in academic articles and their impact?

2 Materials and Method

2.1 Data Source

We analyzed academic data from the PubMed platform, A biomedical literature search system that was classic in research clickbait [8]. Academic article datasets were collected from the PubMed platform through two data collection software (Octopus Collector and Houyi Collector, which fit the structure of this platform), and the capacity for data scraping was 100,000. The variables included in the academic article datasets were: title, PMID, publish date, and citation count.

The title in academic article datasets was searched by line on the Altmetric database which included information related to a single academic article on news sites, blogs, Twitter, Facebook, etc. If an academic article had relevant online media news on the internet, the data for that paper will be retained. If not, the data for that article will be removed. After censoring, 91,376 lines of articles were excluded, and 8,624 remaining papers could be tracked on the database Altmetric with 91,376 lines of news data. The variables included in the news datasets from Altmetric were: post-date and title.

In addition, the variables added in the academic article datasets: number of news, Mendeley index and dimension score. The number of news refers to the amount of news released by the internet platform related to a certain paper from the Altmetric database. The Mendeley Index was the number of readers on the Mendeley platform who had included a paper in their literature database, with a higher Mendeley Index indicating that more users were following the paper's results. From the Dimensions platform, the dimensions score describes one article cited by multiple publications such as books, standards, and patents, reflecting the comprehensive value of an article.

This study focused on English headlines used as the research target, and the news data of non-English content were removed. A language detection algorithm written in Python was used to identify the language of the news headlines. 2,839 news items (5.66%) that were not reported in English were identified, and this part of the news data and the corresponding paper data were removed. 2,616 news items (5.21%) were also excluded from the study, and both the news items and their corresponding papers were removed for the reason of directly citing the title of a paper without adapting. In the end, a total of 44,718 news items and 6,720 papers were obtained. The entire data collection process is illustrated in Fig. 1.

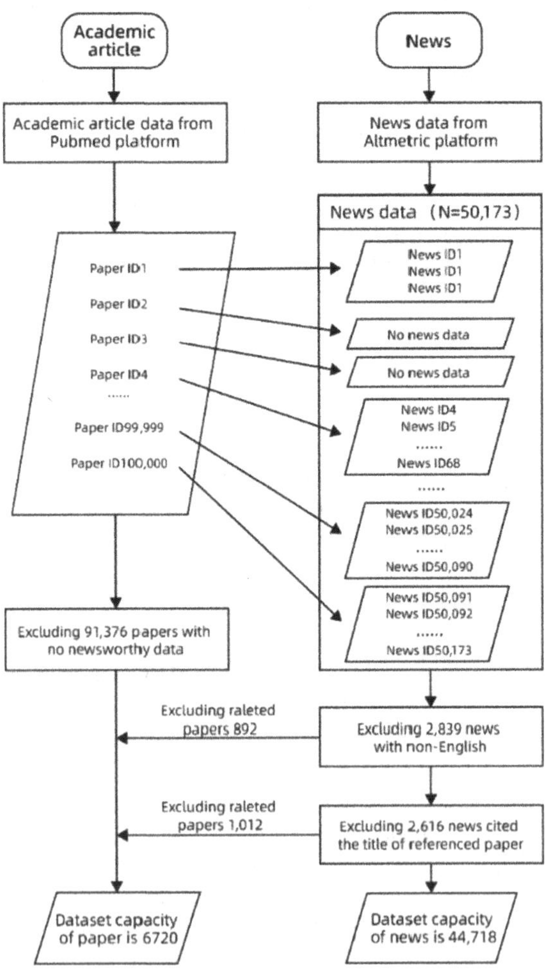

Fig. 1. The process of data collection

2.2 Clickbait Detection

This study identified clickbait in article titles and news headlines through algorithms. The clickbait recognition algorithm had the following requirements: (1) The algorithm was designed to address the English literature; (2) The algorithm should be able to complete the recognition of clickbait relying on the title only; (3) The algorithm needed to have a high accuracy and precision. We compiled a list of publications on the identification of clickbait in English titles [10–15], from which we selected 16 algorithmic models that were reported to perform highly.

This study conducted performance testing on them using an existing English dataset of clickbait, in ensuring the reliability of the 16 algorithms in practical applications. The source of the datasets is Clickbait Challenge 2017 [16] initiated by Bauhaus College in Weimar, Germany. The content in datasets consisted exclusively of news headlines posted on Twitter by news media, showing clear characteristics of news textual features. Besides, the datasets were labelled by multiple annotators and all labelling results were verified by the datasets constructors. The dataset inter-rater agreement Fleiss Kappa for clickbait classification is 0.36(fair agreement) and inter-rater reliability is 0.84 [17], which meets the consistency requirement. The process of choosing detection model is shown in Fig. 2.

Algorithm Performance Evaluation

Clickbait detection is a binary classification recognition problem. Based on the actual values of the test datasets, the test set samples were divided into positive samples (i.e., clickbait data) and negative samples (i.e., non-clickbait data). By comparing the predicted values of the detection algorithm with the actual values of the test set data, the final result of each test sample can only belong to one of these four categories, as shown in Table 1. The algorithm performance can be evaluated through the number of samples in each category.

The commonly used evaluation metrics for classification algorithms include accuracy, precision, recall, F1-score, etc. [18]. Accuracy referred to the proportion of correctly identified samples by the detection algorithm to the total number of samples, as calculated by the formula (1). Precision referred to the proportion of true positive samples to the total predicted positive samples, as calculated by the formula (2). Recall was the proportion of true positive samples to the total positive samples in the actual values, as calculated by the formula (3). F1-score was the harmonic mean of precision and recall, as calculated by the formula (4), which reflects the stability of the algorithm.

$$Accuracy = \frac{N_{tp} + N_{tn}}{N_{tp} + N_{fp} + N_{fn} + N_{tn}} \tag{1}$$

$$Precision = \frac{N_{tp}}{N_{tp} + N_{fp}} \tag{2}$$

$$Recall = \frac{N_{tp}}{N_{tp} + N_{fn}} \tag{3}$$

$$F1 - score = \frac{2 * Precision * Recall}{Precision + Recall} \tag{4}$$

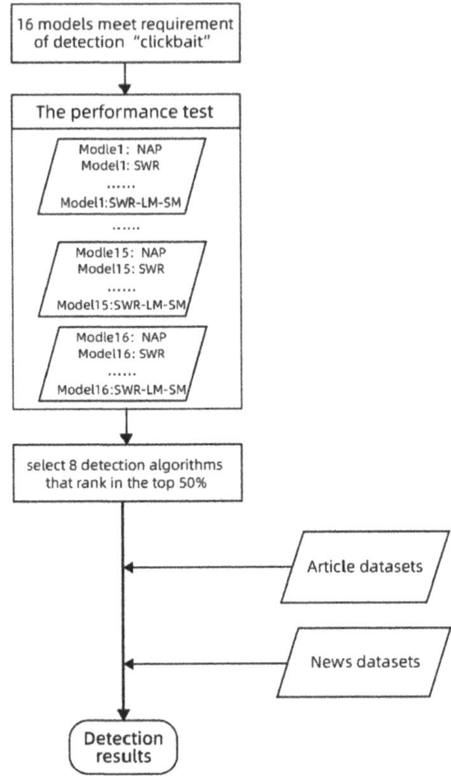

Fig. 2. The process of choosing detection model

Table 1. The prediction results of clickbait detection algorithm

Predicate value	Real value	
	Positive	Negative
Positive	True Positive	False Positive
Negative	False Negative	True Negative

Note: N_{tp}, N_{fp}, N_{fn}, N_{tn} respectively represented the numbers of true positives, false positives, false negatives, and true negatives in the predicted outcomes.

Algorithm Preprocessing Selection

The pre-processing of the organized data was conducted using four methods: no additional pre-processing (NAP), stop word removal (SWR), lemmatization (LM), and stemming (SM). Multiple pre-processing algorithms were employed to process the target data, resulting in eight pre-processed datasets, namely NAP, SWR, LM, SM, SWR -LM, SWR -SM, LM-SM, and SWR -LM-SM. Each detection model required the use of these eight pre-processed datasets for clickbait detection, in selecting the optimal pre-processing conditions for each model.

Algorithm Performance

The results of performance testing for various algorithms were presented in Table 2. The accuracy of the 16 detection models was generally between 75% and 80%. However, there was a variation in the precision of these algorithms, ranging from a minimum of 0.421 to a maximum of 0.656. Algorithms with high accuracy also tend to have higher precision, but there was little difference in precision among algorithms with high accuracy.

Table 2. The performance test results of the clickbait detection algorithms

Model	Algorithm	Classifier	Preprocess	Accuracy	Precision	Recall	F1-Score
1	Bag of words	Extra Trees	LM-SM	0.766	0.575	0.266	0.364
2	Bag of words	Logistic Regression	LM	0.776	0.608	0.309	0.409
3	Bag of words	Naive Bayes	SM	0.764	0.536	0.463	0.497
4	Bag of words	Neural Network	LM-SM	0.740	0.478	0.366	0.414
5	Bag of words	Random Forests	SM	0.765	0.567	0.317	0.376
6	Word2vec	Extra Trees	SM	0.764	0.585	0.214	0.313
7	Word2vec	Logistic Regression	NAP	0.769	0.637	0.189	0.292
8	Word2vec	Naive Bayes	LM-SM	0.729	0.456	0.391	0.421
9	Word2vec	Neural Network	LM	0.775	0.637	0.244	0.353
10	Word2vec	Random Forests	SM	0.764	0.575	0.233	0.331
11	Word2vec + ReLu	Neural Network	LM	0.775	0.646	0.231	0.34
12	TFIDF	Naive Bayes	LM	0.787	0.656	0.413	0.507
13	TFIDF	XC Boost	LM-SM	0.760	0.485	0.352	0.408
14	TFIDF	SVM	LM	0.745	0.512	0.231	0.318
15	TFIDF	Random Forests-grid	LM-SM	0.774	0.462	0.348	0.400
16	TFIDF	Dummy	SM	0.745	0.421	0.195	0.267

Clickbait Detection Result

This study employed multiple algorithms to jointly identify clickbait. We selected 8 detection algorithms that rank in the top 50% in terms of accuracy and had a precision greater than 0.5 to recognize paper titles and news headlines. Referenced to previous research, a consistency standard was established as a reference to obtain a sufficient sample size. The consistency threshold for identification results in this study was set at 75% [11], which meant that a headline was considered clickbait only when six out of the eight algorithms identify it as such.

Table 3. The identification results of the paper and news headlines

Materia	Number of titles	Clickbait	Non-clickbait
Title in article datasets	6,720	1,705	5,015
Title in news datasets	44,718	4,884	39,834

As shown in Table 3, the recognition results of paper titles and news headlines reveal the identification of a total of 6,720 paper titles, among which 1,705 were identified as clickbait, accounting for 25.4% of the total number of papers. Additionally, 44,718 news headlines were recognized, of which 4,884 were identified as clickbait, accounting for 10.9% of the total number of news content. The variables added in the academic article datasets: number of clickbait news, number of news, clickbait identification, and consistency for identification.

3 Result

3.1 Clickbait Current Situation

Online Media News Clickbait

The Altmetric platform was established in 2011. Therefore, this study utilized time series analysis techniques to examine and forecast the annual reporting frequency of clickbait news compiled from news data between 2011 and 2021.

The annual reporting frequency of clickbait news was a non-stationary time series. In addition, logarithmic transformation was applied to it and denoted as $logA$. . Then, according to the results of Augmented Dickey-Fuller (ADF) test, the $logA$ sequence was found to be a stationary sequence ($p = 0.0238$), and the 1-degree difference significance of the Q statistic was observed, indicating non-white noise sequences ($p = 0.032$). The autocorrelation and partial autocorrelation plots of the $logA$, and it was observed partial correlation function truncation at lag 1, that $logA$ followed the 1-degree autoregression or AR (1). The model ($R^2 = 0.482$, $adjusted - R^2 = 0.425$) result demonstrated that the first-order autoregressive parameter was significant (Coefficient = 0.389, Std. = 0.126, $t = 3.099$, $p = 0.013$). In online platforms, the annual reporting frequency of clickbait news exhibited the current year's quantity was significantly influenced by the previous years.

Based on the established model (Fig. 3), we predicted future trends in clickbait news headlines. The predicted trend indicated a steady increase in the annual reporting frequency of clickbait news over time. It was foreseeable that, under the current governance mechanisms of online platforms, the frequency of clickbait news headlines related to research will continue to increase.

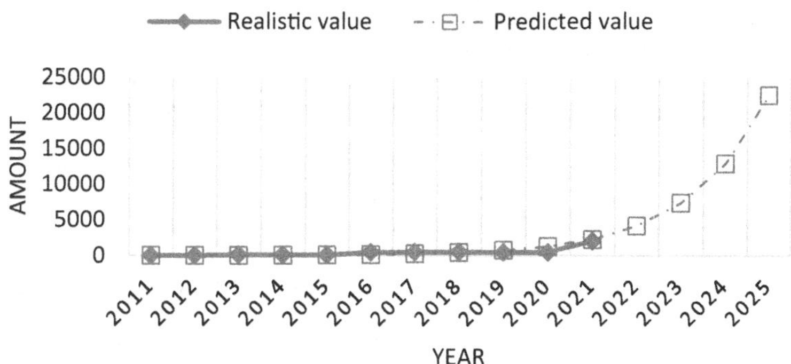

Fig. 3. The forecast chart of clickbait news

Academic Clickbait

Based on the data of PubMed, the annual frequency of academic clickbait was compiled from academic article datasets between 2011 and 2021. Compared with 2011, the annual amount of clickbait in academics increased by 420.51% in PubMed in 2021.

The annual frequency of academic clickbait is a non-stationary time series. In addition, logarithmic transformation was applied to it and denoted as *logB*. Then, according to the results of ADF test and Q-statistic, the *logB* sequence was found to be a stationary sequence ($p = 0.0046$), and the 1-degree difference was observed significance, indicating non-white noise sequences ($p = 0.044$). The partial autocorrelation plots' partial correlation function truncation at lag 1, that *logB* followed the 1-degree autoregression or AR (1). The model ($R^2 = 0.612$, $adjusted - R^2 = 0.568$) demonstrated that the first-order autoregressive parameter was significant (Coefficient = 0.017, Std. = 0.006, $t = 2.623$, $p = 0.028$). In PubMed platforms, the annual frequency of academic clickbait exhibits the current year's quantity was significantly influenced by the previous years.

We made a prediction of future trends in academic clickbait (Fig. 4), and it was evident that the current state of academic clickbait on the PubMed platform exhibited a fluctuating upward development trend. While there might be occasional minor declines, the overall trend was still on the rise. Therefore, we surmised that the academic clickbait on the PubMed platform will continue to expand in quantity without external interventions.

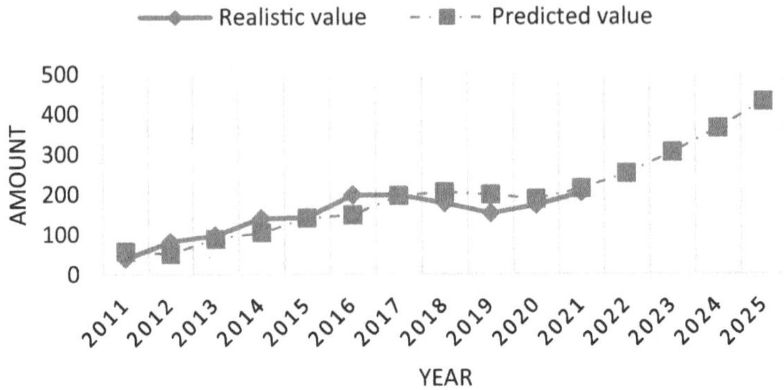

Fig. 4. The forecast chart of academic clickbait

Correlation Between Online Media News Clickbait and Academic Clickbait

In aims to investigate the causes of academic clickbait, we employed a vector autoregressive (VAR) model of multivariate time series analysis to examine the inherent relationship between the annual reporting frequency of clickbait news and the annual frequency of academic clickbait.

It could be inferred from the aforementioned analysis that *logA* and *logB* sequence was found to be a stationary sequence and a non-white noise sequence. Therefore, these were available to utilize VAR model. The VAR lag order selection criteria was calculated, the AIC and SC values of the model are minimized (AIC = 1.660706, SC = 1.792189) when the lag period was 1, indicating that the optimal lag period was 1. To examine the causal relationship between the two-time series, Granger causality tests were performed, and the *logA* series was a Granger cause of the *logB* series ($p < 0.05$). This suggested that the annual reporting frequency of clickbait news was a Granger factor for the annual frequency of academic clickbait. Therefore, VAR model was constructed using the *logA* and *logB* sequence with the lag periods of $t - 1$ and $t - 2$ (Eq. 5). Subscripts t–1 and t–2 were used to represent the values of the *logA* and *logB* sequences in the t − 1 and t − 2 years, respectively.

$$logB_t = 0.393376 * logB_{t-1} + 0.210508 * logB_{t-2} + 0.018901 * logA_{t-1} + 0.034384 * logB_{t-2} + 0.942242 + \varepsilon \quad (5)$$

The absolute reciprocals of the AR unit roots lie within the unit circle respectively which indicated that the established VAR model was stationary. Consequently, the estimated equations derived from the model parameters were also stationary. Converting the estimated equation into the original data format (Eq. 6).

$$B_t = 10^{0.942242} * B_{t-1}^{0.393376} * B_{t-2}^{0.210508} * A_{t-1}^{0.018901} * A_{t-2}^{0.034384} * 10^{\varepsilon} \quad (6)$$

Formula (5) described the regularity of the frequency of academic clickbait, which indicated that the variation in the annual frequency of academic clickbait on the PubMed platform was related to the frequency of previous years, and had a certain numerical correlation with the annual reporting frequency of clickbait news over time.

3.2 Impact of Academic Clickbait

Impact of Academic Clickbait on Media Attention

The level of media attention reflects the degree to which news outlets are interested in a particular academic paper and can be measured by the number of news articles reporting on the paper.

The news data was summarized for each academic paper, and the number of news reports for each paper was counted. Based on whether the paper was an academic clickbait, a total of 1705 academic clickbait data and 5015 non-academic clickbait data were obtained. Then, the Kolmogorov-Smirnov test (KS test) was used to measure the normality of the amount of news in each measure, and the number of news reports for both academic clickbait and non-academic clickbait did not follow a normal distribution and remained non-normal even after necessary transformations such as logarithmic or square root transformations. Levene's test results indicated that the two sets of data pass the test for homogeneity of variances ($F(1, 6718) = 0.362$, $p > 0.05$). The data did not follow a normal distribution, this study used the Mann-Whitney U test to investigate whether there was a significant difference in the number of news articles between academic clickbait and non-academic clickbait. The results of the Mann-Whitney U test indicate that there is no significant difference ($Z = -1.395$, $p = 0.163$) between the mean number of news articles reporting academic clickbait ($M = 6.59 \pm 13.748$) and non-academic clickbait ($M = 6.68 \pm 19.051$). Whether a scholarly article on PubMed was an academic clickbait had no significant effect on having more associated online news.

Impact of Academic Clickbait on Citation Count

The citation count of a paper is an important indicator of the academic impact of the paper. Previous studies showed that certain features in the title of a paper directly or indirectly influence its citation count [19, 20]. This section analyzed the citation counts of academic clickbait and non-academic clickbait based on the academic article datasets from the PubMed platform.

In terms of the citation count of academic papers, time was one of the important influencing factors. Generally, compared to papers published in the last two years, papers published earlier may receive more citations, but sometimes time causes a decrease in its citation count when the information and achievements of a paper become relatively outdated. Time was a plausible influencing factor on citation count, it is imperative to comprehensively examine its impact before exploring the potential influence of academic clickbait on citation count. In this study, we conducted a time effect analysis of the average citation count data of papers on the PubMed platform through the autoregressive integrated moving average (ARIMA) model.

The citation count for each of the 6,720 papers was disaggregated by year, and the annual average citation count for papers on the PubMed platform was calculated, for the period spanning from 2002 to 2021. Visual inspection of the time series plot reveals a clear increasing trend in the average citation count per article throughout the analyzed period of this study.

This study assessed the stationarity of time series data by employing the ADF test on the original data, first-order differenced data, and second-order differenced data, the result provided evidence that the second-order differenced time series data exhibited stationarity. Based on this, the d parameter in the ARIMA (p, d, q) model was set to 2. The second-order difference significance of the Q statistic was observed, indicating non-white noise sequences ($p = 0.032$). The autocorrelation function and partial autocorrelation function plots of the second-order differenced series exhibit truncation at lag 1, suggesting an autoregressive process with parameter $p = 1$ and $q = 0$. Consequently, the final model was specified as ARIMA (1, 2, 0).

The model parameters ($R^2 = 0.\ 985$, $adjusted - R^2 = 0.\ 331$) were calculated. The results of the significance test of the parameters demonstrated that the first-order autoregressive parameter is significant (Coefficient = -–0.682, Std. = 0.249, t = –0.2735, p = 0.015), which demonstrate the number of papers cited is significantly influenced by time with an upward trend (Fig. 5).

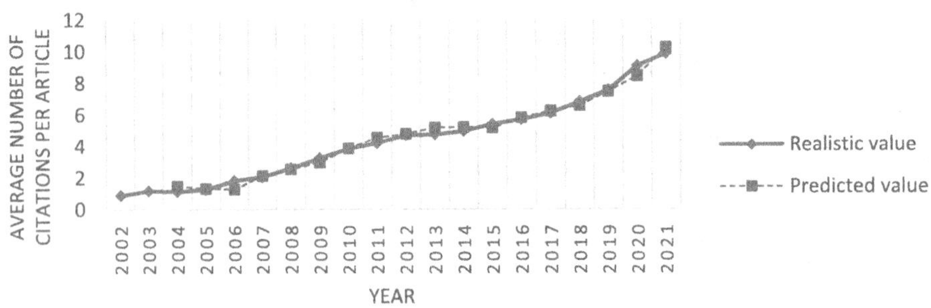

Fig. 5. Average number of citations per article by time

Therefore, when studying the impact of academic clickbait on the citation of papers, it is necessary to include the potential impact of time in the analysis. It was hard to completely consider the title of an article as academic clickbait, and this article used consistency for identification to respect this clickbait phenomenon. Higher consistency for identification corresponded to more likely individual readers to notice the title of the article as an academic clickbait. Simultaneously, consider the impact of media factors on the citation, factor as Dimension score, Mendeley index, number of clickbait news, and number of news were included in the analysis. Shown in Table 4.

Based on SPSS 26.0, we performed a multiple linear regression analysis hypothesis test on the data above, results were as follows:

(1). The dependent variable in this study was the citation, which was a continuous variable and satisfies the hypothesis that the dependent variable is a continuous variable.
(2). The linear relationships existed between each independent variable and citation count, which were visually inspected through generated scatterplots of the five independent variables against the dependent variable.
(3). The assumption of low correlation among the independent variables in multiple linear regression was satisfied. We used Pearson correlation coefficients to examine

Table 4. The data for regression analysis

No	Consistency for identification	Publication duration	Dimension score	Mendeley index	number of news	number of clickbait news	number of non-clickbait news	citation count
1	0.875	8	99	447	1	1	0	37
2	0.75	8	976	2263	91	12	79	410
3	0.25	6	130	128	53	4	49	67
4	0.25	5	25	35	1	0	1	10
5	0.875	7	470	942	4	1	3	175
…	…	…	…	…	…	…	…	…
6719	0.75	6	362	991	41	5	36	171
6720	0.375	7	304	441	10	0	10	181

the relationships between each independent variable, and the results revealed that there was a significant positive correlation between Dimension score and Mendeley index ($r = 0.813$, $p < 0.01$), as well as between the number of clickbait news and the number of non-clickbait news ($r = 0.955$, $p < 0.01$). No significant high correlation was observed among the remaining variables. In consider of high correlation among two or more independent variables may result in multicollinearity problems. Therefore, in this study, we removed Dimension score and number of non-clickbait news form the independent variables. The remaining five independent variables exhibited no significant high correlation.

(4). The assumption of observational independence was met in the data. We constructed a multiple linear regression model and assessed the homoscedasticity of the data by plotting the residuals against the predicted values. The standardized residuals were randomly scattered around the horizontal line of zero residual, irrespective of the predicted values of the dependent variable, indicating the stability of the residual variance and thus supporting the homoscedasticity assumption. Furthermore, the histogram and normal probability plot of the standardized residuals demonstrated an approximate normal distribution, satisfying the assumption of multiple linear regression. We further analyzed the independence of residuals using the Durbin-Watson statistic, and the results indicated that the residual values were independent of each other ($d = 1.970$, $dL = 1.718 < d < 4\text{-}dU = 2.180$).

The test results indicate that the data, with academic clickbait probability, publication duration, Mendeley index, number of news, and number of clickbait news as independent variables, and citation count as the dependent variable, meet the hypothesis of multiple linear regression analysis. The multiple linear regression analysis results ($R^2 = 0.813$, $adjusted - R^2 = 0.661$) presented in Table 5.

66.1% of the total variance in citation counts accounts can be explained by several independent variables. The results of the variance analysis of the regression model indicate that, at a significance level of 0.05, the probability of academic clickbait, the

Table 5. The results of regression analysis

	B	95% Confidence interval	β	t	p
Constant	–9.903	[–12.834, –6.973]		–6.624	0.000
Consistency for identification	–5.737	[–10.739, –0.735]	–0.016	–2.248	0.025
Publication duration	1.454	[1.168, 1.739]	0.072	9.977	0.000
Mendeley index	0.263	[0.258, 0.267]	0.798	109.892	0.000
Number of news	–0.035	[–0.130, 0.059]	–0.007	–0.732	0.464
Number of clickbait news	0.114	[–0.176, 0.405]	0.007	0.770	0.441

duration of publication, and the Mendeley index had significant effects on citation count. In the final regression equation, only these three independent variables were included, as represented by Eq. 7.

$$y = -9.903 - 5.737 * CI + 1.454 * PD + 0.263 * MI \tag{7}$$

Note: y- Citation count; CI- Consistency for identification; PD- Publication duration; MI- Mendeley index

The above model shows that the citation count of PubMed platform articles was mainly influenced by the probability of academic clickbait (standardized regression coefficient [β] = -0.016, p = 0.025), publishing duration (β = 0.072, p < 0.001), and Mendeley index (β = 0.798, p < 0.001). As for the probability of academic clickbait, it had a negative impact on the citation count, and an increase in the probability of academic clickbait leads to a decrease in the citation count of the article. The higher the probability of academic clickbait, the lower its citation count.

4 Discussion

4.1 Clickbait Current Situation

Clickbait in both the news and academics had exhibited an increasing trend over time. Among them, the development of clickbait news had been particularly rapid, showing an exponential growth pattern, and existing measures had failed to curb the spread of clickbait on online platforms [8]. In 2021, the annual volume of clickbait in academic publications on PubMed increased by 420.51% compared to 2011. The number of academic clickbait on the PubMed platform had varied year by year and had shown some numerical regularity with clickbait news over time. One possible explanation for this result is that some research workers, perhaps influenced by clickbait in news headlines, also hope to exhibit humorous personalities in their own research. Indeed, academics should be responsible for their headlines. The exaggeration of a paper's title is likely to lead to exaggerated news coverage related to the paper [9].

Based on the current state of clickbait which coded potentially inaccurate information, our study believed there are two areas that can contribute to preventing clickbait. Firstly, research into how headliners are managed on online platforms would be a way to safeguard user experience [3–6]. Secondly, readers are the last line of defense in screening and defending against clickbait, and it is important to study clickbait prevention measures based on readers' perspectives.

4.2 Impact of Academic Clickbait

Overall, we found academic clickbait given articles a certain "penalty" effect, as it had a negative impact on citation count. Previous research findings demonstrated that the use of academic clickbait had a minimal effect on citation count [21]. Our results indicated that academic clickbait had a negative impact on the citation count for academic papers on the PubMed platform. There were two possible explanations for this result:

Firstly, academic clickbait undermined the credibility of academic papers. Readers of academic papers had high expectations of the content, and academic clickbait was generally perceived content that deviates from the information conveyed in the title, which lowered the credibility of the paper and makes it difficult to be cited by other scholars.

Secondly, locating clickbait by searching the literature using specialist terms was more difficult than a non-clickbait. The readership of academic papers was relatively specialized, consisting mainly of students and research scholars. When searching for academic papers, this group had specific reading needs and often used professional keywords for searching. However, academic clickbait titles rarely contained these keywords, making it difficult to be searched and found.

Currently, the use of positive framing, excessive affirmation, and questioning in titles had become a common approach in cutting-edge psychology research papers [7]. Readers of academic papers had high expectations of the content; even academic clickbait articles received 53% more downloads but 38% fewer citations than other articles [22]. Although some disciplines may gain more citations by using question titles or special punctuation marks, the use of these forms in titles did not influence the success of publication [23]. As a result, using professional conventions to standardize the description of article titles within the relevant field can avoid the "penalty" effect of using clickbait.

5 Conclusion

This study explored the development of clickbait in the context of academic papers on the PubMed platform and online news, and we analyzed whether articles using clickbait gain high influence among academics from the perspective of news. We applied algorithms to detect clickbait content in the titles of academic papers on the PubMed platform and online news, this study found that the amount of clickbait content in both contexts had been increasing yearly and growing trend in clickbait in online news would not be contained under existing governance frameworks. Moreover, academic clickbait had a certain "penalty" effect, as it had a negative impact on citation count. The findings of this study encourage researchers to achieve successful publication without using clickbait.

Acknowledgment. The authors would like to acknowledge the support from National Natural Science Foundation of China (72171030).

References

1. Forman-Katz, N., Matsa, K.E.: News Platform Fact Sheet. https://www.pewresearch.org/journalism/fact-sheet/news-platform-fact-sheet/. Accessed 02 Apr 2023
2. News Feed FYI: Click-baiting. https://about.fb.com/news/2014/08/news-feed-fyi-click-baiting/. Accessed 09 Mar 2023
3. Golman, R., Loewenstein, G.: Curiosity, information gaps, and the utility of knowledge. Inf. Gaps Utility Knowl. (April 16, 2015). 96–135 (2015)
4. Munger, K., Luca, M., Nagler, J., Tucker, J.: The effect of clickbait. Verfügbar unter https://rubenson.org/wp-content/uploads/2018/09/munger-tpbw18.pdf,letzterZugriff. **26**, 2020 (2018)
5. Kirwan, G.H., Fullwood, C., Rooney, B.: Risk factors for social networking site scam victimization among Malaysian students. Cyberpsychol. Behav. Soc. Netw. **21**, 123–128 (2018). https://doi.org/10.1089/cyber.2016.0714
6. Zhang, C., Clough, P.D.: Investigating clickbait in Chinese social media: a study of WeChat. Online Soc. Netw. Media. **19**, 100095 (2020). https://doi.org/10.1016/j.osnem.2020.100095
7. Lockwood, G.: Academic clickbait: articles with positively-framed titles, interesting phrasing, and no wordplay get more attention online. Winnower. **3** (2016). https://doi.org/10.15200/winn.146723.36330
8. Vinkers, C.H., Tijdink, J.K., Otte, W.M.: Use of positive and negative words in scientific PubMed abstracts between 1974 and 2014: retrospective analysis. BMJ **351**, h6467 (2015). https://doi.org/10.1136/bmj.h6467
9. Sumner, P., et al.: The association between exaggeration in health related science news and academic press releases: retrospective observational study. BMJ **349**, g7015–g7015 (2014). https://doi.org/10.1136/bmj.g7015
10. Pujahari, A., Sisodia, D.S.: Clickbait detection using multiple categorisation techniques. J. Inf. Sci. **47**, 118–128 (2021). https://doi.org/10.1177/0165551519871822
11. Shang, L., Zhang, D., (Yue), Wang, M., Lai, S., Wang, D.: Towards reliable online clickbait video detection: a content-agnostic approach. Knowl.-Based Syst. **182**, 104851 (2019). https://doi.org/10.1016/j.knosys.2019.07.022
12. Kumar, V., Khattar, D., Gairola, S., Kumar Lal, Y., Varma, V.: Identifying clickbait: a multi-strategy approach using neural networks. In: The 41st International ACM SIGIR Conference on Research & Development in Information Retrieval, pp. 1225–1228. Association for Computing Machinery, New York, NY, USA (2018). https://doi.org/10.1145/3209978.3210144
13. Liao, F., Zhuo, H.H., Huang, X., Zhang, Y.: Federated Hierarchical Hybrid Networks for Clickbait Detection. http://arxiv.org/abs/1906.00638 (2019). https://doi.org/10.48550/arXiv.1906.00638
14. Zhou, X., Jain, A., Phoha, V.V., Zafarani, R.: Fake News Early Detection: An Interdisciplinary Study, http://arxiv.org/abs/1904.11679 (2020). https://doi.org/10.48550/arXiv.1904.11679
15. Rony, M.M.U., Hassan, N., Yousuf, M.: Diving deep into clickbaits: who use them to what extents in which topics with what effects? In: Proceedings of the 2017 IEEE/ACM International Conference on Advances in Social Networks Analysis and Mining 2017, pp. 232–239. Association for Computing Machinery, New York, NY, USA (2017). https://doi.org/10.1145/3110025.3110054
16. Clickbait Challenge. https://webis.de/events/clickbait-challenge/. Accessed 30 Mar 2023

17. Landis, J.R., Koch, G.G.: The measurement of observer agreement for categorical data. Biometrics **33**, 159–174 (1977). https://doi.org/10.2307/2529310
18. Anand, A., Chakraborty, T., Park, N.: We used neural networks to detect clickbaits: you won't believe what happened next! In: Jose, J.M., Hauff, C., Altıngovde, I.S., Song, D., Albakour, D., Watt, S., Tait, J. (eds.) ECIR 2017. LNCS, vol. 10193, pp. 541–547. Springer, Cham (2017). https://doi.org/10.1007/978-3-319-56608-5_46
19. Subotic, S., Mukherjee, B.: Short and amusing: the relationship between title characteristics, downloads, and citations in psychology articles. J. Inf. Sci. **40**, 115–124 (2014)
20. Powers, D.M.W.: Evaluation: from precision, recall and F-measure to ROC, informedness, markedness and correlation. http://arxiv.org/abs/2010.16061 (2020). https://doi.org/10.48550/arXiv.2010.16061
21. Stremersch, S., Verniers, I., Verhoef, P.C.: The quest for citations: drivers of article impact. J. Mark. **71**, 171–193 (2007). https://doi.org/10.1509/jmkg.71.3.171
22. Jamali, H.R., Nikzad, M.: Article title type and its relation with the number of downloads and citations. Scientometrics **88**, 653–661 (2011)
23. Buter, R.K., van Raan, A.F.: Non-alphanumeric characters in titles of scientific publications: an analysis of their occurrence and correlation with citation impact. J. Informet. **5**, 608–617 (2011)

Author Index

H. Mori et al. (Eds.): HCII 2023, LNCS 14056, pp. 471–472, 2023.
https://doi.org/10.1007/978-3-031-48044-7

Printed in the United States
by Baker & Taylor Publisher Services